Fritz Machlup
Donald M. MacKay
Una Mansfield
Richard Mattessich
Mihajlo D. Mesarović
George A. Miller
Elliott W. Montroll
Hassan Mortazavian
Joel Moses
Allen Newell
Charls Pearson
Alan J. Perlis
Zenon W. Pylyshyn
W. Boyd Rayward
Jesse H. Shera
Vladimir Slamecka
Myron Tribus
Peter Wegner
Patrick Wilson
Vladimir Zwass

THE STUDY OF
INFORMATION

THE STUDY OF
INFORMATION
Interdisciplinary Messages

Edited by

FRITZ MACHLUP AND UNA MANSFIELD

with a Foreword by

GEORGE A. MILLER

A Wiley-Interscience Publication

JOHN WILEY & SONS

New York · Chichester · Brisbane · Toronto · Singapore

Most of the papers included in this volume were obtained
with the support of the National Science Foundation
Grant No. IST-80-08007, A02. However, any opinions,
findings, conclusions, and/or recommendations expressed herein are those of the authors and do not
necessarily reflect the views of the NSF.

Library of Congress Cataloging in Publication Data

Main entry under title:
The Study of Information.

   "A Wiley-Interscience publication."
   Bibliography: p.
   Includes index.
   1. Information science—Addresses, essays, lectures.
I. Machlup, Fritz, 1902–1983. II. Mansfield, Una.

Z665.S826 1983   020   83-12147
ISBN 0-471-88717-X

Printed in the United States of America

10 9 8 7 6 5 4 3 2 1

CONTRIBUTORS

[*Editors' Note:* The following list does not include past affiliations, honors, and awards or major publications of contributors. Many of these publications are included in the Cumulative List of References. Our main objective is to show the major disciplinary commitments of the authors; we therefore include their past and present offices (but not council memberships) in national professional associations, and editorial duties and editorial-board memberships for learned journals and professional periodicals.]

MICHAEL A. ARBIB, Professor of Computer and Information Science, and Director, Center for Systems Neuroscience, University of Massachusetts, Amherst; associate editor, *Cognition and Brain Theory;* member of the editorial boards, *International Journal of Man-Machine Studies, Journal of Mathematical Biology, Journal of Semantics, Journal of Social and Biological Structures,* and *Cybernetics and Systems*

AVRON BARR, Research Associate, Department of Computer Science, Stanford University

DAVID BATTY, President, CDB Enterprises, Inc., Silver Spring, Maryland; Visiting Professor, University of Maryland.

ROBERT D. BEAM, Associate Professor of Economics, and Director of the Center for Economic Education, University of Wisconsin, Superior, Wisconsin

TONI CARBO BEARMAN, Executive Director, National Commission on Libraries and Information Science, Washington, D.C.; former editor, *NFAIS Newsletter;* member of the editorial boards, *Bulletin of the American Society for Information Science, The Network Librarian, Resource Sharing and Library Networks,* and *Serials Librarian*

ROBERT C. BERWICK, Assistant Professor of Computer Science and Engineering, M.I.T. Artificial Intelligence Laboratory, Cambridge, Massachusetts; member of the editorial board, *Linguistic Inquiry*

THOMAS G. BEVER, Professor of Psychology and Linguistics, Columbia University, New York; co-founder and associate editor, *Cognition*

MARGARET A. BODEN, Professor of Philosophy and Psychology, University of Sussex (U.K.); member of the editorial board, *Cognition and Brain Theory;* associate of *Behavioral and Brain Sciences;* member of executive committee of *Mind* Association

v

KENNETH E. BOULDING, Distinguished Professor Emeritus of Economics, University of Colorado, Boulder; Research Associate and Project Director, Institute of Behavioral Science, University of Colorado, Boulder; past president, American Economic Association, and American Association for the Advancement of Science

WALTER BUCKLEY, Professor of Sociology, University of New Hampshire, Durham

C. WEST CHURCHMAN, Acting Chairman, Center for Research in Management, and Professor Emeritus of Business Administration, University of California, Berkeley; past president, The Institute of Management Sciences; former editor-in-chief, *Philosophy of Science,* and *Management Science;* member of the editorial boards, The *Information Society, Journal of Management Studies, OMEGA,* and *Research Policy*

RICHARD H. DAY, Professor of Economics, and Director, Modelling Research Group, University of Southern California, Los Angeles; co-editor, The *Journal of Economic Behavior and Organization;* former associate editor, *Journal of Economic Dynamics and Control*

RAY C. DOUGHERTY, Associate Professor of Linguistics, New York University; former member of the board of editors, *Linguistic Analysis*

MURRAY EDEN, Chief, Biomedical Engineering and Instrumentation Branch, National Institutes of Health, Bethesda, Maryland; Professor of Electrical Engineering, Emeritus, M.I.T.; editor, *Information and Control*

PETER ELIAS, Edwin S. Webster Professor of Electrical Engineering, Massachusetts Institute of Technology; former editor and current member of the editorial board, *Information and Control;* member of the editorial board, *Proceedings of the IEEE;* former member of the editorial board, *SPECTRUM*

MICHAEL S. GAZZANIGA, Professor of Psychology in Neurology, and Director of Cognitive Neuroscience, Cornell University Medical College, New York City

SAUL GORN, Professor, Computer and Information Science Department, Moore School of Electrical Engineering, School of Engineering and Applied Science, University of Pennsylvania, Philadelphia

DOUGLAS R. HOFSTADTER, Associate Professor of Computer Science, Indiana University, Bloomington, Indiana

SAMUEL JAY KEYSER, Professor and Head, Department of Linguistics and Philosophy, and Director, Center for Cognitive Science, M.I.T., Cambridge, Massachusetts; editor, *Linguistic Inquiry*

MANFRED KOCHEN, Professor of Information Science, Research Mathematician, and Adjunct Professor of Computer and Information Systems, University of Michigan, Ann Arbor, Michigan; managing editor, *Hu-*

man Systems Management; former associate editor, *Journal of the ACM* and *Behavioral Science*

RICHARD N. LANGLOIS, Assistant Professor of Economics, University of Connecticut, Storrs

FRITZ MACHLUP (*deceased January 1983*) former Professor of Economics, New York University, and Walker Professor of Economics and International Finance Emeritus, Princeton University; past president, American Association of University Professors, American Economic Association, and International Economic Association; former acting managing editor and member of the editorial board, *American Economic Association;* former member of the editorial boards, *Knowledge: Creation, Diffusion, Utilization, Rivista Internazionale di Scienze Economiche,* and *Public Finance*

DONALD M. MACKAY, Emeritus Professor, Department of Communication and Neuroscience, University of Keele, Staffordshire (U.K.); joint editor, *Experimental Brain Research* and *Biological Cybernetics*

UNA MANSFIELD, Visiting Research Faculty, Department of Economics, Princeton University, Princeton, New Jersey

RICHARD MATTESSICH, Distinguished Arthur Andersen and Company Alumni Professor at the University of British Columbia, Vancouver (Canada); associate editor, *Journal of Business Administration;* member of the editorial board, *Economia Aziendale* (Accademia Italiana di Economia Aziendale)

MIHAJLO D. MESAROVIĆ, Cady Staley Professor, Department of Systems Engineering, Case Western Reserve University, Cleveland, Ohio; member of the editorial boards, *Mathematical Systems Theory* and *Information Sciences*

GEORGE A. MILLER, James S. McDonnell Distinguished University Professor of Psychology, Princeton University; past president, American Psychological Association and Eastern Psychological Association; former editor, *Psychological Bulletin*

ELLIOTT W. MONTROLL, Professor at the Institute of Physical Science and Technology, University of Maryland, College Park; editor, *Journal of Mathematical Physics* and *Studies in Statistical Mechanics;* former member of the editorial boards, *Science* and *Proceedings of the NAS* [National Academy of Sciences]; current member of the editorial board, *Journal of Physics and Chemistry of Solids*

HASSAN MORTAZAVIAN, Research Associate, Department of System Science, School of Engineering and Applied Science, University of California, Los Angeles

JOEL MOSES, Professor and Head, Department of Electrical Engineering and Computer Science, M.I.T., Cambridge, Massachusetts; former editor, *Transactions on Mathematical Software* of the Association for Computing Machinery

ALLEN NEWELL, University Professor of Computer Science, Carnegie-Mellon University, Pittsburgh, Pennsylvania; past president, American Association for Artificial Intelligence

CHARLS PEARSON, President, Catronix Corporation, Atlanta, Georgia; associate editor for empirical semiotics, *Journal of Empirical Esthetics,* and *Mind, Brain, and Machine*

ALAN J. PERLIS, Eugene Higgins Professor of Computer Science, Yale University, New Haven, Connecticut; past president, Association for Computing Machinery; former editor-in-chief, *Communications of the ACM*

ZENON W. PYLYSHYN, Professor of Psychology and Computer Science, and Director of the Centre for Cognitive Science, The University of Western Ontario, London (Canada); past president, Society for Philosophy and Psychology; associate editor, *Behavioral and Brain Sciences;* member of the editorial boards, *Cognitive Science, Cognitive Psychology, Cognition,* and *Artificial Intelligence*

W. BOYD RAYWARD, Professor and Dean, The Graduate Library School, University of Chicago; former editor and current member of the editorial board, The *Library Quarterly*

JESSE H. SHERA (*deceased March 1982*) former Professor and Dean Emeritus, Graduate Library School, Case Western Reserve University, Cleveland, Ohio; past president, Association of American Library Schools and Beta Phi Mu; former editor, *American Documentation, Information Systems in Documentation,* and *Documentation in Action;* former associate editor, The *Library Quarterly* and *Journal of Cataloging and Classification;* former member of the editorial board, *Library Science*

VLADIMIR SLAMECKA, Professor, School of Information and Computer Science, Georgia Institute of Technology, Atlanta, Georgia; former chairman, United States National Committee for FID [Federation for International Documentation]; associate editor, *Information Processing and Management;* member of the editorial boards, *Information Systems, Library Research,* and *International Information and Communication*

MYRON TRIBUS, Director, Center for Advanced Engineering Study, M.I.T., Cambridge, Massachusetts

PETER WEGNER, Professor of Computer Science, Brown University, Providence, Rhode Island

PATRICK WILSON, Professor, School of Library and Information Studies, University of California, Berkeley

VLADIMIR ZWASS, Associate Professor of Computer Science, Fairleigh Dickinson University, Teaneck, New Jersey; editor-in-chief, *Journal of Management Information Systems*

FOREWORD

A nation cannot live merely on victuals, comforts, games, and weapons; a concern with ideas and values is essential, for without them life becomes meaningless.

(Fritz Machlup, *The Production and Distribution of Knowledge in the United States*, 1962)

Communication has become an American obsession. Those who admire it justify the obsession as a necessary precondition for democratic government, or for a free economy; others view it less favorably as a defense against the loneliness of personal independence, or against the insecurity of competitive co-existence. Whatever the reason, the vast communication industries that have sprung up in this century now bathe every willing citizen in a continuous and unprecedented flow of written, spoken, musical, and pictorial messages. The Earl of Chesterfield to the contrary, knowledge of the world can now be acquired in a closet. Social and economic changes that have accompanied this effusion of communication, first in the United States and now worldwide, do clearly signal a New Industrial Revolution.

The Viennese intellectual and economist Fritz Machlup was among those who first recognized and tried to characterize the economic consequences of this revolution. Indeed, his work on the economic role of knowledge may prove to be Machlup's most important intellectual contribution. On his visit to the United States in 1933—a visit that eventually became permanent—he picked up, through reading and discussions at Harvard, an academic interest in the theory of monopolistic or imperfect competition. Then one thing led to another: among the institutions that restrict competition is the patent system; study of the patent system drew his attention to the economic importance of research and development; quality research, in turn, depends on quality education; education leads to the availability of journals and books, which are but part of the vast communication system of the United States. As his topic broadened, Machlup decided that what he came to call the Knowledge Industry deserved comprehensive description and analysis.

In 1959 and 1960 the economic role of knowledge became the subject of a series of five invited lectures, the first at Cornell, the next four at Fordham. Encouraged by their reception, Machlup expanded the lectures into a book that was published in 1962 by the Princeton University Press: *The Production and Distribution of Knowledge in the United States*. The two longest chapters were IV, entitled Education, and V, Research and Development.

The book was immediately recognized as a significant and pioneering work, the first serious discussion of a basic change in American life. In the concluding chapter Machlup stated the clear implication: "If employment opportunities continue to improve for high-level-knowledge-producing labor and to worsen for unskilled manual labor, the danger of increasing unemployment among the latter becomes more serious" (p. 397). Needless to say, the trend has continued: his estimate that knowledge production and distribution accounted for 29 percent of the adjusted gross national product in 1958 was subsequently updated by Marc Uri Porat to 46 percent in 1967. And the unemployment of unskilled labor has indeed become more serious.

In 1971, when he retired as Walker Professor of Economics and International Finance at Princeton, Machlup decided that he had a moral obligation to update his statistical analysis. In addition to his duties as professor at New York University and a full agenda of other research, he undertook an eightfold expansion of the 1962 book: the initial plan was for a series of eight volumes, roughly one volume for each chapter of the earlier book, the whole to be entitled *Knowledge: Its Creation, Distribution, and Economic Significance*, with the Princeton University Press as publisher.

Volume I, *Knowledge and Knowledge Production*, was published in 1980. According to the original plan, the second volume was to survey the branches of learning and the information sciences, and to analyze the economic concept of human capital. As the work progressed, however, it grew into three separate books, expanding the planned series from eight to ten volumes. The first part, *The Branches of Learning*, appeared as Volume II in 1982. Volume III, *The Economics of Information and Human Capital*, was completed only weeks before Machlup died of a heart attack on January 30, 1983, at 80 years of age.

Volume IV was to deal with the information sciences, the remaining part of the originally planned second volume. In preparation, Machlup persuaded 39 information scientists to write a total of 56 essays on their various specialties so that he, in his role as an editor, could go to school under the experts— could "see the stir of the great Babel, and not feel the crowd." The result is the present book, prepared in collaboration with Una Mansfield. It is not Volume IV, of course, but some indications of Machlup's reactions to this heroic exercise can be gathered from the co-authored Prologue and his own Epilogue.

Probably nothing less than a Grand Design could have persuaded anyone, even the enormously energetic Machlup, to organize such an enterprise as this. The information sciences are highly diverse. Someone who speaks of information in his own context may know of someone else who uses it in a different context, yet never find the occasion or the impulse to explore the similarities and differences. Now Machlup has made that exploration for us, and made it with a sensitivity to semantics and logic that few could match. Discourse across these disciplinary boundaries will surely proceed more smoothly in the future. Experts can join with The Celebrated Intelligent Layman in their gratitude for the resulting improvement in mutual intelligibility. The topic is important, sufficiently important that, even if we cannot speak in unison, we should speak as clearly as possible.

Kenneth Boulding once commented that Machlup had what he called the anti-Midas touch—even if he were to touch gold, he would turn it to life. All the contributors to this volume, all who endured his compulsive criticism and enjoyed his appreciative praise as he tried to bring our essays to life, join with Una Mansfield and me in dedicating our efforts here to the memory of our charming friend and mentor, Fritz Machlup.

GEORGE A. MILLER

Princeton, New Jersey
May 15, 1983

PREFACE

Fritz Machlup's pioneering work on *The Production and Distribution of Knowledge in the United States* [1962] did not deal with the academic disciplines that study information, for the simple reason that at the time Machlup was researching and writing his book (mid- to late 1950s), few of them existed. For instance, the concepts of *cybernetics* and *information theory* had been introduced as recently as 1948 by Norbert Wiener and Claude Shannon, respectively, and were still gaining acceptance among scholars. The stored-program digital computer pioneered by John von Neumann in the late 1940s had not yet given rise to the development of *computer science* or its subfield *artificial intelligence*. The movement to develop *general system theory* was spearheaded by Ludwig von Bertalanffy in 1954; and Herbert Simon, a founding father, gives the year of birth of *cognitive science* as 1956. The term *information science* was not used formally until 1958, and the nature of the study area it denotes is still a matter of debate. *Linguistics* and *library science* did exist, but they were not yet regarded as interrelated by virtue of their common interest in studying information.

By 1980, however, Machlup wrote in his introduction to the first volume of the series updating the 1962 work that "a comprehensive work on knowledge could not reasonably disregard the existence and rapid growth of several young disciplines that concern themselves with systems of information and communication." So he planned a volume (Volume IV) on *The Disciplines of Information* that would "explore the interrelations among the numerous disciplines, metadisciplines, interdisciplines, and subdisciplines that deal with *information* as their central or peripheral concern." I had the privilege of collaborating with him on the research for that volume, which included the commissioning of papers from experts in the various disciplines so as to provide a basis for the analysis of interrelations. These papers are presented here, and the Prologue and Epilogue contain their preliminary analysis, which was to be expanded in Volume IV. The intentions of the writers of these pieces will be better understood if I first offer a brief description of the objectives and procedures adopted for the project. I quote from the research proposal of Fritz Machlup in his application to the National Science Foundation in 1979:

> This project is designed to examine the interrelations among a number of disciplines that are now regarded as constituent of, cognate to, or complementary with information science. . . . The views expressed by representatives of

different disciplines are inconsistent and obscure. . . . Specialists in the . . . disciplines will be invited to prepare papers on the intra- and interdisciplinary relationships as they see them. . . . The study is not intended as a mere survey or synthesis of views held in the profession but rather as a serious . . . analysis of the logical and methodological relations among past and present approaches. . . . Whether a particular discipline is regarded as autonomous, superior, subordinate . . . to another discipline is far less important than to illuminate the genuine concerns of each of the fields and the ways in which various idealogical strands are interwoven. . . . There is no specific method of analyzing logical and methodological positions. As in the general philosophy of science, the methodology of particular scientific disciplines calls for an analysis of apparent consistencies and inconsistencies, of the pertinence and relevance of arguments, and of the linkages of pragmatic considerations with philosophical premises . . . .

Nine lead papers and between three and five discussion papers for each of the nine were commissioned. The writers of subsidiary papers were asked to offer critical comments, elaborations, or supplementary observations on the subject of the lead paper. The author of the lead paper would then come back with a rejoinder. This procedure was designed to produce a discussion as lively as a round-table debate and yet as well-thought-out as an argument presented for publication in a learned journal or collective volume. Altogether, 56 contributions from 39 authors, plus an analytical Prologue and Epilogue by the co-editors, resulted from this undertaking. All responses and rejoinders were given titles descriptive of the messages delivered, and the work was divided into nine sections dealing with cognitive science, computer and information science, artificial intelligence, linguistics, library and information sciences, cybernetics, information theory, mathematical system theory, and general system theory. The format of lead paper/comments/rejoinder worked well, except in Section 3 where the four papers were written independently, with "endnotes" rather than a rejoinder by the lead author, and in Section 4, which has no rejoinder.

The interdisciplinary character of the project is evident, whether authors are listed by departmental affiliation or by professed specialty. As a matter of fact, diversity of opinions, especially in matters of methodology, is not confined to diversity of research commitment or of departmental affiliation; disagreements are most conspicuous, and aired with greatest vehemence, among those whose research interests are most alike. All in all, however, more can be learned from the interplay of conflicting ideas, from the arguments and counterarguments on each issue, than from the best-formulated but monolithic expositions of the fields.

In view of our interdisciplinary readership, a few editorial conventions had to be imposed: for instance, technical "jargon" was discouraged and mathematical notation reduced to the necessary minimum. First names were used in the text to introduce scholars who though well known in some disciplines might not be known in others. In citations and quotations, initials of authors with common family names were included for easy reference. The manuscript was virtually complete at the time of Professor Machlup's death, with the exception of his own Epilogue, the Cumulative List of References, and the Index. The parts missing from the Epilogue have been indicated by me in an *Editor's Note* at the point in the text where his outline had placed them; the parts that have been published are exactly as Machlup had written them.

Apart from Fritz Machlup, the information community lost two other outstanding scholars during the course of this research: Colin Cherry died in November 1979, about the time Machlup was inviting him to act as an adviser to the project; and Jesse H. Shera died in March 1982, just a few months after he had submitted his paper in Section 5. Each has left us a rich legacy in his writings.

A project of this magnitude involves the cooperation of many organizations and individuals. Funding for the research was provided by grants from the National Science Foundation to New York University, and from the Spencer Foundation and the Earhart Foundation to Princeton University. Our thanks to these foundations and institutions for their support. Howard L. Resnikoff and his successor as director of the NSF Division of Information Science and Technology, Edward C. Weiss, provided encouragement and guidance to Professor Machlup; and Herbert S. Bailey, Jr., director of the Princeton University Press, and Robert F. Rich, editor of the journal *Knowledge*, were trusted friends whose advice helped shape his plans. Scholars who served as advisers to the project and nominated writers of papers and comments included Russell Ackoff, Saul Gorn, Kenneth A. Klivington, Donald E. Knuth, Lewis Levine, J. C. R. Licklider, Mitchell Marcus, Mihajlo Mesarović, George A. Miller, Alan J. Perlis, Claude E. Shannon, Herbert A. Simon, David Slepian, Don R. Swanson, and Terry Winograd. Four of them—Gorn, Mesarović, Miller, and Perlis—contributed papers of their own, as did the 35 other scholars in the List of Contributors. We are grateful to all of them, especially the authors of lead papers who were willing to have their work "critiqued" so intensively.

Professor Machlup benefited from discussing parts of our Prologue and his Epilogue with several colleagues and family members, among them John Woodland (Woody) Hastings, Richard C. Jeffrey, Richard N. Langlois, Stefan Machlup, George A. Miller, Allen Newell, and Kenneth Stigleitz. He would also want me to express his gratitude to Mary Taylor Huber and Peter Swire, who provided valuable research assistance in the earliest phase of the project, and to Rosa Schupbach for secretarial support throughout its duration. Eliana Covacich and Robert Korchak at New York University were especially helpful to him; and Michael McGill and Helene Ebenfield at NSF showed understanding as program and project officials. As chairman of the economics department, Stephen M. Goldfeld acted as "host" for Professor Machlup's Princeton-based research during his lifetime and bore responsibility for its successful completion after his death. Two good friends of

Machlup's, William J. Baumol and Donald W. King, also were generous with their advice and support in bringing this part of his work to fruition.

The staff at John Wiley & Sons turned a difficult task into a pleasant one. Special thanks are due to James T. Gaughan, the editor in charge of this volume; to Carole Schwager and Christina Mikulak, who showed sensitivity in their management of the copyediting; to Aline Walton for her designing skill; and to Rose Ann Campise, whose cheerful but firm control kept the publication on schedule.

I owe a personal word of thanks to Anthony Debons, whose provocative teaching aroused my own curiosity about the relations among the "information disciplines" and led directly to my collaboration with Machlup. My debt to Fritz Machlup covers much more than gains in scholarship; his friendship and that of his wife Mitzi have greatly enriched my life.

UNA MANSFIELD

Princeton University
October 1983

ACKNOWLEDGMENTS

The authors and editors are indebted to the publishers for their permission to reprint material from copyrighted works, as follows:

In Section 1

Sloan Foundation, Advisors of the Alfred P., "Cognitive Science '78," Report of the State of the Art Committee; passage reprinted by permission of the authors and the Sloan Foundation.

In Section 4

Piatelli-Palmarini, Massimo, ed., *Language and Learning: The Debate between Jean Piaget and Noam Chomsky* [1980]; passages reprinted by permission of the Harvard University Press.
Piaget, Jean, *Genetic Epistemology* [Woodbridge Lectures, 1968], translated by Eleanor Duckworth, copyright © 1970 Columbia University Press; passage reprinted by permission of the Columbia University Press.

In Section 6

Minsky, Marvin L., "Computer Science and the Representation of Knowledge," in Dertouzos, Michael L., and Moses, Joel, eds., *The Computer Age: A Twenty-Year View,* copyright © 1980 Massachusetts Institute of Technology; passage reprinted by permission of the MIT Press.
Wiener, Norbert, *Cybernetics, or Control and Communication in the Animal and the Machine,* copyright © 1948 and 1961 Massachusetts Institute of Technology; passages reprinted by permission of the MIT Press.
Hall, Thomas S., *Ideas of Life and Matter: Studies in the History of General Physiology 600BC-1900AD, Vol. 1: From Pre-Socratic Times to the Enlightenment,* copyright © 1969 by the University of Chicago; passages reprinted by permission of the University of Chicago Press.
Waterman, Talbot H., "Systems Theory and Biology—Views of a Biologist," in Mesarović, Mihajlo D., ed., *Systems Theory and Biology* [1968]; passages reprinted by permission of Springer-Verlag, New York.

Dunlap, Knight, *The Elements of Scientific Psychology,* St. Louis, 1922, The C. V. Mosby Co.; passage reprinted by permission of the publisher.

Bruner, Jerome S., "Introduction" to MacDougall, William, *Body and Mind,* copyright © by Jerome S. Bruner; passage reprinted by permission of Beacon Press.

In Section 7

Tribus, Myron, "Thirty Years of Information Theory," in Levine, Raphael D., and Tribus, Myron, eds., *The Maximum Entropy Formalism Conference, MIT, 1978,* copyright © by the Massachusetts Institute of Technology; paper reprinted by permission of the MIT Press.

CONTENTS

SECTION 3

SECTION 4

SECTION 5

SECTION 6

SECTION 7

SECTION 8

SECTION 9

EPILOGUE

THE STUDY OF
INFORMATION

PROLOGUE

CULTURAL DIVERSITY IN STUDIES OF INFORMATION

Fritz Machlup and Una Mansfield

The idea of two cultures in the academic world has been most forcefully presented by C. P. Snow. According to him, a deep intellectual gulf divides the mathematically minded laboratory-dwellers, engaged in the natural sciences, from the book-loving denizens of the library stacks, the literary intellectuals. [Snow, 1959.] The two cultures, sharing a mutual incomprehension and disrespect of each other, are what now (in violation of semantic tradition) are called science and the humanities. [Machlup, 1980, pp. 62–84.] Snow later became aware of the existence of other fields. He conceded that recognition of the social sciences would present us with "something like a third culture," but he denied the good sense of considering all possible branches and twigs of learning that might give us "two thousand and two" cultures. (Snow, 1964, pp. 66, 70.) We have chosen to deal here with only thirty or forty cultures, a limitation explained by the fact that we are not going to deal with the entire universe of learning but with only that part of it that is characterized by the keyword *information*.

THE PROJECT

Our project is to analyze the logical (or methodological) and pragmatic relations among the disciplines and subject areas that are centered on information. Disciplines (sciences, academic areas of research and teaching) are orderly arrangements (metaphorically called bodies) of coherent thoughts, formulated as propositions, about things (sense-objects or thought-objects) deemed worthy of being known (i.e., being believed with some degree of confidence) and being passed on. In other words, disciplines are what a number of people, respected for having read widely and for being read by other widely read people, have claimed to be disciplines. (We shall return later to the question of how this pronouncement can be made operational.) Relations among different disciplines are therefore relations among the expressed thoughts of selected scholars (scientists). Logical relations among

3

propositions formulated by different people cannot easily be examined unless the same words used by them denote the same meanings and equal meanings are denoted by the same words. Whether this is actually the case in any particular instance cannot simply be assumed but has to be established by scrutinizing the contexts of their messages. If such scrutiny reveals the presence of misleading homonymity and/or expected synonymity, translation becomes a prior task. Translation of discourses by different speakers and writers is not easy and will succeed only if the translators have studied the other fields sufficiently to have become ''multilingual''—even though all is being said in English. Few of those brought up in one of our thirty or forty ''cultures'' have become bilingual or trilingual in our sense, and only very exceptional scholars have succeeded in understanding the communications emanating from all the disciplines involved.

It will now be understood why we have chosen the procedure of inviting representatives of a variety of disciplines to set forth how they see relations between their own specialty and various other disciplines, metadisciplines, interdisciplines, or subdisciplines. Their specialty may be a constituent of a larger discipline; it may share principles in common with cognate specialties or disciplines; it may be complementary with other fields; but whatever interdisciplinary relations our authors see, they should describe. To have such ''interdisciplinary messages'' discussed by others who are working in the same field or a neighboring one, would allow us and our readers to reach at least a fractional understanding of the logical and pragmatic relations among the disciplines involved.

Interdisciplinary Explorations

When we attempted to explain our project of interdisciplinary explorations to various curious people, we received some strange reactions. Many of our listeners could not believe that there were all that many disciplines concerned with information; when we offered a sample of the -ics and -logies, . . . theories, and . . . sciences that had been unknown to them, their faces expressed the mixture of awe and contempt that is characteristic of those suffering from an inferiority complex effectively suppressed by a strong armor of intellectual superiority: ''cybernetics? informatics? cognitive science? semiotics? robotics? artificial intelligence? Never heard of it!''

Others had ''heard of it'' and showed some appreciation for our efforts to find out about the fields of inquiry that seem to form a class of academic subjects dealing with the same object—or at least with something that has the same name, *information*. One easy discovery of the explorer is the fact that he or she finds here a prize example of homonymity: Information is not just one thing. It means different things to those who expound its characteristics, properties, elements, techniques, functions, dimensions, and connections. Evidently, there should be *something* that all the things called information have in common, but it surely is not easy to find out whether it is much more than the name. If we have failed and are still at sea, it may be our fault: Explorers do not always succeed in learning the language of the natives and their habits of thought.

One scholar who is at home in several of the different areas of study—Herbert Simon, spiritus motor in many scientific endeavors—likened our project to an anthropological exploration: We go into areas whose inhabitants speak foreign tongues (with many words sounding like words in our own language but having very different meanings); we try to find some guides to help us learn the meanings of these strange sounds; and we try to make sense of what we see and hear, yet we probably misunderstand much and are bewildered by even much more. Another scholar refused to compare our work to anthropological research, chiefly because anthropologists often have taken vows of intellectual chastity, so that they can embark on their explorations untroubled by prior knowledge, immaculately free from preconceptions, and innocent of philosophical liaisons. What is really needed for a successful inquiry is "an interdisciplinary epistemology . . . integrated with philosophical understanding and with psychological and biological knowledge." We tend to agree with this judgment expressed by Margaret Boden but should quickly admit that the statement, made in her paper in this volume, was meant to refer chiefly to computational insights. We find it equally valid for *all* interdisciplinary inquiries in the fields concerned with information.

The intellectual requirement to break down the barriers between disciplines has long been recognized. In virtually all branches of learning, we can observe an ongoing conflict between specialization and integration, separatism and unificationism, isolationism and scholarly cosmopolitanism, or, in brief, fission and fusion. The warning that we ought not to become *Fachidioten*—the German pejorative word for excessively specialized experts ignorant of things outside their narrow fields—has been sounded in all areas of knowledge, but it is noteworthy that some of the founders of the disciplines of information have been particularly concerned about the scholarly seclusion of their fellow researchers.

Although a call for "mere intellectual communication across the boundaries of these several disciplines is not enough"—to quote again from Boden's paper—listening to interdisciplinary messages is better than plugging one's ears. International and interdisciplinary symposia were organized soon after Norbert Wiener came out with his *Cybernetics* [1948] and Claude Shannon with his paper on "A Mathematical Theory of Communication" [1948]. The First International Symposium on Information Theory was held in London in the summer of 1950. Among the participants were "mathematicians, physicists, engineers, linguists, physiologists, geneticists—in fact folk from almost every branch of science." (MacKay, 1969, p. 9.) All branches of learning mentioned in this quotation are traditional disciplines, represented in the conventional structure of every university. When similar interdisciplinary symposia are held nowadays—32 years after that first

London symposium—many of the participants regard themselves as representatives of new disciplines, specialties, or interdisciplines that did not exist in the early 1950s or at least had not yet been recognized as academic subjects of instruction, not even for courses offered by any of the existing departments or programs.

A Cluster of Disciplines and Specialties

Although an enumeration of these new fields of inquiry and instruction may be a rather unnecessary task for most readers of this volume, some readers may be list-fanciers and may care to see the catalogue. In offering one, we must warn, however, that some of the listed disciplines, hybrid disciplines, or specialties, are challenged by some critics or opponents as illegitimate (in one sense or another); that boundary disputes are unresolved; and that even the major concerns of some of the subjects are controversial. The main purpose of the listing is to impress the semi-informed reader with the lack of order in a set of "bodies of ordered knowledge." After all, it was the lack of order, the jungle of coexisting, apparently interrelated subjects of study, that prompted the undertaking of our inquiry.

We begin our list with designations that contain the letters *i n f o r m:* information theory, information science, and informatics.[1] We continue our list with a similarly primitive scheme of classification: first the disciplines with names ending in *ics,* then those ending in *logy,* followed by those called *science, analysis, theory,* or *research:* bibliometrics, cybernetics, linguistics, phonetics, psycholinguistics, robotics, scientometrics, semantics, semiotics, systemics; cognitive psychology, lexicology, neurophysiology, psychobiology; brain science, cognitive science, cognitive neuroscience, computer science, computing science, communication sciences, library science, management science, speech science, systems science; systems analysis; automata theory, communication theory, control theory, decision theory, game theory, general system theory; artificial-intelligence research, genetic-information research, living-systems research, operations research, pattern-recognition research, telecommunications research. We may add two fields, one no longer fashionable (largely because of its less flashy designation) but once quite respected—documentation; and the other often overlooked (because of its association with classified intelligence-gathering)—cryptography. Having grouped the disciplines or specialties in our list according to the endings of their names, *ics* and *logy* (favored for scientific subjects) or according to appellations like *science, analysis,* and so forth, we

---

[1] We limited ourselves in the preceding to the three best-known designations but may add here another six of lesser currency: informantics, informatistics, informatology, informology, informetrics, and infometrics. We are indebted to Alvin M. Schrader, who not only compiled a long list of designations but also knows the names of the terminologists responsible for coining them. [Schrader, 1984.]

hasten to say that no hierarchical differences should be inferred. Indeed, some who profess a field designated as a science are wont to renounce its claim to this (apparently honorific) generic term, while others who hold a general or empirical theory insist on its being really a science. Discussions of such hierarchical distinctions are usually quite unproductive.

The more than thirty fields of inquiry and instruction included in the preceding catalogue do not exhaust the class of studies of information and knowledge. The field of communication in the sense of mass media has been getting an increasing share of attention. The two keywords, information and knowledge, go together in a large range of fields. This is true for most disciplines dealing with cognition; moreover, almost all social sciences include specialties devoted to the role of information *and* knowledge in society. Sociology of knowledge has long been a specialty in good standing, and sociology of information has emerged more recently. Anthropology and politics have begun to inquire into knowledge and information as increasingly relevant subject matters. The economics of knowledge and information has accumulated a bibliography of far over 20,000 published titles. Social psychology has its own literature on information and knowledge. And we should not miss mentioning social phenomenology of knowledge. [Schutz and Luckmann, 1973, especially chaps. 3, 4.]

This is a forbidding array of disciplines, metadisciplines, interdisciplines, and specialties, far too big to be covered by the interdisciplinary messages prepared for this volume. A few major disciplines of information had to be selected for special emphasis, but the contributors were asked to examine and discuss the methodological and pragmatic interrelations among as many areas in the study of information as they cared to link to their major research interests. They did, and thereby did much to show that disciplinary isolationism is an unsound attitude.

Fences around the Fields

Several analogies have been used to characterize isolationist or parochial attitudes of specialists uninterested in cognate or complementary fields of inquiry. For example, they erect fences around their fields—like unsociable property owners inhospitable to their neighbors. The impediments dividing the universe of discourse need not perpetuate isolation of the specialists; fences can be taken down, or jumped over, and in any case, one may look over the fence to observe what the neighbors are doing. A good many of the originators and innovators of disciplines of information have urged their fellow researchers to promote mutual understanding and collaboration.

Norbert Wiener deplored that there are

fields of scientific work . . . which have been explored from the different sides of pure mathematics, statistics, electrical engineering, and neurophysiology, in which every single notion receives a separate name from each group, and in which important work has been triplicated or quadruplicated, while still other important work is delayed by the unavailability in one field of results that may have already become classical in the next field.

It is these boundary regions of science which offer the richest opportunities to the qualified investigator. (Wiener, 1948, p. 2.)

In the same vein, Ludwig von Bertalanffy, the biologist and one of the pioneers of general system theory, wrote that

science is split into innumerable disciplines continually generating new subdisciplines. In consequence, the physicist, the biologist, the psychologist, and the social scientist are, so to speak, encapsulated in their private universes, and it is difficult to get word from one cocoon to the other. (Bertalanffy, 1968, p. 30.)

And, to quote one more champion of mutual understanding among the representatives of different fields, Kenneth Boulding lamented that

the Republic of Learning is breaking up into isolated subcultures with only tenuous lines of communication between them . . . an assemblage of walled-in hermits, each mumbling to himself words in a private language that only he can understand. (Boulding, 1956b, p. 198.)

However, in his plea for interdisciplinary collaboration, Boulding warned that "it is all too easy for the interdisciplinary to degenerate into the undisciplined." (Ibid., p. 13.)

Some of these pleas go much farther than the plea that specialists learn to know at least what their neighbors are doing. The interdisciplinary messages in this volume are all from disciplines concerned with information, communication, cognition, or knowledge. The hope that representatives of different fields of study may begin to learn each other's vocabularies, and try to comprehend what others are saying, should not be deemed overly ambitious. When the same word, information, is used in a dozen different meanings in different areas of inquiry, one should expect all users of that word to be sufficiently curious to find out what "the others" mean by it. Moreover, when users of the word have come to comprehend that the use of homonyms may make their own communications unintelligible, or at least misleading, to others, they should attempt to guard against misunderstandings, perhaps by careful specification of their terms and by explicit efforts to exclude unintended meanings.

We do not wish to give the impression that most specialists in the fields in question favor isolation and oppose closer interdisciplinary relations. Some, however, want to draw a line between research on *information* and research on *knowledge*. Although they admit that mutual understanding and some joint work may be helpful to specialists researching information-processing and other operations concerned with information, they want to call a halt when it is suggested that the cooperation be extended to the study of knowledge. This limited broadmindedness, which excludes the study of knowledge—although, as a rule, information is designed to effect or affect knowledge—is not much less parochial and isolationist than the decision of an information scientist to learn nothing but how to measure storage capacity or compare the costs of alternative data-retrieval systems.

To be sure, the relative number of researchers who reject a wide lens for their camera and insist on a sharp but narrow focus has been declining—largely because people have become ashamed of their narrowness. Still, many teachers in academic departments, divisions, and schools hold to the view that the narrow focus is science and the wide lens is speculation. Strong support for greater breadth has come from the small team of cognitive scientists, some of whom have progressed from the study of information-processing to the study of knowledge-structures. Indeed, at least one of them has defined cognition as "the activity of knowing: the acquisition, organization, and use of knowledge." (Neisser, 1976, p. 1.) To impose a fixed boundary line between the study of information and the study of knowledge is an unreasonable restriction on the progress of both.

SPLITS AND MERGERS CHANGING THE MAP OF DISCIPLINES

We have enumerated almost forty fields in which information plays a strategic role. Most of these fields made their first appearance on the academic scene during the last three or four decades. Their emergence is remarkable because of the extraordinary bunching of new arrivals of manifestly cognate disciplines (metadisciplines, interdisciplines, and subdisciplines). The evolution of new species of academic subjects is largely a matter of *splits* or *mergers* of existing ones and a subsequent process of *selection* on intellectual and quasi-intellectual (political) grounds. The notions of splits, mergers, and selection call for elaboration.

Fission and Fusion in Academe

Splitting, or fission, of academic disciplines has been observed for over two thousand years. Chemistry, for example, was an early spin-off from physics, both being exhibited as separate sciences in philosophical discussions and classifications of natural philosophy. After various subdivisions had occurred, a merger of parts of physics and chemistry proved expedient: It resulted in physical chemistry. Several splits and mergers—fissions and fusions—have occurred in the life sciences, with biology being divided into several subdisciplines and merged with parts of physics and chemistry. This process led to biophysics and biochemistry, with the latter splitting again into chemical biochemistry and biological biochemistry. [Machlup, 1982, pp. 101, 152.] Similar sequences of splits and mergers have occurred in moral philosophy. Fission is already indicated in Aristotle's work and becomes quite explicit in the writings of the Christian church fathers. In the departmental organization of modern universities, the separations were made in the nineteenth and twentieth centuries. The mergers were usually made through the creation of interdepartmental *programs,* but, in many instances, political forces have led to the creation of interdisciplinary *departments.* Thus, moral philosophy, or social science, was first divided, in several consecutive steps taken during a period of fifty to a hundred years, into cultural anthropology, demography, economics, human geography, political science, social psychology, and sociology. Then all these and several more disciplines were again brought together for area studies, ethnic studies, urban studies, women's studies, and several more problem areas. For example, all social sciences had to be called on for a program or department of Latin American studies, sometimes supplemented by history (cultural, political, and social), languages (Spanish and Portuguese), and law.

As a rule, the reasons for splits and mergers are associated with such philosophical and methodological issues as those encapsuled in pairs of opposites like analysis versus synthesis, abstract versus concrete, and basic versus applied. (Note that we did not include deduction versus induction, those Pandora boxes of confusion.) Analysis, increasing abstraction, and emphasis on basic research dictate splits of disciplines; whereas synthesis, attention to the concrete, and interest in application to real-life problems dictate collaboration and mergers of disciplines. However, to explain the historical facts of fission and fusion of academic disciplines on grounds of sound methodological principles does not mean that actual splits and mergers were always motivated entirely by sound principles; personality clashes, campus politics, institutional funding, and similar less-principled influences have often caused or triggered decisions by faculties and administrations of our universities.

Creation or Emergence of New Fields

These decisions do not, however, create new disciplines—either by splitting existing ones or joining parts of existing ones into new amalgams—but merely ratify a development that has already sufficiently progressed in learned journals, colloquia and symposia, and the invisible college of oral, written, and prepublished communications. This is the place for us to come back to the question of whether a discipline becomes a discipline just because some people say that it is a discipline. We qualified this statement by an essential proviso: that people who say, "Let there be a new science of Aplopathoscopics!"[2] are respected scholars who have read widely and are

---

[2] Aplopathoscopic neumatology was one of the subdivisions of psychology proposed by Jeremy Bentham. [Bentham, 1816; Machlup, 1982, p. 63.]

being read widely by respected scholars who have read widely and are being read widely by respected . . . and so forth—though the circle of scholars need not be large. There are operational tests for the existence of such a consensus among recognized scholars. The tests include such things as references to certain keywords characteristic of the new discipline (or specialty) in subject indexes of recent textbooks and in titles of articles and books; the appearance of survey articles summarizing the contents of publications in the new field; the extension of the classification scheme of a larger discipline in order to provide one or more special headings for listing publications in the new discipline (or specialty); the appearance of books of readings and volumes of conference proceedings focusing on the new discipline (or specialty); and, finally, courses offering instruction in the new subject in universities, first to graduate students, later, perhaps, also to undergraduates.[3]

A novel approach to the identification of specialties that are presumably "ready to become recognized as having arrived" relies on citation analysis. The analyst finds clusters of articles and books linked either by cocitation or by bibliographic coupling. In cocitation, different earlier publications are linked by being cited together in the same new pieces; in bibliographic coupling, different new publications are linked as they cite the same earlier pieces. [Garfield, Malin, and Small, 1978, p. 185.] A similar approach can establish mutual-citation societies by compiling a citation matrix: In a new or emerging field, whom did the writers cite and by whom were they cited? If, however, a small group of people cite one another but cite hardly anyone else, must one not suspect the existence of a club, a cult, or a conspiracy? Perhaps so; yet one should not on this ground deny the group recognition as a bona fide field of study, especially not if some of its members are scholars also respected outside the group.

Reapportionments and Multiple Assignments

That a new discipline is put together entirely by merging selected portions from two or more existing disciplines is no reason for denying it the designation of a science. Portions from several fields may be required for the study of particular phenomena or particular problems. If such multidisciplinary efforts are needed not only temporarily but for prolonged periods of time, an interdiscipline will be established, without any presumption regarding a higher or lower scientific level. If the new interdiscipline is largely concerned with special or concrete problems, its orientation is likely to be more toward applied research.

Some scientists have been taught (or rather mistaught) to restrict the

---

[3] These tests have actually been carried out to ascertain that the economics of knowledge and information has become an established specialty within the field of economics. [Machlup, 1984, chap. 9.] The number of titles published in this specialty exceeds 20,000.

appellation *science* to basic research and deny it to applied research. Such snobbism or bigotry is not compatible with the fact that currently at least 95 per cent of all scientific effort is mission-oriented, that is, designed to produce practically useful knowledge. Let us submit, first, that the merger of parts of several sciences creates a compound discipline no less scientific than the donor disciplines; second, that the parts taken over from existing disciplines and incorporated into new ones are not thereby removed from their original or conventional discipline but belong to both, the old and the new; and thirdly, that any new findings altering the structure of our knowledge or adding to it may enrich both the old and the new fields.

In the title of this section, we have suggested that splits and mergers are changing the map of academic disciplines. This suggestion may be misleading in some respects. It may induce us to think of a process like redistricting—changing the boundaries of election districts in a state—and this would be fallacious. For what is added to one district is taken away from another—something we have just denied with regard to mapping academic disciplines or areas of research.

Fortunately, the philosophers of science who have discussed the boundaries of various disciplines have not drawn maps showing how certain phenomena, problems, concepts, laws, or theories should be appropriately assigned to various disciplines without undue duplication. Any degree of overlapping is acceptable in reapportioning the universe of learning. Multiple assignments of the same tasks (for research or instruction) may be highly productive. And the fact that a discipline imports most of its materials and/or methods from other disciplines does not reduce its significance and should not reduce its scientific respectability.

We have refrained in this section from drawing on Allen Newell's instructive examples of and observations on the emergence of new interdisciplines. Instead of quoting and paraphrasing, we want to call Newell's paper to the reader's special attention. What Newell tells us in his comments on Pylyshyn's lead paper and in his own lead paper on artificial intelligence is most illuminating on the issues we have discussed here.[4]

Science or Nonscience, Is That the Question?

We have discouraged some of our contributors from using much space for discussing whether a particular discipline is true science or something else. Several of them decided, even without our advice, not to expatiate on this sterile topic. We did not, however, wield a red pencil to delete all comments on whether something was a science, or "only" philosophy, speculation, technology, practical art, professional training, and so forth. We knew that

---

[4] Among the most intriguing is Newell's story of neuroscience, "also an interdiscipline—the neuro parts of anatomy, physiology, pharmacology, and biochemistry—just working itself up to disciplinary status," but participating "in the central paradigm of modern biology." (See Newell's paper in Section 1 of this volume.)

many writers in information science had guilt feelings about the fact that this discipline had neither discovered new laws nor invented new theories and therefore did not deserve recognition as a science. Such an inferiority complex is the result of indoctrination with an outmoded philosophy of science, with persuasive (propagandist) definitions of science and scientific method.[5]

The restrictive meaning of science, taught in courses and texts in experimental natural sciences and designed to exclude other academic disciplines from the class of sciences, occurs only in English. Neither French nor German—nor any other language, to our knowledge—has words to express the narrow concept of science or any expressions equivalent to scientific method. [Machlup, 1980, pp. 67–69.] If the restriction of the term to eligible disciplines could serve any scientific purpose, the French, Germans, Russians, Japanese, and others would surely have coined words to express what their English-speaking colleagues had in mind. Still, some contributors to this volume do allude to conflicts between science and philosophy, science and unverified belief, science and art, science and technology, science and profession. These issues are therefore briefly addressed in the Epilogue by Fritz Machlup.

For present purposes, we may confine ourselves to the statement that we do not care, and no one else need care, whether information science, library science, computer science, decision science, system science, or any of the disciplines discussed in this volume, are genuine sciences. Little depends on the decision to deny this honorific designation to a particular discipline.[6] If little or nothing follows from the distinction between science and nonscience, it is not worth investing much time making or defending it. Too bad that even a little time has to be spent showing that the distinction is mischievous.

SOME TRANSDISCIPLINARY ISSUES

The titles of the papers contributed to this volume contain the names of twenty disciplines or subdisciplines. The texts of the papers contain refer-

---

[5] ". . . the attempt to define scientific method or to analyze science is a search for a *persuasive* definition . . . the term 'science' has no definite and unambiguous application." (Black, 1949, p. 69.) "Neither observation, nor generalization, nor the hypothetic-deductive use of assumptions, nor measurement, nor the use of instruments, nor mathematical construction—nor all of them together—can be regarded as essential to science." (Ibid., pp. 80–81.)

[6] If someone points to the differences in salaries of librarians, physicists, and computer specialists, the explanation lies in supply and demand, not in discriminatory designations of their fields. However, it may be possible that agencies and foundations supporting research are persuaded to favor grant applications for supposedly more scientific projects: "The charge of being 'unscientific' is not mere namecalling; it is a charge with financial consequences. It has to do with what research gets funded and therefore with what research gets carried out." (Lakoff, 1978, pp. 267–268.) We suspect, however, that it is not the magic of the word scientific that charms the grantors but rather the lure of research leading to practical findings.

ences to or discussions of innumerable disciplines or subdisciplines; in forty of these, the term *information,* in one of its several meanings, plays a key role. We shall not undertake a survey of the whole lot, but we feel an intellectual obligation to select a few of the fields for commentary in this introductory chapter, because representatives of these fields have expressed conflicting views on their methodological nature, their scope, and pragmatic significance. Our interpretations and suggestions may differ—in some instances quite drastically—from some of the pronouncements of our contributors, notwithstanding the fact that it is thanks to their statements that we have reached our present positions. Indeed, before we studied their papers, we had seen some of the interconnections and relations among the fields in question quite differently from the way we do now. This is especially true with regard to general system theory and should not surprise readers of the papers dealing with this field: They will find that intradisciplinary conflict and controversy are rampant. Intradisciplinary dissension becomes particularly pronounced when representatives of a subject try to clarify its relations to other disciplines.

Before offering our commentaries on selected areas of research and instruction, we shall say a few words on transdisciplinary and interdisciplinary issues.

The Balance between Research and Instruction or Training

Some of the conflicts about the scientific character of a field commonly called science are due to prejudice with respect to a scientist's proper activities. The high priests of the scientific establishment have created a pecking order giving highest rank to the successful researcher, second highest to the plodding researcher (with some publications to his credit), third rank to the teacher (without meritorious publications), and lowest rank to the professional who only practices some of the things (know-how or skill) included in the curriculum of the school, department, or academic program that disseminates the knowledge embodied in the discipline. A fifth category is usually disregarded: those who have studied and mastered the discipline but are not active as researchers, teachers, or practitioners.

Like many or most hierarchical distinctions, ranking the level of science according to the activities in which those trained in the field are engaged is largely a matter of snobbism and arrogance. Should the question of how much of a science a particular discipline is be answered by calculating the proportions of basic researchers, applied researchers, teachers, consultants, and practitioners who have acquired advanced degrees in the discipline? Is biophysics really more of a science than biochemistry just because the proportion of degree holders employed by universities is greater? Does molecular genetics become less of a science when many of its professors move into industry? Is computer science or one of its specialties, such as artificial-intelligence research, downgraded because increasing numbers in the field or specialty are yielding to the pecuniary inducements of nonacademic employment? For many decades, the majority of degree holders in chemistry and geology have been employed in other than academic positions, but have they for that reason regarded themselves as nonscientists? All these questions are rhetorical, inviting, in our opinion, negative replies.[7] If we are right and *the status of a science is not determined by what those who have studied it are doing for a living,* then some of the self-doubts of professors of practical sciences could be removed. Professors in schools of information science, computer science, and/or library science need not forego the self-esteem usually cultivated by "true scientists."

Formal and Empirical Sciences

A more detailed discussion of the distinction between formal (or rational) and empirical sciences will be deferred to the last chapter, but a few words are needed here to introduce our characterization of some of the disciplines discussed in this volume. That logic and pure mathematics are the prototypes of formal science, convey truth by resolution (a priori) and therefore cannot be tested and disproved by experience (a posteriori), and can be applied to propositions about the real world in attempts to test these propositions for consistency and formal validity—all these are verities with which most educated people are familiar. Less well known is the fact that new developments in scientific reasoning can extend the scope of logic as well as mathematics and that some novel disciplines, or some of their parts, belong to the domain of formal science. When purely formal statements (axioms, heuristic postulates, analytical conventions, paradigms, rigid laws, and

---

[7]The issue of practical versus pure sciences is perhaps most easily clarified by contrasting medical science with medical practice. Clearly, medical *research, teaching* medicine, and *practicing* medicine are three different activities. No matter whether students of medicine plan to become researchers, professors, or practitioners, they will have to be educated in several medical and cognate sciences—anatomy, physiology, chemistry, biochemistry, pharmacology, cardiology, ophthalmology, otolaryngology, gynecology, psychiatry, and several others. The majority of medical students plan to take a degree of doctor of medicine and obtain a license to practice medicine. In their capacity as practitioners, doctors are not scientists, though they have mastered a good many sciences. Those engaged in medical research and/or in teaching medicine may spend part of their time as practicing physicians; their scientific work consists of research, publication, and teaching; but many medical doctors double as *scientists and practitioners.* None of the sciences taught in medical schools is less of a science due to the fact that the ratio of those who have studied it and are "only" practitioners is much larger than in other fields. An enthusiastic teacher-scholar may take pride in the fact that a larger percentage of students choose to engage in research rather than in medical practice, but this does not reflect on the discipline professed. Likewise, a medical school that produces relatively large numbers of medical researchers will have a much better reputation than one that produces only practitioners. But this has nothing to do with the scientific character of disciplines taught in medical schools. It is possible, of course, that the *way* the discipline is presented to students is affected by the knowledge of the vocational-career orientation of most students, and, thus, the scientific level of the presentation might be lowered.

scientific research programs) are applied to empirical propositions (based on observations or generalizations), expositors are often misled in their discernment of the analytical or synthetic character, not only of propositions and general theories, but also of entire specialities and disciplines. Whether these areas of inquiries should be assigned to the category of formal sciences or to the category of empirical sciences is sometimes hard to decide. It happens that such doubts prevail regarding the nature of several of the disciplines dealing with information.

Information science is not involved in any such methodological controversy, chiefly because no agreement exists about its object or objects. By and large, information scientists deal with practical matters and, therefore, with the world of experience. *Library science* is clearly empirical in all its aspects: bibliographical work, cataloging, indexing, reference services, management, organization, acquisition, circulation, and all the rest; every phase of research in this field is practical-empirical. The case of *computer science* is not quite so obvious, because there is some formalism behind a few of the research agenda and some innovational projects; still, on closer examination, sound judgment will assign computer science to the category of empirical disciplines. This holds also for its semiautonomous subdiscipline, *artificial intelligence.*

Cognitive science, a recently developed metadiscipline comprising almost a dozen interdisciplines, gives us difficulties, because not all of these subdomains are equally easy to characterize. Among the traditional disciplines that are partly engaged in interdisciplinary bonding is philosophy; it is joined with psychology on the one hand and with linguistics on the other. Should the philosophy of psychology and the philosophy of language be regarded as empirical if only one partner in the joint venture is in the epistemic domain, in the domain of experience and observation? We are inclined to answer affirmatively. Nonempirical reasoning, although not subject to testing and falsification, does not transport the synthetic propositions about observed or experienced phenomena and processes into the domain of pure construction or evaluation. The empirical strain in the pair dominates the nonempirical, which, thus, is the recessive one.

One other subdomain of cognitive science open to question about its methodological status is the interdiscipline formed by the cross-connections between computer science and neuroscience, both of which are clearly empirical fields. Why, then, should any question arise regarding the empirical nature of the joint research efforts of two empirical disciplines? It is the designation given to the interdiscipline that can make us suspicious: The name *cybernetics*—the theory of communication and control—can raise doubts (which will become clear presently when we discuss cybernetics). Our tentative conclusion, at this juncture, is that the name does not fit the interdiscipline in question. Joint research in neuroscience and computer science cannot be anything but empirical. Regarding other subdomains of cognitive science, no doubt about their empirical nature can be entertained.

Semiotics and linguistics, the science of signs and the science of those signs that make up language, respectively, deal with observable objects. Although a good deal of the reasoning in these disciplines is formal and, thus, in the domain of mental construction, the subject matter is no doubt empirical.

We now come to disciplines of a rather different character, and we want to state that we have approached them with a minimum of preconceptions regarding their methodological status. After careful study of the papers in this volume and of some of the earlier literature on *cybernetics* and *general system theory* (including mathematical system theory), we have come to the following conclusions about the relation between these fields and their places in the universe of learning.

Cybernetics is a method of examining interactive parts of any system of communication and control, with particular emphasis on feedback and homeostasis. It is part and parcel of general system theory, which is concerned with these and also other relations among parts of a whole and between the whole and its environment. General system theory, which thus comprises cybernetics, is a method of organizing one's thinking in terms of interrelated elements in closed or open sets. It is part of the general methodology of nomological disciplines. General methodology, which thus comprises general system theory, is "the second part of logic" (sometimes called material logic in contrast to formal logic). (Windelband, 1913, p. 22.)

To summarize, cybernetics is a part of general system theory, which is a part of methodology, which is a part of logic. All of these may be given the designation of disciplines or sciences, though not empirical sciences. Whenever formal sciences are applied to the interpretation of phenomena, or of relations among phenomena, the resulting propositions are parts of the discipline or disciplines that are concerned with the phenomena or relations in question. To offer examples, mathematics and methodology applied to molecular biology yield molecular biology; system theory applied to macroeconomics yields macroeconomics; and cybernetics applied to neurophysiology yields neurophysiology.

More will be said later, both about cybernetics and general system theory in special sections of this introductory essay. Our next question for the present discussion of formal versus empirical science concerns the status of *information theory* in the narrow form of the mathematical theory of communication. With its progenitor, Claude Shannon, and his precursors, Harry Nyquist and Ralph Hartley, all of them researchers at Bell Laboratories doing mission-oriented research on electrical circuitry and signal transmission, one would hardly have any serious doubts about this kind of work being empirical. Yet, we shall argue that the strategic propositions of Shannon's theory are purely formal uses of general probability theory applied to assumed states of assumed objects; they are analytical relations derived from definitions and other resolutions.

This statement may sound strange to ears not attuned to methodological dissonances. Can one reasonably conclude that purely formal propositions, a purely analytical framework, may have a proper place in a practical-empirical discipline? The answer is affirmative; yes, indeed. However, the *use* of formal systems and abstract models in a discipline is not conclusive evidence that the discipline is formal or empirical. We reserve judgment on the methodological status of information theory, especially since information theory comes in numerous dresses and guises, manifestations and incarnations.

PROFILES OF SOME SELECTED DISCIPLINES

If we were to attend to the traditional tasks of introducing a collective volume, we should have to say a few words about each of the papers. We prefer to think that the papers need no introduction. Perhaps we should have offered introductory remarks to each of the nine sections in which the volume is organized; we have decided against this scheme, because the interdisciplinary character of many of our authors' messages makes it more desirable to bring the editors' comments "up front." We shall offer brief sketches, or profiles, of information science, computer science, artificial intelligence, cognitive science, semiotics and linguistics, cybernetics, system theory, and information theory. The sketches are not intended to summarize the messages conveyed in the papers, still less to criticize or take sides. They may, we hope, be of service to readers who are quite unfamiliar with the subject matter.

Information Science

We have detected at least four main uses of the term information science in the literature: (1) In its broadest sense, it stands for the systematic study of information and may include all or any combination of the academic disciplines discussed in this volume; (2) when included in the phrase *computer and information science,* information science denotes the study of the phenomena of interest to those who deal with computers as processors of information; (3) in *library and information science,* it indicates a concern with the application of new tasks and new technology to the traditional practices of librarianship; and (4) in its narrow sense, information science is used as the name for a new area of study that is evolving from the intersection of the other three mentioned areas, with perhaps a special interest in improved communication of scientific and technological information and in the application of well-tested research methods to the study of information systems and services.

The earliest formal use of the term information science in the United States seems to have been in the description of a program in computer and information science at the Moore School of Electrical Engineering, University of Pennsylvania, in 1959. [Wellisch, 1972, p. 164.] However, an Institute of Information Scientists had been formed in the United Kingdom in May 1958, although the use of the term information scientist may have been intended to differentiate *information* scientists from *laboratory* scientists, since the main concern of members was with the management of scientific and technological information. [Farradane, 1970, p. 143.] The level of subject expertise needed to handle this information dictated that it be done by scientists fully qualified in the disciplines concerned, rather than by librarians with a knowledge of only general science terminology.

Cultural Diversity and the Melting Pot

The early work in the broad area of information science is well characterized by the subheading chosen for these paragraphs. Scientists and scholars from a variety of disciplines were attracted to the new area of research and teaching; they brought with them their own research methods and terminology resulting in a Babel of sorts. Librarians found it difficult to interact with mathematicians; cognitive psychologists had problems in dealing with physicists; and social epistemologists considered engineers to be a breed apart. This variety of interests is reflected even today in the membership of the only society in the United States that seeks to cater to all information professionals—The American Society for Information Science. [King, Krauser, and Sague, 1980.]

The great melting pot of information science included, among other things, electrical engineering (e.g., research on signal transmission over noisy channels), computer technology (e.g., research on information-processing by machines), biological sciences (e.g., research on information-processing in living systems), behavioral sciences (e.g., research on cognitive processes), and social sciences (e.g., research on the sociology of knowledge). Not that there were many who engaged in all of these areas of inquiry, but there were some who concentrated on one or two and did so under the banner of information science. However, assembling under a banner is not the same thing as eliminating cultural diversities in the processes ascribed to the melting pot: The diversities remain and no unified science emerges.

The Power of the Plural S

We submit that most of the confusion caused by the use of the term information science in its broadest sense could be avoided by the addition of the plural *s*. The information sciences could then take their place alongside the natural sciences, the social sciences, and other umbrella terms that indicate a grouping of disciplines and fields of study that share a common characteristic. The bond among the information sciences is, of course, their focus on information as the object of study, though it is important to bear in mind that the word *information* is interpreted very differently by various groups of researchers. [For a discussion of "What They Mean by Information," see Machlup's Epilogue.]

The assemblage of different fields under the collective designation would have solved a good many problems or pseudoproblems. Like the natural sciences and the social sciences, the information sciences need no single paradigm, no overarching scientific research program, no common fundamental postulates and axioms, no unified conceptual framework.[8]

Computer and Information Science

The omission of the plural *s* in the combination of computer and information science has also proved misleading. Was it intended to bring two sciences into the same organizational unit or to forge one science out of two? In the latter case, hyphens would have been needed to show that the word *computer* shared with *information* the function of a modifier of *science*: computer-and-information science. On the other hand, if no complete union, but only cohabitation, was intended, the continued coexistence of the two sciences should have been recognized by a plural *s*. This had evidently been in the thoughts of earlier concerned scientists; thus, the Curriculum Committee on Computer Science of the Association for Computing Machinery told us in their report in 1968 that although they had decided to use the term computer science, others, "wishing perhaps to take in a broader scope and to emphasize the information being processed, advocate calling this discipline 'information science' or, as a compromise, 'the computer and information sciences'." (ACM Curriculum Committee, 1968, p. 153.) Note that the plural *s* here is intended to indicate two separate sciences—computer science and information science—and not the information sciences in the sense of an umbrella term. Incidentally, although the use of the compound computer and information science (with or without the plural *s*) is more usual, some authors do use the terms computer science and information science interchangeably. [See, for example, Pylyshyn, 1970, p. 61, and Wegner in this volume.]

There was, of course, a good reason for getting studies of the computer and information under one roof. The interest of computer scientists in information tends to be confined to its role in computer systems and to involve signs, symbols, and so forth (the semiotic approach), and their processors (the informatic approach). [See papers by Gorn, and Pearson and Slamecka in this volume.]

Library and Information Science

What has been said about missing hyphens and the plural *s* holds also for the combination between the study of the library and the study of information.

---

[8] Most schools and even some universities offer courses called *science* and *social science*, evidently presenting surveys of several disciplines under each title. We consider the omission of the plural *s* in these instances as a benighted practice.

One needs to decide whether two separate but cognate subjects ought to be housed under one roof or whether they should be fused into one science with the research effort fully integrated. Most writers and teachers have not made up their minds, and by omitting both hyphens and the plural *s*, they put an unstructured string of words on their letterheads.

The type of information science that grew out of the documentation movement of the 1960s, and is taught mainly in library schools, has a focus different from that of the computer scientists. The emphasis is on better techniques for managing recorded information in whatever medium it resides. There is concern with how the records will be used and, therefore, with their intellectual content. Much of the information-science activity in this field centers on the application of new technology to traditional library functions of acquiring, storing, retrieving, displaying, and disseminating records—in other words, on technically improved librarianship. Thus far, there is little evidence that the new technology has been exploited to produce radically new ways of handling the store of knowledge recorded in library and other materials. But there is no doubt that new tasks have been assigned to librarians, for example, the management of information centers concerned with nonbibliographic information, participation in resource-sharing networks made necessary by the increasing volume of recorded knowledge and dwindling library budgets, retrieval from electronic online databases made possible by the new computer and communications technology, and so on.

The eagerness with which library schools have moved to incorporate the word *information* into their titles is proof that their deans and faculties view the new technological developments in information handling as vital for their growth or even their survival. A recent article pointed out that " 'Information' is now contained in the names of fully 37 of the 70 schools appearing in the most recently revised list of programs accredited by the American Library Association, although only one (Syracuse's School of Information Studies) has forsaken the word 'library' altogether." (Harter, 1982, p. 40.)

But although library schools are quick to enlarge their curricula to include aspects of information studies, there is a question whether this is always a substantive change in disciplinary orientation. Often courses in information science consist merely of teaching students to use a new tool, the computer—something that will eventually be done at earlier stages in the schooling process, at the secondary, if not elementary, level. (Learning to use a computer will soon be regarded as a basic skill.) On a somewhat higher level is teaching data retrieval from online electronic databases, which is now taught and may well remain in the curricula of library schools. Still, this sort of training cannot reasonably be regarded as information science. To qualify for that designation, the respective studies should involve designing, building, and programming the online retrieval systems.

The discipline of library science, or librarianship, onto which this new type of information science is being grafted has a long and proud tradition of service. Its origins and development, and the disciplinary dilemma it faces in this era of information technology, are eloquently described by Boyd Rayward and the commentators in Section 5 of this volume and need not be profiled separately here. [See also Buckland, 1983.]

Narrowly Focused Information Science

We have characterized information science in the broadest sense as a rather shapeless assemblage of chunks picked from a variety of disciplines that happen to talk about information in one of its many meanings. We have then looked at information science oriented toward the needs or interests of computer scientists. The third kind of information science was that which would have an intimate liaison with library science. We shall now ask ourselves whether there can be an independent information science with a narrower focus—the problem of information linked neither to computer science nor to library science and also avoiding the vagueness associated with information science in its broadest sense.

Perhaps such a discipline will evolve, but we doubt that it now exists. Among research projects reported in this narrow field of information science are studies of patterns of communication among scientists and scholars (e.g., cocitation analysis); studies of improved methods of classifying information (e.g., computer-based cataloging of documents); statistical studies of the growth and distribution of the literature (e.g., the area known as bibliometrics); novel methods of information exchange (e.g., electronic information networks, teleconferencing, etc.); control of access to information (e.g., governmental regulation of information transfer, international communications conventions, etc.); modeling and computer simulation of information systems and networks; studies of the characteristics and behavior of users of information systems and services; studies of human factors involved in the design of man/machine systems; and so on.

It is difficult to say whether these types of research constitute an independent discipline or are merely developments that belong in either computer science or library science. There is no doubt, however, that information service and knowledge analysis are growing branches in most developing economies and that there is a need for trained information professionals.[9] But received wisdom suggests that an academic discipline without unique and substantial research objectives would lose its internal dynamism. To generate such a research program, we need professional schools of information sciences (with a plural *s*). Several of these cooperative sciences offer promising opportunities for research. If schools persist in using the singular information science, it is our belief that as subsets of research activities in

---

[9] For a discussion of the concept of the information professional, and the results of a statistical survey of information professionals employed in organizations in the United States, see *The Information Professional: Survey of an Emerging Field*. [Debons, King, Mansfield, and Shirey, 1981.]

the area make significant progress, they will adopt identifying titles of their own, as did the area of artificial intelligence within computer science.

Computer Science

Our first question about computer science is whether its subject is the computer itself, a highly complicated machine, or rather what is being done with computers, namely, the processing of all sorts of information. This is controversial, even among those who teach computer science, with those who favor the information focus recommending that the name of the discipline be *computer and information science* or, better still, following the continental European practice, *informatics*. [See Gorn's lead paper in this volume.]

In their preliminary recommendations for an undergraduate program in computer science, the Curriculum Committee of the Association for Computing Machinery supported the second position:

> Computer Science is concerned with *information* in much the same sense that physics is concerned with energy; it is devoted to the *representation, storage, manipulation* and *presentation* of information in an environment permitting automatic information systems. As physics uses energy transforming devices, computer science uses information transforming devices. (ACM Curriculum Committee, 1965, p. 544.)

The first position has been taken by Anthony Ralston. He insisted that "information is no more uniquely the province of computer science than energy is of physics. . . . The unique aspect of computer science is the computer." (Ralston, 1971, p. 1.) Many authoritative writers in the field concur with this view: "Phenomena breed sciences. There are computers. Ergo, computer science is the study of computers." (Newell, Perlis, and Simon, 1967, p. 1373.)

The machine in question is the general purpose automatic electronic digital computer. Digital computers deal with *discrete* (numeric and nonnumeric) quantities, as opposed to analogue computers, which deal with *continuous* flows.[10] Design of both types of computers was a specialty of the field of electrical engineering, and operating and maintaining analogue computers has remained a subspecialty within that discipline. However, the enormously complex task of designing, programming, operating, and maintaining the all-purpose digital computer gave rise to the development of a separate discipline, *computer science*.

---

[10] "*Digital computers* operate arithmetically, or according to other logical rules, on strings of digits, generally on the BINARY SCALE. . . . As they work by manipulating symbols and not by direct analogues of the quantities represented, their accuracy in numerical work is limited only by the size of their STORE and the nature of the ALGORITHM used, and they are equally capable of operation on nonnumerical information." (Strachey, 1977, p. 122.)

The choice of the name computer for the machine in question has proved to be somewhat misleading. To be sure, the initial applications of these machines were to processing numbers. Digital computers, however, can and do manipulate entities that are *symbolic representations* of other things. We have no estimate, but no doubt a very large portion of their use now is for processing nonnumeric contents (e.g., texts, images, and graphics); therefore, we agree with those who have suggested that symbol manipulator would have been a more appropriate name for the machine. [For example, Ralston, 1971.]

A Mathematical or an Engineering Discipline?

There is no agreement among computer scientists as to whether theirs is a mathematical or an engineering discipline. Some of the protagonists of the thesis that computer science is essentially mathematical may have been motivated by the age-old prejudice that gives scientists superior ranking over engineers. If this is what is behind the controversy, we submit that it is an irrelevancy. Mathematics is no doubt essential in the training and work of computer scientists. The same thing, however, can be said for a large number of other disciplines, in the natural sciences as well as the social sciences. Neither the fact that mathematics is indispensable to the discipline, nor the fact that most of the literature in the discipline makes heavy use of mathematical symbols and equations, is a sufficient criterion for the discipline being *essentially* mathematical. Certainly, it would not be sufficient for regarding it as a branch of mathematics. The use of mathematics in any field makes the field no more a part of mathematics than the use of the English language by the expositors makes the discipline part of English as an academic field.

Having said this, however, we want to stress that certain specialties within computer science, such as *algorithms, automata theory, numerical analysis,* and *symbolic manipulation,*[11] may well be called essentially mathematical. In the case of algorithms, Alan Perlis has provided us with a nice example of where mathematical activity gives way to computer-science concerns:

> The algorithms of computer programming are enormously complex and more specialized than it is the custom of mathematics to treat. It could be argued that the construction and studies of such specialized algorithms is out of place in the

---

[11] Symbolic manipulation is a field "concerned with manipulation of algebraic formulas used in algebra or calculus." (Moses in this volume.) It should not be confused with symbol manipulation, an area that studies physical symbol systems and their processing by computers. "The applications . . . of computers as nonnumeric symbol manipulators are reason enough in themselves to emphasize the symbol-manipulation point of view. Another reason, however, is that this point of view suggests an analogy with human thought processes. The human brain may also be accurately considered to be a symbol manipulator." (Ralston, 1971, p. 4.)

mathematics department; the labor of synthesis being too great for the insight into theory each such study provides. Yet these algorithms . . . deliver the power of the computer to the most demanding applications of our technological society. (Perlis, 1968, p. 71.)

Perhaps we should leave the last word on this subject with Herbert Simon, who has said that the "highly abstractive quality of computers makes it easy to introduce mathematics into the study of their theory—and has led some to the erroneous conclusion that, as a computer science emerges, it will necessarily be a mathematical rather than an empirical science." (Simon, 1969 and 1981, pp. 18–19.)

There is little doubt about the engineering nature of computer science: It designs and builds artifacts for all to see. The structure of a computer system consists of *hardware* (physical components) and *software* (specialized programs for managing the hardware). Hardware comprises electronic, electromechanical, and other devices for switching, storing, and communicating signs and signals (in the form of electrical impulses) within the system. Software consists of "a class of computer programs . . . which are used to aid in the production, debugging, maintenance, and orderly running of the other programs."[12] It may be "more important than computer hardware in determining the productivity of computer installations." (Rosen, 1976, p. 1283.) The production of software for computers has become such a critical and costly activity that in recent times attempts have been made to apply engineering principles to it, with a view to standardization. This has led to the evolution of a new specialty within computer science called *software engineering.* [Wegner in this volume.]

Closely related to engineering is the question of design. In his widely read monograph, *The Sciences of the Artificial,* Herbert Simon argues that "a science of design not only is possible but is actually emerging at the present time. It has begun to penetrate the engineering schools, particularly through programs in computer science . . . ." (Simon, 1969 and 1981, p. 58.) Saul Amarel points to a "fundamental reason for a close coupling between computer science and a science of design. It comes from . . . concern . . . with the information processes of problem solving and goal-directed decision making, which are at the core of design." (Amarel, 1976, p. 314.)

[12]The layman often has difficulty in distinguishing between the hardware, firmware, software, and programs of computer systems. One measure of distinction among them is their degree of modifiability. *Hardware* refers to the material parts of the computer system; it cannot be modified by a user. *Firmware* refers to computer programs (sets of instructions) that have been embodied in a physical device that can form part of a computing machine; it also cannot be modified by a user. *Software* refers to various programming aids that facilitate a user's efficient operation of the computer equipment (examples are assemblers, generators, subroutine libraries, compilers, operating systems, etc.); it is subject to some modification by a user. *Programs* refer to sets of instructions that tell the computer exactly how to handle a problem; they are highly modifiable and are generally tailored to fit specific user needs.

The Theoretical and the Innovational

The main endeavors of computer science are theoretical and innovational. The former builds conceptual frameworks for understanding the workings of the computer. The innovational objective is to explore new computer systems and applications in the light of new insights. Different computer scientists have different priorities. Saul Gorn emphasizes the distinction between knowledge orientation and action orientation, but he is convinced that the interaction between the two will prove most productive. [Gorn in his lead paper in this volume.]

Theoretical work in computer science over the past twenty-five years has developed slowly. The phenomenal growth of the field has drawn heavily on "fundamental research in solid-state physics, electronics, classical numerical analysis, and mathematical logic." (Perlis, 1979, p. 423.) However, there is evidence that theories such as complexity theory (the study of resource requirements of abstract algorithms) have come into existence because of the computer and the variety of tasks it performs, and not in response to problems posed purely in terms of mathematical logic. [Ibid., p. 424.] Amarel lists the following areas of theoretical work in computer science as "concentrating on comprehensive analysis of specific classes of phenomena for which formal models exist . . . theory of computation, automata theory, theory of formal languages, and switching theory" and adds that work in the "new area of analysis of algorithms (which includes important approaches to the study of computational complexity) promises to contribute significant theoretical insights into problems that are in the mainstream of the computer field." (Amarel, 1976, p. 316.)

On another level, Newell and Simon have cited their physical symbol system hypothesis to show that "computer science is a scientific enterprise in the usual meaning of that term: that it develops scientific hypotheses which it then seeks to verify by empirical inquiry." (Newell and Simon, 1976a, p. 125.)

One of the most active areas of computer research has been the development of programming languages and systems. Programming has been described by Donald Knuth as an art rather than a science. [Knuth, 1974a.] Programming *languages* are the media through which humans instruct computers to execute particular tasks. Languages operate on various levels, and versions have been developed for particular groups of users, particular areas of study, and so on. The two best-known computer programming languages are FORTRAN (for scientific applications) and COBOL (for business data-processing). But while new languages continue to be developed, "language invention no longer plays a major role in computer science research." (Perlis, 1979, p. 426.)

Of greater concern now is the development of programming *systems,* which has led to a theoretical approach to the problems of program development that is based on structured programming and the use of mathematical techniques for verification and proof in connection with the production of programs. "The aim is to produce programs that have been proved to be correct before they are tested on a computer and thereby to eliminate much of the program-testing activity." (Rosen, 1976, p. 1285.)

Another major area of innovational research in computer science is information storage and retrieval. This involves the study of efficient methods of storing and processing large quantities of data in a computer and methods of searching for and retrieving these data. It includes the very active field of *database management.*

These, then, are a few of the most publicized areas of theoretical and innovational research in computer science. But perhaps the most challenging—and the most controversial—research area of all is that known as *artificial intelligence,* which is concerned with the means by which computers may perform tasks that would "require intelligence if done by men." [Minsky, 1968.] This area uses most of the traditional research methods of computer science, while adding a few special approaches of its own. (We shall devote a separate section of this chapter to this subdiscipline and no less than five papers in this volume.)

Relations to Other Disciplines

Although computer science is now developing its own research identity, its boundaries are by no means clearly defined, for it overlaps with many established disciplines. Zenon Pylyshyn has said that

> Computer scientists find themselves involved in widely diverse academic areas. They conduct research and publish papers in engineering, mathematics, economics, sociology, psychology, linguistics, philosophy, library science, the biological sciences, business, law, and the humanities, as well as in other cross-discipline areas such as communications and information theory, control theory, and general systems theory. (Pylyshyn, 1970, p. 61.)

Pylyshyn was referring to the disciplines with which computer science shares research interests, and not just to those in which the computer has found fruitful application as a tool. The widespread use of digital computers in virtually all academic disciplines presents a different sort of challenge to computer scientists: The representation of knowledge and problems of the other discipline in forms that are acceptable to computers and the development of computer methods for effectively handling these problems. As computer science becomes more and more involved in the business of other disciplines, a certain amount of transfer occurs. In their paper in this volume, Pearson and Slamecka have enumerated some of these migrations: "information systems and database areas into management science, computer-aided design into mechanical engineering and architecture, . . . and very-large-scale integration (VLSI) onto a new turf shared by physics, electronics, and materials science and engineering."

This leads Pearson and Slamecka to ponder on what will remain in the core of the computer-science curriculum, and they speculate that "the knowledge-oriented component of this core will be concerned principally with the theory of signs, sign structures, sign processes, and algorithms. The disturbing thought is that, if this scenario is correct, the educational programs in today's departments of computer science . . . are not very relevant." (Pearson and Slamecka in this volume.)

Which brings us back to the question with which we started: Whether *information* and its processing, or *the computer* as a configuration of hardware, firmware, software, and programs, is the central object of study in computer science.

Artificial Intelligence

There seems to be general agreement that artificial intelligence (AI) is a part, although an isolated part, of computer science.[13] It has been described as an "audacious effort to duplicate in an artifact what we humans consider to be our most important, our identifying property—our intelligence." (McCorduck, 1979, p. xi.) Marvin Minsky, one of the pioneering researchers in this field, suggests that it shares its goals with other disciplines:

> With computer science we try to understand ways in which information-using processes act and interact. With philosophy we share problems about mind, thought, reason, and feeling. With linguistics we are concerned with relations among objects, symbols, words, and meanings. And with psychology we have to deal not only with perception, memory, and such matters but also with theories of ego structure and personality coherence. (Minsky, 1979, p. 400.)

External Influences

Artificial intelligence benefited from a rich intellectual heritage. Work in *mathematical logic* (mainly by Frege, Whitehead and Russell, Tarski, and Church) had demonstrated that some aspects of reasoning could be formalized. Work on *computation* by Turing and others linked the formalization of reasoning to the computing machines that were ripe for development. And the abstract conception of computation as *symbol processing* had been firmly established: Even before the first computers were designed, Turing had seen that "numbers were an inessential aspect of computation—they were just one way of interpreting the internal states of the machine." (Barr and Feigenbaum, 1981, p. 4.)

The cyberneticists also exerted considerable influence on research in

---

[13] The term *artificial intelligence* was first used formally in the title of the Dartmouth Summer Research Project on Artificial Intelligence, held during the summer of 1956. It is attributed to John McCarthy, an AI pioneer and the principal organizer of that conference. [McCorduck, 1979, p. 96.]

artificial intelligence: They linked ideas about the workings of the nervous system with logic and computation. To quote Minsky again,

> AI grew out of the cybernetics of the 1940s with the hope that the limitations of that methodology might be overcome by the new ideas coming from computation—particularly the recognition that programs themselves, rather than their applications, were objects of scientific interest. . . . The era of cybernetics was a premature anticipation of the richness of computer science. The cybernetic period seems to me to have been a search for simple, powerful, general principles upon which to base a theory of intelligence. (Minsky, 1979, p. 401.)

Computation and Intelligence

Such questions as *can computers think* and *are computers intelligent* can be answered only on the basis of agreed definitions of thinking and intelligence. According to Newell and Simon, who have done ground-breaking work on intelligent systems, "there is no 'intelligence principle,' just as there is no 'vital principle' that conveys by its very nature the essence of life." Rather, they point to structural requirements for intelligence, one of which is the ability to store and manipulate symbols. "Symbols lie at the root of intelligent action, and one of the fundamental contributions to knowledge by computer science has been to explain, at a rather basic level, what symbols are." (Newell and Simon, 1976*a*, p. 114.)

Artificial intelligence has been described as "the study of intelligence as computation." (Hayes, 1973, p. 40.) But there is some controversy as to whether computation may be applied to the cognitive or subcognitive level. [See the papers by Barr and Hofstadter in this volume.]

A distinction has been drawn between artificial intelligence and computational psychology (simulation of cognitive processes). Margaret Boden admits that there is "a difference in emphasis between workers who try to make a machine do something, irrespective of how humans do it, and those who aim to write a program that is functionally equivalent to a psychological theory." But she adds that

> most programs depend, at least in part, on the programmer's intuitive notions (implicit theories) about how people function in comparable circumstances [and] the distinction between these two categories of machine research is becoming less clear and less relevant with increasing appreciation of the difficulties involved in 'powerful' programming, that is, programming that enables the machine to function intelligently. (Boden, 1977, p. 5.)

Programs as Objects of Scientific Interest

Artificial intelligence research is centered on the art and science of computer programming. Indeed, two factors that served to isolate AI within computer science were (1) its choice of *heuristic* programming techniques, as distinct from the algorithms favored by computer scientists; and (2) its development of *list-processing* program languages, when the rest of computer science was moving toward the use of compilers.[14] Allen Newell has pointed to these isolating factors, and added a third, which became apparent as soon as the discipline of computer science identified itself with digital computers, relegating analogue computers to a subsection of electrical engineering: (3) The digital-computer people initially regarded computers as machines that manipulated *numbers*, whereas the group interested in artificial intelligence saw computers as machines that manipulated *symbols*. [Newell in his lead paper in this volume.]

According to Newell, the choice by AI workers of programming systems as the class of systems to describe intelligent behavior, "led to psychologically revealing tasks" and caused the AI group to turn to the discipline of psychology for inspiration. It was a two-way partnership, with AI exerting an influence on psychology, principally in the areas of problem-solving and concept formation. "However, when psychology opted to concentrate on memory structure, psychology and AI went fundamentally separate ways. Psychologically relevant work on memory by AI researchers did exist, but moved out of AI into psychology." (Newell in his lead paper in this volume.)

Connections with Brain Theory

The decision by AI researchers to turn to psychology, rather than neurophysiology, for inspiration was the subject of comment by Michael Arbib:

> Virtually no eminent workers in AI feel it important to relate their research to actual brain mechanisms. Some, like Newell and Simon, are interested in using AI to shed new light on human problem-solving, but such studies are psychological rather than neurophysiological. The brain theorist, on the other hand, studies neural networks, be they representative of actual brain structures, of a regular geometry conducive to simulation or the proving of theorems, or of interest mainly for the way in which their connections change over time. Most of the functions dominating AI work simply are at too high a level for their expression in neural networks to be ripe for study. (Arbib, 1975a, p. 270.)

So the cyberneticists and others work independently of AI researchers in modeling the human brain. Arbib gives us a glimpse of their work in the field of brain theory in his two papers in this volume.

---

[14] "List-processing languages are computer languages that facilitate the processing of data organized in the form of lists. . . . LISP (short for LISt Processing) . . . one of the most popular of such languages . . . was developed by John McCarthy and his associates at M.I.T. during the late 1950s and early 1960s." (Slagle, Dixon, and Jones, 1978, pp. 778–779.) Compiling techniques for computer languages appeared with the advent of algebraic languages in the mid-1950s. They were used originally for numerical computation; almost all of the major computer languages are compiled (COBOL, FORTRAN, PASCAL, etc.).

The Internal Organization of AI

Within AI itself, several subfields evolved, each with its own specific interests, research techniques, and terminology. In addition to work on special programming languages and tools, these included research on natural-language understanding, vision, problem-solving, game-playing, theorem-proving, and so forth. It soon became clear that the main AI programs all used the same fundamental technique—*heuristic search*. [Newell and Ernst, 1965.] However, "as the scope of AI programs seemed to narrow, there arose a belief by some AI scientists that the essence of intelligence lay not in search, but in large amounts of highly specific knowledge, or *expertise*. . . . The subfield called 'expert systems' . . . emerged in the mid-1970s in part as a result of this emphasis." (Newell in his lead paper in this volume.)

As heuristic search with little knowledge of the task domain gave way to knowledge-intensive programs, the area of *knowledge engineering* (computer-based management of given assemblages of "knowledge") was born. This has led to the development of so-called expert systems that can match the diagnostic skills of a human expert in a relatively limited domain. However, it is important to remember that knowledge is here being used in a very restricted sense. To quote from *The Handbook of Artificial Intelligence,* "we often talk of list-and-pointer data structures in an AI database as knowledge per se, when we really mean that they represent facts or rules when used by a certain program to behave in a knowledgeable way." (Barr and Feigenbaum, 1981, p. 143.)

With the development of expert systems on computers, many workers in AI believed that the time had come for them to move away from work on toy tasks (small illustrative tasks, such as manipulation of blocks by a "seeing" computer) and onto work on real tasks (e.g., construction of expert systems for medical diagnosis). Douglas Hofstadter in his paper in this volume suggests that this move is counterproductive for the basic scientific interests of the field.

Robotics

One area of AI involvement in real tasks does not appear to be in dispute. Bertram Raphael has stated that "interest [by AI researchers] in the development of . . . robot-like devices is both a natural consequence of past developments, and a necessary stimulant to future research in the evolution of artificial intelligence and non-numerical problem solving." (Raphael, 1970, p. 455.) He defines a robot as "a computer-controlled mechanism that can interact with its real-world environment in an autonomous, reasonably intelligent manner." (Ibid.) This is in contrast to the relatively simple devices known as industrial robots that can be programmed to perform some repetitive task in a fixed environment. "The initial growth of industrial robots took place largely outside of AI as a strictly engineering endeavor.

. . . [it] tended to minimize the intelligence involved, e.g., the sensory-motor coordination." (Newell in his lead paper in this volume.)

On the other hand, during the late 1960s, three major AI research groups (at Massachusetts Institute of Technology, Stanford Research Institute, and Stanford University) pioneered work on intelligent robots. Vision was coupled with arms and motion and (at one center) with speech, so that "these heuristic robot systems have exhibited behavior more complex than that of any other robot systems in existence." (Raphael, 1970, p. 456.) The renewed association of AI with robotics takes advantage of the continued advance in vision research in AI during the 1970s.

Allen Newell points to the unresolved question of whether robotics is "a central part of AI or only an applied domain . . . . Do graduate students in AI have to understand the underlying science of mechanics and generalized coordinate systems that are inherent in understanding manipulation and motion? Or is that irrelevant to intelligence? Cases can be made either way." (Newell in his lead paper in this volume.)

This unresolved question reminds us that AI does indeed share its goals with other disciplines, as Minksy said. Clearly, a high degree of cooperation among disciplines will be needed to achieve the ambitious goal of automating intelligence. One area that promises to be of special interest to AI researchers is the emerging discipline—or metadiscipline—of cognitive science.

Cognitive Science

This is the youngest of the disciplines featured in this volume. One of its protagonists is not sure whether this new science, or metadiscipline, is still only "a goal rather than a reality." (Pylyshyn in his paper in this volume.) Very real, however, is the fact that a number of distinguished researchers call themselves cognitive scientists, meet in conferences, publish books, and have established a journal named *Cognitive Science;* its first volume appeared in 1977. Yet, this may have been a delayed christening. One of the founding fathers took 1956 "as the year of the birth of cognitive science." (Simon, 1980, p. 34.) A brief description of the new discipline is in order. Such a description may stress the subject matter, the major problems addressed, the techniques of analysis employed, the theoretical formalisms adopted, and a genealogical map showing from which disciplines the new one has descended. [Collins, 1977.]

The Scope and Nature of the New Science

Cognitive science is "the domain of inquiry that seeks to understand intelligent systems and the nature of intelligence. . . . At the root of intelligence are symbols, with their denotative power and their susceptibility to manipulation." (Simon, 1980, p. 35.) Or, more briefly, cognitive science is "the analysis of the human mind in terms of information process." (Ibid., p. 34.)

The first of these definitions refers to intelligent systems, the latter to human mind; the idea is that both human intelligence and computer intelligence are to be studied. (Ibid.) Alternative definitions seem to avoid the terms mind and intelligence and instead refer to cognitive systems and mental faculties. (Sloan Foundation, 1978, p. viii.)

The resumption of studies of the mind constitutes a decisive break with behaviorism in psychology and neopositivism in general methodology, the two *isms* that had banished all nonobservables from the domain of science. The new area of research is the result of collaboration of members of several disciplines—of six wider fields (represented by separate departments in most universities) and eleven interdisciplines (or specialties) that are the outcome of pairwise bonding between several of the major six. As shown in the figure reproduced in the appendix to Pylyshyn's paper, psychology, philosophy, linguistics, anthropology, neuroscience, and computer science are the six fields of departmental rank; computational psychology (or simulation of cognitive processes), neuropsychology, philosophy of psychology, philosophy of language, psycholinguistics, neurolinguistics, computational linguistics, anthropological linguistics, cognitive anthropology, evolution of the brain, and cybernetics are the eleven subdomains of cognitive science. Not that they are all equally active or equally productive; indeed, some of the subdomains live only a token existence.[15]

"The most immediate problem areas" cultivated by cognitive science are "representation of knowledge, language understanding, image understanding, question answering, inference, learning, problem solving, and planning." (Collins, 1977, p. 1.) The favored techniques of analysis "include such things as protocol analysis, discourse analysis, and a variety of experimental techniques developed by cognitive psychologists in recent years." (Ibid.) Somewhat questionable is the following pronouncement about the methodological commitments of the new discipline: "Unlike psychology or linguistics[,] which are analytic sciences[,] and artificial intelligence[,] which is a synthetic science, cognitive science strives for balance between analysis and synthesis." (Ibid., p. 2.) All four disciplines compared and contrasted in this quotation are clearly empirical sciences and as such cannot do without either analysis or synthesis. Even more puzzling is the remark by the editor of *Cognitive Science* that "this discipline might have been called 'applied epistemology'." Epistemology is generally regarded as a major part of metaphysics and hence nonempirical, purely analytical; and "applied" epistemology could in a way fit any branch of knowledge. Fortunately, Pylyshyn in his paper in this volume settles the question of the methodological status of cognitive science when he declares it to be "an empirical natural science."

---

[15] With all these subdomains and contributing disciplines, one hardly expects further additions to the list. Yet some major researchers in the field have proposed additional shareholders in the new enterprise: epistemology (perhaps a stand-in for philosophy) and economics [Simon, 1980, p. 33]; and education [D. G. Bobrow, 1975.]

That cognitive science is considered a discipline with its focus on information and knowledge needs hardly any documentation; but we can profit from quoting some of the fundamental questions on its agenda: "How is information about environments gathered, classified, and remembered? How is such information represented mentally, and how are the resulting mental representations used as a basis for action? How is action coordinated by communication? How are action and communication guided by reason?" (Sloan Foundation, 1978, p. v. This part of the report to the Foundation was drafted by George A. Miller.)

"Representation," a Keyword

One of the keywords in cognitive science is representation. It is not always clear just what is being represented and what is representing.[16] One could imagine our knowledge representing something observed or assumed in the external world or our knowledge being represented by something going on or retained in our brain or nervous system; or our knowledge being represented by some expressions (visual, auditory, and tactile), artifacts (signs, signals, symbols, and codes), or various kinds of action (meaningful and communicable to others). Assuming that the stingy economizers of prepositions mean not representation *by* knowledge but representation *of* knowledge, we rule out the first of the three possible meanings; considering that most users much of the time do their research using computers, we rule out the second meaning. Thus, we conclude that the representations in question are largely in terms of computer programs.[17]

One can get an idea of the role of representation in research and analysis in cognitive science when one realizes the inordinately large number of adjectives employed to modify the noun: In three papers in one volume, we encountered visual representation, multiple representation, exhaustive representation, selective representation, formal representation, semantic-network representation, predicate-calculus representation, procedural representation, declarative representation, analogical representation, propositional representation, semantic representation, syntactic representation, intensional representation, universal-knowledge representation, and ad hoc-knowledge representation. [D. G. Bobrow, 1975; Woods, 1975; R. J. Bobrow and Brown, 1975.]

---

[16]"Through some mapping M, a representation (call it knowledge-state 1) is created which corresponds to world-state 1." Here, knowledge is representing a particular (observed? inferred? imagined?) world state. A little later, the same author speaks of the problematic "simplicity of representing particular knowledge." Here, it is knowledge that is being represented. (D. G. Bobrow, 1975, pp. 2–3.)

[17]"Clearly, the best representation for a body of knowledge depends on how that knowledge is *to be used by the program* . . . ." (R. J. Bobrow and Brown, 1975, p. 104.)

Adaptive Systems, Learning, and Evolution

A delicate philosophical problem in cognitive science is created by the fact that intelligent systems are essentially adaptive "in the face of . . . changing environments [which] creates a subtle problem in defining empirical invariants for them." (Simon, 1980, p. 36.) Simon examines malleability and adaptation on three time scales: the shortest, in which systems "change their behavior in the course of solving each problem situation they encounter"; a somewhat longer one, in which they learn, that is, "make adaptations that are preserved and remain available for meeting new situations successfully"; and the longest, in which "intelligent systems evolve," an evolution that can be biological or social or both. (Ibid., pp. 36–37.)

Realization of the adaptability of the cognitive system, especially through learning, which may be deliberately designed, caused Simon to call cognitive science "a science of the artificial." The term, although it conveys important characteristics of the systems in question, is not self-explanatory and has led many a student astray. Yet, we have to concede the main point of the argument: Cognitive science "is concerned with phenomena that could be otherwise than they are . . . and which will be altered continually as they adapt to the demands of their environments." (Simon, 1980, p. 45.) Incidentally, the fact that learning can be designed and, as a matter of fact, is designed in several ways, blurs, or perhaps destroys, the methodological boundary line between the positive and the normative. Simon is not worried about this (actually inevitable) development. Long before cognitive science, several other areas of study have experienced this boundary conflict; it has been endemic in economics, with its optimization (or economic principle); in psychology, with its positive and prescriptive learning theory; and in linguistics, with its goals of competence and performance. [Ibid., p. 43.]

Motivational and Emotional Processes

The small group of researchers that constitutes the community of researchers in cognitive science consists of dynamic and creative scholars active in this new discipline because they believe in its achievements and its promise. There may be a few outsiders who are critical or skeptical, but we cannot yet find any vociferous dissenters within the group. This makes it difficult to present a profile of this young metadiscipline. We do, however, have a few statements from leaders in the field, where they admit that little progress has been made on (or beyond) some of its frontiers. One of these relates to the understanding of motivational and emotional processes and their interaction with purely cognitive processes. [Norman, 1980.]

The lack of progress on this front is explained by the fact that "the communication codes appear to be so radically different in the affective and cognitive subsystems. Information in the cognitive system (or at least a considerable part of it) is encoded symbolically, while the signaling systems

for motivation and emotion appear much more analogical and continuous.''
(Simon, 1979, pp. 383–384.) Since computer simulation has been the major
research technique in cognitive science but seems unsuitable to research on
affective processes, the slow advance in the study of motivation and emotion is not surprising.

Semiotics and Linguistics

Of the eleven interdisciplines listed as subdomains of cognitive science, no
less than five are areas cognate to linguistics, or rather interdisciplines of
which linguistics is one of the partners: psycholinguistics, neurolinguistics,
computational linguistics, anthropological linguistics, and philosophy of language. Five out of eleven sounds like a large share; however, the subdomains' eligibility for listing was based on *some* research going on in the
subdomains, not on great activity or productivity. It seems, moreover, that
the linguists were, more or less, ''sleeping partners'' in the various under-
takings, or that the joint research was done largely by noncertified or visiting
linguists, that is, by members of the cooperating discipline doubling as linguists. If one asks some academic linguists about cognitive science or any
other of the studies of information, there may be a blank look in the eyes of
some and a disclaimer of interest voiced by others.

In addition to the five interdisciplines that link linguistics with studies of
information and knowledge, there is the metadiscipline of semiotics, the
science of signs, which is ordinarily counted among the subjects within the
wide domain of information science. Indeed, Gorn, and especially Pearson
and Slamecka in their papers in Section 2 of this volume agree that ''informatics is a semiotic discipline.'' Yet, many (perhaps most) traditional linguists reject semiotics as a legitimate member of their family, treating it as a
stepchild, or stepfather, if at all;[18] some of the papers included in Section 4
reflect this attitude.

Perhaps one should understand it as a part of usual academic-political
practice if members of an old established discipline do not easily accept
collaboration with a new fledgling interdiscipline. This cannot explain linguists' lack of enthusiasm for a close link with semiotics, but it may be
pertinent to their attitude toward the subdomains of cognitive science. The

---

[18]To avoid a confusion of historical timing, we should note that, whereas some of the interdisciplines involving linguistics have only recently arrived on the scene, semiotics is by no means a
young subject. ''Signs,'' as distinguished from ''Things'' and ''Actions,'' were among ''the
three great Provinces of the intellectual World'' mapped by John Locke in his famous *Essay*.
[John Locke, 1690.] Locke took the term semiotics from the Greek Stoics; modern semiotics
began with Charles Sanders Peirce. [Peirce, 1867.] The Swiss linguist Ferdinand de Saussure is
credited with important developments. [Saussure, 1916 and 1959.] Most widely quoted is the
exposition by Charles W. Morris. [Morris, 1939.] The studies by Roman Jakobson are cited with
special respect. [Jakobson, 1962; 1971.] A recent survey of the state of the art was published by
Thomas A. Sebeok. [Sebeok, 1976.]

affection of scholars not brought up as traditional linguists is not requited by the proper linguists. This coolness of linguists vis-à-vis their sometimes ardent suitors seeking active collaboration is well described by Allen Newell in the case of psycholinguistics. [See Newell's lead paper on artificial intelligence in Section 3.]

Another gray area within this many-faceted discipline is mathematical linguistics. Perhaps we may quote here an apt comment by Vasilii V. Nalimov, the Russian mathematician and all-round scientist:

> Linguistics, one of the most ancient sciences, is also losing its humanistic appearance. Mathematical linguistics has been created, which, in the manner of Bar-Hillel, can be divided into statistical linguistics dealing with the frequency analysis of symbol systems and structural linguistics dealing with constructing abstract models of language. If the first branch can be regarded as a result of the mathematization of science, the second results from the humanization of mathematics: problems emerging within the humanities are formulated in the frame of mathematics. At any rate, Chomsky's theory of contextfree languages is clearly a mathematical subject generated by linguistic problems.
>
> Linguistics has also acquired some purely engineering aspects. The problems of machine translation, working out languages for computers, and especially the problem of "man-computer dialogue" have added engineering features even to such a purely humanistic field as semantics, though the principal problems of semantics have retained their humanistic core. (Nalimov, 1981, pp. 204–205.)

Semiotics

Realizing that the science of signs includes the science of those signs that make up language, one cannot help seeing in semiotics the wider field that embraces linguistics. This does not imply, however, that every semioticist must be a linguist, nor that every linguist must be a semioticist. Division of labor may be strongly indicated, but one expects that the two groups know what in general the others are talking about and that both avoid using the same terms in different meanings. The second expectation is not fulfilled, in that one of the keywords, syntactic, is ambiguous.

In semiotics, syntactic is the level of sign theory at which the observer finds that he or she has reason to recognize certain things as intended signs but does not understand what they signify. In linguistics, syntactic refers to rules or regularities in grammar regarding the coordination of words and their functions in the structure of a sentence (like subject and predicate). Syntactic analysis in linguistics thus represents a higher level of sign recognition than in semiotics.

Semiotics distinguishes three levels: syntactics, semantics, and pragmatics, dealing with nine kinds of signs (such as tokens, types, and tones on the syntactic level; indexes, icons, and symbols on the semantic level). A presyntactic level (or dimension) has been proposed to cover instances where the observer sees some objects, such as ink marks on paper, patterns of chiseled grooves on rocks or stones, or tree stumps in the woods, but does not know whether they are signs; that is, artifacts that signify something, at least to the person or people who produced them and wanted to communicate to others. [Seiffert, 1968, pp. 80–81.] One speaks of the syntactic dimension when one clearly recognizes that the observed objects are signs but does not know what they signify. When what is spoken, written, or printed is in a foreign language that the observer does not understand, the signs are still in the syntactic dimension. The borderline of the semantic dimension is blurred when communication is in the recipient's own language but on a technical level not comprehensible to him, like an argument in the jargon of another scientific discipline. The reader or listener may understand almost every word, and even its grammatical function in each sentence, but still not grasp the meaning of the sentences. To be at the truly semantic level, those at the receiving end have to be somewhat familiar with the subject matter and/or with the linguistic peculiarities in which it is treated. For example, native Germans with twelve or fourteen years of schooling may fail to understand Kant's *Critique of Pure Reason* if they have had no background in philosophy. While these readers are on the semantic level with regard to the words of the text, they are only on the syntactic level as far as Kant's total message is concerned. [Seiffert, 1968, pp. 84–85.] In the pragmatic dimension, semantic comprehension is associated with action, as when the message is an invoice requiring payment or a summons to appear in court.

What contributions has semiotic research made to either the study of natural language or to studies of information? This question is debated. Views expressed in various papers in this volume show disagreement. Pearson and Slamecka hold that semiotics has promoted progress in informatics. According to a skeptical view, "the accomplishments of the research program in general semiotics . . . have not been spectacular, unless one classifies the achievements of cybernetics under this heading." (Weinreich, 1968, p. 169.) As to linguistics, the same source has this to say: "Although no sign system equals language in the variety and overlapping of semiotic devices employed, it has been instructive to embed the study of natural language in a broader investigation of sign phenomena of all kinds, including substitutes for language (e.g., flag codes) and extension of language (gesture patterns, chemical formalism, etc.)." (Ibid.)

Grammar, Inherited or Learned?

The old controversy about heredity versus environment (nature versus nurture) as major determinant of human intelligence reappeared in the field of linguistics: Was the understanding of, or feeling for, grammar entirely a result of learning or was there a predisposition for it due to genetic evolution? The terms chosen for these notions are strangely different from those customary in other areas of research and debate: Linguists like to speak of "nativism" (for the genetic source) and empiricism (for milieu and learning). The scholars associated with the two sides of the controversy are Jean Piaget, the psychologist who taught us about learning stages in children, and Noam Chomsky, the linguist who developed the theory that an understanding for grammar is an innate characteristic of humans. [Piatelli–Palmarini, 1980.] The controversy is still going on, and some of the papers in Section 4 of this volume include observations on the theme.

Cybernetics

More than any other discipline, cybernetics sprang from the head of one founding father, Norbert Wiener.[19] [Wiener, 1948 and 1961.] He regarded cybernetics as "a new scientific subject," which at the time of the second edition was "an existing science." (Ibid., p. vii.) The question is only whether the scope of that science coincides with that of Wiener's book, in the sense that cybernetics comprises all that is in *Cybernetics,* but not more. Wiener himself held that "the center of interest" in a subject that has "real vitality" is apt to "shift in the course of years." (Ibid.) Hence, cybernetics should not be limited to what Wiener put down in his book. On the other hand, not all that is covered in the book can reasonably be said to be cybernetics, since he devoted many pages and several chapters to applications of cybernetics to various empirical subjects, such as computing machines, psychology, psychopathology, social organization, learning theory, electrophysiology, and what not.

A recent leaflet by the American Society for Cybernetics contains a motley collection of definitions of cybernetics. After giving Wiener's formulation (from the title of his book) and Ampère's obsolete suggestion of the science of government, the leaflet supplies four definitions ranging from epistemology via organization theory and the science of form and pattern to the art of manipulating defensible metaphors.[20]

---

[19] It is easy to show that some of the fundamental ideas presented in Wiener's *Cybernetics*— say, the notion of (though not the term) feedback—had been known to earlier writers about reflexes and related physiological phenomena. Also, Bertalanffy's general system theory, presented in German articles, anticipated Wiener's publication. Still, the exposition of these ideas under the name cybernetics is unquestionably Wiener's.

[20] To quote in full, "For philosopher Warren McCulloch, cybernetics was an experimental epistemology concerned with the communication within an observer and between the observer and his environment. Stafford Beer, a management consultant, defined cybernetics as the science of effective organization. Anthropologist Gregory Bateson noted that whereas previous sciences dealt with matter and energy, the new science of cybernetics focuses on form and pattern. For educational theorist Gordon Pask, cybernetics is the art of manipulating defensible metaphors, showing how they may be constructed and what can be inferred as a result of their existence." (From a leaflet published by The American Society for Cybernetics, 2131 G Street NW, Washington, D.C., 20052.)

Murray Eden in his paper in the present volume considers two related insights as the most important findings of cybernetics: First, that there is an essential unity in the set of problems in communication, control, and statistical mechanics (noisy phenomena), whether they are to be studied in the machine or in living tissue. Second, that "the computing machine must represent almost an ideal model of the problems arising in the nervous system." (Eden in this volume.)

Connections or Applications?

Eden has been able to show connections, including some close ones, between cybernetics, either as a science or (more often) as a viewpoint, and some thirty other disciplines or specialties. This many-sidedness alone should suggest that the connections are not empirical conjunctures of phenomena that are common subjects of observation and explanation by the different disciplines but, instead, that cybernetics offers a technique of analysis applicable to a large variety of phenomena, natural, social, and man-made. Without hinting at the possibility of cybernetics being a methodological research program of wide applicability, Eden comes to this conclusion: "The notions of cybernetics have permeated many disciplines—computer science, information theory, control theory, pattern recognition, neurophysiology, psychophysics, perceptual psychology, robotics, and the like. Having been integrated into them, cybernetics has performed the function for which it was proposed." (Eden in this volume.)

This conclusion sounds as if cybernetics has fulfilled its mission and can be buried—which would not be the appropriate thing to do in the case of a successful and fertile, methodologically sound scientific research program. Perhaps another interpretation offered by Eden as well as by Elias, Arbib, and Mattessich explains the virtual disappearance of cybernetics from the Western academic establishment. According to that interpretation, cybernetics is a part of general system theory and has been completely absorbed by this much broader scientific research program.

When Arbib holds that "the history of cybernetics is, in large part, also the history of cognitive science," one might infer that he sees cybernetics as an empirical discipline like cognitive science. The same impression is conveyed when he reports that members of his research group used "cybernetics to refer to a conjoined study of brain theory and AI"—both clearly subjects of empirical research. On the other hand, Arbib speaks of modern system theory as "the descendant of Wiener's control theory"—and this agrees with our conception.

A Part of System Theory?

Richard Mattessich (in his paper in Section 6) supplies a neat enumeration of what he regards as the basic notions of cybernetics: organization and emergent properties; structure, hierarchy, and evolution; function and goal orientation; information, control, and feedback; environment and its influence; system laws and mathematical homologies. According to Mattessich, cybernetics is most appropriately regarded "as a subset of systems research."[21] We endorse this view.

The tendency to link cybernetics with general system theory and, even further, with information theory began in Europe almost as soon as Norbert Wiener's and Claude Shannon's works were reported. Thus, in a series of conferences held in Paris in the spring of 1950 on *Cybernétique: théories du signal et de l'information,* the first speaker defined cybernetics as "the science of relations, controls, and transmissions of information." (de Broglie, 1951, p. v.) This definition announces the unification of the triad: The science of relations is general system theory, the science of controls is cybernetics proper, and the science of transmissions of information is information theory. The speaker subsumed them all under the name cybernetics.

This merger of the three disciplines under a single name can be seen on the organization charts for the academic enterprise in Europe, but not in the United States. We doubt that most American representatives of general system theory and information theory would be prepared to accept such a take-over offer. On the other hand, a take-over of cybernetics by system theory seems to be more or less a fait accompli.

System Theory

We have long been baffled by the variants we encountered in the literature on systems. Were system theory and systems theory two different fields of study? Was system theory different from general system theory? What distinguished system theory from systems analysis, systems research, the systems approach, and systems science? All these appellations occur not only in the earlier literature but also in papers contributed to this volume. And there is systemics too.

Distinctions and Differences

Some of our contributors hold that genuine differences, either in methods or methodological positions, account for the distinctions. We have concluded that hypotheses about intended meanings of singular versus plural are inter-

---

[21] Some writers go farther and make the two disciplines one and the same: "Cybernetics is the science of general system theory." (Paul E. Martin, 1981, p. 11.) This, however, is the view of a writer based in Central Europe, who thinks that cybernetics serves chiefly to devise systems of "improved, simplified and less costly information handling [by management] in business and government," and that Stafford Beer, who wanted to design the socialist planning system of President Allende in Chile, is "one of the greatest living cyberneticians of our time." (Ibid., p. 14.) As Eden and Elias mention in their papers in this volume, the meaning of cybernetics in the Soviet Union is wider still in that it comprises mathematical economics and econometrics.

esting but not convincing. For we established that the same writers alternated in casual inconsistency between using plural and singular interchangeably in the same papers, chapters, pages, and even paragraphs. (Why were they not queried by their editors? We, too, decided to grant our contributors freedom to be inconsistent in this matter.)[22]

The question which noun is modified by general in general system theory proved even more bewildering. Was it the general theory of systems or the theory of general systems? At one point, we became convinced that the absence of a hyphen between the first two words was not deliberate but mere sloppiness. Our evidence seemed strong: The yearbooks of the Society for General Systems Research have carried the title *General Systems*, and authors wrote of general systems as contrasted with special systems. We were disabused of this conclusion when we saw foreign-language renditions of general system theory—all emphasizing the generality of the theory, not of the systems.[23] We should not be surprised, however, if a parishioner of one of the various denominations of system theory were to castigate us for downgrading the theory of general systems. The ferocity with which different system theorists attack one another's methods and methodological positions has shown us that whatever is said about systems will make some of the partisans very angry.

There is no agreement about definitions of either system or system theory.[24] This need not bother us: Scholars (scientists) may disagree on how to define a term and yet agree on its meaning. They are too proud to imitate the layman's excuse, "You know what I mean," when he is aware of failing to express himself clearly. And scholars are usually able to convey clear meanings without formulating explicit definitions; not so when they speak about systems. Still, three or four notions are mentioned as fundamental by

---

[22] One of the founding fathers of this subject matter, Ludwig von Bertalanffy, in his book on *General System* (singular) *Theory* wrote of the systems (plural) approach, and he reported that the proposed name of the Society for General System (singular) Theory was changed to Society for General Systems (plural) Research. [Bertalanffy, 1968, pp. 4, 15.] In the foreword to his book, *General System* (singular) *Theory*, he used Systems (plural) Theory in the second sentence and in the next sentence, stated that "Systems (plural) Science, or one of its many synonyms, is rapidly becoming part of the established university curriculum." (p. vii.) We can easily confirm this last statement: The system theorist George Klir professes his discipline in a Department of Systems (plural) Science. In support of those who favor the singular, we may mention that the Theory of Games (plural) is always rendered as Game (singular) Theory; likewise, the Theory of Numbers (plural) is transformed into Number (singular) Theory. On the other hand, one speaks of a numbers (plural) game, and economists talk about commodity markets and commodities markets without awareness of a possible distinction.

[23] Five years before his article "An Outline of General System Theory" [Bertalanffy, 1950], Bertalanffy published in German a paper "Zu einer allgemeinen Systemlehre." [Bertalanffy, 1945.] Similarly, we find "La théorie générale des systèmes" in French and "La teoria generale dei sistemi" in Italian.

[24] "Definitions of general systems theory differ. . . . The divergence begins at the very start when attempts are made to define a system." (Rapoport, 1976, p. 11.)

most system theorists: a whole (or assemblage, set, group, etc.), parts (or elements, objects, constituent entities, members, etc.), relations (among the parts), and sometimes, as an afterthought, environment (outside the boundaries of the system or also within it for each entity).

Interactions or Just Any Interrelations?

The biggest question arises with regard to the relations. Some writers specify interactions and thereby restrict the class of possibly relevant relations; others say interdependence, which restricts it less, but some speak of interrelations, which includes much more than interdependence and interactions. Relations among the entities may be of many kinds—for example, logical (contrariety, transitivity, etc.), spatial (next to, below, etc.), comparative (larger, faster, etc.), attitudinal (friendly, uncooperative, etc.), hierarchical (foreman, boss, etc.), kinship (son, sister, etc.)—without necessarily implying particular influences, stimuli, responses, actions, or reactions. Most of the concrete systems and special systems that are presented in the literature (as illustrations of the nature and significance of general systems) feature mutual influences, attractions, communications, and interactions. Exceptions, however, are not infrequent, and when the argument is presented in mathematical language, with any one element changing as a function of changes of all others, one can no longer make out the nature of the interrelated parts and the nature of their interdependence. There may be humans (acting on command, request, advice, or in spite; or in order to gain or to survive); cells (in a living body); neurons (firing at neighboring ones); species of animals (multiplying or dying out or evolving physiological, anatomical, or behavioral traits); molecules in different arrangements (say, in chemical substances); electrical impulses (transmitted over a channel). But the parts of the system may also be shapes and colors (on a canvas or screen); tones in various intervals (in melodic or harmonic consonances and dissonances); ink spots on pieces of paper; all sorts of patterns and configurations, arrangements, and organizations. Indeed, it is the very idea of *a general theory of systems in general* to say something about *all* kinds of entities that are interrelated members of a set (which may be a subset of another set) or of a whole (which may be part of another whole).

The question is whether much of great importance can be said about all possible systems.[25] Important in this context may mean helpful to investigators in several disciplines in their research, analysis, and interpretation; or it may mean helpful to organizers and managers in the practical world of engineering, business, and government; or helpful to philosophically minded scholars in their abstract reflections about the scientific enterprise in general.

---

[25] ". . . all we can say about practically everything is almost nothing." (Boulding, 1956b, p. 197.)

Most writers on system theory see the value of their formal theory in its aid to various other disciplines, formal or empirical. Particularly, general mathematical systems theory is said to provide foundations for other disciplines, to "offer both a conceptual framework and a working methodology." (Mesarović, 1968*b*, p. 60.) According to one authority, the logical connections among phenomena, model, and system are expressed in these two statements: "(a) A theory of any real-life phenomena . . . is always based on an image, termed a model. (b) Without introducing any constraints whatsoever the formal, invariant, aspects of that model can be represented as a mathematical relation. This relation will be termed a system." (Ibid.)

General, Special, and Concrete Systems

We have mentioned general, special, and concrete systems; perhaps we should state what, in our opinion, these adjectives may mean. A *general* system is constituted by the interrelated (interdependent, interactive) elements a, b, c, . . . in an ensemble S. We are not told what the elements are and what the ensemble is—they may be just anything. A *special* system is less abstract, in that we are told that it represents, for example, an economy in which individuals, firms, and perhaps also a government are interacting; or a human body, in which genes, nerves, blood vessels, and so forth, receive stimuli and transmit responses; or a solar system, in which stars, planets, and satellites attract one another; or a machine, in which different parts are doing what the successful designer has contrived for them to do. Specifications about interrelations among the elements of such systems will evidently take account of what the theorists who invented (or discovered?) the system believe to be plausible. The system theorist may still write a, b, c, . . . for the elements of a special system, but he or she will tell the reader whether these letters symbolize people or cells or celestial bodies or machine parts. A *concrete* system refers to presumably observable things, for which data can be procured. Thus, a concrete system is linked to happenings at a particular time in a particular place or at least to so-called records, genuine or invented by statisticians, of so-called observations, actual or inferred. For example, a concrete system of the economy may have real numbers for the money supply in the United States at certain dates and for the gross national product within certain periods. Most of the numbers in economic models are even more fictitious than the statistical aggregates mentioned, so much so that West Churchman in his paper in this volume remarks that "systems information does not correspond to empirical information at all." Such an admission is, of course, in flagrant contradiction of the confidence of mathematical system theorists who believe that there can be real data and exact and complete data that uniquely determine a model (though not in economics).

In any case, concrete systems, with numerical values substituted for all elements and relations, are incorporated into the body of the disciplines that are charged with responsibility for investigating the phenomena or records in question. As we said in an earlier section, system theory provides the principles for the organization of the data. In a similar vein, Talbot Waterman, the biologist, said that, because of their "multivariable and highly interconnected organization, living things require for their effective study some overall strategy like systems analysis." (T. H. Waterman, 1968, p. 1.)[26] Characterizing systems analysis (or system theory) as an overall strategy for studying complex structures is precisely what we meant when we alluded to analytical conventions, scientific research programs, and a few other phrases hinting at the rational, nonempirical nature of system theory and similar formal sciences, particularly methodology.

System Theory and Information Studies

In what sense can system theory or general system theory be regarded as one of the disciplines that study information or as based on such studies or as contributing to them to such an extent that it belongs to that class or family? Several partly overlapping reasons can be culled from the literature or derived from statements not necessarily intended to answer our question.

1. System theory is said to contain (more conspicuously than other disciplines) automata theory, communication theory (in one or more of its meanings), control theory, cybernetics, decision theory, game theory, information theory (in several of its meanings), and operations research, all of which are unquestioned members of the family. [Mesarović, 1968*b*.]

2. Systems composed of discrete components are at the core of computer science. Indeed, the goals of the "systems view of computer science are analogous to the goals of general systems theory." (Moses in his paper in this volume.)

3. With respect to systems of which humans are the essential members and that are designed to aid the study of (either spontaneously developed or deliberately designed) societal organizations, the interrelations are largely in the form of (direct or indirect) communications through meaningful signs, ordinarily through (spoken, written, or printed) verbal messages yielding information (in the semantic sense).

4. Where systems are collections or societies of animals, the interrelations are usually in the form of communications through signals that are interpreted as meaningful messages yielding (nonverbal but still semantic) information.

[26]Waterman went on to say that "[d]epending on the available data and the purpose of the analysis any, or more usually several, of a wide range of specific techniques may be employed ranging from the use of information theory and cybernetics to computer simulation or multivariable statistical analysis." (T. H. Waterman, 1968, p. 4.)

5. In systems whose members are neither humans nor animals, relevant interrelations among the inanimate parts are often characterized as communications that yield information (in a metaphoric, nonsemantic sense).

6. In open systems, where inputs are received from the outside-environment, these inputs are often treated as matter-energy-information-negative entropy. A closed system would gradually run down to a state of maximum entropy; only an open system, receiving inputs of "negentropy," can be maintained (and may even develop). The equivalence (in some respects) of energy and information is the subject of the mathematical theory of communication, widely known under the alias information theory.

7. Among the many kinds of special systems are information systems, designed to optimize the operations of collecting pertinent data, storing them, retrieving them at appropriate moments, processing them in appropriate ways, encoding them, transmitting them over appropriate channels, receiving and decoding them—all this in a fashion that maximizes the surplus of benefits over costs. Systems theory will guide the designing of information systems and many of the activities of system engineers and information professionals.

8. General system theory develops "a framework of general theory to enable one specialist to catch relevant communications from others" and allow knowledge to grow "by the receipt of meaningful information—that is, by the intake of messages by a knower which are capable of reorganizing his knowledge." (Boulding, 1956a, pp. 11–12.)

This is not supposed to be a complete statement of connections between system theory and information. Moreover the various connections should be questioned regarding the compatibility of the terms employed: The meanings of *system* varied somewhat and the meanings of *information* varied in essential respects, indeed so much that one may raise the charge of equivocation unless one charitably accepts a plea of innocent deception. Still, the inclusion of general system theory in the class of disciplines concerned with information seems legitimized.

This should not mean, however, that general system theory has no place outside that class. We would not want the celestial system to be treated as a discipline concerned with information. If general system theory is seen as a part of general methodology, it would be wrong to limit its relevance to studies of information, the empirical phenomenon.

Information Theory

Those who have read ten or more different expositions of this field of research (and have not been influenced by a charismatic teacher) cannot help being uncertain about the field's real subject, it scope, and its name. Information theory is only one of several alternative names of this discipline; among other designations are mathematical theory of communication, communication theory, coding theory, signal-transmission theory, and mathematical theory of information measurement. Is this discipline chiefly about information or about communication or about signals? Is it largely abstract mathematics and mathematical statistics, a branch of probability theory? Is it perhaps a specialty of electrical engineering with emphasis on channel capacity? Is it a part of (or closely allied with) thermodynamics and statistical mechanics, with its focus on physical entropy, or is its major concern telecommunication, with the focus on systems design—or is it general enough to apply to problems of biology, psychology, and the social sciences? Every one of these claims has been made.[27]

Three Senses or Many More

One reason for the diversity of claims is that " 'Information theory' is used in at least three senses. In the narrowest of these senses, it denotes a class of problems concerning the generation, storage, transmission and processing of information [in a very special sense], in which a *particular measure* of information is used." (Elias, 1959 and 1968, p. 253. Emphasis added.) This is essentially Shannon's theory.[28] [Shannon, 1948.] "In a broader sense, infor-

---

[27] Some of these positions may be exemplified here by direct quotation: "Unlike Newton's laws of motion and Maxwell's equations, which are strongly physical in that they deal with certain classes of physical phenomena, communication theory is abstract in that it applies to many sorts of communication, written, acoustical, or electrical. . . . Communication theory proceeds from clear and definite assumptions to theorems concerning information sources and communication channels. In this it is essentially mathematical, and in order to understand it we must understand the idea of a theorem as a statement . . . which must be shown to be the necessary consequence of a set of initial assumptions. This is an idea which is the very heart of mathematics as mathematicians understand it." (Pierce, 1961 and 1965, p. 18.)

On the other hand, one of the contributors to this volume contends that "Shannon's theorem about the existence of codes that make it possible to transmit information at rates that come arbitrarily close to a specified upper limit with arbitrarily low probabilities of undetected error rooted what others called 'information theory' firmly as an engineering discipline." (Kochen in his paper in Section 5.) Strangely enough, the same author a few years earlier had characterized information theory (of the Shannon type) as a mathematical specialty.

In contradistinction to this view, a Russian mathematician stated that "Information Theory is one of the youngest branches of applied probability theory." (Khinchin, 1956; English translation, 1957, p. 30.)

A less apodictic position is taken by another of the contributors to this volume. He holds that after "the popularity of the information-theoretical approach, especially in the 1950s, [the] later disillusionment with that approach, especially among psychologists, stems from an initial lack of public clarity as to the scope and limits of Shannon's theory . . . , and especially from a widespread failure to distinguish the concept of information per se from various measures of its 'amount'. It should be added that some of the most generally useful qualitative concepts of information engineering . . . , such as feedback and feedforward, have quite independent origins and owe nothing to the mathematical theory of information measurement." (MacKay in his paper in this volume.)

[28] "This area is also called 'coding theory' and . . . 'the mathematical theory of communication'." (Elias, 1968, p. 253.)

mation theory has been taken to include any analysis of communications problems including statistical problems of the detection of signals in the presence of noise, that make *no* use of an *information measure*." (Elias, 1959 and 1968, p. 253. Emphasis added.) "In a still broader sense, information theory is used as a synonym for the term 'cybernetics' " and thus includes the theories of servomechanisms, automata, communication, control, "and other kinds of behavior in organisms and machines." (Ibid.)

One can easily extend this list, especially if one includes the meanings intended by users of the name information theory who are not committed to the technical writings on the discipline in the three senses just distinguished. Many who respect the meaning of the word *information* in common parlance, in business, public, social, and private affairs, affirm that any scholarly study of those social, linguistic, and psychological processes and phenomena can reasonably be called information theory. For example, Bar-Hillel and Carnap, concerned exclusively with *semantic information,* regarded themselves as information theorists. [Bar-Hillel and Carnap, 1953*b*.] Likewise, Helmut Seiffert, a German philosopher who wrote one of the most sensible books on information, views information theory through a very wide lens. [Seiffert, 1968.] Dean Jamison distinguishes "six alternative theories of information," all of them semantic, unrelated to electronic processes. [Jamison, 1970, p. 29.] However, such authors are usually not regarded as authentic representatives of information theory, since that designation has been assigned by the academic community to the specialists concerned with what we would prefer to call the mathematical theory of signal transmission.

That the designation information theory has been used in so many senses is, of course, closely connected with the multifarious meanings in which the word information has been used. Although Machlup devotes a special section of the Epilogue to that theme, a few comments on the equivocal use of this word may not be amiss at the present juncture.

Strange Uses of Common Words

Virtually all prominent representatives of the field under discussion have expressed regret about the name under which it has become known and the use of the word *information* for something that is, at best, related to certain aspects of specific techniques of signal transmission. The main protagonist, Claude Shannon, avoided the name *information theory* in his publications; he called it mathematical theory of communication. [Shannon, 1948; 1949.] He also had misgivings about giving a special and uncommon meaning to the word information. Myron Tribus in his paper in the present volume recounts that Shannon had consulted John von Neumann about this nomenclature and von Neumann advised him to call the new thing entropy, which few people could confuse with anything with which they thought they were familiar.[29] Warren Weaver, in his attempt to interpret Shannon's theory, warned his readers that the word information was used here in a "rather strange way, [in] a special sense which . . . must not be confused at all with meaning." (Weaver, 1955, pp. 100, 104.)

Shannon was not the first to use the term in a strange way. Ralph Hartley, one of Shannon's predecessors at Bell Laboratories, had said *information* when he spoke of the successive selection of signs from a given list, regardless of meanings. [Hartley, 1928.] Some authors would like to involve the physicists and insinuate that early writers on thermodynamics had spoken of entropy in terms of information. To be sure, the formula developed by Boltzmann was an early exemplar of the species developed by Shannon, and Boltzmann's subject was entropy; and, of course, he spoke of ordered and not-ordered movements, mixtures, and states. But he did not use the word *information* in the context. [Boltzmann, 1872; 1877; 1886 and 1905a; 1904 and 1905b.] Perhaps one could say that entropy and uncertainty were logically correlated and that uncertainty and information could be logically related by the use of appropriate (special, arbitrary, or contrived) definitions. Still, one cannot in fairness blame physicists for the confusion between signal transmission and information, though some may be blamed for failing to distinguish between information and observation. In any case, the roles of entropy and uncertainty in information theory are complex and controversial, and they involve not only semantic but also methodological considerations.

Communication, one of the possible alternatives for the term *information*, is also a word with multiple meanings, some of which are concerned with making oneself understood. (For example, the statement that a speaker does or does not communicate well refers to his or her capacity to convey to the audience the meaning of what he or she intends to communicate.) Some use *communication* to indicate bilateral or two-way information. [Boulding, 1955, p. 111.] (The idea in this case is not only a meaningful message from a speaker to a listener but a meaningful dialogue between discussion partners.) Yet, there are also senses of the word *communication* that do *not* imply meanings intended by a speaker or writer and understanding by a recipient; communication of heat is one example. There is also communication of liquids or gases between connected vessels; finally, there is the communication of diseases. Thus, unlike information, the term *communication* has for centuries been used without any connotation of transmission of ideas to an understanding recipient.[30] We conclude that Shannon was right in calling his

---

[29] That von Neumann continued to have misgivings about speaking of *information* and *information theory* may be inferred from the fact that he placed quotation marks around "information theory" when he first referred to it in the introduction of his posthumously published booklet *The Computer and the Brain*. [von Neumann, 1958, p. 1.]

[30] "Communicating, from an engineering point of view, means simply moving electronic traffic

results a theory of communication and he should not have allowed his followers to call it information theory.

Regret about the misleading name given to the theory and its keyword is shared by many eminent writers on the subject. It is a pity, said Colin Cherry, "that the mathematical concepts stemming from Hartley have been called 'information' at all." (Cherry, 1957 and 1966, p. 50.) What is really involved in the mathematical theory of communication are signs and signals and their transmission over channels of communication.

Signal Transmission and Channel Capacity

Communication theory was formulated to serve engineers who design telecommunication systems. "Engineers are concerned primarily with the correct transmission of signals, or (electric) representations of messages; they are not commonly interested, professionally, with the purposes of messages" or their meanings. "A message is regarded as the 'selections from the alphabet,' which is then put into physical form (signals) as sound, light, electricity, et cetera, for transmission. . . . The signals reaching the receiver represent instructions to select . . . . All communicable messages (i.e., expressible by signs) may be coded into . . . binary 1, 0 sequences." (Cherry, 1957 and 1966, pp. 168–170.) For example, if the ensemble of messages available for selection contains eight possible messages, three signals suffice to instruct the receiver to select the message that was selected by the sender.[31] An ensemble of 32 messages (letters or signs) requires a sequence of five binary signals, since $32 = 2^5$. To select the correct word from a dictionary with approximately 32,000 words, a communication system would require only 15 binary signals, since $32,768 = 2^{15}$.

For telegraphic communication, sequential discrete signals are transmitted; for telephonic communication, continuous wave forms are transmitted. These wave forms are distinguished by amplitude (measured by the ordinate) and frequency (cycles per second). The "maximum (sinusoidal . . .) frequency which the signals are considered to contain [is called] bandwidth." (Ibid., p. 303.) As a rule, "the longer the duration of a signal, T, the narrower its spectral bandwidth, F, . . . and vice versa." (Ibid., p. 139.) Under certain conditions, signal duration multiplied by effective bandwidth may be treated as constant, which makes for certain upper limits in channel capacity. The apparently continuous wave forms are broken down in some

---

from one place to another. It matters little if the signal represents random noise or a Shakespearean sonnet." (Branscomb, 1979, p. 143.) We wish to record dissent from this statement by a professor of communication engineering: He emphasized that his discipline is very much concerned with the distinction between signals and noise.

[31] The first signal reduces the possible choices from 8 to 4; the second signal, from 4 to 2; and the third signal commands the final selection. That three binary (or *yes/no*) signals suffice to select one message from an alphabet of eight is mathematically expressed by the fact that $8 = 2^3$.

systems into discrete, equally spaced ordinates, and only samples of successive amplitudes are transmitted to the receiver. The composite signal received is, within limits, the same as the unsampled signal supposedly sent. [Ibid., p. 142.] (Do we risk ridicule from experts if we suggest as an analogy the sequence of still photographs in film strips showing apparently continuous movement?)

According to some specialists, the greatest contribution to statistical communication theory was Shannon's capacity theorem, also called the coding theorem, regarding noisy channels. It states that within certain limits, depending on specified channel constraints, it is possible "by using codes of sufficient length to set the input rates arbitrarily close to [the channel's capacity] and yet maintain [despite the noisy channel] the probability of reception error as small as desired." (Feinstein, 1958, p. 43.) Although electrical engineers had known this before Shannon's equations, they agree that the formal and rigorous determination of capacity limits is of fundamental importance.

In these few paragraphs on elements of communication theory—signal transmission and channel capacity—we have avoided using the word *information*, but it is time to explain what the engineers mean by it. They do not mean the *what* that is to be communicated, but, instead, they mean the instruction that the sender, by signals, conveys to the receiver, commanding it (not him or her, but it) to select a particular message from the given ensemble of possible messages. Thus, this information in the engineering sense is an instruction to select.[32] And the rate of information is the rate at which such instructions can be transmitted per signal or per second. [Cherry, 1957 and 1966, pp. 170–180.] However, even the word *instruction* is misleading, in that it may produce an association with *verbal* instructions given to a person equipped with a mind and supposed to engage in a cognitive process. The word *command* has the same semantic defect. *Activation* would be a more appropriate term: Activating impulses are transmitted through the channel to the receiver. Thus, *activation rate* might be a suitable substitute for *information rate*.

The Urge to Measure and the Choice of Words

One may wonder why people other than communication engineers were willing to accept the engineering sense of *information* for contexts where no bandwidth, no signals per second, no channel capacity, no signal/noise ratio,

---

[32] "Mathematical communication theory concerns the signals alone . . . abstracted from all human uses" and apart from all meaning. The signals control selection of signs from the receiver's alphabet, as when "one teletype machine [is] communicating with another. At the transmitting end, the operator selects and presses keys one at a time; coded electrical signals are thereby sent to the receiving machine, causing it to select and depress the correct key automatically. We see the receiver keys going down, as though pressed by invisible fingers." (Cherry, 1957 and 1966, pp. 168–169.)

and so forth, were involved. When scholars were chiefly interested in cognitive information, why did they accept a supposedly scientific definition of "information apart from meaning"? One possible explanation is the fact that they were impressed by a definition that provided for measurement. To be sure, measurement was needed for the engineering purposes at hand; but how could anybody believe that Shannon's formula would also measure information in the sense of what one person tells another by word of mouth, in writing, or in print?

We suspect that the failure to find, and perhaps impossibility of finding, any ways of measuring information in this ordinary sense has induced many to accept measurable signal transmission, channel capacity, or selection rate, misnamed amount of information, as a substitute or proxy for information. The impressive slogan, coined by Lord Kelvin, that "science is measurement" has persuaded many researchers who were anxious to qualify as scientists to start measuring things that cannot be measured. As if under a compulsion, they looked for an operational definition of *some aspect* of communication or information that stipulated quantifiable operations. Shannon's formula did exactly that; here was something *related* to information that was objectively measurable. Many users of the definition were smart enough to realize that the proposed measure—perfectly suited for electrical engineering and telecommunication—did not really fit their purposes; but the compulsion to measure was stronger than their courage to admit that they were not operating sensibly.[33]

A British scientist had also been searching for definitions that permitted measurement of information: Donald MacKay. He came up with three different definitions of measurable information, some of which had been proposed by statisticians and engineers. [Fisher, 1935; Gabor, 1946.] He distinguished the logon content, the metron content, and the selective-information content, the latter being Shannon's measure of information. In his paper in this volume, he writes: "It would be clearly absurd to regard these various measures of 'amount-of-information' as rivals. They are no more rivals than are length, area, and volume as measures of 'size.' By the same token it would be manifestly inept to take any of them as definitions of information itself." With regard to the Shannon definition (in terms of probability or, as MacKay put it, unexpectedness), he has this to say: "To try to translate every reference to information (whether in biology or elsewhere) into a statement about unexpectedness would be as inept, and as conceptually Procrustean, as translating all references to a house into statements about

---

[33] The irrational zeal to measure even where it makes no sense is frankly expressed in the following statement: "In many ways it is less useful to measure the amount of information [in Shannon's sense] than the amount of meaning. In later chapters, however, I reluctantly deal more with measurement of the amount of information than of meaning because as yet meaning cannot be precisely measured." (J. G. Miller, 1978, p. 12.)

its size." MacKay's exposition, however, was not without linguistic infelicities. He was very helpful when he warned—as early as 1950—against confusing information in the original sense of the word (where some meaningful content is expected) with amount-of-information (the latter referring to measurable improbability or unexpectedness of signals from a given set). But then he introduced or accepted the term information-content—which a commonsensible reader would expect to refer to the meaning-content of the information—and wanted that term to denote a measurable *amount* of information-transmission, regardless of any meaning-content.[34] [MacKay, 1951*a*; 1954*b*; 1969, pp. 56, 156–160, 163–167.]

Confusing Explanations

The available expositions of the essential notions of information in the sense of signal transmission are incredibly confusing to a reader who is not satisfied with superficial comprehension but insists on a full understanding of the major aspects of the subject. The reader is constantly confronted with terms that are defined but not made clear. We shall illustrate this with respect to some of the keywords.

Let us begin with *selection*, the act of choosing one of two, several, or many messages (or signals) from a given set (ensemble, source, repertoire, or pool). Who selects and what for? The reader, having been treated to several examples of coin-tossing and dice-throwing, is led to think that the message received, for example, *tails* or *five*, is entirely a matter of chance. This interpretation is reinforced by the next example furnished by virtually all expositors, the case of picking any card, its face down, from a well-shuffled deck of playing cards. So, the selection of the message is a random choice? Hold it! The next example, almost universally, is the game Twenty Questions. Here, the recipient chooses questions not at random but more or less intelligently and receives presumably correct answers of yes or no. If each answer constitutes a transmitted message, it is surely not random, but selected in good faith to the best of the transmitter's knowledge, be he, she, or it a human being or a man-made machine. This example of successive yes's and no's comes closer to what the expositors are trying to show, namely, that a sequence of steps is needed to arrive at the ultimately sought answer. However, the conscientious reader may still be puzzled by the division of labor in selecting in this case: The recipient selects the twenty (or

---

[34] Not only general readers but also logicians mean by contents of information their *semantic* contents. Thus, Bar-Hillel and Carnap held that the terminology and the theorems of telecommunication research were unfortunately applied "to fields in which the term 'information' was used . . . in a semantic sense, that is, one involving *contents* or designata of symbols . . . ." (Bar-Hillel and Carnap, 1953*b*, p. 147. Emphasis added.)

less or more) questions and the transmitters select the answers, though before the questioning begins, they have also selected the correct answer to be guessed. The relevance of all this to the process of signal transmission is not made clear in any expositions that we have read.

The core of the theory is probability, yet few expositors care to state just *what* is probable about a message transmitted. A communication system such as the telegraph or the telephone does not usually transmit messages that tell which side of the coin happened to come up or which number of eyes (or dots or spots) were on the top of the die or which among the playing cards in the deck was picked. Messages conveyed by telegraph are usually in the form of strings of words (in a natural or artificial language) and numbers. It is easy to understand that the signals adopted to represent letters in a telegram should be chosen so that simpler signals stand for the most frequently occurring letters. A coding convention of this sort will reasonably be based on the probability of particular letters being required to compose words—where probability means the frequency of these letters in the English (French, German, etc.) language. (The most frequent are *e* and *t*, then *i*, *a*, *n*, and *m*.)

The frequency of individual letters occurring in an English text (or another language) matters a good deal when engineers designing a telegraph system determine what signals ought to be used in encoding, transmitting, and decoding. The most frequently used letters should be represented by the shortest sequence of signals, with longer sequences of signals reserved for less frequently used letters. In most expositions of the theory, discussion of this encoding problem is followed by a discussion of doublets (digrams) and triplets (trigrams), that is, sequences of two or three letters that occur frequently, infrequently, or never in the particular natural language. The bearing of these different frequencies, however, is less on the assignment of signals to signs, but rather on the ease of detecting errors in scrambled telegrams. (For example, *sck* is not likely to appear in any English word.) Such detection, however, is unlikely to be built into the architecture of the system but rather into the cognitive capability of the human recipient.

Turning from telegraph to telephone communication, the physical signals used to transmit words spoken by a human voice into a microphone and channeled through wires and cables are surely very different, and the probability of particular letters in a written language is no longer significant. Now, differences in pitch may be important. (We have asked ourselves whether a telephone system optimal for Chinese speakers would be the same as one for English.) We can send music over the telephone, and the relative frequency (probability) of very high, very low, very loud, and very soft tones probably matters. These issues, however, are not ordinarily included in elementary expositions of information theory and the so-called amount-of-information transmitted. The illustrations furnished, even by those who repudiate any concern with semantic content, usually employ sentences that *do* have meaning, and this further confuses the reader. For example, when it is pointed out that the probability of a message depends on how many possible messages there are, and when this is followed by an example of two English sentences (widely used in practice manuals for students of typing), the reader will be puzzled about the information contained in either of the two messages that was selected. Was this a selection by chance, and is each of the messages equally probable in any other sense? [Elias, 1959 and 1968, p. 254.]

When we are told about the probability of a message, we remain puzzled about just what is probable about a message. We cannot help (despite all warnings) thinking first of the probability of its proving true, useful, or valuable. Second, we think of the probability of its being selected by a transmitter making a rational choice, either trying to be helpful, perhaps obeying a command, or trying to deceive the recipient. Third, remembering information theorists' advice to forget about meaning and not to forget about the given pool of possible messages, we think of the probability of the message being picked at random from all possible messages. Fourth, having learned about disturbing noise being mixed with genuine signals, we think of the probability of the message reaching the receiver without undue noise and, thus, as it is intended by the sender. Finally, backsliding into the normal attitude of connecting messages with something they are supposed to convey, we think of the probability of the message being understood by the recipient. This half-dozen meanings of the probability of a message does not exhaust the list, and the trouble is that formulations chosen by most expositors do little to help the recipient of their messages grasp the entire exercise.[35]

Information Theory and System Theory

With the difficulties of properly interpreting the many inept and obscure expositions of information theory, added to the fact that there is not *one* information theory but several of different scope and even different objects, it would be an unduly daring attempt to characterize the methodological nature of the insufficiently specified discipline. The question, for example, whether it is an empirical or an entirely analytical theory cannot be answered before one decides just what the theory says and what it denies.

---

[35] In one of Cherry's formulations, we are confronted with three probabilities: "the probability of message x being sent, assessed from past observations of the transmitter"; "the probability of an x being sent, on those occasions when y is received"; and "the likelihood that, if any particular x *had* been sent, the specific y would be received." (Cherry, 1957 and 1966, p. 202.) We interpret this argument as an exercise on deriving the likelihood—that is, the so-called probability of a single event of a specific type—from prior statistical probabilities, as frequencies observed in the past, where the first is the frequency of x alone and the second, the frequency of a conjuncture of x and y.

It is possible to interpret the theory as an auxiliary specialty of electrical engineering or communications technology. Electrical impulses, air waves, microphone vibrations, telegraphs, telephones, radios, television sets, wires, cables, and scores of other things that make up communication channels, encoders, decoders, and all the rest are undoubtedly observable phenomena of the physical world, and any research concerned with such phenomena is empirical (indeed, practical-empirical) in character. On the other hand, much about the analysis of the fundamental processes involved has to do with probability—logical and statistical (and some even subjective)—and this would support the interpretation that the theory belongs to probability theory, either as an integral part or as an application. To the extent that statistical probability is based on observed frequencies of events, the theory has a firm empirical base; to the extent, however, that the relevant observations are merely assumed and included in a general, and therefore abstract, model, the result is analytical. Inasmuch as this analytical-deductive argument is formulated in terms of mathematical equations, the theory may be considered as pure mathematics. Thus, depending on how one looks at information theory, it may be subsumed under very different categories of knowledge, ranging from practical-technological via empirical-statistical to abstract-analytical.

Mihajlo Mesarović in his paper in this volume proposes to equate systems theory with information theory. He does so, however, after redefining both information and information theory. He liberates information from Shannon's construct, which, he thinks, "refers only to the capacity for transmission," and makes it much richer and thereby suitable for use in the context of goal-seeking behavior. Accordingly, he extends information theory enough to make it into a broad theory of information. Then, but only then, may Mesarović be justified in saying, as he does, that "information theory and systems theory are one and the same." What this asserted equality, or statement of identity, amounts to is merely a normative pronouncement— that the two fields *ought* to be the same; or, perhaps, a protest against the actual inequality of what now goes under the name information theory and general system theory. For, in actual academic practice, "Information theory is a set of concepts, theorems, and measures that were first developed by Shannon for communication engineering and have been extended to other quite different fields . . . ." (J. G. Miller, 1978, p. 12.)

This extension of information theory, as developed for communication engineering, to other quite different fields has been a methodological disaster—though the overenthusiastic extenders did not see it, and some of them, who now know that it was an aberration, still believe that they have learned a great deal from it. In actual fact, the theory of signal transmission or activating impulses has little or nothing to teach that could be extended or applied to human communication, social behavior, or psychology, theoretical or experimental.

Addendum to the Prologue:
Letter from George A. Miller

[Editor's note (U.M.): As well as making suggestions for improving various parts of the Prologue, George Miller provided us with a comment on its section dealing with cognitive science. This was contained in a letter to Fritz Machlup dated January 18, 1983, and Professor Machlup's immediate reaction was: "We should publish it as it is." However, he wanted more time to think about it, but he died unexpectedly before we had had a chance to discuss it again. I have decided to be guided by his initial reaction, and Miller has kindly agreed to have the letter published as it is, with only very slight editing.]

Dear Fritz:

It has taken longer than I had hoped to read "Cultural Diversity in Studies of Information" by you and Una. I hope my impressions will still be of some interest to you.

I enjoyed most of it, although at points I must confess that your patience with the territorial claims of the different cultures is greater than mine. I particularly relished your defense of pluralism, and your interest in good ideas regardless of whether they come labeled as "science" or "practice." As one who lives in a marginal science myself, I long ago discovered that attempts to work solely in the manner that I had been taught to regard as characteristic of true science could only stunt my intellectual growth as a psychologist. So I decided to pursue problems wherever they led; if the result was not science, that was unfortunate but not important . . . .

Your discussion of cognitive science seems to me to rely too heavily on the views of those who take computers and artificial intelligence as providing the definitive characteristics of this field. Personally, I find it difficult to communicate clearly my enormous debt to people like Simon, Newell, and Minsky for helping cognitive psychology take a great leap forward, yet at the same time to communicate with equal clarity that the human brain/mind system is enormously more complicated than, and different from, any contemporary computational system.

An interesting point that you make might help me straighten out my difficulties with computer-oriented cognitive science. In my opinion, computer science applied to the problems of cognitive psychology should yield cognitive psychology. The fact that it has not, that it has yielded something novel—concepts of mind and intelligence so abstract that it doesn't matter whether the system possessing them is living or dead—may mean that I have mistakenly regarded computer science as a formal science.

But I suspect that the tensions already tearing the new field apart are worse than that diagnosis might suggest. Contemporary computers manipulate symbols, and symbol manipulation is certainly one kind of intelligence. But whether that kind of intelligence is the only kind remains an open question. I can accept the claim that the brain must be a universal Turing machine, but that tells me almost nothing as long as I don't know what kind of universal Turing machine it really is. (It is like telling me that the correct theory of the brain's function could be written in ink.) Unfortunately, I am convinced the brain is not the same kind of universal Turing machine as are the machines presently merchandised by IBM.

At this point, therefore, I have personally taken refuge in the plural *s* that you endorse so strongly . . . . The cognitive sciences are those scientific disciplines sharing an interest in the representation and transformation of knowledge (read "information" in the present context). But, as you have pointed out some- where, sharing an interest and being a single discipline are very different things. Moreover, my definition of the cognitive sciences is not easily distin- guished from your definition of the information sciences, yet it is plain enough that your information science is a larger, more catholic assemblage than my cognitive science. At which point I merely shrug. You, I believe, feel a com- mitment to rationalizing the difference.

You are certainly right . . . that "representation" is a keyword in cognitive science. Historically, philosophers since Descartes have assumed that the mind somehow copies, reflects, or represents the real world, so representation is hardly a new idea. The philosophers, however, immediately raised the ques- tion of how we can possibly know whether or not the mental representation of the real world is correct, true, valid. At this point Hume, then Kant, then dozens of others were able to create professional philosophy out of the epis- temological (metaphysical) problems that resulted. When cognitive scientists revert to the problem of representation, therefore, one assumes (or at least hopes) they have a better strategy in mind than the philosophers did, that there are other important questions to ask about representations other than their accuracy, since that question is known to lead straight out of empirical science.

The alternative, as I understand it, is that we now have machines capable of interestingly complex representations, and we should use them to learn what- ever we can about representational processes. Perhaps along the way we will notice something that will shed light on the structure and function of mental representations. But I have heard no guarantees, and as the difficulties become more and more apparent, the tendency for the computer exploration to ex- punge psychologism (just as logic did a century earlier) and move off on its own seems stronger and more attractive. That might be a good development, but it would spell the doom of cognitive science as a new discipline encom- passing both artificial intelligence and psychology.

Some of my misgivings are reflected in your comments about motivational and emotional processes. . . . But I (and many other cognitive psychologists) would go further. Consider something like the memory of a pain. If, while you feel the pain, you describe it verbally to yourself, then when you go to a doctor's office you can remember your verbal encoding of the experience. That is the kind of memory that computer-oriented theorists have much to say about. But suppose you forget to encode a description verbally at the time you feel the pain. By the time you arrive at the doctor's office, the original pain experience itself will have faded and your memory of it will have become quite unreliable. That kind of precategorical memory for the "raw feels" of life presumably requires some kind of analogue representation, but whatever it is, contemporary computer science does not help us understand it any better. In other words, the important split here is not cognition vs. conation and emotion, but rather a split within cognition itself: symbolically represented cognition vs. primal, nonsymbolically represented cognition. In short, computer-oriented theories of cognition are not so much wrong as incomplete . . . .

Thank you, both of you, for letting me see this. I hope these random associations will be of some help.

Sincerely,

George A. Miller

SECTION 1

INFORMATION SCIENCE
Its Roots and Relations as Viewed from the Perspective of Cognitive Science

Zenon W. Pylyshyn

INTRODUCTION: THE HISTORICAL LINKS

Arthur Koestler once pointed out that it is commonplace for science to "sleep walk" its way to new stages of development—to progress and achieve dramatic new world views while not fully understanding, or indeed frequently misunderstanding, the nature and significance of work that scientists themselves are doing. Frequently, it is only with the advantage of hindsight that the significance of various developments can be assessed.

There are clear indications in the history of science [e.g., Butterfield, 1957] that periods of progress are coincident with major new technical and conceptual developments or sometimes, as in the case of Galileo's use of geometry, with taking an existing formalism seriously as a way of understanding the world. Similarly, philosophical understanding also rests on available conceptual tools. As Susanne Langer put it, "In every age, philosophical thinking exploits some dominant concepts and makes its greatest headway in solving problems conceived in terms of them." (Langer, 1962, p. 54.)

Several decades ago, the brilliant mathematician and computer pioneer John von Neumann pointed out that in the past, science had dealt mainly with the concepts of energy, power, force, and motion, and he predicted that "in the future science would be more concerned with problems of control, programming, information processing, communication, organization, and systems." (Burks, 1970, p. 3.)

The precise nature of the Weltanschauung that ties together this syndrome of concepts is not yet clear. [See, however, Simon, 1969; Newell and Simon, 1976a.] It seems to represent a move away from the study of material substance toward a more abstract study of form. The new conceptual tools leading up to the development of artificial intelligence and cognitive science are bound up with such notions as mechanism, information, and symbol.

The earliest harbingers of these developments may well have been in symbolic logic, especially the formalist movement in studies of the foundations of mathematics, initiated in the first half of the twentieth century by people like Hilbert, and developed by Russell and Whitehead, Frege, Zermelo, and others. These people began the attempt to reduce the notion of a mathematical proof to that of a game played with tokens of uninterpreted meaningless symbols according to certain purely formal rules—rules whose application depends only on recognizing the occurrence of the type of each token (i.e., in recognizing an x, whenever it occurred, as being an instance of the same particular symbol). No sooner had this goal of formalizing mathematics been formulated than it was discovered to be in principle not achievable. Gödel, Turing, Church, Rosser, Kleene, Post, and others showed that there exist true but formally unprovable propositions, formally insoluble problems, and uncomputable functions. [See the collection of fundamental papers in M. Davis, 1965.]

This work, carried out in the 1930s, was important for many reasons. One is that it made precise the notion of formal mechanism or a mechanism or process that functions without the intervention of an intelligence or any natural being and yet can be understood without knowing about any of its physical properties. In making this notion precise, these studies laid the foundations for a way of conceptualizing a wide range of problems in many different areas of intellectual endeavor—from philosophy of mind and philosophy of mathematics to engineering, and including almost every facet of social and biological science.

Although these foundational mathematical developments of the 1930s were probably the most dramatic signs of a major breakthrough in the understanding of formal symbol systems, they were neither the only such signs nor were they necessarily the most directly influential. For example, there had earlier been a tradition in linguistics called structuralism, which probably originated with the publication of Ferdinand de Saussure's lectures in linguistics in 1916 and soon spread considerably beyond linguistics proper. This movement influenced the allied fields of anthropology (e.g., Levi-Strauss), sociology [Barker and Wright, 1955], and psychology (e.g., Piaget) and even led to what many view as the synthesis of a new interdisciplinary field of semiotics—a term (attributed to Charles Morris) that refers to the study of relations of signs and symbols to behavior.

If we were to try to find the major direct influences on the current Zeitgeist—of the current ways of viewing nonphysical forces that shape our world and our behavior (as von Neumann foresaw, in the statement previously quoted)—we would doubtlessly trace them to a number of technical achievements that emerged during wartime scientific work in the United States and Britain, though it is not clear that World War II actually provided any of the impetus for these developments. [Newell and Simon, 1972.] It is no accident that this work involved many of the same people who contributed to seminal developments in logic and foundational mathematics (particularly Alan Turing and John von Neumann), for the technical developments were very much part of the same intellectual movement. These technical achievements included the following closely related developments:

1. *Control theory,* or the theory of closed-loop feedback systems, was one of the earliest and most far-reaching of the wartime technical developments. The need to develop automated systems for aiming and maintaining the directional stability of radar antennas and artillery on moving vehicles spawned an enormous surge of research and mathematical analysis, involving people like Wiener, Nyquist, Hartley, and others. The broad and profound significance of this work soon became clear [Wisdom, 1970] and led to an important paper by Rosenblueth, Wiener, and Bigelow [1943], which analyzed the philosophically troublesome notion of teleology or purposive behavior in terms of feedback.

2. *Information theory* developed in close parallel with control theory (indeed, Wiener coined the term cybernetics to refer to both as they applied to the analysis of animal and machine behavior). The quantification of information—in terms of the potential of a certain set of events to affect selections—provided an important step in the rigorous analysis of what had hitherto been known only informally to be a central concept in the understanding of animal and machine behavior. Claude Shannon (along with the people mentioned in connection with the study of control theory) showed that there was a well-defined relation between certain general properties of a physical system (notably its bandwidth and signal-to-noise ratio) and the maximum rate at which information could be processed or transmitted through it, regardless of what the information was about and what was to be done with it. [Shannon and Weaver, 1949.]

3. Mathematical *decision theory,* the theory of competitive games, and operations research were important extensions of mathematical analyses to optimization problems in social, industrial, and management situations. [See, for example, Simon, 1957.] Along with cybernetics, these developments represented a new license to apply formal mathematical ideas to the social and biological sciences. These developments also legitimized the notion of decision, just as work in communication and control theory had legitimized the notion of information, by establishing it on a rigorous analytical foundation.

4. The development of *automatic computing machinery* eventually brought all these ideas together by providing an object that was at once a tool for carrying out analyses required by these complex studies and at the same time, an object of theoretical study that involved elements of all these new analytical methods. The appearance of both analogue and digital computers in the late 1940s was an event of inestimable importance in bringing the new view of animal and mechanical commonality into sharp focus. From the very beginning, computers influenced people's thinking about the nature of thought, intelligence, and adaptation and formed the key to the new mechanistic conception of mind, based on a much richer metaphor (though

some, like me, feel that it is much more than a metaphor) than those that had been prevalent in earlier attempts to unite the psychological, biological, and physical modes of explanation. The historical and philosophical issues surrounding this discovery are beyond the scope of this essay; however, they are discussed elsewhere in some detail. [Pylyshyn, 1970; Arden, 1980a; and Pylyshyn, 1982.]

The overlap among these four areas, as measured in terms of the proportion of people who contributed to them, is remarkable. For example, the earliest writings on the theory of interdependent competitive decisions (theory of games), while dating back to the 1920s, became a central concern in the 1940s, about the time when their author, John von Neumann, became involved in designing the earliest stored-program electronic digital computer [Pylyshyn, 1970] and in applying notions of computation to problems of biology [Burks, 1970]. Claude Shannon also wrote some early papers on computing and the use of symbolic logic in the design of switching circuits. Norbert Wiener, who had been a student of Bertrand Russell, contributed to technical developments in both information theory and the theory of control systems. Even more important was Wiener spearheading the rapidly growing view that, at a suitable level of formal abstraction, these ideas were also relevant to understanding any complex system, including social and biological systems. This led to the view that there are important abstract principles that are shared by any highly interacting sets of functional elements, regardless of whether these are sets of cells in a liver or brain, sets of animals in an ecological system or sets of humans in a social system or sets of electronic components wired together to form a complex artifact. This view gave rise to an area of study sometimes referred to as general systems theory.

Analog computation was also closely tied to both control theory and information theory. The mathematical tools for analyzing analog systems— calculus and differential equations—were the ones that were relevant to continuously varying electronic systems such as those that occur in feedback control loops. By contrast, the study of digital computers, decisions, and the parts of information theory having to do with encoding were often discrete. As it turned out, discrete systems were found to be mathematically more tractable and also much more interesting in a number of respects. For example, they appear to be far more general (inasmuch as they contain the class of universal computers, or Turing machines) than continuous ones. The common mathematical tool that was used in these cases was symbolic logic.

Almost all early workers on computers and communication systems were trained in symbolic logic. Indeed, even to this day, mathematical logic has had a central role in developing ways of conceptualizing problems in the entire spectrum of information-related disciplines. Despite some early criticisms of the predominance of logic in the study of artificial intelligence, logic is becoming more central than ever—both for the analysis of programming systems and as a formalism for representing knowledge and even programs themselves.

The one area that has not been mentioned already but which played an important, though initially highly speculative part in these developments, concerns the relation of this network of ideas to understanding human thought and the nature of intelligence. As early as 1950, attempts to apply certain ideas developed in the study of foundations of mathematics (for example, the notion of computational mechanism as exemplified by the Turing machine) to understanding the nature of intelligence were published by Turing, von Neumann, Shannon, and others. But it was with the availability of actual computing devices in the early 1950s that this goal began to be pursued in earnest.

There were two primary strands in this early work. One was directed at the class of self-organizing or adaptive systems and emphasized learning, statistical-pattern recognition, and the modeling of neural networks. This strand frequently associated itself with the term cybernetics. The second strand was more molar. It was directed at understanding problem-solving and thought processes at what we would now call the cognitive or the knowledge level. These two strands were nearly equally represented at a historic symposium held in 1958 at the National Physical Laboratory in England on Mechanization of Thought Processes. In the last fifteen or so years, however, work on the class of approaches that are concerned with self-organizing systems—especially those influenced by speculation about the properties of randomly connected neural networks—has all but disappeared. On the other hand, work on the second class of approaches has grown rapidly and also changed in emphasis in order to reflect a new understanding of the problem of intelligence. The first decade of this work (roughly 1955–1965) was dominated by the search for general problem-solving techniques together with powerful methods called *heuristics* for controlling the breadth of trial-and-error search. This work is well represented by the reports reproduced in a classical book of readings. [Feigenbaum and Feldman, 1963.]

The second decade [described in Minsky, 1968; Feigenbaum, 1969] was, by contrast, more concerned with problems of planning and designing good forms of knowledge representation and the development of high-performance (or expert) systems in narrower domains. The key terms changed from learning, classification, and search to planning, knowledge representation, and semantics. The most recent general picture of the state of the field generally referred to as artificial intelligence can be found in a chapter in the collective volume *What Can Be Automated?* [Arden, 1980a.]

SOME CHARACTERISTICS OF COGNITIVE SCIENCE

In this essay, I am concerned primarily with relations among disciplines and with scientific and technical developments that have shaped and continue to influence the development of the attempt to understand the nature of intelligence. It is not the only form in which the search for an understanding of mind is proceeding. Nor, furthermore, is this effort being carried out in only one academic discipline, for example, the one calling itself cognitive psychology or artificial intelligence. There are many distinct disciplines contributing to the effort. What characterizes this particular class of approaches—which have recently come to be collectively (and somewhat loosely) called cognitive science—is an allegiance to the network of ideas that I roughly outlined and might be summarized as follows:

(a) The approach is formalist in spirit; that is, it attempts to formulate its theories in terms of symbolic mechanisms of the sort that have grown out of symbolic logic.

(b) The level of analysis, or the level at which the explanations or theories are cast, is functional, and they are described in terms of their information flow. What this means in particular is that this approach factors out such questions as how biological material carries out the function and how biochemical and biophysical laws operate to produce the required information-processing function. This factorization is analogous to separating electrical-engineering considerations from programming considerations in computer science. This does not mean that such questions of biological realization are treated as any less important, only that they represent a distinct and, to a large extent, independent area of study.

(c) In addition to factoring out organic questions, this approach is also characterized by the techniques it uses in formulating its theories and exploring the consequences of its assumptions. The most widely used (though not universal) technique is that of computer implementation. Thus, an important methodological goal of cognitive science is to specify symbolic mechanisms that can actually exhibit aspects of the behavior being modeled. Adherence to such a sufficiency criterion makes this approach in many respects like a design discipline rather than a natural science, at least insofar as the latter typically attempts to uncover a small set of fundamental axioms or laws. Its concern with synthesis makes it, to use Herbert Simon's phrase, one of the "sciences of the artificial." [Simon, 1969.] By this, Simon means that the search for ways in which a certain task can be carried out within specified constraints—for example, of time and space—is the mark of a design discipline. Of course, in the case of cognitive science many of the constraints originate with empirical observations. These observations may be not only of what tasks people can carry out, but also of such things as the time it takes people to solve certain kinds of problems, which ones they find most difficult, and so on. Nonetheless, adopting the criterion of constructing a working system as part of the explanatory process makes the cognitive scientist's task less like that of a physicist than a design engineer.

(d) The approach tends to emphasize a strategy sometimes referred to as top-down analysis, where a premium is given to the task of understanding how the general cognitive skill in question is possible (consonant with the constraint of mechanism) in contrast to the task of accounting for empirical particulars. This difference in style contrasts with the traditional approach in experimental psychology, which emphasizes the observational fit of models. The contrast has been carefully examined and discussed. [Newell, 1970; Pylyshyn, 1979; Sloman, 1978a.]

(e) The commitment to the informational level also contrasts the enterprise with the phenomenological approach, where the existential notions of significance, meaningfulness, and experiential content are given a central role in the analysis, and with behaviorism, which attempts to analyze behavior without appealing to internal informational states. The philosophical implications of this point have been treated in recent publications. [Fodor, 1981; Haugeland, 1978; Dennett, 1978a.]

These general characteristics of cognitive science are also shared in various degrees by other scientific disciplines. The formalist or symbol-mechanistic character (a) is deeply entrenched in contemporary linguistics (especially in generative grammar), decision theory, parts of anthropology (e.g., the work of Levi-Strauss), and biology (e.g., the work of Burks). The functionalist perspective (b) is now quite general in psychology and philosophy of mind as well as in technology, where it is referred to as the black-box approach. Both (a) and (b) are fundamental to computer science as well as to any science that concerns itself with such notions as the flow of information or the distribution of control. Such ideas have thus affected everything from engineering to management science—and even political science. [Deutsch, 1963.]

Criteria (c) and (d) are not quite so prevalent as the first two. For example, the desire to synthesize aspects of the phenomena being modeled, as part of the attempt to understand them, is not widespread in the social sciences. Notable exceptions are cognitive psychology and management science (especially the branch of the latter called industrial dynamics, or the even more ambitious world dynamics [Forrester, 1971]). The synthetic approach is also not yet very common in biology. (See Marr's critique of theories in neurophysiology that fail to focus on the constructive computational aspect of biological function [Marr, 1975].) Even modern linguistics, which is, in many ways, a prototypical cognitive science, places little emphasis on the capacity of the theoretical mechanism actually to generate samples of performance. However, more recently examples of the contrary trend can be found. [Marcus, 1980.]

The Representational Metapostulate

Although, as we have seen, there are a number of theoretical and methodological characteristics that pervade a variety of approaches to understanding intelligence and human cognition, there is one overriding theme that more than any other appears to me to characterize the field of cognitive science. There are a number of ways of expressing this theme—for example, as the attempt to view intelligent behavior as consisting of processing information or to view intelligence as the outcome of rule-governed activity. But these characterizations express the same underlying idea: Computation, information processing, and rule-governed behavior all depend on the existence of physically instantiated *codes* or symbols that refer to or represent things and properties outside the behaving system. In all these instances, the behavior of the systems in question (be they minds, computers, or social systems) is explained, not in terms of intrinsic properties of the system itself, but in terms of rules and processes that operate on *representations of extrinsic things*. Cognition, in other words, is explained in terms of regularities in semantically interpreted symbolic representations, just as the behavior of a computer evaluating a mathematical function is explained in terms of its having representations of mathematical expressions (such as numerals) and the mathematical properties of the numbers these expressions represent. This is also analogous to explaining economic activity by referring, not to the categories of natural science (say, speaking of the physico-chemical properties of money and goods), but to the conventional meaning or symbolic value of these objects (e.g., that they are taken to represent such abstractions as legal tender or buying power). Although in both economics and cognitive science, the meaning-bearing objects (or the instantiations of the symbols) are physical, it is only by referring to their symbolic character that we can explain observed regularities in the resulting behavior.

PATTERNS OF COMMUNICATION AMONG
CONTRIBUTING DISCIPLINES

It is difficult to judge the degree of current, as opposed to potential, interrelations among the disciplines that comprise cognitive science or the broader field known as information science. The extent of interest that each field shows in the problems and findings of the other has varied from time to time and from topic to topic. Generally, however, research cross-fertilization, such as that measured by the frequency of citations, has tended to remain largely within traditional disciplinary boundaries: Technical reports tend to refer to other technical reports and empirical studies refer to other empirical studies.

For example, I recently conducted a simple survey to determine the extent of cross-disciplinary citation among several prominent journals in artificial intelligence and cognitive science. For artificial intelligence, I used what is probably the most representative source of papers in this field, the International Joint Conference on Artificial Intelligence (IJCAI) held in 1977 in the United States and two years of the journal *Artificial Intelligence*. A random sample of 528 references cited in that corpus revealed that at least 300 were clearly classifiable as references to other papers in artificial intelligence. Of these references, 56 were to other papers in the IJCAI proceedings; 29 to the AI journal; 16 to the Machine Intelligence series of books; and 157 were to such journals in computer science and engineering as the *Journal* and the *Communications* of the Association for Computing Machinery (ACM), the Institute of Electrical and Electronics Engineers (IEEE), and newsletters of the various Special Interest Groups of ACM (SIGs). There were only 35 citations of books or journals in psychology and 7 of journals in linguistics. Several other applied areas were also only occasionally represented, among them medicine, music, and management science. There were about 160 books, dissertations, and other references that could not be adequately categorized.

The outstanding feature of these tentative figures is the relative rarity of citations of psychological and linguistic papers (or reports in other empirical sciences) and the rather high rate of citations of unpublished works in the form of technical reports and dissertations. The mode of disseminating results in unpublished technical reports is quite characteristic of the field of artificial intelligence and contributes to the difficulty outsiders have in getting a good idea of the current state of research in that field. This style of communication can be attributed to a number of factors. It may in part reflect the fact that up to a few years ago, only a handful of major centers were turning out the bulk of the most influential work. Indeed, until about ten years ago, virtually all the work was being done by a small invisible college of researchers who were known to one another and thus were able to keep in contact adequately through the private distribution of technical reports. In addition to these historical reasons for this mode of communication, however, there is a more substantive reason, one that is related to the nature of the field. A great many of the products of research in artificial intelligence consist of massive computer systems whose contribution cannot be fully evaluated without a great deal of technical detail about their operations and yet whose potential audience is too small to merit publication in book form.

The relative paucity of citations of empirical research in other fields, such as psychology, may in part reflect the fact that much current research in artificial intelligence is concerned with developing computational techniques for information processing (for dealing with problems of representation and control). In addition, most people working in artificial intelligence come

from computer science or engineering backgrounds (though this is changing), and their familiarity and interest in psychological research literature
may be minimal. But there is an even deeper reason that may be relevant to
this tendency to ignore psychological research: Much of what is reported in
psychological literature may be irrelevant to even that part of the artificial-
intelligence community directly concerned with modeling aspects of human
cognition. It is irrelevant because most psychological experimentation is
motivated by the goal of clarifying issues raised in other experiments. It is,
as Newell has very well argued, largely paradigm-driven rather than
motivated by larger theoretical systems. [Newell, 1973b.]

The interest shown in artificial-intelligence research by publications in
psychology journals does not appear to be any greater than what I found for
the converse. A sample of the last two years of the journals *Cognitive Psychology, Cognition,* and *Memory and Cognition,* totaling some 1200 references, revealed that the vast majority (nearly 1000) were to psychological
articles and books. Indeed, looking at the references to psychological papers
alone, I find that the vast majority of them (571 to 133) were what could be
called journals in conventional experimental psychology rather than those
that could be classified as cognitive or information-processing. Of all the
citations, only 50 were of studies of artificial intelligence or computer simulation, while another 70 were of linguistics articles and 16 of papers in
philosophy. The latter two categories were represented almost entirely in
the journal *Cognition,* which especially encourages such cross-disciplinary
work. It would appear from these figures that at present research in cognitive psychology sees itself as being more closely allied with general experimental psychology than with any other subfield of cognitive science.

Despite these rough statistical observations concerning the relative insu-
larity of the two major contributing disciplines of cognitive science, there are
reasons to persist in the view that a major new cross-disciplinary area of
study is developing. For one thing, a somewhat better picture emerges if one
looks at the journal *Cognitive Science,* which is the official journal of the
Cognitive Science Society and is intended to foster cognitive science as an
interdisciplinary venture. Out of 331 citations of the last two years, 110 were
judged to be clearly psychological (31 books and 79 journal articles in psychology, with 29 of the articles in cognitive psychology); 55 were artificial
intelligence papers; 14 were articles in computer science journals; 50 were
citations of other articles in *Cognitive Science* itself; 40 were journal articles
in philosophy and logic; 26 were linguistics papers; 7 were neurophysiology
papers; and the remaining 36 citations were distributed among a variety of
areas, including library science, education, business, anthropology, and
book reviews.

Despite this apparent exception, I believe that the evidence (however
subjective and unreliable it may be) does strongly suggest that from a statistical point of view, cognitive psychology and computational studies of cognition are in fact not yet experiencing a large degree of cross-fertilization. On

the other hand, these indicators pertain to the general population of publications: They say nothing about how the most important and most influential work is being done. Much of the most ground-breaking work is, in my view, clearly cross-disciplinary and has been extremely influential in shaping people's thinking about cognitive science. The reason that this does not show up in statistical patterns of citations is that the number of such seminal works is (still) small. As an example of this, the aggregate statistics presented do not reveal that some important cross-disciplinary works[1] form the bulk of the small set of cross-disciplinary citations in *both* psychology and artificial-intelligence literature. Thus, while the total number of cross-disciplinary citations may not be large in relation to the total number of publications, a few of the clearly cross-disciplinary works have been extremely influential. And that is perhaps to be expected in an area that purports to form a new discipline as opposed to just being an amalgam of existing fields.

The same pattern emerges when one examines various other possible indicators of the relation between cognitive science and its contributing disciplines. For example, membership in various professional societies and on editorial boards of journals indicates that most people who belong to these official bodies belong to the traditional disciplines but that, as in the case of the citation statistics examined, there are a small number of highly influential cross-disciplinary members. Also paralleling the finding for citations, both the editorial board of *Cognitive Science* and the governing body of the Cognitive Science Society contain a broad distribution of members from the contributing fields, especially psychology, computer science, and linguistics.

THE CONVERGENCE TOWARD COGNITIVE SCIENCE

I have examined historical relations among fields that have recently come together as cognitive science and have briefly looked at several indexes of their de facto interrelation in the practice of research in this new field. However, the practitioners of cognitive science have a general view of what disciplines currently house the problems that are at the core of cognitive science. These include such fields as anthropology, computer science, linguistics, neuroscience, philosophy, and psychology. They also include such existing cross-disciplinary areas as cybernetics, neurolinguistics, neuropsychology, computational psychology, computational linguistics, philosophy of psychology, philosophy of language, anthropological linguistics, cognitive anthropology, and brain evolution. A committee appointed by the

---

[1] Prime examples are Newell and Simon's *Human Problem Solving* [1972]; Winograd's *Understanding Natural Language* [1972a]; Ernst and Newell's *GPS: A Case Study in Generality* [1969]; and such collections as Bobrow and Collins's interdisciplinary reader [1975].

Board of the Alfred P. Sloan Foundation (to advise the foundation on fruitful areas of frontier research deserving special support) recently put together an informal internal report on the state-of-the-art in cognitive science.[2]

The introductory section of this report mentions the preceding areas of scholarship as being the contributing fields of cognitive science, while warning that a general integration of the cognitive elements of these distinct disciplines is not yet at hand: Cognitive science is still a goal rather than a reality. However, it is a goal that an increasing number of scholars endorse and has led in the last few years to the creation of several dozen centers of excellence devoted to its pursuit.[3] The portion of the Sloan Report included in the appendix describes in general terms the current vision of the scope of this discipline.

An inspection of the general picture just presented and in the appendix reveals that cognitive science is not identical with what is commonly referred to as information science, inasmuch as it does not mention many fields that are concerned with storing, processing, and communicating information—such as work on information theory (including theories of optimal encoding, cryptography, and information security); information retrieval from large data banks; practical work in network development or library and document-management systems; and many other such research areas that are intimately involved with studying information. None of these studies can be excluded as irrelevant to cognitive science, since any of them could produce insights on the technical aspects of information use in cognitive (i.e., thinking) systems. Nonetheless, these studies are not primarily directed at understanding the nature of human and nonhuman cognition or the exercise of intelligence in the course of relating systems to their environments. Thus, it is fair to view cognitive science as primarily an empirical natural science concerned with a subset of the class of problems in information science, namely, those that bear on the general question of the exercise of intelligence by systems that exist at least partially in an autonomous relation with a natural and social environment to which they are actively adapting.

---

[2] Authors of this report included Michael Arbib, Carl Baker, Joan Bresnan, Roy D'Andrade, Ronald Kaplan, Jay Keyser, George Miller, Donald Norman, Zenon Pylyshyn, Scott Soames, Richard Thompson, Edward Walker, and Edgar Zurif.

[3] Among the North American universities that have established centers for cognitive science are Brown University, University of California at Berkeley, Carnegie-Mellon University, University of Chicago, University of Colorado, Cornell Medical School, University of Illinois, University of California at Irvine, University of Massachusetts, Massachusetts Institute of Technology, University of Michigan, University of Pennsylvania, University of Pittsburgh, Princeton University, University of Rochester, Rutgers University, University of California at Santa Barbara, University of California at San Diego, Stanford University, University of Texas, University of Western Ontario, and Yale University. In addition, a large number of industrial and other research institutions have also developed cognitive science laboratories—among many others, Bell Laboratories, Bolt, Beranek and Newman, Exxon, Fairchild, IBM, Rand, Schlumberger-Doll, Stanford Research Institute, and Xerox.

Appendix

COGNITIVE SCIENCE, 1978

Report of the State of the Art Committee to the Advisors of the Alfred P. Sloan Foundation, October 1, 1978

Introduction

Cognitive science is the study of the principles by which intelligent entities interact with their environments. By its very nature, this study transcends disciplinary boundaries to include research by scholars working in such disciplines as neuroscience, computer science, psychology, philosophy, linguistics, and anthropology. The familiar labels of these disciplines have provided the road map adopted here to explore the state of research in cognitive science.

It is, however, the richly articulated pattern of interconnection among these subdomains which makes explicit the basis for the claim that an autonomous science of cognition has arisen in the past decade. The disciplines contributing to this science, and the major bonds among them, are summarized by the following diagram. Each of the six fields listed is connected to the others by a network of interdisciplinary regimens, some of which represent ancient topics of intellectual concern, others of which raise familiar and important issues which have not yet become the focus of major scholarly effort.

Each of the component fields is tied to two or more of the others by a network of interdisciplinary regimens. Each labeled link represents a well defined area of inquiry which involves the intellectual and physical tools of the two disciplines it ties together. Thus cybernetics uses the concepts developed by computer scientists to model brain functions elucidated by neuroscientists. Similarly, psycholinguistics joins two fields in its concern for the mental apparatus and operations responsible for the acquisition of language and its production and understanding, and the simulation of cognitive processes has combined computer science and psychology in order to formulate explicit theories of thinking and problem solving. Other pairs share similar sets of concerns.

Each of the 11 solid lines in the figure represents a well defined and professionally established domain of interdisciplinary inquiry which may be found within one or more traditional academic departments. Those four links shown as dotted lines in the figure identify a set of issues, some already familiar and important, which have not yet become the focus of formally recognized scholarly effort.

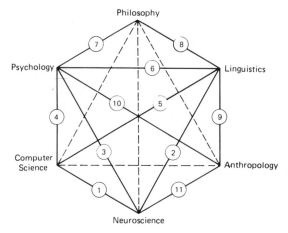

Figure 1. Subdomains of Cognitive Science: 1. Cybernetics. 2. Neurolinguistics. 3. Neuropsychology. 4. Simulation of cognitive processes. 5. Computational linguistics. 6. Psycholinguistics. 7. Philosophy of psychology. 8. Philosophy of language. 9. Anthropological linguistics. 10. Cognitive anthropology. 11. Evolution of brain.

It is possible to consider linked sets of the six major disciplines taken three or more at a time. The triad of philosophy, psychology, and linguistics, for example, represents an old area of inquiry concerned with language and the use of language in cognitive tasks. Each such group represents a valid and increasingly active area of research whose practitioners have been trained in two or more of the fields involved. A major concern of this paper is the argument that the network of interacting disciplines shown here should be considered as a whole under the name cognitive science. That whole cannot yet be integrated successfully, but such an integration is the goal toward which these related groupings are moving.

What the subdisciplines of cognitive science share, indeed, what has brought the field into existence, is a common research objective: *to discover the representational and computational capacities of the mind and their structural and functional representation in the brain.* Cognitive science is already being practiced by workers in the fields and subfields listed above. These workers have accepted the challenge to specify adequate theoretical descriptions of cognitive systems and to test empirically the predictions of these theories. The survey which follows presents some of the examples of their collaboration in research directed toward this objective and provides ample demonstration of the practical necessity of such a coordinated scientific attack. The questions now being addressed in the subfields of cognitive science are fundamentally related; moreover, the theoretical and methodological apparatus of one subfield is being increasingly applied, and sometimes improved, to answer questions in another.

The reader will no doubt want to examine in detail the work within one or more of the subdomains of cognitive science discussed in the survey. Here we turn to a simple, but relatively well worked-out example to illustrate the transdisciplinary nature of research in cognitive science.

Consider the names we give to colors. There would seem to be little to complicate the description of color-naming: there are the perceived colors and words to name them. A child must learn to match the two, and an adult uses this matching to refer reliably to colors. In order to appreciate the serious scientific interest of the matching process, one must consider that color-naming is a special case of more abstractly characterizable cognitive processes.

In particular, how do the people who speak a language decide which objects, events, properties, or relations they will name? Is the set of name-ables a universal property specified by some innate characteristic of the mind, or can people partition and name reality in any way convenient to them? This is not an arbitrary question; it has been the subject of continuing discussion for at least two centuries. Linguists recognized long ago that the active lexicons of languages differ in reflection of the interests and concerns of their speakers.

There are those relativists who feel that culture is free to form any verbal concept and that it forms those which serve the habitual patterns of thought of its members. Universalists, on the other hand, feel that while patterns of usage may differ, the concepts underlying habitual usage are constrained in every human culture by the nature of the physical world and by the innate biological mechanisms that have evolved to cope with that world. Most students of the question feel that some subfields of thought might be best understood in relation to the habit patterns of a particular culture, while biological principles that apply universally to human beings constrain others. Thus, for example, languages differ in surface form sufficiently to require translation but at the same time share the biologically determined universal properties which make translation possible.

At first glance, the domain of color names might seem an ideal place to demonstrate relativism. We know that the range of visible colors from red to blue and from black to white is continuous. It is possible, then, that cultures might divide and label the color continuum as they see fit. Different colors could become salient or memorable in different cultures, for a variety of reasons, and names would arise to label them. In fact, it is common knowledge that the speakers of these languages do draw different boundaries between the color to which their names refer. According to the relativist thesis, people who label the continuum of colors differently reflect different cognitive capacities—learned or innate—for thinking about color. They have different color concepts.

To demonstrate this thesis—that psychological differences are associated with terminological conventions—early experiments tested the color memory of English speakers. An extensively developed European and American color technology made it possible to control and specify color samples precisely, and these calibrated colors were presented to subjects who were asked to remember them and, later on, to select them from a larger set of samples.

The samples for which people have reliably communicable color names (the sort of names which would enable a second person to select the color on the basis of the name assigned) were found to be just those that could be recognized and selected from others after a time interval. Colors without simple names were both difficult to name or describe and difficult to remember.

Such results initially were interpreted to mean that language does constrain thought—in this case, that habits of color-naming determined the accuracy of color memory. This interpretation proved to be inverted. Subsequent studies demonstrated conclusively that particular colors are not distinctive because a culture has given them names. Rather, the colors are given names because they are distinctive.

The evidence comes from several sources. Psychological studies revealed that the primary colors—those which English speakers call red, green, yellow, blue, black, and white—have special status in color discrimination tests. Neurophysiological research demonstrated that the visual system organizes these primaries into opponent pairs—red/green, yellow/blue, and black/white. In other words, the organization of color into primary pairs is an innately given biological property of all humans with normal vision. Furthermore, anthropological studies of peoples whose languages contain fewer color terms than English revealed that, in all cases, the "best instances" of the colors named are close to the psychologically primary colors; that these color terms are directly translatable to English. Finally, when memory tests were conducted on people who spoke a language with only two basic color terms, they remembered primary colors best, even though they had no names for them.

Clearly, some aspects of color-naming are culturally determined: the number of terms does vary. However, the use made of available color terminology is constrained by innate neurophysiological properties and their relation to cognition rather than vice versa. In short, the conceptual capacity underlying color-naming conforms more closely to the universalist than to the relativist position.

Of itself, this conclusion is of no momentous significance: color terms form only a fragment of the lexicon in any language. Our present interest, however, is to demonstrate the kind of interdisciplinary research strategy that is required to establish such a result.

Note first that the intellectual significance of the color-naming studies derives from a general theoretical question about the nature of the human mind, a question which is not properly restricted to any one of the disciplines that contributed to the research just described. We assume that this one research objective of cognitive science is to formulate abstract descriptions of the mental capacities manifested by the structure, content, and function of various cognitive systems. We will refer to the subject matter of this kind of objective as *abstraction*.

Second, note that the research on color-naming would have been impossible without the extensive development of the science and technology of color. This base not only provides the instrumentation needed to carry out the research, but, more importantly, provides the intellectual resources needed to specify alternative models of the color-naming process. Often a cognitive function could be accomplished by a variety of realizable physical systems. We will refer to the systematic exploration of these alternatives as the objective of *instantiation*.

Third, note that not only color technology but psychological, linguistic, and anthropological methods were required to discover how people in various cultures name and think about colors. The data obtained led to the conclusion that one model of the color-naming system more plausibly characterizes that found in humans. That is to say, devices could be designed and implemented either to allow an arbitrary partition of the color space or to give priority to a particular set of colors. It is the latter which more accurately parallels that in humans. We will refer to attempts to characterize the mental processes underlying cognitive function in living organisms as the objective of *plausibility*.

Finally, note that an important element of the explanation of color-naming was a reasonably convincing neurophysiological account of the capacity. For more complex cognitive systems, of course, the neurological basis will be much more difficult to discover and characterize, but the scientific analysis of a cognitive system cannot be considered complete until its biological foundations are understood. We will refer to the study of the neurological mechanisms involved in cognition as the objective of *realization*.

These four objectives are shared by cognitive scientists, and they constitute the general problem areas around which work in the subdomains of the field is oriented. In effect, the result of research directed toward achieving the objectives just outlined is to place constraints on possible theories of cognition and its biological representation; constraints based on the abstract properties of cognitive capacities, the properties of devices for instantiating those capacities, their plausible implementation in living organisms, and their neurological realization.

The field of cognitive science has arisen because these objectives unite the work of scholars in many academic and professional disciplines. The emergence of the field as an empirical science has, however, preceded the development of an institutional framework within which research on such issues could be optimally pursued. Consequently, cognitive scientists all too often find the transdisciplinary interaction that is so vital to the conduct of their work difficult to attain or provide. The incorporation of directly relevant work from another field is sometimes frustrated by the unfortunate impediments to interdisciplinary collaboration in research and training and by the specialized terminology which has been developed within each discipline.

While it is, of course, impossible to guarantee the success of an intellectual undertaking, cognitive science clearly is a field at the brink of rapid, and perhaps significant, change. As the field matures, there is little doubt that great progress will be made in many of the aspects of cognition currently under investigation. Perhaps the single most important contribution which can be made to further this effort would be to introduce centers of research in which active scholars and students might come together for extended collaboration in research and training at all levels. This report is intended to demonstrate the value of, and immediate need for, such a contribution to the field.

COGNITIVE SCIENCE
The View from Brain Theory

Michael A. Arbib

Pylyshyn offers a historical perspective on cognitive science, which sees its roots in mathematical logic, with artificial intelligence at the core of recent developments. In the first section of this comment, I offer a somewhat different history, one that places more emphasis on brain research, and which suggests that cognitive science is *Cybernetics Redux*.

CYBERNETICS AND THE ROOTS OF COGNITIVE SCIENCE

Technology has always played a crucial role in attempts to understand the human mind and body; for example, the study of the steam engine has contributed concepts to the study of metabolism, and electricity has been part of the study of the brain at least since sometime before 1791, when Galvani touched a frog's leg to an iron railing. In 1750, Offray de la Mettrie published *L'homme machine* and suggested that such automata as the mechanical duck and flute player of Vaucanson indicated the possibility of one day building a mechanical man who could talk. [Offray de la Mettrie, 1750.] The automata of those days were unable to adapt to changing circumstances, but in the following century, machines were built that could automatically counter disturbances to restore their desired performance. Perhaps the best known example of this is Watt's governor for the steam engine. This development led to James Clerk Maxwell's paper, "On Governors," which laid the basis for both the theory of negative feedback and the study of system stability. [Maxwell, 1868.] At the same time, Claude Bernard drew attention to homeostasis, observing that physiological processes often form circular chains of cause and effect that could counteract disturbances in such

This paper refers to research supported in part by NIH grant NS 14971 and by A. P. Sloan Foundation grant 80-6-13 to the University of Massachusetts. Portions of this paper appeared in somewhat different form in my article in the *Handbook of Physiology—The Nervous System II. Motor Control* [1981].

variables as body temperature, blood pressure, and glucose level in the blood. [Bernard, 1878–1879.]

The year 1943 was the key year for bringing together the notions of control mechanism and intelligent automata. Kenneth Craik published his seminal essay *The Nature of Explanation.* [Craik, 1943.] Here, the nervous system was viewed "as a calculating machine capable of modeling or paralleling external events," suggesting that the process of paralleling is the basic feature of thought and explanation. In the same year, Rosenblueth, Wiener, and Bigelow published "Behavior, Purpose and Teleology." [Rosenblueth, Wiener, and Bigelow, 1943.] Engineers had noted that if the feedback used in controlling the rudder of a ship were, for instance, too brusque, the rudder would overshoot, compensatory feedback would yield a larger overshoot in the opposite direction, and so on and so on as the system wildly oscillated. Wiener and Bigelow asked Rosenblueth if there were any corresponding pathological conditions in humans and were given the example of intention tremor associated with an injured cerebellum. This evidence for feedback within the human nervous system led the three scientists to urge that neurophysiology move beyond the Sherringtonian view of the central nervous system as a reflex device adjusting itself in response to sensory inputs. Rather, setting reference values for feedback systems could provide the basis for analyzing the brain as a purposive system explicable only in terms of circular processes, that is, from nervous system to muscles to the external world and back again via receptors.

The year 1943 also saw the publication of "A Logical Calculus of the Ideas Immanent in Nervous Activity," in which Warren McCulloch and Walter Pitts offered their formal model of the neuron as a threshold logic unit. [McCulloch and Pitts, 1943.] They were building on the neuron doctrine of Ramon y Cajal and the excitatory and inhibitory synapses of Sherrington. They used notations from the mathematical logic of Whitehead, Russell, and Carnap, but a major stimulus for their work was the Turing machine, a device that could read, write, and move on an indefinitely extendable tape, each square of which bore a symbol from some finite alphabet. Alan Turing had made plausible the claim that any effectively definable computation, that is, anything that a human could do in the way of symbolic manipulation by following a finite and completely explicit set of rules, could be carried out by such a machine equipped with a suitable program. [Turing, 1936.] What McCulloch and Pitts demonstrated was that each such program could be implemented using a finite network (with loops) of their formal neurons. Thus, as electronic computers were built toward the end of World War II, it was understood that whatever they could do could be done by a network of neurons.

These, then, were some of the strands that were gathered in Wiener's book *Cybernetics, or Control and Communication in the Animal and the Machine,* published in 1948, and in the Josiah Macy Jr. Foundation conferences, which, from 1949 on, were referred to as *Cybernetics: Circular Causal and Feedback Mechanisms in Biological and Social Systems.* It is beyond the scope of the present commentary to trace the further evolution of work under the banner of cybernetics. Rather, let us simply note that, as the field developed in the fifties, it began to fragment. Much work in cybernetics now deals with control problems in diverse fields of engineering, economics, and other social sciences, whereas the broad field of computer science has become a discipline in its own right. Here, we briefly cite five subdisciplines that have crystallized from the earlier concern with the integrated study of mind, brain, and machine.

1. *Biological Control Theory.* The techniques of control theory, especially the use of linear approximations, feedback, and stability analysis, are widely applied to the analysis of such diverse physiological systems as the stretch reflex, thermoregulation, and the control of the pupil.

2. *Neural Modeling.* The Hodgkin-Huxley analysis of the action potential, Rall's models of dendritic function, analysis of lateral inhibition in the retina, and the analysis of rhythm-generating networks are examples of successful mathematical studies of single neurons, or of small or highly regular networks of neurons, which have developed in fruitful interaction with microelectrode studies.

3. *Artificial Intelligence.* This is a branch of computer science devoted to studying techniques for constructing programs enabling computers to exhibit aspects of intelligent behavior. Among such intelligent behavior is playing checkers, solving logical puzzles, or understanding restricted portions of a natural language such as English. Although some practitioners of artificial intelligence look solely for contributions to technology, there are many who see their field as intimately related with cognitive psychology.

4. *Cognitive Psychology.* The concepts of cybernetics gave rise to a new form of cognitive psychology that sought to explain human perception and problem-solving not in neural terms but rather at some intermediate level of information-processing constructs. Recent years have seen strong interaction between artificial intelligence and cognitive psychology.

5. *Brain Theory.* Because cybernetics extends far beyond the analysis of brain and machine, the term *brain theory* has been introduced to denote an approach to brain study that seeks to bridge the gap between studies of behavior and overall function (artificial intelligence and cognitive psychology) and the study of physiologically and anatomically well-defined neural nets (biological control theory and neural modeling).

In the 1970s, a new grouping took place, which brought together researchers in artificial intelligence and cognitive psychology with those linguists and philosophers of mind who emphasize symbol-processing. The resulting field is more a loose federation than an integrated discipline, and it is this cognitive science that Pylyshyn describes in his article. Few practitioners are aware of the roots of cognitive science in cybernetics, and most believe that their ignorance of brain research is a virtue and human intelligence can be studied as symbol-manipulation without concern for its embodiment. (John Searle offers a recent critique of this viewpoint. [Searle, 1982a.]) At the same time, all too many neuroscientists see workers in artificial intelligence as simply playing with toys. In the hope of better bridging neuroscience and cognitive science, I offer an integrated perspective on past and potential contributions of brain theory to the analysis of the role of visual information in the neural control of movement. Due to lack of space, I shall not discuss efforts to bring neurologists, psycholinguists, brain theorists, and artificial intelligence workers together to study language, but simply refer to a recent collection of papers [Arbib, Caplan, and Marshall, 1982] and a dissertation [Gigley, 1982].

MAPS AS CONTROL SURFACES

A notable characteristic of the brain is the orderly mapping from one neural layer to another, be it the retinotopic mapping from the retina to the many visual systems or the somatotopic mapping of the motor cortex to the musculature. I briefly look at one hypothesis of how such a map acts as a control surface such that the spatio-temporal patterns in the map provide input to some control system in the brain. Pitts and McCulloch offered a distributed-processing model of the reflex arc that extended from the eyes through the superior colliculus to the oculomotor nuclei, thereby controlling muscles that direct the gaze so as to bring the fixation point to the center of gravity of distribution of the visual input's brightness. [Pitts and McCulloch, 1947.] Pitts and McCulloch noted that excitation at a point on the left colliculus corresponds to excitation from the right half of the visual field and so should induce movement of the eye to the right; gaze is centered when excitation from the left is exactly balanced by excitation from the right. Their model is so arranged, for example, that each motoneuron controlling muscle fibers in the muscles that contract to move the eyeballs to the right should receive excitation summing the level of activity in a thin transverse strip of the left colliculus. This process provides all the excitation to muscles turning the eye to the right. Reciprocal inhibition by axonal collaterals from the nuclei of the antagonist eye muscles, which are excited similarly by the other colliculus, performs subtraction. The quasicenter of gravity's vertical coordinate is computed similarly. Eye movement ceases when and only when the fixation point is the center of gravity.

   This scheme shows how to design a retinotopically organized network in which there is no "executive neuron" that decrees which way the overall system behaves; rather, the dynamics of the effectors, with assistance from neuronal interactions, extract the output trajectory from a population of neurons, none of which has more than local information as to how the system should behave. In other words, the Pitts and McCulloch model of the superior colliculus shows how the organism can be committed to an overall action by a population of neurons, none of which has global information about which action is appropriate.

I have argued that the study of such cooperative computation in somatotopically organized networks provides a central paradigm in brain theory. [Arbib, 1972.] The study of visuomotor coordination in frog and toad provides an area (by no means the only one) rich in experiments that may contribute to our understanding of the neural underpinnings of perceptual structures and distributed motor control. A number of experiments on prey catching and predator avoidance as well as on the modification of behavior by the presence of barriers have led to models of prey selection and prey-enemy pattern-recognition. [Ewert, 1980; Arbib, 1982.] These experiments provide support for the following general conclusions:

1. Analysis of vision must not only study local features and responses to point stimuli, but also develop techniques to analyze structured visual stimuli. Visual processing can be viewed in terms of cooperative computation in somatotopically-organized networks, with overall patterns of activity being generated in neural structures wherein no single neuron has global information as to what course is appropriate. Here, there is a rich area of relevant artificial intelligence totally ignored in Pylyshyn's review, namely, machine vision. For example, Dana Ballard and Christopher Brown approach machine vision in a way that is increasingly based on a brainlike style of cooperative computation. [Ballard and Brown, 1982.] As discussed in my "Cybernetics: The View from Brain Theory" in this volume, there is now developing a general theory of competition and cooperation in neural nets, with applications to prey selection, mode selection, and stereopsis, and with similarities to relaxation techniques used in artificial intelligence. An important bridge between machine vision and human vision is offered by Marr. [Marr, 1982.]

2. It is useful to view a neural map as a control surface providing input to some control system in the brain. In addition to a knowledge of competition and cooperation within the neural nets that constitute each controller, there must be an understanding of the cooperative computation of controllers. This cooperation may entail coordination turning off all but one of the controllers, or it may involve a rich interplay between subsystems, each modulating the other.

THE PERCEPTUAL AND MOTOR SCHEMAS

Pylyshyn has correctly stressed that cognitive science currently tends to formulate its theories in terms of symbol-manipulation and that theories of biological organization are ignored. (Pylyshyn is more diplomatic. His exact words are: "questions of biological realization are [not] treated as any less important, only . . . they represent a distinct and, to a large extent, independent area of study.") In fact, theories apply blinkers to the consideration of relevant facts, and a cognitive scientist who restricts himself or herself to a symbol-manipulation theory will never examine the data on brain function that could show the inadequacy of this approach. Pylyshyn emphasizes the top-down analysis of much cognitive science. However, he has elsewhere given a more subtle analysis of the way in which the data the scientist chooses to examine determine the appropriate grain of the functional architecture of the theory. [Pylyshyn, 1980.] Just consider the very different demands of linguistic models that address the following three kinds of data: judgments of sentence grammaticality, response time and eye-movement data on sentence comprehension, and aphasiological data on the effect of brain damage in language performance.

In the rest of this comment, I want to show how an analysis of perception and motor control in the style of top-down cognitive psychology can fruitfully interact with bottom-up analysis enriched by the analog (rather than symbolic) control theory of cybernetics. The approach grows out of my concern with brain theory, and is developed in more detail in my contribution to the *Handbook of Physiology*. [Arbib, 1981.] However, the neural aspects of the analysis will be played down in the present discussion.

Perceptual Schemas and the Action-Perception Cycle

Human behavior is determined by a far greater knowledge of the environment than afforded by the current stimulation of the retina, especially because so little of that stimulation is foveal. Our actions are addressed not only to interacting with the environment in some instrumental way, but also to updating our "internal model of the world." [Gregory, 1969.] In a new situation, we can recognize familiar things in new relations and use our knowledge of those things and our perception of the relations to guide our behavior in that situation. It thus seems reasonable to posit that the internal model of the world must be built of units, each of which roughly corresponds to a domain of interaction, which may be an object in the usual sense, an attention-riveting detail of an object, or some domain of social interaction.

The notion of schema has been widely used in neurology [Frederiks, 1969]; psychology [Bartlett, 1932; Piaget, 1971]; artificial intelligence, under such names as frames [Minsky, 1975]; and in the study of motor skills.

Where much of cognitive science talks of knowledge in only some abstract realm of symbol-manipulation or problem-solving, I here wish to stress knowledge representations that subserve perception, embedded within the organism's ongoing interaction with its environment. As the organism moves in a complex environment, making, executing, and updating plans, it must stay tuned to its spatial relations with its immediate environment, anticipating objects before they come into view. The information gathered during ego motion must be systematically integrated into the organism's internal model of the world: Information picked up modifies the perceiver's anticipations of certain kinds of information that, thus modified, direct further exploration and prepare the perceiver for more information. Such considerations will, I predict, increasingly engage the attention of cognitive scientists as robotics becomes an increasingly active area of study within artificial intelligence. The problem of controlling robot arms and integrating visual and tactile information will require increasing attention to control theory, cooperative computation, and sensorimotor integration. This will combat the overemphasis on symbolic processes provided by Pylyshyn's paper.

The intelligent organism does not so much respond to stimuli as select information that helps it achieve current goals, although a well-designed or evolved system certainly needs to take appropriate account of unexpected changes in its environment. Planning is the process whereby the system combines an array of relevant knowledge to determine a course of action suited to current goals. In its fullest subtlety, planning involves the refinement of knowledge structures and goal structures as well as action per se.

Novel inputs (e.g., encountering an unexpected obstacle) can alter the elaboration of high-level structures into lower-level tests and actions that, in turn, call on the interaction of motor and sensory systems. Scientists seek to study programs that are part of the internal state of the system and can flexibly guide ongoing action in terms of internal goals or drives and external circumstances. My thesis is that perception of an object (activating appropriate perceptual schemas) involves gaining access to routines for interaction with the object (motor schemas) but does not necessarily involve executing even one of these routines. Although an animal may perceive many aspects of its environment, only a few of these can at any time become primary loci of interaction. Therefore, perception activates (i.e., defines a search space, draws a map), and planning concentrates (lays out the route to be followed).

I use the term *perceptual schema* to denote the process whereby the system determines whether a given domain of interaction is present in the environment. The state of activation of the schema then determines the credibility of the hypothesis that what the schema represents is, indeed, present, whereas other schema parameters represent such properties as size, location, and motion of the perceived object. Consider a schema that represents, say, a chair; also consider an environment that has two chairs in plain view. It is clear that two copies of the chair schema (or at least two separate sets of chair-schema parameters) are required to represent the two chairs. These two copies are separate instantiations of the same schema, each with its own set of parameter values. The internal representation of the environment may thus be viewed as an assemblage of spatially tagged, parametrized schema-instantiations.

Motor Schemas

I have used schema to indicate the type of unit from which the internal representation of the environment can be built. Programs for motor control may themselves be seen as assembled from suitable units, which are referred to as motor schemas. These motor schemas are related to synergies (in the sense of the Russian school founded by Nikolai Bernstein [Bernstein, 1967]). These schemas may exhibit short-term memory. To control properly the motion of an object (the controlled system), the controller must clearly know such relevant parameters of the object as its mass and moment of inertia. However, in the real world the exact values of these parameters are seldom available and may actually change over time. (Compare short-term loading effects on muscles with longer term aging effects and weight changes.) To adapt to such changes, the feedback loop must be augmented by an identification algorithm. The job of this algorithm is to identify more accurately the parameters of the controlled system. To do this, it continually monitors the behavior of the controlled system and compares it with the output that would be expected on the basis of the current estimated parameters. Any discrepancies in the output can be used to obtain more accurate estimates of the parameters that define the controlled system. These updated parameters can then be supplied to the controller as the basis for its state estimation and control computations.

Note well that the identification algorithm can do its job only if the controller is of the right general class. It is unlikely that a controller adapted for guiding the arm during ball-catching would be able, simply as a result of parameter adjustment, to control properly the legs in performing a waltz. Thus, the adaptive controller (controller plus identification procedure) is not to be thought of as a model of the brain; rather, each such control system is a model of a single motor schema that can be activated when appropriate.

This framework for analyzing visually guided behavior of a complex organism is based on four general premises:

1. The action-perception cycle: As the organism moves—making, executing, and updating plans—it must maintain an up-to-date representation of its spatial relations with its environment.

2. The model of the environment is an active, information-seeking process composed of an assemblage of perceptual schemas, each instantiation of which represents a distinct domain of interaction with such relevant properties as size and motion represented by the current values of parameters of the schema.

3. Activation of perceptual schemas provides access to related motor schemas but does not necessarily entail execution of these schemas. Planning is required to determine the actual course of action. The plan is updated as action affords perceptual updating of the internal model.

4. The plan of action is to be thought of as a coordinated control program composed of motor schemas, each viewed as an adaptive controller that uses an identification procedure to update its representation of the object being controlled. Thus, the identification procedure can be viewed as a perceptual schema embedded within a motor schema.

COORDINATED CONTROL PROGRAMS

Karl Lashley laid many of the foundations for neuropsychology, that most cognitive of the neurosciences. In an important critique of stimulus/response theory, he raised questions about serial order in behavior that are answered at the conceptual level as soon as one thinks of the brain's computations not in terms of stimulus/response couplings or chains of associations but, rather, in terms of coordinated control programs. [Lashley, 1951.] Although our knowledge of computer programs removes the conceptual problem of serial order, the question of how such control strategies can be neurally implemented is only beginning to be answered. Much of the neurophysiological analysis of movement has focused on spinal mechanisms (especially feedback mechanisms in posture and locomotion) and on higher level single-cell correlates of stimulus or response. Future research clearly must aim to better analyze the distribution of planning operations within cortical structures and understand the signal flow this planning must impose on the cerebellum and other regions that modulate this planning.

Even though the neural mechanisms for the planned coordinated control of motor schemas seem to be beyond the range of current experimental investigation, I suggest that artificial-intelligence approaches to planning may provide a framework for the development of such investigations in the future.

A pattern of action may be quite complex, with the actions intertwined and overlapping. Simultaneous actions must be coordinated, and successive actions must be smoothly phased, one into the next. In this section, I discuss the concept of a coordinated control program as the type of structure that orchestrates the interwoven activation of motor schemas controlling different actions.

Biological control theory usually studies neural circuitry specialized for the control of a specific function, be it the stretch reflex or the vestibulo-ocular reflex. Yet, most behavior involves complex sequences of coordinated activity of a number of control systems. Thus, I explore the notion of a coordinated control program as a combination of control theory and the computer scientist's notion of a program suited to analyzing the control of movement. Control theorists use a block diagram to represent a system. Each box represents a subsystem that is continually active, whereas the lines linking the boxes illustrate the transfer of data, showing how the output of one system helps determine input to another. By contrast, the boxes in flow diagrams used by computer scientists represent not subsystems but patterns of activation of subsystems. The computer has various subsystems, such as memory registers, arithmetic units, and test units. At any time in a computation, certain data are stored in these subsystems, and one box in the flow diagram is activated in the sense that it is used by the computer to determine what tests and operations are to be carried out by the subsystems and how data are to be transferred among them. The lines of the flow diagram then specify how activation is to be transferred from one instruction to another.

In a coordinated control program, control schemas are so scheduled that simultaneous actions are coordinated and successive actions are smoothly phased one into the next. Although certain basic programs are hard-wired into the organism, most programs are generated as the result of an explicit planning process. A hypothetical program for reaching to a target showed that perceptual schemas need not be defined as a separately specified part of a coordinated control program but may, instead, enter automatically as the identification algorithms that are required to define the appropriate values of the parameters in the motor schemas entering into the program. [Arbib, 1981.]

Concepts from computer science and artificial intelligence have been exposed to little in the way of neuroscientific experiment but may serve to stimulate new models of perceptual structures and their role in planning and controlling movement.

CONCLUSION

I have examined the role of visual information in the control of movement from the perspective of brain theory, seeking to bridge the gap between the cognitive-science topics addressed in Pylyshyn's paper (artificial intelligence and cognitive psychology) and the study of physiologically and anatomically well-defined neural nets (biological control theory and neural modeling).

Complexity seems to demand intermediate levels of analysis to mediate between a top-down analysis of the flexibility of an animal's behavior in a richly structured environment and the data of neuroscience. The environment can be represented in terms of an assemblage of instantiations of perceptual schemas, each instantiation representing relevant parameters of some particular object or domain of interaction relevant to the organism. Artificial intelligence provides techniques for analyzing processes whereby a plan of action is created on the basis of the organism's goals and current perceptions. Cybernetic analyses and Russian studies of skilled movement give the notion of motor schemas as the units from which each plan of action is constituted; the concept of a coordinated control program suggests how motor schemas might be interwoven. Control-theoretic studies of feedforward and identification algorithms are useful in describing the structure of motor schemas at a level that can be connected with neurophysiological investigation. The growing refinement of experiments in the motor-skills literature, especially when coupled with electromyogram recording, begins to let us essay functional accounts of coordinated control programs for a number of behaviors that involve the integration of several motor schemas. However, the neural implementation of such programs, as distinct from the motor schemas themselves, remains elusive.

We thus see that when we turn from abstract problem-solving to the study of perception and movement, we can make use of a spectrum of concepts that ranges from those firmly rooted in the findings of the neuroscientist's laboratory and the control theory descended from Wiener's cybernetics to those that have proved their efficacy in the design of robots. I have also observed that there are whole areas of artificial intelligence, such as machine vision, that are absent from Pylyshyn's picture of cognitive science. More centrally to the present paper, I have suggested that cognitive scientists (those working in vision being the most striking exception) are "blinkered" in their choice of data and thus dismiss neural data as irrelevant, holding that a top-down analysis is necessarily sufficient. Pylyshyn certainly reinforces this perception when he surveys 331 citations in the journal *Cognitive Science* and finds that only 7 were to sources in neuroscience. Another commentator might note that anthropology, too, is still too limited in its impact on cognitive science. The aim of this commentary has been to encourage the cognitive scientist to learn from both brain theorist and experimentalist in developing a theory of the human mind that can benefit from the rich body of data and models on animal behavior, comparative neuroanatomy, neuroethology, and neurophysiology, and the clinical data of the neurologist.

Two last comments: In the diagram provided in the appendix to Pylyshyn's paper, one of the missing links is that between philosophy and neuroscience. Surely this is a mistake. Discussion of the brain-mind problem antedates the current fashion for cognitive science by centuries and is still going strong, as witnessed by the active interest generated by the (in my opinion, mistaken) dualist position of Karl Popper and John Eccles in their volume on *The Self and Its Brain*. [Popper and Eccles, 1977.] I would also draw the reader's attention to Robert Young's *Mind, Brain, and Adaptation in the Nineteenth Century*, which should engender humility in us all by showing how thoughtfully neurologists of the last century considered problems at the center of cognitive science today. [Young, 1970.]

COGNITIVE NEUROSCIENCE
More Plain Talk

Michael S. Gazzaniga

Zenon Pylyshyn has laid out with striking clarity what cognitive scientists do, which is, mainly, test the design of information systems that model aspects of a behavior. That is not what cognitive neuroscientists do, and my bet is that the approach he describes will be inefficient in designating cognitive systems that do accurately describe how *human* minds work. That is the task cognitive neuroscientists have set for themselves, and their objective is to take up the problem experimental psychologists left for neuroscientists but that neuroscientists did not pick up. This is because the current view in neuroscience is that the cellular study of brain function will yield more substantial insights into, well, into something, and the question is what is the something? Accepting completely Pylyshyn's case for the levels-of-analysis approach, cognitive neuroscientists believe that the cellular approach of their colleagues in basic neuroscience will tell us about cells. That is an admirable task, but one that leaves begging the task of understanding human cognition.

In order to compare the approaches, it is helpful to take the example of the problem of memory. The basic neuroscientists, taking the lead from work on brain-damaged humans, have decided to focus a large part of their energies on a brain structure called the hippocampus. This structure, which is implicated in the human memory process, can be removed from experimental animals, placed in tissue culture, and the metabolic and electrophysiological properties of its cells studied. A series of elegant reports has demonstrated that changes in cellular activity occur to repetitive stimulation that are long lasting, indeed, seemingly permanent. The biochemical machinery responsible for this response seems to be in hand and investigations are well on their way to determining the site of morphological changes on the synapse that must occur to explain the long-lasting effect. Nice, perhaps even brilliant, but how such changes connect with how a person remembers a telephone number when it is breezed by at a cocktail party is not even attempted.

At the level of description at which cognitive scientists work, the task is to describe how artifacts and/or humans process information. Over the years, cognitive scientists have established limits on the amount and kind of information that can be apprehended, on strategies that facilitate the acquisition of information, and on the possible different kinds of memory the cognitive system handles. These elegant studies generate data on response characteristics of these human and nonhuman information systems, and theories are constructed about how the system must be organized. What is left open, of course, is whether or not the human brain is organized the way the cognitive scientists think it must be, just as Pylyshyn plainly says.

Alas, the cognitive neuroscientists' approach! The subject for experimental observation is the human with brain disease and/or focal lesion that can be accurately localized and described. The measures are on this human's ability to perform memory tasks of a wide variety. The results allow one to construct theories about how the memory system is organized by considering how systems make errors that are reliably generated by specific pathological states. The approach puts constraints on the theories of the cognitive scientists and the neuroscientists. At the present time, the cognitive neuroscientist is rewriting the backdrop for researchers in both areas. The neuroscientist is being redirected to other brain areas as well as facing the reality that more than one cellular process may be responsible for memory. Cognitive scientists are having to adjust their theories to the fact that there is not one cognitive system that is in charge of all information-processing. Recent developments would suggest that the cognitive system has a modular-type organization and that these modules may have specialized features.

Of course, in reality, all of the approaches seem terribly exciting, and any contemporary scientist must become reasonably conversant in the three fields—cognitive science, basic neuroscience, and cognitive neuroscience—but each of us, happily, has our own preference.

COGNITIVE SCIENCE
A New Patch in the Quilt?

Saul Gorn

Pylyshyn first presents a historical introduction discussing a general ideological drift from material and power concepts to the study of their interactive relations and our symbolization of them. He points out that the resulting paradigms were cybernetic and, finally, also included the study of communication and control of symbol systems (analog and digital computers). These "influenced . . . thinking about the nature of thought, intelligence, and adaptation," to quote Pylyshyn. He distinguishes a cybernetics of continuous processes from one of the discrete, much as Moses, in his comments on my paper in this volume, distinguishes the paradigms of system theory from those of information science. Where the first set of paradigms studied self-organizing and adaptive systems, the second addressed itself to the simulation of thought processes involved in problem-solving, that is, to artificial intelligence.

Pylyshyn's second section discusses what he feels are the more or less common attitudes of the group of disciplines that "attempt to understand the nature of intelligence" (philosophy, linguistics, anthropology, neuroscience, computer science, and psychology—as he points out in his last section and as appears in the appendix from the report to the advisors of the Sloan Foundation). He feels that these shared attitudes are (1) formalist, (2) functional, (3) in the habit of using simulation techniques to "specify symbolic mechanisms that can actually exhibit aspects of the behavior being modeled," (4) addicted to top-down analysis, and hence (5) in sharp contrast with phenomenological and behavioristic approaches. He finds aspect 3 the most characteristic, calling it, I believe, "the representational metapostulate."

Pylyshyn's third section discusses the intercommunication of the parent discipline and the new area by examining citation statistics. He finds that communication is heaviest within the new area and fairly slim across the boundaries.

Finally, Pylyshyn quotes the Sloan report as saying that the integration into one discipline is not yet at hand. In any event, he believes such an integrated discipline would not be identical with information science, because it is not involved with storing, processing, and communicating information or with information retrieval. Hence, he sees "cognitive science as primarily an empirical natural science concerned with a subset of the class of problems in information science."

Anyone looking at both Pylyshyn's paper and mine would immediately recognize many attitudes in common; a large portion of our historical references is (as was to be expected) the same: mathematics, logic, and mechanisms. But where he includes cybernetic history, I stress the semiotic and pragmatic; he includes the neural and psychological generation and recognition of ideas and their symbolism where I stress their linguistic, social, and, perhaps, anthropological generation and recognition. To revert to the pre-Marxian meaning of the word *ideology* that I describe in my paper, both historical approaches, Pylyshyn's and mine, are ideological, he stressing the physical side and I the social. But not only the historical questions we raise are ideological! The very subjects we are discussing are two aspects of what might be called the art, science, and engineering aspects of ideology. Cognitive science is concerned with the generation and recognition of ideas; informatics is concerned with the generation and recognition of symbolizations of ideas. We are both discussing ideology ideologically.

Since each discipline has its own pragmatically (in the technical sense) distinct ideology, will this general theory of ideologies be capable of having a single ideology of its own, or will it have to remain an alliance of disciplines, what I call a superdiscipline, the way I believe history, education, library science, and cybernetics must? Pylyshyn's question of whether there will be a convergence to one cognitive science is a most valid one. I think the answer will depend on what I have called interdisciplinary politics. Will an appropriate brainwashing curriculum for a single major in the subject develop to form what in the United States educational system is called a department? It would have to have courses covering the physical, chemical, biological, psychological, and social generation of the recognitive aspects of cybernetics and explain or describe or model character recognizers, word recognizers, sentence recognizers, concept recognizers, picture recognizers, accepting automata, the variety of technological as well as biological receptors, and the general processes of understanding and problem-solving! Destutt de Tracy's book [1817] on ideology also tried to cover grammar and logic. I am skeptical, and I suspect Pylyshyn is too.

There is one characteristic ideological attitude that both Pylyshyn and I present: What Pylyshyn calls the representational metapostulate, I describe as part of the mass ego of informatics, as follows:

> The very fact, however, that they have symbolisms with well-defined manipulative procedures may make it useful for them to simulate their processes symbolically. It is one of the informatician's basic insights (prejudices, superstitions, ideologic attitudes, or peculiar ways of looking at the world?)

that any process that can be precisely specified is capable of being symbolically simulated . . . . (From my paper in this volume.)

I believe this is not much different from what Pylyshyn says in the second section of his paper. However, I find his item (1) in that section, the attribution of formalist properties (as though it were mathematical) puzzling; for example, artificial intelligence is much more empirical than formal.

In this connection, I have a question to ask Pylyshyn the psychologist rather than Pylyshyn the computer scientist: Are not the semantics of the symbols representing the basic cognitions of most disciplines definitely *not* symbol-manipulative? Do they not refer to what they consider to be *real* things and not symbols? Is it not only the informatician whose basic concepts are about symbol manipulation? Even mathematicians resent being confused with arithmeticians or accountants. How, then, should I interpret this sentence from Pylyshyn's paper: "In all these instances, the behavior of the systems in question (be they minds, computers, or social systems) is explained, not in terms of intrinsic properties of the system itself, but in terms of rules and processes that operate on *representations of extrinsic things*." Is this not a computer scientist talking, rather than a psychologist or a cognitive scientist? Perhaps the title of Pylyshyn's paper should have been reversed to read "Cognitive Science: Its Roots and Relations as Viewed from the Perspective of Information Science."

Finally, a remark on Pylyshyn's analysis of the citation statistics is in order. I believe he uses them as evidence in response to his question about convergence into one discipline. Although I go along with him on the convergence question, I do not think citation indices form conclusive evidence. When a new disciplinary area is being formed, one would naturally expect a transition period during which the fusion process accompanies the fission process by which the new body is separated from its parents. It is precisely when there is a Kuhnian scientific revolution that the new generation breaks contact with the old (which continues to follow its same old paradigms). Is this not the standard way in which a new patch is formed in the patchwork quilt of human lore? In this case, the corners of eight abutting patches (the previously mentioned cognitive disciplines) are cut off and fused to form a new patch. If, then, a convergence is occurring (and, I repeat, I am skeptical), present statistics would still be not only what is expected, but would most likely be misused by the old guard as an argument against the young Turks.

REFLECTIONS ON THE STRUCTURE OF AN INTERDISCIPLINE

Allen Newell

In his "Information Science: Its Roots and Relations as Viewed from the Perspective of Cognitive Science," Zenon Pylyshyn outlines the development of cognitive science, an interdiscipline that lies within something called information science, this latter being too amorphous and wide-ranging to be termed even an interdiscipline. Here follow a few thoughts on the nature of interdisciplines.

COMPLICATIONS

The disciplinary structure of science is a crazy quilt. Disciplines emerge and extend, shrink and disappear, merge and fracture, overlap and surround. However, even by such balkan standards, the intellectual history of cognitive science seems to me especially complicated, although no doubt it is just my professional myopia. Pylyshyn does a good job of making this complexity apparent. I agree with all the historical strands he lists; however, it seems to me he gets only half of the complexity out on the table.

For instance, cognitive science is often taken to have six disciplinary pillars, as in the figure used by the Sloan Committee and reproduced in Pylyshyn's paper: psychology, philosophy, linguistics, anthropology, neuroscience, and computer science. All of these except computer science (which is a stand-in for artificial intelligence) are essentially absent from Pylyshyn's account.

This research was sponsored in part by the Defense Advanced Research Projects Agency (DOD), ARPA Order No. 3597, monitored by the Air Force Avionics Laboratory under Contract F33615-78-C-1551. The views and conclusions contained in the paper are those of the author and should not be interpreted as representing the official policies, either expressed or implied, of the Defense Advanced Research Projects Agency or the United States government.

To take psychology, with which I am somewhat familiar, a good case can be made that the situation described in Pylyshyn's story is right—that psychology was transformed by an external intellectual movement whose central core comprised control theory, information theory, computation, and operational mathematics. However, psychology was not a passive patient; it transformed that transformation and added to it significantly. Some features of the transformed psychology may follow directly and necessarily from the central ideas of information-processing; for example, the acceptance of mental mechanisms in the head and the separation of the study of human and animal behavior. But the same cannot be said of focusing on memory as the important structure to research, which has certainly characterized the main line of the information-processing revolution in psychology. This has its roots, of course, in psychology's long-standing concern with learning. Memory is the internal mental structure that most directly lies behind learning. Indeed, lack of any mechanistic notion of memory blocks the study of learning in process terms, so that learning itself cannot be taken over immediately and made the central object of study in an information-processing psychology.

Another important response of psychology was to fail to develop the study of problem-solving and higher cognitive processes into a really major stream of research. Problem-solving and the use of strategies was a striking feature of early work that influenced psychology, coming partly from game theory but mostly from artificial intelligence. However, higher cognitive processes have remained a relatively minor, although integral and conceptually important, part of modern cognitive psychology. For many cognitive psychologists, the cognitive revolution really starts with Ulric Neisser's *Cognitive Psychology* in 1967, ten years after the usual date of the late 1950s, as pegged by the work of Broadbent, Bruner, Chomsky, Miller, Newell and Simon, and Swets and Tanner. [Neisser, 1967.] Neisser's book explicitly took cognitive psychology to be centered on perceptual and memorial mechanisms. In part, this was due to the emergence in the late sixties of a highly successful mental chronometry, with the work of Neisser, Posner, and Sternberg, which, in concert with the focus on memory, locked psychology into the study of the underlying micro-organization of human cognition.

The continued commitment to a basic experimental methodology was another important internally determined component of psychology's response. Although the amount of theory has gradually increased, the central path to knowledge remains the well-controlled and carefully designed laboratory experiment, generated to test some question or hypothesis arising from prior experimental work. Indeed, it remains the norm that theory and experiment should be coupled in the same person and in the same paper. It is rare for a purely theoretical paper to appear in the major journals of cognitive psychology. This commitment to method may even be taken as an overarching determiner of psychology's response. Scientists are driven by what they know how to do next. However fascinating and beckoning a potential path, if a scientist does not know how to do the next piece of research down that path, he or she will rarely go that way.

The point is that modern cognitive psychology is as much a product of the earlier history of psychology and developments internal to cognitive psychology, as it is of the external ideas of information-processing. In turn, this cognitive psychology is a major determiner of the character of the interdiscipline of cognitive science and cannot be left out of the picture.

The story of linguistics, even more than psychology, seems to me one of internal determination, although I am on less sure ground here. To an outsider, the Chomskian revolution arises from the same general intellectual milieu that Pylyshyn sketches, impacting linguistics rather than psychology. The algebraic character of the new linguistics and the fundamental idea of generative rules characterizing behaving systems—these seem a product of the same intellectual viewpoint of operational mathematics that gave rise to operations research, game theory, and control theory. But to an insider, perhaps to Chomsky himself, the development of the new linguistics looks almost entirely internal. When he traces roots, as in his *Cartesian Linguistics,* it is in terms of internal linguistic history and such general philosophical positions as rationalism and empiricism. [Chomsky, 1966.] It is certainly not the Descartes of analytical geometry that the book's title refers to.

Again, from an internal linguistics perspective, I would suspect that the continued development would be seen mostly as flowing outward. Certainly, one can document a transformation of psycholinguistics in the sixties that flowed directly from linguistics, but left linguistics only modestly changed, if at all. And there has remained a barrier, both intellectual and political, between linguistics and computer science, which has kept computational linguistics in a rather ambiguous status. My concern here is not primarily to assess or evaluate such relations, but only to note how they complicate the already complex picture that Pylyshyn sketches.

Another kind of complexity exists, which can be illustrated by the case of artificial intelligence. Here we have a field that has a fair amount of coherence, but only a short time ago (the sixties) was itself considered an interdiscipline. How come it is now seen as a disciplinary pillar on which one can build a new interdiscipline of cognitive science? Indeed artificial intelligence is not a discipline, in the usual sense of the word, but rather a part of computer science—which itself is newly come to disciplinary status. In their wisdom, the makers of the Sloan figure did put computer science as a node rather than artificial intelligence. But the reality is that almost the entire connection with computer science lies with artificial intelligence. As an indication of how jerry-rigged the structure is, artificial intelligence did not get itself its own national professional society—the American Association for Artificial Intelligence—until after the Cognitive Science Society was formed.

The complexities continue when we consider neuroscience. It also is an interdiscipline—the neuro parts of anatomy, physiology, pharmacology, and biochemistry—just working itself up to disciplinary status, so the remarks about artificial intelligence apply here as well. But much more important, neuroscience does not share a common scientific Zeitgeist with the rest of cognitive science. Rather, it participates in the central paradigm of modern biology—as exciting and dynamic a scientific development as the second half of this century is likely to witness. True, some neuroscientists work across the boundary, and many on all sides have yearnings for a larger integration. But such connections seem unlikely to suffice for an interdiscipline. Indeed, taking Pylyshyn's interconnection statistics seriously, I would expect the cross-referencing to be almost totally disjoint. To pick a random statistic of this kind, there happen to be eight Andersons referenced in the 1981 *Annual Review of Neuroscience,* but among them one does not find any of the four Andersons familiar to cognitive scientists (James A., John R., Norman H., or Richard C.). [Cowan, 1981.]

The complexities continue. Cognitive science shows up as an official interdiscipline about twenty years after the beginnings of the revolution and quite a few years after the major pillars had been transformed or created, each in their various ways (and with much heralding and discussing). So cognitive science is not so much a harbinger or a precipitation point as a consolidation or a mid-course correction. In fact, there do not seem to be any substantive events that mark the creation of cognitive science—no new intellectual discoveries or even changes of perspective. If a scientific historian were given the history since the mid-fifties, with the specific organizing activities of cognitive science deleted, and told to guess when it occurred, almost any time at all would do. Perhaps the one aspect that might serve as a marker is the more active involvement of philosophy, whose engagement with the implications of information-processing systems before the mid-seventies was fairly minimal. This does not, of course, prevent there from being a few seminal individual contributions, such as those of Hilary Putnam. [Putnam, 1960.]

In this respect, there is a fascinating parallel between the history of cognitive science and the history of behavioral science, which came into existence in the mid-fifties. Then it was the Ford Foundation and the pillars were psychology, social psychology, economics, political science, sociology, and anthropology; now, it is the Sloan Foundation and the six fields already mentioned. Then, the argument was whether history was a behavioral science; now, it is whether neuroscience is a cognitive science. Then, even more than now, the pillars had existed for a long time, and no scientific event or breakthough signaled the time for integration but, rather, there was a spreading awareness of the need for integration. Behavioral science is no longer an active organizing focus. However, the loosening up of disciplinary boundaries that occurred then remains, as do some more specific legacies, such as the Center for Advanced Study in the Behavioral Sciences. Behavioral science has become a social institution somewhat more ephemeral than that of an interdiscipline but still more real than information science, which is almost entirely a descriptive term of the analyst. Cognitive science is still on the ascendancy and its fate is not yet revealed to us. But this parallel story indicates that the zoo of social institutions may be more varied than we usually think.

The complexities keep coming. What of semiotics? According to a recent article,

> Semiotics is the study of signs, i.e., of those entities which effect communication between interpreters of signs. Quite a variety of things can function as signs. A word, a sentence, a gesture, a facial expression, a photograph, a diagram, etc., are all signs because we, their interpreters, are more concerned with what they *stand for* or represent than with what they are merely *in themselves*. (Laferrière, 1979, p. 434.)

Surely semiotics is a part of cognitive science—or is cognitive science or includes cognitive science. But we would not know of the existence of semiotics from the cognitive science literature; even the enumeration of all the cross-relations in the Sloan figure leaves it out. Pylyshyn, to his credit, does mention it in passing. But the situation is symmetric. Except for the occasional quotation from great men common to us all (Warren McCulloch and Roman Jakobson), the referenced article bears no witness to either the sources described in Pylyshyn's paper or any of the massive work done since then that cognitive scientists know and love.

All disciplines make claims; we should hardly be surprised at that. Likewise, perhaps, it is in the proper nature of claims to overlap. But the complexities get thicker when multiple fields, here cognitive science and semiotics, claim almost exactly the same intellectual territory and then pass in the night. And the complexity of this labeling phenomenon bedevils the participants in cognitive science as well: Each claims to be the science of much of the same phenomena. Each, of course, has special slants (including methodological ones) to bring to the party; but slants are add-ons to a science, subject to change as the field moves on. Again, the point is not to pass judgment on this situation. It is to note the difficulties that arise in making sense of the state and structure of science in this area. And so it goes. I suspect that when the whole set of papers on the disciplines of information is spread out, along with their multiple commentaries, my few additions will hardly seem the greater part.

IS THE COMPLEXITY REAL?

Perhaps the difficulty is that we are casting the story in terms of the disciplinary structure of science. There are certainly alternative ways to tell the story of an intellectual domain such as information science or cognitive science. Perhaps the situation would not seem so complicated, if we dealt directly in some other coin—in ideas and discoveries or major scientists or the *paradigms* of Thomas Kuhn or the *research programmes* of Imre Lakatos. [T. S. Kuhn, 1962a; Lakatos, 1970.] As we all know, the notion of a discipline continually gets a bad press, especially from academics unhappy with the felt constraints of departments officiating in the name of this or that discipline.

One possibility is to describe the structure in terms of scientists. Pylyshyn himself notes how a few scientists show up repeatedly—Warren McCulloch, George Miller, Herbert Simon, and John von Neumann. But this way lies madness, it seems to me; such people are invariably polymaths. Their intellectual histories are about as intricate and convoluted as can be imagined—a task for the skilled biographer rather than a device for making the structure of fields clear.

Recently, called on to provide some historical background of artificial intelligence, I decided to enumerate the global intellectual issues that have gained prominence over the course of its history. Such issues—procedural versus declarative or serial versus parallel—though usually stated crudely, seem to capture enduring concerns of a field. In another essay for this collection, focusing on artificial intelligence, I lay out these issues, which provide one such alternative description. Alas, one of the most striking features of artificial intelligence is the large number of issues that have been prominent at one time or another and which pile up on each other several deep. Many of the issues there reflect rather directly one or another of the issues raised by Pylyshyn or previously added by me. Additional issues of this list, I suspect, will be identifiable in other essays in this collection.

This list hardly constitutes real evidence, though it is probably a bit better than my Anderson index. Nevertheless, I conclude that the complexity is real. Whether it is more complex than in other fields remains an open question. But it is a crazy enough quilt to require understanding, and we might as well continue to examine it through the lens of disciplinary structure.

WHAT IS A DISCIPLINE?

How are we to understand disciplines, so we may understand interdisciplines? Like so many other things concerning humans, there seems to be both a cognitive dimension and a social/motivational dimension. (For instance, think of task feedback to humans, which can be cast either cognitively, as knowledge of results, or motivationally, as reinforcement.)

Cognitively, a discipline seems to be an interreading population of scientists. Two scientists are in the same discipline if they read the same literature and feel themselves responsible for keeping up with the same set of ideas. The notion is not absolute, of course—specialities are well recognized. However, the notion of a specialty implies a common base. In fact, specialty is to discipline as figure is to ground. The discipline becomes important in defining the intellectual ground against which scientists do their work; that is, pursue their specialties.

Thus, a significant aspect of artificial intelligence not being a discipline in itself and being part of the discipline of computer science is what the scientist in artificial intelligence knows about besides his or her own research, say, on expert systems. If artificial intelligence were a discipline, all the scientist would know about are other aspects of intelligent systems, such as vision, theorem-proving, and natural language. With artificial intelligence part of computer science, the scientist also knows about work on multiprocessing architectures, verification, algorithm analysis, and so on. Correspondingly, of course, he or she knows only a little about what is going on in cognitive psychology and nothing at all about what is going on in social psychology.

If, by some chance of fate or fashion, artificial intelligence had become part of psychology or philosophy or, say, a developed cybernetics, then quite different things would be part of the ground. Advances in behavior modification, phenomenological philosophy, or muscle control, respectively, would be a living part of the artificial intelligence scientist's world. Correspondingly, VLSI (very-large-scale integration) and the structure of protection systems would not.

What intellectual ground a scientist stands on is immensely important. It affects what intellectual resources are drawn on in choosing frameworks for analysis, interpretation of difficulties, sources of inspiration, and the kernel ideas for solutions to conceptual problems. It affects to whom the scientist can talk about his or her problems—namely, those who share common ground—and, therefore, what types of suggestions he or she obtains. In short, though it does not affect the position or velocity of the work, which is determined by the research task itself, the discipline affects all higher derivatives.

One fundamental cognitive reason why disciplines exist seems apparent—it comes from resource limitations to human cognition. There are only so many hours in the day; they can be filled with only so much talk and only so many articles. These limits assure that no scientist will be familiar with more than a small fraction of science; thus, science cannot be the seamless web we all desire. However, such limits do not determine that science will partition itself into (disciplinary) clumps, in which many scientists read approximately the same scientific literature and few read heavily across disciplines. It seems equally plausible that each scientist would trace out an idiosyncratic problem-oriented trajectory through science. The whole of science would then have the appearance of a randomly woven but homogeneous-appearing mat—a crazy quilt at the individual level rather than at the discipline level.

There is an entirely different side to disciplines and their structure, namely, they are social institutions and serve social and motivational needs. They provide the rocks to which scientists attach their identities. "Hello, who are you?'' ''I'm a physicist'' or a philosopher or a biochemist. That people will answer ''I'm a computer scientist'' shows that computer science has become a discipline. Disciplines carry a point of view—to answer ''I'm an anthropologist'' declares the view that culture is an important explanatory ingredient in human affairs. One does not pronounce on another discipline's subject matter without appropriate deferential behavior. This is not just a matter of familiarity, for the hierarchy of the sciences is in part a social-dominance hierarchy. Physicists can pronounce on psychology with less deference than vice versa.

Again, on the surface, there seems little mystery behind the institutional nature of disciplines. They are nurtured by the organization of universities along disciplinary lines into departments, supported by professional societies. Critical to this is the strong tradition of graduate education, localized in the departments, with its almost exclusive command of the young's attention during the period when career identities are shaped. This is compounded by the faculty of a department being composed almost exclusively of scientists with PhDs from the discipline. Thus, from a social viewpoint, there are ample grounds for the disciplinary structure that exists in science perpetuating itself. However, it seems less clear that organizing science according to disciplines has any favored status over other ways of organizing, in terms of social mechanisms. Its emergence may strongly reflect historical factors.

WHAT IS THE ROLE OF INTERDISCIPLINES?

Given the disciplinary structure, as just described, what then is the role (or set of roles) of interdisciplines? There are two obvious ones. First, science is in fact all of a piece; thus, any decomposition into disciplines must necessarily be imperfect. Interdisciplines represent a spillover as groups of scientists with common interests read each other's work and begin to cooperate with each other. In this role, interdisciplines can be permanent and stable institutional structures in science.

Second, the division into disciplines changes with history. Early in the development of science, new sciences precipitate out of a less differentiated scientific and intellectual activity—for example, natural philosophy. The emergence of physics and chemistry as separate disciplines would be an example, or the emergence of statistics. As science matures, all of the territory is covered in one way or another by some science, then new sciences are carved out of existing ones. Interdisciplines are simply early forms of disciplines on the way to existence; biochemistry provides an example.

Other roles are possible: An interdiscipline could be an intermediate stage where part of one discipline moves to another. It could be a temporary scaffolding while some important ideas are transmitted to a set of fields, only to disintegrate when this task has been accomplished. It could simply be a device for periodic widening of scientific awareness, more analogous to a professional meeting (though on a much longer time scale) than a disciplinary structure. Or, it could be similar to a special-interest group, permanently established to signal the importance of some aspect otherwise ignored. Psycholinguistics is perhaps an example of this latter. All of these are cognitively centered roles, but social roles are also possible, such as being a structure within which to provide funding.

So what is true of cognitive science? It seems to me unlikely that it is the nascent form of a new discipline, carved out of psychology, linguistics, computer science, and so forth. The determining factor, it seems to me, is the role of the parts in the parent disciplines, and the determining factor would seem to be the ability of the parts to be excised from their parent disciplines. This would be eased if a part were a specialty or peripheral in some way, easiest perhaps if a strain line already existed along which cleavage could occur. Psychology seems to me the key: The part of psychology included in cognitive science is cognitive psychology, which is the central core of the parent discipline—what experimental psychology was of yore. It seems inconceivable that there could exist a psychology without cognitive psychology; what would it be? And without cognitive psychology, it is inconceivable that there could be cognitive science. For the other parts, the situation is more favorable to founding a new discipline (though with other consequences of course). The linguistics part of cognitive science could just become the new psycholinguistics, and linguistics could proceed without it, more or less as it has without psycholinguistics. Artificial intelligence has a fault line down the middle, separating the concern with engineering and applied systems from the concern with the basic nature of intelligence and human intelligence. This latter half is the part that participates in cognitive science; a split is certainly possible along this cleavage line. Thus, artificial intelligence would not leave computer science, but a part of it would. The other three cognitive science partners—philosophy, anthropology, and neuroscience—seem less critical in determining whether a new discipline will congeal.

It seems much more likely that cognitive science plays one of the other roles. Perhaps, it is a more or less permanent spillover, reflecting imperfections in the particular arrangements of current disciplines concerned with the nature of mind. The imperfections are certainly clear to all. With so many parties to the endeavor, hence, so much need for work at this or that point across a boundary, even if arrangements falter from time to time, they will be continually reactivated.

Pylyshyn notes that cognitive science may not even be much of an interdiscipline. Thus, perhaps even this last position is too strong. Recall, again, behavioral science, which seemed strong in its day, but has faded to much less than an interdiscipline. Pylyshyn bolsters his concern with some simple counts of the extent of intercitation. Despite my slight caricature with the Anderson statistic (because I was too lazy to do better), I am in favor of any attempt to provide some data, however scrappy, for discussions of this sort. In fact, however sketchy Pylyshyn's own data, I find I have little urge to disagree with the pattern revealed. On the other hand, I believe, in fact, that the component fields in cognitive science are strongly interdisciplinary. Thus, it seems necessary to find a plausible interpretation of the pattern Pylyshyn found.

First, I think a set of fields are interdisciplinary to the extent that ideas interpenetrate. The ideas may be any type—theories, data, methods, problems, or perspectives. However, they must receive their development in field X and eventually be used in some form in field Y. Commerce must occur in all directions and continue over some period, thus involving a population of ideas. The citation data presented by Pylyshyn refer to the channels over which the penetration occurs. I find it quite plausible that much of the penetration goes via one or a few seminal publications or works. Scientists in general cite publications that have not only influenced them but that they have read. In general, these will be only the seminal works—they are sufficient to convey the idea. There is no need to examine the original work in the parent field or to follow in detail its continued advancement there. In general, only the gross aspects of an idea—to wit, the idea itself—is useful in the recipient field. Actually, a significant transform is usually necessary to make the idea applicable to the recipient field, which is accomplished by the transferring publication. Thus, there is no reason to go beyond it.

I will not attempt to construct a map to demonstrate the interdisciplinary nature of cognitive science; that is beyond the limits of an already long note. I assert cognitive science scores quite well, with repeated ideas flowing back and forth. The flow is not equal at all times and between all subfields, nor should it be. There will certainly be some patterning to it. But it contrasts strikingly with a unidirectional, one-time penetration, such as that from information theory into psychology in the early 1950s. To take just a single example, that of semantic nets, several ideas have flowed back and forth over a period of 15 years (so far), primarily between psychology and artificial intelligence. In each of the instances, only a couple of publications were involved, and they were each reports of bridging research results. [For example, Quillian, 1968; Anderson and Bower, 1973; Schank and Abelson, 1977.]

This view of the nature of being interdisciplinary seems to make it unlikely that cognitive science is just a more widespread but weaker interreading population of scientists, which is what the spillover role would imply. It is more like an intermittent-communication device, in which the continuous intercommunication, as in common journals and common meetings, is a way of keeping the background level high enough to trigger new ideas occasionally and, although it seems less necessary, for the reception of those seminal publications when they occur.

WHAT WILL HAPPEN TO IT ALL?

I end where I began. The disciplinary picture for cognitive science is a crazy quilt and even more so for information science. I believe it will stay that way almost indefinitely. The intellectual domain of understanding human nature is too extended and admits too many approaches to enforce unification. All that is required to avoid any serious pressure for unification is that endeavors be separate in their problems. Overlapping claims need not violate this, because claims are made by area, but separation is determined by problem. As long as the approaches in a field that answer one problem do not suffice to answer nearby ones, then many approaches can coexist with little pressure to unify them. The progress of an approach taken in isolation is not relevant—it can be real, measurable, and even dramatic, without implying that other approaches to the same arena should be abandoned.

Will it always be this way? That is too far in the future to guess. I believe the essential condition for the gradual simplification of the disciplinary picture for cognitive science lies in the development of techniques that solve well-specified scientific problems and answer scientific questions in routine ways. The phonetic alphabet is a good example; we all depend on linguistics for that. The representations for grammars are another; I believe they will be around and used routinely by all scientists, even when our conceptions of language have evolved considerably. Similarly, from psychology comes signal-detection theory, with the concept of the operating characteristic, and from artificial intelligence comes the LISP programming language. These all become islands of certainty that all disciplines borrow and use when needed. Though sometimes such techniques become irrelevant and drift away, by and large they form a permanent accumulation. They can be expected to increase gradually (and sometimes rapidly) to form a framework that will ultimately force simplification of the disciplinary structure. Until that time, there is no reason for those professing an interdiscipline not to let the crazy quilt continue. Furthermore, there are good reasons to be confident that ideas will continue to move from discipline to discipline.

INFORMAVORES

George A. Miller

Both the human tendency to think analogically and the dangers of reasoning by analogy are familiar themes to students of the history of ideas. One cannot help but wonder what about the human mind compels it to flirt so outrageously with the potentially disastrous consequences of false analogies.

The general pattern of analogical thinking, of course, is to explain something that is poorly understood by noting its similarity to something that is well understood. Thus, it is not uncommon to explain complicated natural phenomena by analogy to human artifacts, since people generally feel that they understand reasonably well those things they themselves have actually manufactured. In the life sciences, one thinks of such examples as explaining the motions of the limbs by analogy with levers, explaining the circulation of the blood in terms of the analogy of the heart to a pump, explaining eyes and ears by analogy to cameras and microphones, or explaining metabolism by analogy to heat engines.

Attempts to understand human cognition have generated their own analogies. The mind has been likened to a cave on whose walls events cast their shadows, to a slate on which experience can write, to a hydraulic system for pumping energy into alternative activities, to a telephone switchboard that connects ideas to one another or responses to stimuli, even to a hologram that stores representations distributively. The current favorite, of course, is the modern, high-speed, serial, stored-program, digital computer, an analogy that has catalyzed the rebirth of cognitive psychology as an active scientific enterprise.

In *What is Life?*, a little book that opened up biology for physicists, Erwin Schrödinger pointed out that organisms survive by ingesting, not food, not calories, but negative entropy. [Schrödinger, 1945.] It is no accident, of course, that the mathematics of entropy are also the mathematics of information. The analogy is obvious: Just as the body survives by ingesting negative entropy, so the mind survives by ingesting information. In a very general sense, *all higher organisms are informavores*.

But how should this suggestive parallel be developed? No sooner was the question asked than computer scientists offered an answer. The computer seemed to provide a precise, well-understood system that could serve as a laboratory for the analysis of all kinds of informavores. The human informavore seemed merely a special case of the more general theory of information processing that remained to be discovered. And so the informavore analogy was transformed almost immediately into the computer analogy.

Perhaps it is unfair to speak of these hypotheses as analogies. To someone caught up in an analogical line of reasoning, the hypothesis under consideration must seem much more than a mere analogy. Unless an analogy is taken very seriously, the motivation to explore its implications will be lacking. Instead of calling the hypothesis an analogy, therefore, it may be promoted to the status of a theory. But calling an analogy a theory does not make it one; only hard, empirical work can accomplish that. (In the study of cognition, an analogical flavor is often preserved in the preference for speaking of models rather than theories.)

Pylyshyn draws an accurate picture of cognitive science today, a picture in which the languages that computer science has provided for formulating cognitive theories and the tests of those theories that computer simulation allows seem to outrun by far any mere analogy. Still, the heart of the matter is the exploration of an analogy.

Which is not a bad thing. To say that modern conceptions of machines will continue to evolve, and that richer cognitive analogies will evolve along with them, is not to criticize the progress that has already resulted from exploiting analogies presently available. It is merely to suggest that current conceptions may still be incomplete.

Consider an analogy between analogies. Insofar as a limb is used as lever, the theory of levers describes its behavior—but a theory of levers does not answer every question that might be asked about the structure and function of the limbs of animals. Insofar as a mind is used to process information, the theory of information processing describes its behavior—but a theory of information processing does not answer every question that might be asked about the structure and function of the minds of human beings.

Or does it? Suppose all psychologists restricted themselves to theories that could be simulated and tested on contemporary computers. Would anything of importance be lost?

Such questions may seem premature while so much still remains to be done to explore the limits of the computer analogy, but it is important to have as clear a perspective as possible on any analogy we happen to be considering. Pylyshyn, in his paper, comments that a "commitment to the informational level" places cognitive science in contrast to "the phenomenological approach, where the existential notions of significance, meaningfulness, and experiential content are given a central role."

To some psychologists, these would be serious losses indeed. If one *defines* psychology as the science that deals with significance, meaningfulness, and experiential content (and some psychologists do), then progress in the information sciences will be bought at the end of this century at the same price progress in formal logic was bought at the beginning of the century—at the price of a total divorce from psychologism.

But the informational level may be richer than we now know. That is to say, computers as we presently know them may prove to be incomplete analogues of informavores. The claim would not be that there is something computable that they cannot compute but simply that evolution may have produced a species of informavore—a kind of special purpose computer—that we as yet have no idea how to construct or imitate.

*   *   *

The opposite of analysis, in one sense, is synthesis. In that sense, the computer analogy offers a priceless antidote to behavioral analysis—the possibility of synthesizing and testing integrated, goal-oriented systems. It is this possibility that is contributing so generously to what Pylyshyn calls "the convergence toward cognitive science."

In another sense, however, the opposite of analysis is acceptance. In that sense, analysis characterizes an active, problem-solving attitude of mind. In the analytic mode, one asks questions that impose analytical categories and symbols on experience; by contrast, in the accepting mode, one accepts each moment as a new miracle and appreciates it with gratitude and wonder. In this sense of analytic, present-day computers may be too analytic to model completely a human mind capable of both modes of learning. It is noteworthy, for example, that information-processing models of human memory have a great deal to say about the storage and retrieval of verbal messages but almost nothing to say about memory of a pain, of the sound of a person's voice, or of the taste of a good wine.

Perhaps the kind of processing that modern computers do so rapidly and so well is not the only thing informavores can do with information. The future of the information sciences may be even brighter than anyone can now foresee.

REPRESENTATION, COMPUTATION, AND COGNITION

Zenon W. Pylyshyn

The five commentaries on my chapter are an excellent sample of the diverse viewpoints that comprise cognitive science. They go a long way toward redressing my own biases in emphasizing certain features of this new discipline or interdiscipline. For this reason, I have little to say to the commentators individually beyond thanking them for their positive contribution. Instead, I take this opportunity to remark in a general way on a number of themes that recurred in much of the discussion. One is the notion of a discipline and the other is the question of the scope and character of cognitive science as explanatory science.

Allen Newell and Saul Gorn both raised the question of whether cognitive science is a discipline, an interdiscipline, or (in Gorn's terminology) an idealogy. Disciplines, in the usual sense of this term, are a lot like academic departments. They can be based on almost any kind of cohesive purpose: a concern with what appear superficially to be similar puzzles (Why do people behave the way they do? What makes it possible for certain organisms to reason and adapt intelligently?); a concern with the same objects of study (people, animals); the use of similar formal techniques (algebra, difference equations, field theories, etc.), similar empirical methods (statistical experimental designs), or even similar physical facilities. In my own university, psychology is considered to be a social science for undergraduate-teaching purposes and a biological science for graduate and research purposes, chiefly because for the latter purposes, it requires specialized laboratory space and facilities. Thus, the survival of cognitive science as a departmentally recognized discipline or even as an interdiscipline depends at least as much on political, economic, and social factors as it does on scientific ones. Clearly, these are not the sorts of issues that concern us in trying to understand the character of cognitive science as a science.

What is really central in that case is the question of whether there can be an explanatory, theoretical science of *cognition*. This is the question whether our present notion of the subject matter of such a science is close to being what philosophers call a natural kind. It has been widely recognized—ever since Plato first drew our attention to it—that in order to develop a successful explanatory system, we must "carve nature at her joints." The way we group and distinguish properties and phenomena is crucial to the success of the scientific project. Thus, for a successful theory of motion, we must not distinguish, as did the ancients, between natural and violent motion, though we do have to distinguish between weight and mass, a distinction with which medieval thinkers struggled but which was not clarified until the seventeenth century. Such distinctions serve to carve out a natural and relatively homogeneous scientific domain within which a set of explanatory principles apply.

It had been assumed for centuries that the appropriate natural domain of study for what we informally call cognition (or higher mental functions) is something like complex biological systems. In the 1940s and 1950s, this domain was expanded beyond biology to include what were called cybernetic systems. Gradually, and through the influence of the sorts of historical developments to which several of the commentators alluded (most particularly the work in artificial intelligence), a picture of natural domain began to evolve. It looked more and more as though the "natural kind" to which the theories would apply were those systems that were governed by representations or by knowledge and goals. Newell, in a similar analysis of the current state of the field, referred to this as the "physical symbol system hypothesis." [Newell, 1980b.]

This was not simply a case of expanding the domain of study by finding increasingly abstract ways of viewing systems (as has sometimes been claimed of general systems theory). The representation view also has a restricting effect. Some of the central concepts of psychology, as George Miller notes, are excluded in the process. For example, while the distinction between conscious and unconscious representations is glossed over, the subjective-feeling component (the "qualia") of mental states falls outside the domain of such cognitivist explanations. Similarly, the physical forms in which representational systems are instantiated becomes a separate field of study. The work of cognitive neuroscientists like Michael Gazzaniga and Michael Arbib is taken to be a contribution to our understanding of how one particular class of machines—the biological one—is able to carry out representation-governed processes. Their work is a study of the underlying functional architecture, not the rule-governed representational processes themselves, since these constitute an autonomous natural domain with regularities that can be captured independently of particular physical instantiations. The domain of *cognition* is thus viewed as a natural kind encompassing all informavores (as George Miller puts it so colorfully) rather than a human or even a biological category of functioning. What is lost in the processes is the concept of a domain of study defined in terms of our naive interests rather than in terms of its scientific tractability. But such losses are routine in scientific evolutions: Astronomy, too, lost much glamor and wonder when it was discovered that astrological questions were not in its purview.

I end with some brief comments prompted by Saul Gorn's remarks concerning the notion of a formal symbol and semantics. Being governed by representations is not the same as being formal and computational. Nonetheless, computation is the *only* model we have of how a physical system can be governed by representation. As such, the computation view of mind is neither a logical necessity nor a metaphor: It is a far-reaching empirical hypothesis. Thus, Saul Gorn is exactly right when he says that I am viewing cognition from the perspective of information science rather than the converse. That is because I believe this is precisely the view that characterizes cognitive science; it is a sweeping reanalysis of the notion of cognition itself. What I called the representational metapostulate is *not* the same as the "basic insight of informatics" that Gorn refers to; namely, "that any process that can be precisely specified is capable of being symbolically simulated." Rather, it is the much stronger hypothesis that cognition *consists in* (not "is capable of being simulated by") manipulating physically instantiated symbols. It is the quite literal proposal that cognition *is* computation.

Because of this postulate, symbols do not have the same status in cognitive science that they have in either physics or semiotics, though for different reasons in the two cases. In physics, symbols represent physical magnitudes and the relations among these: They are a notation for the subject matter only. The symbols themselves are not assumed to have any realization except in the expression of the theory. Thus, the choice of a notation, though it has important consequences for the utility of the theory, does not matter for the empirical truth of the theory. In cognitive science, as in computing, symbols not only refer to some extrinsic domain (say, numbers or beliefs), but they are also real objects in their own right that the machine (or, by hypothesis, the mind) manipulates in a manner that preserves the semantical properties of those symbols. In the case of numerical computation, for example, symbol manipulation is carried out in such a way that when interpreted as numbers according to some uniform scheme, the expressions remain congruent with number-theoretic properties. That is why we can quite literally say that the machine carries out arithmetic processes. According to the view I have been describing, exactly the same story is to be told about cognition in general. Because of this, in cognitive science the notation matters: It constitutes a substantive claim about the cognitive process. Gorn is right in remarking that this is the computer scientist talking, but that is because computer science and cognitive science converge precisely at this point.

Cognitive science is also quite different from semiotics in the kind of symbols that it studies, which may account for the quite wide divergence between the two approaches (as Newell notes). Semiotics is concerned with what might be called secondary symbols. These are the symbols that we humans use in order to convey meanings. They are not symbols that function directly as intrinsic causes of behavior, the way symbols do in computers. The symbols of the semiotician have no meanings and exhibit no behavior unless there is an intelligent, knowing agent to interpret them. These secondary symbols get all their meaning from their social and conventional (and sometimes personal) use. Hence, to study these secondary symbols is to study the body of cultural conventions, intentions, aspirations, and so on, of individuals and groups. By contrast, mental symbols of the sort that concern cognitive science, like computational symbols, have intrinsic meaning (semantics) by virtue of being instantiated in a physical mechanism in such a way that they interact causally with each other and the world outside (through transducers).

These few reactions do not adequately address some of the genuinely contentious issues that several of the commentators raised. My original paper was written in the spirit of investigative and analytical reporting, not in the spirit of scientific imperialism. If it sounded as though I was claiming that the computational perspective of cognitive science is an important new direction in the study of mind, that is because I really do believe that if the representational metapostulate can be empirically sustained, it will prove to be the biggest breakthrough in psychological conceptualization since Descartes. The representational metapostulate will give us not only a handle on the important problem of how intentional rule-governed systems can be compatible with physical causality, but it also comes equipped with a set of working tools for actually building testable theories of the mind.

SECTION 2

INFORMATICS (COMPUTER AND INFORMATION SCIENCE)

Its Ideology, Methodology, and Sociology

Saul Gorn

My task is to discuss my area—computer and information science—and its relations to some neighboring areas, among which I mention library science, information retrieval, information science, cybernetics, cognitive psychology, artificial intelligence, semiotics, and linguistics. I add computer engineering, management, and decision science, even education, and, of course, the field in which I was brought up, pure mathematics. The purpose of this discussion is to distinguish my new area from these others pragmatically and methodologically but especially ideologically.

THE PLAN FOR THIS PAPER

Let me, first of all, choose a shorter expression than *computer and information science*. Like the French (*informatique*) and the German (*Informatik*), let me choose the word "informatics." It contains the idea of information and has an ending like that of *mathematics*, implying a formally based theory. It is too bad that informatics loses the computational component in its name and also leaves no impression of an experimental basis, both of which I consider equally important, as we shall see.

Previous papers of mine on the subject were addressed to applied mathematicians, pure mathematicians, library scientists, logicians, linguists, pedagogues, behavioral scientists, and political scientists. [Gorn, 1965; 1967; 1968.] I even discussed why each audience needed a different presentation. The audience on the present occasion is the mixture of the neighboring areas I mentioned first, and the purpose of this paper and those from the other areas is to help us sort out our separate identities, if they are indeed separate.

I propose to do my part by first discussing my picture of the disciplines of human knowledge and action, their ontogenic development, and resulting

distinct ideological identities and phylogenic relations. Then, I will identify
the ideology and areas of study within informatics and examine its relation to
the other areas; and finally, I will discuss their stability in the social sense.

Let me outline the sections in greater detail. For the section on the disciplines of human knowledge and action, I have an agenda of twelve points: (1)
The social specialization into disciplines and, in particular, the definition of a
discipline and the relation of disciplines to language and the history of disciplines to the genesis of language. (2) The meanings of the word *ideology*. (3)
The dependence of the sciences, arts, and crafts on the extension of human
perceptive and motor ranges and their consequent interdependence with
technology. (4) How this dependence makes empiricism itself dependent on
advanced technology, with many well-known examples from the history of
science. (5) How this dependence creates the ontological commitments that
I have called waves of agreement to perceive; they correspond to Kuhn's
paradigms and occur during his scientific revolutions, especially when they
lead to a social agreement to support the economics of the production of
advanced receptor and effector instruments. (6) The changes in the meaning
of the word *science*. (7) How taking a wave theory rather than a particle
theory of knowledge keeps us from forgetting the pragmatics of symbolism.
(8) The language and the metalanguage developments in disciplines and how
the metalanguage level in symbolic thought can cause a separation of knowledge and action. (9) How mathematics and the physical sciences are supposed to be independent of the pragmatics of their language (where the word
pragmatics is used in a technical sense). (10) How the metalinguistic assumptions of determinism versus free will distinguish the knowledge-
oriented from the action-oriented disciplines, and how the professions try to
tie them together to expand our powers despite our limitations. (11) The
diachronics of the languages of disciplines and the stages at which they
communicate with mathematics and informatics. (12) The mass ego of a
discipline.

In the section called The Informatic Outlook, I shall discuss eight issues:
(1) How symbol-manipulation activity was accelerated by electronic computers because they demand decision-making instructions and common storage of instructions and data. (2) How the programming activity becomes
another symbol-manipulating activity capable of mechanical handling and,
therefore, a self-referencing activity. (3) How the first result is the area of
artificial intelligence, and the second result is the emergence of the principle
of logical equivalence of hardware and software, which yields the characteristic idealized concept of processor and the ambiguous meaning of *assembly*.
(4) The syntactic, semantic, and pragmatic aspects of informatics. (5) The
syntactic aspects—automata theory and formal languages—and the resul-
tant theory of computation with a specification of the limits of computation.
(6) The semantics of symbols versus the semantics of symbol manipulation:
How symbol manipulation simulates the processes symbolized. (7) How to
distinguish disciplines by their ideologies: the differing semantics of physi-

cists, mathematicians, and informaticians. (8) How the areas within informatics will vary from the formal and mathematical, through the empirical and experimental (especially where unsolvable and unsolved problems are concerned), through aesthetic and ethical reactions, into the variety of applied informatics in a number of professional activities.

Finally, the last section, on the intercommunication and stability of disciplines, will deal with seven topics: (1) The two meanings of *ideology* that we are using (as contrasted with the Marxian meaning and its relatives); the sociology of ideas versus the biology and psychology of ideas and their connection because of the need of social support for the advanced technology needed to maintain them. (2) How to compare and contrast the ideologies of disciplines. (3) Cybernetics as a superdiscipline and robotics as a professional activity. (4) The managerial-professional activities related to informatics. (5) Pedagogy as a superdiscipline; the impossibility of a single pedagogic ideology and the similar impossibility of a single ideology for information retrieval. (6) The library profession and its long-range stability: the dependence of the stability of a discipline on both the existence of stable ideologies (to maintain communication) and the existence of unsolvable problems (to prevent technological obsolescence). (7) How the stability of informatics depends on maintaining the interlocking of its scientific, artistic, and professional activities.

DISCIPLINES AND THEIR IDEOLOGIES

We all know that ever since the agricultural and urban revolutions humans have tended to specialize their activities. The result is that, by now, human lore, especially in Western civilization, is a patchwork quilt of areas of activity called arts, sciences, and professions. In spite of such philosophies as operationalism, some of these areas still seem to be mainly knowledge-oriented, such as mathematics, the natural and social sciences, the humanities, and other academic disciplines, while others seem to be mainly action-oriented, like farming, sports, hunting, cooking, mining, manufacturing, constructing, and the like. Still others seem to have as their purpose the transformation of knowledge into action, such as the professions of engineering, medicine, law, education, and so forth. Let me use the word *discipline* to cover them all, since the dictionary gives the following meanings: branch of knowledge involving research; rule or system of rules affecting conduct; and even, training that corrects, molds, strengthens, or perfects.

The patchwork quilt of disciplines is like a series of slightly distorted plane projections that a mapmaker might make of, say, a doughnut-shaped planet. Each, therefore, represents a portion of human activity from a specialized point of view. It seems to me that these specialized representations, especially for the more sophisticated disciplines, are for separate ideologies with definite histories of development and even changes of territory covered; that these histories of development are similar to the diachronic histories of the development of language and are even similar to early stages in the development of linguistic ability in a child; and that the results are rather distinct Weltanschauungen that change in time. [Gorn, 1965; 1967.]

Although a meaning of *ideology* in one of my dictionaries is the integrated assertions, theories, and aims that constitute a sociopolitical program, especially as the word was used by Hegel and Marx, the earlier broader meanings are still recorded: a systematic body of concepts; a manner, or the content of thinking, characteristic of an individual, group, or culture. I believe that Destutt de Tracy also intended it to mean the development and presentation of ideas and would have considered the present developmental psychologists such as Piaget to be direct descendants. [Picavet, 1891 and 1971; Destutt de Tracy, 1817.]

Human knowledge began by being strictly limited by human perceptive devices—the senses—and their limited ranges. We have a limited audio-frequency range and visual-frequency range and similar limited ranges for our other senses as well as for our motor controls. It took technological inventiveness to extend our perceptions and controls and, indeed, the physical ranges in which we could continue to exist. To change, or even to understand, the temperature range of our surroundings already called for controlling fire; the invention of tools, utensils, and containers; the invention of clothing and shelter; and observing the seasons, so that even before the agricultural revolution, technology had begun. The division of labor that followed, leading into the urban revolution, resulted in a variety of arts, crafts, and professions. The more knowledge-oriented disciplines of the type now called physical sciences, however, had to wait for the appropriate technological advances that extended our perceptions beyond the range of our senses. Devices that extended our counting ability, or our ability to measure length, area, and volume, had to appear before arithmetic could develop; the abstractions of number, length, area, and volume could not even exist in the human mind to permit the development of mathematics prior to such technological advance. As we were to see over and over again, our decision in each science of what new things or processes were worth perceiving depended on an advance in technology. [See, for example, John Dewey, 1929.] And, thenceforth, physical scientists and technologists together formed a Jacob's ladder, each bootstrapping the other's knowledge into a more advanced state.

Similarly, even an advanced and sophisticated stage in such arts as sculpture, architecture, painting, and music could not occur without the technology sufficient to standardize—and therefore permit the harmonization of—line, mass, perspective, and color vision and their composition for our eyes, or rhythm, melody, and timbres of sound and their composition for our ears. We had to standardize, not merely our perception of these arts through new measuring devices, but our production of them through new instruments and techniques. In fact, the necessary technology for these arts did not develop until the sixteenth through the nineteenth centuries.

We see, then, that it was only when technology had advanced sufficiently that empiricism could even become conceivable, let alone possible. The human spectra and ranges of perception and control had to be extensible by machines, or there would be no evidence on which to base empiricism. The idea of empiricism may have had early philosophical roots—from Aristotle to Roger Bacon—but it was not until the seventeenth century that Francis Bacon's form of it was expressed, and it took centuries before empiricism could really flourish.

For example, statics and dynamics developed in the time of Archimedes (300 B.C.), together with various hydraulic and ballistic technologies. That was when the concepts of force and weight and pressure outside the human range really became perceptible and measurable. Similar developments tied optics to astronomy and biology before measurement could advance into the macroscopic and microscopic ranges. Certainly, the biological concept of the cell could have no empirical base before then. It took many decades before temperature could be measured and centuries before its relation to mechanics could be appreciated. Thomas Kuhn points out that it is impossible to indicate the moment of discovery of oxygen. Over some decades, Priestley, Lavoisier, Scheele, and others did some individual groping with experiments and technological devices to control the materials and mutual communicating on what to capture and how, before it could be said that anyone knew what oxygen was. [T. S. Kuhn, 1962a; 1977.] It took years for these scientists to decide what it was that ought to be perceived and to extend their senses and controls by technological devices in order to perceive it. This is the social phenomenon that I have elsewhere called a wave of agreement to perceive. And there had to be this social agreement to perceive what was unperceivable before, or else the social expense required to manufacture the artificial effectors and receptors would not be accepted. This is especially marked in twentieth-century physics and its dependence on accelerators.

The basic chemical concept of an element, as it was introduced by Dalton and is thought of today, could not even exist (in spite of the ancient forms of atomism), let alone have an empirical basis, until after a number of occurrences similar to the story of oxygen; the principle that chemicals combine in fixed proportions and the principle of conservation of mass was inconceivable, let alone unmeasurable, until then. Similar things could be said about the concepts of energy in each of the variety of meanings it has had over the millenia. The principle of conservation of energy was inconceivable and inexpressible before the late nineteenth century.

When Thomas Kuhn talks about scientific revolutions, where some of the paradigms of the science are replaced, I interpret this to mean that the community forming that science has decided that something considered worth perceiving before is no longer worth perceiving and is to be replaced by a new basic concept or a new basic principle, using a new insight. [T. S. Kuhn, 1962a.] On a millenial time scale, phlogiston disappeared in a flash, to be replaced by oxygen; on a time scale that could look at day-to-day, week-to-week, and month-to-month changes, phlogiston died hard, and the birth of oxygen was difficult.

Kuhn's analysis is restricted to those knowledge-oriented disciplines called the sciences and, more specifically, the empirical sciences and especially the physical sciences. Machlup has pointed out that for thousands of years, the word *science* referred to the absolutely certain, such as mathematics and logic and metaphysics but excluded natural philosophy; and that it was only in the nineteenth century when an empirical base became a requirement for science that the tables were turned to drive metaphysics out. [Machlup, 1980.] Machlup points out, however, that in languages other than English, the word *science* still includes other disciplines (even law); but I note that all his examples of the term in other languages are what I have called knowledge-oriented as distinguished from action-oriented. It seems to me that even the action-oriented disciplines develop their characteristic concepts, ideologies, Weltanschauungen, and what I have elsewhere called mass egos, in a similar way. I will return to this question shortly. Meanwhile, let me discuss this attitude toward knowledge implied by those concerned with its accumulation.

Those fond of physical metaphors in psychology and epistemology often compare knowledge to physical entities in order to invent methods for weighing and measuring it. They often visualize knowledge as an inert quantity of stuff independent of the knower. (I believe it was Karl Popper who criticized and sharpened this point of view. [Popper, 1968.]) Knowledge is en*light*enment, and those fond of physical imagery, in talking about it, should remember that *light* was not fully understood in the physical sciences until Huyghens's wave theory was developed as well as Newton's particle theory.

Charles S. Peirce pointed out that the study of signs (symbol systems) was not merely about a dyadic relation between the symbol and what it means but was really discussing the triadic relation among symbols, their meanings, and their users or interpreters. (I will come back to this point when I discuss the ideology of informatics.) In a similar way, knowledge, which is what we try to symbolize when we communicate, is not merely a relation between what is known and the knower; knowledge is the result of an attempt to communicate and, therefore, involves a community of knowers as well as what is known. This communication process works like a boundary-value problem among the knowers of the community, and the things and processes the community knows in common result from something like a wave phenomenon. When the concepts of cardinal number, length, area, volume, mass, weight, temperature, energy, element, or cell, or the processes of which they partake, were invented (not discovered!), this was a production of new knowledge that occurred over a period of time. And this social process was what I called a wave of agreement to perceive. This is the process that some historians of science call discovery, and whose retraction and replacement Thomas Kuhn calls the change of paradigm in a scientific revolution. [T. S. Kuhn, 1962*a*.]

Furthermore, the continued transmission of these social agreements to a larger community is the part of the wave of agreement to perceive that we commonly call education, although some call it brainwashing.

It seems to me that this process occurs in all disciplines, not just in the sciences in a restricted sense. But before I go into this question, I want to consider why the division of labor among us has separated knowledge-oriented disciplines from action-oriented ones. Why did understanding divorce itself from purposefulness, knowledge from power? To use the cybernetic terms, why did communication separate itself from control? In Schopenhauer's words, why is the world as "idea" distinguished from the world as "will"? How did aesthetics come to separate itself from ethics, the true and the beautiful from the good?

We have all noticed squirrels alternating active skittering around with passive, quiet observation. The human animal seems to be the only one that has specialized these two states. Perhaps neurophysiologists can tell us if it is characteristic of the chordata phyllum to alternate receptor-signals going to the brain with effector-signals coming from it along the spinal cord. But it would take sociological or anthropological information to tell us why Western civilization used this dichotomy in its division of labor among those professing action-oriented and knowledge-oriented disciplines. Why did Plato consider the question of the usefulness of knowledge demeaning? Why have science and technology become so divorced when the bases of both are so interlaced, as we have already observed? What were the reasons for the sharp separation of pure and applied mathematics, especially in the twentieth century? Why are the words *academic* and *practical* used as mutual insults? Although I agree with operational philosophers like Anatol Rapoport that this separation has had a bad effect, the social phenomenon involved still needs explaining. [Rapoport, 1953 and 1967.]

In the case of those disciplines sophisticated enough to have developed formal symbolic systems, such as mathematics and physics, I offer a partial answer by observing what is required of sentences in their languages, known as laws, ideal laws, logical laws, or analytic sentences in mathematics and material laws, laws of nature, or synthetic sentences in the physical sciences, as observed by the logical positivists. [Carnap, 1939 and 1969.] In any case, they are declarative sentences whose verbs appear in the indicative mood. They must be formed using nouns and verbs for the basic things and relations or processes that are either precisely what those communities decided to be their basic percepts, or else linguistically constructed phrases and clauses that use them in accepted syntactic structures.

The additional concepts must be defined in terms of the basic ones. Carl Hempel tells us that these definitions are rarely simply nominal or real definitions but often employ what Carnap has called reduction to an experiential basis. This means that the definition is not simply the presentation of a necessary and sufficient condition for recognizing the new concept but is preceded by a special condition or is accompanied by special measurement requirements. [Hempel, 1939 and 1969.] It seems to me that these conditions and measurements are concerned precisely with specifications, outside the immediate range of human perceptions, that the discipline has decided to extend itself to. The only syntactically acceptable sentences in these languages are sentences that can be verified as true or tested for falsity by formal logical or standard empirical means. The results are then, first of all, strictly descriptive because they are declarative—hence, knowledge-oriented; second, their acceptance criteria must be independent of the variety of representation systems (or even languages) they are presented in. For example, even as simple a statement in mathematics as the arithmetic one that $7 + 5 = 12$ must have its truth value independent of the notational language for numbers or the addition procedure used. (The puzzle if $7 + 5 = 13$, what is $6 + 8$ is not really a mathematical one.) Similarly, the sentences in physics expressing the motions of a system of, say, twenty bodies or whatever number is used to model the solar system, must be equally valid when translated into another coordinate system. In fact, Einstein used the Tensor notation precisely because a grammatical sentence in it could not be physical nonsense as a result of being essentially dependent on which coordinate system it appears in. A physical law should be the same independently of the language used to describe it! This is a guarantee of objectivity. I submit that it was the quest for objective truth, independent of the knowers, that caused the dichotomization of knowledge and action. [J. Dewey, 1929.]

Thus, the laws of mathematics and physics must be independent of their users or interpreters. To use Charles Morris's interpretation of Peirce's semiotics that I have already mentioned, the symbology of these disciplines must be independent of pragmatics, and possibly even formal. [Morris, 1939 and 1969.]

The very sophistication in the language of the discipline that allows one to define composite concepts and composite processes from the basic ones by some standard assembly method, whether definitions be nominal or real—(or explicatory in Hempel's sense)—refocuses one's attention from the things and processes considered by the discipline to the symbolic expressions and symbolic manipulations needed to express them. One is now becoming involved with the metalanguage of the language of the discipline; that is, one is now not merely talking *in* the language of the discipline, one is talking *about* its grammar as well. The action orientation is now more symbolic than substantive, and the discipline as a whole appears more knowledge-oriented. [See Hermann Hesse on the *Glass Bead Game*, 1949.]

The model I am presenting of the ideological development of disciplines has these disciplines building up special symbolic languages. At their birth, and during revolutions of the Kuhnian type, a number of basic expressions are introduced or replaced; expressions referring to *processes* the community has agreed to perceive are the basic *verbs* of the language. Expressions referring to the *things* the community has agreed to perceive are the basic *nouns* of the language. Definitional habits developed by the community permit it to specify composite processes and composite objects to yield phrases and clauses or new nouns and verbs of the language. Communication habits developed by the community make its members build these syntactic types into sentences and assemblages of sentences.

When the discipline is mainly knowledge-oriented, as in the academic type, the tendency seems to be to have the majority of the sentences in the declarative mood; furthermore, the manner of assembling these sentences is often in deductive or inductive groups, each discipline having its own method of reasoning or argument. For example, mathematics and physics use formal and extensional logic, and the assemblages are definitions and proofs and demonstrations.

When, however, the discipline is mainly action-oriented, the majority of the sentences tend to be imperative, hence, neither true nor false (though possibly good or bad). Moreover, the important assemblages are assignments, allocations, and programs. Assembly grammar is not logic; it uses the methods of programming. Communication is mainly in command languages, as in industrial orders, game rules and protocols, recipes, military commands, or governmental programs. The language is that of management, and the sentences are like legal laws, not natural laws or valid truths. The basic assumption in the action-oriented disciplines seems to be free will, while the basic assumption in the empirical sciences seems to be determinism. I submit that these are presenting laws of nature but belong to the metalanguage of the discipline. They are decisions on how their statements are to be viewed and organized in the language.

Each of the two extreme types of discipline has a few sentences belonging to the other type. Management peppers its prescriptive commands with descriptions of the conditions for alternative actions or initial states or the goal to be achieved. Theoreticians pepper their extensive descriptions of the states of their worlds with verification procedures (specified often in the metalanguage they use in discussing the methods).

Scientists of the operational type demand a better balance. But it is the disciplines called *professions*, whose mission is to transfer knowledge into action, that employ the indicative and the imperative in more equal doses. (But note that even medicine has its surgeons and internists; law, its practitioners and reviewers.)

I have elsewhere detailed the development of disciplines into phases that mainly describe the complexity of the expressions in their languages from the primitive noun system (taxonomic) to the sophisticated metalinguistic expressions (formal deductive or simulative). [Gorn, 1965.] My claim has been that an advanced stage in the development of a discipline's language and symbols makes it develop a contact with mathematics, and an even more sophisticated—in fact, self-conscious—stage brings it into contact with informatics. However, before I consider the ideology of informatics that causes this relation to other disciplines, I should say something about what I have called the mass ego of a discipline.

The claim that every discipline whose language is sufficiently sophisticated (in fact self-conscious) establishes contact with informatics (and many such with mathematics) is not, I feel, merely personal; it is a claim that I believe any informatician would make for reasons I will explain shortly. This is an example of what I would call the mass ego of informatics. Every fairly advanced discipline regards itself as a critically important factor without which the warp and woof of the fabric of human knowledge and action would unravel. Its participants feel that the concepts they have agreed to perceive cover a certain set of dimensions of human perception that no other discipline can do justice to and that all others depend on. Furthermore, it is with its closest neighbors in the topology of disciplines that it is likely to have the severest ideological arguments; after all, it is almost impossible for a microscope to be kept in focus for overlapping views simultaneously. The informatician is no different from the others in these respects, as we shall see.

THE INFORMATIC OUTLOOK

Informatics is concerned with symbolic expressions and their manipulations. Such symbol manipulation, especially in numerical and analytic computations, has been changing slowly over the millenia. Since the Renaissance, and especially after the industrial revolution, it spread over a number of disciplines and accelerated. It was, however, the amplification of this phenomenon of the spreading and changing of symbol manipulations, caused by the appearance of electronic computers, that made the process extremely apparent, because its pace had become visible on a day-to-day basis.

Such symbolic manipulation had already transcended numerical computation in the calculus, with formal differentiation and integration, and in symbolic logic, especially because of the school of formalists at the turn of the century, but even with Aristotle when he discussed syllogisms.

When, however, the electronic speeds of the new computers required decision-making instructions and a programming process separated from the time of computation and when the necessary program occupied the same storage as the numerical data, it became obvious that most of the programming process itself was just another symbol manipulation that the same machine could accomplish. It then became clear that numerical computation was a very special example of a much broader concept of computation, one that included the linguistic process of programming. Furthermore, the common storage of instructions and data made the language of programming capable of self-referencing operations.[1] Programs could possess some of the

---

[1] I have called this property of some machines and their languages unstratified control. The metalanguage of programming is contained in the object language. Hofstadter calls this property "a strange loop." [Hofstadter, 1979.]

self-referencing subtleties we had thought to be characteristic of speech and thought, and, hence, what we previously thought to be unmechanizable.

The result was not only the design of more sophisticated programming languages more suited to human use but the design of programs of the type now known as possessing *artificial* intelligence. In fact, some informaticians are trying to make natural language reveal more mechanism, and some keep trying to make mechanical languages more natural.

Also any instruction, and, hence, any set of instructions, could either be wired into the circuitry or placed in the storage. The difference between hardware and software disappeared as a logical distinction—as the very peculiar words *hardware* and *software* indicate.

So far, everything I have said about computation is action-oriented and tied to the computer. But prior to the appearance of digital computers, a *theory* of computation had already appeared. [Kleene, 1979.] Symbolic logicians had already investigated the logical limits of computation; Turing had analyzed computation, designed the universal Turing machine, and proved the unsolvability of the halting problem; Gödel had shown the limits of formalism with his undecidability theorems; Church, Kleene, and Curry had analyzed computation in recursive-function theory and combinatory logic; Thue and Post, and, most recently, Markov, had presented general computation as word problems; and most important, all these approaches were shown to be equivalent. Thus, when computers appeared, Noam Chomsky's discussion of natural linguistics was in terms of computation, and a new computational view of psycholinguistics was introduced. [Chomsky, 1963; Chomsky and Miller, 1963; Miller and Chomsky, 1963; and Fodor, 1980.] This new development produced linguistic descriptions of programming processes, a mathematical automata theory, and formal languages. These, in turn, affected the design of programming languages and machines. In short, the presence of the machines amplified and made tangibly and visibly apparent what had been a slow process of development in symbol manipulation before their appearance.

We now perceive informatics as concerned with the synthesis *and* analysis of systems of *symbolic expressions and* the synthesis *and* analysis of *processors* that interpret, translate, and manipulate such expressions. More prosaically stated, informatics is concerned with the study, design, and use of data structures and their transformation by mechanical means, as a recent text has put it. [Tremblay and Sorenson, 1976.]

In its present youthful stage, this new discipline covers the art, science, *and* profession of symbol manipulation. The action-oriented *and* the knowledge-oriented aspects of computation are less likely to move apart, because the description of symbolic expressions remains tied to the prescriptive language of its interpreting processors. In other words, the knowledge-oriented concept of data structures and the action-oriented concept of data-processors remained harnessed instead of going through the usual polarization. I prefer to speak of mechanical languages and their interpreting processors rather than data-structure systems and data-processors. And the new concept of processors that the informaticians have agreed to perceive in a new ontological commitment is, as I see it, a blending together into one entity of mechanisms (hardware), programs (software), and rigidly controlled human procedures (in symbol manipulation). The assembly of a processor can be performed equally well in assembly language by using as software the program that is known as the assembler, or by wiring machines together (whether big or small—chips in fact), and only our decision as to which method happens to be more efficient determines the choice. This is what I have called the principle of logical equivalence of hardware and software; I believe that it is part of the peculiar ideology of informatics.

The concept of *assembly* in informatic systems refers equally to such activities as splicing programs, wiring mechanisms together, calling programs that are stored in mechanisms, or having people push buttons, punch cards, or type instructions and follow procedures specified explicitly by machine outputs. These combinations of machines, programs, and algorithmized people are the "users and interpreters" of symbolic expressions that Charles S. Peirce considered to be the third element in the triadic relation evoked by symbolism. In the study of symbols that Charles Morris called semiotics, he referred to the relations of symbolic expressions to their users and interpreters as *pragmatics*. [Morris, 1939 and 1969.]

Informatics must concern itself precisely with these pragmatic questions, where, as we have seen, mathematics and the physical sciences must be independent of them, certainly in their products if not in their methods. In this respect, informatics is more like linguistics, psychology, the behavioral sciences, philosophy, and the professions. This pragmatic tie between symbolic expressions and the design of symbol manipulators, the processors forming the basic concept that informaticians have agreed to perceive, is likely to keep *both* the science and technology harnessed together, as I have already remarked.

The study of relations among, and operations with, symbolic expressions independent of their semantic content or pragmatic context is called syntactics. It is in the study of syntactic questions that informatics is most formal and closely related to mathematics and its methods. The study of relations between symbolic expressions and their meanings, independent of their method of use or interpretation, is called semantics.

I have stressed from the beginning of this paper that the different disciplines are distinguished from one another, especially if they are sophisticated enough to have well-developed symbolic systems, by having ideologically distinct types of semantic concepts. The very fact, however, that they have symbolisms with well-defined manipulative procedures may make it useful for them to simulate their processes symbolically. It is one of the informatician's basic insights (prejudices, superstitions, ideologic attitudes, or peculiar ways of looking at the world?) that any process that can be precisely specified is capable of being symbolically simulated, because a precise specification is already a symbolic simulation. Notice that the symbol system need not be numbers; it could consist of analytical expressions from mathematics or physics; formulae in one, two, or three dimensions from chemistry; graphic representations of polypeptide chains; double-helix representations of genes; graphic representations of communication systems; symphonic scores; choreographic scores in laban-notation; or even animated motion pictures; wiring diagrams; specifications for chip designs in microprocessors; architectural drawings in animated graphics; photographs for pattern recognition in artificial intelligence; or actual people being viewed and heard. And the symbolic medium could be holes punched in cards, electronic signals, magnetic signals, visual signals, sounds, even speech, or whatever. Adding receptors and effectors simulating or going beyond human ranges to the input/output devices could extend applications beyond symbol manipulation to be fully cybernetic in the design of robots.

This symbolic mass ego of informatics is not a schizophrenic dream. Most sophisticated disciplines, even action-oriented ones concerned with games, agree that the informatician has this useful power and maintain contact with him or her in spite of the fact that their own semantics, when they use their symbols, are different from those of the informatician.

The informatician's machines may deal with real semantics if they have the appropriate sensors and effectors, but the informatician can always deal with the real semantics of symbol manipulation by using the unstratified control in his or her machines. This difference between semantics in different disciplines can create confusing arguments, especially when, as we have seen, the concepts they symbolize are closely related.

It is not difficult to distinguish the biologist's meaning of the English word *function* from the mathematician's, but see how different our interpretation of the analytical expression $1 - \frac{1}{2}gt^2$ is when we are thinking like physicists, mathematicians, or informaticians. In the first case, t might mean time and g the acceleration of gravity, and the formula might represent the trajectory of an object being dropped from an elevated moving vehicle—a physical process. To the mathematician, on being told that $g = 32.2$, symbol t is almost meaningless, and any other free variable would serve as well. On being told that its domain is real numbers, he or she sees not a physical trajectory but a static set of ordered pairs of numbers that is all there at once; he or she might visualize it as a graph, but a static one, and not a moving point. Furthermore, the formula $(1 - \sqrt{\frac{1}{2}g}\, t)(1 + \sqrt{\frac{1}{2}g}\, t)$ would be to him or her, another representation of exactly the same function. Finally, the informatician would see the two formulae as crude descriptions of two different computational processes that would only yield the same value for the same value of t under very special representations of t; to the informatician, real time is represented not by t, but the access of the value of t from storage and the time of interpretive computation—in this case, calculation.

Having run through the syntactic, semantic, and pragmatic aspects of the symbol-manipulating activity with which informatics is concerned, we can now see how different people in the field were able to stress different kinds of activity.

The formal theoretical aspects close to logic and mathematics cover such topics as the theory of computation, the analysis of algorithms, switching theory, automata theory [Hartmanis, 1979], the study of formal languages [Greibach, 1979], the study of data structures, and the syntactic representation of semantics. Among these topics, one learns what can and what cannot be computed and for those problems that can be computed, what varieties demand what kinds of computing rhythms and storage controls and at what cost. One also learns the capabilities of various programming techniques, the symbol-manipulative aspects of formal logic and theorem-proving, and the formal techniques of program verification. [Ibid.]

The informatic activity that is empirical and experimental rather than formal turns up in modeling human symbolic behavior in heuristic searching and problem-solving. [See Newell and Simon, 1976a.] Whenever theory informs us that some class of problem is unsolvable, we immediately search for subclasses of problems that are solvable and do so by experimenting with new solution methods until our theoreticians can prove to us that the methods we find are obvious, limited, or fallacious. Even when theory informs us that a general-solution method exists but is very costly, we thrash around for heuristic procedures that may fail to be universally successful (these are called algorithms) but are likely to succeed much sooner. Much of this modeling of human problem-solving behavior that remains empirical is the subject of the area called artificial intelligence. [See also Amarel, 1976; Newell and Simon, 1976a; Salton, 1976; Simon, 1976; and Pearson and Slamecka, 1976.] This part of informatics is the part that is applied to the area of engineering called robotics.

This empirical side of informatics, together with the theoretical side called analysis of algorithms, is the area some call a major portion of informatics; it is known as the design of algorithms. If we note that these procedures called algorithms have equivalent representations in software and hardware, we recognize our basic concept of processor again; this area is, therefore, what I called the synthesis and analysis of interpreting processors. However, we should not forget that in addition to the algorithms, there are devices that feed them and collect their results, which are similar to human receptors and effectors. These input and output devices can extend the semantics of the symbol systems being processed to the various extensions of our senses and motor controls needed in robotics. Thus, the various studies in graphics, vision, and speech recognition, and their use in image processing and pattern recognition, are also extensive portions of empirical informatics.

So far, we have examined the areas of informatics that are most scientific in the recent English sense of the word. In both the theoretical and empirical portions, people are concerned with truth—the truth about symbol manipulation. But many are engaged in informatic activity because of aesthetic or ethical reactions. Some are attracted to the beauty, and some, especially those with professional interests in applications, are interested in the good things that can be achieved and the further increase of our powers, while others are appalled by the stupid or evil applications that are possible. [Weizenbaum, 1976.] The information-handling machines have been called intelligence amplifiers. It is true: They are, but they are also stupidity amplifiers. They are symbol-manipulation amplifiers that can be used for good or ill.

Knuth's Turing lecture presented the aesthetic view. He talked about beautiful and clearly understandable programs. [Knuth, 1974a.] And we can readily imagine that most of the designers of processors, hardware, software, or systems may react aesthetically, especially now that microprocessor chips can be designed for production by automatic VLSI (very-large-scale integration) techniques and produced without exorbitant capital investment (unlike cyclotrons). The ranks of hardware designers may become almost as populous as those of the software engineers and, in fact, may largely overlap them. Because of the principle of logical equivalence of hardware and software, the machine designer and programmer did not have to have different aptitudes. Now it will be much more usual for them to be one and the same person.

These aesthetic and ethical views of professional aspects of informatics have been there from the beginning, connected first with formal aspects of logic design, then with structured programming rules for software engineers [e.g., Dijkstra, 1976], and finally with the variety and value of the applications, especially as they begin to transcend the symbol-manipulative.

It is, however, this area of applications to all other disciplines that should absorb the vast majority of professional informaticians. These professionals would apply their knowledge of informatics to the production of programs, programming aids, and programming systems—or their hardware equivalents—for the other disciplines. For example, these professionals might design processors called simulators—psycholinguistic simulators, economic-system simulators, traffic simulators, management-information systems, military-information systems, science-information systems, report generators, inventory-control systems, and so forth.

In any case, the application to the other discipline would require that its own personnel and informaticians dredge up the basic concepts from the mass ego of that discipline and model its language syntactically in its simulators. The model might even be semantically based if the appropriate receptors and effectors are available, as they might be in robotics.

This sums up my picture of the ideology of informatics and its practitioners, whether they behave as formal theorists (such as pure mathematicians), empirical scientists, or professionals with aesthetic or ethical goals in a variety of applications. I believe it is the ontological commitment deeply entrenched in this ideology that keeps knowledge-oriented and action-oriented behaviors harnessed together and makes the complete separation of pure informatics from applied informatics less likely. However, the variety of applications is so tremendous, even more than in the case of mathematics, because of the pragmatic aspects of the subject, that it is quite likely that a number of distinct professions will spin off, whereas mathematics only produced an amorphous community of applied mathematicians.

This leads me to consider community relations between informatics and other disciplines and especially its immediate neighbors.

THE INTERCOMMUNICATION AND STABILITY OF DISCIPLINES

I remarked early in this paper that the word *ideology* has acquired a number of meanings; I have been using two of those meanings. The first refers to a systematic body of concepts, especially as applied to a manner or the content of thinking characteristic of an individual, group, or culture; in our case, the relevant groups or cultures are called disciplines, and the body of concepts includes what Thomas Kuhn calls paradigms. The second meaning is that of Destutt de Tracy[2] and the *ideologues* [Picavet, 1891 and 1971] around the time of Napoleon. This meaning was the study of the development of ideas from sensations, especially in humans; the ideologues intended ideology to be a branch of zoology, specifically of human biology, particularly neurology and psychology. Destutt de Tracy's [1817] book on ideology acknowledges descent from Condillac and has a second part on grammar and a third part on logic. Clearly, he would have included today's psycholinguists and such developmental psychologists as Piaget among the ideologues. He believed, for example, that ideas were initiated by direct perception and extended by inner perceptions called memory, judgments (the comparison of outer perceptions with memories), and will (the perception of desires and action caused by this perception).

Our description of informatics and its relation to other disciplines, in fact, of the generation of ideologies of disciplines and their Kuhnian transformations, extends the basis in perception that the ideologues insisted on to a basis in the extended perceivers and controllers beyond the human spectrum, one that is provided by technology. In the case of informatics, it is the electronic computer that provides this extension, just as it is the accelerator in modern physics, the electron microscope in material science and biology, and similar devices and techniques in genetics and anthropology and as it was the microscope and telescope in the time of Galileo.

A true unification of human knowledge (such as the sciences) and action (such as the arts and professions) would call for the ability to patch the variety of ideologies together when they have been generated by extensions in many directions beyond the human range. Such patchwork is going on in a

---

[2] I am indebted to Bertrand de Jouvenel for pointing out to me that my method of identification of informatics was ideological in this sense.

large variety of interdisciplines, such as biophysics, biochemistry, sociobiology, ecology, bionics, the aforementioned psycholinguistics; and in such superdisciplines as cybernetics, history, anthropology, philosophy, and pedagogy.

This process of mapping all of human lore has been going on since the urban revolution, and the system of disciplines has moved around and changed kaleidoscopically. We have been filling in and constantly modifying this map. I believe this to be a more realistic model than the nineteenth-century model of science progressing by indefinite accretion; such an infinitely progressing model is obviously unstable, even apart from the criticisms of Thomas Kuhn and Karl Popper. Historians, philosophers, and sociologists of science would mainly concern themselves with our first meaning of ideology but would also be concerned with Destutt de Tracy's meaning in order to understand the way the first develops.

Stable disciplines have distinct ideologies, and we can, therefore, distinguish them from one another by contrasting those ideologies. For instance, in my presentation of the ideology of informatics, I showed that it was not a branch of mathematics by, for example, pointing out that it must concern itself with pragmatic questions where mathematical concepts must be independent of them. Another way of distinguishing disciplines is by examining their proportions of descriptive, prescriptive, and professional activities (those translating knowledge into action).

Let us use these methods to discuss some of the variety of neighboring disciplines and subject areas, specifically cybernetics, robotics, communication theory, library science, information retrieval, information science, management-information systems, decision science, and management science.

As Norbert Wiener defined it, cybernetics is the study of "communication and control in the animal and the machine"; I have already called it a superdiscipline. Wiener intended cybernetics to include neurology, communication theory, control theory, what is now called general systems theory, and bionics. Informatics, I think, is included because it concerns itself with communication by explicitly designed symbolic systems and the control of such communication by mechanisms, procedures, algorithmized people, or suitably assembled systems of these (what I have called processors). If input/output devices attached to computers are extended to include more general receptors and effectors, the resulting extension of the field would include robotics and also be a part of cybernetics. However, although robotics makes use of the area of informatics known as artificial intelligence, it is clearly involved with concepts and principles of the sciences related to extended perceptions provided by the receptors and effectors used, and robotics is pragmatically concerned with actions needed in processes for which robots are designed. In short, robotics is mainly concerned with translating from the knowledge of a number of disciplines (informatics included) into action; it is a professional activity. Whether robotics will develop a unified ideology, and, therefore, become a single discipline, will be determined by its practitioners. If its members set up a tight communication system and decide that their new recruits need a standardized curriculum in their education, robotics will, indeed, become a separate discipline. Cybernetics is likely to contain a number of disciplines, and informatics is likely to have a number of such professional disciplines developing from its applications. The areas variously called decision science, management-information systems, medical-information systems, and management science are other examples of professions of the cybernetic kind neighboring on informatics. If the word *science* in some of these titles remains attached to them, even if only as a convenience in obtaining economic supports, then that word *science* will have gone through still another stage in its evolution. I would tend to call these disciplines professions rather than sciences, because their emphasis is on system design rather than being strictly knowledge-oriented. That is my interpretation of the present meanings of the words *science* and *profession*. Thus, the designers of medical-information systems would be applying knowledge of medicine and informatics to a particular management area.

The professional activity of the pedagogues, in this country known as the field of education, is another example of what I have called a superdiscipline. Each discipline, in order to educate its newcomers, develops a complicated curriculum in order to imprint its ideology. I have heard some talk in the past of having universal pedagogic techniques independent of the subject matter taught. I am skeptical, for pragmatic reasons, that such tools can be sufficient. Distinct ideologies requiring, as they do, different habits of thought must, it seems to me, call for different pedagogic techniques.

The pedagogue must be able to recognize when a pupil understands a subject and to generate such understanding when it does not exist. He or she must, therefore, have a technique to elicit activity from the student, either to reveal the state of the student's understanding or to generate such. Different ideologies of different disciplines demand different techniques, and the pedagogue who introduces one must be steeped in it himself or herself. One cannot expect the majority of pedagogic techniques, which must ipso facto be pragmatic to suit human users and interpreters, to be pragmatically independent of the ideologies of the disciplines taught.

It seems to me that the area of information retrieval makes a similar pragmatic demand. In order to retrieve relevant information, one must understand the structure in which it is stored—usually in accordance with the ideology of the storer—and compare it to the ideology of the purpose for which it is to be retrieved. Hence, I believe that this pragmatic dependence on the ideology of the subject applies not merely to the superdiscipline called pedagogy, but also to that most ancient profession of library management and the area related to informatics known as information retrieval.

Because the different disciplines of knowledge and action will keep changing their scope, knowledge about each discipline will never be needed in the same order or in exactly the same language in which it was produced. Thus, the organization of disciplinary information as it is produced will never be the same as the appropriate organization needed to recall it efficiently for future use. It follows that the organization of the library will always need changing and, hence, the problems of library organization will never be solved once and for all. Thus, the library profession will never be static enough to be totally mechanizable. Each generation of librarians may suffer a certain amount of technological obsolescence, but the profession as a whole never can. Since its main problem is unsolvable, it is guaranteed to be a stable profession.

In fact one can say, conversely, that only *those* professions will be stable and, at long range, safe from technological obsolescence whose problems are unsolvable. For example, physicians, whose main duty is to keep us from dying, will always be with us. Similarly for teachers, whose job it is to keep mankind from becoming stupid; or mass-communication professionals, who must keep us informed.

It is attempts to solve new problems, especially the unsolvable ones, that are responsible for establishing new disciplines and their ideologies, especially the stable ones. The application of computers to these problems is, therefore, likely to present symbolic simulations of their pragmatic demands, hence, of their ideologies. I would therefore expect a number of professions to keep spinning off from informatics.

As a young discipline, however, theoretical aspects are still closely connected with the action-oriented design and handling of computational and linguistic mechanisms. Fundamental results from the mathematical theory of computation present a host of provably unsolvable problems of symbol manipulation and a host of impracticable solutions to overly general problems together with proofs that they cannot be improved. They mark the limits of computation that every professional informatician must be aware of, as well as the unsolvable areas that can be conquered only by subdivision. This essential tie of the knowledge-oriented base to action-oriented aspects and the consequent empirical activity may succeed in keeping informatics from separating into distinct knowledge-oriented disciplines, the way mathematics did after the Pythagoreans and Plato; grammar, after the Stoics; and logic, after the logistic and formalist schools. This fact, coupled with the host of unsolvable problems, may maintain informatics as a stable discipline without its unravelling into separate sciences, arts, and professions. If such is the case, informatics will not become a metascience, as did the just-mentioned disciplines, or, for that matter, metaphysics.

In short, we should not try to separate computer science from information science but should try to maintain one discipline of informatics. Any attempt to cause such a separation by, for example, trying to create another metascience [see Otten and Debons, 1970] would separate the action from the knowledge, as has happened with Pythagorean mathematics, Sophistic rhetoric, Aristotelian metaphysics and the Aristotelian organon, Stoic grammar, and the logic and grammar of the logical positivists. Such a separation would cause the cessation of the very effervescence that the mixture of knowledge and action maintains. In the case of the library profession, even nonpragmatists and extreme idealists would agree that this is the wrong way to go. [See Wright, 1979.][3]

[3] For further insights, see Furth [1974], Heilprin [1974], D. Hillman [1977], Kochen [1974], Otten [1974], Sager [1977], Slamecka and Pearson [1977], Whittemore and Yovits [1974], and Yovits, Rose, and Abilock [1977].

PERSPECTIVES ON INFORMATICS AS A SEMIOTIC DISCIPLINE

Charls Pearson and Vladimir Slamecka

The purpose of this paper is to analyze the logical and methodological relations between information science and computer science and some of the other subject areas that contribute to the scientific study of information. Gorn proceeds toward this destination in two stages. First, he develops two main theses: (1) Informatics (encompassing information and computer science, engineering, and technology) is a semiotic discipline; and (2) information science and information engineering should not and perhaps cannot be separated very much. These theses provide a perspective that is then used to analyze the relation between informatics and several neighboring disciplines.

The gist of our comments may be summarized as follows. We are in full agreement with the first thesis—that informatics is a semiotic discipline. Given this perspective, we also fully concur that most of the neighboring disciplines (including robotics, cybernetics, what is currently called information science, etc.) are professions or technologies rather than sciences and that most uses of the word science in this area are honorific rather than scientific. On the other hand, we are not convinced that information science and informatic engineering should never be separated and that the honorific use of the term science by information professions and technologies will necessarily persist.

Our sympathetic regard for viewing informatics as a semiotic discipline is easily explained: This view has been the common denominator of the academic programs of Georgia Tech's School of Information and Computer Science since its establishment in 1964, and a major if not central thrust of its research programs. [Slamecka and Gehl, 1978.] Thus, Gorn's and our views have largely coincided for nearly two decades [see Gorn, 1963; Slamecka, 1968]; and our research interests contributed to several of the topics mentioned in his paper, notably the theorem of hardware-software equivalence [Poore, Baralt-Torrijos, and Chiaraviglio, 1971], logic of plans and programs [Baralt-Torrijos, 1973], and particularly empirical semiotics [Pearson, 1977]. Our comments on Gorn's first thesis are thus largely an amplification of his views, as well as an argument for a broader interpretation of the domain of semiotics relevant to information science.

ON THE SEMIOTIC NATURE OF INFORMATICS

Discussions of semiotics are often buried in linguistic analyses; for this reason, we first discuss the semiotic background and then comment from its perspective on several positions in Gorn's paper. In the following development of the topic, we make use of a language developed specifically for use in the empirical analysis of meaning and information, called the Language of Menetics. [Pearson, 1977.] Much of the origins of this language stems from Charles Peirce, Charles K. Ogden and Ivor A. Richards, Rudolf Carnap, and Charles Morris.

In order to perform an information experiment, it is necessary to control all known variables and sources of variation for the purpose of analyzing unknown sources of variation and the relations among them. This implies the idealization and simplification of an information situation into its minimal atomic units and the selection—or design—of one such unit for observation or study. To use an example from physics, it is possible to measure the heat equivalent of energy by shaking the Golden Gate Bridge with giant machines and measuring the temperature rise across the span. This would be a most inefficient way of carrying out such an experiment and unthinkable, of course, in a modern physics laboratory. If we are interested in better *understanding* (Gorn's knowledge-orientation) the relation between mechanical energy and thermal energy, we would idealize the situation down to a single controllable and analyzable source of mechanical energy, boundary conditions that control the flow of heat, and a means for measuring temperature rise. Similarly, in the study of information, we must simplify our messages and communication situations—the things the information community has agreed to perceive—down to their minimal atomic units and assemble them in simple, controllable, and analyzable configurations, so as to be able to study the unknown sources of variation among them and the relations among these sources.

In the information and communication situation, the minimal atomic elements are called signs. Thus, signs are the elementary carriers of meaning and information, and the basic science of information concerns the structure of signs—how they carry information and meaning and how they are processed. This study has been called semiotics[1] (in various forms of the word)

---

[1] The word semiotics should not, however, be attributed to the American philosopher, Charles Morris. Morris never called the discipline semiotics; he consistently called it semiotic, as did also the founder of modern semiotics, the American logician and philosopher, Charles Peirce. Modern usage of the term *semiotic* stems from its reintroduction into philosophy by the British philosopher John Locke. The expression *semiotics* came only later, and Morris himself noted that someone else had called the discipline semiotics. The anthropologist Margaret Mead is often given credit for coining this term.

since the times of the pre-Socratic philosophers. Gorn is eminently correct in his assessment of the role that semiotics plays in the study of information.

Charles Peirce divided the structure of all signs into three dimensions dealing with (1) the medium, body, or existence of the sign; (2) the object or designation of the sign; and (3) the interpreter, interpretation, or interpretant of the sign. Later, Charles Morris found all signs to have these same three dimensions and gave them their currently accepted names: syntactic, semantic, and pragmatic dimensions. Although this can be viewed as Morris's interpretation of Peirce, Morris developed it before he read Peirce. (Peirce's work was not publicly available until several years later.)[2]

Signs also have both an internal structure and an external structure in all three dimensions. The external structure is observable (e.g., the shape of a sign, its medium or embodiment, or the interpreter of a sign). The external components of a sign are its information generators, and the various measures of information (in the empirical sense—the term *information measure* also has a distinct mathematical sense) are the empirically interesting observable aspects of these information generators or external components.

The internal structure of a sign is theoretical rather than observable; an example would be the intension of a sign. The internal components of a sign are its meaning components. Extension and intension are semantic components of meaning. Morris, who originated the term *semantics* (apart from a completely different use for the same word by Breál), defined semantics as the study of relations between signs and their objects (this object is to be understood here in its ideal, theoretical sense).

The division of semiotics into syntactics, semantics, and pragmatics allows us to classify the various kinds of signs. Peirce's most famous classification was a three-way semantic classification into indexes, icons, and symbols. Indexes have extension and object as their only semantic structure—apart from any syntactic or pragmatic structure they may have. Icons have extension, intension, object, and ground in their semantic structure. And symbols have extension, intension, cognision, object, ground, and cognitive mentellect in their semantic structure. (Peirce originally used his philosophical categories of firstness, secondness, and thirdness to draw this distinction.) Another well-known three-way classification of signs is a syntactic one into tokens, types, and tones. Peirce sometimes used the terms *sinsign, legisign,* and *qualisign* to draw this same distinction using his philosophical categories. A final three-way classification of signs involves the pragmatic dimension: Pragmatically, signs can be divided into rhemes, phemes, and dolemes.

There are, thus, nine elementary kinds of signs: tokens, types, tones, indexes, icons, symbols, rhemes, phemes, and dolemes. Since a sign must fall into one of each of the syntactic, semantic, and pragmatic categories, the

---

[2] It may be of interest in this regard to note that Morris was a student of George Herbert Mead, who worked quite closely with John Dewey at the University of Chicago and that Dewey, if not actually a student of Peirce's, studied him quite thoroughly.

actual structure of a sign must be a combination of three of these elementary kinds.

This classification scheme helps us to understand the relation between semiotics and informatics. Accordingly, in its concern with semiotic structure, informatics is concerned with not only symbolic expressions and their manipulations (as Gorn suggests) but with all elementary kinds of signs; symbols are just one of the nine such kinds of semiotic structure. Along the same line of reasoning, Gorn's definition of *semantics* as the study of relations between symbolic expressions and their meanings would seem to neglect syntactic meaning, pragmatic meaning, external semantics, and the semantics of nonsymbolic signs (the semantics of a string quartet, for instance). Peirce and Morris both recognized their versions of semiotic as the study of all signs, not just symbols; for instance, in one paper on aesthetics, Morris has analyzed the meaning of icons.

Having clarified the semiotic background, we are now in a position to comment on several other statements in Gorn's analysis. One comment concerns the distinction between the indicative and imperative moods. The distinction is important for the subject at hand, because one of the distinguishing features of science and technology concerns the essential role played in science by declarative sentences and in technology by imperative sentences. Gorn is aware of this role and of the role the attitude of the interpreter plays in distinguishing between scientific text and technological text (thus confirming his agreement with the basic triadic nature of information and the sign). Mood is the syntactic encoding of a pragmatic attitude. It is a grammatical device that indicates the relation between the interpreter of a sentence and his or her attitude toward the propositional content of the sentence (e.g., indicative, imperative, interrogative, etc.).

Another related comment refers to the essential existence of nouns and verbs. The statement that sentences in disciplines sophisticated enough to have developed formal symbolic systems *must* be formed using nouns and verbs does not indicate an essential nature of information, since nouns and verbs are not universal semiotic categories. The existence of nouns and verbs in all of the sentences under discussion only indicates the Indo-European origins of such formal systems and the reliance of current methods of formalization on the grammatical structure of the Indo-European languages, especially ancient Greek and late Latin. Incidentally, current research in semiotics or information science seems to neglect this interesting relation between the grammatical structure of natural language and the resulting structure of the methods of formalization adopted by various intellectual communities within the society of that language's speakers. On the other hand, the fruitful analogy suggested by Gorn between languages in the conceptual study of a discipline and coordinate systems in the mathematical study of a discipline has been given some attention. [Pearson, 1977.]

The suggestion that the symbology of mathematics and physics is *possibly* formal deserves comment for two reasons. First, the symbology of mathematics *is* formal because mathematics is the formalization of the syntactic encoding of our reasoning processes. The symbology of physics, on the other hand, can never be completely formal, because of the semantic nature of physics and, indeed, of all the sciences—including information science.

Two other semiotic comments that share a specific relation to logic, or the methods of reasoning, are in order. In addition to the two methods (the deductive and inductive) of manipulating information in the style called reasoning, listed by Gorn, mention may be made of what Peirce called the most important method of reasoning—the abductive method, now more often called retroductive. This is the method of *inventing* hypotheses that, if true, would explain some known results. Abduction is absolutely indispensable for investigation in all disciplines called nomological sciences.

Gorn's insightful comparison of the action-oriented technologies with the knowledge-oriented sciences acknowledges the role that imperative sentences play in technology, and the role that the indicative mood plays in the sciences. This suggests to us that research into the nature of the sentential mood and the development of a logic of the sentential mood will be important for obtaining a better understanding of information science and the other semiotic sciences. Consider, for example, Gorn's suggestion that since imperative sentences are neither true nor false, good and bad may be used as alternatives. However, acceptable/unacceptable and practical/impractical are other equally important pragmatic alternatives; so are beautiful/ugly and moral/immoral, though not as pure alternatives to true/false. This example indicates the increased complexity pragmatic structure bears relative to semantic structure.

KNOWLEDGE- VERSUS ACTION-ORIENTED INFORMATICS

The main issue of the paper, as far as the purposes of the entire study are concerned, is the relation between informatics and some of the other disciplines that contribute to the scientific study of information. Gorn draws a distinction between the knowledge-oriented component of informatics (information-and-computer science) and its action-oriented component (information/computer engineering).

The inseparability of information science and computer science is well worth emphasizing. Even though a few scholars, including Gorn, have viewed this field in such a way for years, it is only recently that the similarity or identity of goals and approaches has begun to surface (attested to, for example, by the 1982 Symposium on Empirical Foundations of Information and Software Science). Referring to our earlier comments, a note is appropriate, however, regarding the scope of information and computer science. Gorn refers to information-handling machines as symbol-manipulating amplifiers, a definition that would seem to restrict such machines to digital computers only—a restriction probably not intended. While symbols may play some role in many analog computers, it is the iconic structure that plays the essential role; analog computers are icon-manipulating amplifiers. Similarly, simulators (in the engineering-training, not the software sense of the term) are indexical information processors or index-manipulating amplifiers.

A key point of Gorn's paper is that the knowledge-oriented and the action-oriented components of informatics cannot and should not be separated. The arguments supporting this belief need to be carefully assessed. Informatics is perceived, in a fashion more characteristic of information engineering, as being concerned with synthesis and analysis of symbolic expressions and processors. The action-oriented (technological) and the knowledge-oriented (scientific) aspects of computation are said to be less likely to move apart, because the description of symbolic expressions remains tied to the prescriptive language of its interpreting processors, hence, invariably forming a pragmatic tie.

Two comments seem appropriate here. First, the merger of the knowledge- and action-oriented components of informatics is a historic fact. The mixture of knowledge and action does, indeed, maintain a pregnant environment that can be harmed by forcing their separation; the late Mortimer Taube, perhaps the first philosopher of informatics, was fond of saying that there is no such thing as pure and applied science, only good and bad science.

On the other hand, the merger of knowledge- and action-oriented components of informatics is not absolutely necessary. The pragmatic tie between them refers to the pragmatics of *doing* technology, not to the pragmatics *studied* by a triadic science. At times, such a separation may be necessary for the major idealizations and abstractions characteristic of the great advances in science to take place. To argue as Gorn does that such a separation will of necessity "cause the cessation of the very effervescence the mixture of knowledge and action maintains," is to argue that the separation of mechanical engineering and physical thermodynamics in the nineteenth century was also a similar mistake. While the original inventions of the steam engine and the internal-combustion motor were made by practitioners, no one would argue today against the drastic revolution in the level of technology enabled by the pure knowledge-engendered advances made in physical understanding by such action-indifferent scientists as Gibbs, Maxwell, Helmholtz, Kelvin, and others. This is effervescence at its best!

In informatics, such advances may be sought by standing back from the interpreting process to look at the prescriptive language of interpreting processors, and then describing abstractly what it is they do. This, in fact, is one reason for the necessity of introducing semiotic analysis into informatics—to abstract from the study of pragmatic structure and to describe it indicatively.

Gorn is entirely correct in his assessment of other informatics-related disciplines as being largely professions. The interesting movement we are beginning to note is the emigration of areas from informatics to other professions: information systems and database areas into management science; computer-aided design into mechanical engineering and architecture; artificial intelligence into such problem-solving fields as chemistry and medicine; and very-large-scale integration (VLSI) onto a new turf shared by physics, electronics, and materials science and engineering. This trend—if it is a trend—is comforting in at least two ways: It documents the utility of the concepts engendered by informatics, and it preserves the relative stability and natural evolution of scientific disciplines.

As the "informationalization" of other sciences, professions, and technologies continues, it is interesting to ponder what will eventually remain in the core of *information and computer science* and how extensive that core and its community of practitioners will be. Our perceptions lead us to speculate that the knowledge-oriented component of this core will be concerned principally with the theory of signs, sign structures, sign processes, and algorithms. The disturbing thought is that if this scenario is correct, the educational programs in today's departments of computer science and information science are not very relevant.

THE ROLE OF INFORMATION IN COMPUTER SCIENCE

Alan J. Perlis

Saul Gorn's paper treats the relation of computer-and-information science to some of its neighboring areas, for example, library science, information retrieval, information science, cybernetics, cognitive psychology, artificial intelligence, semiotics, linguistics, computer engineering, management, decision science, education, and pure mathematics. He seeks to distinguish the former from the latter ideologically. His choice of the word informatics as a convenient replacement for computer-and-information science is an interesting one and fits well with the views he develops but also leads to a deemphasis of the key role played by the computer; that is, the consequence of the ubiquitous, high-speed, and almost effortless *execution* of our symbolic systems. While informatics is a newly synthesized and pleasantly neutral word, it accents information, which is definitely not the key concept involved in issues treated in Gorn's paper. The key, in fact, is the computer—as silicon and metal, as metaphor, as silent servant—and it accounts for most of the phenomena treated by Gorn. It particularly accounts for the incredible dynamism that sharpens distinctions between computer-and-information science and its neighbors.

Consider Gorn's treatment of disciplines and their respective ideologies. He points out that human knowledge develops as the available perceptive devices extend and refine our range of distinguishable sensation. Because of their almost arbitrary complexity, we are forced to translate these accumulated sensations into symbolic models whose properties and consequences precipitate further extension and improved control of sensation. The sheer bulk of accumulated sensation-extension, and its manipulation and control, can only be managed by specialization. As these artificial things become visible, they become knowable, usable, and suggestive. It is the dynamics of sensation perception that matters, and from that appreciation springs the importance of the processes by which we alter the focus of our individual and cultural perceptions. Social agreement to perceive and social commitment to invest arise because of present traffic and future prospects, and all is greased by the recognition of metaperceptions, the symbolic processes.

Gorn points out that human beings, and, hence, their disciplines, alternate between states of perception and analysis and those of synthesis and action.

The forms of representation and communication within their languages tend to differ between the two state-sets. Once a discipline extends its concerns beyond the senses, a notion of truth is needed that operates on symbolic use of language and has important properties invariant of representation. In time, every notion of truth becomes dynamic and leads to the development of metanotions, envelopes within which we manipulate our symbol systems. We might ask: "What are the corresponding notions for dealing with the representational and invariant properties of synthesis and action?"

It is here that the contact of all other disciplines with computer science becomes pronounced. Gorn calls this claim a consequence of the mass ego of computer science, much as reductionism is attributed to the mass ego of physics. The representation of our syntheses as computer programs, their experimental study as the execution (action) of these programs, and the observations of the effects of these "runs" on our world (real and symbolic) now constitute a major paradigm in our quest to extend sensation. The widespread adoption of this paradigm is being accompanied by enormous expansion in the computer itself. The expansions have become less functional and more concerned with increases in redundancy and ability to communicate between machines and processes, their software counterparts. It is a continual game of musical chairs in which at each stage either man, computer, or symbolic process is unsatisfied, and an assault to stabilize is launched, whose success merely shifts the dissatisfaction to an ensuing stage.

Gorn makes the interesting observation that those disciplines that deal with unsolvable problems flourish. The social commitment and the willingness to perceive are preserved because unsolvability is indefinitely postponed by creating new perspectives that give the illusion that their solution either gets us closer to that of the original problem or suggests a different problem equally fundamental and, hence, unsolvable. Computer science revels in unsolvable problems. One of its important subareas, artificial intelligence, in seeking symbolic models linking thinking to program execution, is concerned only with unsolvable problems.

In summation, the Gorn paper presents an accurate picture of the interfaces between computer-and-information science and other disciplines, but the dynamics of the flows across the interfaces are less well treated because, in this reviewer's opinion, the computer is not put forth as generator and pump but only as transformer. *Informatics* is too weak a word to identify the rich dynamics of computer-and-information science. For that matter, *computer science* alone is quite adequate as an identifying term and does not gain clarity or accuracy by including the word *information*. Computer science does not deal with information differently than any other field. This can be seen from the fact that it treats its own information in much the same way as biologists or educators do theirs.

Though it shares little in methodology, notation, tools, training, and problem focus, biology is closer to computer science than any of the areas listed by Gorn, because of their mutual preoccupation with growth, evolution, reproduction, and the complexity of ramifying "cell" structures.

THE PROVINCE
OF COMPUTER SCIENCE

Vladimir Zwass

I am dividing my comments on Saul Gorn's paper into three parts. In the first part, I shall discuss the definition of computer science; in the second, I shall reflect on the epistemological domain of this discipline; and in the third, I shall assess the place of computer science among the family of disciplines concerned with the study of information.

ON THE DEFINITION OF THE DISCIPLINE

The domain of computer science may be viewed either in relation to the active object of its investigation, the computer, or in relation to the purpose of computer operations, that is, deriving information. The proponents of the second approach, notably Gorn and Slamecka, merge computer science with information science. [Gorn, 1967 and also in this volume; Slamecka and Gehl, 1978.] I shall argue that the two definitions may be seen to converge, but that the point of convergence requires closer study.

Since *information* has no generally accepted definition at this time, we may accept the operational meaning implicit in the preceding paragraph or, following Börje Langefors, consider information to be an increment of knowledge. [Langefors, 1977.]

Gorn offers several definitions of *informatics,* the term he uses in the continental European fashion for the unified computer-and-information science. According to his initial definition, as a discipline concerned with manipulating symbolic expressions, informatics would include formal logic and mathematics—surely too broad a scope. In Gorn's paper, the definition is sharpened subsequently by relating symbolic expressions to their processors and treating both as objects of research. This definition is congruous with the one I will advocate for computer science.

Computer science is concerned with the limits and methods of processing symbolic information by a synthetic processor and with synthesizing effective processors. It then appears that the definition of the discipline has to focus on the processor, since it is the general capabilities of the processor that delimit the discipline's domain. The essential commitment of the discipline is to study computing within these limits.

Computer science is thus defined here as a study of the manipulation of symbolic information by synthetic processors, called computers, and, hence, the investigation of effective algorithms, processors, and representation of information for such manipulation.

The word *effective* in this definition stresses the fact that the discipline investigates goal-oriented human activity to a larger extent than natural phenomena, and thus we are discussing one of the sciences of the artificial, to use the phrase coined by Herbert Simon. [Simon, 1969 and 1981.] Computer science was originally defined in terms of the computer. [Newell, Perlis, and Simon, 1967.] A definition of a scholarly discipline in terms of a single artifact appears justified by the almost universal information-processing capabilities of the computer. In this definition, the computer is not a certain physical implement, but an ensemble of well-defined capabilities.

Indeed, in the development of the field, the fundamentals of the theory of computation preceded the appearance of the stored-program computer. However, if we take away the computer as a technological phenomenon, knowledge gained in the theoretical domains of this science may be accommodated within the family of older disciplines, such as mathematics, logic, or linguistics. In fact, some of the fundamental work was originally done in mathematics. [Turing, 1936; Church, 1941.]

To remind ourselves that we are discussing a very young science, it is well to consider the (perhaps harsh) words of Christopher Strachey about the "pitiably small body of generally accepted fundamental laws and principles" it has formulated. (Strachey, 1977, p. 124.)

THE EPISTEMOLOGICAL DOMAIN OF COMPUTER SCIENCE

As just defined, computer science aims not only at gaining knowledge of existing natural phenomena, but, in the first order, at investigating the possible in the artificial. Theoretical investigations are combined with empirical findings, with the latter dominating. [Newell and Simon, 1976a.] The science is strongly influenced by computer technology and the practice of computing. *Homo faber,* the technologist of computer science, and *homo cogitans,* the pure scholar in search of knowledge, are often one and the same person. This person assumes the role of technological expert/leader, to use Znaniecki's typology of "men of knowledge." [Merton, 1973.] Only the scholarly rigor of a specific investigation makes the Ryleian know-what stand out from the know-how.

If the definition I have offered is accepted, the following major areas of computer science may be distinguished:

1. *Theory of Computation.* A combination of formal disciplines employing deductive reasoning, this field includes the theories of automata and formal languages and investigates algorithmic complexity, program verification, and the limits of automatic computability.

2. *Syntactics, Semantics, and Pragmatics of Program Specification.* Broadening the framework of the study of programming languages, this area investigates the means for specifying tasks to the computer, the translation (interpretation) of this specification, and the execution processes arising from the specification. An evolution, or rather a build-up for a discontinuity (as posited by Thomas Kuhn), has been taking place: a departure from the sequential prescriptive languages of the von Neumann machine toward stronger descriptive languages, possibly giving rise to parallel processes. [Winograd, 1979.] The aim is to bridge the semantic gap between the person specifying the task and the computer, with the level of the bridge adjusted to that of the semantic domain of the person providing the specification. Alternatives for expressive specification range from querying by example [Zloof, 1977] to functional programming [Backus, 1978].

3. *Architecture of Processors.* This investigation of the effective combination of hardware, software, and communications needed to create a desired computing environment is strongly influenced by the underlying technologies. A shift from centralized to distributed processing has already occurred; the distribution vector has been a subject of significant theoretical and empirical research.

4. *Synthesis and Analysis of Algorithms.* A combination of science with craft, this area has deep foundations in theoretical computer science.

5. *Representation of Information.* The study of data structures, reflecting largely the physical aspects of data representation (efficient placement of data in computer memories), has become a component of a larger discipline, seeking to provide representational models of real-world entities and relations among them, whose structure possibly varies over time.

A particular promise in the last area is held out by artificial intelligence, an area of research in computer science whose immediate goal is to devise computer-based systems for some of the tasks generally considered to require human intelligence. The larger concern of artificial intelligence is to establish a theory of intelligence based on the information-processing paradigm. Thanks to these approaches, "computer science makes it possible to manipulate ideas as though they were things." (Minsky, 1979, p. 392.)

These research areas are interrelated with technology to organize user systems, such as management-information systems, computer-aided design and manufacturing (including robotics), or information storage and retrieval systems.

The predominantly empirical nature of computer science is reflected by its typical research cycle, usually following these steps, which closely correspond to Karl Popper's theory of knowledge acquisition [Popper, 1972]:

A set of concepts is formed that is related to expanding the functionality of computing in a certain direction (this often occurs in response to technological innovations).

An invisible college of investigators refines and expands the conceptual basis, often with the use of mathematical and simulation models, and formulates the basic hypotheses to be tested in an operational system incorporating the proposed ideas.

An exemplar, to use Thomas Kuhn's terminology, is built. (Often several alternative exemplars are studied.)

Experimentation and modification of the exemplar lead to generalizations. The original concepts, often significantly reformulated, enrich the body of computer science and may gain acceptance in the practical environment.

An excellent example of such research is the development of the working-set theory of virtual-memory management, well documented by its originator. [Denning, 1980.] A larger, paradigmatic change, which has been maturing over the last decade, is the predicted rejection of the von Neumann computer architecture, centered on a single processor with linear memories that store programs and data interchangeably, in favor of data-flow architecture. [Dennis and Misunas, 1975.] Taking advantage of opportunities offered by the very-large-scale integration (VLSI) technology, data-flow architecture offers the promise of a high degree of operational parallelism and is suitable for powerful functional programming.

To conclude, computer science is one of the fields where "external social need" (T. S. Kuhn, 1962a and 1970, p. 19) influences many developmental directions. The Platonian ideal of a disinterested search for knowledge is one of the (weaker) motors of the disciplinary development; Juris Hartmanis, for example, stresses the strategic role of the marketplace. [Hartmanis, 1981.]

COMPUTER SCIENCE AMONG RELATED DISCIPLINES

To appreciate the specific nature of computer science, we need to look at its position in the family of disciplines.

"There have been signs in the past decade that the rather artificial separation of disciplines may be coming to an end," observed Noam Chomsky a decade ago. [Chomsky, 1968 and 1972.] This statement may be well supported in the case of computer science. To gain a perspective on the separation of disciplines, we have to realize that it has occurred largely in the last century and a half.

Computer science has an individual profile as well as close ties with other disciplines. Gorn suggests that we not try to separate computer science from information science. Though an intimate relation exists between the two, the specific investigative domain of computer science previously discussed requires, I believe, that we treat this science as a separate field of inquiry.

To understand the relation between these two sciences, we need to analyze the domain of information science. A number of scholars define information science as a metascience striving to develop fundamental theories of information phenomena, ultimately couched in semiotics. Tefko Saracevic claims that this science has no interest in the computer itself or no pragmatic concerns in general. [Saracevic, 1970.] If we accept this interpretation, avoided by Gorn, computer science could become a beneficiary of fundamental theories of information science, offering in return, theoretical insights into artificial processing of information and the design of information systems.

Machlup's definition of information science as a study of processes and systems of knowledge-transfer implies a far broader relation with computer science. [Machlup, 1979a.] Many aspects of computer use would fall into the domain of information science, so defined. But computers are increasingly used to extend knowledge; computerized systems assist people not only by accelerating cognitive processes, but also by augmenting them or substituting for a specific process. It appears then that computer science and information science have partially overlapping concerns: first, with artificial processing of information and second, with the nature of information and processes of its transfer.

Computer science is related to almost all other disciplines in multiple ways. These relations may be classified as follows:

1. *Sciences that furnish computer science with paradigms of conceptual thinking.* These disciplines include systems theory, which investigates concepts of wholeness and organization; cybernetics, a science of systems, communication among systems, and regulation of systems; and information theory, particularly later attempts to link it to semantic information. A clear demarcation separating these disciplines would be difficult; they investigate behavior of systems using different paradigms. Cybernetics has gained scant acceptance in this country, but it has given impetus to the development of artificial intelligence.

2. *Sciences that share areas of inquiry with computer science.* Because of the interdisciplinary nature of computer science, its practitioners deal with fields carved out by other established disciplines. This research ranges from socioeconomic studies of computing [Kling, 1980] through work shared with information science to cognitive psychology. The latter discipline,

applied together with the methods of artificial intelligence and linguistics, provided the foundation for cognitive science, which investigates problems of knowledge, understanding, inference, and learning.

3. *Sciences that share methods of inquiry with computer science.* The most prominent example is, of course, mathematics; the close relations between the mathematical and computer cultures have been probed by several scholars. [Wegner, 1970; Knuth, 1974b; Arden, 1980a.] Another such discipline is the mathematical theory of communication. [Shannon and Weaver, 1949.]

4. *Sciences that are influenced by the use of computer techniques.* It would be difficult to find a field of inquiry that has not been influenced by the computer. The early concern of George Kistiakowski, that computers would change scientific research by biasing the nature of the problems selected for study, has not been justified. Computers make an entire range of research problems more tractable. In a deeper sense, pointed out by Gorn, they serve sciences by furthering information-oriented thinking.

There remains no doubt that all fields of inquiry (and many other pursuits) have been affected by computers. It is also evident that virtually all disciplines have benefited from both computer science and information science and that few, if any, have suffered undesirable dislocations due to their influence.

COMPUTER SCIENCE AS THE SCIENCE OF DISCRETE MAN-MADE SYSTEMS

Joel Moses

I am pleased to have been given the opportunity to review Saul Gorn's paper on informatics and present some of my own views on computer science and its relation to its neighboring disciplines. It is surprising to me that there have been relatively few attempts to define such an important and fast-growing field as computer science and contrast its approaches with those of mathematics, engineering, the physical sciences, and so forth.

STATIC AND DYNAMIC ASPECTS

We are well beyond the period (1930–1960) when people were fascinated by the sheer fact that man-made artifacts could be general computing engines. This fascination led to an overemphasis on the logical and dynamical aspects of information processing. The fact that computers actually performed computations by manipulating numbers and other symbols, led some theoreticians to studies of the logical limits of various computing machines (e.g., finite-state machines, Turing machines), and others to philosophical exploration of the meaning of certain computational devices such as assignments of values to variables. In the last two decades, the emphasis on the dynamics of computation led to studies of how fast one can perform certain computations such as multiplication or to what extent one can trade space for time in a variety of algorithms.

While these studies have been interesting, their relevance to the practice of computing has been limited except in special areas. I view the rise of software engineering, led largely by Edsger Dijkstra, as a reaction to much of the research on computational dynamics. The position I take here is largely a systems view of computer science that is characteristic of the undergraduate program in computer science at the Massachusetts Institute of Technology. In this approach, large software systems are seen as relatively static objects that are worthy of serious study. Experience shows that the cost of designing, modifying, and maintaining large systems grows nonlinearly with the size of the system. Furthermore, large systems that one wishes to remain viable must be changed constantly as the environment in which they operate changes. Methods for coping with the complexity that is often present in large systems, and, hence, for easing the process of embedding changes in specifications of these systems, are among the key issues in static analyses of systems.

Although I emphasize here the static aspects of computation, it is not my intent to imply that other aspects, such as the dynamic or aesthetic, of the field should be entirely ignored. Efficiency, or dynamic issues underlying a given system, should be dealt with *after* the static structure has been defined. Making it easier for someone to use man-made systems involves a variety of what are often aesthetic issues. Such issues are dealt with by disciplines other than computer science, such as art, linguistics, and psychology. Computer scientists have increasingly been getting involved in such work, often in collaboration with those in the other disciplines.

A view of computer science that emphasizes the static rather than the dynamic aspects of computation yields distinctions different from those Gorn proposed between computer science and its neighboring disciplines. Computer science is clearly not a physical science. The physical sciences are concerned with discovering the principles of the design of a single system, namely God's. Computer science deals with principles for creating new, large man-made systems and is not limited to studying computer systems. God's system is indeed complex, but new approaches for reducing complexity that are absent in God's original design are not of much interest to physical scientists.

ABSTRACT ENGINEERING AND ABSTRACT MANAGEMENT

Software engineers who are, in the main, very close to the systems view espoused here, seem to claim an affinity between computer science and engineering. Clearly, they have a point, but the analogy ought not to be stretched too far. Engineers certainly try to create new man-made systems; they are, however, limited by the properties of the physical world. They spend most of their time figuring out ways to circumvent limitations in materials or mechanical and electrical devices. Computer scientists are in the enviable position of being given primitives (i.e., instruction sets) that can usually be considered to work perfectly, without the interference of the demons that God has placed in the primitives with which engineers must cope. If computer science is to be viewed as a branch of engineering, it should be considered as *abstract engineering*, largely unconstrained by limitations of the physical world.

Physical scientists and engineers are making increasing use of computation in their work. The reason for this is that computers can make highly accurate discrete approximations to the continuous models used in the physical sciences and engineering. It has been clear for some time that the techniques associated with numerical analysis are not at the core of computer science. Rather, the core of computer science deals with problems associated with systems composed of discrete components (e.g., processors, procedures, and instructions). That some such systems mimic the behavior of solutions of nonlinear differential equations is interesting, but it does not shed light on the fundamental system issues of complexity, robustness, modifiability, and so forth. Certainly, modern airplanes and electric-power systems are very complex systems. Their complexity, however, is derived in large part from the need of these systems to perform effectively in the physical world with its continuous phenomena. The study of such complex systems is not of much interest to a computer scientist.

The goals of my systems view of computer science are analogous to the goals of general systems theory. The weakness of the analogy is that general systems theory uses continuous models and usually studies control issues in continuous systems rather than information flow in discrete systems, which is the domain of computer science.

Many have noted the analogy between computer systems and the human organizations that are the domain of management science. Human organizations can be viewed as systems composed of discrete components (i.e., people) with discrete information-flow. Managers have an obvious problem in dealing with primitives that are as ill-understood as individual human beings. Thus, computer science can be viewed as the study of *abstract management.*

PURE MATHEMATICS

There is one field that is as abstract, in fact, more abstract than the picture I have painted of computer science; that field is pure mathematics. Mathematics missed out on being the science of man-made systems for several reasons. The four main areas of pure mathematics are algebra, analysis, geometry, and topology; the last three of these all deal with continuous rather than discrete models. Abstract algebra, to which I shall return later, has been used as a tool in the other areas and usually not as a model of discrete systems. The three areas in mathematics (i.e., elementary number theory, combinatorics, and logic) that have been applied to discrete systems have not been at the core of modern mathematics. These areas have, in fact, been heavily used in the dynamical and logical models of computer science.

The second failing of modern mathematics was its general lack of interest in issues of efficiency that are at the core of the dynamical view of computation and of great importance in man-made systems. Thus, investigators in computer science and operations research have had to develop new mathematics for discrete systems, with relatively little support from mathematicians.

Mathematics could have become the underlying theory of man-made systems as well as the theory of God-made systems. That it did not develop in this fashion is a result of historical accidents as well as ideological decisions, as Gorn has noted. Nor do we see engineers or management scientists developing a powerful theory of discrete man-made systems, because they have to cope with their primitives. Hence, if such a theory is to be developed in the coming decades, computer scientists are in the best position to develop it. In fact, they must develop it!

DISCRETE MAN-MADE SYSTEMS

I now proceed to discuss in general terms what I perceive are some of the core issues arising in large, discrete man-made systems. The principle issue is the control of complexity. Something is complicated, the dictionary says, when it has a large number of interconnected parts. Thus, complexity is a function of the static nature of a system. It is unfortunate that theoreticians in computer science use the term *complexity theory* for the theory that deals with such issues as the minimum time or space needed to solve specific problems. Such a dynamic theory ought to have been called a theory of difficulty, but, one supposes, such a term is not as exciting as complexity theory. In any case, apparently difficult problems, such as factorization of integers into primes, need not be complex and vice versa.

If complexity is measured by the number of interconnections, then the obvious way to achieve simplicity is to reduce the number of interconnections a system requires. There is a limit to such a reduction when the number of components (procedures, people, transistors, musical notes, etc.) has to be large in order to achieve the desired functionality. The real key to reducing complexity in large systems is to introduce additional structure or regularity when this is possible. When the interconnections possess some structure, one is capable of modeling the systems using abstractions. In a more abstract setting, the number of components and their interconnections is much reduced. For example, if one recognizes that the same process is being performed in many parts of the system, one can introduce a single new procedure. Similarly, if the same action is being performed on a number of elements, one can organize the elements into a vector. In the first case, we have a procedural abstraction, in the second, a data abstraction.

An instance of an organizational structure of relatively low overall complexity is that of a pyramid or tower of linguistic abstractions. For example, computer systems are often organized as layers of languages: a language (actually, a family with restricted interconnections) of electronic components, a microprogramming language, an assembly language, and a higher level language. Application programs can also often be designed in such a pyramidal fashion; unfortunately, this is not always possible. For example, sorting-routines are in general too combinatorial in nature to permit such restructuring. Nevertheless, I believe it would be wise to consider such designs as objectives for large systems.

TOP-DOWN DESIGN METHODS

Top-down design methods are currently popular. A problem is broken down into a few components; each component is broken down again and so on. Top-down design is very general—it can be applied to most problems without too much difficulty. It possesses, however, an inherent bias toward increasing the overall complexity of the design. Unless one is exceedingly careful, there is a tendency in top-down design to duplicate parts of the design in the overall system. I am reminded of the air force general who claimed that a database system consisting of several million lines of code could not have been written unless they used top-down design. I assume that millions of lines of code would have been saved had there been more coordination in the project than is likely to exist with a top-down approach.

Considerations of efficiency also cause an increase in complexity in many cases. If one knows how to solve a problem directly, one tends to avoid going through channels. As a result, when one retires or goes on vacation, one's replacements may be unable to get the job done because they lack knowledge of the special arrangements. Furthermore, one may be unable to cope with new directives, because keeping up with all the special arrangements has become a full-time job in itself. Top-down design results in systems, I believe, that tend to force such special arrangements and their resulting increase in complexity.

The organization of large enterprises has many features in common with the organization of large software systems. To a first order of approximation, American firms are organized in a top-down fashion and Japanese firms in a more abstract, layered fashion. American firms give the appearance of great flexibility, as in all top-down designs. Actually, the complexity of such organizations reduces their flexibility enormously. Japanese firms, with their careful attention to cooperation and coordination, appear to have much less flexibility. In fact, the much lower overall complexity that results from such coordination greatly increases the Japanese organization's actual flexibility. We may conclude that the way to reduce the overall complexity of a system is to introduce greater local coordination and more abstract links, with all of the local increase in complexity that such a principle entails. The alternative principle, practiced in American firms, of keeping local interaction as simple and clear as possible, tends to increase global complexity due to effects akin to the "tragedy of the commons." [Hardin, 1968.]

THE COMPUTER IN COMPUTER SCIENCE

As can be seen from the preceding discussion, my view is that the science underlying computer science has little to do with computers. Rather, it is the systematic study of issues related to the design of discrete man-made systems. Small systems are often of little interest in such studies, since one has far less difficulty in designing them, except when circumventing the vagaries of nature or in producing some pleasing effect.

Gorn makes the distinction between knowledge-oriented disciplines and action-oriented disciplines. Action-oriented disciplines involve the creation, and, hence, the design, of systems for accomplishing certain actions. A surprising number of Gorn's knowledge-oriented disciplines have a large component of design. Musical compositions and novels (as well as religious texts and law books) are all man-made designs involving discrete components. There are several maxims that are said to hold in such disciplines: One is that you should read before you write; another is that you cannot teach design. I agree with the former but only partially with the latter. For example, it may turn out that mankind will not discover powerful principles underlying aesthetics. On the other hand, mankind will be in serious straits if it does not discover powerful principles underlying the design of large man-made systems. Such principles ought to help composers as well as the designers of the next set of encyclopedias.

SYMBOLIC MANIPULATION

My technical field within computer science is called symbolic manipulation. It is concerned with manipulation of algebraic formulas used in algebra or calculus. The irony is that Gorn equates informatics or computer science with symbolic expressions and their manipulation. A main lesson of the past two decades of activity in symbolic manipulation is the critical importance of proper abstract data structures. Abstract algebra had discovered these structures and especially their interrelations as layers in a tower, which has, of course, led to my interest in the static structure of systems. Algorithms that manipulate data structures can be much more flexible (and less complex) when the appropriate abstract structure is used. This is a point in which computer scientists are only lately becoming interested in the context of data abstraction.

The view I have espoused here is not widely held by the computer science community at this time. In fact, the continuing hardware revolution, as exemplified by the growth in personal computing, is creating increasing interest in relatively small systems. Yet, there is no escaping the problems of large systems. Hardware designers are interested in placing ever larger designs on a chip, and the newest microprocessors permit one to use large programs. As a result, owners of personal computers will soon be using much larger programs than heretofore. It is a natural tendency for a field to work on the problems that are most amenable to a solution. Eventually, the core issues posed by large systems will have to be faced once again. The sooner this reality is recognized, the better off the field of computer science will be.

PARADIGMS OF INFORMATION ENGINEERING

Peter Wegner

Information science (computer science) is a young discipline striving to gain the kind of respectability possessed by physics, mathematics, and engineering. It is therefore not surprising that computer scientists have modeled their research on paradigms in the tradition of the experimental, mathematical, and engineering disciplines. Definitions of computer science that embody each of these traditions are reviewed. Attention is then focused on engineering paradigms, and in particular on the paradigms of software engineering and the emerging subdiscipline of knowledge engineering. It is predicted that knowledge engineering will emerge as a central subdiscipline in the 1990s with paradigms, such as the knowledge-graph paradigm, that will emphasize interactive man-machine cooperation in the management, learning, and use of knowledge.

Paradigms are described by Thomas Kuhn as "oustanding achievements that serve as a model for research by a community of researchers." [Kuhn, 1962*a* and 1970.] He asserts that normal science in a mature discipline is generally based on a paradigm that prescribes acceptable research and influences our interpretation of phenomena. Scientific revolutions such as the transition from Ptolemaic to Copernican astronomy or from Newtonian to relativistic physics result in a change of paradigm. The term paradigm will be used here to denote a model for undertaking and evaluating research even when there is no associated outstanding achievement.

Information science currently has several paradigms that coexist with and complement each other. The coexistence of multiple paradigms is, in Kuhn's view, a characteristic of pre-science rather than normal science. This view suggests that computer science might not yet be sufficiently mature to support a single paradigm. However, an alternative explanation is that information science is not a single discipline like physics, but a collection of disciplines like the physical sciences and that the flourishing of many paradigms is a sign of health and vigor rather than of immaturity.

PARADIGMS AND IDEOLOGY

In his paper, Gorn examines the roles of ideology, methodology, and sociology in the development of disciplines. He points out the close relation between ideologies (systematic bodies of concepts) and paradigms. He distinguishes between knowledge-oriented activities such as mathematics, action-oriented activities such as farming, and activities that transform knowledge into action, such as education and engineering. He suggests that sciences cannot flower independently of technology and in particular that informatics (computer-and-information science) could not begin to flower before the technology of computing was developed. Informatics was initially action-oriented (practical) and has achieved a fusion of action-oriented and knowledge-oriented activities as it has matured. This balance is one of the strengths of computer science in that practical results suggest relevant theory, and theoretical results can increase the effectiveness of action. Gorn warns that a divorce of action-oriented from knowledge-oriented activities could lead to disaster.

Gorn's choice of ideology, methodology, and sociology as characterizing attributes of disciplines is unconventional but suggestive. These attributes are independent of particular disciplines and are applicable in characterizing any discipline or human activity. The ideology of a discipline determines its paradigms and its criteria for evaluating the quality and relevance of contributions to the discipline. Its methodology is the principles that underlie the tools and techniques used in pursuing the goals determined by an ideology. Its sociology includes social interactions among practitioners of the discipline and the social impact of its concepts and products on society. Thus, the ideology, methodology, and sociology associated with a discipline may be thought of as its paradigms, underlying principles, and impact on people.

Ideologies are associated with young people and young disciplines. Computer science became an academic discipline in the mid-1960s with the emergence of the first departments of computer science and the publication of a comprehensive undergraduate curriculum. [ACM Curriculum Committee, 1968.] The search for an identity led to a number of alternative definitions of computer science, associated with different paradigms for judging the value of research. In Gorn's terminology, these definitions express alternative ideologies.

1. Computer science is the study of phenomena related to computers. [Newell, Perlis, and Simon, 1967.]
2. Computer science is the study of algorithms. [Knuth, 1968.]
3. Computer science is the study of information structures. [ACM Curriculum Committee, 1968; Wegner, 1970.]
4. Computer science is the study and management of complexity. [Dijkstra, 1972.]

The first definition reflects an empirical view, since it asserts that computer science is concerned with the study of classes of such man-made phenomena as computers, programming languages, algorithms, and data structures. The second and third definitions reflect a mathematical tradition, since algorithms and information structures are two abstractions that determine different paradigms for modeling the phenomena of computer science. The fourth definition takes the viewpoint of engineering and reflects the great complexity of problems of information engineering encountered in developing complex hardware-software systems.

Each of these definitions has motivated valuable contributions, and they should be regarded as complementary rather than mutually exclusive. The first was dominant in the 1950s and is experiencing a resurgence with the increasing fashionability of empirical computer science. [Feldman and Sutherland, 1979.] The second led to the flowering of research in the areas of analysis of algorithms and computational complexity in the late sixties and early seventies. [Arden, 1980a.] The third has motivated the study of semantic models of programming languages, also in the late sixties and early seventies. The fourth has led to software engineering, which emerged as a subdiscipline in the late 1960s and became a dominant research area in the mid-1970s.

The first view of computer science is action-oriented, the second and third are knowledge-oriented, and the fourth (software engineering) represents a synthesis of both approaches. Thus, the dominant paradigm was action-oriented in the 1950s, knowledge-oriented in the late 1960s and early 1970s, and evolved as a fusion of the two in the late 1970s and 1980s. Computer science was action-oriented in the period immediately following the birth of computer technology, as there were no theories to support the new technology. The development of a theoretical foundation led to a brief period of dominance of theoretical approaches, followed by the current period in which the ideal, not always realized, is research that combines theory and practice.

These four definitions span a variety of views of computer science. We must ask whether this variety is a manifestation of the confusion of a young discipline or whether a variety of paradigms is an inherent (permanent) feature of computer science. My view is that variety is both inherent and intrinsically healthy (many flowers should continue to bloom). The information sciences will blossom into a broad spectrum of mathematical, experimental, and engineering subdisciplines. By the year 2000, many universities may have a school of information sciences with several departments sharing a common set of core requirements, just as schools of engineering currently include departments of electrical, mechanical, and civil engineering.

Schools of information sciences will contain information engineering as a major component; information engineering will, in turn, contain software engineering and knowledge engineering as two subdisciplines. Software engineering is concerned with managing the complexity of software, while knowledge engineering is concerned with the computer-based management of knowledge. Software engineering was born in the late 1960s and has within the short span of 15 years generated a cohesive body of knowledge that combines theory and practice. Knowledge engineering, in the sense that this term is used here, is currently in the process of being born. Its growth will be intimately bound up with the technology of powerful graphics-based personal computers which, by increasing the bandwidth of man-machine communication by several orders of magnitude, provide a technological base for extending man's mental abilities in much the same way that mechanical machines have extended man's physical abilities.

The remaining sections of this paper examine the paradigms and ideology of these two branches of information engineering.

THE EVOLUTION OF SOFTWARE ENGINEERING

During the period 1950–1980, there have been radical changes in the economics of information processing. The cost per executed instruction of computer hardware has decreased by a factor of two every two or three years, while the complexity and total cost of computer applications has increased by several orders of magnitude. The cost of software as a proportion of total computing cost has increased from under 20 per cent in 1960 to over 80 per cent in 1980.

Programming languages such as FORTRAN, originally developed for numerical problems with several hundred lines of code, proved to be inadequate for large applications, with real-time requirements and hundreds of thousands of lines of code, concerned with controlling the operation of ships, airplanes, banks, or chemical plants. Large software projects in the 1960s and 1970s frequently failed to meet schedules, were subject to enormous cost-overruns, and sometimes had to be abandoned because their complexity became unmanageable.

In the late 1960s, it was recognized that there was a software crisis and progress in software technology required the development of systematic techniques for managing the complexity of large software systems. [Naur, Randell, and Buxton, 1976.] The discipline of software engineering was born with the aim of providing a technological foundation for the development of software products analogous to that provided by conventional engineering for the development of physical products.

Software engineering exemplifies the fusion of action-oriented and knowledge-oriented activities. It is motivated by the economic considerations of making software cheaper and more reliable. This contrasts with the scholarly motivations traditionally associated with empirical and mathematical paradigms. However, economic motivations are not necessarily inferior to scholarly motivations as a basis for research. On the contrary, economically motivated paradigms provide stronger incentives for the fusion of action-oriented and knowledge-oriented activities than purely scholarly motivations and should, therefore, be regarded as a source of strength. Software engineering has motivated research on program specification and verification and on modularity and abstraction. It provides scope for the creative practical application of theoretical ideas and is a prime example of the synergy that can be generated by the fusion of theory and practice.

Software engineering, like other branches of engineering, is concerned with developing a technology for the cost-effective production of a particular kind of economically valuable product. It differs from other branches of engineering because of the unique nature of software products. Physical products like cars or television sets have a nonnegligible unit production cost, requiring both labor and raw materials. In contrast, software costs are concentrated entirely in producing the initial prototype, with negligible costs in producing additional copies. Software does not wear out, although it may become obsolete. Reliability is determined by logical features, such as correctness and robustness, rather than by the physical endurance of raw materials.

Software is a conceptual rather than a physical product. Constructing software is in many respects more like constructing a mathematical proof than building a house or a television set, since we are concerned with the logical properties of the program rather than with the physical constraints of materials. However, the fact that software products are judged by their usefulness in problem-solving rather than by an abstract correctness criterion requires engineering as well as mathematical standards to be applied in their construction. Further discussion of the nature of the software problem and research directions in software engineering can be found in a recent volume on software technology. [Wegner et al, 1979.]

The paradigms of software engineering are those of conventional engineering modified to take into account the fact that software is a conceptual rather than a physical product. Many of the terms used in software engineering are modeled on those of engineering. The term *software* is modeled on the term *hardware* and reflects the fundamental insight that any behavior realized by software may in principle be realized by hardware. The fundamental notion of a software life cycle, which provides a basis for modeling software systems, is borrowed from the engineering notion of a system life cycle. The term *software factory* is used to describe systematic production techniques for software components and application generators.

The ideology of software engineering is motivated by economic considerations and is rooted in that of engineering. Software engineering's methodology for managing the complexity of computer systems, an outgrowth of this ideology, is concerned with systematic principles for the construction, maintenance, and enhancement of composite software systems from software components, such that cost is a linear rather than an exponential function of program size. The problems of management and technology transfer in a rapidly changing field present formidable sociological challenges. Mechanisms for the systematic introduction of new technologies must be tried that minimize the pain of obsolescence and encourage a cooperative attitude toward technological innovation.

ADA—A CASE STUDY IN TECHNOLOGICAL INNOVATION

The interplay of ideology, methodology, and sociology in software engineering may be illustrated by considering the development and technological exploitation of the programming language ADA. ADA was developed in the late 1970s in response to the software crisis in order to reduce the cost and improve the reliability of software. The motivation (ideology) for ADA's development was economic, but it has stimulated worthwhile research in software technology, language design, and system implementation in its pursuit of practical objectives. ADA was designed to support a new software methodology for constructing large programs from modular components. Its use will require a new approach to programming very different from that of current assembly-language or FORTRAN programming. The problems of retraining and technology transfer for the large and growing number of potential ADA programmers are not only technical but also political and sociological.

The development of ADA is a self-conscious, well-documented case study of a large-scale project involving the creation, dissemination, and effective use of a new body of knowledge. Each stage of its development was surrounded by public debate among leading programming-language experts and representatives of the user community. The evolution of the language requirements during 1975–1978 and of the language design during 1977–1980 is well documented. Currently, there is public debate about how the novel concepts of ADA should be taught so that practicing programmers can internalize new methods of program design and problem-solving. ADA illustrates both the transformation of an ideology into a body of knowledge based on a new methodology and the sociological concerns that must be addressed in the process of technology transfer.

The history of programming languages has given rise to a number of distinct ideologies and methodologies, each associated with different paradigms of problem-solving and methods of programming. FORTRAN, COBOL, PASCAL, and APL each have a characteristic programming ideology that is fervently advocated by their respective user communities. Every successful programming language spawns a dedicated community of users who would rather fight than switch, illustrating that dedication to an existing paradigm may cause resistance to a new paradigm.

The ADA Joint Program Office, which is coordinating the development and introduction of ADA, is keenly aware that acceptance and cost-effective use of ADA requires a new ideology, methodology, and sociology on the part of its users. It is sponsoring not only language design and implementation but also the study of methodology, education, and technology transfer. For example, I am developing guidelines for education and technology transfer that will include recommendations on how to teach novel language features; structure ADA courses for managers, programmers, and other constituencies; and introduce ADA into industrial, military, and university programming environments. [Wegner, 1982.] This task is difficult since there are no guidelines for developing such guidelines. (Who will guide the guides?) My approach is to provide information about current education and technology-transfer efforts and draw attention to issues without necessarily resolving them.

ADA has, within the short period of five years, generated a subculture of tens of thousands of devoted adherents throughout the world. Hundreds of companies are involved in a variety of ADA-related activities ranging from implementation to education. The rapid spread of ADA at a time when it is not yet implemented and its methodology is not yet tested illustrates Thomas Kuhn's assertion that inadequacy of a current paradigm provides fertile ground for new paradigms.

THE INFORMATION REVOLUTION

The parallelism between software engineering and conventional engineering is part of a wider parallelism between the information revolution and the industrial revolution. The industrial revolution, which occurred in the period 1750–1950, was concerned with harnessing energy to serve man. The information revolution, which started around 1950 and is currently in full swing, is concerned with harnessing information to serve man. The industrial revolution was concerned with developing machines to replace manual labor, while the information revolution is concerned with developing machines that replace mental labor. [Machlup, 1962.] There are striking similarities between industrial and software technologies that stem from the fact that both are concerned with enhancing and amplifying man's ability to control the environment. There are also fundamental differences that stem from the differences between energy and information and differences in the nature of the products produced by manual and mental labor.

The industrial revolution resulted in radical changes in technology and the economics of production. It caused changes in life style from a predominantly rural to a predominantly urban society and a shift in political power from a landed aristocracy whose power was based on the ownership of land to an industrial (capitalist or socialist) establishment whose power was based on controlling the mechanisms for industrial production.

The information revolution is causing changes in technology and life style as radical as those caused by the industrial revolution. The computer industry has, during the last twenty years, grown from insignificant beginnings to become one of the largest employers of labor and of capital. The nature of computer applications is changing from primarily numerical applications, which compute a numerical result, to data management and embedded computer applications, whose objective is to control a larger system whose purpose is not primarily computational. Computer control is playing a larger and increasingly important role in the management of society. Power is shifting from the industrial establishment to those who control the dissemination and distribution of information.

Computers are playing an increasing role not only in the management of society but also in the management of knowledge. After many false starts, artificial intelligence is finally reaching a level that allows building expert systems whose performance is competitive with human experts. Personal computers are becoming cheaper and more powerful, to the point where everyone soon will be able to afford a pocket computer that executes a million instructions a second, has a large memory bank extensible with cassettes, and supports graphical and voice communication. The combination of greater power and greater accessibility will entirely change the relation between man and computers, so that computers will no longer be merely problem-solving tools. They will become an extension of man's intellect and serve to amplify intellectual capability in the same sense that conventional machines amplify man's physical ability. The new role of computers will give rise to new paradigms for managing and using knowledge and to a new subdiscipline of computer science, which I will refer to as knowledge engineering.

KNOWLEDGE ENGINEERING

Knowledge engineering may be defined as the application of systematic techniques to the management and use of knowledge. It is, in this sense, as old as knowledge itself. Euclid's *Elements* is an example of a magnificent piece of knowledge engineering that provided a basis for managing geometrical knowledge, while the classification techniques of Linnaeus are an important example of knowledge engineering in botany and biology. Many of the milestones in the development of science are as important for their contributions to the management of knowledge as for their contributions to knowledge itself.

Widespread availability of powerful graphics-based personal computers will cause fundamental changes in our methods of managing, learning, and using knowledge. It will result in new ways of representing and organizing knowledge and in the conscious development of paradigms and methodology in an area that has traditionally been considered an art rather than a science. It is predicted that by the 1990s, knowledge engineering will be as important a subdiscipline of computer science as software engineering is today. Some of the characteristics of the emerging field of (computer-based) knowledge engineering follow.

Computer-based knowledge engineering depends on the representation of knowledge by information structures inside a computer. The principle that knowledge as well as numbers can be represented in a computer was recognized right at the outset and led to work in artificial intelligence, natural-language translation, and information retrieval in the 1950s. However, the advent of cheap powerful graphics-based personal computers, which may be carried in a briefcase or a pocketbook and used on a day-by-day basis as an extension of the human intellect, will entirely change the relation between people and computers. Computer-based knowledge engineering could not reach critical mass before the 1980s, because of inadequate technology.

Knowledge engineering bears the same relation to the management of knowledge that software engineering bears to the management of software. An item of knowledge, like an algorithm, is an inherently conceptual object that can be given a concrete representation by an information structure and manipulated, used, or displayed by a computer. The creation of computerized knowledge structures representing substantial bodies of knowledge requires techniques for managing information complexity similar to those required for a large program. The common ancestry of software engineering and knowledge engineering as branches of information engineering is reflected in their sharing certain methodological principles. The information revolution is likely to spawn many different kinds of information engineering, just as the industrial revolution generated many different kinds of physical engineering disciplines. The different kinds of information engineering will share with software engineering and knowledge engineering the idea of representing a class of conceptual objects by concrete information structures and the need to manage complexity when structures become large and may evolve over time.

The term knowledge engineering was introduced by Feigenbaum in the context of artificial intelligence and defined as "the art of bringing the tools and principles of artificial intelligence to bear on application problems requiring the knowledge of experts for their solution." [Feigenbaum, 1977.] This definition views knowledge engineering as the art of representing knowledge so that it can be used by computers to perform intelligent tasks.

The present view of knowledge engineering is broader, since it includes building knowledge structures to aid human understanding. Knowledge engineering for human understanding is motivated by an ideology (paradigm) different from that which motivates the development of expert systems. Its goal is to amplify human intelligence rather than substitute computer intelligence for human intelligence. Its methodology involves educational technology, cognitive science, and human-factors research. The technology of managing the modular presentation of complex knowledge structures has some of the flavor of software engineering but requires consideration of human factors associated with animation, user interaction, multiple windows, and other techniques for increasing the effectiveness of man-machine communication.

Knowledge representations should facilitate display for the benefit of users, including multiple views and other forms of redundancy, rather than efficiency and precision for the benefit of computers. Whereas knowledge structures for computer understanding must be very detailed and precise, knowledge structures for human understanding are concerned, not with the precise specification of a computational task, but with organizing knowledge for human readers who possess considerable contextual understanding and are capable of conceptualizing at a level far above that of the computer.

Restructuring existing knowledge so that it is more accessible to humans involves more than putting existing knowledge repositories such as the Library of Congress on computers and accessing them through information-retrieval systems. It involves restructuring existing knowledge so that it can be flexibly presented in different formats for different contexts of use. The technology for such restructuring is not well understood, but its nature can be illustrated by considering recent developments in computerized printing technology and computer-based learning.

Computers are revolutionizing printing technology and allow high-quality text to be quickly and cheaply produced. Word-processing systems provide authors with much greater control over production, layout, and modification of text. Soon computers will be used not only for writing and printing books but also for reading them. Book-size computers with flat panel displays will make electronic books a reality. The greater bandwidth of man-machine interfaces will qualitatively change the nature of man-machine communication and make communication of knowledge by reading computer books more effective than conventional communication by reading hard-copy books.

Whereas hard-copy books consist of a linear sequence of pages, materials intended to be read on a computer may have a graph structure with different entry points for readers with different backgrounds. Multiple windows allow the reader to pursue several lines of thought simultaneously or view a given object at several levels of detail. Interactive responses by the user can be used by the computer to tailor the mode of graph traversal to the interests and skill level of the student. Each mode of the graph structure can include dynamically animated pictures, texts, and programs. For example, the mathematician may wish to animate the development of a proof, while the computer scientist may wish to animate the process of program development and execution.

An electronic book represents a family of different hard-copy books that could be obtained by printing out nodes of the graph structure in a particular linear order for particular kinds of students. It is conjectured that flexibility in adapting the pace and order of presentation of information to the student, combined with the power of animation (possibly augmented by voice input and output) can, if properly used, enormously increase the student's capacity to absorb and understand both elementary and advanced knowledge.

Knowledge graphs that may be entered at different points and traversed in different ways represent a paradigm for knowledge engineering that imposes a modular, interactive, discipline on both creators (authors) and users (students). Knowledge graphs are a basic representation not only for electronic books, but also for computer games such as Adventure, which derive their fascination from the fact that they allow players to explore new graph-structured worlds. We do not yet have much experience with building large knowledge graphs, since the hardware technology to support effective use of such graphs is only now being developed. Some features of such graphs are briefly described.

Knowledge graphs should have a domain-independent interconnection structure that facilitates several modes of graph traversal, such as browsing, retrieval, learning, reference, authoring, and so forth. Each node will have a domain-dependent internal structure containing objects such as programs, when representing knowledge about programming, and proofs, when representing knowledge about mathematics. Creators and users of a graph will have available to them a domain-independent set of operations for navigating in the graph and domain-dependent operations for manipulating objects in each domain. The ZOG system is probably the best known current example of a general-purpose system of this kind. [Robertson, McCracken, and Newell, 1981.]

This discussion only scratches the surface of potential developments in knowledge engineering. We must wait for at least a decade to know whether its potential will be realized and to gain a better understanding of its paradigms. However, I believe that during the next decade, knowledge engineering will begin to realize its potential for amplifying man's intellectual reach and that within twenty years, personal computers will be as indispensable to scholarly research as libraries are to the scholars of today.

Computer-based learning is likely to become an important subfield of knowledge engineering. Its paradigms, methodology, and sociology are briefly discussed.

COMPUTER-BASED LEARNING

A new computer-based educational technology based on the knowledge-graph paradigm will emerge in the next decade. Better man-machine communication will increase the effectivness of computer-aided educational technology to the point where it dominates technologies based on traditional books. Teachers may find that computer-aided supplements to classroom teaching will, during the next decade, become both more effective and more accessible than conventional books.

The new educational technology will have both a technical and a social impact on the process of textbook writing. Technical computer writing style is likely to differ from that for traditional textbooks, being more modular and more interactive. Organization of large knowledge domains as a graph structure of text modules is a challenge comparable to that of writing a traditional text on the same subject matter but will require authors to organize the material in new ways. The modular approach has the disadvantage that it may violate the natural continuity of the subject matter but the advantage that it requires authors systematically to decompose knowledge into manageable modules.

Creators and readers of a computer textbook form a social community whose members can communicate directly with each other via a computer message system. Authors can incrementally make the text available, receive instantaneous feedback from readers, and rapidly respond to such feedback. Man-machine communication may be used not only for machine display of knowledge, but also for communication among its community of creators and users. Such social interaction will permeate all work in knowledge engineering and may fundamentally affect the sociology of all disciplines by providing a new mode of communication among scholars.

Computers will not only help students to learn more effectively, but also help authors to write more effectively. Conventional printing technology permits only very costly enhancement of a book by means of new editions. Computer technology permits continuous incremental enhancement after development of the book has been completed, thereby permitting improvements in quality and flexible adaptation to changing requirements that would previously have been impossible.

The advantages of incremental enhancement can be illustrated by drawing an analogy between the life cycle of a program and a book. Studies have shown that 80 per cent of the effort of supporting a program over its life cycle is in maintenance and enhancement. With conventional printing technology, the only form of maintenance and enhancement is printing a second edition, which is time-consuming and expensive. By allowing cheap incremental maintenance and enhancement, computer printing technology could completely change the role of authors in the life cycle, allowing them to play a much more active role in both the production and enhancement process.

A computer support system for a community of authors and students involved in creating, disseminating, and learning a body of knowledge will be called an educational environment. An educational environment should support not only individual students but also communication among the community of students and authors. An educational environment should provide interactive feedback to students using the system and interactive feedback to authors concerning the effectiveness of the system. It should be concerned not only with technical issues of knowledge representation but also with social issues of communication among a community of users with different goals. As the man-computer interface becomes more powerful and computers are increasingly used for communication among humans, social issues and human factors for effective communication will become increasingly important.

An educational environment must provide an author environment that helps authors create and enhance text modules, a student environment that allows students to learn effectively and receive adequate interactive feedback, and a testing environment that provides statistics concerning the effectiveness of learning and allows hypotheses to be tested. We can think of the environment as consisting of a database of text modules with different but overlapping views provided for authors, students, and testing.

Experience with such computer-aided instruction systems as PLATO [Bitzer, 1976] is relevant to the development of a computer-based education environment. But progress in personal-computer technology and developing environments as portable collections of software tools (such as UNIX [Bell Laboratories, 1978]) makes it possible to create educational environments with much greater power than PLATO.

Computer-based learning is a subfield of knowledge engineering that provides a concrete illustration of its paradigms, methodology, and potential social impact. Its paradigms are concerned with fundamentally increasing the capacity of man to master knowledge, both quantitatively and qualitatively. Its methodology involves educational techniques, software methodology, cognitive science, and artificial intelligence. Its sociology involves synergy among a community of authors, teachers, and students in developing and using an open-ended computer-based educational system.

CONCLUSION

Gorn's concern with the ideology, methodology, and sociology of information science reflects an unconventional but worthwhile perspective on the creation, diffusion, and use of knowledge in the computer field. The helpfulness of this perspective is illustrated by applying it to subdisciplines like software engineering and large-scale case studies like ADA. However, the impact of information science on our methods of learning, working, and thinking, illustrated here by our discussion of knowledge engineering, is an even more important topic, which Gorn has not addressed. Information science has a special, intimate relation to knowledge, both because subdisciplines like artificial intelligence are concerned with the mechanistic modeling of knowledge and because knowledge engineering provides a tool for managing knowledge that offers our only hope for controlling the knowledge explosion. Moreover, computers provide a new dimension for communication among a community of scholars that could fundamentally change the sociology of creating and using knowledge in all academic disciplines.

A PRAGMATIST REPLIES

Saul Gorn

In the spectrum of comments on my paper, the one that was furthest removed from my point of view was that of Joel Moses. He remarks on the irony of his individual interest being symbolic manipulation when he cannot accept my making symbolic manipulation a central issue of computer science.

I gather that he wants to identify the field as being concerned with the analysis, design, and management of large, complex, discrete, man-made systems. He would, therefore, expect it to include certain chunks of cybernetics, especially of systems science, systems engineering, decision science, and management science. The involvement of computers, on the one hand, and symbol manipulation, on the other, may be absolutely essential in handling problems but are not, from his point of view, the central issue. To him, a part of what I have called informatics that is more characteristic of the area he is discussing would be software engineering. Peter Wegner in his comments also seems to consider this to be the most characteristic area of informatics; I will comment on this later.

Now, whether the area described by Moses will actually crystallize into what I have called a discipline will, of course, depend on such social phenomena as the development of a single new ideology and a few paradigms. In his discussion of what could be considered an outline of such an ideology, I found a few of his attitudes a bit puzzling. First of all, what led him to think that I called the arts and crafts knowledge-oriented disciplines? Secondly, Moses claims that it is the static structure of the large, discrete, man-made systems with which he is concerned, when it is their maintenance and robustness and modifiability in a constantly changing environment that is on his mind. I can only assume that Moses believes it is the *stability* of the system that is the central issue. Finally, and most important, I am puzzled by his claim to be pragmatic while making a sharp distinction between engineering for God's system (i.e., the physical world) and engineering for man-made systems. Moses's assumption seems to be that there is only one world out there, with only one proper perception of it—a point of view I would call *monoideological*; I think such an assumption is held by many materialists, idealists, positivists, and "unified-scientists" and results in rather complicated methodological positions.

However, there are billions of possible perceptions and their possible outlines beating on our senses and even more on the technological extensions of our senses that we have developed, whether they depend on very short-range or very long-range sampling in the human time-scale. We must choose at any moment which to outline and perceive and in so doing, must shut out the others—hence, the different disciplines. Is this not also man's system as well as God's? On the other hand, having chosen what to perceive from our variety of methods of interpretation, our physical and biological interpretive behavior intervenes. Is this not also God's system and not just man's?

From this pragmatic point of view, the distinction between the two worlds is a red herring drawn across the trail. Plato (the extreme idealist) also felt that there is only one world out there, and we only see its shadow on the wall of our cave. I feel that whether there is only one world out there or not, different people, by extending their perceptions and motor controls in different dimensions, are viewing different shadows in the different disciplines. My type of pragmatism is essentially *polyideological,* with the university structures of Western culture as a kind of pantheon. If, indeed, the stability of man-made systems is Moses's concern, I wonder how stable the area he outlines can be.

I believe that, by and large, Alan Perlis, on the contrary, understands me very well, and I even agree with him that the name *informatics* is weak. I have found, of course, that my personally preferred expression, mechanical pragmatics, fails to arouse understanding, let alone enthusiasm, although the more philosophic in the audience understand cybernetic pragmatism as my point of view. In my local environment, *computer and information science* served very well, especially in view of our sharing activities in cognitive science.

I certainly agree with Perlis that the electronic computer had a striking effect that was critical in the development of informatics. The computer (and, still more, the computer network) has changed our visualization of the historical fluidity of symbol-manipulation systems from the viscous to the effervescent, from being apparent only to the time-accelerating minds of philosophers and historians to being obvious to the frequent user. In short, the electronic computer itself was certainly a time-collapsing catalyst to our understanding of symbol manipulation but is still only half the story; understanding and designing and using symbolic systems being the other and older half.

Perlis says that the computer scientist does not deal differently with information than the scientist in any other field does. This I deny. I hold that the computer scientist's semantic interpretation of symbols belonging to other fields is essentially more muted and less real than that of a person in any of the other fields, because it remains strictly at the metalevel. A person in another field views its symbols as representing a living reality and the appropriate laws, natural or ethical. He or she will be more sensitive than the computer scientist to both the axiomatic principles and the characteristic methodological arguments justifying the methods, especially the paradigms of his or her field. This is why designers of expert systems in the knowledge engineering discussed by Wegner are teams of informaticians and people in the appropriate disciplines, who describe, analyze, and program the protocols that those in the discipline express when they think aloud (thereby revealing the particular logical methods belonging to the discipline's paradigms). This is what I called dredging up the basic concepts from the mass ego of that discipline. (See my discussion in my paper in this volume of the professional aspects of informaticians and their relation to education.) Wegner discusses this also in his section on computer-based learning. Evidently Feigenbaum, in the paper quoted by Wegner, maintains that such an activity demands the involvement of people in that discipline as well as computer people.[1]

In studying the design and use of symbolic systems, it is important to study many, and not merely those that might be considered good but also those that might be called bad, if only to be able to recognize the symptoms of ill effects when they occur. For example, it is quite possible that the phenomenon called *information overload* in people might not only be not alleviated but actually catastrophically aggravated by the use of computers. This is a possibility that Wegner should also consider in his enthusiastic discussion of knowledge engineering and computer-based learning.

The effervescence caused by computers and other extenders of our sensors and effectors should not only extend our sense of power but also increase our humility; for these devices by which we feel we have extended our perceptions and capabilities are so prosthetic that we can, in their use, acquire no more grace than a dog walking on its hind legs or a man walking on stilts, while our capacity for catastrophic misjudgment is tremendously amplified. Misuses of computers, like misuses of atomic energy, space technology, genetics, medications, and the pollution of knowledge generally can easily lead to human disaster. This is, of course, an old and often-repeated message: Pandora's box, *Frankenstein,* The Sorcerer's Apprentice, *Dr. Faustus, Paradise Lost,* Icarus and Daedalus, the tower of Babel, *Dr. Jekyll and Mr. Hyde,* and in a hidden way, *Prometheus.*

I would, therefore, hesitate to imply in the name to be given to the discipline that processors alone are its subject. The substance being processed and transformed is to be equally investigated in order to provide a picture of professional possibilities to the rest of humanity, who, even more than we informaticians, must evaluate and choose, for good or ill.

Vladimir Zwass, unlike Perlis, proposes that perhaps the study of the

---

[1] In this connection, it is interesting to go back to the Proceedings of the Western Joint Computer Conference 1961, whose theme was *Extending Man's Intellect* and look at the papers by Herbert Simon, Edward Feigenbaum, and Julian Feldman. [Western Joint Computer Conference, 1961.]

computer as "the active object under investigation" is not identical to studying the "purposes of computer operations, much as the two studies may overlap". I agree that such areas might, indeed, be separated, but I think that it would be unfortunate if they were, as I have stated in my paper. I return to this question later. However, I disagree with some of the reasons for, and modes of, separation that Zwass suggests.

First of all, I do not agree that the study of the manipulation of symbolic expressions includes formal logic and mathematics. It includes the study of syntactic methods employed in their notational systems, and only some of these syntactic methods have invariant mathematical and logical significance. But by and large, mathematicians and logicians would consider such pragmatic symbolic properties to belong to their methodological questions and, hence, strictly speaking, to be outside the range of their subject proper. For example, a discussion of the clumsiness of a notational system is not considered a mathematical or logical question. Again, courses in analysis do not spend time proving that the formal differentiation process for analytic expressions, whatever the notation happens to be, must conclude without the possibility of continuing indefinitely, even though the method of proof is an example of a mathematical method applied to their notational systems. Similarly, Herbrand's syntactical attack on the study of first-order logic needs an argument to show that the particular notation used is irrelevant as far as the logic is concerned, because the properties discussed are notationally invariant. Mathematics or logic is concerned with the common semantics of the variety of notations, and not with their syntax. And these disciplines are certainly not interested in those syntactic properties that vary with the notation, such as the connectivity of subexpressions, which I call pragmatic accidents of the notational system.

On the other hand, a significant portion of the theoretical aspects of informatics uses mathematical methods and, therefore, is an example of applied mathematics, just as the methodological discussion of mathematical and logical notation is applied informatics. The interesting fact is that some of these mathematical methods in informatics actually serve to keep action-oriented aspects tied to the knowledge-oriented. For example, the techniques of formal verification of programs or their logically equivalent machines can be viewed as interlocking a *description* of the machine in the form of a state diagram at a cogently chosen level of detail with a *prescription* of the program in the form of a flowchart at the same level.

When Zwass says that "Computer science is concerned with the limits and methods of processing symbolic information by a synthetic processor and with synthesizing effective processors," we seem to be agreeing, although I would not insist on the word *synthetic* and, hence, would include more than the sciences of the artificial. However, when Zwass goes on to interpret a synthetic processor as among those called computers, and stresses the effectiveness of their algorithms, it becomes clear that I have not succeeded in conveying the idea of interpreting processor as abstracting the common essence of machines, programs, and symbolic processes. Thus, the principle of logical equivalence of hardware and software no longer appears to be a basic tautology, and the design paradigm applying equally to the architecture of processors and the synthesis and analysis of algorithms does not come across. (See, for example, the mathematical method that I have just described in the preceding paragraph.) Zwass can, therefore, misinterpret me as defining this scholarly discipline by its relation to a single artifact. It is exactly the fear of this kind of misinterpretation that is the basis of my departure from the view of the field in the letter by Newell, Perlis, and Simon to which Zwass refers. [Newell, Perlis, and Simon, 1967.] The misinterpretation is there in spite of Zwass's qualification that "the computer is not a certain physical implement, but an ensemble of well-defined capabilities."

Thus, my view of computer science is broader than Zwass gives it credit for being, while my view of information science is not so all-embracing as he thinks. On the other hand, the picture Zwass gives of a separate information science seems to me to cover all the cognitive sciences, which I am not convinced will crystallize into one discipline. For I believe they are coextensive with what I would be tempted to name general ideology, returning to the original sense of that word.

In the areas of applications, Zwass presents an interesting classification of the sciences by the type of relation they have with computer science. I would like to see this classification extended to include action-oriented disciplines and the professions.

Whereas Perlis thinks that I have overemphasized information science and Zwass thinks that I have forced it into a marriage with computer science, Charls Pearson and Vladimir Slamecka agree somewhat with my harnessing them together. They hold, however, that the result should include more semiotic studies and not force the marriage with information engineering. I am in general agreement with Pearson and Slamecka on the first point, although I do not know how to set the boundary in order not to include all of the cognitive sciences. In particular, I also agree that the variety of meanings of *meaning* should be considered in informatics. In talking about semantics, I have been using the word *meaning* in the sense of the object symbolized and have let the word *pragmatics* carry the others, where, as Pearson and Slamecka point out, its meaning is much, much broader. Also other mood effects should be studied besides the indicative and the imperative, and even there we need more application studies of deontic, temporal, and dynamic logic. Furthermore, I am glad Pearson and Slamecka brought up the fact that the syntactic types *noun* and *verb* are not linguistic universals; it adds emphasis to my stressing the importance of pragmatic effects of language. I am also glad that they mentioned Peirce's concept of abduction, which can be so important in modeling goal-seeking behavior in artificial intelligence. However, it was my intention to emphasize that each discipline has its own flavor of reasoning and these flavors may be a major concern of methodology; I have mentioned this in connection with expert systems.

Pearson and Slamecka are also correct about my not intending to restrict attention to the digital in symbol manipulation. I have always felt that analog machines should also be involved. They are better suited and faster in imitating by feedback the adaptive and conditioning type of learning, because they do not proliferate memories to be retrieved. Robotic sensors and receptors can obviously use them.

When Pearson and Slamecka object to my saying that the symbology of mathematics and physics *may* be formal, they forget, on the one hand, that the intuitionists in mathematics do not accept formalist views and, on the other, that rational mechanics is considered part of physics in the United States but part of mathematics in Europe.

Pearson and Slamecka find that harnessing knowledge and action is related to pragmatics merely in "doing technology, not to the pragmatics *studied* by a triadic science." But does not the action force the selection of such using and interpreting behavior as is relevant to the symbology? In this connection, I was surprised to see Helmholtz listed as an action-indifferent scientist. His study of the adaptation time required in using prismatic lenses was a direct study of the pragmatic effects of perception on action and a model for psychologists.

We are agreed, however, that the professional aspects of informatics go well with the theoretical, though we may argue about how separate they are and for how long. Not only do I insist, as Pearson and Slamecka do, that pragmatic questions should be an object of study within the field, but I submit that professional aspects must also be included in such studies. It is very much to the point, for example, that a contextfree language cannot be interpreted by a finite-state machine but also needs a pushdown store. To me, this is not merely a theorem in automata theory and formal languages but also a fact of mechanical pragmatics; for it clearly states a relation between a set of symbolic expressions and its mechanical user or interpreter.

As for the possibility of a number of professional aspects having their pilot studies within informatics and then graduating into separate disciplines with related ideologies but different paradigms, I find Pearson and Slamecka's description and examples very well put. Except for the VLSI (very-large-scale integration) example, they belong to the area of knowledge-engineering discussed by Wegner.

Wegner remarks early in his comments that knowledge-oriented, action-oriented, and professional aspects of informatics have different paradigms; and I have to agree that such radically different orientations must differ in their paradigms. I believe, however, that a shared ideology is enough to keep them in a single community. I therefore disagree with Thomas Kuhn that the mark of a single discipline (physical science, in his case) is a single paradigm;

a single ideology suffices, and major revolutions in a discipline are changes in ideology, in which case the paradigms must follow suit. After all, paradigms are social decisions on the courses of action that are proper for the given ideology. The community may agree completely on what is worth perceiving and yet vary in deciding what to do about it, without necessarily losing touch with one another.

In the case of informatics, Wegner describes this variety, and I agree with him that it is a sign of health, although I doubt that its members form the neat time-packages he describes. For that matter, although software engineering, as Wegner describes it, fits neatly into informatics, I consider its scope too narrow. Its title, already a decade old, is unfortunate because it tends to negate the ideological identification of hardware and software. Will the system design of software be so very different from that of hardware in a world of data distributed in networks and of microprocessors assembled in VLSI components? Will methodological arguments produce different paradigms? I would guess that they would not precisely because of the logical-equivalence idea that I have already described.

As for these areas and the ones spinning off knowledge engineering to form a school of information sciences, Wegner seems to agree with Pearson and Slamecka, though he stresses different areas. Various areas of applied mathematics have formed such alliances in the past, and very successful ones, as Wegner, Pearson, and Slamecka know better than most. But the spread of applications of mathematics became too varied for all to fit into anything smaller than a university. The spread of applied informatics will be even broader, because of its pragmatic aspects. I would think that institutes smaller than complete universities would be built around closely allied ideologies and paradigms. The cognitive sciences alone would have to be as ambitious as most schools of education, covering as they do the survey of ideologies and their maintenance. And is not the idea of an institute of knowledge engineering a description in modern dress of a school of education, emphasizing modern educational techniques?

SECTION 3

INTELLECTUAL ISSUES
IN THE HISTORY OF
ARTIFICIAL INTELLIGENCE

Allen Newell

Science is the quintessential historical enterprise, though it strives to produce at each moment a science that is ahistorical. With a passion bordering on compulsion, it heeds the admonition that to ignore the past is to be doomed to repeat it. Science has built its main reward system around discovering and inventing, notions that are historical to the core. Thus, writing about science in the historical voice comes naturally to the scientist.

Ultimately, we will get real histories of artificial intelligence (henceforth, AI), written with as much objectivity as the historians of science can muster. That time has certainly not come. We must be content for a while with connections recorded in prefaces, introductions, citations, and acknowledgments—the web that scientists weave in their self-conscious attempt to make their science into a coherent historical edifice. So far, only a few pieces, such as *Machines Who Think,* provide anything beyond that, and they still have no deliberate historiographic pretensions. [McCorduck, 1979.]

This essay contributes some historical notes on AI. I was induced to put them together originally in response to a request by some of our graduate students in computer science for a bit more historical perspective than is usual in their substantive fare. It is to be viewed as grist for the historian's mill but certainly not as serious history itself. The attempt to define and document all of what I put forward is beyond my resources for the moment. This essay's claim to accuracy, such as it is, rests on my having been a

I thank Elaine Kant and Stu Card for comments on an earlier draft and Paul Birkel and Marc Donner for leading me to write the paper. Note: This research was sponsored in part by the Defense Advanced Research Projects Agency (DOD), ARPA Order No. 3597, monitored by the Air Force Avionics Laboratory under Contract F33615-78-C-1551. The views and conclusions contained in the paper are those of the author and should not be interpreted as representing the official policies, either expressed or implied, of the Defense Advanced Research Projects Agency or the United States government.

participant or an observer during much of the period. As is well known to historians, the accuracy of the participant-observer is at least tinged with bias, if not steeped in it. The situation is worse than that; I am not just a participant but a partisan in some of the history here, including parts still ongoing. Reader beware.

HOW IS THE HISTORY OF A SCIENCE TO BE WRITTEN?

Human endeavors are indefinitely complex. Thus, to write history requires adopting some view that provides simplification and homogenization. The standard frame for the history of science is in terms of important scientific events and discoveries, linked to and by scientists who were responsible for them. This assumes that scientific events declare themselves, so to speak. In many respects this works, but it does so best when the present speaks clearly about what concepts have won out in the end, so that we can work backward through the chain of antecedents, adding only a few dead-ending branches to flesh out the story.

With fields in an early state—and AI is certainly one—critical events do not declare themselves so clearly. Additional frameworks are then useful. Obvious ones of general applicability are proposed theories and research methodologies; neither is very satisfactory for AI. The theoretical ideas put forth have, especially when successful, been embedded in computer systems (usually just as programs but sometimes including special hardware). Often, the systems speak louder than the commentary. Indeed, a common complaint of outsiders (and some insiders) is that there is no theory in AI worthy of the name. Whether true or not, such a perception argues against taking theories as the unit in terms of which history is to be written. As for research methodology, AI as a whole is founded on some striking methodological innovations, namely, using programs, program designs, and programming languages as experimental vehicles. However, little additional methodological innovation has occurred within the field since its inception, which makes for lean history.

Similarly, the more sophisticated units of historical analysis, such as the *paradigms* of Kuhn or the *research programmes* of Lakatos, provide too course a grain. [Kuhn, 1962a; Lakatos, 1970.] It can be argued that AI has developed and maintained a single paradigm over its short lifetime, or at most two. Similarly, it has contained at most a small handful of research programmes. But units of analysis work best with enough instances for comparative analysis or for patterns to emerge. There are certainly too few paradigms for an internal history of AI. The same is probably still true of research programmes as well, though it would be of interest to attempt such a description of AI.

Useful frameworks for historical analysis can often be based on the organization of subject matter in a field. AI proceeds in large part by tackling one task after another, initially with programs that can accomplish them crudely, followed gradually by successive refinements. Game-playing, theorem-proving, medical diagnosis—each provides a single developmental strand that can be tracked. Thus, a history of AI as a whole could be written in terms of the geography of tasks successfully performed by AI systems. Almost orthogonal to this task-dimension is that of the intellectual functions necessary for an intelligent system—representation, problem-solving methods, recognition, knowledge acquisition, and so forth—what can be termed the physiology of intelligent systems. All these functions are required in any intellectual endeavor of sufficient scope, though they can be realized in vastly different ways (i.e., by different anatomies), and tasks can be found that highlight a single function, especially for purposes of analysis. Thus, a history can also be written that follows the path of increased understanding of each function and how to mechanize it. Both of these structural features of AI, and perhaps especially their matrix, provide potentially fruitful frameworks for a history. Their drawback is just the opposite from the ones mentioned earlier, namely, they lead to histories that are almost entirely internal, shedding little light on connections between AI and neighboring disciplines.

I settle on another choice, which I will call *intellectual issues*. It is a sociological fact of life that community endeavors seem to polarize around issues—fluoridation versus ban fluoridation, liberal versus conservative. Such polarizing issues are not limited to the purely political and social arena but characterize scientific endeavors as well—heliocentrism versus geocentrism, nature versus nurture. Intellectual issues are usually posed as dichotomies, though occasionally three or more positions manage to hold the stage, as in the tussle between capitalism, socialism, and communism. Intellectual issues are to be distinguished from issues in the real world of action. No matter how complex and ramifying the issues of individual freedom and state control that lie behind a fluoridation campaign, the passage or defeat of an ordinance banning fluoridation is a concrete act and is properly dichotomous. But with nature versus nurture, the dichotomy is all in the eye of the beholder, and the real situation is much more complex (as is pointed out ad nauseum). The tendency to polarization arises from the way people prefer to formulate intellectual issues.

Scientifically, intellectual issues have a dubious status at best. This is true even when they do not have all the emotional overtones of the previous examples. Almost always, they are defined only vaguely, and their clarity seldom improves with time and discussion. Thus, they are often an annoyance to scientists just because of their sloganeering character. Some time ago, in a conference commentary entitled You Can't Play Twenty Questions with Nature and Win, I myself complained of the tendency of cognitive psychology to use dichotomies as substitutes for theories (e.g., serial versus parallel processing, single-trial versus continuous learning). [Newell, 1973*b*.]

Intellectual issues surely play a heuristic role in scientific activity. However, I do not know how to characterize it, nor am I aware of any serious attempts to determine it, though some might exist. Of course, large numbers of scientists write about issues in one way or another, and almost all scientists of an era can recognize and comment on the issues of the day. Were this not true, they could hardly be the issues of the particular scientific day. From a historical and social standpoint, of course, intellectual issues have a perfectly objective reality. They are raised by the historical participants themselves, and both the existence of intellectual issues and the activity associated with them can be traced. They enter the historical stream at some point and eventually leave at some other.

Whether intellectual issues make a useful framework for a scientific history seems to me an entirely open question. Such a history does not at all substitute for histories based on events and discoveries, laid down within a framework drawn from the substantive structure of a field. Still, ever since that earlier paper in 1973, I have been fascinated with the role of intellectual issues. Recently, I even tried summarizing a conference entirely in terms of dichotomies. [Newell, 1980a.] Withal, I try it here.

THE INTELLECTUAL ISSUES

I will actually do the following: I will identify, out of my own experience and acquaintance with the field, all of the intellectual issues that I believe have had some prominence at one time or another. Although I will take the field of AI as having its official start in the mid-1950s, the relevant intellectual issues extend back much earlier. We surely need to know what issues were extant at its birth. I will attempt to put a date both on the start of an issue and on its termination. Both dates will be highly approximate, if not downright speculative. However, bounding the issues in time is important; some issues have definitely gone away and some have come and gone more than once, though transformed each time. I will also discuss some of the major features of the scientific scene that are associated with a given issue. I will often talk as if an issue caused this or that. This is in general illegitimate. At best, an issue is a publicly available indicator of a complex of varying beliefs in many scientists that have led to some result. Still, the attribution of causation is too convenient a linguistic practice to forego.

Table 1 lays out the entire list of intellectual issues. In addition to the short title of the issue, expressed as a dichotomy, there is an indication of an important consequence, although this latter statement is necessarily much abbreviated. The issues are ordered vertically by date of birth and within that by what makes historical sense. All those born at the same time are indented together, so time also moves from left to right across the figure; except that all the issues on hand when AI begins in 1955 are blocked together at the top. Issues that show up more than once are multiply repre-

Table 1. The Intellectual Issues of AI

1640–1945	Mechanism versus teleology: settled with cybernetics
1800–1920	Natural biology versus vitalism: establishes the body as a machine
1870–	Reason versus emotion and feeling #1: separates machines from men
1870–1910	Philosophy versus the science of mind: separates psychology from philosophy
1910–1945	Logic versus psychologic: separates logic from psychology
1940–1970	Analog versus digital: creates computer science

 1955–1965 Symbols versus numbers: isolates AI within computer science
 1955– Symbolic versus continuous systems: splits AI from cybernetics
 1955–1965 Problem-solving versus recognition #1: splits AI from pattern recognition
 1955–1965 Psychology versus neurophysiology #1: splits AI from cybernetics
 1955–1965 Performance versus learning #1: splits AI from pattern recognition
 1955–1965 Serial versus parallel #1: coordinate with above four issues
 1955–1965 Heuristics versus algorithms: isolates AI within computer science
 1955–1985 Interpretation versus compilation: isolates AI within computer science
 1955– Simulation versus engineering analysis: divides AI
  1960– Replacing versus helping humans: isolates AI
  1960– Epistemology versus heuristics: divides AI (minor); connects with philosophy
 1965–1980 Search versus knowledge: apparent paradigm shift within AI
 1965–1975 Power versus generality: shift of tasks of interest
 1965– Competence versus performance: splits linguistics from AI and psychology
 1965–1975 Memory versus processing: splits cognitive psychology from AI
 1965–1975 Problem-solving versus recognition #2: recognition rejoins AI via robotics
 1965–1975 Syntax versus semantics: splits linguistics from AI
 1965– Theorem-proving versus problem-solving: divides AI
 1965– Engineering versus science: divides computer science, including AI
  1970–1980 Language versus tasks: natural language becomes central
  1970–1980 Procedural versus declarative representation #1: shift from theorem-proving
  1970–1980 Frames versus atoms: shift to holistic representations
  1970– Reason versus emotion and feeling #2: splits AI from philosophy of mind
   1975– Toy versus real tasks: shift to applications
   1975– Serial versus parallel #2: distributed AI (Hearsay-like systems)
   1975– Performance versus learning #2: resurgence (production systems)
   1975– Psychology versus neuroscience #2: new link to neuroscience
    1980– Serial versus parallel #3: new attempt at neural systems
    1980– Problem-solving versus recognition #3: return of robotics
    1980– Procedural versus declarative representation #2: PROLOG

sented in the table, according to the date of rebirth, and labeled #1, #2, and so forth. When the ending date is not shown (as in *Reason versus Emotion and Feeling #1: 1870–*   ), then the issue still continues into the present.

The issues are discussed in historical order, that is, according to their order in the table. This has the advantage of putting together all those issues that were animating a given period. It has the disadvantage of mixing up lots of different concepts. However, since one of the outcomes of this exercise is to reveal that many different conceptual issues coexisted at any one time, it seems better to retain the purely historical order.

Mechanism versus Teleology: 1640–1945

We can start with the issue of whether mechanisms were essentially without purpose. This is of course the Cartesian split between mind and matter, so we can take Descartes as the starting point. It is an issue that can not be defined until the notion of mechanism is established. It is and remains a central issue for AI, for the background of disbelief in AI rests precisely with this issue. Nevertheless, I place the ending of the issue with the emergence of cybernetics in the late 1940s. If a specific event is needed, it is the paper by Rosenblueth, Wiener, and Bigelow, which puts forth the cybernetic thesis that purpose could be formed in machines by feedback. [Rosenblueth, Wiener, and Bigelow, 1943.] The instant rise to prominence of cybernetics occurred because of the universal perception of the importance of this thesis. (However, the later demise of cybernetics in the United States had nothing whatsoever to do with any change of opinion on this issue.) AI has added the weight of numbers and variety to the evidence, but it has not provided any qualitatively different argument. In fact, from the beginning, the issue has never been unsettled within AI as a field. This is why I characterize the issue as vanishing with cybernetics. It does remain a live issue, of course, in the wider intellectual world, both scientific and nonscientific, including many segments of cognitive science. Above all, this issue keeps AI in perpetual confrontation with its environment.

Intelligence presupposes purpose, since the only way to demonstrate intelligence is by accomplishing tasks of increasing difficulty. But the relation is more complex the other way around. While purpose could hardly be detected in a device with no intelligence, that is, with no ability at all to link means to ends, no implication follows about the upper reaches of intelligence. Animals, for instance, are obviously purposive yet exhibit strong limits on their intelligence. Thus, settling the question of artificial purpose does not settle the question of artificial intelligence. The continuation of this basic controversy throughout the entire history of AI over whether intelligence can be exhibited by machines confirms this separation. Yet, historically it is not right to posit a separate issue of mechanism versus intelligence to contrast with mechanism versus teleology. No such distinction ever surfaced. Instead, there is an underlying concern about the aspects of mentality that can be exhibited by machines. This shows itself at each historical moment by denying to machines those mental abilities that seem problematic at the time. Thus, the argument moves from purpose in the 1940s to intelligence in the 1950s. With the initial progress primarily in problem-solving, we occasionally heard in the 1960s statements that machines might solve problems but they could never really learn. Thus, the basic issue simply endures, undergoing continuous transformation.

Natural Biology versus Vitalism: 1800–1920

A critical issue for AI that had come and gone long before AI really began is the issue of vitalism—do living things constitute a special category of entities in the world, inherently distinct from inanimate physical objects. As long as this issue was unsettled, the question of whether the mind of man was mechanical (i.e., nonspecial) was moot. It is difficult to conceive of concluding that the animate world does not generally obey the laws of the physical world but that the mind is an exception and is entirely mechanical. Thus, only if vitalism has been laid to rest for our bodies can the issue be joined about our minds.

The vitalist controversy has a long and well-chronicled history. Retrospectively, it appears as an inexorable, losing battle to find something special about the living, though the issue was joined again and again. Organic matter was just a different kind of matter from inorganic matter—an issue laid to rest finally with the synthesis of urea, an indisputably organic material, from inorganic components in 1828 by Wohler. Organisms had their own inherent internal heat—an issue laid to rest in the work of Bernard by the mid-1800s. For our purposes, the starting and ending dates of the issue are not critical. Vitalism's last champion may be taken to be the embryologist Hans Driesch at the turn of the century, who proposed that organisms develop only by virtue of nonmaterial vital principles, called *entelechies*. [Driesch, 1914.] Issues almost never die, of course, as the continued existence of the Flat Earth Society should remind us. Nevertheless, no substantial intellectual energy has been focused on vitalism in more than fifty years. That the human body is a physical machine, operating according to understood physical laws and mechanisms, sets the stage for considering the mechanistic nature of thought and intelligence.

Reason versus Emotion and Feeling #1: 1870–

The basic separation of the heart from the head occurred long ago and is a fundamental part of Christian folk psychology. It is background. What concerns us is the ascription of reason (cold logic) to machines and the belief that a machine could have no heart—no feelings or emotions—to ever conflict with its reason. I do not seem to find any good way to fix the initiation of this issue. The striking characteristic of the golem of Rabbi Loew in 1580 seemed to have been literal-mindedness, not heartlessness. And nineteenth-century artificial humans seemed to combine all the human attributes, as did, for instance, Frankenstein's constructed monster. [Shelley, 1818.] But by the twentieth century, certainly in *R.U.R. (Rossum's Universal Robots)*, we clearly have the intelligent robot, who is without soul, hence, without emotions or independently felt wants. [Čapek, 1923.] So I have split the latter two dates and taken 1870 as the start.

The relevance of this for AI is in providing a basis for separating machines from humans that is different from the issue of purpose. Although a birthright issue of AI, it does not play a major role. That the issue is there can be seen clearly enough in the paper on "Hot Cognition" by Abelson, which put forth some proposals on how to move machine intelligence in the direction of having affect. [Abelson, 1963.] The lack of prominence stems in part, no doubt, from the strong engineering-orientation of AI, which emphasizes useful mental functions (e.g., problem-solving and learning). In agreement with this, Abelson is one of the few social psychologists associated with AI, and the paper was given at a psychology conference. Thus, this issue remains in the background, waiting to become prominent at some future time.

Philosophy versus The Science of Mind: 1870–1910

For science as a whole, the separation from philosophy and the acceptance of empiricism as a fundamental tenet occurred centuries ago. For psychology, this occurred very recently, in the last decades of the nineteenth century. Indeed, psychology celebrates the establishment of the first experimental laboratory (Wundt's in Leipzig) in 1879. It was not an especially difficult passage for psychology, given the rest of science as a model. It can be considered complete by the rise of behaviorism, say, by Watson's classic paper. [Watson, 1913.] Thus, this issue emerged and vanished before AI began. The residue was a continuing tradition in philosophy concerned with mind, which was completely distinct from work in psychology and, even more so, from technology. This issue ensured that when AI did emerge, which happened instantly on computers becoming sufficiently powerful,[1] it would be without more than peripheral involvement of the philosophy of mind.

Logic versus Psychologic: 1910–1945

We continue to lay out the issues—and their resolutions—that were in effect at the birth of AI. This issue concerns whether symbolic logic was to be taken as revealing how humans think or whether humans use some sort of unique "psychologic." It surely started out with logic identified with

---

[1] A case can be made that serious AI started as soon as computers attained 4K of random-access primary memory.

thought, as Boole's classic monograph entitled *The Laws of Thought* testifies. [Boole, 1854.] But logic was rapidly transformed from an explication of the possible varieties of thinking to a device for probing the foundations of mathematics. We can take the *Principia Mathematica* of Whitehead and Russell as marking the completion of this transformation. [Whitehead and Russell, 1910–1913.] The effect was to separate logic from psychology (and also from the philosophy of mind, although that is a more complex story).

Modern logic, of course, was integrally involved in the development of the digital computer, and, thus, it enters into the history of AI. But logic did not enter AI at all as the logic of thought; that separation remained. Logic was part of the underlying technology of making mechanisms do things. In fact, it was precisely the split of logic from thought that set logic on the path to becoming a science of meaningless tokens manipulated according to formal rules, which, in turn, permitted the full mechanization of logic.

Thus the issue was really settled by 1910, and the status in the first half of the century was that psychologic was not a significant item on the agenda of any science. This, of course, was due to behaviorism's restriction of psychology's agenda. I have placed a date of 1945 for the ending of this issue; this is really an ending of the phase of separating logic from thought. The nerve-net model of McCulloch and Pitts can be used to mark this, along with the work of Turing on which it depended. [Turing, 1936; McCulloch and Pitts, 1943.] They attempted to show that physical systems that echo the structure of the brain could perform all computations, which is to say, all logical functions. Whether this is seen as saying more about the brain or more about logic can be argued; in either case, it brought them back into intimate contact. We might think that the ending of one phase of the issue (the stable separation of logic from thought) should initiate a new phase, namely, a new controversy over the exact nature of the connection. But it did not happen that way. Rather, the issue was not discussed, and basic questions about the mechanization of mind took the form of other issues. The reason that happened cannot be explored here. In part, it comes from the shift with AI from the characterization of the brain in computational terms to the digital computer, where logic played a completely technical and engineering role in describing sequential and combinational logic circuits.

Analog versus Digital: 1940–1970

When computers were first developed in the 1940s, they were divided into two large families. Analog computers represented quantities by continuous physical variables, such as current or voltage; they were fast, operated simultaneously, and had inherently limited accuracy. Digital computers represented quantities by discrete states; they were slow, operated serially, and had inherently unlimited accuracy. There was a certain amount of skirmishing about which type of computer was better for which type of job. But the technical opinion-leaders maintained a view of parity between the two families—each for its own proper niche. Inevitably, there arose hybrid computers, which claimed to have the best of both worlds: digital control and memory coupled with analog speed and convenience.

It was all over by 1970. The field of computers came to mean exclusively digital computers. Analog systems faded to become a small subpart of electrical engineering. The finish was spelled not just by the increased speed and cost-efficiency of digital systems, but by the discovery of the Fast Fourier Transform, which created the field of digital signal processing and thus penetrated the major bastion of analog computation. The transformation of the field is so complete that many young computer scientists hardly know what analog computers are.

The main significance of this issue, with its resolution, was to help create the discipline of computer science and separate it from electrical engineering. Its effect on AI lies mostly in the loss of an analytical point of view, in which the contrast between analog and digital computation is taken as the starting point for asking what sort of information-processing the nervous system does. An admirable example of this point of view can be seen in the notes for von Neumann's Silliman Lectures, published posthumously. [von Neumann, 1958.] This style of analysis belongs to the world of cybernetics and not to that of AI. I doubt if many young AI scientists have read von Neumann's little book, though it was highly regarded at the time, and von Neumann was one of the towering intellects of the computer field.

Symbols versus Numbers: 1955–1965

We now come to the first of the issues that characterizes AI itself, as opposed to the background against which it emerged. The digital-computer field defined computers as machines that manipulated numbers. The great thing was, its adherents said, that everything could be encoded into numbers, even instructions. In contrast, scientists in AI saw computers as machines that manipulated symbols. The great thing was, they said, that everything could be encoded into symbols, even numbers. The standard measure of a computation at the time was the number of multiplications it required. Researchers in AI were proud of the fact that there were no multiplications at all in their programs, though these programs were complex enough to prove theorems or play games. The issue was actively pursued as a struggle over how the computer was to be viewed. However, it was joined in an asymmetric way. The bulk of the computer field, and all its responsible opinion-leaders, simply adopted the view that computers are number manipulators. There was no attempt to argue against the view that computers are symbol manipulators. It was just ignored, and the standard interpretation maintained. Researchers in AI, on the other hand, were actively engaged in promoting the new view, considering the standard one to be a radical misreading of the nature of the computer and one that provided a significant barrier to the view that computers could be intelligent.

The result of this clash of views was to isolate AI within computer science. AI remained a part of computer science, but one with a special point of view that made it somewhat suspect, indeed somewhat radical. This isolation is important historically, for it has affected the professional and disciplinary organization of the two fields. It derives ultimately, no doubt, from a basic divergence of views about whether computers can or cannot exhibit intelligence. This overarching issue, of course, continued to be important on its own, as witnessed by the debates that occurred throughout the 1950s on whether machines could think. But the more specific issues that it spawned also had independent lives.

The issue of symbols versus numbers did not arise until after the first AI programs came into existence, circa 1955. Before that time, programs were classified as numerical versus nonnumerical. This latter class was a miscellany of all the things that processed data types other than numbers—expressions, images, text, and so forth.[2] This included the few game-playing and logic programs but much else as well. The symbols-versus-numbers issue emerged only when a positive alternative became formulated, that is, symbolic manipulation. This was not a synonym for nonnumerical processing, for it laid the groundwork for the separation of image- and text-processing from AI. Indeed, the work on machine translation, which started in the early 1950s, was initially considered as one strand in the development of intelligence on machines. [Locke and Booth, 1957.] But that effort became concerned with text and not symbols and developed its own identity as computational linguistics. (All of this, of course, was before text processing in its current meaning emerged—an event that bore no significant relation to the development of computational linguistics.)

I have placed the ending of this issue at about 1965, although I do not have a significant marker event for its demise. The issue is certainly not alive now and has not been for a long time. In part, this is due to the prominence of many nonnumerical data types in computer science generally, such as text and graphics. These make the characterization of computers as number manipulators no longer ring true. In part, it is due to the shift within theoretical computer science to algebraic and logical formalisms, with the concurrent retreat of numerical analysis from its early dominant role. In part, of course, it is due to the success of AI itself and the demonstrations it brought forward of the symbolic character of computation. It is tempting to say that the cause was simply the growth of scientific understanding—but such reasons do not fare well in historical accounts. In any event, my recollection is that the symbols/numbers issue was no longer prominent by the late 1960s, though a little historical digging might place it five years later.

Symbolic versus Continuous Systems: 1955–

An important characterization of a science, or an approach within a science, is the class of systems it uses to construct its theories. Classical physics, for

---

[2]The concept of data type did not arrive in clear form until much later.

instance, viewed systems as being described by systems of differential equations. Given a new phenomenon to be explained, a physicist automatically, without a thought, used differential equations to construct his or her theory of that phenomenon. Mathematical psychology in the 1950s and 1960s could be characterized by its acceptance of Markov processes as the class of systems within which to seek theories of particular phenomena.

The issue is within what class of systems should a description of intelligent systems be sought. On one side were those who, following the lead of physical science and engineering, adopted sets of continuous variables as the underlying state descriptions. They adopted a range of devices for expressing the laws—differential equations, excitatory and inhibitory networks, statistical and probabilistic systems. Although there were important differences between these types of laws, they all shared the use of continuous variables. The other side adopted the programming system itself as the way to describe intelligent systems. This has come to be better described as the class of symbolic systems, that is, systems whose state is characterized by a set of symbols and their associated data structures. But initially, it was simply the acceptance of programs per se as the theoretical medium.

Adopting a class of systems has a profound influence on the course of a science. Alternative theories that are expressed within the same class are comparable in many ways, but theories expressed in different classes of systems are almost totally incomparable. Even more, the scientist's intuitions are tied strongly to the class of systems he or she adopts—what is important, what problems can be solved, what possibilities exist for theoretical extension, and so forth. Thus, the major historical effect of this issue in the 1960s was the rather complete separation of those who thought in terms of continuous systems from those who thought in terms of programming systems. The former were the cyberneticians and engineers concerned with pattern recognition; the latter became the AI community. The separation has been strongly institutionalized. The continuous-system folk ended up in electrical-engineering departments; the AI folk ended up in computer-science departments. (It must be remembered that initially computer-science departments were almost exclusively focused on software systems and almost all concern with hardware systems was in electrical-engineering departments.)

I believe this issue largely explains one peculiar aspect of the organization of the science devoted to understanding intelligence: By almost any account, pattern recognition and AI should be a single field, whereas they are almost entirely distinct. By now, in fact, due to another important historical twist, many people in computer science work in pattern recognition. But if such people also know traditional pattern recognition, they are seen as interdisciplinary.

Another interesting implication is buried here. The issue is not properly dichotomous, for there exist other classes of systems within which to search for intelligent systems. One obvious candidate is logic.[3] Were there not

---

[3] In fact, there are additional possibilities. [Newell, 1970.]

scientists who believed that logic was the appropriate class of systems? And if not, why not? First, by logical systems is meant the class of systems that do logical operations, such as AND, OR, NOT, and so forth.[4] This is the class corresponding to the logic level in the hierarchy of computer structures. The logic level is located between the circuit level and the program (symbol) level. All three levels are equally comprehensive and provide three possibilities for ways of describing intelligent systems. Indeed, circuit and program levels correspond exactly to the continuous and symbol positions of the issue under discussion. Now, in fact, in the early days, there were attempts to build logic machines and discuss the behavior of systems directly in terms of logic circuits. The classical neural networks of McCulloch and Pitts were an effort at modeling the neural system at the logic level. [McCulloch and Pitts, 1943.] But all these efforts rapidly died out and were all but gone by the mid-1960s. My own guess about why this happened is that the hierarchy of computer levels indicated quite clearly what to do with a logic level—namely, compose a higher level system. But this implied simply reproducing existing program-level systems, at least without some new organizational ideas at the program level. But the logic level provided no such ideas, nor could it. Thus, there was nowhere to go. In fact, the history of these efforts seems quite obscure, and tracing the demise of logic as a system language for intelligent systems would be a substantial, though rewarding, undertaking.

Problem-Solving versus Recognition #1: 1955–1965

An interesting issue grew up in association with the continuous/symbolic split. Those thinking within the framework of continuous systems concentrated on pattern recognition as the key type of task for machines to do—character recognition, speech recognition, and visual-pattern recognition. They also often concentrated on learning (as noted in the following paragraphs), but it was almost always a recognition capability that was being learned. The Perceptron of Rosenblatt can be taken as paradigmatic here. [Rosenblatt, 1958.] Contrariwise, those thinking within the framework of symbolic systems concentrated on problem-solving as the key type of task for machines to do—game-playing, theorem-proving, and puzzle-solving.

This separation of tasks reinforced the split between these groups. To the AI community, the intellectual depth of the tasks performed by the pattern-recognition systems seemed relatively trivial compared with the problem-solving tasks done by the programming systems. But just because of that, a myth grew up that it was relatively easy to automate man's higher reasoning functions but very difficult to automate those functions man shared with the rest of the animal kingdom and performed well automatically, for example,

---

[4]It might also mean the class of theorem-proving systems using logical calculi; but this is really a subclass of symbol systems.

recognition. Thus, work on recognition was at the foundation of the problem of intelligence, whereas work on problem-solving was an add-on.

The symbolic/continuous split and the problem-solving/recognition split are organically related. Each task is the one most easily approached in terms of the class of systems adopted. However, that does not make the two intellectual issues the same. Scientists can hold quite different attitudes about the two splits, and the two issues can become uncoupled in a different era under different conditions. Both these issues emerged in the late 1950s concurrently with the birth of AI. By 1965 the two fields of AI and pattern recognition had separated rather completely and taken up distinct, relatively permanent institutional roles. The conflict could be considered to have reached a resolution. However, it was to become unstuck again almost immediately.

Psychology versus Neurophysiology #1: 1955–1965

Strongly coordinated with the issues of symbolic versus continuous systems and problem-solving versus recognition was another, conceptually distinct issue, namely, whether AI would look to psychology or to neurophysiology for inspiration. That human intelligence was to be both guide and goad to engineering intelligent systems was clear. However, this did not discriminate between psychology and neurophysiology. As is well known, these two disciplines speak with entirely separate, though not necessarily contradictory, voices. In general, those concerned with continuous systems and pattern recognition looked to neurophysiology; those concerned with symbolic systems and problem-solving (i.e., AI) looked to psychology. Evidence of the exclusive attention of early AI to psychology (in contradistinction to biology) is amply provided by the two major sets of readings of those years. [Feigenbaum and Feldman, 1963; Minsky, 1968.] By 1965, this issue was no longer a live one, and the cast for AI was set.

The split between neurophysiology and psychology did not dictate the split between symbolic and continuous systems; if anything, it was the other way around. Neurophysiology, of course, was linked to continuous variables, with its signals, networks, and geometry. But experimental psychology was not linked at all to symbolic systems. The dominant class of systems in psychology at the time was that of stimulus/response (S/R) systems, an abstract form of inhibition-and-excitation network. The only alternatives were the continuous fields of Gestalt theory or the pseudo-hydraulic systems of Freudian psychology (both only vaguely defined, though that is irrelevant here). In fact, the class of symbolic systems was discovered within AI and imported into psychology. [Newell and Simon, 1976a; Newell, 1980b.] Thus, the choice of psychology by AI was made because the class of systems that AI took to work with, that is, programming systems, led to psychologically, not physiologically, revealing tasks.

Neurophysiology played a key role in keeping continuous systems from suffering the same fate as logic systems. Whereas with logic systems there was nowhere to go except toward program-like organizations, with continuous systems there was the brain to model. We need not demand an answer to what the higher organization would be, we could just take as guide the brain as revealed in current neurophysiological work. It is true, of course, that in the late 1940s and early 1950s, the discrete approximation to the nervous system (neurons as digital threshold devices) promised to provide neurophysiological inspiration for the class of logic systems. But under a barrage of criticism, even the engineers came to accept the nervous system as too complex to be modeled by logic-level systems, which is to say, its continuities had to be taken seriously. Thus, without any source of inspiration, logic-level systems faded away as a separate language for modeling intelligence, but continuous systems remained.

Performance versus Learning #1: 1955–1965

Yet another issue can be identified that is coordinated with the issue of symbolic versus continuous systems. AI concentrated on creating performance systems, that is, systems that performed some task demanding intelligence. Cybernetics and pattern-recognition research concentrated on creating systems that learned. Indeed, another subfield grew up that called itself self-organizing systems. [Yovits, Jacobi, and Goldstein, 1962.] In practice, self-organizing systems largely overlapped with the work in pattern recognition and it had common roots in cybernetics. But self-organizing systems took the problem of learning as the central focus rather than the problem of recognition. For instance, within self-organizing systems, there was considerable interest in embryology, even though it had little to do with recognition at the time.

Through the early 1960s, all the researchers concerned with mechanistic approaches to mental functions knew about each other's work and attended the same conferences. It was one big, somewhat chaotic, scientific happening. The four issues I have identified—continuous versus symbolic systems, problem-solving versus recognition, psychology versus neurophysiology, and performance versus learning—provided a large space within which the total field sorted itself out. Workers of a wide combination of persuasions on these issues could be identified. Until the mid-1950s, the central focus had been dominated by cybernetics, which had a position on two of the issues—using continuous systems and orientation toward neurophysiology—but no strong position on the other two. For instance, cybernetics did not concern itself with problem-solving at all. The emergence of programs as a medium of exploration activated all four of these issues, which then gradually led to the emergence of a single composite issue defined by a coordination of all four dimensions. This process was essentially complete by 1965, although I do not have any marker event. Certainly by 1971, at the second International Joint Conference on Artificial Intelligence in London, it was decided that henceforth the conference would not accept pure pattern-recognition papers, an act which already reflected an existing state of affairs.

Serial versus Parallel #1: 1955–1965

It is worth noting for future reference that most pattern-recognition and self-organizing systems were highly parallel network structures. Many, but not all, were modeled after neurophysiological structures. Most symbolic-performance systems were serial programs. Thus, the contrast between serial and parallel (especially highly parallel) systems was explicit during the first decade of AI. The contrast was coordinated with the other four issues I have just discussed. However, I do not recollect it playing nearly as active a role as any of the other four, so I have simply added it on as a comment.

Heuristics versus Algorithms: 1955–1965

These issues were not the only ones that emerged in the first decade of AI's existence, nor the most important. A candidate for the most important initial issue was AI's development of heuristic programs in contradistinction to algorithms. Algorithms were taken to be programs that guaranteed that they would solve a problem or solve it within given time bounds. Good programs were algorithmic, and if not, the fault lay with the programmer, who had failed to analyze his or her problem sufficiently—to know what the program should do to solve this problem. Heuristic programs, on the other hand, were programs that operated by means of heuristic rules of thumb— approximate, partial knowledge that might aid in the discovery of the solution but could not guarantee to do so. The distinction implied that intelligent problem-solving could be attained by heuristic programs. For a short while, one name for the field of AI was heuristic programming, reflecting, in part, a coordination with such subfields as linear programming and dynamic programming (which were also just then emerging).

An important effect of this issue was to isolate AI within computer science but along a different dimension than the issue of symbols versus numbers. Heuristic programming indicates a commitment to a different course than finding the best engineering solution or mathematical analysis of a problem. According to the standard engineering ethos, the proper use of the computer requires the engineer or analyst to exert his or her best intellectual efforts studying the problem, find the best solution possible, and then program that solution. Providing a program with some half-baked, unanalyzed rules seemed odd at best and irrational, or even frivolous, at worst. A good example of this tension can be found in the work of Wang, whose theorem-proving program performed much better than the LOGIC THEORIST. [Newell, Shaw, and Simon, 1957; Wang, 1960.] The thrust of Wang's position was that much better theorem-provers could be built if appropriate results in mathematical logic were exploited. The defense by the AI commu-

nity stressed finding how humans would solve such problems, in effect denying that the fullest analysis of experimental tasks was the object of the
investigation. Another important example was the MACSYMA project to
construct an effective computer system for physicists and engineers to do
symbolic manipulation of mathematical expressions. Although this work
grew out of two prior efforts in AI, it was cast by its leaders as "not part of
AI," but, rather, as part of an area of computer science called symbolic
manipulation, which took a thoroughgoing engineering and analytical attitude. [Slagle, 1963; Moses, 1967.]

I have put the demise of the issue at the mid-1960s; the issue gradually
ceased to be discussed, though the distinction continues to be made in
textbooks and introductory treatments. Once the field was underway, with
lots of AI systems to provide examples, the point at issue became transpar-
ent. Moreover, the distinction has difficulty in being transformed into a
technical one, because it is tied to features external to the procedure itself,
namely, to the problem that is supposed to be solved and the state of knowledge of the user of the procedure.

Interpretation versus Compilation: 1955–1985

A third issue served to separate AI from the rest of computer science, in
addition to the issues of symbols versus numbers and heuristics versus
algorithms. AI programs were developed in list-processing languages, which
were interpretive, whereas the mainstream of language development was
moving irrevocably toward the use of compilers. Prior to the mid-1950s,
programming languages beyond assemblers were interpretive. The major
turning point in compilers, FORTRAN, was developed in the mid-1950s,[5]
and it determined the direction of programming-language development
(though, of course, not without some controversy). Speed of execution was
the consideration uppermost in the minds of the programming fraternity. In
contrast, AI took the interpretive character of its languages seriously and
declared them to be necessary for attaining intelligent systems. This was
epitomized by the use of full recursion, but it penetrated throughout the
entire philosophy of language design, with the attractive idea of putting
intelligence into the interpreter.

This separation of AI programming from mainline high-level language
programming, which started immediately at the birth of AI, has persisted to
the present. Its effects go much deeper than might be imagined. This separation has played a major role in determining the heavy AI involvement in
interactive programming, which contrasts with the minimal involvement of
the central programming-languages, with their adherence to the compile-

---

[5] In fact, the first report of FORTRAN at a scientific meeting occurred at the same session as the
first report of a list-processing language. [Backus et al., 1957; Newell and Shaw, 1957.]

and-run operating philosophy. Just for fun, I have indicated the end of this issue in 1985, on the assumption that the coming generation of powerful personal computers will finally force all languages to come to terms with full dynamic capabilities in order to permit interactive programming. But this is pure conjecture, and the separation may now be wide enough to require a generation to heal.

The grounds for this issue can be traced to demands for efficiency on the one hand versus demands for flexibility on the other; perhaps the issue should have been so labeled. For instance, the main programming community in the late 1950s also had a strong negative reaction to list-processing, because of its giving up half the memory just to link the actual data together. But, although the general efficiency issue was always on the surface of discussions, the total situation seems better described in terms of distinct structural alternatives, that is, interpreters versus compilers, list structures versus arrays, and recursion versus iteration.

Simulation versus Engineering Analysis: 1955–

One issue that surfaced right from the start of AI was whether to make machines be intelligent by simulating human intelligence or by relying on engineering analysis of the task. Those who were primarily trying to understand human intelligence inclined naturally to the simulation view; those who were primarily engineers inclined to the pure task-analysis view. The principle was frequently invoked that we do not build a flying machine by simulating bird flight. On the simulation side, there was more than one position. The majority took the view that casual observation and casual introspection was the appropriate approach—that is, the human was a source of good ideas, not of detail. A few, usually with strong psychological interests or affiliations, took the view that actual experimental data on humans should be examined.

This issue seems never to have produced any important crises or changes of direction in the field; however, it has probably decreased the amount of mutual understanding. There seems to be little movement in a scientist's position on this issue. Each investigator finds his or her niche and stays there, understanding only superficially how those with different approaches operate. The position adopted probably reflects fairly deep attitudes, such as determine whether a scientist goes into an engineering discipline or a social/behavioral discipline in the first place. This is to be contrasted with many fields where methods are effectively neutral means to ends, to be used by all scientists as the science demands. There is little indication of diminution of this issue over the years, although starting in the 1970s, there has been some increase in the general use of protocols to aid the design of AI systems, even when there is no psychological interest.

This completes the set of new issues that arose coincident with the birth of AI. Five of them—symbolic versus continuous systems, problem-solving versus recognition, psychology versus neurophysiology, performance versus learning, and serial versus parallel—separated AI from other endeavors to mechanize intelligence. But the goal of mechanizing intelligence bound all of these enterprises together and distinguished them from the greater part of computer science, whose goal was performing tasks in the service of mankind. Three issues—symbols versus numbers, heuristics versus algorithms, and interpreters versus compilers—clustered together to make AI into a relatively isolated and idiosyncratic part of computer science. Finally one—simulation versus engineering—was purely internal to AI itself.

Replacing versus Helping Humans: 1960–

An issue that surfaced about five years after the beginning of AI was whether the proper objective was to construct systems that replace humans entirely or to augment the human use of computers. The fundamentally ethical dimension of this issue is evident. Yet, it was not overtly presented as an issue of social ethics but, rather, as a matter of individual preference. An investigator would simply go on record one way or another, in the prefaces of his or her papers, so to speak. Yet, there was often an overtone, if not of ethical superiority, of concordance with the highest ideals in the field. Those whose inclinations were toward AI did not so much meet this issue head on as ignore it. Indeed, it was perfectly possible to take the view that work in AI constituted the necessary exploration for man/computer symbiosis. [Licklider, 1960.]

A relatively weak issue such as this could not really become established unless man/machine cooperation offered technical possibilities and challenges as exciting as constructing intelligent machines. Thus, the beginning of this issue coincides with the appearance of interesting interactive systems, such as SKETCHPAD, which had an immense influence on the field. [Sutherland, 1963.]

Artificial intelligence scientists have had a relatively large involvement in the development of user/computer interaction throughout the history of computer science; for example, in time-sharing in the 1960s and 1970s, in making languages interactive in the 1970s, and in developing personal machines in the early 1980s. One explicit justification given for this involvement was that AI itself needed much better programming tools to create intelligent programs—a reason quite independent of the issue presented here. However, it is not possible to untangle the relations between them without some rather careful historical analysis.

Many of those who opted for working in user/computer cooperation tended not to become part of AI as the latter gradually evolved into a field. However, as I have already noted, it was entirely possible to work in both AI and user/computer cooperation. Still, the net result was an additional factor of separation between those in AI and those in neighboring parts of computer science.

Epistemology versus Heuristics: 1960–

It is easy to distinguish the knowledge that an intelligent agent has from the procedures that might be necessary to put that knowledge to work to exhibit the intelligence in action.[6] The initial period in AI was devoted almost exclusively to bringing into existence modes of heuristic processing worthy of consideration. In 1959, John McCarthy initiated a research position that distinguished such study sharply from the study of appropriate logical formalisms to represent the full range of knowledge necessary for intelligent behavior. [McCarthy, 1959.] This study was clearly that of epistemology—the study of the nature of knowledge. It bore kinship with the subfield of philosophy by the same name, although, as with so many other potential connections of AI and philosophy, the orientation of the two fields is highly divergent, although the domain of interest is nominally the same.

There has been little controversy over this issue, although the two poles led to radically different distributions of research effort. Work on epistemology within AI has remained extremely limited throughout, although recently there has been a substantial increase. [D. G. Bobrow, 1980.]

Search versus Knowledge: 1965–1980

In the first years of AI, through the early 1960s, AI programs were characterized simply as highly complex programs, without any particular notion of common structure. For instance, the field was also called *complex information processing* as well as *heuristic programming*. By 1965, however, it had become clear that the main AI programs used the same fundamental technique, which became known as *heuristic search*. [Newell and Ernst, 1965.] This involves the formulation of the problem to be solved as combinatorial search, with the heuristics cast in specific roles to guide the search, such as the selection of which step to take next, evaluation of a new state in the space, comparison of the present state to the posited goal-state, and so on. As the scope of AI programs seemed to narrow, there arose a belief in some AI scientists that the essence of intelligence lay not in search, but in large amounts of highly specific knowledge, or *expertise*. This issue was well enough established by the mid-1970s to occasion the declaration that a paradigm shift in AI had already occurred, the original paradigm having been heuristic search with little knowledge of the task domain and the new paradigm being knowledge-intensive programs. [Goldstein and Papert, 1977.]

It may be doubted that these changes amounted to an actual paradigm *shift*. What clearly did happen was a major expansion of AI research to

---

[6]Said this way, the connection of this issue to the competence/performance issue discussed later would seem to be overwhelming. However, the research programmes associated with the two issues have never made common cause.

explore systems that included substantial domain-specific knowledge. The subfield currently called expert systems, which includes many of the attempts at constructing applied AI systems, emerged in the mid-1970s in part as a result of this emphasis. However, it became clear that heuristic search invariably continued to show up in these programs. Whenever it did not, the problems being solved by the AI system were extremely easy relative to the knowledge put into the system.

It is useful to see that two types of searches are involved in intelligence. The first is the search of the problem space, that is, heuristic search, which is combinatorial. The second is the search of the system's memory for knowledge to be used to guide the heuristic search. This memory search is through a pre-existing structure that has been constructed especially for the purpose of being searched rapidly; it need not be combinatorial. Both types of searches are required of an intelligent system, and the issue of search versus knowledge helped to move the field to a full consideration of both types. The net result was not so much a shift in the paradigm as a broadening of the whole field. This had become clear enough to the field so that by 1980 the issue can be declared moot.

Power versus Generality: 1965–1975

Another way to characterize the major early AI programs is that they took a single well-defined difficult task requiring intelligence and demonstrated that a machine could perform it. Theorem-proving, chess and checkers playing, symbolic integration, IQ-analogy tasks, and such management-science tasks as assembly-line balancing—all these fit this description. Again, there was a reaction to this. Although AI could do these sorts of tasks, it could not do the wide range of presumably trivial tasks we refer to as having common sense. The need was for generality in AI programs, not power.

This call had been issued early enough. [McCarthy, 1959.] However, it was really not until the mid-1960s that a significant shift occurred in the field toward the generality and commonsense side. This gave rise to using small constructed puzzles and artificial problems to illustrate various components of everyday reasoning. A typical example was the monkey-and-bananas task, patterned after simple tasks solved by Köhler's chimpanzee, Sultan. Whereas such problems would have seemed insignificant in the early years, they now became useful, because the goal of research was no longer power, but understanding how commonsense reasoning could occur.

By 1975, this shift had run its course, and new concerns for working with relatively large-scale real problems took over with the development of expert systems already mentioned. As could have been expected, the end of this period of emphasis did not mean a shift back to the original issue. Although expert systems tackled real problems and, hence, were obviously powerful, they did not achieve their power by the heuristic-search techniques of the early years; instead they used large amounts of domain-specific knowledge (coupled, sometimes, with modest search).

However, as is usual in the history of science, work on powerful AI programs never stopped; it only diminished and moved out of the limelight. By 1975, highly successful chess programs emerged, built on heuristic-search principles, with an emphasis on large amounts of search—a million positions per move in tournament play—and good engineering. Thus, intellectual issues shift the balance of what gets worked on but rarely shut off alternative emphases entirely.

Competence versus Performance: 1965–

The Chomskian revolution in linguistics also started in the late 1950s. It was, along with AI, just one of many similar and interrelated developments in engineering, systems, and operational analysis. Although each of these developments had a particularly intense significance for some particular field, for example, linguistics or computer science, they all formed a common interdisciplinary flux. Gradually, these activities sorted themselves into separate subfields or disciplines, developing opposing positions on the issues previously laid out, as we have seen for AI vis-à-vis cybernetics and pattern recognition.

In many ways, linguistics was a special case. It was already a well-formed discipline, and the revolution was at the heart of the discipline, not in some peripheral aspect that could have split off and aligned with other intellectual endeavors. Furthermore, only very few linguists participated in the general flux that was occurring in the world of engineering and applied mathematics. Linguistics was culturally and organizationally quite distinct, having strong roots in the humanities. In fact, it probably made an immense difference that Noam Chomsky became affiliated with the Massachusetts Institute of Technology (MIT).

It was not until the mid-1960s that issues emerged that determined relations between linguistics and other subfields and disciplines. A principal issue was the distinction between competence and performance, which was moved to a central position in the new linguistics by Chomsky. [Chomsky, 1965.] Linguistic competence was the general knowledge a speaker had of the language, in particular, of the generative grammar of the language. Performance was the actual production of utterances, which could be affected by many additional factors, such as cognitive limits, states of stress, or even deliberate modifications for effect. The distinction made useful operational sense for linguistics, because there were two sources of evidence about human-language capabilities, the actual utterance and the judgment of grammaticality—a sort of recall/recognition difference, although that analogy was never exploited.

This distinction might seem innocuous from the standpoint of science history, that is, purely technical. In fact, it served to separate quite radically the sciences concerned primarily with performance, namely AI, computational linguistics, cognitive psychology, and psycholinguistics, from linguistics proper. Linguistics itself declared that it was not interested in performance. More cautiously said, competence issues were to have absolute priority on the research agenda. But the effect was the same: Work in any of the performance fields was basically irrelevant to the development of linguistics. There could be a flow from linguistics to these other fields, and, indeed, there was an immense flow to psycholinguistics, but there could not be any significant flow in the other direction.[7]

A more effective field-splitter would be hard to find. It has remained in effect ever since, with the competence/performance distinction being extended to other domains of mentality. This has certainly not been the only significant cause of the separateness of AI from linguistics. There are important isolating differences in method, style of research, and attitudes toward evidence. Many of these other issues share substance with the competence/performance distinction and affect the separation between psychology and linguistics much more than that between AI and linguistics. Thus, perhaps these issues can be left to one side.

Memory versus Processing: 1965–1975

During the immediate postwar decades, the mainstream of individual human psychology was strongly influenced by the general ferment of engineering, system, and operational ideas (as I have previously termed it). This involved human factors and information theory in the early 1950s; and signal-detection theory, control theory, game theory, and AI in the mid-1950s. As with linguistics in the period of 1955–1965, all these ideas and fields seemed to mix while matters sorted themselves out. By the mid-1960s, psychology had focused on memory as the central construct in its view of man as an information processor. Short-term memory and the visual iconic store combined to provide an exciting picture of the interior block-diagram of the human mental apparatus (what would now be called the architecture). This settled what the main lines of investigation would be for the field; the marker event for this conviction is Neisser's book, *Cognitive Psychology*. [Neisser, 1967.]

This settlement is important for the history of AI, because AI's influence on psychology in the 1955–1965 period was primarily in the area of problem-solving and concept formation. With psychology opting for memory structure, psychology and AI went fundamentally separate ways. Although the work on problem-solving remained a common concern, it was a sufficiently minor area in psychology, so that it exerted only a modest integrating effect. AI itself during this period had little interest in memory structure at the block diagram level. Psychologically relevant research on memory by AI researchers did exist but moved out of AI into psychology; for example, the

---

[7]This is not the whole story of the relations of linguistics with other fields; for example, there have been important contacts with logic and philosophy.

work on EPAM (Elementary Perceiver and Memorizer). [Simon and Feigen-baum, 1964.]

In the second half of the 1960s came another major advance in cognitive psychology, namely, the discoveries of how to infer basic processes from reaction times. [Neisser, 1963; Sternberg, 1966.] This insight promised even greater ability to dissect human cognitive processes and confirmed the basic choice of psychology to analyze the block-diagram level of cognition. This insight also broadened the analysis from just memory structure to the stages of information-processing. In this respect, it might seem better to call the issue under discussion one of system levels: AI focusing on the symbolic level and psychology focusing on the architecture,[8] that is, the equivalent of the register-transfer level. However, the concern with memory so dominates the years prior to 1965, when this issue was being sorted out, that it seems preferable to label it memory versus processing.

Long-term memory has been absent from the previous account. During this period, AI was certainly concerned about the structure of long-term memory, under the rubric of semantic memory. This would seem to provide common ground with psychology, yet initially it did not do so to any great extent. Two factors seem to account for this. First, in psychology, the new results, hence the excitement, all involved short-term memories. The established theory of learning, interference theory, against which these new ideas about memory made headway, assumed a single memory, which was in essence long-term memory. Second, the memory that psychology considered was episodic—learning what happened during an episode, such as learning what familiar items were presented at a trial. This stood in marked contrast with semantic memory, which appeared to be a timeless organization of knowledge. Only gradually did the psychologically relevant work on semantic memory by a few investigators capture any significant attention within cognitive psychology. The seminal publication of Anderson and Bower's *Human Associative Memory* can be taken as a marker of the beginning of this attention. [Anderson and Bower, 1973.]

Problem-Solving versus Recognition #2: 1965–1975

In 1965, AI took back the problem of recognition that had become the intellectual property of the pattern-recognition community. This can be marked rather precisely by the work of Roberts on the recognition of three-dimensional polyhedra. [Roberts, 1965.] The essential features were two: First, recognition was articulated, that is, the scene had to be decomposed or segmented into subparts, each of which might need to be recognized to be a different thing. Thus, the result of recognition was a description of a scene rather than just an identification of an object. But a description is a symbolic

---

[8] Although the term *architecture* is just now coming into common use in psychology.

structure that has to be constructed, and such processes were quite outside the scope of the pattern-recognition techniques of the time, though exactly of the sort provided by AI. Second, a major source of knowledge for making such recognitions came from adopting a model of the situation (e.g., it consists only of polyhedra). This made recognition processes strongly inferential, again fitting in well with work in AI, but not with work in pattern recognition.

By the late 1960s, work on vision was going on throughout AI, but the transformation went further than just vision. Three laboratories (at MIT, Stanford, and the Stanford Research Institute) started major efforts in robotics. Vision was to be coupled with arms and motion and in at least one AI center (Stanford), with speech. The entire enterprise was radically different in its focus and problems from the research in pattern recognition that was still going on in parallel in departments and research centers of electrical engineering. In fact, there was little actual controversy to speak of. Both groups simply did their thing. But likewise, there was no substantial rapprochement.

Syntax versus Semantics: 1965–1975

The Chomskian revolution in linguistics was strongly based on theory. Built around the notions of generative and transformational grammar, it posited three distinct components (or modules) for phonology, syntax, and semantics, each with its own grammar. The initial emphasis was on syntax, with work on semantics much less well developed.[9] Despite cautions from the competence/performance distinction, the inference was clear from both the theory and practice of linguistics—syntactic processing should occur in a separate module independently of semantic processing. Indeed, what computational linguistics there was in association with the new linguistics involved the construction of programs for syntactic parsing.

In the late 1960s, a reaction to linguistics arose from within the AI and computational linguistics communities. It took the form of denying the separation of syntax and semantics in the actual processing of language. The initial analysis of an utterance by the hearer was as much a question of semantics as of syntax. Language required an integrated analysis by the hearer and, hence, by the theorist. This reaction can be marked by the work of Quillian, whose introduction of semantic nets was a device to show how semantic processing could occur directly on the surface structure of the utterance (though presumably in conjunction with syntax). [Quillian, 1968.]

This reaction was grounded more broadly in the assertion of the importance of processing considerations in understanding language, the very thing

---

[9]There was work on phonology, but the domain lay outside the range of interest of AI and, in fact, of psychology as well.

denied by the competence/performance distinction. It sought to put processing considerations into the mainstream of linguistic studies, the latter being
owned, so to speak, by the linguistics community. One result, as might have
been expected, was to compound the separation between linguistics, on the
one hand, and computational linguistics and AI, on the other. Another was
to create a stronger independent stream of work on language in AI with its
own basis.

Theorem-Proving versus Problem-Solving: 1965–

Theorem-proving tasks have always been included in the zoo of tasks
studied by AI, although the attention these tasks received initially was
sporadic. However, some logicians and mathematicians worked on theorem-
proving in logic, not just as another task, but as the fundamental formalism
for understanding reasoning and inference. In the last half of the 1960s, with
the development of a logical formalism called resolution, this work in
theorem-proving took center stage in AI. [Robinson, 1965.] It seemed for a
time that theorem-proving engines would sit at the heart of any general AI
system. Not only was their power extended rapidly during this period, but a
substantial amount of mathematical analysis was carried out on the nature of
theorem proving in the predicate calculus. Even further, theorem-proving
programs were extended to handle an increasing range of tasks, for example,
question-answering, robot-planning, and program-synthesis.

A consequence of this success and viewpoint was that theorem-proving
was taken to be a fundamental category of activity distinct from other problem-solving, with its own methods and style of progress. A good indicator
of this is Nilsson's AI textbook, which divides all problem-solving methods
of AI into three parts: state-space search, problem-reduction (i.e., subgoals),
and predicate-calculus theorem-proving. [Nilsson, 1971.] It is not clear
whether this issue has been laid to rest by now or not. As recounted in the
following section, under the procedural/declarative issue, theorem-proving
has become much less central to AI since the mid-1970s. But theorem-
proving and problem-solving still remain distinct research strands.

Engineering versus Science: 1965–

Computer science is torn by a fundamental uncertainty over whether it is an
engineering or science discipline. There is no doubt about the engineering
side; computer science designs and creates artifacts all the time. The doubt
exists on the nature of the science involved. Computer science certainly
studies intellectual domains that are not part of other disciplines. The question is whether or not they have the character of a science. However, the
dichotomy need not be accepted: A third alternative is that the unique intellectual domain of computer science is part of mathematics. Computer science would then join other engineering specialties, such as control theory

and information theory, which have their own characteristic mathematical development.

Much rests on the putative outcome of this issue: What should computer science be like in the future? Should departments of computer science be part of the college of engineering or the college of arts and sciences? What status should be accorded to various subdisciplines in computer science? Can a thesis involve just a design? And more. The start of this issue coincides with the creation of departments of computer science in the mid-1960s, which served to raise all these questions. Whether the issue will ever be laid to rest is unclear, but it is certainly unlikely while the whole field grows dynamically, with a continuing flood of new and destabilizing notions.

Artificial intelligence participates along with the rest of computer science in the uncertainties over whether it is an engineering or science discipline. However, the issue for AI has its own special flavor. AI participates with many disciplines outside computer science in the attempt to understand the nature of mind and intelligent behavior. This is an externally grounded scientific and philosophic goal, which is clearly not engineering. Thus, the nature of the science for AI is not really in doubt as it is for the rest of computer science. However, this does not end the matter, for interactions occur with other issues. For instance, to the extent that we are oriented toward helping humans rather than replacing them, we may not wish to accept the understanding of the nature of mind as a scientific goal, but only as a heuristic device.

The orientation toward engineering or science can have major consequences for how a field devotes its energies. Currently, for example, an important divergence exists in the subfield of computer vision. Should the nature of the environment be studied to discover what can be inferred from the optic array (a scientific activity); or should experimental vision systems be constructed to analyze the data they generate within the framework of the system (an engineering activity)? That both activities are legitimate is not in question; which activity gets the lion's share of attention is in dispute. And there is some indication that an important determiner is the basic engineering/science orientation of a given investigator.

Language versus Tasks: 1970–1980

The 1970s saw the emergence of concerted efforts within AI to produce programs that understand natural language, amounting to the formation of a subfield, lying partly in AI and partly in computational linguistics. The key markers are the works of Woods and Winograd. [Woods, 1970; T. Winograd, 1971]. This issue had been building for some time, as we saw in the issue of syntax versus semantics.

The emergence of such a subfield is in itself not surprising. Natural language is clearly an important, even uniquely important, mental capability. In addition to AI, there existed another relevant field, computational linguistics, concerned generally with the application of computers to linguistics. Neither is it surprising that this subfield had almost no representation from linguistics, although, of course, linguistics was of obvious central relevance.[10] The syntax/semantics issue, which had reinforced the separation of linguistics from AI, was a primary substantive plank in the programme of the new subfield.

What is interesting was the creation of another attitude within a part of AI, which can be captured by the issue of language versus tasks. Studying the understanding of language was seen as a sufficient context for investigating the nature of common sense. An important discovery was how much knowledge and inference appeared to be required to understand even the simplest sentences or short stories. Thus, the very act of understanding such stories involved commonsense reasoning and, with it, the essence of general human intelligence. Programs could be interesting as AI research, so the attitude went, without doing any other task in addition to understanding the presented language input. The effect of this strategic position was to separate the work in natural-language processing from the tradition in AI of posing tasks for programs to do, where the difficulty could be assessed. The issue did not occasion much discussion, although its effects were real enough. The issue was masked by the fact that understanding by itself was a difficult enough task for AI research to make progress on. No one could object (and no one did) to not adding what seemed like an irrelevant second difficult task for the system, which would simply burden the research endeavor.

Procedural versus Declarative Representation #1: 1970–1980

Recall that resolution theorem-proving flourished in the late 1960s and bid fair to become the engine at the center of all reasoning. In fact, it took only a few years for the approach to come up against its limitations. Despite increases in power, relative to prior efforts, theorem provers were unable to handle any but trivial tasks. Getting from logic to real mathematics—seen always as a major necessary hurdle—seemed as far away as ever.

The reaction to this state of affairs became known as the procedural/ declarative controversy. Theorem provers were organized as a large homogeneous database of declarative statements (clauses in resolution), over which an inference engine worked to produce new true statements to add to the database. This was the essence of a declarative representation of knowledge and its attractions were many. Its difficulty lay in the costs of processing. The inference engine treated all expressions in the database alike or, more precisely, without regard for their semantics. There also seemed no

---

[10] Among the contributors to the first conference on Theoretical Issues in Natural Language Processing, a series that became the forum for this subfield, I can identify only one mainstream linguist. [Schank and Nash-Webber, 1975.]

way for a theorem prover to be given information about how to solve problems. These two features added up to a major combinatorial explosion. The remedy—the procedural side of the issue—lay (so it was claimed) in encoding information about the task in procedures. Then knowledge would be associated directly with the procedures that were to apply it; indeed, the procedures would embody the knowledge and, thus, not have to be interpreted by another inference engine. This would permit the appropriate guidance for problem-solving and, thus, keep the combinatorial explosion under control.

There are irremediable flaws in both sides of the argument whether knowledge should be coded in procedural or declarative form, just as there are irremediable flaws in both sides of the argument whether a program is heuristic or algorithmic. Both procedural and declarative representations are necessary to make any computation at all happen. In consequence, arguments over the issue were largely inconclusive, although they produced the closest thing to a public issue-controversy in AI's short history. However, the effect on the course of AI research was enormous. First, work on theorem-proving shrank to a trickle, with what remained mostly devoted to nonresolution theorem-proving. Second, so-called planning languages emerged as a result—PLANNER, QA4, CONNIVER, POPLAR, and so forth. [Bobrow and Raphael, 1974.] These programming-language systems were intended to provide a vehicle for writing the sorts of domain-dependent, procedure-oriented theorem provers called for in the debate. While that did not quite happen, these languages in themselves provided a major conceptual advance in the field. The effects of this issue had about run their course by 1980.

Frames versus Atoms: 1970–1980

In a paper that circulated widely before it was published in the mid-1970s, Marvin Minsky raised the issue about the size of representational units in an intelligent system. [Minsky, 1975.] Knowledge should be represented in *frames,* which are substantial collections of integrated knowledge about the world, rather than in small atoms or fragments. The basic issue is as old as the atomistic associationism of British empiricism and the countering complaints of the Gestaltists. How are the conflicting requirements for units of thought and contextual dependence to be reconciled?

This issue had hardly surfaced at all in the first decade of AI. List structures, the basic representational medium, were in themselves neither atomistic nor wholistic but adaptable to whatever representational constructs the designer had in mind.[11] But the coming to prominence of resolution-theorem-

---

[11] This is because list structures approximate general symbolic systems. The neutrality is easily confirmed in the continued and universal use of list-processing languages to realize systems of all kinds along this dimension.

proving in the late 1960s brought with it as a side effect the *clause* as the unit of representation. The clause was a primitive assertion that could not be broken down into a conjunction of other assertions—primitive predicates P, negations of primitive predicates $\sim P$, disjunctions P or Q, implications P implies Q, and so forth. The total knowledge of the system was to be represented as the conjunction of clauses—that is, to use the old Gestaltist phrase, as an *And-sum* of separate bits of knowledge.

Thus, the issue of size of representational unit grew out of the same ground as the procedural versus declarative controversy, and, indeed, it was articulated by the same group at MIT who had made most of the latter issue. As is always the case, concern was, in fact, widespread but had been subordinated to other concerns. [Abelson, 1973; Norman, 1973; Schank, 1973.] Minsky was the first one to give clear voice to the concern. The effect of the paper was dramatic, despite the fact that the paper itself was entirely speculative and discursive. Throughout AI, the concept of the frame as the appropriate data structure was widely embraced. By 1980, frame systems were an established part of AI, and a very substantial fraction of the work in knowledge representation was involved in such systems.

Much follows on this development (in conjunction with the procedural/declarative issue)—the rise of substantial research effort in knowledge representation and the strengthening of renewed ties with philosophy. [Brachman and Smith, 1980.] These efforts conjoin with those of AI epistemology, discussed earlier. They raise some new issues, such as the relation of philosophic work on meaning to directly inspired computational models. But these issues have not yet jelled enough to be included in their own right.

Reason versus Emotion and Feeling #2: 1970–

Philosophy has a long-standing concern with the mechanization of mind. Indeed, under the rubric of the mind/body problem, it can be said almost to own the problem, it having been bequeathed to philosophy by Descartes. In its genesis, AI had very little involvement with philosophy, beyond the background awareness that comes from participation in the general intellectual culture. No philosophers of mind were involved and no technical philosophical issues were dealt with. A glance at the content of the two fields provides one obvious clue. The phenomena attended to in philosophy are sensations as subjective experiences—*raw feels,* to use a bit of philosophic jargon. A typical article is entitled "The Feelings of Robots." [Ziff, 1959.] Thus, though AI and philosophy of mind ostensibly deal with the same problem, in fact they go after largely distinct phenomena.[12]

---

[12] Another example is the problem of induction, where philosophy is concerned with the certainty of induction and AI is concerned with performing the inductions. [Newell, 1973c.]

The issue has not been especially active, but it has been raised. [Gunderson, 1971.] It is argued that performance functions (i.e., those functions AI currently deals with, called *program-receptive* functions) can be mechanized; but that sentient functions (i.e., feelings, called *program-resistant* functions) cannot. Whether this will ever grow to a substantial controversy is hard to tell at this point. It is certainly available as a reserve position that can serve to separate AI from the philosophy of mind. It adds to the general background concern, discussed in the first occurrence of this issue, of the absence of emotion and feeling in the development of intelligent systems.

Toy versus Real Tasks: 1975–

As noted in the power/generality issue, the field took a shift in the mid-1960s away from powerful programs toward programs that could exhibit common sense. Further, as noted in the language/tasks issue, this line further transmuted to being concerned with understanding via the understanding of natural language. Concomitantly, programs were often built to work on small simple illustrative tasks or environments, usually puzzles or made-up situations.

By the mid-1970s some systems had been developed that worked with real tasks that had substantial intellectual content, to judge from their role in the real world. The initial such system can be taken to be DENDRAL, which determined the structural formula for chemical molecules, given the data on the mass spectrogram.[13] [Lindsay, Buchanan, Feigenbaum, and Lederberg, 1980.] DENDRAL began in the late 1960s and grew in power throughout the early 1970s. It was joined in the mid-1970s by several systems that performed competently in real medical-diagnosis tasks, of which MYCIN was the paradigm. [Shortliffe, 1974.] This was the immediate locus of expert systems, which, as previously noted, grew up as part of the general emphasis on knowledge in contrast to search. With it grew an attitude that AI in general should no longer work on small illustrative, artificial tasks but that it was time to work on real tasks. The simple artificial tasks came to be called toy tasks, not just because the term conveys the contrast between childish and grown-up pursuits, but also because stacking children's blocks had become a favorite illustrative task environment.

The tension between basic research and application exists in all sciences at all times. Sciences sometimes build institutional structures to contain the tension. As we saw in the issue of science versus engineering, computer science has kept its basic and applied components mixed together in a single discipline, thus exacerbating the tension. The tension was, in fact, especially

---

[13] The other system often mentioned similarly is MACSYMA, the highly sophisticated program at the Massachusetts Institute of Technology for doing symbolic mathematics. As mentioned earlier, it had deliberately removed itself from being an AI program.

severe for AI during the decade of the 1970s. The climate in Washington was not benign for basic research in general, and there was sustained pressure from AI's primary government funding agency (DARPA—Defense Advanced Research Projects Agency) to make AI pay off. That said, however, the distinction between toy versus real tasks is not solely the distinction between basic and applied research. Tasks taken from the real world and performed by intelligent humans as part of their working lives carry a prima facie guarantee of demanding appropriate intelligent activity by systems that would perform them. It can be argued that such tasks are the appropriate ones for AI to work on, even if the goal is basic research. Thus, the toy-versus-real-tasks issue stands ambiguously for both meanings—basic versus applied and irrelevant versus relevant basic science.

Serial versus Parallel #2: 1975–

By the mid-1970s, computer science had for some time been seriously exploring multiprogramming and multiprocessing. These provided the groundwork for considering parallel systems for doing AI. A major instigation occurred with the development of the Hearsay-II model of speech understanding. [Lesser and Erman, 1977.] Hearsay-II comprised a number of knowledge sources (acoustic, phonetic, phonological, lexical, syntactic, semantic, and pragmatic), each working concurrently and independently off a common blackboard that contained the current working state about the utterance and each contributing their bit to the evolving recognition and reacting to the bits provided by the others.

The Hearsay-II structure was certainly a parallel one, but it was at a level of parallelism quite different from earlier network models, namely, a modest number (tens) of functionally specialized processes. Furthermore, individual processes remained fundamentally symbolic (even though lots of signal-processing was inherent in the speech-recognition task). Hearsay-II was only one of several efforts to pursue the notion that an intelligent system should be thought of in terms of communicating subprocesses rather than as an individual serial machine. A metaphor arose for thinking about an intelligent system—the scientific community metaphor—which took the operation of science, with its notion of cooperation, publication, experiment, criticism, education, and so forth, as the appropriate model for intelligent activity. Gradually, a group of people emerged interested in working on distributed AI.

Performance versus Learning #2: 1975–

As noted earlier, learning was generally associated with work on pattern recognition. With the split between problem-solving and recognition, work on learning within AI declined. As always, it never stopped entirely. Indeed, such is the basic fascination with learning processes, and with the belief that they hold the key to intelligence, that each learning program that was constructed received substantial attention.[14] [Samuel, 1959; D. A. Waterman, 1970; Winston, 1970; Sussman, 1975.] However, each learning system was relatively idiosyncratic, with its own interesting lessons, so that the whole did not add up to a coherent effort for the field.

A reversal of this state of affairs developed by the late 1970s. It was triggered by the spread of a class of programming systems, called production, or rule-based systems, which are used for both constructing expert systems and analyzing human cognition. [Waterman and Hayes-Roth, 1978.] To appreciate their role in the resurgence of work on learning, we must take a step back. To create a learning system requires solving two research problems. First, a space of potential performance programs must be created, in which learning will constitute moving from one program to another, searching for programs with better performance. If the space of programs is too vast and irregular, then learning is, in effect, automatic programming, and it becomes extremely difficult. If the space is too limited, then learning is easy, but the performance programs are of little significance. Determining the right space is, thus, a critical research activity. Second, given the space, it is still necessary to design an interesting learning system, for the space only lays out the possibilities. Thus, inventing the learning system is also a critical research activity. A major reason why early AI learning-systems seemed so idiosyncratic was that each made unique choices on both these dimensions. Most important, doing research on learning was doing a double task and taking a double risk.

A production system is composed entirely of a set of *if-then* rules (if such and such conditions hold, then execute such and such actions). At each instant, the rules that hold are recognized, and a single rule is selected to execute. In such a system, the natural space of performance programs consists of subsets of if-then rules, and the primitive act of learning is to add a new rule to the existing set (or sometimes to modify an existing rule in some simple way, such as by adding another condition). This space of performance programs is neither too limited nor too open, since it is easy to restrict the rules to be learned to a special class. As a consequence, the first research choice is essentially made for the researcher, who can then concentrate on constructing an interesting learning program. Moreover, learning programs will have much in common, since they now use similar spaces of performance programs. Indeed, this is just what happened in the late 1970s as researchers began to construct a wide variety of small learning systems, all built around variants of the production-system formalism. [Michalski, Carbonell, and Mitchell, 1983.] It must be realized, of course, that such focusing of effort does not remove the collective risk. If production systems

---

[14] Some other systems were built, which might have been viewed as learning systems, but, instead, were taken simply to be performance programs in specialized task environments, for example, induction programs.

are the wrong program organization to be exploring, then the entire field is moving down an unproductive path.

Psychology versus Neuroscience #2: 1975–

AI would appear to be at the mercy of the immense gulf that continues to separate psychology and the biology of the brain. As each field continues to progress—which both do dramatically—hopes continually spring up for new bridging connections. No doubt at some point the permanent bridge will be built. So far, although each increment of progress seems real, the gap remains disappointingly large.

It is possible that AI has a major contribution to make to this by exploring basic computational structures at a level that makes contact with neural systems. In the early instance of psychology versus neurophysiology (which was before the term *neuroscience* had been coined), that possibility seemed quite remote. The theoretical structures that did make contact with neurophysiology were remote from the computational structures that preoccupied AI researchers. Then the split occurred, with pattern recognition all but moving out of computer science.

In the mid-1970s, a new attempt began to connect AI with neuroscience, initiated by the work of David Marr. [Marr, 1976.] The emphasis remained on vision, as it had been in the earlier period. But the new effort was explicitly computational, focusing on algorithms that could perform various low-level vision functions, such as stereopsis. Although Marr's effort was new in many ways, and based on specific technical achievements, most of the global issues of the earlier time reappeared. This work has now expanded to a larger group, which calls its work, among other things, the new connectionism, and promises to be a substantial subfield again, this time within AI.

Serial versus Parallel #3: 1980–

The new wave of neuroscience-inspired AI contains, of course, a commitment to highly parallel network structures. The issue of serial versus parallel merits a separate entry here to maintain a clear contrast with the distributed AI effort, which defined the second wave of concern with parallel systems. In this third phase, the degree of parallelism is in the millions, and computing elements in the network have modest powers; in particular, they are not computers with their own local symbols. In the new structures, computation must be shared right down to the roots, so to speak. The interaction cannot be limited to communicating results of significant computations. Furthermore, the communication media between elements are continuous signals, and not just bits. However, unlike the earlier work, these new computational systems are not to be viewed as neural nets; that is, the nodes of the network are not to be put in one-to-one correspondence with neurons, but, rather, with physiological subsystems of mostly unspecified character.

Problem-Solving versus Recognition #3: 1980–

Robotics has returned to AI after having left it for most of the 1970s. Perhaps it is unfortunate to call the issue problem-solving versus recognition, since recognition is only one aspect of robotics. The main sources of the new wave of effort are external to AI—industrial robotics plus the concern of the decline in American productivity and the trade position of the United States vis-à-vis Japan and West Germany. The initial growth of industrial robotics took place largely outside of AI as a strictly engineering endeavor. As a result, the initial growth tended to minimize the intelligence involved, for example, sensory-motor coordination. One component of the new association of robotics with AI is the coupling of significant amounts of vision with manipulators, reflecting the continued advance of vision capabilities in AI throughout the 1970s. (Touch and kinesthetic sensing is increasingly important, too, but this does not build so strongly on prior progress in AI.) Importantly, along with industrially motivated aspects, there is also a revival of basic research in manipulation and movement in space and over real terrains.

It might seem that this is just another purely technical progression. But with it has returned, as night follows day, the question of the relation of AI and robotics as disciplines, just as the question was raised in the issue of problem-solving versus recognition during the late 1960s. Is robotics a central part of AI or only an applied domain? Do graduate students in AI have to understand the underlying science of mechanics and generalized coordinate systems that are inherent in understanding manipulation and motion? Or is that irrelevant to intelligence? Cases can be made either way. [Nilsson, 1982.]

Procedural versus Declarative Representation #2: 1980–

In the late 1970s, a new programming system called PROLOG emerged, based on resolution-theorem-proving and constituting, in effect, a continuation of the effort to show that declarative formulations can be effective. [Kowalski, 1979.] The effort is based primarily in Europe, and it is a vigorous movement. The attack is not occurring at the level of planning languages, but at the level of LISP itself. Over the years, LISP has established itself as the lingua franca of the AI community. Even though various other programming systems exist, for example, rule-based systems of various flavors, practically everyone builds systems within a LISP programming environment. The planning languages (PLANNER, CONNIVER, etc.), which showed how to effect another level of system organization above LISP, have not proved highly effective as a replacement, and they receive only modest use. As already noted, their contribution has been primarily conceptual. Thus, although the original attack on theorem-proving was in terms of the planner languages, the modern counterattack is at the level of LISP. By being centered in Europe, with very little attention paid currently to

PROLOG in the major AI centers in the United States, the issue takes on additional coordinated dimensions. The outcome is far from clear at this juncture.

DISCUSSION

It should be clear by now why I entered the caveats about historical accuracy at the beginning. Each of the issues raises serious problems of characterization and historical grounding. No attempt has been made to define an intellectual issue, so that some modestly objective way could be found to generate a complete set of issues, for example, by placing a grid over the literature of the field. Several additional issues might well have emerged, and some of those presented here might not have made the grade. Thus, the population of issues exhibited must be taken, not just with a pinch of salt, but soaked in a barrel of brine. Similar concerns attend dating the issues and my interpretation of them; nevertheless, some comments about the total picture seem worthwhile.

What Is Missing?

I do know why some issues did not make it. Three examples will illustrate some reasons. The first is the broad but fundamental issue of the ethical use of technology and the dehumanization of people by reduction to mechanism. This issue engages all of technology and science. It seems particularly acute for AI, perhaps, because the nature of mind seems so close to the quick. But the history of science reminds us easily enough that at various stages astronomy, biology, and physics have seemed special targets for concern. There has been continued and explicit discussion of these issues in connection with AI. [Taube, 1961; Weizenbaum, 1976; McCorduck, 1979.] I have not included them in the list of intellectual issues because they do not, in general, seem to affect the course of the science. Where some aspect does seem to do so, as in the issue of helping humans or replacing them, it has been included. However, the broader issue certainly provides a thematic background against which all work goes on in the field, increasing its ambiguity, and the broader issue undoubtedly enters into individual decisions about whether to work in the field and what topics to select.

The second example involves Hubert Dreyfus, who has been a persistent and vocal critic of AI. [Dreyfus, 1972.] He has certainly become an issue for the field; however, this does not necessarily produce an intellectual issue. Dreyfus's central intellectual objection, as I understand him, is that the analysis of the context of human action into discrete elements is doomed to failure. This objection is grounded in phenomenological philosophy. Unfortunately, this appears to be a nonissue as far as AI is concerned. The answers, refutations, and analyses that have been forthcoming to Dreyfus's writings have simply not engaged this issue—which, indeed, would be a novel issue if it were to come to the fore.

The third example involves the imagery controversy, which has been exceedingly lively in cognitive psychology. [Kosslyn, Pinker, Smith, and Shwartz, 1979.] The controversy is over the nature of the representations used by humans in imagining scenes and reasoning about them. There is no doubt about its relevance to AI—the alternatives are a classical dichotomy between propositional (symbolic?) representations and analog ones. Thus, at heart, it is a variant of the issue of analog-versus-digital representation, which has received mention. But for reasons that are quite obscure to me, the imagery issue has received hardly any interest in the AI community, except where that community also participates in cognitive psychology. As things stand at the moment, this would be an issue for cognitive science, but it is not one for AI.

Though enumerating intellectual issues exposes a certain amount of the history of a field, even if only from particular viewpoints, some important parts can be missed. These seem to be endeavors that were noncontroversial or where the controversies were merely of the standard sort—of what progress had been made, what subfields should get resources, and so forth. Thus, work on program synthesis and verification goes unnoticed. Also, the major effort in the 1970s to construct speech-understanding systems is barely noticed. Perhaps this is not a valid point about the basic historical scheme but reflects only the unevenness of my process of generating issues. Certainly, there were issues in speech-recognition research both in the 1960s, when Bell Laboratories decided to abandon speech recognition as an inappropriate task, and in the 1970s, when a substantial effort sponsored by DARPA to construct speech-understanding systems was dominated by AI considerations over speech-science considerations. Perhaps intellectual issues are generated from all scientific efforts in proportion to the number of scientists involved in them (or to their square?); all we need to do is look for them.

Characteristics of the History

Turning to what is revealed in Table 1, the most striking feature, to me at least, is how many issues there are. Looked at in any fashion—number active at one time (fifteen on average) or total number of issues during AI's quarter-century lifespan (about thirty)—it seems to me like a lot of issues. Unfortunately, similar profiles do not exist for other fields (or I do not know of them). Perhaps the situation in AI is typical, either of all fields at all times or of all fields when they are getting started. In fact, I suspect it is due to the interdisciplinary soup out of which AI emerged. [See my paper "Reflections on the Structure of an Interdiscipline" in this volume.] Many other related fields were being defined during the same post-World-War-II era—cybernetics, operations research, management science, information theory, control theory, pattern recognition, computer science, and general systems theory. Even so, I do not see any easy way of pinning down a correct interpretation of why there are so many issues.

Issues are not independent; they come in clusters, which are coordinated. Researchers tend to fall into two classes, corresponding to one pole or another on all issues in the cluster. Clusters that occur in this history are as follows (where polarities of subissues have been reoriented, if necessary, to make them all line up together, corresponding to the superordinate issue):

AI versus Cybernetics

> Symbolic versus continuous systems
> Problem-solving versus recognition
> Psychology versus neuroscience
> Performance versus learning
> Serial versus parallel

AI versus Computer Science

> Symbols versus numbers
> Heuristics versus algorithms
> Interpretation versus compilation
> Replacing versus helping humans
> Problem-solving versus theorem-proving

Problem-Solving versus Knowledge Search

> Heuristics versus epistemology
> Search versus knowledge
> Power versus generality
> Processing versus memory

Linguistics versus AI and Cognitive Psychology

> Competence versus performance
> Syntax versus semantics

Engineering versus Science

> Engineering analysis versus simulation
> Engineering versus science
> Real versus toy tasks

Wholes versus Atoms

> Procedural versus declarative representation
> Frames versus atoms

A cluster might seem to define a single underlying issue, which can then replace component issues. However, the fact that issues are coordinated does not make them identical. Some scientists can always be found who are aligned in nonstandard patterns. In fact, some of the clusters seem much more consistent than others. Thus, the multiplicity of issues keeps the scientific scene complex, even though, because of clustering, it appears that it should be clear and simple. In fact, many of the groupings are more easily labeled by how they separate fields than by any coherent underlying conceptual issue.

Clustering of issues does seem to be a common occurrence; for instance, a standard advanced text on learning in psychology begins with a list of seven dichotomous issues that characterize learning theories. [Hilgard and Bower, 1948 and 1975, pp. 8–13.] The first three—peripheral versus central, habits versus cognitive structures, and trial-and-error versus insight—form a coordinated cluster that characterizes stimulus/response theories versus cognitive theories (to which could even be added tough-minded versus tender-minded, the contrast William James used to distinguish the two main types of psychologists). One possible source for such coordinated clusters is the attempt to find multiple reasons to distinguish one approach from another. The approach comes first and the issues follow afterward. Then the issues take on an autonomous intellectual life and what starts as rationalization ends up as analysis.

A major role of the issues here seems to be to carve up the total scientific field into disciplines. AI, computer science, logic, cybernetics, pattern recognition, linguistics, and cognitive psychology—all these seem to be discriminated in part by their position on these various issues. The issues, of course, only serve as intermediaries for intellectual positions that derive from many circumstances of history, methodological possibilities, and specific scientific and technical ideas. Still, they seem to summarize a good deal of what keeps the different fields apart, even though the fields have a common scientific domain.

Is the large burst of issues that occurred at the birth of AI just an artifact of my intent to gather issues for AI? If the period just before AI began, say from 1940–1955, were examined carefully, would many more issues be added? The relevant question should probably be taken with respect to some other field as a base. Would a burst like this be found for cybernetics, which started in 1940–1945? My own suspicion is yes, but I have not tried to verify it.

Perhaps then the situation of AI could turn out to be typical. We would find a plethora of issues in any science if we would but look and count; the list from Hilgard and Bower might serve as a positive indicator. However, before rushing to embrace this view, some counterevidence should be examined. An interesting phenomenon in this same postwar period was the emergence of several one-theorem fields. Game theory, information theory, linear programming, and (later) dynamic programming—all had a single strong result around which the field grew.[15] Certainly, each also provided a novel formulation, which amounted to a class of systems to be used to theorize about some field. But initially there was only one striking theorem to justify the entire field. It gave these fields a curious flavor. My personal recollection is that all these fields, while exciting, profound, and (sometimes) controversial, had none of the complexity of issues that we find in Table 1.

Intellectual Issues and Progress

There is a natural temptation to use the history of intellectual issues to measure progress, once it has been explicitly laid out. It is true that some issues have vanished from the scene, such as symbols versus numbers; that seems, perhaps, like progress. It is also true that other issues seem to recur, such as problem-solving versus recognition; that seems, perhaps, like lack of progress. Neither interpretation is correct, I think. Rather, the progress of science is to be measured by the accumulation of theories, data, and techniques, along with the ability they provide to predict, explain, and control. This story is not to be told in terms of such intellectual issues as populate this paper. It requires attention to the detailed content, assertions, and practice of the science itself. True, at the more aggregate level of the *paradigms* of Kuhn or the *programmes* of Lakatos, whole bodies of theory and data can become irrelevant with a shift in paradigm or programme. But on the scale of the twenty-five years of AI research (1955–1980), the story is one of accumulation and assimilation, not one of shift and abandonment. It is not even one of settling scientific questions for good.

What then is the role of intellectual issues in the progression of science? To echo my earlier disclaimer, I can only conjecture. Intellectual issues seem to me more like generalized motivators. They evoke strong enough passions to provide the springs to action, but they are vague enough so that they do not get in the way of specific work. They can be used to convey a feeling of coherence among investigations in their early stages, before it is known exactly what the investigations will yield.

Evidence for this is that issues do not really go away; they return and return again. Repetition is abundant in Table 1. The model that suggests itself immediately is the spiral—each return constitutes a refined version of the issue. Though the issues are certainly not identical each time, it seems difficult to construe the changes as any sort of progressive refinement; some seem more like wandering (e.g., the serial/parallel issue). A more plausible explanation (to me) is that intellectual issues reflect perennial unanswerable

---

[15] Another field, general systems theory, also had a single idea around which to build—that there are common laws across all levels of systems from the atomic through cellular through societal through astronomical. But there was no central result available, only the system view, and this field has been markedly less successful than others in its growth and health.

questions about the structure of nature—continuity/discontinuity, stasis/ change, essence/accident, autonomy/dependence, and so forth. Whenever in the course of science one of these can be recognized in the ongoing stream of work, an appropriate intellectual issue will be instantiated, to operate as a high-level organizing principle for a while. To be sure, this picture does not capture all that seems to be represented in our population of intellectual issues. But it seems substantially better than viewing science as progressively resolving such issues.

CONCLUSION

Putting to one side questions about the accuracy of the particular set of issues displayed in Table 1, of what use is a history of a scientific field in terms of intellectual issues? To repeat once more: It cannot substitue for a substantive history in terms of concepts, theories, and data; however, it does seem to capture some of the flavor of the field in an era. It is clearly a component of the paradigm of a field or of research programmes within a field. And, let us confess it, intellectual issues have a certain spiciness about them that makes them fun to talk and write about. Perhaps it is the sense of touching fundamental issues. But perhaps it also echoes Bertrand Russell's famous aphorism that dealing with intellectual issues has all the advantages of theft over honest toil.

METHODOLOGICAL LINKS BETWEEN ARTIFICIAL INTELLIGENCE AND OTHER DISCIPLINES

Margaret A. Boden

Whether our interest is in psychology, philosophy, or linguistics, there is no question but that artificial intelligence (AI) has given us a new standard of rigor, and a new appreciation of the importance of mental *process*. Linguistics already had rigor but not process; psychology had little of either; and philosophy had less of each. AI provides a range of precisely definable computational concepts, specifying various symbolic representations and transformations, with which to conceptualize the mind. And the technology of programming makes manageable a degree of theoretical complexity that would overwhelm the unassisted human brain. So the inadequacy of theoretical approaches that fail to recognize the complexity of mental structure and process is now evident, and psychology and the philosophy of mind have been influenced accordingly.

One example of a class of empirical psychological work partly inspired by AI ideas is microdevelopmental research [e.g., Karmiloff-Smith and Inhelder, 1975; Karmiloff-Smith, 1979], which studies the dialectical interplay between the child's action sequences and changing cognitive representations (theories, models, heuristics, and choice-criteria). The specifics of action are emphasized on the assumption that procedural details of performance (not only its overall structure) give clues to the underlying competence. However, the degree of procedural detail—though high relative to more traditional forms of experimentation in psychology—is inadequate for expressing a complete computational model of the psychological processes concerned. It is not a straightforward matter to assess such studies in computational terms, and we need to learn how to refine the theories and methodology of these studies so as to facilitate such assessment.

This case exemplifies the general point that, if we ask whether AI has given us new discoveries as well as a new approach, the reply might be that it has not been so helpful to working psychologists as its supporters initially hoped. There has been an increasing amount of computationally influenced empirical research in cognitive, developmental, and educational psychology. But (with the arguable exception of vision) we have gained little new insight into the actual details of mental life, as opposed to the *sorts* of questions that it may be appropriate to ask.

Is this because psychologists have not yet learnt how to apply AI fruitfully to further their research or because (as some critics claim) it is in principle unsuitable for psychological modeling? This question raises a number of methodological difficulties and conceptual unclarities in applying AI ideas to other disciplines. Some of these involve commitments to basic theoretical or philosophical issues and call for cooperative research by people in various specialties.

There is much disagreement—and not a little skepticism in some quarters—about the extent to which empirical psychological work should or can be planned and assessed in the light of computational ideas. It is not even agreed whether or not psychologists sympathetic to the computational approach should seek to express their theories in programmable (or programmed) terms, as opposed to merely bearing computational issues in mind in their work. Some AI workers even believe that doing psychological experiments is not an intellectually justifiable exercise in our present state of ignorance, arguing that we should concentrate on clarifying the range of possible computational mechanisms before trying to discover which ones are actually used by living creatures.

Correlatively, there is disagreement over the psychological relevance of specific examples of work within AI. Some of this disagreement is grounded not in detailed objections, but in broad philosophical differences over the potential psychological relevance of facts about neurophysiology or hardware.

For instance, there are two streams of work within AI vision research, each of which has spurred psychological experimentation. The theoretical emphases of these two streams are different, and, to some degree, opposed. One is focused on low-level computational mechanisms, while the other is focused on higher level, top-down processes in scene analysis. The former (especially in the work of David Marr and his group) takes account of psychological optics and neurophysiology in some detail. [Marr, 1982.] But the latter considers optics only in very general terms and ignores neurophysiology on the principled ground that physiological (hardware) implementation is theoretically independent of questions about computational mechanisms.

This last is a widely shared view in AI (in some quarters approaching the status of a dogma), and one that has caused many physiologically minded psychologists to doubt the usefulness of AI work. It is a position that is correct in principle but possibly sometimes misleading in practice. In an abstract theoretical sense, all computing devices are equivalent, just as all programming languages are. But to ignore the varying computational powers of distinct (electronic or physiological) hardware may be as stultifying in practice as to try to use a single programming language for all programs.

Differences between programming languages often matter: A computation that can be expressed easily if we use the representational potential of one language may be difficult, or even practically infeasible, if we rely on another. Clearly, further computationally informed work on neurophysiological mechanisms is needed. It may be that physiology is relevant to the relatively peripheral processing but irrelevant at higher levels, but the precise points at which we may expect physiology to have a casting vote are controversial. (Some of Marr's earlier work on the cerebellum, for instance, is now attracting interest within AI.)

If we could prove that a particular computation simply could not be carried out in real time by any existing cerebral mechanism, then the use of alien computer hardware to effect it would be psychologically irrelevant. However, our ignorance of both computational and neurophysiological constraints preempts such proofs. Nor can we prove that only mechanisms like those in our brains are capable of certain computations. The most that can be claimed as physiological support of a programmed model is that it is consonant at some significant level with neurophysiology.

This claim is made, for example, in support of a very recent advance in the computational modeling of vision. [Hinton, 1981.] G. E. Hinton's work is focused on low-level, dedicated hardware, mechanisms that are capable of cooperative computation or parallel processing. Although it is not a simulation of detailed neurophysiology, Hinton believes it to be a prime strength of his model that it is compatible with what is known about nervous function. For instance, his model relies on excitatory and inhibitory connections between computational units on various levels that appear to have an analogue in the nervous connectivity of our own visual system.

Critics of AI often complain that one program does not make a theory, any more than one swallow makes a summer. That is, AI is accused of being empirical in the sense in which much of medicine is—it achieves practical results by methods it does not understand and which it, therefore, cannot responsibly generalize. This is, indeed, a methodological shortcoming of much AI work—but not of all. Thus, Hinton's research is especially interesting because it provides not only an *example* of a program that achieves a desired result (the perception of shape), but also a *general proof* that results of this class can be computed by computational systems of this form that are within specific size constraints. In brief, he has proved that many fewer computational units are necessary for the parallel computation of shape than we might initially have supposed. This proof lends some more physiological weight to the model, since the human retina apparently has enough cells to do the job.

Because Hinton's model of vision uses a type of computation fundamentally different from that of traditional AI, it raises the question of just which psychological phenomena AI can be used to illuminate and which it cannot. Hinton's results suggest that parallel-processing systems can perform shape discriminations—such as recognition of an overall Gestalt—commonly believed (even within AI) to require relatively high-level interpretative processes. Hinton's results suggest also that the way in which an object is represented may be radically different depending on whether it is perceived as an object in its own right or as part of some larger whole. This might account for the phenomenological differences between perceptual experiences of which we are reminded by those philosophers (e.g., Dreyfus [1972]) who argue that AI is essentially unfitted to model human minds. In general, commonly expressed philosophical criticisms of AI and cognitive psychology that assume serial processing may be invalidated by these recent developments.

This would be doubly true if computational techniques of this work on vision can be generalized to other domains. Hinton believes, for example, that his computational model of spatial relations enables motor control to be understood in a new way, one that is significantly analogous to mechanisms of muscular control in the human body. Phenomenologically influenced philosophers, as well as scientists concerned with the psychophysiology of movement, commonly complain that AI does not—or even cannot—model the body. Many philosophers and psychologists argue that human intelligence is rooted in our embodiment as material beings situated in a material world and see AI as, therefore, radically irrelevant. Most current computers do not have bodies that can move in and manipulate the external world, and even robots are currently very crude in their motor abilities. But Hinton's preliminary work on motor control suggests an efficient way of computing a jointed limb's movements and pathway through space (a problem that can be solved by traditional computing techniques only in a highly inefficient manner).

Even where psychologists deliberately match experimental results against theories expressed in programmed form (e.g., the work of Newell and Simon on problem-solving), the psychological relevance of the computational model is debatable. [Newell and Simon, 1972.] It is not always clear just which aspects of a program we might plausibly expect to be open to empirical test. Some aspects are not intended to have any psychological reality but are included merely to produce a program that will run. However, we cannot be sure that none of these last have any psychological significance, since it is a prime claim of AI that it can highlight procedural lacunae in our theories and offer us new concepts with which to jump the gap. Nor is the methodology of protocol-matching unproblematic: What are we to conclude from the fact that *no* behavioral protocol is observed to match a specific process posited by the programmed theory or that some matching protocol *is* observed? These problems (which have analogous forms to trouble all experimental psychologists) have been discussed by both proponents and opponents of AI, but there is no consensus about the extent to which they cast doubt on a computational approach to empirical psychology.

Of the many people who would concede that certain aspects (at least) of vision, language-use, and problem-solving might yield to an AI approach, some may feel that social psychology, for instance, has nothing to gain from computational insights [e.g., Gauld and Shotter, 1977]; this should not be too hastily assumed, however. Work within AI on the structure of action and the attribution of intentions is relevant to theoretical discussions in social psychology. In general, AI supports the view that there may be generative rules underlying social interaction or that social perception is a structured interpretative activity. But although these ideas are essentially consonant with a computational viewpoint, specifying them in a particular case is a notoriously difficult matter.

A general account of what sorts of psychological phenomena are or are not grist for the AI mill would, of course, be very useful. But firm intellectual ground could be provided for such an account only by a systematic theory of representation. Philosophical discussions of the nature of intentionality are clearly relevant [e.g., Fodor, 1981; Dennett, 1978b]. Some philosophers [e.g., Searle, 1980] argue that AI cannot model *genuine* (biological) intentionality, although discussions in recent issues of the peer-commentary journal *Behavioral and Brain Sciences* show this claim to be highly controversial. But even John Searle admits that it can provide a scientifically useful metaphor for intentionality. This is why AI is potentially relevant to studies that are normally thought of as being humanistically oriented, such as social and clinical psychology. [Boden, 1972.] Given that representational processes in computer models can function as heuristically fruitful analogues of representational processes in our minds, the problem remains of providing an account of the range and efficacy of such processes.

Artificial intelligence has shown that distinct representational forms affect and effect inference in significantly different ways. Hinton's work previously mentioned is one of many examples that addresses such issues. Another is Saul Amarel's [1968] comparison of solutions to the "missionaries and cannibals" problem, grounded in six representations of increasing power; and a third is Aaron Sloman's [1978b] discussion of analog representations, which are interpreted by exploiting the similarity between their own structure and that of the thing represented. However, there is—as yet—little systematic understanding of the power and limitations of different representations. Work in computational logic is pertinent if it can show whether or not a certain type of representation or computational process is, in principle, capable of modeling a specific type of knowledge or simulating a given class of psychological process.

General results in the philosophy of science apply to AI-based psychology no less than to noncomputational theories. Some such results provide for a rebuttal of common criticisms of the computational viewpoint. For instance, even were it to turn out that AI is not appropriate for modeling many psychological phenomena, we should not forget the Popperian point that we would still have learnt something by the enterprise. Science involves conjecture and refutation, and it is an advance to know that a specific conjecture has been empirically rejected. Nor should we forget that some tricky methodological problems apply not only to AI-based psychology but to other theories too. Thus, critics of AI often remark—rightly—that we cannot conclude from the fact that a computer program achieves a result in a certain way that the mind achieves it in the same way. This is a special case of the general truth that if our theory fits the facts, it may not be the only one to do so. Because of this, conclusive verification of *any* scientific theory is in principle impossible.

Work in AI concerns the nature and functioning of knowledge, and we may hope for an increasing degree of cooperation between AI researchers and philosophical epistemologists. Traditional approaches to reasoning (whether deductive, inductive, or probabilistic) are overidealized. They ignore epistemologically important features of intelligent inference, features that apply to all finite minds and cannot be dismissed as mere psychologism irrelevant to normative epistemology. AI offers richer and more rigorous descriptions of various data and procedures that comprise knowledge and of the computational constraints that necessitate this rich variety.

Current AI research into the logic of nonmonotonic reasoning and truth-maintenance, for example, asks how a belief system can be organized to cope with the fact that a proposition may intelligently be proved to be true yet turn out later to be false. Traditional logicians may wince at this description, but finite minds have to construct their knowledge under this epistemic constraint. Closely related work on frames considers the ways in which single exemplars or stereotypes can be used in a flexible fashion for intelligent (though fallible) reasoning. Current discussion of naive physics examines the everyday (pretheoretical) understanding of concepts such as *cause, shape, thing, pathway, inside, fluid,* and so forth, and should help clarify traditional problems concerning concepts like these. [P. J. Hayes, 1979.]

As these examples suggest, AI calls for a closer relation between epistemology and empirical science than is usually thought proper by philosophers. Work on nonmonotonic reasoning can correctly be described as a logical enquiry and, in principle, could have arisen in a noncomputational context. In practice, however, it is AI that has enabled us to recognize the complexity of problems involved in formalizing everyday inference and has extended traditional formal approaches by offering new (computational) concepts suited to expressing epistemic matters. Developmental psychology (both Piagetian and non-Piagetian) has much to say on what might be called naive physics—as also do studies of the perceptuomotor basis of language (such as the psycholexicology of George Miller and Philip Johnson-Laird [1976]). Biological and physiological considerations are relevant in view of the sensorimotor ground of our knowledge, and there is a growing recognition of the extent to which the newborn baby is already equipped with computational structures and procedures fitted to the interpretation of its life-world. Some recent work in the philosophy of mind [Churchland, 1979] similarly argues that epistemology cannot ignore our material and biological embodiment—but it suffers from a failure to consider the computational point of view.

Thus, we need an interdisciplinary epistemology in which computational insights are integrated with philosophical understanding and psychological and biological knowledge. Indeed, the need for a genuine interdisciplinarity is a prime lesson of the computational approach. Workers in AI have much to learn from the insights of psychologists, linguists, physiologists, biologists, and philosophers, who, in turn, can benefit from their computationally informed colleagues. [Boden, 1981b.] Mere intellectual communication across the boundaries of these several disciplines is not enough. We also need mutually cooperative research by people who (albeit specializing in one area) have a familiarity with other fields and a commitment to their intellectual integration. This vision of cognitive science will require modifying current educational practices, so that students are no longer socially separated—and even intellectually opposed—by traditional academic labels.

Reference to education reminds us of the pragmatic, as opposed to the methodological, implications of AI. I have in mind here not primarily the many commercial and administrative *applications* of AI, though these will radically affect our social relations and institutions. Rather, I mean the way in which the spread of computer analogies of the mind may influence the way people think about themselves and society. As I have argued elsewhere, AI is not only not dehumanizing but—potentially—is positively rehumanizing. [Boden, 1977, chap. 15.] There are at least two senses in which this is so.

First, the view of intelligence springing from AI is active and constructive rather than passive and defeatist like that which all too commonly informs current educational (and mental-testing) practices. For example, the AI-grounded educational approach developed by Seymour Papert deliberately fosters constructive self-criticism, so that children concentrate on the specifics of how to get better at doing something rather than giving up in despair at their lack of talent. [Papert, 1980.] Again, AI-based CAI (computer assisted instruction) focuses on the pupil's active construction and exploration of the relevant domain of knowledge. [Sleeman and Brown, 1982.] In this, it differs significantly from the mechanistic approach of traditional teaching machines.

Second, because AI deals with representational systems, it has a conceptual base that can admit discussion of human subjectivity. This is why, as I remarked earlier, social and clinical psychology can make use of the computational approach. In general, this approach is consonant with humanistic or hermeneutic (interpretative) theories of psychology rather than with those psychological theories, such as behaviorism, grounded in the objective natural sciences. Correlatively, hermeneutic or intentionalist philosophies of mind are closer in spirit to AI than most of their proponents believe.

This remains true even if we accept the claim of some philosophers (e.g., Searle) already mentioned that processes in computer programs are not *really* representations and do not *really* possess intentionality but that these terms as used by the computer scientist are parasitic on their use in the human psychological context. The point is that the representational *metaphor* (for such it is, in this view) is one that is suited to express psychological phenomena (which alone are *truly* representational or intentional) precisely because it is drawn from those parts of our everyday conceptual scheme that concern these matters. For concepts to be fruitful in the theory and methodology of an empirical psychology, it is not required that they be interpreted as literal descriptions of the phenomena, just as we need not see the atom as *literally* a solar system in order to benefit from the notion of planetary electrons. So, whether computer programs specify representational processes or merely "representational" ones, they are conceptually close to hermeneutic forms of psychology rather than to those forms that ignore subjectivity.

Educational projects within society at large are needed to alert people to these facts, for most people associate computers with relatively stupid brute-force programs (such as those used to calculate gas bills) and think of them as machines and, therefore, as mechanistic. Most people fail to realize that computational machines are radically different from noncomputational machines and that they are not mechanistic in the sense that implies a denial of subjectivity. The mistaken, though widespread, assumption that AI models of human beings are mechanistic in this sense may make people experience a threat to—or even an undermining of—their personal autonomy and moral responsibility. Behaviorism in psychology and the philosophy of mind has been often, and justly, criticized for its underestimation or denial of these psychological characteristics. But the computational approach, if properly understood, is not open to such criticisms. To realize this is to disarm the computational bogeyman.

ARTIFICIAL INTELLIGENCE
Cognition as Computation

Avron Barr

The ability and compulsion to *know* are as characteristic of human nature as our physical posture and our languages. Knowledge and intelligence, as scientific concepts, are used to describe how an organism's experience seems to mediate its behavior. This paper discusses the relation between artificial intelligence (AI) research in computer science and the approaches of other disciplines that study the nature of intelligence, cognition, and mind. The state of AI after twenty-five years of work in the field is reviewed, as are the views of its practitioners about its relation to cognate disciplines. The paper concludes with a discussion of some possible effects on our scientific work of emerging commercial applications of AI technology, machines that can know and can take part in human cognitive activities.

ARTIFICIAL INTELLIGENCE

Artificial intelligence is the part of computer science concerned with creating and studying computer programs that exhibit behavioral characteristics we identify as intelligent in human behavior—knowing, reasoning, learning, problem-solving, understanding language, and so on. Since the field came into being in the mid-1950s, AI researchers have designed dozens of programs and programming techniques that support some sort of intelligent behavior. Although there are many attitudes expressed by researchers in the field, most are motivated in their work on intelligent computer programs by the thought that this work may lead to a new understanding of mind:

> AI has also embraced the larger scientific goal of constructing an information-processing theory of intelligence. If such a *science of intelligence* could be developed, it could guide the design of intelligent machines as well as explicate intelligent behavior as it occurs in humans and other animals. (Nilsson, 1980, p. 2.)

Whether or not it leads to a better understanding of the mind, there is every evidence that current work in AI will lead to a new *intelligent technology* that may have dramatic effects on our society. Already, experimental AI systems have generated interest and enthusiasm in industry and are being developed commercially. These experimental systems include programs that: solve some hard problems in chemistry, biology, geology, engineering, and medicine at human-expert levels of performance; manipulate robotic devices to perform some useful sensory-motor tasks; and answer questions posed in restricted dialects of English (or French, Japanese, etc.). Useful AI programs will play an important part in the evolution of the role of computers in our lives—a role that has changed in our lifetime from remote to commonplace and if current expectations about computing cost and power are correct, is likely to evolve further from useful to essential.

The Origins of Artificial Intelligence

> Scientific fields emerge as the concerns of scientists congeal around various phenomena. Sciences are not defined, they are recognized. (Newell, 1973*c*, p. 1.)

The intellectual currents of the times help direct scientists to the study of certain phenomena. For the evolution of AI, the two most important forces in the intellectual environment of the 1930s and 1940s were *mathematical logic,* which had been under rapid development since the end of the nineteenth century, and new ideas about *computation.* The logical systems of Frege, Whitehead and Russell, Tarski, and others showed that some aspects of reasoning could be formalized in a relatively simple framework.

> The fundamental contribution was to demonstrate by example that the manipulation of symbols (at least *some* manipulation of *some* symbols) could be described in terms of specific, concrete processes quite as readily as could the manipulation of pine boards in a carpenter shop . . . .
>
> Formal logic, if it showed nothing else, showed that ideas—at least some ideas—could be represented by symbols, and that these symbols could be altered in meaningful ways by precisely defined processes. (Newell and Simon, 1972, p. 877.)

Mathematical logic continues to be an active area of investigation in AI, in part because general-purpose, logico-deductive systems have been successfully implemented on computers. But even before the advent of computers, the mathematical formalization of logical reasoning shaped people's conception of the relation between computation and intelligence.

Ideas about the nature of computation, due to Church, Turing, and others, provided the link between the notion of formalization of reasoning and the computing machines about to be invented. What was essential in this work was the abstract conception of computation as *symbol-processing.* The first computers were numerical calculators that did not appear to embody much intelligence at all. But before these machines were even designed, Church and Turing had seen that numbers were an inessential aspect of computation—just one way of interpreting the internal states of the machine.

> In their striving to handle symbols rigorously and objectively—as objects— logicians became more and more explicit in describing the processing system that was supposed to manipulate the symbols. In 1936, Alan Turing, an English logician, described the processor, now known as the *Turing machine,* that is regarded as the culmination of this drive toward formalization. (Newell and Simon, 1972, p. 878.)

> The model of a Turing machine contains within it the notions both of what can be computed and of universal machines—computers that can do anything that can be done by any machine. (Newell and Simon, 1976a, p. 117.)

Turing, who has been called the father of AI, not only invented a simple, universal, and nonnumerical model of computation, but also argued directly for the possibility that computational mechanisms could behave in a way that would be perceived as intelligent.

> Thought was still wholly intangible and ineffable until modern formal logic interpreted it as the manipulation of formal tokens. And it seemed still to inhabit mainly the heaven of Platonic ideals, or the equally obscure spaces of the human mind, until computers taught us how symbols could be processed by machines. A.M. Turing . . . made his great contributions at the mid-century crossroads of these developments that led from modern logic to the computer. (Newell and Simon, 1976a, p. 125.)

As Allen Newell and Herbert Simon point out in the "Historical Epilogue" to their classic work *Human Problem Solving,* there were other strong intellectual currents from several directions that converged in the middle of this century in the people who founded the science of artificial intelligence. [Newell and Simon, 1972.] The concepts of cybernetics and self-organizing systems of Wiener, McCulloch, and others dealt with the macroscopic behavior of locally simple systems. The cyberneticists influenced many fields, because their thinking spanned many fields, linking ideas about the workings of the nervous system with information theory and control theory as well as with logic and computation. Their ideas were part of the Zeitgeist, but, in many cases, the cyberneticists influenced early workers in AI more directly—as their teachers.

What eventually connected these diverse ideas was, of course, the development of computing machines themselves, conceived by Babbage and guided in this century by Turing, von Neumann, and others. It was not long after the machines became available that people began to try to write programs to solve puzzles, play chess, and translate texts from one language to another—the first AI programs. What was it about computers that triggered the development of AI? Many ideas about computing relevant to AI emerged in early designs—ideas about memories and processors, systems and control, and levels of languages and programs. But the single attribute of the new machines that brought about the emergence of the new science was their inherent potential for *complexity,* encouraging (in several fields) the development of new and more direct ways of describing complex processes—in terms of complicated data structures and procedures with hundreds of different steps.

> Problem solving behaviors, even in the relatively well-structured task environments that we have used in our research, have generally been regarded as highly complex forms of human behavior—so complex that for a whole generation they were usually avoided in the psychological laboratory in favor of behaviors that seemed to be simple . . . .
>
> The appearance of the modern computer at the end of World War II gave us and other researchers the courage to return to complex cognitive performances as our source of data. . . . a device capable of symbol-manipulating behavior at levels of complexity and generality unprecedented for man-made mechanisms.
>
> This was part of the general insight of cybernetics, delayed by ten years and applied to discrete symbolic behavior rather than to continuous feedback systems. (Newell and Simon, 1972, pp. 869–870.)

Computers, Complexity, and Intelligence

As Pamela McCorduck notes in her entertaining historical study of AI, *Machines Who Think,* there has been a long-standing connection between the idea of complex mechanical devices and intelligence. [McCorduck, 1979.] Starting with the fabulously intricate clocks and mechanical automata of past centuries, people have made an intuitive link between the *complexity* of a machine's operation and some aspects of their own mental life. Over the last few centuries, new technologies have resulted in a dramatic increase in the complexity we can achieve in the things we build. Modern computer systems are more complex by several orders of magnitude than anything man has built before.

The first work on computers in this century focused on the kinds of numerical computations that had previously been performed collaboratively by teams of hundreds of clerks, organized so that each did one small subcalculation and passed his or her results on to the clerk at the next desk. Not long after the dramatic success demonstrated by the first digital computers with these elaborate calculations, people began to explore the possibility of more generally intelligent mechanical behavior—could machines play chess, prove theorems, or translate languages? They could, but not very well. The computer performs its calculations following the step-by-step instructions it is given—the method must be specified *in complete detail.* Most computer scientists are concerned with designing new algorithms, new languages, and new machines for performing tasks like solving equations and alphabetizing lists—tasks that people perform using methods they can explicate. However, people cannot specify in detail how they decide which move to make in a game of chess or how they determine that two sentences mean the same thing.

The realization that the detailed steps of almost all intelligent human activity were unknown marked the beginning of artificial intelligence as a separate part of computer science. AI researchers investigate different types of computation, and different ways of describing computation, in an effort not just to create intelligent artifacts, but also to understand what intelligence is. A basic tenet is that human intellectual capacity will best be described in the same terms as those invented to describe artificial intelligence researchers' programs. However, researchers are just beginning to learn enough about those programs to know how to describe them scientifically— in terms of concepts that illuminate the program's nature and differentiate among fundamental categories. These ideas about computation have been developed in programs that perform many different tasks, sometimes at the level of human performance, often at a much lower level. Most of these methods are obviously not the same as those people use to perform the tasks—some of them might be.

The Status of Artificial Intelligence

Many intelligent activities besides numerical calculation and information retrieval have been accomplished by programs. Many key aspects of thought—like recognizing people's faces and reasoning by analogy—are still puzzles; they are performed so unconsciously by people that adequate computational mechanisms have not been postulated. Some of the successes, as well as some of the failures, have come as surprises. I will list here some of the aspects of intelligence investigated in AI research and try to give an indication of the state of progress.

There is an important philosophical point here that will be sidestepped: Doing arithmetic or learning the capitals of all the countries of the world, for example, are certainly activities that *indicate* intelligence in humans. The issue here is whether a computer system that can perform these tasks can be said to *know* or *understand* anything. This point has been discussed at length [e.g., Searle, 1980 and appended commentaries] and will be avoided here by describing the *behaviors* themselves as intelligent without commitment on how to describe the machines that produce them.

Problem Solving

The first big successes in AI were programs that could solve puzzles and play games like chess. Techniques, such as looking ahead several moves and

dividing difficult problems into easier subproblems, evolved into the fundamental AI techniques of *search* and *problem reduction*. Today's programs
play championship-level checkers and backgammon, as well as very good
chess. Another problem-solving program that performs symbolic evaluation
of mathematical functions has attained very high levels of performance and
is being widely used by scientists and engineers. Some programs can even
improve their own performance with experience.

As discussed in the following sections, the open questions in this area
involve capabilities that human players exhibit but cannot articulate, such as
the chess master's ability to see the board configuration in terms of meaningful patterns. Another basic open question involves the original conceptualization of a problem, called in AI the choice of problem representation.
Humans often solve a problem by finding a way of thinking about it that
makes the solution easy; AI programs, so far, must be told how to think
about the problems they solve (i.e., the space in which to search for the
solution).

Logical Reasoning

Closely related to problem- and puzzle-solving was early work on logical
deduction. Programs were developed that could prove assertions by manipulating a database of facts, each represented by discrete data-structures just
as they are represented by formulas in mathematical logic. These methods,
unlike many other AI techniques, could be shown to be complete and consistent. That is, given a set of facts, the programs theoretically could prove all
theorems that followed from the facts, and only those theorems. Logical
reasoning has been one of the subareas most persistently investigated in AI
research. Of particular interest are the problems of finding ways of focusing
on only the relevant facts in a large database and of keeping track of
justifications for beliefs and updating them when new information arrives.

Programming

Although perhaps not an obviously important aspect of human cognition,
programming itself is an important area of research in AI. Work in this field,
called *automatic programming,* has investigated systems that can write
computer programs from a variety of descriptions of their purpose: examples of input/output pairs, high-level language descriptions, and even English descriptions of algorithms. Progress has been limited to a few fully
worked-out examples. Automatic-programming research may result not only
in semiautomated systems for software development, but also in AI programs that learn (i.e., modify their behavior) by modifying their own code.
Related work in the theory of programs is fundamental to all AI research.

Language

The domain of language-understanding was also investigated by early AI researchers and has consistently attracted interest. Programs have been written that retrieve information from a database in response to questions posed in English, translate sentences from one language to another, follow instructions or paraphrase statements given in English, and acquire knowledge by reading textual material and building an internal database. Some programs have even achieved limited success in interpreting instructions that are spoken into a microphone rather than typed into a computer. Although these language systems are not nearly so good as people are at any of these tasks, they are adequate for some applications. Early successes with programs that answered simple queries and followed simple directions, and early failures at machine-translation attempts, have resulted in a sweeping change in the whole AI approach to language. The principal themes of current language-understanding research are the importance of vast amounts of *knowledge* about the subject being discussed and the role of *expectations,* based on the subject matter and the conversational situation, in interpreting sentences. The state of the art of practical language programs is represented by useful "front ends" to a variety of software systems. These programs accept input in some restricted form—they cannot handle some of the nuances of English grammar and are useful for interpreting sentences only within a relatively limited domain of discourse. Although there has been very limited success in translating AI results in language- and speech-understanding programs into ideas about the nature of human language *processing,* the realization of the importance in language-understanding of extensive background knowledge and the contextual setting and intentions of the speakers has changed our notion of what language or a theory of language might be.

Learning

Certainly one of the most salient and important aspects of human intelligence is our ability to learn. However, this is an example of cognitive behavior that is so poorly understood that very little progress has been made in achieving it in AI systems. Although there have been several interesting attempts, including programs that learn from examples, from their own performance, or from advice from others, AI systems do not exhibit noticeable learning ability.

Robotics and Vision

One area of AI research that is receiving increasing attention involves programs that manipulate robot devices. Research in this field has looked at everything from the optimal movement of robot arms to methods of planning a sequence of actions to achieve a robot's goals. Some robots "see" through a television camera that transmits an array of information back to the computer. Processing visual information is another very active, and very difficult, area of AI research. Programs have been developed that can recognize objects and shadows in visual scenes and even identify small changes from one picture to the next, for example, for aerial reconnaissance. The true potential of this research, however, is that it deals with *artificial* intelligences in perceived and manipulable environments similar to our own.

Systems and Languages

In addition to work directly aimed at achieving intelligence, the development of new tools has always been an important aspect of AI research. Some of the most important contributions of AI to the world of computing have been in the form of spin-offs. Computer-systems ideas like timesharing, list processing, and interactive debugging were developed in the AI research environment. Specialized programming languages and systems, with features designed to facilitate deduction, robot manipulation, cognitive modeling, and so on, have often been rich sources of new ideas. Most recent among these has been the plethora of knowledge-representation languages. These are computer languages for encoding knowledge and reasoning-methods as data structures and procedures, developed over the last five years to explore a variety of ideas about how to build reasoning programs. Terry Winograd's article, "Beyond Programming Languages," discusses some of his ideas about the future of computing, inspired in part by his research on AI. [Winograd, 1979.]

Expert Systems

Finally, the area of expert or knowledge-based systems has recently emerged as a likely area for useful applications of AI techniques. [Feigenbaum, 1977.] Typically, the user interacts with an expert system in a "consultation dialogue," just as he would interact with a human expert in a particular area: explaining his problem, performing suggested tests, and asking questions about proposed solutions. Current experimental systems have achieved high levels of performance in consultation tasks like chemical and geological data-analysis, computer-system configuration, completing income tax forms, and even medical diagnosis. Expert systems can be viewed as intermediaries between human experts who interact with the systems in *knowledge acquisition* mode and human users who interact with the systems in *consultation* mode. Furthermore, much research in this area of AI has focused on endowing these systems with the ability to explain their reasoning, both to make the consultation more acceptable to the user and to help the human expert locate the cause of errors in the system's reasoning when they occur.

Because I am most familiar with this area of AI research, and because its imminent commercial applications are, I feel, indicative of important changes in the field, much of the ensuing discussion of the role of AI in the study of mind will refer to expert-systems research. The fact that these systems represent vast amounts of knowledge obtained from *human* experts; are used as *tools* to solve hard problems using this knowledge; can be viewed as *intermediaries* between human problem-solvers; must *explain* their thought processes in terms that people can understand; and are worth a lot of *money* to people with real problems are the essential points that, I will argue, will be true of all of AI someday—in fact, of computers in general—and will change the role that AI research plays in the scientific study of thought.

Open Problems

Although there has been much activity and progress in the twenty-five year history of AI, some very central aspects of cognition have not yet been achieved by computer programs. Our abilities to reason about others' beliefs; know the limits of our knowledge; visualize; be reminded of relevant events; learn; reason by analogy; make plausible inferences; realize when they are wrong, and know how to recover are not at all understood.

It is a fact that these and many other *fundamental* cognitive capabilities may remain problematic for some time. But it is also a fact that computer programs have successfully achieved a level of performance on a range of intelligent behaviors unmatched by anything other than the human brain. The failure of AI to achieve some seemingly simple cognitive capabilities in computer programs becomes, according to the view of AI presented in this paper, part of the set of phenomena to be explained by the new science.

ARTIFICIAL INTELLIGENCE AND THE STUDY OF MIND

Artificial intelligence research in problem-solving, language processing, and so forth, has produced some impressive and useful computer systems; it has also influenced, and been influenced by, research in many fields. What, then, is the relation between AI and other disciplines that study the various aspects of mind, for example, psychology, linguistics, philosophy, and sociology?

AI certainly has a unique method—designing and testing computer programs—and a unique goal—making those programs seem intelligent. It has been argued from time to time that these attributes make AI independent of other disciplines: "Artificial intelligence was an attempt to build intelligent machines without any prejudice toward making the system simple, biological, or humanoid." (Minsky, 1963, p. 409.) But we do not start from scratch in building the first program to accomplish some intelligent behavior; the ideas about how that program is to work must come from somewhere. Furthermore, most AI researchers *are* interested in understanding the human mind and actively seek hints about its nature in their experiments with their programs.

The interest within AI in results and open problems of other disciplines has been fully reciprocated by interest in and application of AI research activity among researchers in other fields. Many experimental and theoretical insights in psychology and linguistics, at least, have been sparked by AI techniques and results. Furthermore, I argue later on, this flow is likely to increase dramatically in the future; its source is the variety of new phenomena displayed by AI systems—the number, quality, utility, and level of activity of which will soon greatly increase. But first let us examine what kind of interactions have taken place between AI and other disciplines in the last 25 years.

The Language of Computation

As I defined it at the outset, AI is a branch of computer science. Its practitioners are trained in the various subfields of computer science: formal computing theory, algorithm design, hardware and operating-systems architecture, programming-languages, and programming. The study of each of these subareas has produced a language of its own, indicating our understanding of the important known *phenomena* of computing. The underlying assumption of our research is that this language (which involves concepts like process, procedure, interpreter, bottom-up and top-down processing, object-oriented programming, trigger, etc.), and the experience with computation that it embodies, will, in turn, assist us in understanding the phenomena of mind.

Before I go on to discuss the utility of these computational concepts, it should be stated that, in fact, our understanding of computation is quite limited. John von Neumann dreamed of an information theory of the nature of thinking:

> . . . that body of experience which has grown up around the planning, evaluating, and coding of complicated logical and mathematical automata will be the focus of much of this information theory. . . .

> it would be very satisfactory if one could talk about a "theory" of such automata. Regrettably, what at this moment exists—and to what I must appeal—can as yet be described only as an imperfectly articulated and hardly formalized "body of experience." (von Neumann, 1958, p. 2.)

And ten years later, in their superb treatise on perceptronlike automata, Minsky and Papert lament:

> We know shamefully little about our computers and their computations . . . . We know very little, for instance, about how much computation a job should require . . . .
>
> The immaturity shown by our inability to answer questions of this kind is exhibited even in the language used to formulate the questions. Word pairs such as "parallel" vs. "serial," "local" vs. "global," and "digital" vs. "analog" are used as if they referred to well-defined technical concepts. Even when this is true, the technical meaning varies from user to user and context to context. But usually they are treated so loosely that the species of computing machine defined by them belongs to mythology rather than science. (Minsky and Papert, 1969, pp. 1–2.)

There is still no adequate theory of computation for understanding the nature and scope of symbolic processes, but there is rapidly accumulating experience with computation of all sorts—useful new concepts continually emerge.

The Computational Metaphor

The discipline most closely related to AI is cognitive psychology. Both deal primarily with the same kinds of behavior—perception, memory, problem-solving—and they are siblings. Modern cognitive psychology emerged from its behavior-oriented precursors in conjunction with the rise of AI. That there might be a relation between the new field of AI and traditional interests of psychologists was evident from the beginning:

> Our fundamental concern . . . was to discover whether the cybernetic ideas have any relevance for psychology. The men who have pioneered in this area have been remarkably innocent about psychology . . . . There must be some way to phrase the new ideas so that they can contribute to and profit from the science of behavior that psychologists have created. (Miller, Galanter, and Pribram, 1960, p. 3.)

What in fact happened was that the existence of computing served as an inspiration to traditional psychologists to begin to theorize in terms of internal, cognitive mechanisms. Using the concepts of computation as metaphors for processes of the mind strongly influenced the form of modern theories of cognitive psychology—for example, theories expressed in terms of memories and retrieval processes.

> Computers accept information, manipulate symbols, store items in "memory" and retrieve them again, classify inputs, recognize patterns, and so on. Whether they do these things just like people was less important than that they

do them at all. The coming of the computer provided a much-needed reassurance that cognitive processes were real. (Neisser, 1976, p. 5.)

The metaphorical use of the language of computation in describing mental processes was found to be, at least for a time, quite a fertile ground for sprouting psychological theories:

During a period of concept formation, we must be well aware of the metaphorical nature of our concepts. However, during a period in which the concepts can accommodate most of our questions about a given subject matter, we can afford to ignore their metaphorical origins and confuse our description of reality with that reality. (Arbib, 1972, p. 11.)

When pioneering work by Newell, Shaw, and Simon, and other research groups showed that "programming up" their intuitions about how humans solve puzzles, find theorems, and so forth, was adequate for getting impressive results, the link between the study of human problem-solving and AI research was firmly established.

Consider, for example, computer programs that play chess. Current programs are quite proficient—the best experimental systems play at the human expert level, but not so well as human chess masters. The programs work by searching through a space of possible moves, that is, considering alternative moves and their consequences several steps ahead in the game, just as human players do. These programs, even some of the earliest versions, could search through thousands of moves in the time it takes human players to consider only a dozen or so alternatives. The theory of optimal search, developed as a mathematical formalism (paralleling, as a matter of fact, much work on optimal decision theory in operations research), constitutes some of the core ideas of AI.

The reason that computers cannot beat the best human players is that looking ahead is not all there is to chess. Since there are too many possible moves to search exhaustively, even on the fastest imaginable computers, alternative moves (board positions) must be evaluated without knowing for sure which move will lead to a winning game, and this is one of those abilities that human chess experts cannot make explicit. Psychological studies have shown that chess masters have learned to see thousands of meaningful configurations of pieces when they look at chess positions, which presumably helps them decide on the best move, but no one has yet suggested how to design a computer program that can identify these configurations.

Due to the lack of theory or intuition about human perception and learning, AI progress on computer chess was virtually stopped, but it is quite possible that new insights into a very general problem were gained. The computer programs had pointed out more clearly than ever what kinds of things it would be useful for a cognitive system to learn to see. It takes many years for a chess expert to develop expertise, ability to understand the game in terms of these concepts and patterns that he or she cannot explain easily, if at all. The general problem is of course to determine what it is about our experience that we apply to future problem-solving: What kind of *knowledge* do we glean from our experience? The work on chess indicated some of the demands that would be placed on this knowledge.

Language Translation and Linguistics

Ideas about getting computers to deal in some useful way with the human languages, called natural languages by computer scientists, were conceived before any machines were ever built. The first line of attack was to try to use large bilingual dictionaries stored in the computers to translate sentences from one language to another. [Barr and Feigenbaum, 1981, vol. 1, pp. 233–238.] The machine would just look up the translation(s) of each word in the original sentence, figure out its meaning (perhaps expressed in some *interlingua*), translate the words, and produce a syntactically correct version in the target language.

It did not work. It became apparent early on that processing language in any useful way involved understanding, which, in turn, involved a great deal of knowledge about the world—in fact, it could be argued that the more we know, the more we understand each sentence we read. And the level of world knowledge needed for any useful language-processing is much higher than our original intuitions led us to expect.

There has been a serious debate about whether AI work in computational linguistics has enlightened us at all about the nature of language. [See Dresher and Hornstein, 1976; and replies by Winograd, 1977; Schank and Wilensky, 1977.] The position taken by AI researchers is that if our goal in linguistics is to include understanding sentences like *Do you have the time?* and *We'll have dinner after the kids wash their hands,* which involve the total relationship between the speakers, then there is much more to it than the syntactic arrangement of words with well-defined meanings; that although the study in linguistics of systematic regularities within and between natural languages is an important key to the nature of language and the workings of the mind, it is only a small part of the problem of building a useful language processor and, therefore, only a small part of an adequate understanding of language.

> For both people and machines, each in their own way, there is a serious problem in common of making sense out of what they hear, see, or are told about the world. The conceptual apparatus necessary to perform even a partial feat of understanding is formidable and fascinating. (Schank and Abelson, 1977, p. 2.)

> Linguists have almost totally ignored the question of how human understanding works. . . . It has nevertheless been consistently regarded as important that

computers deal well with natural language. . . . None of these high-sounding things are possible, of course, unless the computer really "understands" the input. And that is the theoretical significance of these practical questions—to solve them requires no less than articulating the detailed nature of "understanding." If we understood how a human understands, then we might know how to make a computer understand, and vice versa. (Ibid., p. 8.)

This idea that building AI systems requires the articulation of the detailed nature of understanding, that is, that implementing a theory in a computer program requires us to work out our fuzzy ideas and concepts, has been suggested as a major contribution of AI research.

Whenever an AI researcher feels he understands the process he is theorizing about in enough detail, he then begins to program it to find out where he was incomplete or wrong. . . . The time between the completion of the theory and the completion of the program that embodies the theory is usually extremely long. (Ibid., p. 20.)

And Newell, in a thorough discussion of eight possible ways we might view the relation of AI to psychology, suggests that building programs "forces psychologists to become operational, that is, to avoid the fuzziness of using mentalistic terms." (Newell, 1970, p. 365.)

Certainly the original conception of the machine-translation effort, although it seemed intuitively sensible, fell far short of what would be required to enable a machine to handle language, indicating a limited conception of what language is. It is in the broadening of this conception that AI has contributed most to the study of language. [Schank and Abelson, 1977, p. 9.] Thus, AI can show, as illustrated in the examples of chess and language understanding, that intuitive notions and assumptions about mental processes just do not work. Furthermore, analyzing the behavior of AI programs implemented on the basis of existing, inadequate concepts can offer hints on how the concepts of the theory affect its performance and on why the theories do not work.

Scientific Languages and Theory Formation

Laurence Miller, in an article that reviews the dialogue between psychologists and AI researchers about the contribution of AI to the understanding of mind, concludes that

the critics of AI believe that it is easy to construct plausible psychological theories; the difficult task is demonstrating that these theories are true. The advocates of AI believe that it is difficult to construct adequate psychological theories; but once such a theory has been constructed, it may be relatively simple to demonstrate that it is true. (L. Miller, 1978, p. 113.)

And Schank and Abelson agree:

> We are not oriented toward finding out which pieces of our theory are
> quantifiable and testable in isolation. We feel that such questions can wait.
> First we need to know if we have a viable theory . . . . (Schank and Abelson,
> 1977, p. 21.)

Just as AI must consider the same issues that are addressed in psychology
and linguistics, other aspects of knowledge, dealt with by other traditional
disciplines, must be considered. For example, current ideas in AI about
linking computing machines together into coherent systems or cooperative
problem-solvers forces us to consider the sociological aspects of knowing. A
fundamental problem in AI is communication among many individual units,
each of which knows some things relevant to some problems as well as
something about the other units. The form of communication between units,
the organizational structure of the complex, and the nature of the individuals' knowledge of each other are all questions that must find some engineering solution if the apparent power of distributed processing is to be realized.

These issues have been studied in other disciplines, albeit from very
different perspectives and with different goals and methods. We can view
the different control schemes proposed for interprocess communication, for
example, as attempts to design *social systems* of knowledgeable entities.
Our intuitions, once again, form the specifications for the first systems. Reid
G. Smith has proposed a *contract net* where individual entities *negotiate*
their role in attacking the problem via requests for assistance from other
processors, proposals for help in reply, and contracts indicating agreement
to delegate part of the problem to another processor; and W. Kornfeld and
Carl Hewitt have developed a model explicitly based on problem-solving in
the scientific community. [R. G. Smith, 1978; Kornfeld and Hewitt, 1981.]
Only after we have been able to build many systems based on such models
will we be able to identify key factors in the design of such systems.

There is another kind of study of the mind, conducted by scientists who
seek to understand the workings of the brain. The brain is a "mechanism"
that has been associated with computing machines since their invention, and
that has puzzled computer scientists greatly:

> We know the basic active organs of the nervous system (the nerve cells). There
> is every reason to believe that a very large-capacity memory is associated with
> this system. We do most emphatically *not* know what type of physical entities
> are the basic components for the memory in question. (von Neumann, 1958,
> p. 68.)

If research on AI generates a language for describing what a computational
system is doing, in terms of processes, memories, messages, and so forth,
then that language may very well be the one in which the function of the

neural mechanisms should be described. [Lenat, 1981; Torda, 1982.] And, as Herbert Simon points out, this functionality may be shared by nature's other brand of computing device, DNA:

> It might have been necessary a decade ago to argue for the commonality of the information processes that are employed by such disparate systems as computers and human nervous systems. The evidence for that commonality is now overwhelming, and the remaining questions about the boundaries of cognitive science have more to do with whether there also exist nontrivial commonalities with information processing in genetic systems than with whether men and machines both think. (Simon, 1980, p. 45.)

One more example of the overlap of concerns between AI and related disciplines: Enabling an individual to know something about what another knows, without actually knowing it, involves defining the nature of what is known elsewhere—who are the experts on what kinds of problems and what might they know that could be useful. This is related directly to the kind of categorization of knowledge that is the essence of library science. But instead of dealing with categories in which static books will be filed, AI must consider the dynamic aspects of systems that know and learn.

The relation, then, between AI and disciplines like psychology, linguistics, sociology, brain science, and library science is a complex one. Certainly, our current understanding of the phenomena dealt with by these disciplines—cognition, perception, memory, language, social systems, and categories of knowledge—has provided intuitions and models on which the first AI programs were built. And, as has happened in psychology and linguistics, these first systems may, in turn, show us new aspects of the phenomena that we have not considered in studying their natural occurrence. But most importantly, the development of AI systems, of useful computer tools for knowledge-oriented tasks, will expose us to many new phenomena and variations that will force us to increase our understanding.

THE PRACTICE OF ARTIFICIAL INTELLIGENCE

Artificial intelligence and computer science in general employ a unique method among disciplines involved in advancing our understanding of cognition—building computers and programs and observing and trying to explain patterns in the behavior of these systems. Programs are the phenomena to be studied:

> Conceptual advances occur by (scientifically) uncontrolled experiments in our own style of computing . . . the solution lies in more practice and more attention to what emerges there as pragmatically successful. (Newell, 1981, p. 4.)

Observing our own practice—that is, seeing what the computer implicitly tells us about the nature of intelligence as we struggle to synthesize intelligent systems—is a fundamental source of scientific knowledge for us. (Ibid., p. 19.)

Thus, AI is one of the "sciences of the artificial," as Herbert Simon has defined them in an influential paper—half of the job is designing systems so that their performance will be interesting. [Simon, 1969 and 1981.] There is a valuable heuristic in generating these designs: The systems that we are naturally inclined to want to build are those that will be useful in our environment. Our environment will shape them, as it shaped us. As Simon described the development of time-sharing systems:

Most actual designs have turned out initially to exhibit serious deficiencies, and most predictions of performance have been startlingly inaccurate.

Under these circumstances, the main route open to the development and improvement of time-sharing systems is to build them and see how they behave. (Ibid., p. 21.)

Genus Symbol Manipulators

Newell and Simon's psychologically phrased idea of observing the behavior of programs follows from their twenty-five-year research program in what they have named "information processing psychology." Newell and Simon developed, in the early years of this enterprise, some of the first computer programs that showed reasoning capabilities. This research on chess-playing, theorem-proving, and problem-solving programs was undertaken as an explicit attempt to model corresponding human behaviors. But Newell and Simon took the strong position that these programs were not to serve simply as metaphors for human thought, but were themselves theories. In fact, they argued that programs were the natural vehicle for expressing theories in psychology.

An abstract concept of an information processing system has emerged with the development of the digital computers. In fact, a whole array of different abstract concepts has developed, as scientists have sought to capture the essence of the new technology in different ways. . . .

With a model of an information processing system, it becomes meaningful to try to represent in some detail a particular man at work on a particular task. Such a representation is not metaphor, but a precise symbolic model on the basis of which pertinent specific aspects of the man's problem solving behavior can be calculated. (Newell and Simon, 1972, p. 5.)

Taking the view that artificial intelligence is theoretical psychology, simulation (the running of a program purporting to represent some human behavior) is simply the calculation of the consequences of a psychological theory. (Newell, 1973c, p. 47.)

. . . a framework comprehensive enough to encourage and permit thinking is offered, so that not only answers, but questions, criteria of evidence, and relevance all become affected. (Ibid., p. 59.)

Newell and Simon, in their view that computer programs are a vehicle for expressing psychological theories rather than just serving as a metaphor for mental processes, were already taking a strong position relative to even the new breed of cognitive psychologists who were talking in terms of computerlike mental mechanisms. As Paul R. Cohen puts it, in his review of AI work on models of cognition:

We should note that we have presented the strongest version of the information-processing approach, that advocated by Newell and Simon. Their position is so strong that it defines information-processing psychology almost by exclusion: It is the field that uses methods alien to cognitive psychology to explore questions alien to AI. This is an exaggeration, but it serves to illustrate why there are thousands of cognitive psychologists, and hundreds of AI researchers, and very few information-processing psychologists. (Cohen, 1982, p. 7.)

However, Newell and Simon did not stop there. A further development in their thinking identified brains and computers as two species of *physical symbol system*—the type of system which, they argue, *must* underlie any intelligent behavior.

At the root of intelligence are symbols, with their denotative power and their susceptibility to manipulation. And symbols can be manufactured of almost anything that can be arranged and patterned and combined. Intelligence is mind implemented by any patternable kind of matter. (Simon,1980, p. 35.)

A physical symbol system has the necessary and sufficient means for general intelligent action. (Newell and Simon, 1976a, p. 116.)

Information processing psychology is concerned essentially with whether a successful theory of human behavior can be found within the domain of symbolic systems. (Newell, 1970, p. 372.)

The basic point of view inhabiting our work has been that programmed computer and human problem solver are both species belonging to the genus IPS. (Newell and Simon, 1972, p. 869.)

It is this view of computers—as systems that share a common, underlying structure with the human intelligence system—that promotes the behavioral view of AI computer research. Although these machines are not limited by the rules of development of their natural counterpart, they will be shaped in their development by the same natural *constraints* responsible for the form of intelligence in nature.

The Flight Metaphor

The question whether machines could think was certainly an issue in the early days of AI research, although dismissed rather summarily by those who shaped the emerging science:

> To ask whether these computers can think is ambiguous. In the naive realistic sense of the term, it is people who think, and not either brains or machines. If, however, we permit ourselves the ellipsis of referring to the operations of the brain as "thinking," then, of course, our computers "think" . . . . (McCulloch, 1965, p. 368.)

Addressing fundamental issues like this one in their early writing, several researchers suggested a parallel with the study of flight, considering cognition as another natural phenomenon that could eventually be achieved by machines.

> Today, despite our ignorance, we can point to that biological milestone, the thinking brain, in the same spirit as the scientists many hundreds of years ago pointed to the bird as a demonstration in nature that mechanisms heavier than air could fly. (Feigenbaum and Feldman, 1963, p. 8.)

It is instructive to pursue this analogy a bit farther. Flight, as a way of dealing with the contingencies of the environment, takes many forms—from soaring eagles to hovering hummingbirds. If we start to study flight by examining its forms in nature, our initial understanding of what we are studying might involve terms like feathers, wings, weight-to-wing-size ratios, and probably wing-flapping, too. This is the *language* we begin to develop—identifying regularities and making distinctions among the phenomena. But when we start to build flying artifacts, our understanding changes immediately.

> Consider how people came to understand how birds fly. Certainly we observed birds. But mainly to recognize certain phenomena. Real understanding of *bird flight* came from understanding *flight;* not birds. (Papert, 1972, pp. 1–2.)

Even if we fail a hundred times at building a machine that flies by flapping its wings, we learn from every attempt. And eventually, we abandon some of the assumptions implicit in our definition of the phenomena under study and realize that flight does not require wing movement or even wings.

> Intelligent behavior on the part of a machine no more implies complete functional equivalence between machine and brain than flying by an airplane implies complete functional equivalence between plane and bird. (Armer, 1963, p. 392.)

Every new design brings new data about what works, what does not, and clues as to why. Every new contraption tries some different design alternative in the space defined by our theory-language. And every attempt clarifies our understanding of what it means to fly.

But there is more to the sciences of the artificial than defining the true nature of natural phenomena. The exploration of the artifacts themselves, the stiff-winged flying machines, because they are useful to society, will naturally extend the exploration of various points of interface between the technology and society. While nature's exploration of the possibilities is limited by its mutation mechanism, human inventors will vary every parameter they can think of to produce effects that might be useful—exploring constraints on the design of their machines from every angle. The space of "flight" phenomena will be populated by examples that nature has not had a chance to try.

Exploring the Space of Cognitive Phenomena

This argument, that the utility of intelligent machines will drive the exploration of their capabilities, suggests that the development of AI technology has begun an exploration of cognitive phenomena that will involve aspects of cognition that are not easy to study in nature. In fact, as with the study of flight, AI will enable us to see natural intelligence as a limited capability, in terms of design tradeoffs made in the evolution of biological cognition.

> Computer science is an empirical discipline. . . . Each new machine that is built is an experiment. . . . Each new program that is built is an experiment. It poses a question to nature, and its behavior offers clues to an answer. . . .
>
> We build computers and programs for many reasons. We build them to serve society and as tools for carrying out the economic tasks of society. But as basic scientists we build machines and programs as a way of discovering new phenomena and analyzing phenomena we already know about. . . . the phenomena surrounding computers are deep and obscure, requiring much experimentation to assess their nature. (Newell and Simon, 1976a, p. 114.)

For what will AI systems be useful? How will they be involved in the economic tasks of society? It has certainly been argued that this point is one that distinguishes biological systems from machines:

> The human is a physical symbol system, yes, with a component of pure cognition describable by mechanisms. . . . But the human is more: The human is an animate organism, with a biological basis and an evolutionary and cultural history. Moreover, the human is a social animal, interacting with others, with the environment, and with itself. The core disciplines of cognitive science have tended to ignore these aspects of behavior . . . . (Norman, 1980, pp. 3–4.)

The difference between natural and artificial devices is not simply that they are constructed of different stuff; their basic functions differ. Humans survive . . . . (Ibid., p. 10.)

Tools evolve and survive based on their utility to the people who use them. Either the users find better tools, or their competitors find them. This process will certainly continue with the development of cognitive tools and will dramatically change the way we think about AI.

We measure the intelligence of a system by its ability to achieve stated ends in the face of variations, difficulties and complexities posed by the task environment. This general investment of computer science in attaining intelligence . . . becomes more obvious as we extend computers to more global complex and knowledge-intensive tasks—as we attempt to make them our agents, capable of handling on their own the full contingencies of the natural world. (Newell and Simon, 1976a, pp. 114–115.)

In fact, this change has already begun in AI laboratories, but the place where the changing perception of AI systems is most dramatic and accelerated is, not surprisingly in our society, the marketplace.

AI, INC.

To date, three of the emerging AI technologies have attracted interest as commercial possibilities: robots for manufacturing, natural-language front-ends for information-retrieval systems, and expert systems. The reason that a company like General Motors invests millions of dollars in robots for the assembly line is not scientific curiosity or propaganda about "retooling" their industry. General Motors believes these robots are essential to its economic survival. AI technology will surely change many aspects of American industry, but its application to real problems will just as surely change emerging technology—change our perception of its nature and its implications about knowledge. The remaining discussion focuses on this issue in the context of expert systems.

Expert Systems

With work on the DENDRAL system in the mid-1960s, AI researchers began pushing work on *problem-solving* systems beyond constrained domains like chess, robot planning, blocks-world manipulations, and puzzles: They started to consider symbolically expressed problems that were known to be difficult for the best human researchers to solve. [Lindsay, Buchanan, Feigenbaum, and Lederberg, 1980.]

One needs to move toward task environments of greater complexity and open-ness—to everyday reasoning, to scientific discovery, and so on. The tasks we tackled, though highly complex by prior psychological standards, still are sim-ple in many respects. (Newell and Simon, 1972, p. 872.)

Humans have difficulty keeping track of all the knowledge that might be relevant to a problem, exploring all alternative solution-paths, and making sure none of the valid solutions is overlooked in the process. Work on DENDRAL showed that when the human expert could explain exactly what he or she was doing in solving problems, the machine could achieve expert-level performance.

Continued research at Stanford's Heuristic Programming Project next produced the MYCIN system, an experiment in modeling medical diagnostic reasoning. [Shortliffe, 1976.] In production rules of the form *if ⟨condition⟩ then ⟨action⟩*, Shortliffe encoded the kind of information about their rea-soning process that physicians were most able to give—advice about what to do in certain situations. In other words, the *if* parts of the rules contain clauses that attempt to differentiate a certain situation, and the *then* part describes what to do if we find ourselves in that situation. This production-rule knowledge representation worked surprisingly well; MYCIN was able to perform its task in a specific area of infectious-disease diagnosis as well as the best experts in the country.

Furthermore, the MYCIN structure was seen to be, at least to some extent, independent of the domain of medicine. So long as experts could describe their knowledge in terms of *if-then* rules, the reasoning mechanism that MYCIN used to make inferences from a large set of rules would come up with the right questions and eventually, a satisfactory analysis. MYCIN-like systems have been successfully built in research laboratories for appli-cations as diverse as mineral exploration, diagnosis of computer-equipment failure, and even for advising users about how to use complex systems.

Transfer of Expertise

There is an important shift in the view of expert systems described in the preceding paragraph, which illustrates the changing perspective on AI that I have suggested will take place as it becomes an applied science. Early work on expert systems, building on AI research in problem-solving, focused on representing and manipulating facts in order to get answers. But through MYCIN, whose reasoning mechanism is actually quite shallow, it became clear that the way that these systems interacted with people who had knowl-edge and those who needed it was an important, deep constraint on the system's architecture—knowledge representations and reasoning mecha-nisms.

A key idea in our current approach to building expert systems is that these programs should not only be able to apply the corpus of expert knowledge to specific problems, but they should also be able to interact with the users and experts just as humans do when they learn, explain, and teach what they know. . . . these *transfer of expertise* (TOE) capabilities were originally necessitated by "human engineering" considerations—the people who build and use our systems needed a variety of "assistance" and "explanation" facilities. However, there is more to the idea of TOE than the implementation of needed user features: These social interactions—learning from experts, explaining one's reasoning, and teaching what one knows—are essential dimensions of human knowledge. They are as fundamental to the nature of intelligence as expert-level problem-solving, and they have changed our ideas about representation and about knowledge. (Barr, Bennett, and Clancey, 1979, p. 1.)

Randall Davis's TEIRESIAS system, built within the MYCIN framework, was the first to focus on *transferral* aspects of expert systems. [Davis, 1976.] TEIRESIAS offered aids for experts who were entering knowledge into the system and for the system's users. For example, in order for an expert to figure out why a system has come up with the wrong diagnosis or is asking an inappropriate question, he or she has to understand its behavior in his or her own terms: The system must explain its reasoning in terms of concepts and procedures with which the expert is familiar. The same type of explanation facility is necessary for the eventual user of an expert system, who will want to be assured that the system's answers are well founded. Expert-systems technology had to be extended to facilitate these kinds of interactions, and in the process, our conception of what constituted an expert system has changed. No longer did the systems simply solve problems; they now transferred expertise from people who had it to people who could use it.

We are building systems that take part in the human activity of *transfer of expertise* among experts, practitioners, and students in different kinds of domains. Our problems remain the same as they were before: We must find good ways to represent knowledge and meta-knowledge, to carry on a dialogue, and to solve problems in the domain. But the guiding principles of our approach and the underlying constraints on our solutions have subtly shifted: Our systems are no longer being designed solely to be expert problem solvers, using vast amounts of encoded knowledge. There are aspects of "knowing" that have so far remained unexplored in AI research: by participation in *human* transfer of expertise, these systems will involve more of the fabric of behavior that is the reason we *ascribe* knowledge and intelligence to people. (Barr, Bennett, and Clancey, 1979, p. 5.)

The Technological Niche

It is the goal of those who are involved in the commercial development of expert-systems technology to incorporate that technology into some device that can be sold. But the environment in which expert systems operate is our own cognitive environment; it is within this sphere of activity—people solving their problems—that the eventual expert-system products must be found useful. They will be engineered to our minds!

> With these systems, it will at last become economical to match human beings in real time with really large machines. This means that we can work toward programming what will be, in effect, "thinking aids." In the years to come we expect that these man-machine systems will share, and perhaps for a time be dominant, in our advance toward the development of "artificial intelligence." (Minsky, 1963, p. 450.)

It is a long way from the expert systems developed in research laboratories to any products that fit into peoples' lives; in fact, it is even hard to envision what such products will be. Egon Loebner of Hewlett-Packard Laboratories tells of a conversation he had many years ago with Vladimir Zworykin, the inventor of television technology. Loebner asked Zworykin what he had in mind for his invention when he was developing the technology in the 1920s—what kind of product did he think his efforts would produce. The inventor said that he had had a very clear idea of the eventual use of TV: He envisioned medical students in the gallery of an operating room getting a clear picture on their TV screens of the details of the operation being conducted below them.

We cannot, at the outset, understand the application of a new technology, because it will find its way into realms of application that do not yet exist. Egon Loebner has described this process in terms of the technological niche, paralleling modern evolution theory. [Loebner, 1976; Loebner and Borden, 1969.] Like the species and their environment, inventions and their applications are codefined—they constantly evolve together, with niches representing periods of relative stability, into a new reality. "Moreover, the niches themselves are . . . defined in considerable measure by the whole constellation of organisms themselves. There can be no lice without hairy heads for them to inhabit, nor animals without plants." (Simon, 1980, p. 44.) Thus, technological inventions change as they are applied to people's needs, and the activities that people undertake change with the availability of new technologies. And as people in industry try to push the new technology toward some profitable niche, they will also explore the nature of the underlying phenomena. Of course, it is not just the scientists and engineers who developed the new technology who are involved in this exploration: Half of the job involves finding out what the new capabilities can do for people.

The commercial application of TV technology was foreseen by David Sarnoff, according to the model he had used for the radio broadcasting industry. It is important to note that the commercial product that resulted from TV technology, the TV-set receiver, was only part of a gigantic system that had to be developed for its support (actually imported from radio, with modifications and extensions), involving broadcast technology, networks, regulation of air waves, advertising, and so forth. Loebner refers to this need for system-wide concern with product development as the Edisonian model of technological innovation: Edison's achievement of the invention of the long-life, commercially feasible light bulb was conducted in parallel with his successful development of the first dynamo for commercially producing electric power and his design and implementation of the first electric-power distribution network.

The Knowledge Industry

Among the scientific disciplines that study knowledge, the potential for commercial applications of artificial intelligence presents unique opportunities. In order to identify and fill the niches in which intelligent machines will survive, we must ask questions about knowledge from a rather different perspective. We must identify the role that various aspects of intelligence play, or could play, in the affairs of people, in such a way that we can identify correctable shortcomings in the way things are done.

There is no question that the current best design of an intelligent system, the human brain, has its limitations. Computers have already been used to aid people in dealing with such shortcomings as memory failure and confusions, overloading in busy situations, their tendency to boredom, and their need for sleep. These extended capabilities—total recall, rapid processing, and uninterrupted attention—are cognitive capabilities that we have been willing to concede to the new species in *genus symbol manipulators*. They have helped us do the things we did before and have made some entirely new capabilities possible; for example, airline reservation systems, 24-hour banking, and Pac-Man (although the truly challenging computer games are yet to come!). Intelligence is also going to be present in this new species, as envisioned twenty years ago by Marvin Minsky: "I believe . . . that we are on the threshold of an era that will be strongly influenced, and quite possibly dominated, by intelligent problem-solving machines." (Minsky, 1963, p. 406.) Finding a way to apply this new intellectual capability, for effectively applying relevant experience to new situations, is the task ahead for AI, Inc. It may be a while in coming, and it may involve a rethinking of the way we go about some cognitive activities. But it is extremely important that the development of intelligent machines be pursued, for the human mind is not only limited in its storage and processing capacity, it also has known bugs: It can easily be misled, stubborn, and even blind to the truth, especially when pushed to the limits.

And, as is nature's way, everything gets pushed to the limits, including humans. We must find a way of organizing ourselves more effectively, of bringing together the energies of larger groups of people toward a common goal. Intelligent systems, built from computer and communications technology, will someday know more than any individual human about what is going on in complex enterprises involving millions of people, like a multinational corporation or a city. And intelligent systems will be able to explain each person's part of the task. We will build more productive factories this way and maybe someday, a more peaceful world. We must keep in mind, following our analogy with flight, that the capabilities of intelligence as it exists in nature are not necessarily its natural limits: "There are other facets to this analogy with flight; it, too, is a continuum, and some once thought that the speed of sound represented a boundary beyond which flight was impossible." (Armer, 1963, p. 398.)

ARTIFICIAL INTELLIGENCE
Subcognition as Computation

Douglas R. Hofstadter

The philosopher John Searle has recently made quite a stir in the cognitive-science and philosophy-of-mind circles with his celebrated "Chinese room" thought experiment, whose purpose is to reveal as illusory the aims of artificial intelligence (AI), and particularly to discredit what he labels "strong AI"—the belief that a programmed computer can, in principle, be conscious. [Searle, 1981.] Various synonymous phrases could be substituted for "be conscious" here, such as: "think," "have a soul" (in a humanistic rather than a religious sense), "have an inner life," "have semantics" (as distinguished from "mere syntax"), "have content" (as distinguished from "mere form"), "have intentionality," "be something it is like something to be" (a somewhat ponderous yet appealing phrase due to philosopher Thomas Nagel), "have personhood," and others. Each of these phrases has its own peculiar set of connotations and imagery attached to it as well as its own history and proponents. For our purposes, however, we shall consider them all as equivalent and lump them all together, so that the claim of strong AI now becomes very strong indeed.

At the same time, various AI workers have been developing their own philosophies of what AI is and have developed some useful terms and slogans to describe their endeavor. Some of them are: *information processing, cognition as computation, physical symbol system, symbol manipulation, expert system,* and *knowledge engineering.* There is some confusion as to what words like *symbol* and *cognition* actually mean, just as there is some confusion as to what words like *semantics* and *syntax* mean.

It is the purpose of this paper to try to delve into the meanings of such elusive terms and, at the same time, shed some light on the views of John Searle, on the one hand, and Allen Newell and Herbert Simon, on the other hand—visible AI pioneers who are responsible for several of the terms in the previous paragraph. The thoughts expressed herein were originally triggered

I would like to thank Daniel C. Dennett and Marsha J. Meredith for their careful reading of, and valuable comments on, earlier drafts of this paper.

by the preceding paper called "Artificial Intelligence: Cognition as Computation" by Avron Barr. However, they can be read independently of that paper.

The questions are obviously not trivial and certainly not resolvable in a single paper. Most of the ideas in this paper, in fact, were stated earlier and more fully in my book *Gödel, Escher, Bach: an Eternal Golden Braid.* [Hofstadter, 1979.] However, it seems worthwhile to extract a certain stream of ideas from that book and enrich it with some more recent musings and examples, even if the underlying philosophy remains entirely the same. In order to do justice to these complex ideas, many topics must be interwoven, and they include the nature of symbols, meaning, thinking, perception, cognition, and so on. That explains why this paper is not three pages long.

COGNITION VERSUS PERCEPTION: THE 100-MILLISECOND DIVIDING LINE

In Barr's paper, AI is characterized repeatedly by the phrase "information-processing model of cognition." Although when I first heard that phrase years ago, I tended to accept it as defining the nature of AI, something has gradually come to bother me about it, and I would like to try to articulate that here.

Now what's in a word? What's to object to here? I won't attempt to say what's wrong with the phrase so much as try to show what I disagree with in the ideas of those who have promoted it; then, perhaps, the phrase's connotations will float up to the surface, so that other people can see why I am uneasy with it.

I think the disagreement can be put in its sharpest relief in the following way. In 1980, Simon delivered a lecture that I attended (the Procter Award Lecture for the Sigma Xi annual meeting in San Diego), and in it he declared (and I believe I am quoting him nearly verbatim): "Everything of interest in cognition happens above the 100-millisecond level—the time it takes you to recognize your mother." [Simon, 1981.] Well, our disagreement is simple; namely, I take exactly the opposite viewpoint: Everything interesting in cognition happens *below* the 100-millisecond level—the time it takes you to recognize your mother. To me, the major queston of AI is this: "What in the world is going on to enable you to convert from 100,000,000 retinal dots to one single word *mother* in one-tenth of a second?" Perception is where it's at!

THE PROBLEM OF LETTERFORMS: A TEST CASE FOR ARTIFICIAL INTELLIGENCE

The problem of intelligence, as I see it, is to understand the fluid nature of mental categories; to understand the invariant cores of percepts such as your mother's face; to understand the strangely flexible yet strong boundaries of concepts such as chair or the letter *a*. Years ago, long before computers, Wittgenstein had already recognized the centrality of such questions in his celebrated discussion of the "nonpindownability" of the meaning of the word *game*. [Wittgenstein, 1922.] To emphasize this and make the point as starkly as I can, I hereby make the following claim: The central problem of AI is the question: "What is the letter *a*?" Donald Knuth, on hearing me make this claim once, appended, "And what is the letter *i*?"—an amendment that I gladly accept. In fact, perhaps the best version would be this: The central problem of AI is: "What are *A* and *I*?" By making these claims, I am suggesting that for any program to handle letterforms with the flexibility that human beings do, it would have to possess full-scale general intelligence.

Many people in AI might protest, pointing out that there already exist programs that have achieved expert-level performance in specialized domains without needing general intelligence. Why should letterforms be any different? My answer would be that specialized domains tend to obscure rather than clarify the distinction between strengths and weaknesses of a program. A familiar domain such as letterforms provides much more of an acid test.

It is strange that AI has said so little about this classic problem. To be sure, some work has been done. There are a few groups with interest in letters, but there has been no all-out effort to deal with this quintessential problem of pattern recognition. Since letterform understanding is currently the ultimate target of my own research project in AI, I would like to take a moment and explain why I see it as contrasting so highly with domains at the other end of the expertise spectrum.

Each letter of the alphabet comes in literally thousands of different official versions (typefaces), not to mention millions, billions, trillions, of unofficial versions (those handwritten ones that you and I and everyone else produce all the time). There thus arises the obvious question, "How are all *a*'s like each other?" The goal of an AI project would be, of course, to give an exact answer in computational terms. However, even taking advantage of the vagueness of ordinary language, we are hard put to find a satisfactory intuitive answer, because we simply come up with phrases such as "they all have the same shape." Clearly, the whole problem is that they *don't* have the same shape. And it does not help to change "shape" to "form" or to tack on phrases such as "basically," "essentially," or "at a conceptual level."

There is also the less obvious question, "How are all the various letters in a single typeface related to each other?" This is a grand analogy problem if ever there was one. We are asking for a *b* that is to the abstract notion of *b*-ness as a given *a* is to the abstract notion of *a*-ness. We have to take the qualities of a given *a* and, so to speak, "hold them loosely in the hand," as we see how they "slip" into variants of themselves as we try to carry them over to another letter. Here is the very hingepoint of thought, the place where one thing slips into alternative, subjunctive, variations on itself. Here, that "thing" is a very abstract concept—namely, the way that this particular shape manifests the abstract quality of being an *a*. The problem of *a* is, thus, intimately connected with the problems of *b* through *z* and with that of stylistic consistency.

The existence of optical character readers might lead us to believe at first that the letter-recognition problem has been solved. If we consider the problem a little more carefully, however, we see that the surface has barely been scratched. In truth, the way that most optical character-recognition programs work is by a fancy kind of template matching, in which statistics are done to determine which character, out of a fixed repertoire of, say, 100 stored characters, is the "best match." This is about like assuming that the way I recognize my mother is by comparing the scene in front of me with stored memories of the appearances of tigers, cigarettes, hula hoops, gambling casinos, and can openers (and of course all other things in the world simultaneously) and somehow instantly coming up with the "best match."

THE HUMAN MIND AND ITS ABILITY TO RECOGNIZE AND REPRODUCE FORMS

The problem of recognizing letters of the alphabet is no less deep than that of recognizing your mother, even if it might seem so, given that the number of Platonic prototype items is on the small side (26, if we ignore all characters but the lowercase alphabet). We can even narrow it down further—to just a handful. As a matter of fact, Godfried Toussaint, editor of the pattern-recognition papers for the *IEEE Transactions,* has said to me that he would like to put up a prize for the first program that could say correctly, of 20 characters that people easily can identify, which are *a*'s and which are *b*'s. To carry out such a task, a program cannot just recognize that a shape is an *a*; it has to see *how* that shape embodies *a*-ness. And then, as a test of whether the program really knows its letters, it would have to carry "that style" over to the other letters of the alphabet. This is the goal of my research: To find out how to make letters slip in "similar ways to each other," so as to constitute a consistent artistic style in a typeface—or simply a consistent way of writing the alphabet.

By contrast, most AI work on vision pertains to such things as aerial reconnaissance or robot-guidance programs. This would suggest that the basic problem of vision is to figure out how to recognize textures and how to mediate between two and three dimensions. But what about the fact that although we are all marvelous face-recognizers, practically none of us can draw a face at all well—even of someone we love? Most of us are flops at drawing even such simple things as pencils and hands and books. I personally have learned to recognize hundreds of Chinese characters (shapes that involve neither three dimensions nor textures) and yet, on trying to reproduce them from memory, find myself often drawing confused mixtures of characters, leaving out basic components, or, worst of all, being unable to recall anything but the vaguest "feel" of the character and not being able to draw a single line.

Closer to home, most of us have read literally millions of, say, k's with serifs, yet practically none of us can draw a k with serifs in the standard places. (This holds, of course, for any letter of the alphabet.) I suspect that many people—perhaps most—are not even consciously aware of the fact that there are two different types of lowercase a and of lowercase g, just as many people seem to have a very hard time drawing a distinction between lowercase and uppercase letters, and a few have a hard time telling letters drawn forwards from letters drawn backwards.

How can such a fantastic "recognition machine" as our brain be so terrible at rendition? Clearly, there must be something very complex going on, enabling us to *accept* things as members' categories and to perceive *how* they are members of those categories, yet not enabling us to reproduce those things from memory. This is a deep mystery.

In his book *Pattern Recognition,* Mikhail Bongard concludes with a series of 100 puzzles for a visual pattern-recognizer, whether human, machine, or alien, and, to my mind, it is no accident that he caps off his set with letterforms. [Bongard, 1970.] In other words, he works his way up to letterforms as being at the pinnacle of visual recognition ability. There exists no pattern-recognition program in the world today that can come anywhere close to doing those Bongard problems. [Ibid.] And yet Barr cites Simon as writing the following statement:

> The evidence for that commonality [between the information processes that are employed by such disparate systems as computers and human nervous systems] is now overwhelming, and the remaining questions about the boundaries of cognitive science have more to do with whether there also exist nontrivial commonalities with information processing in genetic systems than with whether men and machines both think. (Simon, 1980, p. 45.)

I find it difficult to understand how Simon can believe this in an era when computers still cannot do basic kinds of subcognitive acts (acts that we feel are unconscious, acts that underlie cognition).

In another lecture in 1979 (the opening lecture of the first meeting of the Cognitive Science Society, also in San Diego), I recall Simon proclaiming that despite much doubting by people not in the know, there is no longer any question as to whether computers can think. If he had meant that there should no longer be any question about whether machines may *eventually* become able to think or whether we humans are machines (in some abstract sense of the term), then I would be in accord with his statement. But after hearing and reading such statements over and over again, I don't think that's what he meant at all. I get the impression that Simon genuinely believes that today's machines are intelligent and that they really do think (or perform "acts of cognition"—to use a bit of jargon that adds nothing to the meaning but makes it sound more scientific). I will come back to that shortly, since it is in essence the central bone of contention in this article but first, a few more remarks on AI domains.

TOY DOMAINS, TECHNICAL DOMAINS, PURE SCIENCE, AND ENGINEERING

There is a tendency in AI today toward flashy, splashy domains—that is, toward developing programs that can do such things as medical diagnosis, geological consultation (for oil prospecting), designing experiments in molecular biology, molecular spectroscopy, configuring Vax installations, designing VLSI (very-large-scale integration) circuits, and on and on. Yet, there is no program that has common sense; no program that learns things that it has not been explicitly taught how to learn; no program that can recover gracefully from its own errors. The "artificial expertise" programs that do exist are rigid, brittle, and inflexible. Like chess programs, they may serve a useful intellectual or even practical purpose, but despite much fanfare, they are not shedding much light on human intelligence. Mostly, they are being developed simply because various agencies or industries fund them.

This does not follow the traditional pattern of basic science. That pattern is to try to isolate a phenomenon, to reduce it to its simplest possible manifestation. For Newton, this meant the falling apple and the moon; for Einstein, the thought experiment of the trains and lightning flashes and, later, the falling elevator; for Mendel, it meant the peas; and so on. You don't tackle the messiest problems before you've tackled the simpler ones; you don't try to run before you can walk. Or, to use a metaphor based on physics, you don't try to tackle a world with friction before you've got a solid understanding of the frictionless world.

Why do AI people eschew toy domains? Once, about ten years back, the MIT "blocks world" was a very fashionable domain. Roberts and Guzman and Waltz wrote programs that pulled 3-D blocks out of 2-D television-screen dot matrices. Patrick Winston, building on their work, wrote a program that could recognize instantiations of certain concepts compounded from elementary blocks in that domain (arch, table, house, and so on). Terry Winograd wrote a program that could "converse" with a person about activities, plans, past events, and some structures in that circumscribed domain. Gerald Sussman wrote a program that could write and debug simple programs to carry out tasks in that domain, thus effecting a simple kind of learning. [Winston, 1975; Winograd, 1972a; Sussman, 1975.] Why, then, did interest in this domain suddenly wane?

Surely no one could claim that the domain was exhausted. Every one of those programs exhibited glaring weaknesses and limitations and specializations. The domain was phenomenally far from being understood by a single, unified program. Here, then, was a nearly ideal domain for exploring what cognition truly is—and it was suddenly dropped. Researchers at Massachusetts Institute of Technology were at one time doing truly basic research on intelligence and then quit. Much basic research has been supplanted by large teams marketing what they vaunt as "knowledge engineering." Firmly grounded engineering is fine, but it seems to me that this type of engineering is not built on the solid foundations of a science, but on a number of recipes that have worked with some success in limited domains.

In my opinion, the proper choice of domain is the critical decision that an AI researcher makes when beginning a project. If you choose to get involved in medical diagnosis at the expert level, then you are going to get mired down in a host of technical problems that have nothing to do with how the mind works. The same goes for the other earlier-cited ponderous domains that current work in expert systems involves. By contrast, if you are in control of your own domain, and can tailor it and prune it so that you keep the essence of the problem while getting rid of extraneous features, then you stand a chance of discovering something fundamental.

Early programs on the nature of analogy [Evans, 1968], sequence extrapolation [Simon and Kotovsky, 1963, among others], and so on, were moving in the right direction. But then, somehow, it became a common notion that these problems had been solved. Simply because Thomas Evans had made a program that could do some very restricted types of visual-analogy problem "as well as a high school student," many people thought the book was closed. However, we need only look at Bongard's 100 to see how hopelessly far we are from dealing with analogies. [Bongard, 1970.] We need only look at any collection of typefaces (look at any magazine's advertisements for a vast variety) to see how enormously far we are from understanding letterforms. As I claimed earlier, letterforms are probably the quintessential problem of pattern recognition. It is both baffling and disturbing to me to see so many people working on imitating cognitive functions at the highest level of sophistication when their programs cannot carry out cognitive functions at much lower levels of sophistication.

AI AND THE TRUE NATURE OF INTELLIGENCE

There are some notable exceptions. The Schank group at Yale, whose original goal was to develop a program that could understand natural language, has been forced to retreat, and to devote most of its attention to the organization of memory, which is certainly at the crux of cognition (because it is part of subcognition, incidentally)—and the group has gracefully accommodated this shift of focus. [Schank, 1982.] I will not be at all surprised, however, if eventually the group is forced into yet further retreats—in fact, all the way back to Bongard problems or the like. Why? Simply because their work (on such things as how to discover what "adage" accurately captures the "essence" of a story or episode) already has led them into the deep waters of abstraction, perception, and classification. These are the issues that Bongard problems illustrate so perfectly. Bongard problems are the idealized ("frictionless") versions of these critical questions.

It is interesting that Bongard problems are in actuality nothing other than a well-worked-out set of typical IQ-test problems, the kind that Lewis Terman and Alfred Binet first invented 60 or more years ago. [Terman, 1916; Binet, 1916.] Over the years, many other less talented people have invented similar visual puzzles that had the unfortunate property of being filled with ambiguity and multiple answers. This (among other things) has given IQ tests a bad name. Whether or not IQ is a valid concept, however, there can be little question that the original insight of Terman and Binet—that carefully constructed simple visual-analogy problems probe close to the core mechanisms of intelligence—is correct. Perhaps the political climate created a kind of knee-jerk reflex in many cognitive scientists, causing them to shy away from anything that smacked of IQ tests, since issues of cultural bias and racism began raising their ugly heads. But we need not be so Pavlovian as to jump whenever a visual-analogy problem is placed in front of us. In any case, it will be good when AI people are finally driven back to looking at the insights of people working in the 1920s and 1930s, such as Wittgenstein and his "games," Köhler and Koffka and Wertheimer and their "gestalts," and Terman and Binet and their IQ-test problems. [Ibid.; Wittgenstein, 1922; Wertheimer, 1925; Köhler, 1929; Koffka, 1935.]

I was saying that some AI groups seem to be less afraid of toy domains, or, more accurately put, they seem to be less afraid of stripping down their domain in successive steps, to isolate the core issues of intelligence that it involves. Aside from the Schank group, N. Sridharan at Rutgers University has been doing some very interesting work on prototype deformation, which, although it springs from work in legal reasoning in a quite messy real-world domain, has been abstracted into a form in which it is perhaps more like a toy domain (or, perhaps less pejorative-sounding, an idealized domain) than at first would appear. [Sridharan, 1980.] The Lindsay-Norman-Rumelhart group at San Diego has been doing work for years on understanding errors, such as grammatical slips, typing errors, errors in everyday physical actions (such as winding your watch when you mean to switch television channels), for the insights it may offer into the underlying (subcognitive) mechanisms. [Norman, 1981.]

Then there are those people who are working on various programs for perception, whether visual or auditory. One of the most interesting was Hearsay-II, a speech-understanding program developed at Carnegie-Mellon University, Simon's home. It is, therefore, very surprising to me that Simon, who surely was very aware of the wonderfully intricate and quite beautiful architecture of Hearsay-II, could then make a comment indicating that perception and, in general, subcognitive (under 100 milliseconds) processes, have no interest. [Reddy, 1976.]

There are surely many other less publicized groups that are also working on more humble domains and on more pure problems of mind, but from looking at the proceedings of AI conferences, we might get the impression that, indeed, computers must really be able to think these days, since, after all, they are doing anything and everything cognitive—from opthalmology to biology to chemistry to mathematics—even discovering scientific laws from looking at tables of numerical data, to mention one project ("Bacon") that Simon has been involved in.

EXPERT SYSTEMS VERSUS HUMAN FLUIDITY

The problem is that AI programs are carrying out all these *cognitive* activities in the absence of any *subcognitive* activity. There is no substrate that corresponds to what goes on in the brain. There is no fluid recognition and recall and reminding. These programs have no common sense, little sense of similarity or repetition or pattern. They can perceive some patterns as long as they have been anticipated—and, particularly, as long as the *place* where they will occur has been anticipated—but they cannot see patterns where nobody told them explicitly to look. They do not learn at a high level of abstraction.

This style is in complete contrast to how people are. People perceive patterns anywhere and everywhere, without knowing in advance where to look. People learn automatically in all aspects of life. These are just facets of common sense. Common sense is not an area of expertise, but a general— that is, domain-independent—capacity that has to do with fluidity in representation of concepts, an ability to sift what is important from what is not, an ability to find unanticipated analogical similarities between totally different concepts (reminding, as Schank calls it). We have a long way to go before our programs exhibit this cognitive style.

Recognition of one's mother's face is still nearly as much of a mystery as it was 30 years ago. And what about such things as recognizing family resemblances between people, recognizing a French face, recognizing kindness or earnestness or slyness or harshness in a face? Even recognizing age—even sex!—these are fantastically difficult problems! As Donald Knuth has pointed out, we have written programs that can do wonderfully well at what people have to work very hard at doing consciously (e.g., doing integrals, playing chess, medical diagnosis, etc.)—but we have yet to write a program that remotely approaches our ability to do what we do *without* thinking or training—things like understanding a conversation partner with an accent at a loud cocktail party with music blaring in the background, while at the same time overhearing wisps of conversations in the far corner of the room. [Knuth, 1974a.] Or perhaps finding our way through a forest on an overgrown trail. Or perhaps just doing some anagrams absentmindedly while washing the dishes.

Asking for a program that can discover new scientific laws without having a program that can, say, do anagrams, is like wanting to go to the moon without having the ability to find your way around town. I do not make the comparison idly. The level of performance that Simon and his colleague Langley wish to achieve in "Bacon" is on the order of the greatest scientists. It seems they feel that they are but a step away from the mechanization of genius. After his Procter Lecture, Simon was asked by a member of the audience, "How many scientific lifetimes does a five-hour run of 'Bacon' represent?" He replied, "Probably not more than one."

ANAGRAMS AND EPIPHENOMENA

Well, I feel we're much further away from human-level performance than Simon does. I, for one, would like to see a program that does anagrams the way a person does. Why anagrams? Because they are a toy domain where some very significant subcognitive processes play the central role.

What I mean is this. When we look at a "jumble" such as *telkin* in the newspaper, we immediately begin shifting around letters into tentative groups, making such stabs as *knitle, klinte, linket, keltin, tinkle*—and then we notice that, indeed, *tinkle* is a word. The part of this process that I am interested in is the part that precedes the recognition of *tinkle* as a word. It's that part that involves experimentation, based only on the style or "feel" of English words—using intuitions about letter affinities, plausible clusters and their stabilities, syllable qualities, and so on. When we first read a jumble in the newspaper, we play around, rearranging, regrouping, reshuffling, in complex ways that we have no control over. In fact, it feels as if we throw the letters up into the air separately, and when they come down, they have somehow magically "glommed" together in some English-like word! It's a marvelous feeling—and it is anything but cognitive, anything but conscious. (Yet, interestingly, we take credit for being good at anagrams, if we are good!)

It turns out that most literate people can handle "jumbles" (my term for single-word anagrams) of five or six letters, sometimes seven or eight letters; with practice, maybe even ten or twelve. But beyond that, it gets very hard to keep the letters in our head. It is especially hard if there are repeated letters, since we tend to get confused about which letters there are multiple copies of. (In one case, I rearranged the letters *dinnal* into *nadlid*—incorrectly. You can try *raregarden* if you dare.) Now in one sense, the fact that the problem gets harder and harder with more and more letters is hardly surprising. It is obviously related to the famous "7 plus or minus 2" figure that psychologist George A. Miller first reported in connection with short-term memory capacity. [Miller, 1956.] But there are different ways of interpreting such a connection.

One way to think that this might come about is to assume that concepts for the individual letters get "activated" and then interact. When too many get activated simultaneously, then we get swamped with combinations and we drop some letters and make too many of others, and so on. This view would say that we simply encounter an explosion of connections, and our system gets overloaded. The view does not postulate any explicit storage location in memory—a fixed set of registers or data structures—in which letters get placed and then shoved around. In this model, short-term memory and its associated magic number is an *epiphenomenon* (or innocently emergent phenomenon, as Daniel Dennett calls it [Dennett, 1978a]), by which I mean it is a consequence that emerges out of the design of the system, a product of many interacting factors; something that was not necessarily known, predictable, or even anticipated to emerge at all. This is the view that I advocate.

A contrasting view might be to build a model of cognition in which we have an explicit structure called short-term memory that contains about seven (or five, or nine) "slots" into which certain data structures can be fitted, and when it is full, well, then, it is full and we have to wait until an empty slot opens up. This is one approach that has been followed by Newell and associates in work on production systems. The problem with this approach is that it takes something that clearly is a very complex consequence of underlying mechanisms and simply plugs it in as an explicit structure, bypassing the question of what those underlying mechanisms might be. It is difficult for me to believe that any model of cognition based on such a "bypass" could be an accurate model.

When an operating system begins thrashing at around 35 users, do you tell the systems programmer, "Hey, go raise the thrashing number in Tenex from 35 to 60, okay?"? The number 35 is not stored in some magic location in Tenex, so that it can be modified; that number comes out of a host of strategic decisions made by the designers of Tenex and the computer's hardware, and so on. There is no "thrashing-threshold dial" to crank on an operating system, unfortunately. Why should there be a short-term-memory-size dial on an intelligence? Why should 7 be a magic number built into the system explicitly from the start? If the size of short-term memory really were explicitly stored in our genes, then surely it would take only a simple mutation to reset the dial at 8 or 9 or 50, so that intelligence would evolve at ever-increasing rates. I doubt that AI people think that this is even remotely close to the truth; and yet they sometimes act as if it made sense to assume it is a close approximation to the truth.

It is standard practice for AI people to bypass epiphenomena (collective phenomena, if you prefer) by simply installing structures that mimic the superficial features of those epiphenomena. (Such mimics are the "shadows" of genuine cognitive acts, as John Searle calls them in his provocative paper "Minds, Brains, and Programs." [Searle, 1981.]) The expectation—or at least the hope—is for tremendous performance to issue forth; yet, the systems lack the complex underpinning necessary.

The anagrams problem is one that exemplifies mechanisms of thought that

AI people have not explored. How do those letters swirl among one another, fluidly and tentatively making and breaking alliances? "Glomming" together, then coming apart, almost like little biological objects in a cell. AI people have not paid much attention to such problems as anagrams. Perhaps they would say that the problem is already solved. After all, a virtuoso programmer has made a program print out all possible words that anagrammatize into other words in English. Or perhaps they would point out that in principle, you can do an "alphabetize" followed by a "hash" and thereby retrieve from any given set of letters all the words they anagrammatize into. Well, this is all fine and dandy, but it is really beside the point. It is merely a show of brute force and has nothing to contribute to our understanding of how we actually do anagrams ourselves, just as most chess programs have absolutely nothing to say about how chess masters play (as Adriaan de Groot, and later, William Chase and Herbert Simon have pointed out). [de Groot, 1965; Chase and Simon, 1973.]

Is anagrams simply a trivial, silly, "toy" domain? Or is it serious? I maintain that it is a far purer, far more interesting domain than many of the complex real-world domains of the expert systems, precisely because it is so playful, so unconscious, so enjoyable for people. It is obviously more related to creativity and spontaneity than it is to logical derivations, but that does not make it—or the mode of thinking that it represents—any less worthy of attention. In fact, because it epitomizes the unconscious mode of thought, I think it more worthy of attention.

In short, it seems to me that something fundamental is missing in the orthodox AI "information-processing" model of cognition, and that is some sort of substrate from which intelligence emerges as an epiphenomenon. Most AI people do not want to tackle that kind of underpinning work. Could it be that they really believe that machines already can think, already have concepts, already can do analogies? It seems that a large camp of AI people really do believe these things.

NOT COGNITION, BUT SUBCOGNITION, IS COMPUTATIONAL

Such beliefs arise, in my opinion, from a confusion of levels, exemplified by part of the title of Barr's paper, "Cognition as Computation." Am I really computing when I think? Admittedly, my neurons may be performing sums in an analog way, but does this pseudo-arithmetical hardware mean that the epiphenomena themselves are also doing arithmetic or should be—or even can be—described in conventional computer science terminology? Does the fact that taxis stop at red lights mean that traffic jams stop at red lights? We should not confuse the properties of objects with the properties of statistical ensembles of those objects. In this analogy, traffic jams play the role of thoughts, and taxis play the role of neurons or neuron-firings. It is not meant to be a serious analogy, only one that emphasizes that what you see at the top level need not have anything to do with the underlying swarm of activities bringing it into existence. In particular, something can be computational at one level but not at another level.

Yet, many AI people, despite considerable sophistication in thinking about a given system at different levels, still seem to miss this. Most AI work goes into efforts to build rational thought (cognition) out of smaller rational thoughts (elementary steps of deduction, for instance, or elementary motions in a tree). It comes down to thinking that what we see at the top level of our minds—our ability to think—comes out of rational "information-processing" activity, with no deeper levels below that.

Many interesting ideas, in fact, have been inspired by this hope. I find much of the work in AI to be fascinating and provocative, yet somehow I feel dissatisfied with the overall trend. For instance, there are some people who believe that the ultimate solution to AI lies in getting better and better theorem-proving mechanisms in some predicate calculus. They have developed extremely efficient and novel ways of thinking about logic. Some people—Simon and Newell, particularly—have argued that the ultimate solution lies in getting more and more efficient ways of searching a vast space of possibilities. (They refer to selective heuristic search as the key mechanism of intelligence.) Again, many interesting discoveries have come out of this.

Then there are others who think that the key to thought involves making some complex language in which pattern-matching or backtracking or inheritance or planning or reflective logic is easily carried out. Now admittedly, such systems, when developed, are good for solving a large class of problems, exemplified by such AI chestnuts as the missionary-and-cannibals problem, "cryptarithmetic" problems, retrograde chess problems, and many other specialized sorts of basically logical analysis. However, these kinds of techniques of building small logical components up to make large logical structures have not proven good for such things as recognizing your mother or drawing the alphabet in a novel and pleasing way.

One group of AI people who seem to have a different attitude consists of those who are working on problems of perception and recognition. There, the idea of coordinating many parallel processes is important, as is the idea that pieces of evidence can add up in a self-reinforcing way, so as to bring about the locking-in of a hypothesis that no one of the pieces of evidence could on its own justify. It is not easy to describe the flavor of this kind of program architecture without going into multiple technical details. However, it is very different in flavor from ones operating in a world where everything comes clean and precategorized—where everything is specified in advance: "There are three missionaries and three cannibals and one boat and one river and . . . ," which is immediately turned into a predicate-calculus statement or a frame representation, ready to be manipulated by an "inference engine." The missing link seems to be the one between perception and cognition, which I would rephrase as the link between subcognition and cognition, that gap between the sub-100-millisecond world and the super-100-millisecond world.

Earlier, I mentioned the brain and referred to the "neural substrate" of cognition. Although I am not pressing for a neurophysiological approach to AI, I am unlike many AI people in that I believe that any AI model eventually has to converge to brainlike hardware or at least to an architecture that at some level of abstraction is isomorphic to brain architecture (also at some level of abstraction). This may sound empty, since that level could be anywhere, but I believe that the level at which the isomorphism must apply will turn out to be considerably lower than (I think) most AI people believe. This disagreement is intimately connected to the question of whether cognition should or should not be described as computation.

PASSIVE SYMBOLS AND FORMAL RULES

One way to explore this disagreement is to look at some of the ways that Simon and Newell express themselves about symbols.

> At the root of intelligence are symbols, with their denotative power and their susceptibility to manipulation. And symbols can be manufactured of almost anything that can be arranged and patterned and combined. Intelligence is mind implemented by any patternable kind of matter. (Simon, 1980, p. 35.)

From this quotation and from others, we can see that to Simon and Newell, a symbol seems to be any token, any character inside a computer that has an ASCII code (a standard but arbitrarily assigned sequence of seven bits). To me, by contrast, *symbol* connotes something with representational power. To them (if I am not mistaken), it would be fine to call a bit (inside a computer) or a neuron-firing a symbol; however, I cannot feel comfortable with that usage of the term.

To me, the crux of the word *symbol* is its connection with the verb *to symbolize,* which means to denote, to represent, to stand for, and so on. Now in the preceding quotation, Simon refers to the denotative power of symbols—yet, in another part of his paper, Barr quotes Newell and Simon as saying that thought is "the manipulation of formal tokens." [Newell and Simon, 1976a.] It is not clear to me which side of the fence they really are on.

It takes an immense amount of richness for something to represent something else. The letter *I* does not in and of itself stand for the person I am or for the concept of selfhood. That quality comes to it from the way that the word behaves in the totality of the English language. It comes from a massively complex set of usages and patterns and regularities, ones that are regular enough for babies to be able to detect, so that they, too, eventually come to say "I" to talk about themselves.

Formal tokens such as *I* or *hamburger* are in themselves empty; they do not denote. Nor can they be made to denote in the full rich intuitive sense of the term by having them obey some rules. You can't simply push around some Pnames of LISP atoms according to complex rules and hope to come out with genuine thought or understanding. (This, by the way, is probably a charitable way to interpret Searle's point in his previously mentioned paper—namely, as a rebellion against claims that programs that can manipulate tokens such as *John, ate, a, hamburger* actually have understanding.) Manipulation of empty tokens is not enough to create understanding— although it is enough to imbue them with meaning in a *limited* sense of the term, as I stress repeatedly in my book *Gödel, Escher, Bach: an Eternal Golden Braid*. [Hofstadter, 1979, particularly chaps. 2–6.]

ACTIVE SYMBOLS AND THE ANT COLONY METAPHOR

So what is enough? What am I advocating? What do I mean by *symbol*? I gave an exposition of my concept of active symbols. [Ibid., chaps. 11–12.] However, the notion was first presented in that book in the Dialogue "Prelude, Ant Fugue," which revolved about a hypothetical conscious ant colony. [Hofstadter, 1979, pp. 311–336.] The purpose of the discussion was not to speculate about whether ant colonies are conscious or not, but to set up an extended metaphor for brain activity—a framework in which to discuss the relation between holistic, or collective, phenomena, and the microscopic events that make them up.

One of the ideas that inspired the Dialogue has been stated by Edward O. Wilson in his book *The Insect Societies* this way: "Mass communication is defined as the transfer, among groups, of information that a single individual could not pass to another." (E. O. Wilson, 1971, p. 226.) We have to imagine teams of ants cooperating on tasks and that information passes from team to team that no ant is aware of (if ants indeed are "aware" of information at all—but that is another question). We can carry this up a few levels and imagine hyperhyperteams carrying and passing information that no hyperteam, not to mention team or solitary ant, ever dreamt of.

I feel it is critical to focus on collective phenomena, particularly on the idea that some information or knowledge or ideas can exist at the level of collective activities while being totally absent at the lowest level. In fact, we can even go so far as to say that *no* information exists at that lowest level. It is hardly an amazing revelation, when transported back to the brain: namely, that no ideas are flowing in those neurotransmitters that spark back and forth between neurons. Yet, such a simple notion undermines the idea that thought and "symbol manipulation" are the same thing, if by *symbol* we mean a formal token such as a bit or a letter or a LISP Pname.

What is the difference? Why couldn't symbol manipulation—in the sense that I believe Simon and Newell and many writers on AI mean it— accomplish the same thing? The crux of the matter is that these people see symbols as lifeless, dead, passive objects—things to be manipulated by some overlying program. I see symbols—representational structures in the brain (or perhaps someday in a computer)—as active, like the imaginary hyperhyperteams in the ant colony. *That* is the level at which denotation takes place, not at the level of the single ant. The single ant has no right to be called "symbolic," because its actions stand for nothing. (Of course, in a real ant colony, we have no reason to believe that teams at *any* level genuinely stand for objects outside the colony (or inside it, for that matter)— but the ant colony metaphor is only a thinly disguised way of making discussion of the brain more vivid.) [Wheeler, 1911; Marais, 1937; Meyer, 1966.]

WHO SAYS ACTIVE SYMBOLS ARE COMPUTATIONAL ENTITIES?

It is the vast collections of ants (read *neural firings*, if you prefer) that add up to something genuinely symbolic. And who can say whether there exist rules—formal, computational rules—*at the level of the teams themselves* (read *concepts, ideas, thoughts*) that are of full predictive power in describing how they will flow? I am speaking of rules that allow us to ignore what is going on "down below" yet still yield perfect or at least very accurate predictions of the teams' behavior.

To be sure, there are phenomenological observations that can be formalized to sound like rules that will describe, very vaguely, how those highest-level teams act. But what guarantee is there that we can skim off the full fluidity of the top-level activity of a brain, and encapsulate it—without any lower substrate—in the form of some computational rules?

To ask an analogous question, what guarantee is there that there are rules at the cloud level (more properly speaking, the level of cold fronts, isobars, trade winds, etc.) that will allow us to say accurately how the atmosphere is going to behave on a large scale? Perhaps there are no such rules; perhaps weather prediction is an intrinsically intractable problem. Perhaps the behavior of clouds is not expressible in terms that are computational *at their own level,* even if the behavior of the microscopic substrate—the molecules—is computational.

The premise of AI is that thoughts themselves are computational entities at their own level. At least, this is the premise of the information-processing school of AI, and I have very serious doubts about it.

The difference between my active symbols (teams) and passive information-processing symbols (ants, tokens) is that the active symbols flow and act on their own. In other words, there is no higher-level agent (read *program*) that reaches down and shoves them around. Active symbols must incorporate within their own structures the wherewithal to trigger and cause actions. They cannot just be passive storehouses, bins, or receptacles of data. Yet to Newell and Simon, it seems, even so tiny a thing as a bit is a symbol. This is brought out repeatedly in their writings on physical symbol systems.

A good term for the little units that a computer manipulates (as well as for neuron firings) is *tokens*. All computers are good at token manipulation; however, only some—the appropriately programmed ones—could support active symbols. (I prefer not to say that they would carry out symbol manipulation, since that gets back to that image of a central program shoving around some passive representational structures.) The point is, in such a hypothetical program (and none exists as yet), the symbols themselves are acting!

A simple analogy from ordinary programming might help to convey the level distinction that I am trying to make here. When a computer is running a LISP program, does it do function calling? To say yes would be unconventional. The conventional intuition is that *functions* call other functions and the computer is simply the hardware that *supports* function-calling activity. In somewhat the same sense, although with much more parallelism, symbols activate or trigger or awaken other symbols in a brain.

The brain itself does not manipulate symbols; the brain is the medium in which the symbols are floating and in which they trigger each other. There is no central manipulator, no central program. There is simply a vast collection of "teams"—patterns of neural firings that, like teams of ants, trigger other patterns of neural firings. The symbols are not "down there" at the level of the individual firings; they are "up here" where we do our verbalization. We feel those symbols churning within ourselves in somewhat the same way we feel our stomach churning. We do not *do* symbol manipulation by some sort of act of will, leave alone some set of logical rules of deduction. We cannot decide what we will next think of nor how our thoughts will progress.

Not only are we not symbol manipulators; in fact, quite to the contrary, we are manipulated by our symbols! As Scott Kim has put it, rather than speak of "free will," perhaps it is more appropriate to speak of "free won't." This way of looking at things turns everything on its head, placing cognition—that rational-seeming level of our minds—where it belongs, namely, as a consequence of much deeper processes of myriads of interacting subcognitive structures. The rational has had entirely too much made of it in AI research; it is time for some of the irrational and subcognitive to be recognized (no pun intended) for its pivotal role.

THE SUBSTRATE OF ACTIVE SYMBOLS DOES NOT SYMBOLIZE

"Cognition as computation" sounds right to me only if I interpret it quite liberally, namely, as meaning "cognition is an activity that can be supported by computational hardware." But if I interpret it more strictly as "cognition is an activity that can be achieved by a program that shunts around meaning-carrying objects called symbols in a complicated way," then I don't buy it. In my view, meaning-carrying objects won't submit to being shunted about (it's demeaning); meaning-carrying objects carry meaning only by virtue of being active, autonomous agents themselves. There can't be an overseer program, a pusher-around.

To paraphrase a question asked by neurophysiologist Roger Sperry, "Who shoves whom around inside the computer?" (He asked it of the cranium.) [Sperry, 1965, p. 79.] If some program shoves data structures around, then you can bet it's not carrying out cognition; or more precisely, if the data structures are supposed to be *meaning-carrying,* representational things, then it's not cognition. Of course, at *some* level of description, programs certainly will be shoving formal tokens around, but it's only agglomerations of such tokens en masse that, above some unclear threshold of collectivity and cooperativity, achieve the status of genuine representation. At that stage, the computer is not shoving them around any more than our brain is shoving thoughts around! The thoughts themselves are causing flow. (This is, I believe, in agreement with Sperry's own way of looking at matters. [See, for example, Sperry, 1965.]) Parallelism and collectivity are of the essence, and in that sense, my response to the title of Barr's paper is no, cognition is *not* computation.

At this point, some people might think that I sound like Searle, suggesting that there are elusive causal powers of the brain that cannot be captured computationally. [Searle, 1981.] I hasten to say that this is not my point of view at all! In my opinion, AI—even Searle's "strong AI"—is still possible, but thought will simply not turn out to be the formal dream of people inspired by predicate calculus or other formalisms. Thought is not a formal activity whose rules exist *at that level.*

Many linguists have maintained that language is a human activity whose nature could be entirely explained at the linguistic level—in terms of complex grammars, without recourse or reference to anything such as thoughts or concepts. Now many AI people are making a similar mistake: They think that rational thought simply is composed of elementary steps, each of which has some interpretation as an atom of rational thought, so to speak. That's just not what is going on, however, when neurons fire. On its own, a neuron firing has no meaning, no symbolic quality whatsoever. I believe that those elementary events at the bit level—even at the LISP function level (if AI is ever achieved in LISP, something I seriously doubt)—will have the same quality of *having no interpretation.* It is a level shift as drastic as that between molecules and gases that takes place when thought emerges from billions of in-themselves-meaningless neural firings.

A simple metaphor, hardly demonstrating my point but simply giving its flavor, is provided by Winograd's program SHRDLU, which, using the full power of a DEC-10 computer, could deal with whole numbers up to ten in a conversation about the "blocks world." [Winograd, 1972a.] It knew nothing—at its cognitive level—of larger numbers. Alan Turing invents a similar example, a rather sly one, where he has a human ask a computer to do a sum, and the computer pauses thirty seconds and then answers incorrectly. [Turing, 1950.] Now this need not be a ruse on the computer's part. It might genuinely have tried to add the two numbers at the *symbol level* and made a mistake, just as you or I might have, despite having neurons that can add fast.

The point is simply that the lower-level arithmetical processes (the adds, the shifts, the multiplies, etc.) out of which the higher level of any AI program is composed are completely shielded from its view. To be sure, Winograd could have artificially allowed his program to write little pieces of LISP code that would execute and return answers to questions in English such as "What is 720 factorial?" but that would be similar to our trying to take advantage of the fact that we have billions of small analog adders in our brain some time when we are trying to check a long grocery bill. We simply don't have access to those adders! We can't reach them.

SYMBOL TRIGGERING PATTERNS ARE THE ROOTS OF MEANING

What's more, we *oughtn't* to be able to reach them. The world is not sufficiently mathematical for that to be useful in survival. What good would it do a spear thrower to be able to calculate parabolic orbits when in reality there is wind and drag, and the spear is not a point mass—and so on? It's quite the contrary: A spear thrower does best by being able to imagine a cluster of approximations of what may happen and anticipating some plausible consequences of them.

As Jacques Monod in *Chance and Necessity* and Richard Dawkins in *The Selfish Gene* both point out, the real power of brains is that they allow their owners to simulate a variety of plausible futures. [Monod, 1971; Dawkins, 1976.] This is to be distinguished from the *exact* prediction of eclipses by iterating differential equations step by step far into the future, with very high precision. The brain is a device that has evolved in a less exact world than the pristine one of orbiting planets, and there are always far more chances for the best-laid plans to "gang agley." Therefore, *mathematical simulation* has to be replaced by *abstraction*, which involves discarding the irrelevant and making shrewd guesses based on analogy with past experience. Thus, the symbols in a brain, rather than playing out a scenario precisely isomorphic with what actually will transpire, play out a few scenarios that are probable or plausible or even some scenarios from the past that may have no obvious relevance other than as metaphors. (This brings us back to the "adages" of the Yale group. [Schank, 1982.])

Once we abandon perfect mathematical isomorphism as our criterion for symbolizing and suggest that the value of symbol-triggering patterns comes largely from their suggestive value and their metaphorical richness, this severely complicates the question of what it means when we say that a symbol in the brain symbolizes anything. This is closely related to perhaps one of the subtlest issues, in my opinion, that AI should be able to shed light on, and that is the question "What is meaning?" This is actually the crucial issue that Searle is concerned with in his earlier-mentioned attack on AI; although he camouflages it, and sometimes loses track of it by all sorts of evasive maneuvers, it turns out in the end that what he is truly concerned with is the idea that computers have no semantics—and he of course means computers do not now have, and never will have, semantics. [Searle, 1982.] If he were talking only about the present, I would agree. However, he is making a point in principle, and I believe he is wrong there.

Where do the meanings of the so-called active symbols, those giant clouds of neural activity in the brain, come from? To what do they owe their denotational power? Some people have maintained that it is because the brain is physically attached to sensors and effectors that connect it to the outside world, enabling those clouds to mirror the actual state of the world (or at least some parts of it) faithfully and to affect the world outside as well through the use of the body. I think that those things are *part* of denotational power, but not its crux. When we daydream or imagine situations, when we dream or plan, we are *not* manipulating the concrete physical world, nor are we sensing it. In imagining fictional or hypothetical or even totally impossible situations, we are still making use of, and contributing to, the meaningfulness of our symbolic neural machinery. However, the symbols do not symbolize specific, real, physical objects. The fundamental active symbols of the brain represent *semantic categories*—classes, in AI terminology.

Categories do not point to specific physical objects. However, they can be used as masters off of which copies—instances—can be rubbed, and then those copies are activated in various conjunctions. These activations then automatically trigger other instance-symbols into activations of various sorts (teams of ants triggering the creation of other teams of ants, sometimes themselves fizzling out). The overall activity will be semantic— meaningful—if it is isomorphic, not to some actual event in the real world, but to some event that is compatible with all the known constraints on the situation.

Those constraints are not at the molecular or any such fine-grained level; they are at the rather coarse-grained level of ordinary perception. They are to some extent verbalizable constraints. If I utter the Schankian cliché, "John went to a restaurant and ate a hamburger," there is genuine representational power in the patterns of activated symbols that your brain sets up, not because some guy named John actually went out and ate a hamburger (although, most likely, this is a situation that has at some time occurred in the world), but because the symbols, with their own "lives" (autonomous ways of triggering other symbols) will if left alone cause the playing-out of an imaginary yet realistic scenario. [Note added in press: I have it on good authority that one John Findling of Floyds Knobs, Indiana, did enter a Burger Queen restaurant and did eat one (1) hamburger. This fact, though helpful, would not, through its absence, have seriously marred the arguments of the present paper.]

Thus, the key thing that establishes meaningfulness is whether or not the semantic categories are "hooked up" in the proper ways, so as to allow realistic scenarios to play themselves out on this inner stage. That is, the triggering patterns of active symbols must mirror the general trends of how the world works as perceived on a macroscopic level rather than mirror the actual events that transpire.

BEYOND INTUITIVE PHYSICS: THE CENTRALITY OF SLIPPABILITY

Sometimes this capacity is referred to as *intuitive physics*. Intuitive physics is certainly an important ingredient of the triggering patterns needed for an organism's comfortable survival. John McCarthy gives the example of persons able to avoid moving their coffee cups in a certain way, because they can anticipate how they might spill and coffee might get all over their clothes. Note that what is computed is a set of alternative rough descriptions for what might happen rather than one exact trajectory. This is the nature of intuitive physics.

However, as I stated earlier, there is much more required for symbols to have meaning than simply that their triggering patterns yield an intuitive physics. For instance, if you see someone in a big heavy leg cast and they tell you that their kneecap was acting up, you might think to yourself, "That's quite a nuisance, but it's nothing compared to my friend who has cancer." Now this connection is obviously caused by triggering patterns having to do with symbols representing health problems. But what does this have to do with the laws of motion governing objects or fluids? Precious little. Sideways connections like this, having nothing to do with causality, are equally essential in allowing us to *place situations in perspective*—to compare what actually is with what, to our way of seeing things, might have been or might even come to be. This ability, no less than intuitive physics, is a central aspect of what meaning is.

This way in which any situation that is perceived seems to be surrounded by a cluster, a halo, of alternative versions of itself, of variations suggested by slipping any of a vast number of features that characterize the situation, seems to me to be at the dead center of thinking. Not much AI work seems to be going on at present (Schank's and Sridharan's groups excepted, perhaps—and I ought to include myself as another maverick investigating these avenues) to mirror this kind of "slippability." This is an issue that I covered in some detail in *Gödel, Escher, Bach* under various headings such as "slippability," "subjunctive instant replays," "'almost' situations," "conceptual skeletons and conceptual mapping," "alternity" (a term due to George Steiner), and so on. [Hofstadter, 1979; Steiner, 1975; Hofstadter, 1981; 1982a.]

If we return to the metaphor of the ant colony, we can envision these "symbols with halos" as hyperhyperteams of ants, many of whose members are making what appear to be strange forays in random directions, like flickering tongues of flame spreading out in many directions at once. These tentative probes, which allow the possibility of all sorts of strange lateral connections as from kneecap to cancer, have absolutely no detrimental effect on the total activity of the hyperhyperteam. In fact, quite to the contrary: The hyperhyperteam depends on its members to go wherever their noses lead them. The thing that saves the team—what keeps it coherent—is simply the regular patterns that are sure to emerge out of a random substrate when there are enough constituents; statistics, in short.

Occasionally, some group of wandering scouts will cause a threshold of activity to be reached in an unexpected place, and then a whole new area of activity springs up—a new high-level team is activated (or, to return to the brain terminology, a new symbol is awakened). Thus, in a brain as in an ant colony, high-level activity spontaneously flows around, driven by the myriad lower-level components' autonomous actions.

THE GOAL OF AI SHOULD BE TO BRIDGE THE GAP BETWEEN COGNITION AND SUBCOGNITION

Let me, for a final time, make clear how this is completely in contradistinction to standard computer programs. In a normal program, you can account for every single operation at the bit level, by looking "upwards" toward the top-level program. You can trace a high-level function call downwards: It calls subroutines that call other subroutines that call this particular machine-language routine that uses these words and in which this particular bit lies. So there is a high-level, global *reason* why this particular bit is being manipulated.

By contrast, in an ant colony, a particular ant's foray does not achieve some global purpose. It has no interpretation in terms of the overall colony's goals; only when many such actions are considered at once does their statistical quality then emerge as purposeful, or interpretable. Ant actions are not the translation into machine language of some "colony-level" program. No one ant is essential; even large numbers of ants are dispensable. All that matters are the statistics: Thanks to them the information moves around at a level far above that of the ants; ditto for neural firings in brains. Not ditto for most current AI programs' architecture.

AI researchers started out thinking that they could reproduce all of cognition through a 100 per cent top-down approach: functions calling subfunctions calling subsubfunctions, and so forth, until it all bottomed out in some primitives. Thus, intelligence was thought to be hierarchically decomposable, with cognition at the top driving subcognition at the bottom. There were some successes and some difficulties—difficulties particularly in the realm of perception. Then along came such things as production systems and pattern-directed inference. Here, some bottom-up processing was allowed to occur within essentially still a top-down context. Gradually, the trend has been shifting, but there still is a large element of top-down quality in AI.

It is my belief that until AI has been stood on its head and is 100 per cent bottom-up, it won't achieve the same level or type of intelligence as humans have. To be sure, when that kind of architecture exists, there will still be high-level, global, cognitive events—but they will be epiphenomenal, like those in a brain. They will not in themselves be computational. Rather, they will be constituted out of, and driven by, many many smaller computational events rather than the reverse. In other words, subcognition at the bottom will drive cognition at the top. And, perhaps most importantly, the activities that take place at that cognitive top level will neither have been written nor anticipated by any programmer. [Hofstadter, 1982*b*; 1982*d*.]

Let me then close with a return to the comment of Simon's: "Nothing below 100 milliseconds is of interest in the study of cognition." [Simon, 1981.] I cannot imagine a remark about AI with which I could more vehemently disagree. Simon seems to be most concerned with having programs that can imitate chains of serial actions that come from verbal protocols of various experimental subjects. Perhaps, in some domains, even in some relatively complex and technical ones, people have come up with programs that can do this. But what about the simpler, noncognitive acts that in reality form the substrate for those cognitive acts? Whose program carries those out? At present, no one's. Why is this?

It is because AI people have, in general, tended to cling to a notion that in some sense, thoughts obey formal rules at the thought level, just as George Boole believed that "the laws of thought" amounted to formal rules for manipulating propositions. [Boole, 1854.] I believe that this Boolean dream is at the root of the slogan "cognition as computation"—and I believe it will turn out to be revealed for what it is: an elegant chimera.

ENDNOTES TO THE PAPERS ON ARTIFICIAL INTELLIGENCE

Allen Newell

The four papers in this volume devoted directly to artificial intelligence (AI) are all quite independent of each other, having been generated by a process that did not quite live up to the ideal envisioned by the editors, namely, a main paper plus commentaries. Thus, there is no organic reason for a response. Nevertheless, in the interests of good form, I will make a few comments. Since structurally they cannot be footnotes, let them be endnotes. They are just what strikes me as worth noting about the four pieces.

THE NEWELL PAPER

Relative to my own contribution, I find the other papers useful as a reminder of additional intellectual issues that should have been considered. Boden's paper contains an emphasis on *Humanizing versus Dehumanizing*. Although this has an echo in the issue *Replacing versus Helping Humans,* Boden's issue is clearly more fundamental and sweeping. Barr quotes Laurence Miller on the differing attitudes of AI scientists and psychologists about the difficulty of *Constructing versus Testing Psychological Theories*. I agree with the importance of the intellectual issue, and it probably should have been included in my list. It clusters with another issue in separating psychology from AI, namely, *Memory versus Processing,* but it is conceptually quite distinct. However, Miller's emphasis on the issue as the major explanation for the differing evaluations of the contribution of AI would not be supported by the substantially more complex situation that my own paper documents. [L. Miller, 1978.] Barr's quotation from Minsky and Papert complaining about the nontechnical status of words such as parallel and

This research was sponsored in part by the Defense Advanced Research Projects Agency (DOD), ARPA Order No. 3597, monitored by the Air Force Avionics Laboratory under Contract F33615-78-C-1551. The views and conclusions contained in the paper are those of the author and should not be interpreted as representing the official policies, either expressed or implied, of the Defense Advanced Research Projects Agency or the United States government.

analog, not only fits in with the overall picture I drew of the nature of intellectual issues, but reinforces the existence of several particular issues. Such quotations are data points for an objective determination of what intellectual issues existed for AI over time. Finally, Hofstadter's paper makes use of an issue of *Unitary Objects versus Statistical Aggregates* (probably not quite the right moniker), which coordinates with other issues I did include, such as *Serial versus Parallel,* but is not the same. Hofstadter's paper also exemplifies discourse at the level of intellectual issues, but that will come up in my notes on his paper.

THE BODEN PAPER

Margaret Boden has provided another essay that continues to establish her as one of the most knowledgeable and sympathetic critical observers of AI. The themes she plays out here are ones she has been concerned with for some time, and their development can be followed in her recently published collection. [Boden, 1981a.] Especially worthy of attention is her concern over the issue of whether AI is humanizing or dehumanizing. She argues clearly for the possibility that AI is humanizing, against the cultural stereotype that equates mechanization with dehumanization. As already noted, this is an intellectual issue, as that term is used in my paper. Her discussion reveals an important aspect of behavior with respect to intellectual issues, namely, reasoning with generalized concepts. Thus, computers are mechanical, mechanical means nonhuman, therefore computers are dehumanizing, which makes it difficult for considerations of a different flavor to get a hearing, such as those that Boden introduces—active intelligence and the potentialities of computer representation for exploring the nature of subjectivity. Of course, little progress would be made if one instance of slogan reasoning simply replaced another, for example, computers have internal representations, internal representations permit subjectivity, the subjective is part of the humanistic tradition, therefore computers are humanizing. We need to find ways to convert discussion at the level of intellectual issues into scientific studies of the effects (and potential effects) of our artifacts on our culture.

In this regard, the comments of Boden about the potential relevance of AI to social psychology need to be underlined. In my own view, the best bet to unravel the skein of substantive issues about whether complex artifacts, such as the computer, are humanizing or dehumanizing lies in understanding in detail social perception and interpretation and the processing that attends them. Actually, there exists an active, substantial subpart of social psychology called *social cognition,* whose expressed intent is to bring over into social psychology modern cognitive theories and results. [Clark and Fiske, 1982; Nisbett and Ross, 1980.] Cognitive psychology is not AI, and this group is not directly dedicated to bringing over the results of AI into social psychology. However, AI is one of the sources that created modern cognitive theory. I for one would expect the effect of AI on social psychology to occur largely through such an indirect path.

I seem to be arriving at a view of intellectual issues as having substantial ideological content—that one of their dysfunctional aspects is that they permit discourse to stay focused on highly general concepts with ill-defined semantics. Boden's comment on another issue reinforces this conclusion, namely, the psychological relevance of attempts to match experimental results against theories expressed in programmed form, which she labels as debatable. She identifies the basis for the debate to be the uncertain boundary between what aspects of the program are intendedly psychologically relevant and what aspects are not. Boden has also made this point in her early writings about the field. [Boden, 1972.] Indeed, concern with this problem of the boundary was rampant in the 1960s. [Reitman, 1965, chap. 1.]

My point is that this issue has both ideological and scientific components. It participates in an intellectual issue about the possible forms for theories of human behavior—programs versus mathematics versus no-formalism. As an indicator of its ideological character, the issue of surplus meaning of all scientific theories has long been noted both negatively (unjustified incorporation) and positively (novel implications that prove out). With respect to the latter, theoretical physicists positively rhapsodize on letting the elegance of the mathematical formulation lead the way. Yet, the aspect of this perennial problem that is always brought to bear on AI programs as theories is the negative side, as if this were a special feature of these AI theories. A little later in her essay, Boden notes this tendency to apply to AI with a special intensity concerns that afflict all science. It would seem that this phenomenon is not peculiar to AI, but is an aspect of intellectual issues generally.

There are also scientific issues involved here, and genuine advance is possible in resolving them. In fact, this occurred in the mid-1970s. [Newell, 1973a; Anderson, 1976; Pylyshyn, 1978.] Ideally, an information-processing theory posits a *cognitive architecture* for the subject; this is psychologically significant, just like the posits of any theory. An architecture provides symbolic structures for specifying behavior—called programs, plans, behavior schemas, methods, or whatever. Such structures are psychologically significant even in their details, because the claim that a given architecture is operative entails the twin claims that (1) the person's behavior is specified by such structures and (2) any such structures that can be created by the processes of the architecture can govern behavior. Such a technical advance provides a principled way of stating exactly the theoretical significance of the parts of a program proposed as a theory. However, as we saw before, it will hardly settle the total issue, which is fueled by a larger set of concerns.

THE BARR PAPER

Barr attempts what I would call an internal mainstream description of AI—one consonant, say (though naturally enough), with the *Handbook of*

Artificial Intelligence. [Barr and Feigenbaum, 1981.] The picture comes through fairly well. However, I think he has some problems that stem from AI not being isolated enough for such an internalist description to be stable. Barr keeps having to describe AI in relation to other fields, and these descriptions often come through as incomplete.

One place where Barr offers a unique perspective is in respect to the growing emphasis in AI on applications. I believe he is right when he argues the importance of the current development of AI applications to all of AI, although I may locate their importance at a different place than Barr. He seems to place the emphasis on particular system characteristics (e.g., his list of five in the section on The Status of Artificial Intelligence); I see more diffuse but perhaps pervasive effects.

Let me sketch one potential effect of particular interest from the perspective of this volume. This is an enhanced development of an internal history of AI that is less influenced intellectually by other fields than has been the case heretofore. It is not that AI has failed so far to develop a strong identity. Quite the contrary, the possession of the computer as a unique powerful methodological tool and source of theoretical concepts has produced a field brash enough to make its neighboring fields uncomfortable and a bit sniffy on occasion. But coincident with this have been strong couplings with these other fields—with the rest of computer science, psychology, logic, and linguistics. Each of these relations shows a different pattern of symbiotic, competitive, and parasitic elements. But they all characterize a field that has not been left to itself intellectually. For instance, in the 1960s, a substantial segment of the attention of AI researchers was diverted for several years to the development of time-sharing systems, and an analogous shift is now occurring with respect to personal computers and VLSI (very-large-scale integration) design. Without the strong coupling of AI and computer science, this sort of switch could not happen. Its effect is to keep AI's history intermingled with that of mainstream computer science. This intermingling is pervasive, and the evidence for it can be found throughout the *Handbook* as well as in Barr's paper.

However, AI application systems are of AI's own making. They provide a locus for advances made within AI to fold back into new advances within AI, without the involvement of other fields. The interest here is not whether such a development would be a good thing or not, or whose norms should be used to measure it, but how it would affect the character of AI. Because this internal history would grow in an application milieu, the view of AI as an engineering discipline would grow as well. Its bonds with computer science would strengthen; its interest in the primeval problem of the nature of mind would wane. This would probably strengthen cognitive science as a discipline rather than an interdiscipline, since some people in AI with strong concerns about mind and human intelligence would find the application-orientation too uncongenial and would shift their energies to cognitive science.

Alternative futures are possible, of course, even given the continued growth of a robust AI applications field. One is that the interdisciplinary mishmash, so admirably exemplified by this volume, will simply continue to expand and intermix. All attempts of manageable disciplines to congeal will fail, destroyed by the continued emergence of highly significant research results from remote regions. We might be tempted to call the whole thing a superdiscipline; however, it will be a most untidy affair. Most scientists will feel inadequate most of the time, because of their inability to maintain any reasonably comprehensive view or acquire and maintain all the tools they need. Such a state of affairs would hardly be unprecedented. For instance, it occurs whenever fields are invaded from without by radically new, highly technical tools. This happened in the mathematization of economics and psychology, to mention just two that I happen to have witnessed. However, these were transients. A permanent state of conceptual disarray and instability would be a novel experience for science.

The happiest alternative, of course, would be the development of a unified theory of information-processing that would be applicable to everyone's intellectual concerns—in fact and not just in theory (sic). Although many hope for such a thing (including myself), the sprawling character of the intellectual terrain will surely make such a development tortuous and long in coming, even after the essential elements of the successful synthesis have surfaced.

THE HOFSTADTER PAPER

It is now necessary to turn to the paper by Douglas Hofstadter. It is not evident to me why Hofstadter chose this forum to launch a substantive argument, as opposed to commenting on the field's structure. In fact, the somewhat polemical and diffuse character of the paper makes it a little difficult to ascertain all his intentions.

One of the most elegant and gracious institutional mechanisms of science is the principle of public silence. All scientists are obligated to present their work in public forum before their peers, but there is no corresponding obligation to respond. If you use a fellow scientist's work, then you must acknowledge him or her appropriately. But if his or her work is irrelevant to your own progress, then it may simply be ignored—met with silence. Further, the criterion of relevance is not simply that the work speak to the same topic but that it contribute to the actual body of science involved. Thus is prevented endless and socially destructive rounds of evaluation and disputation. What is valuable is winnowed from the chaff; what fails to attract continued attention falls by the wayside and is forgotten with a minimum of pain and fuss. A scientist may feel ignored, but energy is devoted to making progress rather than to criticism, and civility is much increased.

The present forum has a structure that does not permit the public silence that is my instinctive reaction as a scientist to Hofstadter's paper. In the jargon of AI, a slot is provided in which comments on each paper are expected. This expectation means that remaining silent receives a special interpretation, though an ambiguous one. Thus, I make a few comments about the paper to meet my obligations to the reader and the editors.

Hofstadter's paper shows the difficulty with attempting to operate at the level of intellectual issues. The issue-complex he discusses is clearly identified in my "Intellectual Issues" paper by the cluster made up of *Symbolic versus Continuous Systems, Problem-Solving versus Recognition, Psychology versus Neuroscience, Performance versus Learning,* and *Serial versus Parallel.* Elements of all of these issues can be found in Hofstadter's paper, with an emphasis on recognition and parallelism and the addition, as previously noted, of a concern with what might be called a statistical mechanics of the mind.

What is striking in Hofstadter's paper—and what seems to me typical of discussions centered on intellectual issues—is the abundance of strong opinion and argumentation from general conceptual considerations and the absence of concrete scientific data or theory to build on. There is an abundance of attacks on the general opinions of others, with a corresponding promotion of the general opinions of self. There is strong concern with what other people believe and assert, and weak concern with what is true of the scientific phenomenon under discussion, independent of who said it. In short, there is disputation.

A scientific discussion of the relative roles of mechanisms with time constants *less than* rather than *more than* 100 milliseconds would focus on what functions are accomplished by mechanisms at the different durations, how to characterize them theoretically, and what is the evidence for them. The scientific discussion would focus on formulating a question about the relative roles that would add something to our scientific characterization of the mind and its operation. It would not focus in any serious way on what other scientists said, especially in their summary or epigrammatic statements. What counts is what the theory and the data say and why they say it, not what scientists say.

Theories and data are surrounded at all times by a cloud of commentary— that is how we all struggle to communicate and understand the substance of the science we are generating. Intellectual issues seem to be one of the ways of generating this cloud of commentary that accompanies scientific work. Hofstadter, as any other scientist, is free to use all the commentary he wants in his paper, which certainly includes using other scientist's commentary as agreement or foil. This will help to orient us to his work and let us understand it. The problem with the present paper is that, in a poor paraphrase of Gertrude Stein, there is no work there that works. Less epigrammatically, Hofstadter's paper is a (tiny) example of the scientific process gone awry, in which (on the evidence of the text) a paper was written to accomplish science entirely by means of commentary.

I cannot leave Hofstadter's paper without warning the reader about its level of scholarship. I will only select one instance, which is of some importance both to me and the argument in his paper; numerous additional examples, both large and small, occur in the text. Hofstadter devotes a section, Passive Symbols and Formal Rules, to examining the position of Simon and myself on the nature of symbols and contrasting this position in stark terms with his own view (the whole contrast being cast in a peculiarly personal idiom). Since his paper is available in this same volume, it is not necessary to quote extensively. However, a quote from the opening paragraph of that section will help to convey the content of the section:

> We can see that to Simon and Newell, a symbol seems to be any token, any character inside a computer that has an ASCII code (a standard but arbitrarily assigned sequence of seven bits). To me, by contrast, symbol connotes something with representational power. To them (if I am not mistaken), it would be fine to call a bit (inside a computer) or a neuron-firing a symbol; however, I cannot feel comfortable with that usage of the term. (Hofstadter in his paper in this volume.)

Hofstadter is indeed mistaken, absolutely and unequivocally. My concern here is that the reader not take seriously any of Hofstadter's characterizations of our position. Simon and I have written extensively about the nature of symbols, and many of these writings are well known. [Newell and Simon, 1972; Newell and Simon, 1976a; Newell, 1980b.] Here are quotations from the latter, entitled "Physical Symbol Systems," in which I devoted the entire paper to going on record as clearly as I knew how as to our (AI researchers') understanding of the nature of symbols, circa 1980:

> The most fundamental concept for a symbol is that which gives symbols their symbolic character, i.e., which lets them stand for some entity. We call this concept *designation*, though we might have used any of several other terms, e.g., *reference, denotation, naming, standing for, aboutness*, or even *symbolization* or *meaning*. (p. 156.)

> Representation is simply another term to refer to a structure that designates . . . . (p. 176.)

> The usual formulations of universal machines also tend to use the term *symbol* for the alphabet of distinctive patterns that can occur in the memory medium (e.g., the 0 and 1 tape symbols for our Turing machine). As defined, these entities are not symbols in the sense of our symbol system. They satisfy only part of the requirements for a symbol, namely being the tokens in expressions. It is of course possible to give them full symbolic character by programming an accessing mechanism that gets from them to some data structure. (p. 158.)

These quotations are simply the parts of the paper that address directly and unequivocally the characterization that Hofstadter's quotation presents.

The rest of my paper on symbol systems deals at length with the positive characterization of how symbols represent in general, and how this can happen by means of finite mechanisms. The treatment is entirely consistent with Simon's and my other writings on symbols. The point here is not whether this theory is known to be right, only that the description of it in Hofstadter's paper bears little relation to its actual form.

A FINAL WORD

The only final remark I would make about the collection of papers is that the historical pictures they all draw of the field seem roughly consonant (though their evaluations are not necessarily so). To first order, they seem to be talking about the same history. This is true also of the paper by Pylyshyn about cognitive science. [Pylyshyn in this volume.] However, I have not yet seen the other papers in the volume. It will be interesting to see the extent to which quite different views exist of the total historical framework and to discover the sources of such differences.

SECTION 4

LINGUISTICS AND ITS RELATIONS TO OTHER DISCIPLINES

Thomas G. Bever

Language is central to our conception of what it means to be human. Linguistics, the science of language, has been an influential discipline for many years. As speakers, we have strong intuitions about what a satisfactory linguistic theory must include. Linguistic theories have presented precise versions of different scientific approaches to the description of all behavior and knowledge. The dominant philosophy of behavioral science between 1920 and 1960 was an extreme form of operationalism, *behaviorism*. Behaviorism required that all abstract terms of a theory be resolvable into observable stimuli or responses. Thirty years of linguistic investigation clarified the limits of such a framework. In the late 1950s, a leading researcher on animal behavior, B. F. Skinner, published a definitive behaviorist treatment of the psychology of language. [Skinner, 1957.] His book was reviewed by a linguist, Noam Chomsky, who summarized the weaknesses of the behaviorist explanation of grammatical structures. [Chomsky, 1959.] The main point was that behaviorist restrictions on theoretical terms make it impossible to describe structural facts about language. Chomsky argued that abstractness of theoretical devices is not only normal in science, it allows for greater descriptive adequacy in the case of language. This review, and the concomitant development of nonbehaviorist grammars for describing sentences, signaled a revolution in linguistics that has had broad implications for other behavioral and social sciences. The overall effect of discoveries in linguistics has been to raise the possibility that the evolution and contemporary nature of symbolic behavior involves highly specific mechanisms of learning and representation.

LINGUISTICS—THE SCIENCE OF LANGUAGE

Language is a symbolic structure that humans use as a means of communicative and personal representation of the world. Two central aspects of this structure carry meaning: reference and propositional relations.

Reference

Words refer to objects in the world or mind. Prima facie, such reference is an obvious and straightforward kind of relation between a symbol and the world; *dog* refers to four-footed canines, *bachelor* to unmarried human males, and so on. Consideration of the symbol/referent relation has been a central concern of the philosophy of language, since it bears directly on how humans represent and know the world around them. The relation between reference and meaning is not so simple as it seems. We cannot define the symbolic meanings of words as the sum of their referents, since that would incorrectly imply that a trivial change in the referent (e.g., in the number of dogs in the world) would change the meaning of a word. Furthermore, certain words have no external reference, for example, *unicorn,* and certain words seem to be defined only in terms of their effects on other words, for example, *not, did*. [Frege, 1879; Katz, 1971.]

Such facts demonstrate that knowing a language involves something other than simply knowing a large number of symbol/referent associations. This is also attested by the fact that many animals can master many such associations: A skilled shepherd dog can distinguish a large number of different commands involved in moving a herd of sheep. Yet, we do not conclude that such a dog has mastered a language.

Propositional Relations

Languages involve the relation of individual words in meaningful propositions. For example, in the sentence *dogs bark*, there is a relation between *dogs* and *bark* that transcends the separate references that each word might have. This relation is that between an agent of an action and the action itself. Similarly, in *dogs bite cats*, the third word is the object of the action; in *dogs often bite cats*, the second word specifies an aspect of the action. In general, words are set in such relations to each other within meaningful propositions that apply to entire events or states in the world. That is, utterances have meanings that are independent of the reference of the individual words.

The Generative Model of Linguistic Structure

Sentences are the smallest units of language that present well-formed propositions that can relate meanings and references. For this reason, current linguistic investigations focus on the sentence as the major unit of investigation. Within a particular language, sentences have distinct structural properties. For example, in English, *the dog chased the cat* means something different from *the cat chased the dog* but is very similar in meaning to *the cat was chased by the dog*.

The goal of linguistic research is, in large part, to discover the model that describes sentences and their interrelations. In this essay, I present an outline of the model as it is widely accepted, though it must be emphasized that its status and details are always subject to change in interpretation. Three features of linguistic descriptions have remained invariant over many decades. First, languages are characterized as having a number of *levels of representation*. Each level is delimited and defined by a particular set of *units and relations*. The levels are related by *mapping rules* that express well-formed configurational relations between particular structures at each level. [For a general review of the recent history of linguistics, see Newmeyer, 1980.]

A simple example from the English sound system clarifies these notions. Sound sequences are analyzed at two primary levels—an internal array of schematic units and an external string of actual acoustic/articulatory units. Consider the word *bitter*. When the word is pronounced slowly, we can isolate the individual sounds that correspond to the internal array, consisting of /b/,/i/,/t/,/er/. This differentiates the word at both levels from other words, such as *bidder* (/b/,/i/,/d/,/er/). If the words are pronounced quickly, they begin to converge onto the same acoustic sequence. In particular, the middle consonants /t/ and /d/ can be pronounced identically (as a flap of the tongue against the roof of the mouth). Yet, even when rapidly spoken, the two words can still be correctly differentiated. Close analysis shows that one acoustic difference between the two rapidly spoken words is in the length of the vowel that precedes the middle consonant—when the consonantal sound corresponds to /d/ the preceding vowel is longer than when the consonantal sound corresponds to /t/. That is, we *hear* a difference between two consonants, which is acoustically signaled by the length of the preceding vowel.

This simple fact reveals a great deal about what we know when we know English sound regularities; this knowledge is schematized below. Words have an inner level of representation of sound sequences and a set of rules that map them onto an outer level representing the actual acoustic sequences:

Inner sound sequences for lexical items: for example, B I D R; B I T R.

Rules that map inner sequences onto acoustic/articulatory sequences, for example: (1) Vowels are lengthened before voiced consonants; and (2) in rapid speech, voiced and unvoiced consonants between vowels are spoken without voicing.

Rule 1 explains the difference in vowel length between words like *hit* and *hid*, or *back* and *bag*. It also explains why the first vowel in *bidder* is longer than that of *bitter*. Rule 2 explains why the second consonant in those two words sounds alike when they are pronounced rapidly. The ordering of rules 1 and 2 explains why the first vowel in rapidly spoken *bidder* is longer than that of *bitter*, even though the two middle consonants are identical after rule 2 applies to them. The logical ordering of the rules guarantees that the vowel preceding /d/ will be lengthened, before the /d/ loses its voicing. [Chomsky and Halle, 1968.]

Levels of Representation

This example displays a typical mapping relation between two levels of representation in language. Each level captures certain kinds of facts about our knowledge. The inner sound level represents the categorical knowledge of words, expressed in terms of sound schemata; the outer level represents how the words are actually pronounced, expressed in sequences of acoustic/articulatory units. Mapping rules represent relations that the language allows between these two levels.

The interrelation of distinct levels of representation is also part of the description of sentences. The units at each level are the constituent phrases, groupings of adjacent words and symbols into syntactically relevant units. For example, in the sentence *the dog often chased the cat*, the constituent phrases are *the dog*, *often chased*, *the cat*. Such phrases are postulated as components of the outer level of sentence representation, in part because they represent the natural units of phrasing in normal pronunciation. (Try pronouncing the sentence with pauses between the phrases and contrast that with pausing after every odd word.) They also represent the kinds of units out of which the surface sequence is composed.

Phrase constituents are more abstract than lexical items but can serve the same function as different kinds of lexical items. In the example sentence, *the dog* and *the cat* are classified as *nounphrases*, since the main content word of each is a noun; *often chased* is a *verbphrase* for the corresponding reason. This kind of designation allows the description of structural similarity among sentences that differ in other superficial properties. The preceding example has the same structure of the major surface constituents as both of the following: *dogs, chase, cats*; *the domestic canine, with considerable frequency chases, the domestic feline*. Each of these two sentences consists of a nounphrase, a verbphrase, and a nounphrase. Variation in length reflects the fact that constituents can contain constituents within themselves. Certain constituents can contain constituents of the same type: This makes those constituents *recursive*. For example, one type of nounphrase can itself be an entire proposition, underscored in *Harry believes that Bill is a fool*. Such recursion can repeat, for example, allowing *Harry believes that Sam knows that Bill is a fool*. The creative component of sentence structure is represented in the way in which phrase constituents can continually be elaborated: Sentences of arbitrary length and complexity can be represented as results of such self-embedding constituents.

Constituents are most salient in the surface structure of sentences, the level that presents their actual order and arrangement. Sentences are also described at inner levels of representation, where the arrangement of constituents reflects more abstract properties. For example, in *the dog often chased the cat*, the first phrase is defined by its structure and position as the grammatical subject and the last, as the grammatical object.

The differentiation of syntactic levels allows the description of various surface arrangements of constituents that correspond to the same inner arrangement. For example, *the cat chased the dog often* has the same abstract relations between constituents as the preceding case, as does *often the dog chased the cat*. In each case, *often* is arranged as part of the verbphrase in the inner structural level, while appearing in different positions in the outer structure. As in the sound system, the inner structure is mapped onto the outer structure by a set of rules. The particular orders and arrangements that are allowed in a language are the result of several sets of such rules. For example, transformations are rules that arrange an inner structure into a particular surface order. Such rules can rearrange the position of a verb modifier like *often* to appear in a position not adjacent to the verb. The passive transformation arranges the grammatical subject to precede the verb and the grammatical object to follow it, while introducing other words.

When first proposed, these mapping transformations were one of the main objects of linguistic investigation. The goal was to determine the set of transformations for each language and the universal laws that govern how they operate to map the inner syntactic level onto the outer syntactic level. It is important to note that the inner forms are all abstract—that is, they do not correspond to some actual sentence. This is tantamount to the claim that when speakers know a language, they know an abstract property for which they are given no specific example.

As it stands, the model assigns an inner and outer structure to a sentence but does not provide the meaning. The model is an account of structurally well-formed sentences regardless of what they mean (if anything). The model makes it possible to specify exactly what syntactic information contributes to the meaning of a sentence. An initial proposal was that the meaning of a sentence is determined entirely by its inner structure. This captured the intuition that surface variations in constituent order (as between the active and the passive) did not vary propositional relations between constituents.

The Development of the Model

Subsequent developments in the model have turned on two questions: What are the levels that contribute to meaning? What is the relative descriptive importance of transformations and constraints on how they apply? The relation of the model to meaning has been interpreted in two distinct ways by different theories. In one case, generative semantics, it was proposed that the inner structure of a sentence *is* the meaning without any further interpretation. This set up an appealing model in which the inner structure of a sentence is its meaning, and transformations map it directly onto actual sequences. [Lakoff and Ross, 1976.] There were a number of difficulties with this model; most notable was the fact that, as the notion of meaning was broadened, the corresponding range of possible inner structures had to be enriched. If two sentences have the same meaning, then on this model it must be represented by their having an identical inner structure. Simple examples demonstrate how unwieldy this proposal is. Consider the sentences "John is an unmarried eligible human male" and "John is a bachelor." They clearly have the same meaning, yet construction of a transformation to relate them involves great complexity.

A further difficulty with the unification of *inner* structure and meaning was that certain aspects of meaning appeared to be contributed by *surface* structure. For example, different interpretations of *one boy ate each jelly bean* and *each jelly bean was eaten by one boy* are reflected directly in their surface order. Such examples motivated an expansion of what information contributes to meaning to include surface structure as well as inner structure.

This change occurred at roughly the same time that it was noticed that outer and inner constituent arrangements are limited to the same configurations in any given language. [Emonds, 1970.] That is, even though the possible transformations that apply to inner structures could conceivably produce many varieties of surface arrangements, most of this power is never actually used within a language. This motivated the generalization that every surface structure must be potentially generated by some arrangement of inner structure constituents. Transformations became correspondingly simplified to the point at which there is only one transformation, which maps surface structures from underlying structures, namely, the rule *move-X* (where *X* is either an entire clause or a nounphrase). Conditions on possible transformations have been enriched, so that the possible surface configurations are restricted in the right way.

With such developments, it is harder to identify a unique syntactic level as the primary abstract structure. Viewed intuitively, the first version of the syntactic model generated surface sequences by applying various transformations to the inner syntactic structure; in general, the resulting sequences were always possible sentences. In its current manifestation, the model describes many surface sequences that do not correspond to sentences: They are filtered out by conditions of various kinds, ranging from limitations on particular surface properties to conditions on possible relations between surface and inner structures. In this way, the focus of linguistic investigation has shifted from discovering the transformations to discovering the conditions of well-formed structures at each level. An important hypothesis (not yet conclusively proven) is that the conditions are the same for every level of representation. [Chomsky, 1981.]

The Interpretation of Such Models and Facts They Explain

The essential goal of syntactic description is to generate descriptions for the well-formed sentence in a language. The syntactic model provides for every sentence a description consisting of several levels of representation and rules interrelating the levels. A sentence is marked as well formed only if it corresponds to a well-formed description in the model. The postulation of various levels of representation also allows for the structural differentiation of types of sentences. In particular, it allows us to make claims about unacceptability of different kinds. For example, sentences may be unacceptable because they are meaningless (*good is a sugar*), unusable (*the oyster the oyster the oyster split split split*), or ungrammatical (*Harry and Bill didn't know that each other was there*). Such differences show that there is a distinction between acceptability of a word sequence and its grammatical status. Sequences can be acceptable and grammatical, and unacceptable and ungrammatical. But both of the other combinations exist as well—a sequence can be ungrammatical but acceptable, and the converse. This clarifies an important empirical interpretation of the grammar: It describes what sentences are grammatical, not which sequences are acceptable.

LINGUISTICS AND COGNITIVE PSYCHOLOGY

Cognitive psychology is the study of the acquisition and memory of knowledge and beliefs. There are three main current themes in this field. The first explores the span of consciousness, the second is concerned with the form of mental representations, and the third focuses on learning as a special kind of problem-solving. In each case, linguistics has made specific contributions by providing a precise and rich formal description of a complex behavior.

Language and the Psychological Present

For several decades, a major concern has been the transformation of information during the first phases of acquiring knowledge. This study involves the borderlines between processes of attention, perception, and recognition. When we perceive an object in the world, we use a series of retransformations of the stimulus input, starting with the most peripheral sensory representation and moving to the most abstract. We can interpret each stage of representation as a level of consciousness; the span of attention increases in their time range and complexity as it shifts from dependence on one kind of representation to another. Experimental techniques intrude on the ordinary flow of information, showing which points are under conscious control and which are not. This provides a picture of consciousness that is somewhat fragmented. Stable representations of information hop from stage to stage via brief unconscious periods of transformation.

In most cases, the study of this serial process involves information that is itself of little interest, as the perception and retention of letter groups. Such stimuli have little internal structure that might yield information on the kind of transformations that can occur at each stage. A related problem is that the stimuli do not comprise a natural subset of the world that could call on psychologically indigenous processes. Language is such a behavior, and linguistics offers a rich fund of information about possible kinds of representations.

The study of how listeners comprehend speech corresponds to the studies of how information is transformed during immediate encoding. The plausible view of a retransformation is that listeners first transform the acoustic structure into a sequence of separate sounds, which are grouped into words and then into phrases and sentences and, finally, into meanings.

Careful research on comprehension processes has shown that the successive-stage model of encoding is incorrect; rather, the levels of language representation interact directly during comprehension. We can use our high-level expectations about meaning to guide our low-level expectations about sounds. Of course, the points at which such information can be related between levels depend on the presence of complete representations at the separate levels. This gives special status to points in a sentence that correspond to complete units at more than one level of representation; for example, the end of a clause is also typically the end of a meaning proposition and the end of a constituent. Accordingly, numerous studies show that at such points listeners integrate the meaning of a sentence with other aspects of it and its contextual role.

Most important is the fact that sentence comprehension clarifies certain aspects of consciousness. First, we seem to understand sentences directly as we hear them, even though our understanding itself modifies the sounds that we perceive. Various experiments demonstrate that an enormous amount of computational activity occurs during sentence comprehension, but we are conscious only of the unified output—the pairing of a sound sequence with a meaning. This simple fact tells us a great deal about the relation between separable unconscious processes and their unification within consciousness.

In the case of sentences, the unity of conscious experience can even be observed in contrast with the duration of the sentence itself. Consider the sentence you are reading right now. When did it begin as a conscious experience as a sentence? After the first word? The second? In fact, it appears to have begun at the beginning and to have ended exactly at the end. In this sense, sentences are impenetrable units of conscious experience. Since they can be quite long, and still be perceived as sentences, one consequence of language is that it expands the range of our momentary conscious experience. Rather than being limited to six items, a sentence expands our momentary span to 20 words, or 100 sounds! [G. A. Miller, 1956.]

It does so, of course, by utilizing the unconscious mechanisms for rapid calculation of structural organization. This allows us to use language as a case study in the role of structures in expanding the domains of conscious activity.

The Relation between Knowledge and Behavior

A second problem of cognition has been the relation of knowledge to behavior. For example, humans know many things to be true about logic and integers but make characteristic kinds of mistakes in everyday reasoning and mathematics. The systematic nature of such mistakes reveals specific mechanisms for implementing knowledge. This is reflected in three experimental domains of cognitive psychology: memory, perception, and behavior-production. In each case, the development of generative linguistic theory has stimulated new research and a general controversy over how directly the grammar of a language is involved in ongoing behavior.

This controversy first expressed itself in the study of human memory for sentences. The accepted view of memory in general is that it uses canonical schemata, such as a typical face or a typical bird, as basic representational schemata. Individual experiences are retained in terms of such schemata and variations on them. Linguistic research stimulated considerable investigation of sentence memory by providing a number of levels of representation at which such canonical schemata can be stated. Shortly after the emergence of generative grammar, it was natural to investigate the possibility that it is the inner structures of sentences that we retain when we remember them. If true, this would offer a precise theory of the canonical memory structures, and a theory of how they are mapped onto external forms. It was exciting to think that formal linguistic analysis could provide results that would be immediately integrated with psychological investigations of a traditional problem such as memory. This interaction between linguistics and psychology became the cornerstone of a new interdisciplinary field, psycholinguistics. [G. A. Miller, 1962.]

The initial results were encouraging: It appeared to be the case that sentences that are more complex in their grammatical description are harder to remember. For example, a passive construction involves more transformations than an active construction and is, indeed, harder to recall. Such facts, however, turned out to be due to other factors, such as the relative infrequency of the construction and the fact that it presents the major phrases out of the typical subject-verb-object order. When meanings and order are carefully contolled, transformational complexity does not predict memory difficulty. [Fodor and Garrett, 1967.]

There are two ways to resolve such a discrepancy between a formal theory of behavior and direct behavioral evidence. We can argue that the link between the formal theory and the behavior is extremely abstract and that specific behavioral facts might not directly reveal the formal theory. Alternatively, we can argue that behavioral disconfirmations actually disconfirm the linguistic theory itself: If the behavioral predictions are wrong, then the formal theory is wrong. Most scholars took the first course, assuming that the failure of behavioral predictions based on transformational analyses was due to the lack of a theory of how the formal theory is utilized in behavior. This interpretation presumed a distinction between competence (the formal theory) and performance (behavior). Such a distinction allowed a retrenchment of the field of psycholinguistics: Linguistic analyses were invoked as describing the structure of the language but not necessarily the structure intrinsic to language behavior. The role of linguistics was to provide structural analyses of sentences. The role of psychology was to explore which of the analyses actually play a part in speech behavior. [Bever, 1970; Fodor et al., 1974.]

The distinction between competence and performance seemed clear in the case of memory, since there are many ways we can choose to memorize and many different reasons to do so. Speech comprehension and production, however, offer fewer choices—we generally have one purpose in comprehension, to understand ideas; and generally one purpose in talking, to express ideas. We might expect that a grammar would express itself more directly in such behaviors, because there is less opportunity to impose behavior-specific strategies. However, both behaviors appear to use heuristics for interrelating sound and meaning: Heuristics are responsive to certain structural properties of sentences but to other factors as well.

Consider, for example, the usual arrangement of actor, action, and object. In English, this is the normal order. Various perceptual studies suggest that listeners impose such an interpretation on sentences as a preliminary (and unconscious) hypothesis. Clearly, such a strategy is a powerful simplifying device but has nothing directly to do with a formal grammatical property: Most clauses do conform to this pattern, but not all.

Despite the clear evidence that certain aspects of talking and listening depend on nongrammatical patterns and processes, some linguists have adopted the position that the failure of a grammar directly to predict all behavioral facts invalidates that grammar. One proposal, in particular, is that transformations fail to correspond directly to behavioral data because language is not transformational. According to this view, individual lexical items carry sufficient structural information to map directly onto meanings. [Bresnan, 1978.] It is beyond the scope of this paper to present the linguistic arguments that might bear on such a question. However, it clarifies what remains an open issue on the relation between formal grammar and speech behavior: Which properties of behavior directly reflect grammatical knowledge and which reflect properties of perception and behavior production.

General and Specific Learning Mechanisms

The final area of interaction between linguistics and cognitive psychology involves how the formal grammar is learned. Within current cognitive psychology, the issue involves the specificity of mechanisms that learn and process any skill. In one extreme view, all learning is carried out by a general-purpose processing mechanism that applies equally to the learning of language and other abilities. In the alternative view, learning is carried out by a set of innate mental "modules," each highly specialized for its task; the mind would be a federation of such distinct modules.

These two views can agree that the adult mind is highly differentiated into component capacities; the views oppose each other with regard to the nature of learning. The computational model was the dominant theory in the psychology of learning for many years: All learning was held to be the association of stimuli and responses—intelligence consisted of the ability to form large numbers of such associations. This view was an important rationale for studying learning in animals, since human mechanisms of skill acquisition were assumed to be the same, only more capacious. A similar computational view is now held by many researchers in computer science. The computer is viewed as a minor brain that can represent the essential features of the child's mind. Although the processes may be richer than simple association of stimuli and responses, the basic claim about learning is the same as that of the traditional stimulus/response learning theorists: Learning results from the application of general mechanisms to specific experiences. In particular, language would be learned as the result of general problem-solving capacities that children (or computers) apply to the language they experience. [Minsky, 1968; Simon, 1969 and 1981.]

Modular theorists argue that speech data the child hears are always too impoverished to account for what is learned. Therefore, children must have a particular capacity, innately tailored to learn language; otherwise they could not extrapolate from limited data to the correct complete knowledge of their language. The general claim of such theorists is that only artificial and uninteresting skills are truly learned by the application of general intelligence. [Chomsky, 1980a.]

This has brought back into psychology an old controversy over whether the mind is a collection of separate faculties or whether it depends on the deployment of nonspecific intelligence. All parties to the controversy agree that some highly specific processes are innate and that there is some capacity for nonspecific learning. The empirical question involves the nature and relative importance of the two kinds of processes.

LINGUISTICS AND THE BIOLOGY OF COMMUNICATION

The contrast between general and specific bases for language is central to biological considerations: Is language the result of a linguistically isolated evolutionary change, or did it become possible as the result of some general mutation? Evolutionary speculation about a behavior pattern is limited by lack of direct records. What we can do is reason from contemporary morphological and behavioral facts. Three biological properties of language are particularly relevant: the morphology of the vocal tract and attempts to teach animals a language that is visual; the possibility of a maturationally determined critical period for language acquisition; and the neurological specialization of the left hemisphere of the brain for language.

Language Without Mouths

One aspect of language that differentiates it from other animal activity is the richness of its acoustic structure. This depends on an articulatory apparatus that allows for a moving occlusion (produced by the tongue) that separates two relatively independent chambers in front of and behind it. An ape's mouth, for example, simply cannot differentiate the variety of acoustic resonances that are characteristic of language: The jaw is too recessed to allow the tongue to separate two large vocal cavities. Paleontological evidence suggests that relatively recent hominids still had a recessed jaw, which would not allow for phonological variety. This would mark the evolution of language capacity as very recent, perhaps less than 100,000 years. [Lieberman, 1968.]

It is startling to think of the evolution of language as so recent and so dependent on a peripheral physiological change. Furthermore, the existence of sign languages in the deaf suggests that vocal expression is not intrinsically necessary for language to emerge. One line of investigation concerns whether sign language is itself a distinct language or whether it is a visual subset of spoken languages. The research to date suggests that it is an independent language with rules and properties of its own that are not dependent on phonetic-based language. Most interesting is the fact that sign language also appears to respect the more abstract universals of language, such as the separation of levels of analysis. [Klima and Bellugi, 1979.]

Of course, so far as we know, sign language emerged after spoken language, and may be historically parasitic on it in certain ways. One direct test of the phonetic basis for linguistic evolution would be to train an animal to use signs: The most obvious animal is an ape because of its intelligence and closeness to human beings. If the training were successful, then we would have some basis for claiming that the particular articulatory developments in humans might, indeed, have been solely responsible for linguistic capacity.

Teaching apes to talk has, of course, broader implications for our understanding of information and its transmission. A number of recent studies have attempted to teach chimpanzees sign language or the use of computer-controlled abstract symbols. [Gardner and Gardner, 1971; Terrace et al., 1979; Premack, 1976.] The achievements of the chimps are considerable, but there is no convincing evidence that they learn language structure. Rather, like shepherd dogs, they can be taught specific sequences and specific relational symbols; the capacity to generalize from such training to sentences in general appears to be lacking. At the moment, such studies have the ambiguity of experimental failures: All we can be absolutely sure of is that existing techniques have failed to teach apes to talk. We can also be reasonably sure that if some method is found that is more successful, it will involve a learning environment that is highly contrived. It will be radically unlike the environment that stimulates language learning in children.

The Critical-Period Hypothesis

Children acquire the language of the community in which they grow up. This is obvious evidence in favor of the hypothesis that language is learned. The acquisition of behavior patterns by animals shows similar learning, for example, a gosling acquires a permanent attachment to its own parent. This apparent learning turns out to be highly constrained: During a specific phase of growth, the gosling becomes parentally fixated on any object that has approximately the right size and the right speed of movement. This is a typical example of a "critical period," during which specific experiences must occur. After the period has passed, the ability of the animal to learn is closed off. [K. Lorenz, 1965.]

One argument for the biological specificity of language would be that it also has a critical period. The strongest test of this would be to expose certain children to language at different ages to see if their learning ability changes. This ethically unacceptable experiment has been simulated in a few instances in which children brought up in isolation or by animals are discovered in adolescence. A recent case study is Genie, a girl isolated until age 11. Her linguistic ability is still minimal after a number of years of intensive training. This does not prove that there is a critical period for language, since many of her other social and cognitive skills are abnormal as well. [Fromkin et al., 1973.]

Nature occasionally performs a different kind of experiment, in which the brain is injured during childhood. This gives an opportunity to observe the speed with which language function recovers. If there were a critical period, we would expect injury after a certain age to involve categorically greater loss of language. Clinical surveys have found evidence consistent with this; injury after age twenty is often followed by long-lasting aphasia, while injury before age ten is not. [Lenneberg, 1967.] The interpretation of such facts, however, is not unequivocally in support of a critical period for language-learning. First, the critical age would seem to extend for ten years, which is rather unconvincingly critical. Second, recovery of a function by an injured brain is not the same as original acquisition of that function. It has long been known that a seriously injured brain can operate by compensatory functions, not necessarily replacement of damaged structures with identical ones. [K. Goldstein, 1948.] Accordingly, the loss of plasticity of neural recovery for speech may reflect a general loss of plasticity. In particular, it has not been shown that the loss of language-recovery plasticity at age twenty is any greater than the loss of plasticity for other capacities of similar complexity.

A supplementary approach has been to explore the evidence for a critical period in the ability to learn second languages. If such a critical period existed, it would be consistent with the view that language-learning is dependent on specific maturational mechanisms that automatically deteriorate after a certain age. Despite the frequent intuition that learning a second language in adulthood is difficult, research on the topic is not unequivocal. What differences there are might be attributed to a loss of motivation, or of general memory capacity, as opposed to a specific loss of linguistic capacity.

Cerebral Asymmetries

The left hemisphere of human brains is relatively specialized for language. This is simply demonstrated by the fact that injury to that hemisphere results in aphasia, while injury to the right hemisphere rarely does so. Furthermore, children with only a left hemisphere learn language better than children with only a right hemisphere (these children having had the other hemisphere surgically removed). Such a lateral coincidence with language is consistent with the view that the left hemisphere is biologically predisposed for language. Clinical facts, indeed, suggest that such a predisposition must exist but leave open the question of how specific to language the predisposition is. For example, if the left hemisphere is predisposed for all processing that involves interrelations of parts and wholes, then language might emerge in that hemisphere, since sentence-processing always involves interrelating words and phrases with an entire meaning.

A growing body of research is consistent with this view: The left hemisphere appears to be the more frequent seat of relational activities of a variety of kinds. Accordingly, its specialization for language does not show that language is uniquely formed by the hemisphere itself. [Levy, 1972; Bever, 1980a.]

LINGUISTICS AND PHILOSOPHY

Language is the most salient vehicle for human knowledge and judgment. Accordingly, it is often treated as central to issues involving the philosophy of mind. Indeed, certain periods in philosophy have been dominated by the view that in solving linguistic problems, we can solve fundamental problems concerning epistemology and truth. Modern linguistics bears on three main issues: the biological basis of knowledge, reductionism as the standard form of scientific explanation, and the existence of Platonic a priori structures.

Empiricist and Nativist Theories of Mind

The source of human knowledge is one of the oldest problems of philosophy. The question is whether we represent the world as it is or whether we impose our own structure on reality. Empiricism—taken as a theory of learning rather than as a method for advancing knowledge—is the extreme view that categories of experience are derived from experience of the world; nativism is the alternative view that forms of experience are innately determined and actual experience merely provides specific content for the innate forms. Language provides certain critical examples for this debate.

One issue concerns analytic truths, that is, sentences that are true by definition. For example, both sentences that follow are true and have always been so in our experience, but the first could change, while the second could not without a change in the meaning of the words: (1) *Human bachelors are between the height of 1 foot and 9 feet*, and (2) *Human bachelors are unmarried males*. The truth of the second sentence is categorical, rooted in the very meaning of the words. There is no amount of contingent experience that could account for the child's discovery of the categorical nature of such a truth—yet children do discover such distinctions between necessary and contingent truths. This would seem definitively to disprove the empiricist's position, since the distinction must be innate if it is not learned. Empiricists, however, have countered in a number of ways. The most obvious way is to deny that the analytic/synthetic distinction really exists and have it reduced to the distinction between truths that are held with different strengths of belief: Some are held very strongly, some less so. [Quine, 1953.]

We might reply that the justification of the categorical distinction is not at issue, since, in any case, we must account for the untutored belief that it exists. This, however, pushes the problem out of the realm of explaining knowledge into the behavioral domain of explaining the acquisition of false and true beliefs. Since false beliefs exist in any case, the claim that the categorical distinction is false serves as a philosophical coup for empiricists that moves the problem into psychology.

The acquisition of linguistic structure itself is not so easily dealt with by empiricists. Children appear to acquire intricate knowledge about distinct kinds of linguistic facts without receiving explicit training and often without very many speech data. This shows that the child must contribute a great deal of structure to what he or she learns. This observation has been turned into a nativist syllogism by Chomsky and others:

1. To be proven: language is innate.
2. Language has property P.
3. P cannot be learned.
4. Therefore P is innate.
5. Therefore language is innate.

There are numerous properties P that might be invoked. The fact that different kinds of knowledge contribute to the usability of a sentence itself might be undiscoverable from actual data given. How does the child actually learn that certain uses of a sentence are acceptable for pragmatic as opposed to structural reasons? It seems unlikely that all children receive explicit training in the different ways that sentences can be used. No explicit information tells a child that sentences can be used ironically to have the opposite of their ostensible meaning, yet the child acquires this distinction.

Linguists tend to cite more technical properties of linguistic structure as unlearnable by standard learning theories. For example, the restriction that transformational rules must apply to the highest level constituent of a given type is never explicitly presented to the child. Clearly, the child must apply some pattern-recognition strategies to the data as given and impose on them the presumption that such a condition exists. But this imposition itself can draw on only hypotheses internal to the child: Hence, the concept of such a condition on rules must be an innate hypothesis.

The accumulation of such arguments adds up to the claim that the interesting formal properties of language are all innate. To paraphrase Chomsky, there is a "language-learning organ" that can extrapolate a full grammar from extremely scanty data. Language is not learned but rather grows in the mind, much as the liver or kidney grows in the body. [Chomsky, 1981.]

This nativist claim, of course, is itself open to empirical investigation: What children have learned when they use language appropriately is an object of psychological inquiry. Chomsky, however, puts the nativist claim in a context that confronts empiricism in its broader sense: He extrapolates from the relatively narrow claims about language development to broader claims about all human knowledge. He suggests that there is a general theory-forming capacity that is itself an innate mental organ.

The clarity of this attack on empiricism has created a rare situation. A philosophical issue involving the nature of knowledge might actually be resolved in part by appeal to empirical data. In this case, critical data are the patterns of language acquisition: If children can be shown to use gradually some general pattern-learning skills to learn language, then the specific nativist claim is weakened; conversely, insofar as children can be shown to extrapolate creatively beyond speech data in ways that express idiosyncratic formal linguistic universals, the nativist claim is strengthened. At the moment, the weight of evidence from language acquisition is in favor of the nativist position. This, however, may be related to the fact that no strong theory of pattern acquisition has been proposed that might explain language acquisition as a special case. No one has yet shown that such a theory is impossible in principle. [Slobin, 1971 and 1979.]

Reductionist and Functionalist Explanations

The second issue concerns what counts as an explanation in psychological theories. The classical position is reductionism, the view that a true explanation of a behavior is couched in terms of independently motivated laws applying to a level that is mapped onto the behavior. In the case of language, an obvious goal in this tradition would be to explain linguistic knowledge in terms of neurophysiological mechanisms that cause it. The problem is that the phenomenon itself is both highly structured and behavioral, not physical. This allows us to speculate that the same behavioral pattern can be related to a variety of different kinds of physical events. The ready availability of computer programs as models stimulates the view that causal reductionism is not a necessary position: Rather than viewing linguistic structure as caused by neurological structures, we can opt for a weaker reductionism, for example, the position that functional and physiological mechanisms correspond without a unique causal relation between them. On this view, a correct explanation of language involves the specification of rules, not how those rules are physiologically instantiated. As in other cases, language is not unique in this, but it is the most elaborate indigenous behavior we know of and thereby highlights the problems for the reductionist most poignantly. [Fodor, 1980.]

Psychological and Platonic Interpretations of Language

The third philosophical problem concerns the ontological status of linguistic structure. Is it truly a unique expression of human psychology, or is it an abstract structure without cause? We can observe such a contrast between color vision (clearly physiological in origin) and formal logic. The latter is a branch of mathematics and clearly not simply a codification of human reasoning. The truths of logic are true independent of any human cause, though which truths we happen to know may of course be due to human perspectives and limitations. Is language like color vision, or is it like logic?

At first, it might seem obvious that language is like color vision in that it has unique and universal properties that seem to have no general psychological motivation; it is learned with little training and from impoverished data. Such facts as these, however, bear directly on the claim that there is a special psychological capacity to learn language of a particular form; these facts do not speak unambiguously to the question what is the actual cause of the form of language itself.

Certain features of language seem to have properties analogous to logic and mathematics. For example, the concept of true-by-definition is itself internal to language. Whether naive people are able or not to differentiate analytic from synthetic truths, most linguists agree that the distinction is intrinsic to language itself. There is no clear extrinsic cause for the existence of such definitional concepts within a language; they simply are true of the language itself, independent of who knows it or why.

APPLICATIONS OF LINGUISTICS

Language is central to many human activities. Accordingly, there are numerous ways in which attempts have been made to apply linguistics to practical and theoretical problems. Today, computers are the most salient devices for practical implementation of linguistic models. In the classroom, such problems as language-learning and reading involve a mixture of theory and practice. Finally, linguistics has been taken as a model for studying other human symbolic activities.

Computer Science

One of the frequently proposed tests for the adequacy of a computer model of human thought is whether we could tell that it were not human simply by interacting with it through language. If the computer model responds in a humanly plausible manner, success has been achieved. [Turing, 1936.] This operational test is surprisingly easy to achieve if the communication context is restricted. For example, a well-known computer program simulates the conversational activity of an analyst. This program is effective just because the analyst it simulates provides little new information in a therapy session. Rather, the program reformulates statements typed in by the user and turns them into corresponding questions. This leads us to conclude that the program is not a successful replication of a human being, even though it might be hard to detect the difference in the restricted context.

We must treat every language capacity in a computer relative to its application. Three major kinds of applications have been attempted during the past few decades: automatic translation, automatic comprehension, and special-purpose implementations.

Automatic translation would seem to be an obvious candidate for computer processes. After all, much of translation involves word-by-word mapping from one language to another. Computers can certainly implement bilingual dictionaries with great speed. This does not, however, guarantee good translation; in fact, it often produces completely incomprehensible sequences in the target language. This is partly because words in sentences represent meaning by virtue of their interaction together; partly because there are numerous multiword idioms in every language; and because correct interpretation of a sentence often involves an understanding of its relation to other sentences in the same discourse and to the nonlinguistic context in which it is used. Human translators bring their knowledge of the world to bear as they translate, something that a computer cannot do, no matter how sophisticated its linguistic program.

Machine translation dominated attempts to apply computers to language for several decades, but there has been no general solution. Limited successes can transfer sentences in scientific documents from one language to another, but human readers are expected to compensate for the occasional mistakes that appear in even this highly restricted context. There is no reason, however, why moderately good translation should be impossible in principle. As computers become more powerful and have more storage, "brute force" solutions become possible, that is, solutions that involve a great deal of memorized whole-sentence transfer from language to language. Such devices are unlikely to replace translators for artistic and diplomatically sensitive translation but may serve many useful functions. As the programs depend increasingly on such brute solutions, they will depart from implementing linguistic theory itself. This is not to say that humans do not use memorized sentences and phrases in translation; rather, it reflects the fact that language activity is not the same as linguistic structure. The role of linguistics is to provide a set of descriptive constructs that may be used by the programs but that may also not be used.

One result of attempts to create automatic translation programs was the realization that translation necessarily involves some comprehension. That is, we often can translate a sentence only after we have understood it in the original language. This focuses attention on the problem of comprehension itself: Can we construct a computer program that understands sentences in English? The notion of what counts as understanding must itself be specified. If understanding means construction of a human representation, then it is unlikely that a program can be a general solution. However, we may define understanding itself in terms of some limited objectives. For example, the program can be attached to some physical device that carries out English commands. Understanding is then defined in terms of correct behavior by the device. Such devices and programs have been developed that meet with the same kind of limited success as translation programs. [Winograd, 1972b.] Given a limited physical world and a limited vocabulary, limited success is always likely. Again, most existing programs make only haphazard use of linguistic theory itself. Indeed, this is currently a subject of controversy in the field of computational linguistics, the discipline devoted to automatic use of language. Some argue that incorporating linguistic theory is most likely to lead to an ultimately successful comprehension system. Others argue that linguistic theory is irrelevant to comprehension activity just as physical theory is irrelevant to playing billiards.

Comprehension programs generally avoid the problems of acoustic analysis of speech by starting with typewritten text. There have been, however, repeated attempts to construct a voice-typewriter, a machine that would produce a phonetic (or conventionally spelled) output from normal speech. Such programs have failed so far, though limited success is likely via brute-force methods.

The creation of "visible speech" has long been a concern of those interested in aiding the deaf. This led to the search for acoustic invariants in the speech signal that could be used as building blocks for recognition. The simple example previously presented of the English sound system illustrates one of the primary difficulties in this approach: Phonetic units do not consistently correspond to the same representational units of sound, either in content or in serial location. In the words *bitter* and *bidder*, the distinction between /t/ and /d/ is not acoustically reflected in a medial consonant but in the *relative* length of the preceding vowel. The amount of computation required to untangle just this simple problem is prodigious. Such language-specific processes combine with universal aspects of speech production to make the general problem even more difficult. The physical structure of sounds is heavily determined by the sounds that surround them, just because they are produced by continuously moving organs that adjust current activity as a function of what came before and what is to come afterward. This serial blending of sounds creates a nearly intractable problem for automatic recognition that is based on linguistic theory.

The problem may ultimately be solved in other ways; for example, a large memory for an individual speaker's phonetic style will make possible the automatic recognition of speech by that speaker. Practical success, however, may or may not involve linguistic theory itself. We can treat the problem as a special case of signal processing and entirely ignore the linguistic attributions of phonetic segmentation and structure. To date, such programs have not been successful, but there is no reason in principle why they should not be.

The underlying issue will remain the same—even accurate dictation involves knowledge of the language and the world. Imagine the difficulty of taking dictation in a language we do not know about problems we do not understand. Even if the phonetics were identical with English, many odd and undiscoverable mistakes would be made.

Linguistic theory may be of some direct application to special-purpose devices that involve language. One area is in programming languages themselves. It is of course possible to restrict the comprehension problem to the application of programs. Ideally, we could construct programs by writing normal English sentences that specify the steps. The possibility of this is limited by the fact that programming operations themselves often involve technical operations and relations between operations that are not a part of normal experience or language. Thus, programming in English would necessarily involve highly specialized formulations. A more general role of linguistic theory is to provide constraints on the kinds of programming languages we construct that will make these languages easier to learn and use. The reasoning is that insofar as programming languages have universal properties of natural language, they will be easier to manipulate. In actual practice, most programming languages reflect only very elementary properties of natural language—basically a semantic-based context-free structure, with minimal rules of ordering and embedding.

The most fruitful areas of application involve special-purpose devices that carry out limited language functions. For example, speech-production devices are of great practical importance, especially for the handicapped. At the moment, several commercially available machines allow us to type in normally spelled English and hear comprehensible pronunciations of it. These devices incorporate models of the vocal tract as well as some language-specific sound rules like the ones previously presented. Ultimately, general mastery of normal intonation and rhythmic patterns seems achievable. Of course, here, too, the perfect solution would involve *understanding* the utterance; but much of practical value can be achieved by computer-generated speech, just because human listeners compensate for its imperfections.

Linguistics in the Classroom

Two out of the traditional pedagogic three *R*s involve language. Accordingly, it would seem reasonable that a correct understanding of what language is would be important for education. One rationale is that a correct understanding of language would help students use it in reading and writing. Linguistic theory has often been applied by the creators of reading texts. Before 1960, the theory involved primary focus on sound-to-phoneme correspondences and the distribution of words and phrases. Reading texts were constructed with the rationale that students had to build up sound-phoneme correspondence units and master typical phrase patterns. With the advent of transformational grammar, certain texts focused on training the reading of whole sentences and their relation to other sentences. Indeed, at least one set of texts was developed to teach junior-high-school students linguistic theory itself.

Research on the effectiveness of such efforts is hard to carry out. To date, there is no clear evidence that understanding linguistic theory leads to more effective reading or writing. There is no doubt that knowledge of language behaviors can be used by text writers to improve the way that language skills are taught. However, as has been a repeated theme in this essay, the relation between linguistic theory and behavior is itself a matter of controversy. In particular, reading and writing may be skills that depend primarily on behavior-specific mechanisms quite independent of language. The role of linguistics would again be to provide consistent theoretical analyses of sentences in a language. Which of those analyses is relevant to which behaviors is still an empirical question.

THOUGHT, LANGUAGE, AND COMMUNICATION

George A. Miller

The average American has always been more interested in communication than in language. (More interested in communication than in thought, some would say.) People can be persuaded that speech is an important form of communication and that language is the competence underlying speech, but it is difficult for most people to hold that perspective. George Herbert Mead's pragmatic approach feels more comfortable. According to Mead, the exigencies of living in groups created a need to communicate; language evolved in order to meet that need; then language made it possible to think in abstractions, to develop a concept of the self, and to behave purposefully. But language is what it is, not because the human brain is what it is, but because social interactions are what they are.

This relativistic, empiricist vision of human nature and human culture as shaped by environmental pressures has always been attractive to American psychologists—and was once attractive to American linguists. Reduced to absurdity, of course, it becomes the strict behaviorism of B. F. Skinner, who would explain speech as a chain of conditioned reflexes established by environmentally controlled reinforcements and elicited by the occurrence in the environment of the appropriate discriminative stimuli. But there is a broader, pragmatic conception of human nature, one in which the human brain itself has been shaped by the social environment in which it evolved. A careful historian would not dismiss as a behaviorist everyone who was influenced by this pragmatic vision.

An alternative view is that the nature of human language has nothing to do with any need for social communication.[1] Any complex organism—an ape, say—must possess highly developed information-processing capacities in order to survive in an unpredictable environment. Plans must be formulated, alternatives evaluated, data collected and stored, responses made, and consequences noted. Precisely how the nervous system coordinates the flow of

---

[1] I am indebted to Dan Sperber for suggesting this way of stating the alternative view.

information required to keep this system functioning is not yet well understood, but some theorists have spoken, not entirely metaphorically, of the languages of the brain. The basic communicative process is self-regulatory, not social.

According to this view, the unique event in human evolution occurred when our ancestors somehow became able to use the languages of the brain for social communication. Some mutation made it possible to externalize the internal information-processing—some kinds of internal processing, at least—in vocal noises. Thus, human patterns of thought did not await the evolution of language but preceded it. Social cooperation based on the fragmentary clues to thought normally expressed in human speech would seldom succeed if the internal information-processing were not closely similar from one individual to the next; such uniformity is not characteristic of the environments in which people live, but it could be achieved genetically. In short, language is what it is, not because social interactions are what they are, but because the brain is what it is.

People frequently have trouble understanding spoken messages that they do not expect, even when the acoustic signal is loud and clear. The reliance on expectations is sometimes called top-down processing of speech, by contrast to bottom-up processing that begins with the acoustic signal, segments it, then filters and classifies the segments. Engineers who have tried to build speech-recognition systems have had their greatest success with bottom-up approaches, from which it is sometimes hastily concluded that the importance of top-down processing has been vastly overrated. A more prudent conclusion would be that engineers have not yet been able to simulate top-down processing very well, a conclusion that would follow from decent respect for the complexity of neural information-processing and our ignorance of how it is done. Everything a person knows about another person's situation, past or present, can be used to limit what that other person could be expected to say and so make perception of what they do say easier. That kind of coordination is possible because different people think the same way, but no machine has yet been programmed to think as people do.

Part of the internal information-processing that all people do by virtue of being human is described by the universal properties and principles of levels of syntactic representation. The good news is that it has been possible to characterize even a fragment of this internal processing. The bad news is that that is but a small part of the system that psychologists eventually hope to understand.

CURRENT VIEWS OF LANGUAGE AND GRAMMAR

Ray C. Dougherty

A basic problem in linguistics is to define the processes by which a child acquires a language on the basis of exposure to adult speakers of the language. In 1957, Noam Chomsky published *Syntactic Structures* and defined a language as a set of sentences, and a grammar as a device for defining the sentences of a language. [Chomsky, 1957.] In most linguistic representations, a grammar is a combination of algebraic devices that defines all of the sentence types (active, passive, question, etc.) of a language and enumerates all of the individual sentences. The linguist's formal grammar is considered to be a representation of a person's knowledge of his or her language.

Viewed in this perspective, the questions asked in linguistics are: How can a child, exposed to sets of sentences, acquire a grammar? What is the algebraic form of the grammar? What type of data must be presented to a child for the child to acquire a grammar? It is traditional to say that a child "learns" a language on the basis of exposure to sets of sentences. Current linguistics has developed a biological perspective which permits us to consider a grammar as an information-engine that is resident in an information-processing host. An information-engine, of which a grammar is one example, is a highly structured body of knowledge that has the capacity to form a copy of itself in an information-processing host identical with the one in which it finds itself. One might think of a grammar as a computer program and a host as a type of symbol-processing computer. Grammar reproduction is the process by which a computer program (a grammar) in one host can form a copy of itself in another, identically structured host.

FOUR POSITIONS

One can obtain an understanding of the basic problems, if not the solutions, by considering recent works in which four distinct positions have been discussed. One position, the empiricist view, characterized by one author cited later as a mere recording of observations without a structuring activity on

321

the part of the subject, governs little current research. Each of the three remaining positions has its champions.

Chomsky, who has formulated most of the issues defining the biological perspective, presents an "innatist," or, as Piaget calls it, "preformationist" view, according to which all of the basic linguistic structures are precoded into the genetic constitution of a human being and triggered by experience.

Jean Piaget presents a "constructionist" view, which claims that the basic properties of a grammar are neither implicit in the data to which a child is exposed nor innate in the mental organization of a child. Constructivism assumes that grammatical structures emerge as constructions developed by general sensorimotor processes when applied to language data. A child learning a language essentially creates a grammar anew by general processes of sensory perception and motor coordination that are not language-specific.

Seymour Papert has recently developed a computational approach, called Project LOGO, which is closer to Piaget's constructivism than to Chomsky's innatism. Papert has attempted to develop a computer-based model of learning that uses mechanisms developed in computer science to characterize neurological structures. Papert developed the computer language LOGO in order to model the information processes that function to characterize knowledge and the mechanisms by which knowledge is reproduced in a new brain. Papert assumes that one could better understand the processes of grammar and language if one had more understanding of the nature of machines that learn and machines that learn how to learn. He uses LOGO to design such machines and model the neurological processes involved.

THE INNATIST VIEW

In the following passage, Chomsky outlines the biological perspective and his innatist views. He indicates his skepticism concerning constructions of sensorimotor intelligence.

It is a curiosity of our intellectual history that cognitive structures developed by the mind are generally regarded and studied very differently from physical structures developed by the body. There is no reason why a neutral scientist, unencumbered by traditional doctrine, should adopt this view. Rather, he would, or should approach cognitive structures such as human language more or less as he would investigate an organ such as the eye or heart, seeking to determine: (1) its character in a particular individual; (2) its general properties, invariant across the species apart from gross defect; (3) its place in a system of such structures; (4) the course of its development in the individual; (5) the genetically determined basis for this development; (6) the factors that gave rise to this mental organ in the course of evolution. The expectation that constructions of sensimotor intelligence determine the character of a mental organ such as language seems to me hardly more plausible than a proposal that the fundamental properties of the eye or the visual cortex or the heart develop on this basis. Furthermore, when we turn to specific properties of this mental organ, we find little justification for any such belief, so far as I can see. (Chomsky, 1980a, p. 37.)

Chomsky believes that the structures of language and the complex processes of grammar development could not arise from organism/environment interaction alone. Grammar is species-specific and genetically determined. Chomsky elaborates:

> I have touched on only a few examples. In each case, when we investigate the particular properties of human cognition, we find principles that are highly specific and narrowly articulated, structures of a marvelous intricacy and delicacy. As in the case of physical organs, there seems to be no possibility of accounting for the character and origin of basic mental structures in terms of organism-environment interaction. Mental and physical organs alike are determined, it seems, by species-specific, genetically determined properties, though in both cases interaction with the environment is required to trigger growth and will influence and shape the structures that develop. Our ignorance— temporary, let us hope—of the physical basis for mental structures compels us to keep to abstract characterization, in this case, but there is no reason to suppose that the physical structures involved are fundamentally different in character and development from other physical organs that are better understood, though a long tradition has tacitly assumed otherwise. (Ibid., pp. 51– 52.)

THE CONSTRUCTIVIST VIEW

At the same conference where Chomsky offered these views, Piaget defined constructivism as an alternative to both empiricism and innatism (or preformationism). Said Piaget:

> Fifty years of experience have taught us that knowledge does not result from a mere recording of observations without a structuring activity on the part of the subject. Nor do any a priori or innate cognitive structures exist in man; the functioning of intelligence alone is hereditary and creates structures only through an organization of successive actions performed on objects. Consequently, an epistemology conforming to the data of psychogenesis could be neither empiricist nor preformationist, but could consist only of a constructivism, with a continual elaboration of new operations and structures. The central problem, then, is to understand how such operations come about, and why, even though they result from nonpredetermined constructions, they eventually become logically necessary. (Piaget, 1980, p. 23.)

Piaget defines what he sees as the basic problem of research into the nature of language and grammar: To choose between constructivism and preformationism. He also considers empiricism and preformationism equally vacuous.

> The problem is therefore to choose between two hypotheses: authentic constructions with stepwise disclosures to new possibilities, or successive actualization of a set of possibilities *existing from the beginning*. (Ibid., p. 25.)

> In a word, the theories of preformation of knowledge appear, for me, as devoid of concrete truth as empiricist interpretations, for the origin of logicomathematical structures in their infinity cannot be localized either in objects or in the subject. Therefore, only constructivism is acceptable, but its weighty task is to explain both the mechanisms of the formation of new concepts and the characteristics these concepts acquire in the process of becoming logically necessary. (Ibid., p. 26.)

THE COMPUTATIONAL VIEW

Papert's project LOGO can be understood as having developed out of, or at least having been inspired by, many of Piaget's ideas about the genetics of grammar reproduction. Piaget's book, *Genetic Epistemology*, the published version of the Woodbridge Lectures he delivered at Columbia University in 1968, discusses *self-regulation* of the growing knowledge in a new brain:

> These few examples may clarify why I consider the main problem of genetic epistemology to be the explanation of the construction of novelties in the development of knowledge. From the empiricist point of view, a "discovery" is new for the person who makes it, but what is discovered was already in existence in external reality and there is therefore no construction of new realities. The nativist or apriorist maintains that the forms of knowledge are predetermined inside the subject and thus again, strictly speaking, there can be no novelty. By contrast, for the genetic epistemologist, knowledge results from continuous construction, since in each act of understanding, some degree of invention is involved; in development, the passage from one stage to the next is always characterized by the formation of new structures which did not exist before, either in the external world or in the subject's mind. The central problem of genetic epistemology concerns the mechanism of this construction of novelties which creates the need for the explanatory factors which we call *reflexive abstraction* and *self-regulation*. However, these factors have furnished only global explanations. A great deal of work remains to be done in order to clarify this fundamental process of intellectual creation, which is found at all the levels of cognition, from those of earliest childhood to those culminating in the most remarkable of scientific inventions. (Piaget, 1970, pp. 77–78.)

The mechanisms of self-regulation discussed by Piaget provided only global explanations not specific ones. Papert's project LOGO is an attempt to make many of the ideas of Piaget's genetic epistemology concrete. Papert, in discussing one of his examples, indicates how Piaget influenced his work: "When I read Piaget this incident served me as a model for his notion of assimilation, except I was immediately struck by the fact that his discussion does not do full justice to his own idea." (Papert, 1980, p. vii.) Papert mentions that Piaget's ideas gave him "a new framework" for examining his observations. (Ibid., p. viii.) Papert's project LOGO is a version of constructivism and opposed to both empiricism and preformationism. Papert states:

> Noam Chomsky believes that we have a language acquisition device . . . I do not . . . [share] his view of the brain as made up of specialized neurological organs matched to specific intellectual functions. I think that the fundamental question for the future of education is not whether the brain is "a general purpose computer" or a collection of specialized devices, but whether our intellectual functions are reducible in a one-to-one fashion to neurologically given structures.

> It seems to be beyond doubt that the brain has numerous inborn "gadgets." But surely these "gadgets" are much more primitive than is suggested by names like Language Acquisition Device and Math Acquisition Device. I see learning language or learning mathematics as harnessing to this purpose numerous "gadgets" whose original purpose bears no resemblance to the complex intellectual functions they come to serve. (Papert, 1980, p. 220.)

EXPERIMENTAL ANALYSIS

Much of the excitement of research into the structure of language and the genetic processes governing grammar reproduction derives from the fact that the results of research bear directly on traditional questions about the structure of knowledge and the mechanisms by which it is communicated from the older to the younger generations. In linguistics, traditional philosophic questions can be posed in sufficient detail that they can be subjected to experimental analysis.

RULES AND PRINCIPLES
IN PHONOLOGY AND SYNTAX

Samuel Jay Keyser

The following piece attempts to do two things. First, it attempts to show why linguists suppose that mastery of a language is tantamount to mastery of a system of rules rather than, say, memorization of a very large number of words, phrases, sentences, and so on. Second, it draws attention to a major difference that has emerged in recent years between the rule systems of phonology and the rule systems of syntax and speculates on the significance of this difference.[1]

WHY RULES?

A fundamental tenet of linguistic theory is that what people know when they know how to speak is a system of rules. The argument goes as follows:

1. People have, in principle, the ability to produce an infinite number of sentences; thus, consider the following sentences:

   (a) John said that Bill is here.
   (b) John said that Frank said that Bill is here.
   (c) John said that Mary said that Frank said that Bill is here.
   (d) John said that Ned said that Mary said that Frank said that Bill is here.

2. Beginning with (a), note that each subsequent sentence is longer than the preceding one by the addition of the phrase *that (someone's name) said* after the first occurrence of the verb form *said*. However, this process, repeated three times, can be repeated any number of times. Each time it is repeated, a new sentence is produced. Since there is no upper limit on the number of times the phrase *that (someone's name) said* can be introduced into a sentence like (a), there is no upper limit on the number of English sentences that can be produced in this fashion.

---

[1] The author is indebted to Morris Halle and James Higginbotham for a discussion of some of the issues raised in this piece.

3. The argument in (1) shows that there can be no upper limit on the number of sentences in English. However, we know that the human brain, the repository of linguistic ability, is finite. Even if we were to assign one sentence to each atom of gray matter in the brain, we would run out of atoms long before we ran out of sentences.

4. If knowledge is represented mentally and if we have the ability to produce an infinite number of sentences, then how can we represent this infinite knowledge in a finite space?

5. The answer is to assume that the knowledge that enables us to produce an infinite number of sentences is not a representation of each individual sentence, but rather a set of rules, finite in number, whose output is, in principle, infinite.

6. Therefore, what we know when we know how to speak is, among other things, a set of rules.[2]

This argument is based on syntax. However, the ability to speak a language goes beyond syntax to include phonology as well. People know how to pronounce words as well as how to arrange them into sentences. Bever notes, in this regard, that "Words have an inner level of representation of sound sequences and a set of rules that map them onto an outer level representing the actual acoustic sequences." (Bever in his paper in this volume.)

It is not immediately obvious, however, that knowledge of how to pronounce words requires knowledge of rules. Let us consider, then, whether phonological knowledge must also be represented by rules.

WHY PHONOLOGICAL RULES?

We have seen in syntax that rules are required since speakers know, in principle, an infinite number of sentences. However, in phonology we might argue that since the number of morphemes and words is finite, there is nothing incoherent about supposing that a speaker simply memorizes the phonetic makeup of each word. How might this work?

Consider the well-known fact that regular English plurals are pronounced in three separate ways: either as the syllable [ɪz] as in *kisses* or as the consonant [s] as in *hits* or as the consonant [z] as in *dogs*. We might say that when a child learns the English plural, the child simply memorizes these facts. In other words, just as a child must remember that the plural of *mouse* is *mice*, the child must also remember that the plural of *spouse* is *spouses* and not, say, *spice*. Such a model is theoretically possible, since the number of words in English is finite.

---

[2]This argument makes use of that property of natural language that Bever calls "the creative component of sentence structure."

The Novel Form Argument

One way to argue for the view that phonology is rule-governed is to show that novel forms do not present a problem for speakers. That is to say, speakers are able to treat novel forms as if they were not novel at all. Suppose, then, we were to ask someone to provide us with the plural form of a word that ended in a consonant sound that was not a normal English consonantal sound. Thus, consider the sound [χ], which terminates the name *Bach*; that is [baχ].[3] Even though this sound is not an English sound, a native speaker of English would always pronounce the plural of this word with an [s] and not with an [ɪz] or a [z]. This response can easily be verified by asking native speakers of English whether they have ever heard the word before and, if not, what they suppose its plural to be. Moreover, this response can only be understood if we assume that part of a native speaker's knowledge of the English plural is knowledge of a rule and not knowledge of pairs of singular and plural forms. Thus, if there were no rule, it would be an incredible coincidence that all English speakers treat the plural of *Bach* as [s] and not, for example, [baχɪz]. Notice that both forms are easily pronounceable in English, and, were there no rule, we would have to assume that at least one speaker would opt for [baχɪz]. This, in fact, never happens.[4]

We saw that in syntax the argument in favor of rules was based on the need for an infinite output. We have just seen how in phonology the argument in favor of rules is based on novel forms. However, both of these arguments are, in fact, based on the same property, namely, novelty. Thus, for speakers who have never heard the name *Bach* before, the name constitutes a novel word whose plural will, nonetheless, be obvious to them. Similarly, a sentence patterned after those in the preceding example that is, say, three times as long as (d), or even ten times as long, will be a novel sentence to anyone with the patience to put such a sentence together. Nonetheless, such a sentence, despite its novelty, will easily be recognized as being a perfectly grammatical one in English by anyone who knows the language.

Words Are Not Finite

It is not hard to show, however, that the premise on which the ruleless hypothesis is based, namely, that the number of words in English is finite, is itself incorrect. Consider, for example, the words *lion* and *hunter*. English

---

[3] This is the voiceless, velar sound that occurs in German words like *ach*.
[4] We will not pause here to provide a formal statement of the English plural rule. However, several accounts can be found in contemporary literature. For one that also includes an account of its historical evolution, the reader is referred to Keyser and O'Neil [1980].

has a process called compound formation whereby these words can be put together to form a single new word, *lion hunter* meaning a hunter who hunts lions.[5] Notice that if we can add a word to the word *hunter* once, there is no reason why we cannot perform the same operation twice. Thus, suppose we now add the new word *lion hunter* to the word *hunter* to produce another new word, namely, *lion hunter hunter*. This is not only an acceptable word in English, it is also perfectly clear what it must mean. A *lion hunter hunter* means a hunter who hunts lion hunters.

We have now constructed an argument that is formally identical with that in the first set of sentences. We must have phonological rules because our knowledge of words, like our knowledge of sentences, is infinite. This is the novel-form argument for rule-based linguistic systems. Indeed, all novel forms can be construed as evidence in favor of the view that rule systems underlie our linguistic competence.[6]

PHONOLOGICAL AND SYNTACTIC RULE SYSTEMS COMPARED

Even though syntax and phonology share the property of creativity (see footnote 2), there is an interesting difference between the two components. In his subsection on "General and Specific Learning Mechanisms," Bever makes reference to modular versus general purpose models of learning. The modularity hypothesis assumes that "learning is carried out by a set of innate mental 'modules,' each highly specialized for its task . . . ." In this view, the mind is a "federation of such distinct modules."

The modular model of mental representation describes the current state of affairs in linguistic theory as well. This change toward modularity in linguistic theory has come about over the past few years. Noam Chomsky, in his recent monograph, puts the matter in the following terms: "There has been a gradual shift of focus from the study of rule systems, which have increasingly been regarded as impoverished (as we would hope to be the case), to the study of systems of principles, which appear to occupy a much more central position in determining the character and variety of possible human languages." (Chomsky, 1982, pp. 7–8.)

---

[5]Even though we tend to write such compound words with space between them, this orthographic convention should not mislead us into thinking that we are not dealing with a single word. For one thing, this word takes plural endings just like other single words. Just like other single words, we cannot put things inside it. Thus, words like *taffeta* cannot be interrupted and neither can words like *lion hunter*. Hence, we cannot say *lion big hunter* even though we can say *big hunter*. Moreover, we cannot place the plural ending inside the word; that is, the plural of *lion hunter* is *lion hunters* and not *lions hunter*. We see, then, that in a number of ways *lion hunter* behaves like a single word.

[6]Novel forms come from a variety of sources. Errors that speakers make is one common source. Thus, when a child assumes that the plural of *mouse* is *mouses* and not *mice*, the child's behavior can best be understood as resulting from an overgeneralization of the rule for the regular formation of plurals in English.

Linguistic theory is now characterized by levels of representation and principles appropriate to those levels. Within this framework the principles act like filters on representations, indicating whether a given representation is well formed or not.[7] Consider the following sentences by way of illustration:

(a) *Mary bought a hat.*

(b) *What did Mary buy?*

(c) *What$_i$ did Mary buy* [t$_i$]?

(d) *Mary mentioned that Sally bought a hat.*

(e) *What$_i$ did Mary mention that Sally bought* [t$_i$]?

(f) *Mary mentioned the fact that Sally bought a hat.*

(g) **What$_i$ did Mary mention the fact that Sally bought* [t$_i$]?

Note, first, that (b) is related to (a). In particular, (b) contains a fronted question word *what*. However, while this word appears at the front of the sentence, it is, nonetheless, the object of the verb *buy*. To capture this intuition, we place an abstract element called a trace (= t) where the object of *buy* normally appears, and we index the question word and the trace to indicate the relationship that exists between them. This is indicated in (c), which therefore constitutes the appropriate representation of the question corresponding to (a) at one level of grammatical representation.[8] Consider, now, the question that corresponds to (d) at this same level of representation, namely, the sentence indicated in (e). Here, too, a trace element relates the fronted question word *what* with the position that the object of *buy* normally occupies. This brings us to the final pair of sentences, namely (f) and (g). Notice that whereas (f) is a perfectly well-formed sentence in English, it does not have a corresponding question form of the pattern indicated in the earlier questions, namely, in (c) and (e). When we attempt to reproduce that pattern, we get an ungrammatical sentence such as that in (g). On the surface of things this is a remarkable fact. Why, after all, should it not be possible to question (f) just as it was possible to question (a) and (d)? To account for this fact, a principle is assumed to apply at the level of structure corresponding to (g). This principle, called subjacency, states that a fronted element may not occur too far away from its original position (where, for purposes of the present exposition, we leave unspecified what too far away means formally):

Subjacency: In a sentence that contains question words and traces, the question word may not occur "too far" away from its trace.

---

[7] The shift from rules to principles in no way undermines the argument in (1) that knowledge of a language means knowledge of a grammar. Rather the argument goes through but with principles replacing rules as the dominant mechanism of grammatical knowledge.

[8] This level is called *S*-structure, and it corresponds roughly to the notion of surface structure.

The role of subjacency is as follows: Given a representation such as that in (g), the principle checks to see whether the distance between a questioned element and its trace is too great. If it is, the representation is treated as ungrammatical. In this sense, the principle acts as a filter on the level of representation of (g).

The model of syntax that emerges from this example is one that is static in nature. According to this model, there are levels of representations, and there are principles (or filters) that apply to representations at those levels. If the principles are met, the representation is well formed; if they are not, it is not. While this static model appears to be true of syntactic and even semantic levels of representation, it is not true of the phonological level. The latter level is, in marked contrast, characterized by rules and not by filters. Moreover, these rules perform a wide variety of functions. Thus, there are rules that (1) insert sounds, (2) delete sounds, (3) relate sounds to one another in a variety of ways, (4) change values of phonological features, and (5) add new phonological features to a representation.[9]

In short, while the higher levels of contemporary linguistic theory have become much more static in character, the lower levels—specifically, the phonological and phonetic levels—have become much more dynamic in character. Even though there is not sufficient space to illustrate this difference between the various levels of linguistic theory, the difference is one that contemporary researchers in the field would probably not find controversial.

Why the Difference?

The final portion of this piece is devoted to a speculation about why phonological and phonetic components are dynamic in character while the higher levels are static in character. One possible answer to this question lies in the fact that the phonological component is deeply embedded in the physiological mechanisms of the vocal tract and auditory system. For example, crucial to phonological theory is the notion of distinctive features, and these features correspond in a rather direct way to gestures of the vocal tract. Thus, the feature nasality plays a prominent role in the phonology of most of the languages of the world. This feature refers specifically to whether the velum is open or closed during any given speech gesture.[10] For example, the velum is open during the first sound of the word *man* and it is closed in the first sound of the word *can*. The active character of the phonological component may well be a direct consequence of phonological theory being closely related to the mechanisms that actually produce the sounds of language.

[9] This brief enumeration barely does justice to the active character of the phonological component.

[10] The velum is the soft fleshy valve at the roof of the mouth, which, when shut, closes off the nasal cavity and, when open, allows the nasal cavity to resonate.

The situation is quite different when we come to syntax and semantics. Here, there is absolutely no notion at all of what the mechanisms are that correspond to such entities as nounphrase, verbphrase, sentence, complementizer, and specifier (such as articles and adjectives). While we have a clear idea of what the feature *nasal* refers to, namely, the position of the velum, we have no clear idea of what *grammatical category* might refer to in the brain. Similarly, there is no clear idea of what the mechanisms might be that correspond to such notions as coindexing traces with question words as was illustrated in (c) and (e).

CONCLUSION

I conclude with a question. Higher levels of grammatical theory have not yet achieved the marriage of the formalism with the mechanism that phonology has at least begun to achieve. As we learn more about mental mechanisms, will syntactic and semantic theory change in ways that will reflect those mechanisms just as phonological theory has done, or is the present nature of syntax and semantics reflective of those mechanisms already?[11] If a final speculation is in order with respect to this piece, then that speculation would be that syntax and semantics will follow phonology as more is learned about higher order mechanisms of the brain. Given the rightness of this speculation, we can expect radical changes in syntactic and semantic theory to confront us in the future.

POSTSCRIPT

Before his sudden and unexpected death, Fritz Machlup requested that I might add a word about the relationship between my remarks here and studies in the information sciences such as those represented in the present volume. At the risk of going beyond the space limitations imposed on me by the editors, I would like to attempt to comply with his request.

During the past quarter of a century, the study of linguistic theory has, to a great extent, been carried on independently of the study of the computational mechanisms that enable the sentences of a language to be both produced and recognized. Thus, linguistic theory studies human language *competence*, while the study of computational mechanisms, which might be

---

[11] James Higginbotham (personal communication) has suggested that the static character of higher level components has resulted from a shift away from conditions on rules (a dynamic device) to filters, or conditions on well formedness at a linguistic level (a static device) as a mechanism of grammatical description. This shift has come about for reasons internal to linguistic theory itself; in particular, because of the ease of description that results from the use of filters as opposed to rules. Phenomena under current study would require significantly more complicated statements if formulated in terms of rules rather than filters.

supposed to instantiate this competence, deals with human language *performance*. In recent years, however, a trend has been mounting that suggests that these studies should no longer be carried out independently of one another. Rather, the view is growing that each study can, in fact, illuminate the other.

There are at least two reasons why this trend is desirable. The first is an intellectual one. The question of how human knowledge is represented mentally is a profound and important one. The more we understand about what grammars are, the more we will come to understand what we are, since grammatical knowledge is at the very heart of human mentality.

The second reason is a practical one. The introduction of the personal computer has brought to light the fact that computers are, for the most part, very difficult to use without a great deal of training and sophistication. We have only to consider how easy it is to master driving an automobile to see that the computer has a long way to go before it can be equally accessible. One way to facilitate this process might well be to endow the computer with a language that resembles our own as much as possible. This means that we need to understand how parsing mechanisms can best be implemented in computers. However, it may well be that the best way to understand how to build parsers into computers is to understand how parsers are already built into people. The study of how to make computers more accessible is, in other words, a form of applied cognitive science and the more we understand how we work linguistically the better we may be able to design computers for us to work with.

COMPUTATION DOES MATTER
TO LINGUISTICS

Robert C. Berwick

A view widely held by academics over the past few decades has been that computer science and modern linguistic theory do not mix. Several years ago, so the story goes, linguists driven by Noam Chomsky's distinction between linguistic competence and linguistic performance proposed that the study of what people know about their language should take precedence over the study of how people actually process or produce utterances or actually learn language. This distinction between *what* and *how* has attained a kind of self-perpetuating status as the driving wedge between linguistics on the one hand and artificial intelligence and computer science on the other—see Newell's characterization of it as a "field-splitter." [Newell in his lead paper in Section 3 of this volume.]

But times change. I would like to argue that we would be hard pressed to find a more complementary marriage of disciplines than that between linguistics and computer science and that such a marriage has recently borne and will continue to bear great fruit. Linguistics and computer science are partners of a very special kind, because the study of human cognition is now widely equated with the study of information-processing models. But, as every computer scientist knows, such models consist of algorithms that juggle very specific information structures. Algorithmic procedures for using knowledge do not make sense without a specification of the form in which that knowledge is couched. Similarly, an understanding of how language is used hinges on an understanding of what that knowledge looks like—the way it is represented. So the joint work of linguistics and computer science is like the partnership between data structures and the algorithms that use them. In the remainder of this paper I would like to make plain just what the nature of that partnership is and what one can expect to gain from it.

When talking about a living organism—any organism—there are two broad kinds of "how" questions, and each has its place in the explanation of human information-processing abilities. The first of these questions, raised in Dougherty's paper, is couched at the level of the species: How is what the individual organism knows (a body of information) passed on to its descendants? Or, to put the question from the perspective of the offspring, how is knowledge of language acquired? This is a particular kind of *performance* that is rarely mentioned by researchers concerned with the analysis of the day-to-day use of language—for example, it is not even mentioned in Newell's lead paper in this volume as a goal of the computational study of linguistic performance. The second kind of *how* is, in fact, just this more familiar one of individual language use: How do people actually use information about language to speak or understand sentences?

The linguist's answer to both questions, as exemplified in the papers by Bever, Dougherty, and Keyser, is to characterize what an individual knows about language as a system of rules, a grammar. As an example of what a part of a grammar looks like, consider the following sentences (like those described in Keyser's paper):

(a)   *I believe Mary likes Bill.*
(b)   *Who do I believe Mary likes?*

Now, as Keyser observes, what modern linguistic theory does is tell one that (b) really has the underlying form,

(c)   *Who do I believe Mary likes* [t]?

where [t] acts like a variable bound to the value of *who*, so that the question is really to be construed as,

For which X, X *a person, do I believe Mary likes* X?

Further, what people seem to know about forming questions is that one can take a statement like (a) and turn it into a question by imagining that *who* is the object of *like*:

I believe Mary likes who.

and then moving *who* to the front of the sentence, inverting the auxiliary verb and subject, and leaving behind the (unpronounced) variable X. Apparently, though, we cannot move *who* very far. We can move it out of a lower sentence (for example, *Mary likes who*) into the next higher sentence but no farther. Look what happens when we try to move *who* out of a sentence that is in turn embedded in a nounphrase, *the claim that* . . . :

I believe the claim that Mary likes who →
Who do I believe the claim that Mary likes [t].

The sentence is ill-formed, and we know this, even though we can make out what it would mean if we could say such a thing. This is part of our knowledge of English, part of our grammar. Because this knowledge has the effect of restricting the radius of action of the movement of *who*, we might call it a locality principle, P1:

Who cannot be moved across more than one sentence boundary.

Now, so far, all this is a fairly abstract characterization of what people know. The burning question for the computationalist is whether all this machinery—the notion of leaving behind variables and moving elements—is actually involved when people use language. Or is it all just a picturesque metaphor, useful for exposition perhaps, but not really a part of what people actually do?

It is here that computational arguments come to the fore. The beauty of computer science is that it gives us a useful way of looking at complex *how* questions. It is an approach that is perhaps best illustrated by a simpler but more familiar computational problem.

Consider the following task. Suppose we wanted to add up the first 100 integers, $1 + 2 + \ldots + 100$. Let us call this the abstract description of a computational problem. We have described what the problem is, not how to solve it. Now let me give two simple algorithms for solving the abstract problem. The most obvious way to proceed would be to add 1 to 2 and get the sum 3; then add the next integer 3 to this sum, and get 6; add 4 to this, and so on. On the other hand, if I were clever, I could pair up 1 and 100, 2 and 99, 3 and 98, . . . , 50 and 51, noticing that each of these 50 pairs add to 101. So all I have to do is to multiply 101 by 50.

The point is that any single abstract computational problem could have more than one algorithmic solution. Further, it is plain that the two algorithms just given differ greatly in the kind and number of operations that they use. Algorithm 1 uses 99 additions, while Algorithm 2 uses just one multiplication. While the second seems vastly superior to the first in terms of the amount of time it would take to carry out, the specific or particular algorithm we actually use depends on the nature of the machinery at our disposal. In general, there could be many ways of carrying out or implementing one and the same algorithm, and implementation details could make a difference to how fast the algorithm works. Suppose, for example, that we had a pocket calculator with a working addition button but a broken multiplication button. Now, in order to carry out Algorithm 2, we would have to add 101 up 50 times—still better than Algorithm 1 but not by so wide a margin.

What this means is that a complete computational analysis depends on juggling at least three levels of theory: the abstract characterization, the algorithm, and the implementation. (This way of analyzing computational problems has been most clearly stated by Marr and Poggio. [Marr and Poggio, 1977.]) While theoretical analysis of each level cannot be isolated from the others, logically the specification of the abstract problem is prior to that of the algorithmic level or a detailed implementation. Once the basic outline of all three levels has been determined, then we can use what we know about the implementation and algorithmic constraints to tell us something about the abstract problem, and vice versa.

Turning now to the situation of language, the first thing we notice is that what plays the role of the abstract computational problem are forms such as (c). If one thing that we do in order to understand a sentence is to recover its underlying form, then we must convert the string of words,

(d) *Who does Mary like?*

into the form

Who does Mary like [t]?

That is, linguistic theory tell us what the abstract computational problem is, since it tells us what the units of representation are that must be recovered. Now let us consider the *how* of it all. Just as with the 100-integers problem, there could be many ways of actually performing the computations required to get to the underlying form. And there is one additional factor to consider: While we are free to speculate about algorithms and implementation methods to solve the integers problem, in the case of linguistic algorithms and implementations we are shackled not by our own creativity but by Nature's—at least if we want to explain what it is that people do. The chains are wound doubly tight because what we know about the machinery that the brain has at its disposal is quite limited; we know that it does not have *add* and *multiply* buttons, but we know very little more than that.

Even so, we can still advance computational arguments for and against certain ways of characterizing the *what* of linguistic theory. Let me give just one example of this style of argumentation here, an example showing that there is some computational evidence for the abstract form (c) posited by modern transformational grammar. In passing, the argument will illustrate one way in which a theory of computation can support the study of linguistics.

To begin, consider the following two algorithms (machines) for analyzing sentence (d). Each machine takes as input the sentence to be analyzed and writes as output a desired underlying form corresponding to the input sentence.

Algorithm 1. Imagine sliding a window across the input sentence. Depending on what it sees in the window, the analysis machine makes a decision as to what output to produce next. The window is fixed in width, in the sense that it can hold a finite number of words (such as *did*) or phrases (such as a sentence or nounphrase) but no more. This means that we can express the operations of the machine in terms of finite patterns and actions, where a pattern is simply a finite string of words or phrases, and an action is what the machine writes as output. In our example, if the window of the machine holds the items

Who does Mary like?

then the machine writes out the same string as it sees, with the [t] marker inserted as desired

Who does Mary like [t]?

It is important to observe that the representation of the operating rules must be finite if they are to be literally stored in a finite machine.

Algorithm 2 works differently. It assumes an underlying form distinct from that described by (c). Instead of inserting the element [t], suppose that we simply put back the displaced *who*, relocating it in its original position:

Who does Mary like? →
Does Mary like who?

Computationally, this form demands a very different algorithm than that of Algorithm 1. As we "read in" the input sentence, we save *who* in a special memory location, set aside for that purpose. The remainder of the sentence is simply written out directly, word for word. Then, when we reach the word *like* followed by the end of the sentence, we retrieve the saved *who* and literally place it after *like*—as desired.

Which method most accurately reflects what people actually do? I would argue that the second algorithm does not mirror what people do when they process language as accurately as does the representation posited by current transformational grammar combined with Algorithm 1. Simply put, if representation (c) and Algorithm 1 are assumed, then we should expect a locality principle like P1. In contrast, there is no such expectation with the memory-store representation. To the extent that computational Theory 1—representation plus Algorithm 1—explains this descriptive fact about human language, and computational Theory 2 does not, Theory 1 is to be preferred.

The reason for the difference is simple. Recall that Algorithm 1 demands that operating rules be stated in a literally finite pattern-action format, so that the rules can be stored in a physically finite machine. But this means that there can be no rules that move elements in one fell swoop across an unbounded number of sentences—lest the associated pattern be infinite in length. Therefore, given that pattern-action rules are literally stored and that the [t] elements are (properly) inserted by their operation, we would expect that their radius of action should be strictly limited. That is to say, we would expect the existence of something like principle P1. But there is no such distance barrier with the memory-store method, and so there is no reason for a locality principle. Since the *who* can be stored away indefinitely, we can wait forever before putting it back. Therefore, if this method were actually in use, there should be no reason, at least on grounds of sentence analysis, why the following sentence should not be permitted:

Who do I believe the claim that Mary likes?

In short, we have used computational methods about *how* something might be computed to argue for a particular kind of linguistic theory about *what* is represented.

Let me summarize the main point. Assume that what we know about language includes, for example, knowledge that the underlying form of *Who do I believe Mary likes* is

Who do I believe Mary likes [t]?

and that this knowledge is quite literally engaged in computational processes when sentences are analyzed. These two assumptions, combined with the functional (computational) demand that people be able to process sentences of their language efficiently, are sufficient to derive the existence of locality principles that are actually observed. In contrast, under alternative conceptions of what this knowledge of language looks like and how it is put to use—the memory-store method—the reason for the existence of such principles remains a mystery. (Of course, there could be another functional argument for these principles—in particular, they could make learning easier. But that would be another story. See Berwick and Weinberg [1983] for a full account.)

My tentative conclusion, then, is that rules and representations—the "stuff" of modern transformational linguistics—are quite real, since by assuming that they are engaged in mental computations, we can actually explain part of what we observe to be true about our linguistic behavior. It is important to note that we achieve this explanation only by marrying specific linguistic results about *what* with specific computational techniques about *how*. It is time, then, to put to rest the shopworn slogan that linguistics and computer science are at odds with one another. At least for the study of human cognition, they are, and ought to be, inseparable.

SECTION 5

LIBRARY AND
INFORMATION SCIENCES
Disciplinary Differentiation, Competition, and
Convergence

W. Boyd Rayward

The purpose of this paper is to explore some of the relations between librarianship, bibliography, documentation, library science, and information science. All are considered part of a historical process that has led to different ways of envisaging, creating, and investigating the interrelations and relative effectiveness of formalized modes of access to recorded knowledge.

Underlying this approach are two observations. First, libraries represent long-established and complex arrangements of a variety of these formalized modes of access to knowledge. Second, not long after librarianship emerged as a profession whose practitioners were chiefly absorbed by the administrative and operational challenges presented by libraries, there arose a countervailing resistance to the conceptual narrowness that such a professional preoccupation involved. Important as libraries had become, historically they represented only a partial solution to the constellation of problems related to the conservation, organization, and diffusion of recorded knowledge and information. If libraries were to be improved or if other solutions to the problems for which they presented partial solutions were to be invented and tested, then it seemed necessary continually to seek new ways of looking at libraries themselves and at the broader environment of which they are only a part. Librarianship, bibliography, documentation, library science, and information science may be considered as incorporating modes of study and investigation that not only express subtle occupational distinctions, but also represent attempts at obtaining these new and increasingly general perspectives.

In the second part of this paper, I examine five developments in the field that have occurred in the United States in the last ten to fifteen years. I suggest that these developments, relatively insignificant in themselves, are important as indicators that librarianship and information science, the latter arising in part from the documentation movement, have certain formal connections. These connections may well imply that there has been a disciplinary convergence of librarianship toward information science. The developments to be examined in this connection are some recent changes in the names of library schools; the employment of librarians in information centers and other less conventional contexts; the growth in the number and the diversification of the specialized content of journals in librarianship and information science; the appearance of an important body of new terminology in librarianship; and finally, the formal structural recognition of mutual interests that has taken place within the major professional associations in librarianship and information science.

In relating the first part of the paper to the second, I take the somewhat simplistic view that the prominence of the computer in the last ten or fifteen years has given librarians themselves a new power of seeing beyond the conventional boundaries of their thinking and activities traditionally imposed by their concern for individual libraries. Because of the increasing sophistication and accessibility of computer technology, librarians have been able to develop library and information services and to organize, manage, and exploit library and information resources in a manner and to an extent not possible before.

It is also my view that information science—almost a phenomenon of the computer age—represented in part, at least initially, systematic attempts to generalize from and to explore in as rigorous a manner as possible questions and answers that were expressed in what had become accepted library organization and practice. This was not at first clearly recognized or at once accepted.

In the third and final part of this paper, asking a question posed by Don Swanson [1980b]—What are the problems libraries were created to solve?—I try briefly to show that there is a disciplinary continuum between librarianship and information science with no easily identifiable boundary separating them, though the difference between the extreme ends of the continuum are clear and even dramatic. I also suggest that the disciplinary movement toward more general and inclusive perspectives discussed in the historical part of this paper may still continue to express itself in a tendency to seek a redefinition of the objects of study of information science.

Underlying this paper is a simplification, which emerges in various ways, that should be acknowledged at the outset. I consider the formation of stable, long-lived scholarly and professional associations and societies as key events. They are culminations in a developmental process of differentiation in librarianship, bibliography, documentation, library science, and information science that I single out from a complex history that involves much more than them. On the whole, I view the fields designated by these appellations in terms of the occupational characteristics, and a related scholarship, of various organized groups of individuals. I focus on some of the changing structural and organizational expressions of relations between these groups and the scholarship to which they lay claim, rather than on the content of the scholarship itself. By confining myself to a general discussion of research and scholarship and to the nature of scholarly and professional literature in the field, I deliberately eschew discussions of whether, or to what degree or according to which criteria, library science and information science can be considered science.

LIBRARIANSHIP

Let us now turn to a historical analysis of the emergence of a group of related but, at least initially, self-consciously separate disciplinary and professional trends. Librarianship, an ancient occupation, clearly should be the first of these to be dealt with. Its origins lie close to the origins of writing, to the discovery of relatively permanent media on which writing could be inscribed, and above all to the social and economic pressures that led to the preparation, preservation, and retrieval of permanent written records. These were necessary to processes of stable government and commerce, to organized religions with commonly accepted rituals and beliefs, and to the cumulation and transmission of the knowledge of the times. Thus, we may speak of librarianship in the ancient world as well as in the modern world.

Nevertheless, it was not until the last quarter of the nineteenth century that modern librarianship began to emerge as a professional occupation. As such, it was characterized by the invention of tools, techniques, and organizational structures that were widely adopted in the then rapidly multiplying university, college, public, school, and special institutional libraries. Strong formal associations of librarians were created at this time. Indeed, we may date the beginning of the professionalization of modern librarianship as an occupation in the English-speaking world from the foundation of the American Library Association (ALA) in 1876 and the Library Association (of the United Kingdom) in 1877. Among the responsibilities of these associations were the oversight and continuing modification and refinement of codes of accepted practice and dissemination of commonly held beliefs about the goals and functions of various kinds of libraries. These associations helped provide a context for the emergence of an apparatus of systematic professional communication: regular conferences, journals, a small monographic literature in which knowledge in the field was codified, disseminated for use, and made available for public discussion. Processes of formal professional education were created, institutionalized, and gradually standardized.

BIBLIOGRAPHY

But within a generation, it became clear that neither libraries nor the existing organizations of librarians were able to initiate or even contribute usefully to the study of solutions to certain general bibliographic problems that lay outside the walls of these individual libraries. This was as true in the United Kingdom as in the United States. Thus, the creation of the Bibliographical Society in 1892 was proposed and discussed at the Library Association meeting in 1891. An issue debated at length was just what the relation of the Bibliographical Society of Chicago, founded in 1899 (to become the American Bibliographical Society in 1904) would be with the American Library Association (ALA); indeed, the fourth general session of the 1902 conference of the ALA was placed "in charge" of the Bibliographical Society of Chicago for a discussion of the founding of a Bibliographical Institute.[1]

These several bibliographical societies were interested in bibliography as an intrinsically rewarding area of study that had produced notable achievements in its already distinguished history. Bibliography as these societies conceived it had broad consequences for scholarship quite apart from libraries. In England, there was in the early days of the Bibliographical Society the intoxicating idea of such a society creating a great catalog of English literature and preparing a revision and supplement to Hain's *Repertorium Bibliographicum*. [Copinger, 1892; Rayward, 1967a.] In both England and the United States, membership in these early bibliographical societies comprised, certainly at first, many librarians but also, and perhaps predominantly as time went by, book collectors, antiquarians, professional literary and historical scholars, and amateur men of letters who incorporated the results of their specialized research in arcane papers that were communicated to each other at meetings and in the journals of their societies. Gradually, interest in what we would today call general issues of bibliographic control tended to subside in these societies, though never completely in the American Bibliographical Society, to be replaced by a scholarly preoccupation with books as physical objects.

The history of books, printing, and publishing, the description of old and rare books, special collections of books and manuscripts, the implications of the physical characteristics of codices and books for various disciplines, and perhaps above all problems in the transmission of texts, such as the relation of manuscript to printed versions—these gradually became the preoccupation of the members of these societies. As specializations of a highly technical kind developed, *bibliography* unadorned became too vague, too much a portmanteau term to be useful. Nowadays, the scholarly activity of bibliographers is labeled descriptive, historical, analytical, or critical bibliography according to particular, perhaps not precisely or consistently distinguished, criteria of interest, affiliation, and technique.

Bibliographers asserted the overall independence of their own area of intellectual endeavor in new journals, among which *The Library* in Great Britain, the *Papers of the Bibliographical Society of America* in the United States, or, later, the *Proceedings of the Bibliographical Society of Virginia* are important. Such journals help to define the boundaries between biblio-

---

[1] *Yearbook of the Bibliographical Society of Chicago* 1901–1902, p. 26.

graphical scholarship and librarianship, and the continuing existence of the journals asserts their continuing importance and separateness. The early specialized bibliographical journals very soon abandoned discussions of general library problems and issues and even bibliography itself broadly conceived; increasingly they reported the narrowly focused and highly specialized scholarship previously described.

At the turn of the nineteenth century, then, librarianship was differentiated from a certain kind of variously designated bibliographic scholarship, though some librarians have always maintained a close contact with it. Indeed, nowadays, aspects of it are sometimes studied in library schools. Nevertheless, differences in orientation between librarians and bibliographers became clear very early. The professional interests of librarians tended to be of a practical kind, firmly focused on the functions and operational requirements of libraries, the organizations within which librarians were employed. Bibliographers, however, tended to be unconstrained by such organizations and cultivated a general academic orientation toward books as complex cultural, intellectual artifacts. This difference in orientation was reflected, for example, in this remark made at the time the transformation of the Chicago Bibliographical Society into a national body was contemplated: "Only a limited number of librarians of the country are likely to become members of any organization whose aim is other than a purely practical one. It has also been pointed out it would be more difficult, if not well nigh impossible, to bring the scholars of the country into membership in a section of a popular organization like the American Library Association."[2]

DOCUMENTATION IN EUROPE

A different view of bibliography, one that resembles our notion of bibliographic control, was held at the turn of the century by Paul Otlet and his colleagues in Brussels. They had founded the International Institute of Bibliography in 1895 to create a universal bibliographical catalog organized on new lines. Eventually Otlet developed his idea of bibliography in a series of now neglected but seminal papers into what he called "documentation." His concern was not to limit bibliographical control to cataloging books in local institutions, but to find a way of creating a universal index of all documents that constituted records of knowledge; books, yes, but also parts of books, journal articles, brochures, industrial catalogs, patents, certain kinds of administrative records of governments, the archives of municipalities, photographs, post cards, newspapers. The problem was to find out what each contributed to the sum of knowledge, what each contained of potentially

---

[2] *Yearbook of the Bibliographical Society of Chicago* 1901–1902, p. 48.

useful information, and to express and connect this flexibly, creatively to what already existed. Otlet had a clear idea of what he wanted from libraries in the new bibliographical order he was attempting to create. He believed that if the bibliographical apparatus or equipment of individual libraries were inproved, better books could be created. Thus would libraries actively contribute to the advancement of knowledge. Otlet wanted libraries to cease being mere depositories and to become vital institutes of documentation providing special information services on all matters of interest to all members of the public who might wish to use them. He wanted to see all libraries transformed into what he called offices of documentation and these to be joined together in a national and international system of communication for sharing all existing resources, an international documentary network. He envisaged an important role for microfilm in this. (His earliest paper on microfilm, libraries, and scholarship was published in 1906. [Otlet and Goldschmidt, 1906.]) A central preoccupation of his voluminous writing was the delineation of documentation as a separate and developing field of study that might ultimately lead to a transformation in the ways in which information was generated, recorded, transmitted, organized, and used. [Otlet, 1903; Rayward, 1975.]

In the view of Otlet and his colleagues, though general bibliographic organization and control—what they tended to designate as the new field of documentation—encompassed traditional librarianship, it went far beyond it. Traditionally, libraries were concerned with only a portion of the documentary record; for documentalists, the whole of the record lay within their scope. The methods to be used to exploit the record, and the institutional settings in which this work could take place, they believed could be more various and innovative than conventional libraries.

Librarians reacted to the apparent competition and threat of assimilation by what was much touted as a new discipline essentially by denial. In continental Europe, just after the first World War, social relations between librarians and documentalists broke down; they have never been fully repaired. [de Costa, 1982; Rayward, 1967b; 1977b.] In England, there was some mild general interest by librarians before the war in continental European documentalists and their work. This became stronger after the war, with the foundation in 1927 of an English member-organization of the International Institute of Bibliography: the British Society for International Bibliography. The English special library movement, which culminated in the foundation of the Association of Special Libraries and Information Bureaus (ASLIB) in 1924, shared many interests with British documentalists, and in 1937, the British Society for International Bibliography was absorbed by ASLIB. Thus, in England, the documentation and special-library movements were mutually reinforcing, had an early accommodation, and operated quite independently of the more traditional interests and activities of the Library Association.

LIBRARY SCIENCE

In the United States, the situation was a little more complex. Here, dissatisfaction with traditional practices of librarianship led not merely to what might be called academic bibliographic scholarship, on the one hand, and to the special-library movement with its interest in the special information needs of business and industry (which I neglect in this paper [see Johns, 1968]), on the other; it also led to the creation of what was called library science.

Appalled by the absence of rigorous research useful to libraries, C. C. Williamson in 1930 asked "Can it be that there are no problems in library service that call for scientific research? Nothing more to learn? No unsolved problems?" (Williamson, 1931, p. 9.) And he quoted and slightly modified John Dewey in describing how a library science might emerge:

> There is no subject matter intrinsically marked off, earmarked so to say, as the content of *library* science. Any methods and any facts and principles from any subject whatsoever that enable the problems of administration and *service* to be dealt with in a bettered way are pertinent. . . . It may be doubted with reference to some aspect or other of *library service* there is any organized body of knowledge that may not need to be drawn upon to become a source of *library science* . . . ." (Ibid., p. 12.)

In effect, the idea of a library science dates from the late 1920s and specifically from the founding of the Graduate Library School at the University of Chicago. This school was established in order to bring the best standards of higher education to bear on the education of librarians and, through the introduction of the PhD degree and the work of the school's faculty, to promote research in the field. In a statement of policy for the school, Douglas Waples listed what the faculty considered to be the distinctive functions of the school:

> 1. The most important single responsibility of the school is to meet the standards of scholarship and research maintained by other graduate departments of the university, both in the character of work undertaken by the staff and by the research interests of its graduates. 2. The major aim is research, defined as "extending the existing body of factual knowledge concerning the values and procedures of libraries and their many aspects, and including the development of methods of investigation whereby significant data are obtained, tested, and applied. . . ." 6. Not all of the studies undertaken by the school need be confined to research in its restricted meaning of "search for abstract principles." In many instances, they may more properly be called service studies, studies intended to increase the effectiveness of library service. . . . 9. An important function of the school is the preparation, collection, and publication of monographs whereby the results of significant studies are made available to the library professions. (Waples, 1931, pp. 26–27.)

It is not by chance, either, that a minor classic of librarianship was written by an early member of the faculty of the Graduate Library School—Pierce Butler's *Introduction to Library Science*. [Butler, 1933.]

Certainly, there was an attempt at the Graduate Library School to find new perspectives from which to study libraries and their problems. These perspectives were provided by the rigorous, academically respectable methods of the social sciences and historical scholarship. These methods were introduced to challenge the existing reliance on shared practical experience as the basis for the field's professional knowledge, with all that this reliance implied of a stultifying orthodoxy of dogma and belief. The importance in the United States of the Graduate Library School for the professionalization of—and the appropriate institutionalization of an educational apparatus in the nation's universities for—librarianship has been widely acknowledged. [Carroll, 1970, pp. 50–56, 264–266; White, 1976, pp. 231–237; Churchwell, 1975, pp. 60–61, 98–101.]

The Graduate Library School embodied what was for a time a unique and controversial approach to professional education; its professors and students steadily produced a formidable body of research where before practically none existed. The school issued the first scholarly journal in the field, *The Library Quarterly,* and graduated those who became influential librarians or faculty members in other library schools. It was not until the late 1940s that two other library schools introduced doctoral studies in librarianship—the Universities of Illinois and Michigan. The 1950s saw a fairly rapid increase in doctoral programs. These programs by definition emphasized the importance of research, as opposed to training practitioners, and increased the volume and quality of the field's literature by reporting this research. Thus, the idea of a library science is hardly more than fifty years old, and any great volume of research in the field is relatively recent.

It should be noted that the approach to creating a library science outlined by Williamson some fifty years ago still obtains: It is still to take the substantive problems of libraries and librarianship and apply to them research methods that seem appropriate from other disciplines. Much of the research in the field has employed, and continues to employ, the methods of the social sciences or is historical in nature. Latterly techniques of systems engineering and mathematical modeling or analysis (such as the techniques of operations research and the related and sometimes overlapping area of bibliometrics) have proved invaluable in conceptualizing library problems in a new way and providing powerful new techniques for analyzing research data.

While the idea of a library science is now widely accepted within the library profession as desirable, it is only a little exaggerated to say that we do not yet have an extensive, distinctive, coherent, well-integrated or systematized and scientifically derived body of theoretical and practical knowledge in librarianship. This leads to criticism of library science as a science and to suspicion of librarianship as a profession. [Rayward, 1980b.] That it is, however, exaggerated should be acknowledged because of the existence of cumulatively important subsets of library literature in the areas, for example, of systems engineering, operations research, use and user studies, classification and indexing, management, and measuring effectiveness, among others.

Nevertheless, it seems clear to me, despite the research that exists and the academic location of professional education, that the empiricism of nineteenth-century librarianship—which the new library science was to test and perhaps ultimately supersede—remains strongly present in the library profession today. That is to say, much of the librarian's knowledge continues to be arrived at, and quite generally accepted, in a pragmatic way through library practice and the shared experience of librarians. Our cataloging codes and major classification systems, for example, are of this nature. It is probably true that the central core of knowledge underlying librarianship is still of this empirical kind and that consequently library science has failed to lead to an extensive and solid corpus of objectively derived, systematically examined and accumulated knowledge. Whatever knowledge of this kind exists, it may be thought of as peripheral or incidental to the central business of librarians—continuing to try, against increasing odds, to keep their organizations running reasonably effectively.

DOCUMENTATION AND INFORMATION SCIENCE

In 1933, Watson Davis proposed that a scientific information institute be set up to help foster communication among scientists and improve existing methods of bibliographical control of scientific literature. [W. Davis, 1935; Schultz and Garwig, 1969.] Such an institute would, toward these goals, especially exploit the developing technology of microphotography. His proposal elicited widespread comment at home and from the European documentalists. As nothing came of his proposals, he created in 1935 a Documentation Institute within Science Service, an agency for the popularization of science, of which he was the director. He used the word documentation to include "all phases of issuance, use and interchange of recorded information." The word attracted him as a term because it had a wide circulation in Europe as a result of the work of Otlet and his documentalist colleagues, while having no particular meanings associated with it in the United States.[3] The American Documentation Institute was created in 1937 as a kind of club to involve—through their directors or other senior officers—a wide range of libraries, learned societies, and government agencies in microfilm and other projects at first insufficiently supported and then more or less repudiated by Science Service.

Though founded in 1937, the American Documentation Institute became a

---

[3] I owe much of this information to the unpublished work of Irene Farkas-Conn, a doctoral student in the University of Chicago Graduate Library School.

professional and scholarly force only with the publication of its journal *American Documentation* in 1950 and with the institute's transformation into a general-membership organization in 1953. Nevertheless, the early emphasis on technology, scientific communication and publication, and new services offered through new kinds of institutions, anticipated later developments within the institute. Here, essentially, was an attempt, stimulated by technological innovation, to place library and library-related problems in the context of scientific communication.

Vernon Tate's editorial description of the scope of *American Documentation* makes it clear that he, like Davis, saw the European documentation movement as at last crossing the Atlantic to the United States and, from his point of view, finding in the journal a vehicle that would ensure its subsequent development. [Tate, 1950.] The journal was to deal with "The totality of documentation," and the definition of documentation given was that which had been accepted, Tate noted, by the International Federation for Documentation,[4] for which the American Documentation Institute had become the American affiliate. "The term documentation refers to the creation, transmission, collection, classification, and use of 'documents'; documents may be broadly defined as recorded knowledge in any format." Tate also went on to observe of the new work being done by documentalists: "Traditional methods of communicating and recording knowledge are being studied, reorganized and supplanted and in some cases revolutionized." [Ibid., p. 3.]

In the following decades, it became clear that the documentalists considered themselves a breed quite apart from librarians. Unlike librarians, they were not institution-bound. They belonged to a different environment; they came to documentation from a wide variety of scientific and technical fields. They were responding exuberantly to powerful social forces. As Jesse Shera has said of this period: "First of all interest in the problem of information on the part of the scientific world and the federal government reached an unprecedented level. Coupled with this was a period of accelerated technological development." (Shera and Cleveland, 1977, p. 258.) The exploding world of scientific literature; new communications and information-processing technology; mammoth programs of governmental research calling for new systems of information organization, storage, and retrieval—these were the winds and waves of these new mariners, the documentalists, and the information scientists they formally became in 1968, when the American Documentation Institute became the American Society for Information Science. They invented a new language in which to discuss their work. They became increasingly involved with the computer and mathematics. Machine-stored, manipulated, and transmitted data inevitably involved a reassessment of what constituted a document and what documentation was. The computer raised the possibility of a wide range of indexing and retrieval experiments

---

[4]The new name that The International Institute of Bibliography adopted in 1937.

hardly possible before. And, indeed, it may well be that retrieval experiments in the 1960s constitute a first flowering of information science as a science.

Certainly, information science as a discipline nourishing certain professional activities developed rapidly in the 1960s. In 1965, the first *Annual Review of Information Science and Technology* appeared. It is of particular interest because it represents a relatively early survey of the literature of the field and its segmentation into what appeared at that time to be the accepted major disciplinary components. These components vividly exemplified the importance of the computer in giving shape and direction to both discussion and research in the field. The following chapters were written explicitly in relation to the computer: "File Organization and Search Techniques," "Automated Language Processing," "New Hardware Developments," "Man-Machine Communication," "Information-System Applications," and "Library Automation." Two chapters were concerned with aspects of indexing and abstracting: "Content Analysis, Specification and Control," and "Evaluation of Indexing Systems." Another chapter was on "Information Centers and Services," central to which was a comparison of work carried out in special libraries; one was on "Professional Aspects of Information Science and Technology," in which were examined problems of terminology (briefly) and developments in educational programs (at length); and finally, there was a chapter on "National Information Issues and Trends."

The change of the name of the American Documentation Institute to the American Society for Information Science was intended to reflect the changing orientation of the society's members. The adoption of the slippery term *information* led to many theoretical and frequently tortuous attempts at definitions. During the decades of the 1960s and the 1970s, there was also much discussion about what an ideal curriculum for information science might look like as opposed to those already in existence for librarianship.

Many of the developments of the late 1960s may be interpreted as the latest culmination of ongoing attempts to create a more general understanding of how to facilitate access to recorded knowledge than was possible in librarianship, which was perceived as being limited to creating collections of books and related library materials and to managing libraries, or to documentation, which focused on a more abstract notion of records of knowledge or documents. In its turn, information science represented an approach to an even more abstract level of analysis; it included books and documents while not being limited to them. Information science has permitted the development of research that is more generally cumulative and generalizable, more readily enriched by importations from other disciplines. It has led to the development of new options, procedures, and organizational arrangements for facilitating access to information recorded, or manipulated, in new ways.

Let us say that by 1970 this was the situation. On the one hand was a vigorous librarianship, its practitioners still blissful in their relatively undisturbed pragmatism, despite the existence of an important scholarly apparatus for the profession involving, in part, the nation's graduate library schools and despite increasing lip service to the importance of research for the development of their field. Their journal and monographic literature had become voluminous, though fragmented. They were organized into a number of large, well-established, professional associations with a wide range of competing, sometimes conflicting, professional functions. On the other hand was the new, equally vigorous discipline of information science, with a strong research orientation underlying its professional and service components, its own small fairly homogeneous learned society, a generalized field of study (whose precise boundaries, however, were in constant dispute), and a recently established bibliographical and educational apparatus. How did what was a certain combativeness on the part of information scientists and librarians change, insofar as it has changed, to mutual accommodation?

DISCIPLINARY CONVERGENCE

It is too simple to say that library schools, aware of the limitations of library science and recognizing that information science might provide a more respectable disciplinary base for the profession of librarianship, enticed or co-opted information scientists as faculty. Or that it was hoped that if a little information science were added to their library studies, library-school graduates might find the job market opening up. Or that information scientists could not really find a more congenial academic home (or parking lot) in engineering or computer science or mathematics departments than in library schools. There may be some truth in all of these statements.

I attribute a disciplinary convergence, insofar as it has occurred, to essentially two factors. The first was the thoughtful recognition by leaders in the fields of library science and information science that they were committed to finding solutions to the same general problems, despite differences in terminology and orientation. The second was the increasing importance of the computer in libraries; the need to exploit computers has brought about a convergence in language and orientation discussed in the next part of this paper.

In the 1950s, Jesse Shera and Margaret Egan, students of the work of Bradford and the European documentalists, in a series of still valuable papers developed new ideas about librarianship, bibliography, and information. [Shera and Egan, 1953.] They spoke of bibliographic organization [Shera and Egan, 1951], speculated about classification, sought an intellectual foundation for librarianship and bibliography in a theory of social epistemology [Egan and Shera, 1951], and tried to understand the significance and implications of the rapidly changing information technology of the times. [Shera, 1953.] During his tenure at Western Reserve University and later, Shera was a witty, thoughtful observer of new applications of the computer to information handling. He was a librarian eager to reconcile what seemed unnecessarily divergent movements; he was a synthesizer, a gadfly, a theoretician. He held librarianship, documentation, and information science together intellectually in a broad and scholarly perspective and encouraged their joint institutionalization in the library school at Western Reserve, of which he became dean. [Shera, 1968.]

In 1963, Don Swanson, a physicist who had become an information scientist, was appointed dean of the Graduate Library School at Chicago. In 1964, he organized the 29th annual conference of the Graduate Library School on the subject of the intellectual foundations of library education. In his introduction to the conference, he observed:

> The fields of information science, information technology, information retrieval and documentation will not be treated as separate topics but rather as an integral part of library science, . . . thus we shall not be concerned with whether information science is part of library science or vice versa, but rather we shall assume that the educational process in a graduate library school must adequately take both into account. (Swanson, 1965, p. 2.)

Swanson then went on to outline a group of substantive questions that might affect the immediate future of library education and research and that encompassed much of what information science dealt with at the time.

These two instances, and I should stress that many more could be adduced, are of leaders in the field alive to new possibilities. They were indifferent to, or at least undisturbed by, jurisdictional disputes between certain librarians of the time who were fearful of computers and scientific method and some information scientists who were disdainful of the pragmatism and apparent parochialism of librarians. These leaders had a broad, generalized perspective that allowed them to discern the general but common problems that underlay librarianship and the new developments in information processing that were sparked by the computer revolution.

The computer eventually gave their arguments overwhelming force in two ways. Its exploitation in individual libraries led to an almost universal interest of librarians in systems analysis that required identifying and recording library operations at a level of detail appropriate for possible computerization. And this inevitably called into question much of the conventional wisdom underlying library organization and administration. [Flood, 1965.] The development of the Online Computer Library Center (OCLC) and later of other bibliographic utilities and networks and online indexing search services (Dialog, Bibliographical Retrieval Services (BRS), etc.) required librarians to move beyond the confines of their own libraries, using a sophisticated electronic technology. Moreover, it became clear that problems involved in creating and exploiting these systems both locally and centrally were of a complexity and magnitude and yet of a solvability previously unparalleled in librarianship.

Of course, the computer in and of itself was not responsible for these developments. The exploitation of the computer in developing new institutional relations between libraries and in improving local library processes and procedures was encouraged by the growing volume and complexity of materials that had to be dealt with and by a fiscal plight that has become increasingly severe. Nowadays, computer-based systems that have been created as a response to these pressures have become one of the major foci of developments in librarianship. Technical requirements, operational refinement, and improvement of various systems have brought professional librarians and professionally active information scientists together in a way that makes them virtually indistinguishable. Librarianship as librarianship in this context typically concerns itself with the organizational, political, jurisdictional, and economic aspects of the problems that these systems create and to which, in part, they attempt to respond.

DEVELOPMENTS IN LIBRARIANSHIP

Let us now examine five developments that have taken place in librarianship during the last several decades. These developments support the idea that, at least from the librarian's point of view, there is an emergent disciplinary integration between librarianship and information science, the historical divergence and subsequent accommodation of which were discussed in the preceding section of this paper.

Name Changes

First, and perhaps most superficial, are changes in the way library schools name themselves. Recently, the Library School at the University of Illinois changed its name to Graduate School of Library and Information Science. At Denver, the school became the Graduate School of Librarianship and Information Management. At Brigham Young University, the school is called the School of Library and Information Sciences. At Berkeley, it is the School of Library and Information Studies, while at Chicago, though a range of information science courses is taught and the school is reported as one of the first to attempt the systematic integration of a library-and-information science curriculum [Taylor, 1966], the school continues to be called the Graduate Library School. Despite these differing appellations, collectively, we still tend to call all of these schools library schools, but that is no longer precisely accurate in terms of their interests and scope and how they wish to present themselves to the rest of academe. The importance of the name changes lies in what they represent—a shift of emphasis from libraries to something more general. The curriculum in most of these schools now includes courses dealing with computers and computer programming; database creation, management, and development; information storage and searching more generally; and behavioral characteristics of various groups and kinds of information producers and users.

Employment Trends

The changes in the names of library schools reflect, in part, another contemporary trend. The graduates of our library schools as well as becoming librarians now frequently go into information processing or information management, and they are called information specialists, analysts, or consultants. This is the second development I wish to mention. To conventional library jobs, librarians now sometimes add aspects of records management, special indexing services, media management, and research analysis, and they often work in what is called an information center. It has become fairly generally accepted that there is a wide range of professional library and librarylike work that library-school graduates can perform successfully outside conventional library settings. [Sellen, 1980.]

Journal Proliferation

The next change I want to mention is the enormous proliferation of journals in the library and information science fields. Some of these journals have gone through interesting name changes: *Information Storage and Retrieval* has become *Information Processing and Management; American Documentation* has become the *Journal of the American Society for Information Science; UNESCO Bulletin for Libraries* has become the *UNESCO Journal of Information Science, Librarianship and Archives Administration*. One group of new journals is clearly library related: *Collection Management, The Serials Librarian, The Behavioral and Social Sciences Librarian, Public Library Quarterly, Library Research,* and the *Journal of Academic Librarianship*. Other journals, of no less interest to librarians, have in their titles the new language of information work: *On-Line, On-Line Review, Program,* and *Data Base.*

This phenomenon of a rapidly growing number of journals, insofar as it does not represent some form of collective madness, given the economic conditions of the times, must mean something. We can argue that the phenomenon is, in part, the result of the commercial exploitation of institutional pressure on librarians and library-school faculty to increase their publishing activities in order to achieve academic and professional respectability. But we may also argue that this literature suggests that a closely related range of subspecializations has developed and, in librarianship especially, achieved a certain maturity—a range that progresses from matters of quite conventional librarianship through key areas in information science. Journals that tend to draw the boundaries of the fields as a whole, such as the *Library Quarterly* or the *Journal of the American Society for Information Science,* include articles over the whole range of issues and problems dealt with by separate journals, though we assume that there are different frequency distributions of papers across the subspecializations included in the general journals. Neither the field of librarianship nor information science, given this variety and overlapping of journals, can be perceived as unitary and strictly exclusive of the other. Rather, each is an agglomeration of parts, many of which may be regarded as common to both.

Terminology

The new language of librarianship is important because it is a terminological reflection of all the changes that have been occurring. It is this body of relatively new terminology that constitutes the fourth change that I wish to identify. Fifteen years ago, when we spoke of a catalog, we meant sometimes a book but usually a card catalog. We looked to the Library of Congress to supply catalog copy in the form of cards or proof sheets. Now we speak, in addition, of COM (Computer Output Microform) and online public-access catalogs, of MARC (Machine Readable Cataloging) data disseminated on magnetic tapes. In the mid-1960s, new technology consisted of keypunch machines, sorters, printers, and a monstrous engine called a computer, to which indirect access was had in batch mode. Nowadays, there is an increasingly large group of librarians who can speak with some familiarity of CPUs (Central Processing Units) and peripherals; mainframe, mini- and microcomputers; Baud rates and memory capacity; hard discs and floppy disks; and bubble memory. Reference librarians, sensitive to the importance of understanding database structures and search strategies because of new kinds of cost considerations, are expected routinely to conduct what is variously called online or machine-assisted searching of bibliographic and nonbibliographic databases, access to which is purchased from database vendors in dial-up mode using the Tymnet or Telenet communications systems. Other librarians buy software and hardware and turnkey systems from commercial vendors who are part of something we now designate as the information industry. Once, cooperative schemes led to shared storage facilities and union catalogs that were kept up to date and reasonably complete only with enormous difficulty and at a prohibitive cost. Now, we have bibliographic utilities and networks for which the Union Catalog function is but one, and that more or less incidental, of a great range of capabilities. The new language is essentially derived from computer applications in libraries and, as a consequence, is frequently the same as, or at least similar to, that used by information scientists, for whom, historically it can be argued, the computer provided a major disciplinary impetus. The shared language has helped identify shared technical and professional problems.

Structure of Associations

The final development to which I wish to refer is the structural recognition within the formal professional association in both librarianship and information science of major areas of both common and divergent interests. As early as 1951, the Special Libraries Association established a Documentation Division; this division is now the Information Technology Division. The Special Libraries Association has a wide range of specific subject divisions and a Publishing Division as well. In 1962 the American Library Association created an Interdivisional Committee on Documentation, which became, in 1966, the Information Science and Automation Division, now the Library and Information Technology Division. For most of its life, the Resources and Technical Services Division has had a Section for Classification. In 1968, when the American Society for Information Science set up Special Interest Groups (SIGs), one of the first was for Library Automation and Networks and another for Classification Research. Some of the Special Interest Groups, particularly in scientific and technical subject areas, paralleled subject divisions in the Special Libraries Association. Most recently, while the number and configuration of subject areas that are the object of Special Interest Groups have changed, the Library Automation and Network Group and the Classification Research Group have been maintained. Among new groups are those for Community Information Services, Computerized Retrieval Services, Nonprint Media and Reprographics, and Information Generation and Publishing. These all have counterparts within library associations. The Public Library Association of the American Library Association, for example, has a Community Information Section; the Reference and Adult Services Division has a Section for Machine Assisted Reference (also called Computerized Search Services); the Resources and Technical Services Division has a Reproduction of Library Materials Section; the Library Information Technology Division has sections for Information Science and Automation (the old name of the division), Audio Visual Materials, and Video and Cable Communications. These all reflect developing areas of mutual interest between librarians as an occupational group and information scientists.

The formal associations also reveal areas that do not overlap in so direct or important a way. The differences are clearest where library associations focus on quite specific library matters. These are represented structurally within the American Library Association, for example, by the type-of-library divisions. On the other hand, the information science association seems most different when it focuses on information and information processing in a most general way: represented structurally within the American Society for Information Science, for example, by special interest groups on numeric databases, the foundations of information science, and information analysis or evaluation. But librarians increasingly consider that they must be able to use effectively nonbibliographic databases; that the foundations of information science must inevitably encompass recorded information and its "potentiation" for society in organizations such as libraries. Information analysis or evaluation may well deal in a generalized way with issues that a large literature in evaluating library and information services has already attempted to deal with.

A DISCIPLINARY CONTINUUM

In the preceding sections of this paper, I discussed first the emergence of four major disciplinary trends that represent, in the case of documentation and information science especially, attempts to find an increasingly general perspective from which to conceptualize, investigate, and find new and improved operational responses to problems that underlie libraries and librarianship. Next, I described certain contemporary phenomena that suggest a convergence of librarianship toward what has become known as information science. In the third section of the paper, I want to take a more speculative approach to the relation between the definition of librarianship and information science.

As a point of departure, it is useful to examine the question posed by Swanson: What are the problems libraries are intended to solve? [Swanson, 1980a.] An immediate implication of this question is that, despite their antiquity, libraries may not be the only, the best, or even a lasting solution to these problems. Furthermore, if there are other solutions imaginable, it is important to be able to assess their relative effectiveness in the endless search for an optimal configuration of solutions.

Libraries may be regarded as a major institutionalized response to the problems of providing generalized access to the record of what is known. They are a complex organization of access mechanisms. A collection of books and other traditional library materials organized according to the conventions of librarianship by a specially trained and deployed staff for the use of a defined clientele—this is a typical way in which libraries provide access to a portion of the record of knowledge. The explicit or implicit definition of a clientele provides boundaries as to what will be collected and how what is collected will be organized and made available. In addition, an individual library usually provides a range of staff, a variety of bibliographic and other tools, and creates formalized procedures for gaining both bibliographic access and sometimes physical access to that portion and form of the documentary record that is not directly incorporated into the library.

As time has gone by, the ways in which what is known has been recorded, on the one hand, and what constitutes effective access to this record, on the other, have changed. As well as the variety of forms of printed record, there are now other formats in which knowledge or information is recorded; perhaps the latest of these are electronic. Access is required not merely to conventional library materials or to other formats of the record, but to what they contain as well, to their components, or elemental parts that can be described as facts, ideas, data, information. In some circumstances, access is provided not merely on demand but in anticipation of demand through selective dissemination of information (SDI) services. Furthermore, access is also seen as increasingly desirable in a limited number of areas of knowledge to the restructured content of what has been recorded in these areas. The need to provide this kind of access has led to setting up information-analysis centers and social-science-data archives, for example, and employing research analysts. This kind of access has, as a rule, required the participation of kinds of personnel different from those traditionally employed professionally in libraries; special training in the disciplines involved and in computer-based statistical procedures have been thought to be necessary. Schools of library-and-information science nowadays, however, can and do provide some of this training.

As the volume, complexity, and variety of formats of the record of knowledge or recorded information have increased and the number of users and the range of potential requirements of access to this record have expanded, a variety of responses to these circumstances has occurred. Some of the responses have been made commercially by what we now call the information industry, which creates and sells bibliographic services and products to libraries, which constitute a major segment of their market, and also independently of libraries. Libraries have been organized locally, regionally, and nationally into an enormously various range of configurations of systems, networks, and consortia. Developments in telecommunications capabilities have been seized on as facilitating new kinds of institutional arrangements for providing different levels of access both through libraries and outside of them, as in the experimental home-based VIEWDATA or PRESTEL systems. New kinds of organizations have been created to provide new kinds of access, such as information centers and data archives.

A narrow and conventional definition of a library expresses a limited view of the format of the records involved and modes of access provided to them. But if these limitations are abandoned, libraries may be thought to embrace not only the arrangements and services of traditional libraries but of information centers and data archives as well. Traditional libraries fall into place on a historical continuum that has arisen as institutionalized responses to the need to provide access to information in recorded form have been developed, examined, and modified.

Such an approach to a definition may seem too broad to be useful. It includes bookstores and office-filing and records-management systems. It may be argued that it extends to genetics and incorporates museums. While bookstores, office-filing and records-management systems involve what may be described as librarylike documents, they have in the past tended to fall outside the scope of librarianship. In none of these cases were the systems for, and modes of, access particularly complex and interesting. In bookstores, in addition, access is consummated only on a basis that librarians have tended to repudiate (except in the case of the rental collections some public libraries still maintain)—the payment of a fee. Nevertheless, as book jobbers, for example, have developed extensive librarylike systems essentially for the use of libraries, book jobbers have become less like bookstores and more like the libraries they serve. And insofar as in hospitals, law firms, and other institutional settings, filing and records systems have grown in scope and complexity and in the sophistication of the technology through which they are maintained, they have begun to attract the interest of librarians and information scientists.

It is not implausible, either, to think of a museum as a library of artifacts. Suzanne Briet, writing from the point of view of the European documentalists, espouses a definition of documentation almost as broad as this. "An antelope that has been 'cataloged' [in a zoo] is a primary document and other documents are secondary and derivative." (Briet, 1951, p. 8.) It seems more clearly figurative to speak of chromosomes as libraries of genetic information: Certainly neither man nor nature promises generalized access to the information they contain, despite the advances that have been made in genetic engineering.

But it is at this point of seeking appropriate definitions for libraries, documentation, and information science and of exploring their ramifications that we may suggest the continued relevance of the historical development explored earlier by asking the question: What are the phenomena that information science studies? The preceding discussion has focused on a changing understanding of the scope and limits of a professional occupation that attempts to provide information services through relatively permanent and formal structures. What underlies these changes has been an increasingly complex and sophisticated view of what constituted recorded information. First came books; they are documents, and documents contain information, and access to information is provided for by the systematic manipulation of the contents of documents and books. Despite all the unknowns, such relations are relatively clear, and the study of the processes involved and the larger environment in which they take place are relatively well circumscribed.

When, however, the focus becomes not library and information *work,* but information *science,* the clarity, such as it is, is lost. Information becomes a phenomenon for scientific investigation, and the contexts within which it is examined and the investigative techniques to be employed depend very largely on how information is defined. Information as electrical impulses in the brain or as represented by certain biochemical phenomena or as the content of disciplines—this set of different meanings raises a serious problem of disciplinary encroachment. When is *information science* information science and not epistemology, psychology, biopsychology, physiology or physics or journalism or the sociology of groups or anthropology?

Thus, an ultimate consequence of the process of seeking an ever more general perspective for information science, for the problems of access to recorded and potentially consultable or public information underlying the creation and development of libraries, may be the loss of all sense of disciplinary coherence in the field. We might argue from the point of view of the continuum I described earlier that at one end is the librarian constructing a catalog of books; at the other, because of the way in which information can now be conceived, is the genetic engineer consulting the information recorded in and then restructuring DNA. Perhaps, however, there is a discontinuity between the two involving notions of symbolic representation and public consultation that more careful analysis and definition would reveal.

The point here is not so much the difficulty of definition or the slipperiness of terminology as the implication that the generalizing process described early in this paper may still be at work. It is a source of innovation and strength, but it blurs traditional distinctions and can unsettle professional convictions.

KNOWLEDGE AND PRACTICE IN LIBRARY AND INFORMATION SERVICES

David Batty and Toni Carbo Bearman

Librarianship, as Boyd Rayward says, is an ancient profession, as old as Babylon. But the government of society and its commerce has depended on the collection and use of information for just as long—from Babylon through the Domesday Book to the United States Census and beyond. Is not then information science equally ancient? We know about the Babylonian libraries by their catalogs; we know about the use of information in government and commerce from the existence of inventories. The principal characterizing principle of the organization of information seems to be list-making; that is, we might say that the kind of list-making characterizes the kind of general information activity. This thesis will be addressed passim in the paper.

Rayward quite rightly describes the recent convergence of hitherto disparate disciplines or practices, but in referring to library and information science and bibliographers and documentalists, he seems to present a picture that does not always do justice to the complexity of the nature of the component forces. Further, his historical backdrop, with 1876 as the beginning of formal librarianship and the founding of the Graduate Library School in Chicago as the beginning of research in library science, does not really allow a large enough stage to accommodate the true range of significant characters.

In short, while we agree with Rayward's general thesis, we would like to extend it, with reference to some earlier history and other phenomena in the last century. We would like to begin by making a few formal points:

There was a long-standing library tradition before 1876, admittedly (unashamedly?) pragmatic, of academic libraries, and later, subscription and circulating libraries. Those in charge of libraries like the Smithsonian (Jewett), the British Museum (Edwards, Panizzi), and the Boston Athenaeum (Cutter) were learned and articulate.

There was a long-standing bibliographical tradition, which began in the late renaissance, was cultivated in the eighteenth century, flourished in the nineteenth century, and continues today. But the concern of classical bibliographers (for example, McKerrow) has always been for scholarly description of books in such detail that individual copies could be identified.

Scientists in the late nineteenth century quite outside either bibliographic or library traditions were already compiling indexes and catalogs of scientific material, because neither librarians nor bibliographers provided them. These were the protodocumentalists—they were not bibliographers.

From the eighteenth century onward, new libraries and new library practices veered between the bibliographic and documentalist traditions, as they tried, on the one hand, to be scholarly in their catalog descriptions and, on the other, to provide easily used "finding-tools" for their patrons.

Rayward is quite right when he says that "[librarianship's] origins lie close to the origins of writing." However, we should remember that the earliest writings were inventories—of property, goods, and laws in Babylon, Mycenae, and so forth. Early library catalogs were only another form of inventory—even the celebrated Alexandrian catalog of Callimachus. Similarly, in the Middle Ages, monasteries kept inventories of their collections and sometimes used them as catalogs. Even as late as the end of the eighteenth century, libraries kept an internal inventory and perhaps an internal slip catalog arranged by author/title and occasionally published a meager author/title entry catalog for the library patrons. For example, between 1667 and 1840, even Harvard College produced a public catalog only three times. [Weber, 1964.]

The library catalog as we know it was really the product of the book trade: Aldus Manutius and his contemporaries in the late fifteenth century for bibliographic description; Andrew Maunsell and the English booksellers of the early seventeenth century for the subject catalog; and the early eighteenth-century Paris booksellers like Marchand and Brunet, for the idea of a general bibliographic classification.

We should not assume, however, that booksellers gave rise to the bibliographic tradition. Their aim was to sell books, which they did successfully by grouping similar books and subjects together in their catalogs and describing them explicitly and practically to their customers. On the other hand, the classical bibliographer's delight is to record the diversity and differences of books in order to identify individual copies. Indeed, Rayward says, "These several bibliographical societies were interested in bibliography as an intrinsically rewarding area of study that had . . . broad consequences for scholarship quite apart from libraries." Of course they were interested—the eighteenth century had been a century of gentleman's individual scholarship. Now there was a hope of institutionalism—perhaps even a society like the Royal Society.

Rayward asserts that "we may date the beginning of . . . modern librarianship . . . in the English-speaking world from the foundation of the American Library Association (ALA) in 1876 and the Library Association (of the United Kingdom) in 1877. . . . But within a generation, it became clear that neither libraries nor the existing organizations of librarians were able to initiate or even contribute usefully to the study of solutions to certain general bibliographic problems that lay outside the walls of these individual libraries. This was as true in the United Kingdom as in the United States."

This is an almost Hegelian interpretation of library history. For the American Library Association to be formed in 1876 meant the coming together of a large number of like-minded professionals. What had Charles Jewett, Charles Cutter, Justin Winsor, and Melvil Dewey been doing in the years before 1876? What had Edward Edwards, Antonio Panizzi, and Andrea Crestadoro been doing in England before 1877? Britain had passed a Public Libraries Act nearly thirty years before. The years 1876/1877 do not mark the beginning of librarianship; they mark its formalization in two national associations after at least a generation of practice. The international conference of 1877 was a declaration of the existence of a solid body of knowledge and experience.

Jewett had already laid out in the 1840s the three factors essential for solving the problem of universal bibliography: access to material, reproduction technology, and consistent descriptive practice. [Jewett, 1851.] Jewett, and later, Dewey and Cutter, tried to solve the problem from within the library world. Rayward ignores the very real efforts made toward the standardization of bibliographic description by librarians like Panizzi, Jewett, Cutter, and others.

It is true that conventional libraries did not produce a solution to general bibliographic problems in the last quarter of the nineteenth century—nor did bibliographers. The reason was not a failure due to any one part of our general profession, but the effect of historical development—Jewett's three problems were never all solved satisfactorily at the same time.

Indeed, as the bibliographers delved even more into the scholarly minutiae of the differences between copies of early printed books, they inhibited the production of large-scale scholarly catalogs. It fell to the very different documentalists (sometimes called scientific bibliographers, to add to the confusion) to try to collect and organize all the citations in the scientific literature.

Bibliographic control has never been a central interest of classical bibliography. Classical bibliographers are concerned with differences between copies of a published work, whereas librarians are concerned with similarities in order to collect them into subject groups on shelves and into author/title and subject groups in catalogs and indexes. Documentalists have always been concerned with specific detail but have customarily used librarylike techniques to organize their material. They are on the other side of the librarian from the bibliographer but perhaps not so far away.

As Rayward says,

> In the view of Otlet and his colleagues, though general bibliographic organiza-
> tion and control—what they tended to designate as the new field of documenta-
> tion—encompassed traditional librarianship, it went far beyond it. Tradi-
> tionally, libraries were concerned with only a portion of the documentary
> record; for the documentalists, the whole of the record lay within their scope.
> (Rayward in his paper in this volume.)

We should remember that, although Otlet certainly addressed general
bibliographic control in 1895, so had Melvil Dewey, as evidenced in the
preface to the first edition of his classification scheme in 1876. [Dewey,
1876.] Actually the problem had been that librarians, influenced by classical
bibliographers, wanted to include a kind of formalized record in the manner
of the bibliographers. This had begun under the influence of Panizzi's cry for
"a full and accurate catalog" [*Report of the Royal Commission,* 1850] and,
by 1908, with the joint Anglo-American code [*Cataloguing Rules,* 1908], was
somewhat divorced from the indexing tradition of Poole's *Index* [Poole,
1882], and so forth. Early documentalists wanted comprehensive coverage,
sufficient (i.e., perhaps minimum) record, and precise location.

Unfortunately, in his discussion of library science, Rayward neglects special libraries, the true inheritors of the documentalist tradition. In the United
Kingdom at least, in the 1920s/1930s (precisely the period Rayward addresses), there were strong forces binding together the disparate elements of
scientific and technological information and formal (mostly public and special) libraries. Regional networks like Sheffield Interchange Organization
(SINTO), Liverpool and District Scientific, Industrial, and Research Libraries Advisory Council (LADSIRLAC), and so forth, were based in public
libraries (with the public library seen as a kind of honest broker) and linked
all kinds of library and information units for the exchange of nonbibliographic as well as bibliographic information. To understand the true
significance of these networks, and the position of the public library within
them, the reader should realize that for at least the first half of this century,
public libraries in the United Kingdom represented the most powerful sector
of the library profession. It was not unusual to find city reference libraries
richer in their collections and more active in their reference service than
university libraries in the same cities.

Rayward's suggestion that the formation of a theory of librarianship and
library research began with the founding of the Graduate Library School in
Chicago seems less cause and effect than a *post hoc ergo propter hoc* argument. There had been many scholars, thinkers, and workers concerned with
many aspects of library science between 1840 and 1940, most of whom owed
no debt to the Graduate Library School. It is true that Jewett, Cutter, Bliss,
Sayers, and Ranganathan addressed individual aspects (although Cutter and
Ranganathan came close to addressing the whole field). It is probably true to

say that they did not develop a theory of librarianship—but we wonder if one has ever been enunciated. It is true also that much of the work in the late nineteenth century addressed practical aspects of library science—but there are many fields in which research customarily addresses practical aspects of the discipline.

We have mixed feelings about some of the customary attitudes toward or definitions of research especially in library-and-information science. Library-and-information science is in an uncomfortable position vis-à-vis research for two reasons: The discipline is structural rather than substantive, and (partly for this reason and partly for historical reasons), it never amassed, or had time to amass, a solid quantitative base of empirical observations in a period of its development early enough to avoid doubts being cast on that kind of research or observation. Librarians and information scientists very soon found themselves alongside researchers in other disciplines who had that quantitative base and who were now exploring theoretical implications. The profession may do itself a disservice if it seeks to emphasize only "respectable" research. Rayward alludes somewhat disparagingly to the empiricism of the nineteenth century—yet, like medicine and law, we are a profession with a job to do. We hope to improve by learning from research, but we can also improve through carefully considered practice.

The best hope we have is precisely the tenor of Rayward's paper: That we are now seeing the convergence of closely related bodies of knowledge and practice that for long, like siblings with territorial problems, have viewed each other at best with suspicion and at worst with outright paranoia. Information has already become the late twentieth century's biggest industry. With a clear view of the nature, origin, and potential of the components (that may include ourselves), we may see our way to the best resolution.

LIBRARY SCIENCE AND INFORMATION SCIENCE

Broad or Narrow?

Manfred Kochen

It is tempting to begin with a discussion of the nature of information and some elementary distinctions. The disciplines of information are still in too early a stage of development for any kind of consensus on this question to exist. Yet, it may help for the purpose of discussion to offer at least my own views as working definitions. To those of us who were educated in mathematics, physics, chemistry, mathematical social sciences, or engineering since the middle of this century, the concept of information was associated with entropy, order, energy, organization, and control. It aroused our scientific curiosity and excited our imagination as being a concept at the frontier of the unknown. We thought its explication might for the first time unlock some deep secret of nature—how organized systems are formed and maintain themselves—and shed light on tantalizing mysteries of life and mind.

I believe that this curiosity accounted for the unexpected popularity of Wiener's highly technical *Cybernetics* and the enthusiastic reception of the mathematical theory of communication. [Wiener, 1948 and 1961; Shannon, 1948.] Program-steered electronic computers, which made their appearance as practical devices about that time also, were regarded as logical, symbol-processing information engines. Their enormous potential for revolutionizing our conceptions of problem-solving and information-processing also stimulated a great deal of speculation and research.

It is fruitless to engage in semantic disputes over when a discipline of information is not epistemology, psychology, biopsychology, and so forth. What matters is that investigators who identify with the information disciplines formulate researchable problems and make discoveries, and contribute insights that clarify the nature and dynamics of information and knowledge. Their identification with a scientific community that calls itself information science may, presumably, provide them with ideas, methods, paradigms, and interactions. It may lead to success in ways that have not succeeded in other communities of inquiry. To suggest that the primary focus of information science should be library and information *work* is stifling and unproductively restrictive. It is not likely to attract scientists with imagination, ambition, and attitudes similar to those of the best scientists in other areas.

The conceptualization of information[1] as the reduction of uncertainty by a receiver about which message, from an ensemble of messages, was transmitted over a noisy transmission channel was a major scientific achievement. The identification of uncertainty with entropy, and Claude Shannon's theorem about the existence of codes that make it possible to transmit information at rates that come arbitrarily close to a specified upper limit with arbitrarily low probabilities of undetected error, rooted what others called information theory firmly as an engineering discipline. It placed information, in its technical sense, in the repertoire of major concepts of modern science. In this sense, it was definitely divorced from meaning and the less precise interpretations that could connect it to uses such as information in books or documents.

Shortly after large-scale computers began to challenge the talents of engineers, mathematicians, and others—those who later called themselves computer scientists—to explore and realize their potential, information retrieval became one of the first application areas. It was a solution in search of a problem, motivated by the urge to explore all possible uses of computers. It required a broadening of the information concept to include its semantic, pragmatic, and syntactic aspects. Very few of these precomputer-scientists/engineers were affiliated with the American Documentation Institute (ADI) in the mid-1950s. Taffee T. Tanimoto and Hans Peter Luhn were the exceptions, and many of the early pioneers, such as Calvin C. Mooers, still are not active in the American Society for Information Science (ASIS), the present name of ADI.

In 1960, as a research mathematician at the IBM Research Center, I was asked by the director of research to participate in a team to survey the possibilities of automation at the Library of Congress. We became deeply immersed in the problems of librarianship. We came to appreciate them as real problems to which the use of computers, among other possible solutions, might be applicable. For the first time, excepting the problems of intelligence, we reversed the pattern of a solution in search of a problem.

Also for the first time, we became aware of the difference in attitude between professional librarians and ourselves. They had to maintain such standards as the print quality of catalog cards and descriptive and subject cataloging, and the librarians expected the use of computers to increase their productivity, decrease the time it takes to produce cards, and increase the volume and quality of books cataloged. We were looking for greater

---

[1] According to Myron Tribus in his contribution to this volume, Shannon had serious misgivings about using such an overworked term and did so against his better judgment.

justification than that to spend $60 million on powerful computing systems. The tool or solution was far more powerful than that needed to solve such problems, and in another sense, it was not appropriate. Somewhere in the contents of the library's totality of books must be a treasure, a potential synthesis of knowledge so valuable that with the help of computers, it could make a major difference.

It was during the discussions in 1960–1962 about these potential functions of an automated Library of Congress that the idea of a continually updated, on-line encyclopedialike knowledge-base occurred to me. [G. W. King, 1963, p. 22.] Herbert Bohnert pointed me to H. G. Wells's 1936 world encyclopedia proposal, and I began to see an intellectual path—from Wells to Vannevar Bush, Alvin Weinberg, Watson Davis, and Charles Van Doren—that pointed toward what I felt should be a reversal of the priorities then in force. These priorities had stressed improved general access to the record of knowledge by specialists.

It became clear that the needs of our age intersected with the potentials of emerging information technologies in stressing screening, evaluation, and synthesis of what is known and ensuring that continual additions to knowledge fit into a coherent image that can be brought to bear on the day-to-day problems of all people. Such services are active rather than only passive. They intervene when intervention is needed. The new priorities stressed a kind of system that *primarily* teaches, is a work of electronic art, espouses a human viewpoint, addresses and arouses the curious average person, stimulates his or her curiosity, and aims to improve the world. Only secondarily does such a system seek to inform, perform a reference function, aim at the specialist, and accurately reflect the knowledge, opinions, prejudices of the time. The proposed system, now called WISDOM (Worldwide Information Service for the Development of Omniscience in Man), is still an idea, though pilot versions have been implemented.[2] As a system, it is a social organ that is eventually to supplant the minds of individuals, a kind of community mind that may be the next stage in the evolution of mind. But WISDOM is also an emerging movement for the previously mentioned reversal of priorities, and several organizations have been created to further this movement.

Paul Otlet may have had a similar vision in 1895. Indeed, some documentalists and information scientists, such as Eugene Garfield, embraced variants of the idea underlying WISDOM in independent discovery, which led to contributions of revolutionary impact, such as citation indexing and clusters based on coupling profiles (bibliographic coupling plus cocitation

[2]The system was at first called WISE [Kochen, 1972] and elaborated subsequently at a Symposium of the American Association for the Advancement of Science. [Kochen, 1975.] WISE was changed to WISDOM at the suggestion of C. T. Larson, who has been working toward various concrete versions of this idea, such as networks of centers for monitoring and assessing the state of the built environment, exchanging data, ideas, reports of exemplary practices and research results in a coherent, integrated form that will lead to improvement, based in part on his 1953 work with Lonberg-Holms on *The Development Index*.

coupling). Such techniques apply not only to documents that comprise the written record but also to the individuals who use knowledge as well as to the fields of knowledge themselves that are only partially embodied in the record.

Librarianship, library science, documentation, bibliography, and information science in the narrow sense used by Rayward, have in common a focus on the written record and the physical documents—books, journals, manuscripts, musical scores, prints, and so forth—that it comprises. Librarians are concerned with organizing collections of such documents and facilitating their use by library patrons. As such, they need to cope with at least three tasks: (1) continually selecting from the growing record what to collect (possibly weeding little-used items to make room if there are space limitations); (2) bibliographic control or organizing and maintaining the collection as well as maintaining the tools enabling them and their patrons to determine at any time what is in the collection and where it is; and (3) reference, to guide patrons in their use of records in the library's collection.

Information science, in the broader sense in which I interpret it, is, in contrast, concerned with information, knowledge, understanding, and wisdom. Here, *information* is used in its technical, scientific sense to denote what is transmitted over a communication channel to remove a receiver's uncertainty about an ensemble. It is both a flow and a pattern that flows over a channel. This channel may have a memory that stores the encoded information pattern of bits as meaningless codes. The channel may contain a transducer and transformer that rearrange, encode, decode, or otherwise process patterns of bits, as in a computer. As a flow, information is a temporal change in a pattern. To be informed is to experience a change in some cognitive structure; to inform is to effect such an experience.

Information becomes knowledge when it is given meaning, usually by a human mind. A person (or machine) may be said to *know* the answer to a previously unencountered question that is not merely a syntatic transformation of the statement through which that knowledge was acquired. Knowing something requires the existence of a knowledge space containing niches for concepts, ideas, facts, and so forth, that are acquired. These niches are organized into a web, and the way a niche is embedded into this structure, relating it directly to many other niches and indirectly to many more, is what gives it meaning at any time. Knowledge is stock; it may accumulate, but mere accumulation of knowledge is neither understanding nor wisdom. It is the latter that can help us to survive and learn to improve our lives.

Knowledge becomes understanding when it contributes to changes in a knowledge space, adding new connections among niches and new niches, perhaps revising the entire or large parts of the structure. Certain new items of knowledge enable the knower to think of and ask questions never thought of before; they lead to awareness that not all is known and important new knowledge is needed. Understanding leads to deeper answers to questions regarding how and why, while knowledge is mostly know-what and know-how.

Wisdom, in one sense the ultimate purpose of our intellect and the scientific enterprise, and therefore of central concern to information disciplines, means bringing knowledge and understanding to bear on shaping our world for human ends by human means. Wisdom governs communication of information for purposes of control. It includes know-when, that is, the choice of strategic times for action based on or justified by knowledge and understanding.

Clearly, this emphasis is far from concern with access to the written record and even further from understanding such institutions as libraries, media centers, and so forth. That understanding is certainly necessary but it is far from sufficient as a professional and scientific foundation for the knowledge industries. The convergence hoped for by Rayward is certainly desirable, but it is not feasible so long as schools of library science take an attitude of the kind expressed in the following quotation from a resolution by the faculty of a school of library science:

In its *Standards for Accreditation, 1972,* the American Library Association's Committee on Accreditation (ALA/COA is the only group which the Council on Postsecondary Accreditation [COPA] recognizes for purposes of accreditation in librarianship) defines libraries and librarianship in the "broadest sense as encompassing the relevant concepts of information science and documentation," including "media centers, educational resource centers, information, documentation, and referral centers." . . . The School is now actively looking into additional means of enhancing the information science aspects of the AMLS program . . .

These are parts of a resolution passed unanimously by the faculty of the School of Library Science at the University of Michigan on October 19, 1978, in formal opposition to informal suggestions for establishing a campus-wide doctoral program in the information disciplines with the broader and deeper interpretation sketched here.

In doing this, the faculty erroneously judged my interpretation of information science to be consonant with that of the Council on Postsecondary Accreditation and the American Library Association's Committee on Accreditation. Note also the phrase, "information science aspects of the ALMS program," an exceedingly narrow topic of no interest or relation to the information disciplines. It is a typical instance of the confusion generated by superficial interpretations of "information science and documentation" in its popular sense and with reference to such institutions as libraries or media centers. It is also the typical defensive response of an institution that feels threatened with extinction. Whether that fear is justified or paranoid depends on the ability of such institutions to adapt, as in the case of the

Baxter School of Library and Information Science at Case Western Reserve University.

In conclusion, I suggest that the present state in the development of the five fields under discussion is characterized by strongly divergent orientations to information science. Mine differs greatly from the library and information sciences in the title of Rayward's paper. I may have been among the first to use the term *information science* in the previously mentioned broader sense. [Kochen, 1965.] It may be true that many information scientists, however they interpret their field, found welcome homes in library schools. Librarians and library scientists are an amiable group, and the meetings of the American Library Association are full of vitality and excitement. Their hospitality to, and acceptance of, information scientists should certainly be gratefully acknowledged even if there are barriers to understanding and attitude.

If people trained in physical sciences do not borrow models and paradigms from their colleagues in librarianship, library science, documentation, or bibliography, then this is reciprocated. A recent survey of librarians' attitudes toward technology showed that they like technologies but not technologists. [Galvin, 1981.] The forces leading to this state were the relatively slow rate of progress in basic information science, the correspondingly slow development work in the field, the slow growth of the American Society for Information Science, the search by information scientists for appropriate intellectual homes, the expanding need for graduates of library schools during the 1960s, and the need to adapt to new technologies and new ways of thinking.

These forces have now subsided. Replacing them is the more rigorous development of database-management systems, expert-knowledge systems, the use of distributed networks and parallel arrays by computer scientists. Graduates of library schools are no longer in great demand; public libraries, competing for increasingly scarce municipal funds with police, fire, and other vital services, are not receiving enough support to stay even, much less keep up with the growth of the written record at inflated prices. Publishers can no longer count on libraries as certain minimal markets for books and journals. Some employers who support library schools are demanding that graduates be trained in wholly new ways—with stress on the broader interpretation of information science, and some even request that *library* be entirely deleted from the name of the degree.

The trend is almost certainly away from access to such physical items as printed paper or microforms and away from emphasis on bibliographic control of a physical inventory. Printed paper will probably continue to coexist with alternative forms of recorded knowledge but lose its predominance. [Kochen, 1982.] We can no longer refer to electronically recorded databases as the written record except in a most general sense. To be sure, it is as necessary to organize knowledge in the newer recorded form as it is in traditional forms, but the principles of cataloging or indexing taught in library schools may no longer apply.

Attention will, I hope, shift to key problems in information science. More and better researchers may be attracted to information science, and their contributions will lead to vigorous enterprises offering new products and services that meet the needs of knowledge-based societies. When the growing demand for a firm professional and scientific foundation underlying the information sectors of such societies is recognized, those engaged in information will occupy numerous and leading roles and contribute to increasing the productivity of those sectors.

LIBRARIANSHIP AND INFORMATION SCIENCE

Jesse H. Shera

As I anticipated, Boyd Rayward has written an excellent general statement, well documented, of the historical development of librarianship in relation to the emergence of documentation and the transformation of the latter into information science. Therefore, about the most that I can do is to amplify certain points he presents and add some commentary of my own. Admittedly, the commentary is highly subjective and based mainly on more than fifty years of experience in library practice and teaching. Moreover, it at times represents a point of view that is not universally held by librarians and so-called information scientists.

I shall not deal with the stubborn problem of what constitutes a discipline. Suffice it here to say that it is difficult to deal with the interdisciplinary relation between librarianship and information science until a decision has been reached as to whether these areas of activity are, in themselves, true disciplines. Though, over the years, I have referred to librarianship as a discipline, I did so mainly because I did not know how else to classify what librarians do and the technologies by which they have striven to achieve their ends. Information science has yet to prove itself as a discipline. Like librarianship, it is still largely an agglomeration of technologies drawn from other areas of study, particularly, in the case of information science, from mathematics and electrical engineering. In the final analysis, we are still compelled to say, I think, that librarianship is what librarians do and information science is defined by the operations of the information scientist. We could say with, I think, some degree of accuracy that librarianship is a service and information science is an area of inquiry that seeks to measure and improve the efficiency of the librarian; but such a statement is inadequate because information science deals with only a part of what the librarian does.

Viewed from the perspective of history, then, as admirably presented by Rayward, Paul Otlet and his associates who formed the Brussels Institute

Some parts of this paper were used in an article entitled "Information Science and the Theory of Librarianship," published in the Indian journal, *International Information and Communication*, vol. 1 (March 1982), pp. 3–15.

and subsequently the International Federation for Documentation (FID), were basically librarians. Librarianship has always been interdisciplinary in that its goal was to make the total record of the human adventure readily accessible to all. Otlet and his followers merely strove to expand the area of library activity to encompass a wider range of materials and improve access to those records by using a new technology. They adopted the classification scheme devised by Melvil Dewey to form the Universal Decimal Classification (UDC) and supplemented it by using certain signs and symbols of interdisciplinary relations. Neither traditional librarians nor these innovators exemplified a new field of academic endeavor; both were essentially centripetal—drawing to themselves the products of scholarship and the accumulated recorded knowledge of many fields. Thus, these pioneers relied on librarianship for their basic principles and structures. They elaborated what had already been done. That they called themselves documentalists and their field of activity documentation did not change their basic objectives. When the documentation movement came to the United States, American librarians rejected the UDC even though it was based on Dewey's system, because they believed it to be too complex; they turned, instead, to microphotography as a technology that would improve the accessibility and availability of graphic records as well as provide a substantial reduction in costs. Librarians even foresaw a time when microfilm would replace the conventional book. On this side of the Atlantic, documentalists were mainly librarians who had adopted a new technology; there was no alteration in the basic goals.

Because these American documentalists, most of whom were librarians, based their technology on the science of photography, they tended to regard themselves as scientists, tended to avoid the term *librarian,* and formed the American Documentation Institute (ADI). Thus began the fragmentation that has plagued librarianship ever since.

By mid-century, microphotography had become firmly established as an important addition to the librarian's arsenal of technologies, and most of the members of the American Documentation Institute had turned to other interests. Those few who retained their concern for the further development of microphotography seceded to form the National Microfilm Association, composed mainly of commercial interests organized for the promotion and manufacture of photographic equipment.

The remaining members of the ADI turned to new techniques for the organization of library materials—which they characterized as information retrieval. These new interests were largely devoted to the application of electronic and mechanical systems for improving the accessibility of graphic records. Thus, there evolved such systems and mechanisms as Calvin Mooers's Zato coding, Mortimer Taube's coordinate indexing, Ralph Shaw's rapid selector, and the searching selector fabricated by J. W. Perry and Allen Kent at Western Reserve University. The ADI was then largely composed of librarians, with the addition of a number of commercial organizations, such as Eastman Kodak, Remington Rand, and General Electric, which had research resources far beyond those of librarians. The line of demarcation between documentalists and librarians was even then beginning to be drawn, and there were some suggestions that library schools should change their names to schools of documentation. Librarianship was becoming a tarnished word, and many wanted to dissociate themselves from it as much as possible.

This movement was intensified by the influence of Claude Shannon and Warren Weaver and their work at the Bell Telephone Laboratories on the communication of information. The term *information* was misleading, but it was used by members of the American Documentation Institute as being descriptive of their major concern. Again, the influence of Shannon and Weaver became prominent in attracting mathematicians to their field, creating such technologies as bibliometrics and citation analysis. These phenomena had long been known to librarians, but their rebirth gave the phenomena an air of novelty and innovation.

By the late 1960s, the term *documentation* had become old hat, and the ADI changed its name to the American Society for Information Science. Today, even the Special Libraries Association, founded in 1909 by John Cotton Dana (librarian of the Newark, New Jersey Public Library) to serve the bibliographic needs of business and industry, is contemplating a change of name to something akin to an association of information managers. The flight from *library* goes on, leaving the old and respected name to typify, in the main, public library service. The trend would make an interesting study in linguistic deterioration. It is quite evident that information science is rooted in attempts to extend the boundaries of library technology and give it revived respectability by endowing it with a unique name.

The American Society for Information Science and its preceding organization, the American Documentation Institute, could provide an excellent subject for the study of that peculiar amalgam that is librarianship-information science. Unfortunately, a thorough inquiry of this kind has not yet been made. However, in 1979, Donald W. King and two graduate students at the library school at Drexel University interrogated the entire membership of ASIS in an attempt to provide a profile of the membership of that organization. [King et al., 1980, pp. 9–17.] The study does provide some interesting insights. Of the 3894 regular members of the association, 52 per cent responded. Of the respondents, 24.2 per cent, the largest single group, were engaged in library administration. The second largest group was 20.3 per cent, composed of managers, directors, or coordinators. Information technologists, analysts, and scientists came third, with 18.6 per cent, at which point the percentages drop off sharply. Unfortunately, comparable data are not available for the early years of the American Documentation Institute, but I can testify from my own knowledge that the configuration of the membership was quite different. Most of us would have characterized ourselves, without hesitation, as librarians.

It is also interesting to note that in the survey of the primary employers of ASIS members, 35.6 per cent were from industry, 26.9 per cent were from colleges or universities, and 12.1 per cent were from the federal government. In the sample, 56 per cent were women, while in the earlier ADI years, there was no more than a handful of women. Whether or not these statistics reflect the actual situation is problematical in that women may be more responsive to questionnaires than are men, but it does indicate that the new technology is increasingly of interest to women.

In an editorial on the study, Donald King points out that ASIS members are concerned with four primary professional areas: operational information functions, including searching, preparing, and analyzing data on behalf of others—1490 ASIS members; management of information operations, programs, services, or databases—1160 members; information science and technology, including research and development, systems analysis, and systems design—530 members; and educating or training information professionals or other workers—360 members. [King, 1980.] We somewhat glibly assert that librarianship is a field of practice whereas information science is an area of research—and it was in the early days. But today, if the membership of ASIS is indicative, information science is approaching an area of service not unlike that of librarianship. Both activities are concerned with the transfer (I prefer the term *communication*) of certain types of information (and again, I prefer *knowledge*). Information science, however, gets bigger headlines because of its use of engineering and mathematics in its technology.

I have indulged myself in this recapitulation of Rayward's historical summary of the origins of information science in part to amplify some of the points he makes and also to set the stage, so to speak, for some of my own argument.

In his summation, Rayward evinces a certain doubt in his own mind about an organic interdisciplinarity between librarianship and information science. Thus, he writes: "When, however, the focus becomes not library and information *work,* but information *science,* the clarity, such as it is, is lost . . . [Immediately there arises the] problem of disciplinary encroachment. When is *information science* information science and not epistemology, biopsychology, physiology or physics or journalism or the sociology of groups or anthropology?" When he sees information science broadly defined, he discovers a loss of all disciplinary coherence. He goes on to see this library/information science relation as a continuum with

> at one end . . . the librarian constructing a catalog of books; at the other, because of the way in which information can now be conceived, . . . the genetic engineer consulting the information recorded in and then restructuring DNA. Perhaps, however, there is a discontinuity between the two involving notions of symbolic representation and public consultation that more careful analysis and definition would reveal.

The point here is not so much the difficulty of definition or the slipperiness of terminology as the implication that the generalizing process described earlier in this paper may still be at work. It is a source of innovation and strength, but it blurs traditional distinctions and can unsettle professional convictions. (Rayward in his lead paper in this volume.)

Twenty years ago, I thought of what is now called information science as providing the intellectual and theoretical foundations of librarianship, but I am now convinced that I was wrong. A building is not a library, and its organization, operations, and services not a machine. I seriously question whether there is a true interdisciplinary relation between librarianship and information science; rather, it is only a series of borrowings of the technology of one for the use of the other. Because librarianship is much more than the mechanized access to data banks or networks that provides efficient access to institutional borrowing, we must look to other disciplines for its interdisciplinary relations and the core of its theory.

The enthusiasm with which many librarians, especially academic librarians, rushed to embrace new technologies with only the most casual consideration of their appropriateness seemed to substantiate Kaplan's "Law of the Instrument." Simply stated, this so-called law holds that people tend to formulate their problems in such a way as to make it seem that the solution to the problem demands precisely what they happen to have at hand. He illustrates this law by saying that a small boy given a hammer immediately concludes that everything needs pounding. [Kaplan, 1964, p. 303.] A more sophisticated example might be that an executive who has acquired a photocopying machine almost inevitably concludes that all of his or her immortal prose should be distributed throughout the organization in multiple copies.

There are times when it seems that the goal of science is not to know or to understand but to use. In the American character, there has been a strong strain of utilitarianism, or, rather, pragmatism, and this is perhaps no more clearly evident than in librarianship. The major figures in the history of American librarianship were doers rather than thinkers; they were concerned with process rather than purpose. They devised and taught in their library schools routines and procedures, and with the advent of online networks and access to data banks, they are doing it more than ever today. We need not be surprised, therefore, that librarians rushed to embrace science and began to talk glibly of library science, turning their backs on the library's humanistic origins. Librarians even went so far as to evolve a new discipline called information science. They misinterpreted Shannon and Weaver's specialized use of the noun *information* and assumed that it related to the communication of knowledge rather than the transmission of signals. Information theory, in contrast to the theory of librarianship, is severely limited in its communicative potential. Its objective is to provide the librarian with a system giving functional or operational access to the contents of documents. Information scientists give all of their attention to design, production, implementation, and control of the system. Thus, as H. Curtis Wright has so well pointed out, our schools of library science are busily engaged in producing "control artists," technicians and mechanics who tinker with information systems but are unable to solve the problems of access and retrieval because they cannot control ideas. These control artists constantly mistake the symbol for reality and believe that counting or figuring with these symbols solves the bibliographic access problem. [Wright, 1981.] This confusion between data and ideas leads to the confusion between data systems and idea systems. Our so-called information systems are actually nothing but data systems. Thus, Wright is close to what Robert Fairthorne has called "marking and parking" in document retrieval rather than information or knowledge retrieval.

Librarians have become so concerned with process that they have confused substance with instrumentation. Processing data can be performed by machine, but only the human mind can process knowledge or even information. Information science is based on data and their manipulation, not on ideas.

Science deals with *things,* things that can be measured, weighed, poured, fastened, or mixed together, whereas librarians are dealing only incidentally with things but primarily with ideas, concepts, and thoughts. Librarians are, or should be, characterized by their knowledge, not by their instrumentation. We conventionally say that the computer is here to stay and we must learn to adapt to its powers and capabilities. I submit that the situation is quite the reverse: The computer is here to stay, therefore *it* must be made to adapt to the librarians' problems and needs. It must be kept in its proper place as a tool and a slave, or we will become sorcerer's apprentices, with data data everywhere and not a thought to think.

Librarians, ever sensitive to the somewhat meager social esteem accorded their activities, devised the term *library science* and eagerly seized *information science* as potential supports to their claims to professionalism. But science does not a profession make, and an overlay of scientific operations is not a sine qua non for professionalism. The term *profession* derives, of course, from the root verb *to profess, to believe in,* and etymologically, a professor is one who acts according to his or her beliefs or convictions. Wright has recently reviewed the development of the concept from the Greek *arete,* which meant skill or proficiency in a particular job and a knowledge of the job in hand, to the well-known characteristics of a profession as enunciated by Abraham Flexner. [Flexner, 1915.] Wright cites Socrates to the effect that if we wish to know what a good shoemaker is and wish to be a good shoemaker, the first essential is to know what a shoe is and what the purposes of the shoe are. Only then can we decide what materials are best for making shoes and what tools should be employed and the best techniques and methods for using these materials and tools. But such skills and techniques cannot be successful without an understanding of what is to be produced and what functions it is supposed to perform. Wright quite properly sees a direct connection between knowledge of a task and its performance, citing the so-called Socratic paradox that "virtue is knowledge," which was interpreted by his contemporaries to mean that we cannot be efficient unless we take the trouble to learn our job. Stripped of the verbiage that has accumulated around the paradox over the centuries, what Socrates meant was that when there is a specific occupational function to perform, the worker must perform that function knowing what the task is, what its purpose is, and the best way of performing it. This, says Wright, is the true basis of professionalism. [Wright, 1980.] We might also cite the statement attributed to Michelangelo, that the apprentice sculptor should learn anatomy thoroughly and then forget it. By this admonition, he enunciated the belief that a piece of sculpture should not do violence to anatomical laws, but, at the same time, it should be more than an exercise in anatomy. He was subordinating process to purpose. Librarians would do well to remember occasionally *Moses* or a *Pietà* and think somewhat less frequently of Shannon and Weaver.

What, then, is the "shoe" that is the end product of the "shoemaker," the professional librarian. I submit that there are three components in the concept of a library. First, there is *acquisition,* which involves knowing what to acquire for a given clientele and how to acquire it. Acquisition implies substantive knowledge of the materials and the uses to which that knowledge can and should be put. The second is *organization,* that is, ways in which the accumulated materials can be arranged and processed for maximum convenience and efficiency of use. It is here, and only here, that information science makes its contribution to librarianship. The third is *interpretation and service,* which is the raison d'être of the library, and it is here that information science reveals its greatest threat of dehumanizing the library's function. To express the same idea in another way, the library can be seen as three interrelated spheres: the sphere of optimum content; the operational or mechanistic sphere; and the sphere of maximum context. If librarians persist in sublimating librarianship to the lure of the machine and the all importance of data retrieval their "shoes" will be very uncomfortable to the user, and they will leak at certain vital points.

Janus-like, the library looks in two directions simultaneously. It looks toward the social sciences, because it is a creature of society, evolved to meet the needs of human beings working toward the solution of certain problems. Thus, the library qualifies as a social agency or instrumentality. But the library is also humanistic in that its characteristics, modes of access to its resources, uses, and values are humanistic. It is not, and never has been, a scientific enterprise. Except for some tinkering with its processes, scientific technology has made but little contribution to the development of the library. A catalog entry on the face of a cathode ray tube is essentially the same entry devised by Charles A. Cutter, and the fact that it has been transmitted across the continent in a fraction of a second may be a convenience to the user, but it does not alter the character of librarianship or transform it into a science.

Of the importance of the humanities to a world of science, a professor of history at the University of Michigan has recently written: "Our society is a seamless web, and ultimately science and technology share the same values and are dependent upon the purposes which derive from the study of what it means to be human. The neglect of the humanities will bring in its train inevitably the decay of science." He goes on to characterize an excessive dependence on science alone as "the higher barbarism, unless there is some human purpose that looks beyond the immediate technical and economic applications. The day will come when the hand will lose its cunning and life be found to be devoid of purpose. We are more dependent upon our poets than we realize."[1]

It is perhaps reassuring that all of us know successful scientists who enrich their professional reading with generous additions from the humanities; who are accomplished amateur musicians; or who, like the distinguished astronomer Fred Hoyle, have made reputations in creative writing.

Information theory is severely limited in its communicative potential. Its only *aim* is to provide efficient access to knowledge, but the design of mechanisms, their production, and use of the system are its areas of concentration. We are, as Wright has emphasized, turning out control artists and data mechanics. This confusion of ideas with data can be dispelled only by distinguishing between data systems and idea systems. Thus, it follows that information science cannot qualify as a theoretical base for librarianship, and calling it bibliometrics or informatics does not alter the situation. We librarians must constantly remind ourselves that our concern is with sociological and psychological phenomena, not physical objects and processes. Moreover, information science itself does not know what it is or where it is going. It cannot tell whether it belongs in a school of library science, engineering, management, operations research, or some loosely defined area of its own. There is already distinct evidence that the American Society for Information Science is fragmenting itself into a variety of activities, some of which are mutually contradictory.

I submit that librarians must look to "symbolic interactionism" for the proper foundation of a theory of librarianship. This term, first named by Herbert Blumer in 1937, is rooted in the social psychologies of William James, Charles S. Peirce, Charles H. Cooley, John Dewey, and George Herbert Mead.

The term *symbolic interaction* refers to the process by which people relate to their own minds and the minds of others; the process by which individuals take account of their own or others' needs, desires, means and ends, knowledge, and like motivations. Among sociologists this phenomenon is frequently known as social interaction. In the definition of symbolic interaction, the word *mind* denotes instrumental activities that animals as well as human beings direct toward their environment. These instrumental

[1] Stephen J. Tonsor, letter in *Wall Street Journal*, August 31, 1981, p. 13.

activities, sometimes referred to as action or as psychological activities, are related to the organism's requirements and the conditions and resources in the environment that are relevant to meeting those requirements. The term *symbolic* includes the representation of those requirements through a system of commonly understood linguistic, or other representational activities, such as gestures, whereby the content of the communicated message is transmitted to, and understood by, the intended recipient.

Such a discipline of symbolic interaction reminds librarians that their area of concern is based on social phenomena and it provides for the contributions of philosophy, linguistics, and psychology in the formulation of its unique purpose. That purpose is to make accessible the graphic records of human culture, so that people may understand the totality of the environment in which they find themselves and their own place in it.

In summary, we who are librarians must constantly remind ourselves that information science is an area of inquiry, of research. It is not, as is librarianship, a service or a practice. Information science can provide the librarian with some important and useful tools to expedite library services, but the ability to communicate a message with incredible speed over long distances through the use of glass fiber bundles or laser beams or to store vast quantities of recorded knowledge in computerlike mechanisms does not in any way alter the purpose of the library. That the internal-combustion engine can move vast quantities of materials and people over longer distances and with greater efficiency than the horse does not alter the need for transportation. The social purpose of the library remains unchanged—to bring the human mind and the graphic record together in a fruitful relation—for the growth of knowledge is still the goal. Administration, management, architecture, and many other disciplines can contribute to the effectiveness of the library, but they are not librarianship.

We who are engaged in library education must be aware that the librarian needs to attain certain specific skills in the *use* of the tools that all of these disciplines, including information science, have given us. But the hard core of librarianship remains basically as it has always been—the mastery of the substantive content of graphic records. Librarians should be characterized by their knowledge and not by their instrumentation. The most effective librarians enter the profession armed with broad generalized knowledge or with knowledge in a chosen field. Librarians must remain the guides to the mastery of the substantive content of graphic records. The idea, not the process, is our primary concern.

The great danger with which information science threatens librarianship is the loss of control of the library profession to other and less competent hands. Of the dangers inherent in this threat, we do not now seem to be fully aware. The basic purpose of librarianship is not encompassed in the machine, and there is much more to librarianship than is envisaged in information science. If we permit ourselves to be mesmerized by the gadget, if we accept the flickering image of data on a fluorescent screen as knowledge, we will soon become like those mythical people of many centuries ago who mistook for reality the passing shadows reflected on the walls of a cave. So I conclude with the words of that distinguished librarian of Stanford and subsequently dean of the library school at Berkeley, Ray Swank: "The long experience and tested values of librarianship are still our most reliable and sophisticated resources for the solution of information-handling problems in most contexts whatever additional help may now be needed." (Swank, 1981.)

BIBLIOGRAPHICAL R&D

Patrick Wilson

Boyd Rayward says that librarianship has converged toward information science, which was born in the 1960s out of documentation by the computer. That is not how I would describe the situation. To show what I think wrong with his story and what I think the correct story is, I will have to go over some of his ground again, redescribing the situation from a somewhat different angle and with a different distribution of emphasis.

Let me use the phrase *the bibliographical sector* for the assemblage of institutions and organizations that collectively take the output of the publishing industry and try to make it accessible for public use. This sector includes the wholesale and retail book trade, libraries, and various agencies— scholarly, professional, and commercial—that produce such bibliographical instruments as abstracting and indexing services, general periodical indexes, lists of newly published books and books in print. The job of making the output of the publishing industry accessible has two logically distinct parts: first, making it possible to discover the existence of a publication; and second, making it possible to get our hands on a copy of the publication. The first is the problem of intellectual access, the second that of physical access. Until the middle of this century, the bibliographical sector was a relatively tranquil sector of society, but soon after World War II it became an agitated and problem-ridden one. First, the spectacular growth of science and technology led to a vast expansion of the output of scientific and technical literature, constituting what was frequently referred to as an information explosion. To some, it appeared that traditional methods of providing intellectual access to scientific and technical literature were incapable of working adequately in the changed circumstances. Second, the equally spectacular growth of higher education put great strains on libraries in colleges and universities and made it imperative that new methods of handling very large amounts of bibliographical information be developed. Happily, the concurrent development of computer technology promised to provide the necessary new technology to solve the problems of both the size of scientific and technical literature and the pressures on academic libraries.

RESEARCH AND DEVELOPMENT ON BIBLIOGRAPHY

During the last 25 years, an increasing number of people went to work on research and development centering on the problems of the bibliographical sector and focused mainly on libraries and bibliography-producing agencies, to the exclusion of the book trade. Pending a later discussion of the right name for this group, let us call it for now the bibliographical R&D group. Some of the members of this group came from the library profession and its educational institutions (the library schools), others from the group calling itself documentalists or documentation specialists (but considered to be simply special librarians by other librarians). But a large number came from outside: from the fields of mathematics, logic, physics, chemistry, linguistics, industrial engineering, electrical engineering, computer science, and so on. They worked in various settings: some in newly created research institutes affiliated with universities, some as members of newly created R&D or "systems" staffs in libraries and bibliography-producing agencies, some in independent research organizations and industrial organizations, some as faculty members of library schools or engineering schools or computer science departments. The entrants from other fields naturally brought their tools with them as well as their expectations about the proper way of tackling problems in the bibliographical sector. They did not, of course, bring with them an information science, for none existed. They hoped to create one. The question is whether or not they did. To answer this, let us start by sorting out the different kinds of work done by the bibliographical R&D group over the last quarter-century. The work falls roughly into six categories, of which three are of special interest.

First Category

The first and most successful category includes work aimed at improving the means of storage, manipulation, transmission, and display of bibliographical information, based on the application of computer technology. Recent years have seen the development of important new products, systems, and services, such as computer-based services for literature search, computer-produced citation indexes, and computer-based support systems for cataloging. While it is impossible to draw a sharp line between research and development work, it seems clear enough that the work done by the R&D group leading to such new products, systems, and services has been predominantly development work. It is work for the designer of computer systems and the programmer. It is technology, not science; the goal has been, not to produce true statements about the world, but to produce better devices and systems offering new or better services—product and process innovations. There are plenty of published documents describing the work, but the documents are incidental. The literature resulting from this work, like the literature resulting from work on improving technology generally, is not a body of *findings* but of reports of *makings*. The work has increased the available stock of know-how, much of it embodied in devices and systems.

Second Category

The second category includes work aimed at improving techniques for creating the bibliographical information to be manipulated, stored, transferred, and displayed. The improved products and processes already mentioned are advances in operation on *given* bibliographical information. Attempts to improve processes of *originating* the information have been strenuous but much less successful. At the technical heart of the job of providing intellectual access to publications are the operations of bibliographical description (description of everything but the content of a publication) and content representation through indexing, abstracting, and classification. Work on problems of bibliographical description has been essentially organizational or managerial: trying to get agreement on international standards for description and trying to reduce unnecessary duplication of effort. Work on problems of content representation has been theoretical and experimental rather than managerial: trying to find new principles and radically different techniques for the analysis and representation of intellectual content. Attempts first to evaluate and then to improve on the performance of traditional methods of content representation have been frustratingly difficult and on the whole disappointing. Experimental attempts at computer-based automatic indexing and classification have so far led to some advances in understanding but few practical applications. (Computer-produced indexes where words in titles and abstracts are taken as content indicators without further analysis are simply ways of avoiding the problem of content representation.) Abstract analysis of indexing, employing probability and utility theory, has resulted in formulations of normative conditions for optimal indexing, but not in altered practices. Improvement in techniques for the representation of intellectual content is fundamentally different in character from, and enormously more difficult than, improvement in manipulating strings of characters after it is decided what the strings are to be. Strings of characters can be manipulated, transmitted, and displayed without any attention whatever to the meanings they convey; producing a correct representation of semantic content essentially requires understanding the content at some level. Indexing and classification still depend on the rapid intuitive grasp of the scope of the intellectual content of a text. Numerous novel indexing and classification schemes for displaying the results of that intuitive grasp of content have been devised, and many of them put into effect, but it is still true that the subject indexing and classification schemes most widely used by libraries are those proposed, and already well developed, a hundred years ago. It is commonly agreed that these old schemes do not work very well, but improving on them in practice would seem to require some improvement of, or substitute for, that intuitive grasp of intellectual content, and no one has good practical ideas about how that might be done.

Third Category

The third kind of work done by the bibliographical R&D group is not normative but descriptive, devoted to studying some of the characteristics of the literature that constitutes the input to the bibliographical sector and the use of that literature. Much of this is quantitative in character, consisting of bibliometric studies and studies using citation analysis; for example, studies of the size and growth rates of bodies of literature, concentration and dispersal of literature of various subjects in a population of serial publications, and obsolescence or decline in use of literature over time. Bibliometrics and citation analysis are relatively straightforward unobtrusive measures of some aspects of human communication behavior. [Webb et al., 1966.] Other quantitative but obtrusive studies of communication behavior are based on observation, questionnaire, or interview; for instance, the number of hours spent reading, sources from which people learn of publications useful to them, the use made of library catalogs, and so on.

There are those who think, or once thought, that such work would lead to the discovery of laws governing information behavior, such as "laws according to which different kinds of information lose their meaning, validity, relevance, or value" (Zunde and Gehl, 1979, p. 69); or laws governing the growth of knowledge; or laws that would stand to information retrieval as physics stands to engineering. [Weiss, 1977, p. 2.] I take it that we can safely say that no laws have been discovered: interesting empirical regularities, yes (Bradford's Law of Scattering being the most prominent example) but laws, no. [Bookstein, 1976.] A natural law expresses a constraint, a natural necessity; it tells us what in some sense (hard to clarify precisely) must happen, and what cannot happen. Simple statements of empirical regularity do not do that. And it is no more likely that information laws will be discovered by looking at observable features of documents and uses of documents than that sociologists or political scientists will discover laws of social and political behavior by looking at what people say and do. [P. Wilson, 1980.] It is more reasonable, if much more modest, to look on these studies of documents and communication behavior as a form of social intelligence, useful to those concerned with the workings of the bibliographical sector for the enlightenment they give, if for no other reason. Social intelligence is unlikely to be directly applicable in the development of new products or processes, but it can, in the form of market research, indicate the likely reception of a new service. It can help identify lacunae in services, suggest places where practical improvements are desirable, give at least rough guidance in the formation of plans and policies, and spot social changes that are likely to have an impact on the workings of the sector. Research of the sort indicated here can, of course, be undertaken for its own sake, simply because it is interesting. There is, in that case, no external criterion of significance, one fact being as good as another if found to be as interesting. If undertaken to provide social intelligence to the bibliographical sector, however, research has an approximate criterion of importance, namely, how much difference it makes to our plans or expectations or simple understanding of the situation in which we work. On that criterion, it would have to be admitted that much of the work actually done is of little or no significance, but that is hardly unique to the work of this group.

The gathering of social intelligence quite clearly overlaps with work done by other researchers unconnected with, and only incidentally interested in, the bibliographical sector. Both in techniques used and in phenomena investigated, this work is similar to work done by some sociologists and communications researchers. More generally, it can be seen as belonging to the sociology of knowledge. The sociology of knowledge was for a long time too closely identified with the work of Karl Mannheim to be very productive; more recently its interests have widened, and a good deal of sociological inquiry is directed at questions that are also of interest to those gathering social intelligence for the bibliographical sector. [Holzner and Marx, 1979; T. D. Wilson, 1981.] Of course, sociologists are not the only social scientists interested in information and its producers and consumers. How could there be a branch of the study of social life that did not, sooner or later, have to investigate information and communication? And bibliographical R&D might overlap with work in any of the social sciences; as time goes on, we would expect more overlapping, not less.

Fourth, Fifth, and Sixth Categories

The last three categories can be very briefly described as consisting of studies of the bibliographical sector itself as it has been, as it now is, and as it ought to be. Actually, the fourth category, which includes historical studies, contains a great deal of work consisting of the study of old books as physical objects, but it does also include studies of the history of libraries, publishing, and bibliography. The fifth category includes analysis and description of present conditions in the bibliographical sector, much of which is simply social reporting, useful since few people are in positions to know much at first hand about the actual workings of the sector as a whole. Outsiders, or occasional temporary members of the bibliographical R&D group, have made important contributions to this category, notably of economic analysis. [For example, Machlup and Leeson, 1978–1980; Baumol and Marcus, 1973.] The sixth and final category includes studies aimed at improving the organization and management of the sector (apart from its central bibliographical components) and analysis of alternative policies for service. The bibliographical R&D group is certainly not unified by shared problems or methods, but is divided into numerous small groups working in very different ways at strikingly different sorts of tasks.

CONVERGENCE OF LIBRARY SCIENCE AND INFORMATION SCIENCE?

Now we are in a better position to assess the merits of Rayward's claims. Is it correct to say, as Rayward does, that librarianship is converging toward information science? The question would have been easier to answer if Rayward had said instead that library *science* was converging toward information science. Let us see why. Rayward tells us surprisingly little about information science. But if it is, indeed, a separate discipline, as he thinks, and if its content is approximately represented by the *Annual Review of Information Science and Technology,* as he suggests, it is certainly not the only discipline concerned with information. Computer scientists think they are concerned with information, as do cognitive psychologists, communications researchers, and numerous others. We have to say that if Rayward's information scientists are correctly named, they have a generic claim to the title but not a specific claim. They may be information scientists, but they are not the only ones; they constitute only a particular species of the genus information science. Now in that sense, library scientists, if there are any, might also claim to be information scientists; library science would be the name of the species, information science the name of the genus. Then Rayward's thesis could be expressed as follows: One species of information science, namely library science, was converging toward another species, as yet unnamed. This might mean that library scientists were increasingly imitating the research style of the unnamed information scientists or perhaps that they were one by one joining the other group. This would be understandable and might be true. But this is not what he claims is happening. It is the profession, librarianship, not its corresponding science, that he has doing the converging. Presumably, this does not mean that librarians are ceasing to be members of a service profession and are taking up scientific research; rather, it must mean that librarians increasingly look to this unnamed branch of information science rather than to library science for guidance and help. This interpretation seems consistent with what Rayward says of library science: that there were attempts to create such a science but, to put it crudely, library science was a flop. Information science looked vigorous and apt to provide "a more respectable disciplinary base for the profession of librarianship," so library science was dethroned and information science installed in its place.

Is that what has happened? I do not think so. We have to face squarely the question of the actual content of the unnamed branch of information science. For some, this is unproblematic; it is the second of our six research categories, mainly concerned with content representation, and might best be named information-storage-and-retrieval theory. For others, it is equally unproblematic but the third rather than the second category, empirical, looking for behavioral laws rather than practical rules. For still others, it is the first category, principally design of computer-based information systems. Now let us agree that there is a difference, however hard to define exactly, between research and development and between science and engineering and that the largely developmental and engineering-oriented first category cannot furnish the scientific content for a discipline, however practically important and useful it is. No one calls the work in our fourth, historical, category by the name information science, nor are the fifth or sixth categories likely to be so identified. So if this branch of information science can be identified by its subject matter, it must be the subject matter of categories two or three or both. But the work done in these categories is done both by people calling themselves information scientists and people calling themselves librarians (*not* library scientists—I know of no one who calls himself or herself a library scientist).

Content representation is a major practical and theoretical concern for librarians, and quantitative studies of the literature and its users have long been established topics of investigation in librarianship—Bradford of Bradford's Law was a librarian, even if a special librarian. So information science (or this species of it) cannot be distinguished from library science by its special subject matter. Perhaps it cultivates a shared subject matter in a distinctive way? Perhaps the work done by information scientists is theoretical while that done by librarians is not? Or mathematical while that of others is not? Or experimental? Or exact? Or simply, good? No, none of these, not even the last one, will provide a clear criterion for demarcation. No methodological or topical criterion will provide a clear division between work done by those who think of themselves as librarians and those who think of themselves as information scientists. Of course, we are at liberty to say that it matters not at all what people call themselves or how they think of themselves; we can simply define information science by reference to specified subject matter and methods. Anyone can do that if he or she wishes, but there does not seem to be any general agreement on how to draw the boundaries. And doing so turns an empirical question about the relations of two groups into a matter of definition. Some library science will turn out to be information science, and some information scientists' work will turn out to be library science, thus yielding a convergence by definition. But then we are no longer talking about history. Since Rayward was talking about history, I take it that he would not want to take this line.

THE TRANSFER OF RESEARCH STYLES

The fact is that those newcomers to the bibliographical R&D community from mathematics, physics, and other fields brought their characteristic techniques and expectations and enlarged the available repertory of research styles in the community, styles that were then available for others to borrow or copy. The newcomers naturally affiliated themselves with documentalists rather than with librarians, since their initial interest, like that of the documentalists, was in problems of access to the scientific literature. At first, they were, indeed, a distinct group, socially as well as intellectually, from the (relatively few) people doing library-related research. As time has gone on, though, the distinctions have become blurred. It is harder, not easier, to tell the difference between a piece of information science and a piece of library science. [It is useful to look at Peritz, 1980–1981 in this connection.] Information science did not gel into a distinctive, coherent research area with its own subject matter and research methods. In particular, it did not arrive at a distinct "solid corpus" of " scientifically derived" theoretical and practical knowledge. And it did not replace library science as the disciplinary base for the profession of librarianship. That profession has no unique disciplinary base but draws whatever it finds useful from research anywhere in the bibliographical R&D sector and anywhere outside—sociology, management science, communication, and other fields. At it happens, librarianship can draw only a small amount from the research done in categories two and three; as noted earlier, practical applications from category two have been few. Working professionals want practically usable results, but those have been few in the categories that are the chief contenders to constitute the content of information science. So, despite Rayward's evidence from name changes in library schools and the like, I think this convergence of librarianship is mythical.

Shall we say, instead, that library science has converged toward information science? I think that could be made out if all it meant were that styles of work in library science had been influenced by the work of those newcomers. But I would much prefer to avoid talk that suggests two distinct and distinguishable groups. The bibliographical R&D community is not composed of two groups, information scientists and library scientists. It is a single but wildly heterogeneous group, a motley lot of engineers, technicians, professional librarians, historians, classification-and-indexing theorists, and the like. Its work is similarly motley in character. That is what we should expect of people studying and trying to improve different aspects of the operations of a practical sector of society like the bibliographical sector. And we should also expect that this group would have complex relations with other research groups concerned in one way or another with information. As we have seen, its work overlaps, in part, with the social sciences; it is itself, in part, an area of social science research and can make use of work done in other areas of the social sciences. As a branch of technology, the group is a borrower, not a contributor to other branches, dependent on developments in computer technology, telecommunications, and the technology of reprography in particular. Its historical parts are simply specialized branches of intellectual or social history, and the history of technology.

The second research category, content representation, is related to, and stands to gain from advances in, linguistics, cognitive psychology, and artificial intelligence, but help may be a long way in the future. It seems that there ought to be a close relation with linguistics, but linguists' lack of success in dealing with semantics, and their fixation on the single sentence rather than long discourse (a situation that shows signs of changing), do not encourage much optimism about help from that quarter. Cognitive psychology is still so primitive a subject that we cannot expect usable results for a long while. Artificial intelligence seems hardly more likely to help. What we would like, for its possible help in improving techniques for content representation, is deeper understanding of the phenomenon of understanding itself and computer systems that at least simulate understanding at a sophisticated level. We are not likely to get them soon.

COHERENCE: TOO LITTLE OR TOO MUCH?

The information explosion is now in the past, leaving us at a much higher plateau in terms of volume of publication. There are still plenty of problems for research and development in the bibliographical sector. At present, the chief motivation for support of bibliographical R&D is cost containment or reduction. Rayward's fears that information science might lose "disciplinary coherence" seem to me unfounded; the whole bibliographical R&D group is already without disciplinary coherence, but its main practical effort is in product and process development, and I see no reason why that should not continue. Given the rather disappointing results of research in content representation, I should think that the worry would be over too much coherence, that is, continued concentration on a few unsuccessful lines of work. We should rather hope for a profusion of attempts to go in new directions. As for the empirical study of published documents and their use, while it is certainly futile to pursue these studies in the hope of discovering information laws, there is plenty to be learned that might contribute to the development of a really interesting sociology of knowledge.

LIBRARIANSHIP AND INFORMATION RESEARCH

Together or Apart?

W. Boyd Rayward

Some of the assumptions that underlie my paper, assumptions essentially of a simplifying nature, have quite properly caused its commentators some misgivings. I have taken the view that the formation at various times of institutions, associations, and societies, especially those that have proved to be relatively permanent, represents important historical culminations of scholarly and professional activity. Insofar as these bodies can be shown to be related in terms of memberships and missions, I also infer from them the existence of an increasingly complex historical development, of which they represent notable stages. My initial points of reference, then, were the formation of the American Library Association, the Library Association (of Great Britain), various bibliographical societies, the International Institute of Bibliography, the Graduate Library School at the University of Chicago, and the American Documentation Institute (later the American Society for Information Science). I did not intend to present a more general history and, indeed, explicitly eschewed discussions of the special libraries movement in the United States (the Special Libraries Association, still very active, was founded in 1909) and Great Britain (save for a reference to ASLIB, founded in 1924).

DAVID BATTY AND TONI CARBO BEARMAN

Batty and Bearman are troubled by my restricted palette and small canvas, and they sketch in some of the historical detail I neglect. Elsewhere, however, I have discussed at some length certain general bibliographical developments in Great Britain through the latter part of the nineteenth century [Rayward, 1967a], the work of a number of individual bibliographers [Rayward, 1977a; 1981b], of the Royal Society for Scientific Bibliography [Rayward, 1976], and a number of relevant international trends, to which changing notions of bibliographical control of scientific literature especially were central. [Rayward, 1980*a*; 1981*b*.] My present concern is only to suggest a framework, a perspective, for examining and suggesting the interrelations of certain occupational developments over a period of a hundred or more years. I could perhaps have taken one or more different or complementary approaches. I could have examined, for example, professional or scholarly work of significant figures or developments relating to certain phenomena such as subject analysis and indication or other bibliographic practices. I chose instead to confine myself to organizational culminations as reflecting occupational and scholarly or disciplinary maturations.

One apparent misapprehension, however, in Batty and Bearman's comments should receive attention. Given my connection with the Graduate Library School at the University of Chicago, I am very much aware that any discussion that I offer of its past or present may appear if not self-serving, at least necessarily biased. I have, however, alluded to some general studies of education for librarianship that analyze its role in bringing to the phenomena of interest in librarianship the attitudes and techniques of the social sciences and historical scholarship. I nowhere suggest that the school attempted to arrive at "a special theory of librarianship and library research," as my commentators allege. In the United States, in the period following the school's foundation, librarians and others praised or vilified the school according to their point of view for its emphasis on rigorous critical enquiry. To recognize this is in no way to minimize the contributions of those figures, from Jewett to Sayers and Ranganathan, whom Batty and Bearman identify as active between 1840 and 1940. The point might be made in this connection, however, that for all their writing on bibliographical description and classification, none of these figures could remotely be described as having taken a scientific approach to their subject. In taking this approach, the Graduate Library School represented a new attitude and spirit, though, of course, it, too, like all of the other phenomena mentioned in my paper, did not spring full-formed, as Minerva did, from the brow of Jove. Richardson has explored the background to the school's foundation, the crises—some nearly fatal—of its adolescence, and he soberly attempts to assess its contributions through 1951. [Richardson, 1982.] Karetsky has recently examined a notable body of research produced by the school's early faculty and students. [Karetsky, 1982.]

MANFRED KOCHEN

Kochen is writing in a long and distinguished tradition. He tells us that he was influenced by H. G. Wells's "world brain" idea, and he adverts to the influence of some of the early documentalists and pioneers in information science on his thinking, He mentions Paul Otlet but seems to underrate the influence of Otlet's ideas in Europe and those of men like Watson Davis in the United States. And, of course, the paths of Otlet and Wells (and Watson Davis) intersected on at least one notable occasion: The World Congress on Universal Documentation held under the auspices of the Institute for Intellectual Cooperation in Paris in 1937.

But no doubt, Leibniz was a forerunner; in the last third of the seventeenth century, he was struggling to find a universal characteristic, devise a calculus of reason, and create an encyclopedia that would "be the great instrument of bringing civilization to its highest powers." (McRae, 1957, p. 38.) In this encyclopedia were to be unified all the arts and sciences; the encyclopedia would not be merely "the elaboration of an ordered inventory of various intellectual possessions. It was absolutely essential for the radical reform and advancement of the sciences." (Ibid. p. 42.) Similar to the world brain and Leibniz's encyclopedia was the notion of an Office of Publick Addresse that animated a group of men of letters in mid-seventeenth-century London at the time of the Civil War and the Commonwealth. How at last to create Bacon's House of Solomon; how to mobilize the intelligence of the day, what we now generically call information, for purposes of social amelioration; how to coordinate, unify, and allow for the orderly progression of the sciences; above all, how to bring about the city of God on earth— these were among the many religious, scientific, political, and social matters that Samuel Hartlib, William Petty, and John Drury, among the forerunners and founders of the Royal Society, wrote about and discussed among themselves and with the great Comenius, visiting London from Bohemia. The many functions of the Office of Publick Addresse that they variously described were a fascinating combination of a modern employment bureau, the yellow pages of the telephone directory, classified advertisements in newspapers, the community information service offered today by many public libraries, an information analysis center, a research library, a publishing house, and a residential institute of advanced study. [Turnbull, 1947; Webster, 1970.]

Kochen's WISE and WISDOM schemes are related to a long tradition of utopian concern for the unification and mobilization of knowledge, of speculation about ideal forms and uses of encyclopedia. Kochen, however, has turned away, it seems—with what comes across as dismissive impatience— from recorded or public knowledge and from systems to make it accessible. Unlike Leibniz and that group of energetic, enlightened men of the English Commonwealth, unlike Otlet and Wells, his concern is not with what is known and publicly available in a readable format in books, scientific papers, documents, or even by extension on magnetic tapes, not with the objective information they contain. His interest is aroused by something more abstract and subjective, a particular, hitherto elusive quality of the knower—wisdom. Moreover, he deals with the idea of wisdom in no traditional way; his is not the Socratic ideal. For him, wisdom is the product of a system. WISDOM is a system that will have the capability of making men, presumably with or without their assent, all knowing and wise, within, we assume, the constraints of the system. There is something chilling, Orwellian about the notion of a wisdom system; can it, we wonder, entertain doubt, as men do, as to what ultimately is wise and what foolish. Kochen, however, speaks of the system as being able eventually "to supplant the minds of individuals, a kind of community mind that may be the next stage in the evolution of mind." "Wisdom," he observes later, "governs communication of information for purposes of control." While it is difficult to know what much of this actually means, it provides a glimpse of a nightmare world of social and psychological engineering.

Some of Kochen's incidental comments suggest that statements I had framed with some care are not clear. I do not suggest, for example, that information science *should* focus primarily on library-and-information work. I note only that information *science* raises problems of definition that information *work* does not. A number of his comments also suggest that my conclusion that "a certain combativeness" on the part of information scientists and librarians has changed, is not justified in his case. He notes the declining opportunities for library-school graduates, the fiscal plight of public libraries, the declining importance of libraries as publishers' markets, the existence of new kinds of information jobs, the calls that have been made for library schools to remove *library* from their names, and trends towards a "paperless" society. I myself alluded to some of these complex matters when I affirmed that change and accommodation were occurring. Kochen, however, refers to them in such a way, and without much-needed explanation or further interpretation, that they seem like shots from an arsenal of antilibrarianship rhetoric. Presumably, these matters are intended to show that library schools are just about finished—unless they cease being *library* schools; that information scientists in the company of librarians, amiable and hospitable though librarians be, are strangers in a strange land; and above all, that librarians do not, indeed cannot, partake of the central mysteries of WISDOM. This last is explicit. Ultimately, we are told, "concern for the written record," and "understanding of such institutions as libraries, media centers, etc.," are remote from "bringing knowledge and understanding to bear on shaping our world toward human ends by human means." This, in Kochen's view, is the central thrust of the information disciplines. The information disciplines (it is comforting that there is more than one) constitute, it seems, a new "pansophia" and in themselves presumably will be able to do what in the past a multitude of special disciplines separately aspired to.

JESSE SHERA

Shera provides a welcome relief from this kind of thinking. His comments, graceful and penetrating, amplify the historical perspective I attempted to provide and offer some interesting data about the composition of the membership of the American Society for Information Science. Shera's chief concern is to assert the importance of libraries in just those areas that Kochen denies them relevance, at just the point where WISDOM, a kind of deus ex machina, supervenes. The library, in Shera's view, is a social agency, an instrument of social communication; it is also humanistic in that its "characteristics, modes of access to its resources, uses, and values are humanistic." Shera is as disillusioned with information scientists as Kochen is disdainful of librarians. Both scholars, it seems to me, adopt a narrow, perhaps stereotyped, certainly prejudicial view, which I had hoped the perspective I attempted to provide might obviate. The reasons that Shera gives for abandoning his early hope that information science would provide "an intellectual and theoretical foundation" for librarianship seem to me not to be particularly convincing. They are related to the uses to which the computer has been put. Certainly, Shera seems to agree that the advent of the computer precipitated the rapid development of information science and was welcomed by many librarians. But he cites gloomily Kaplan's Law of the Instrument and further suggests that information scientists are preoccupied with the "design, production, implementation, and control of the system." Under their influence, library schools have lost their sense of the historic and humanistic mission of the library; they are turning out "control artists" and "data mechanics." Insofar as this has been true (and I am not sure that it has been), it need not continue. Shera is offering more of a warning than an argument, for he does accept that librarianship as a form of service—a practice—does interrelate with information science as "an area of inquiry, of research."

Libraries are concerned with "sociological and psychological phenomena not with physical objects and processes," Shera asserts. Their goal is the growth of knowledge, and a theory of librarianship, he believes, should be founded on the concept of "symbolic interactionisms." If Shera's position is at all tenable, then as information science moves beyond data systems, beyond the gadget and the flickering image, from the thing to the idea, from information to a concern for understanding and knowledge, it approximates closer and closer Shera's ideal librarianship. We are presented with the irony that Kochen's WISDOM system may be no more than an idealized description of the library, perhaps the library of the future, as Shera conceives it. Here, then, in the terms of my paper, is a convergence with a vengeance.

Shera's final warning that control of librarianship as a profession is threatened by information science does not seem to me to be justified. In a way, Kochen's and Shera's papers are complementary in illustrating the misunderstanding, hostility, even a certain rivalry, that have existed between library and information scientists, for reasons that I find difficult to understand; there seem to be class or status elements of an interesting kind involved. In any case, these two papers reaffirm my view, speaking from the standpoint at least of librarians, that broader perspectives are needed to help librarianship and the enormously wide variety of libraries that now exist to adapt, change, grow, even further diversify. Such perspectives will help them in experimenting with, and in incorporating, new kinds of expertise and technology; in taking shape according to new and reevaluated old philosophies and ideals of service; and in drawing on a more developed kind of scholarship. Let all of these come from where they may.

PATRICK WILSON

Before commenting specifically on Patrick Wilson's paper, I should make it clear that my view of information science and of librarianship is not that of one hoping to make rigorous distinctions between professional occupation, basic and applied research, science, and technology. I do not think of information science or library science as scientific disciplines. (Wilson suggests I think of information science in this way.) I speak of occupations and a related scholarship, of disciplines nourishing professional activities. Thus, I have no quarrel with Wilson's rather elaborately conducted refinement of my argument to show that it is library science, not librarianship, that may be conceived of as converging toward information science. He supports this with a historical argument similar to mine.

Wilson, in effect, starts from an unusual and very general perspective. He eschews various traditional distinctions that had to some degree been my concern and puts forward the notion of the existence of an overarching bibliographic R&D community. This is a striking and useful idea. Wilson's analysis of the kinds of work carried on within this community is masterly, and the six categories of work he describes help organize conceptually a scattered and confusing literature. He concludes that the R&D group is "not unified by shared problems or methods, but is divided into numerous small groups working in many different ways at strikingly different sorts of tasks." He is concerned "to avoid talk that suggests two distinct and distinguishable groups, . . . information scientists and library scientists. It is a single but wildly heterogeneous group, a motley lot of engineers, technicians, professional librarians, historians, classification and indexing theorists, and the like. Its work is similarly motley in character." It has not attained, nor need it fear attaining, disciplinary coherence; its aim is mainly practical, "product and process development."

This notion of Wilson's deserves looking into. In effect, he uses it to avoid any real definition or description of information science in general. He has some fun distinguishing the kinds of information scientists whose work is represented in the *Annual Review of Information Science and Technology* from other species of the genus. Eventually, he argues that a branch of information science that I refer to but do not name cannot be effectively distinguished from library science. Within the bibliographic R&D community, however, it seems to me, are firmly located the various groups I discussed. Note that save for the engineers and technicians (and then presumably not all of them), those whom he mentions in that wildly heterogenous group would probably describe themselves as librarians or information scientists. In schools of library and information science (as well as outside of them, of course) work is regularly conducted in all of the areas Wilson identifies. But is there more? Wilson speaks of the complex disciplinary relations members of this group have with others concerned with information and of what may and may not be hoped from the latter who are clearly not members of the bibliographic R&D community; they are those concerned with more conventionally conceived sciences and engineering. Their interest in information seems to complicate for Wilson the question of definition, or perhaps, more accurately, "designation."

It seems to me that members of the bibliographic R&D community are principally library and information scientists, that those who work within it, whatever their origins, have come to be so designated. The literature proliferating within it, whether reporting research or development, furnishes the basis for a multifaceted discipline. Many of those working in the community have affiliated themselves in the ways I have described. In my view, this community is not so unorganized, so apparently chaotic as Wilson suggests. Its research component struggles to cumulate more and better data about a range of constantly evolving problems, refine our understanding of these problems, and translate what is known into better practice. (This is more than process and product development.) Wilson raises, but does not solve, the problem of how library-and-information science, whatever the extent of its development, interpenetrates and is developed by the bibliographic R&D community. It is not enough simply to say or imply that the problem does not exist. The existence of this community—insofar as the disparate elements Wilson describes are not so disparate as to make the idea of a community a ludicrous fiction—does not obviate the various concerns I dealt with in the last part of my paper; it simply provides a different context for them. The existence of such a community raises questions of definition, historical issues of growth and change, contemporary problems of disciplinary assimilations, and so on. There are, too, occupational issues of how the bibliographic R&D community, and bibliographic R&D itself, are related to professional practice in libraries and other institutional settings. Wilson's is a provocative paper built on an intriguing notion. For a community to exist, let its members work on as many different problems, employing as many different methods as they can devise, the presence of certain commonalities is required: shared beliefs as to how the problems interrelate, some sense of common goals, however complex and fragmented. Wilson stresses differences. The question of similarities is ignored. Maybe Wilson is simply providing his own name for what nowadays would be otherwise described as library-and-information science (and technology)!

SECTION 6

CYBERNETICS

Murray Eden

Norbert Wiener, in his book entitled *Cybernetics, or Control and Communication in the Animal and the Machine,* did not define explicitly the word he believed he had coined. [Wiener, 1948 and 1961.] It had, in fact, been used before: by André-Marie Ampère in his *Essai sur la philosophie des sciences.* [Ampère, 1838 and 1843.] Ampère, in a work typical of the impulse for classification that motivated natural scientists of his day, exhibited a taxonomy of "all human knowledge" and in the same spirit provided neologisms for the sciences he derived in his classification.[1] However, Ampère, despite his statement that he was generalizing the concept of steering, was not aware that it could be extended to the regulation of organismic behavior. He assigned to cybernetics the role of a subscience of government. His classification of biology contained no niche for control, nor for that matter did his classification of physics.

In the introduction to his intensely personal book, Wiener presented his rationale for choosing to name a particular "no-man's land between the various fields [of science]":

> There are fields of scientific work, . . . which have been explored from the
> different sides of pure mathematics, statistics, electrical engineering, and

---

[1]Ampère gave the following description of what he meant by cybernetics: *"Cybernetics* [cybernétique]. Relations between peoples, the subjects of study within the two sciences discussed earlier [international law and diplomacy] are only a small part of that with which a good government must concern itself. Maintenance of public order, administration of laws, equitable distribution of taxes, selection of the people it must employ, and all the other considerations that may contribute to improving the state of society require the continual attention of government. Choices must constantly be made, among diverse measures, about which measure is most appropriate to achieve the desired goal. Only by intensive study and comparison of the various elements that, for each choice, are provided by a knowledge of all that is relevant to the nation—its character, customs, opinions, history, religion, way of life and property, institutions, and laws can government create the general rules of conduct that must guide it in regard to each particular case. Therefore, it is only after all the sciences that are concerned with these various factors that one must place the science in question here. I would call this science *cybernetics* from the word κυβερνήτης. From the restricted definition for the art of steering a vessel, cybernetics took on a meaning—even among the Greeks—of the art of steering in general." (Ampère, 1838 and 1843, pp. 140–141; my own translation—M. Eden.)

409

neurophysiology; in which every single notion receives a separate name from each group, and in which important work has been triplicated and quadruplicated, while still other important work is delayed by the unavailability in one field of the results that may have already become classical in the next field. (Wiener, 1948 and 1961, p. 2.)

CHIEF ELEMENTS OF WIENER'S CONCEPTION

In an historical account, Wiener enumerated the ingredients that led to his notion of cybernetics, which forms the nexus for their application to descriptions of animate and inanimate systems. I sketch the line of his interests and disciplines he coopted along the way. It begins in the late thirties by reason of his association with the neurologist, Arturo Rosenblueth. In 1940, the war required that he turn his attention to "the development [by Vannevar Bush] of computing machines for the solution of partial differential equations" and the design of electric networks [in collaboration with Yuk Wing Lee]. Wiener concluded that scanning as employed in television was destined to be useful to engineering, especially for the representation of functions of more than one variable. In modern parlance, it might well be called image analysis or graphics. These interests taken together led him to the notion of "the modern ultra-rapid computing machine." Another war project, the prediction of aircraft flight paths, led him to work on the theory and technology of prediction [with Samuel Caldwell and Julian Bigelow], hence, to the generalization of the notion of feedback and the belief that control theory was applicable to the explanation of neuromuscular behavior. During the course of this work, it became clear to Wiener and Bigelow "that the problems of control engineering and of communication engineering were inseparable . . . ." (Ibid. p. 8) Wiener and Bigelow focused on the "fundamental notion of message . . . precisely what is called a time series by the statisticians. . . . The solution of the problem of optimum prediction was only to be obtained by an appeal to the statistics of the time series to be predicted . . . ." (Ibid., pp. 8–9.) And a bit later: "It occurred to us . . . that there was a whole region of engineering work in which similar design problems could be solved by the methods of the calculus of variations." (Ibid., p. 10.)

Wiener and Bigelow often found value in the concept of "a message contaminated by extraneous disturbances which we call *background noise*." And thus, "we have made of communication engineering design a statistical science, a branch of statistical mechanics." This notion "attaches itself very naturally . . . to entropy" and to the second law of thermodynamics. The second law enters "in the study of enzymes and other catalysts, and their study is essential for the proper understanding of such fundamental phenomena of living matter as metabolism and reproduction. The third fundamental phenomenon of life, that of irritability, belongs to the domain of communication theory." (Ibid., p. 11.)

We may criticize Wiener for claiming too much in the way of priority for himself and his collaborators. Here and there, he cites collateral and earlier contributors, but he was not writing a history of scientific ideas. The progression was natural enough for a mathematician and statistician in that time. His continuing interest in biology and neurology—almost an avocation—led him to the connections that are so obvious nowadays. They may not have been obvious in the early 1940s when he was meeting with biologists and physicians in the Josiah Macy Jr. Foundation meetings.[2]

At various places in his book, Wiener provides statements of immediate relevance to the question of interdisciplinary points of contact:

Symbolic logic and semeiology:

> If I were to choose a patron saint for cybernetics out of the history of science, I should have to choose Leibniz. The philosophy of Leibniz centers about two closely related concepts—that of a universal symbolism and that of a calculus of reasoning. From these are descended the mathematical notation and the symbolic logic of the present day. (Wiener, 1948 and 1961, p. 12.)

Automata theory:

> The newer study of automata, whether in the metal or in the flesh, is a branch of communication engineering, and its cardinal notions are those of message, amount of disturbance or "noise"—a term taken over from the telephone engineer—quantity of information, coding technique, and so on. (Ibid., p. 42.)[3]

Ergodic theory and group theory:

> . . . in order to appreciate the real significance of ergodic theory we need a more precise analysis of the notion of *invariant,* as well as the notion of *transformation group*. These notions were certainly familiar to Gibbs, as his study of vector analysis shows. Nevertheless, it is possible to maintain that he did not assess them at their full philosophical value. (Ibid., p. 50.)

---

[2] Ludwig von Bertalanffy the biologist and inventor of the term *general system theory* has a somewhat different perspective. [Bertalanffy, 1968.] "It is true that cybernetics was not without precursors [in biology]. Cannon's concept of homeostasis became a cornerstone in these considerations. Less well-known, detailed feedback models of physiological phenomena had been elaborated by the German physiologist Richard Wagner in the 1920s, the Swiss Nobel prize winner W. R. Hess (1941, 1942) and in Erich von Holst's *Reafferenzprinzip*. The enormous popularity of cybernetics in science, technology and general publicity is, of course, due to Wiener and his proclamation of the Second Industrial Revolution." (Bertalanffy, 1968, p. 16.)

[3] Wiener was a bit wide of the mark here. The current progress of automata theory is to a very large extent austerely mathematical and draws most heavily on mathematical logic and the theory of computation.

The computer as a model for the nervous system:

> . . . it became clear to us [N. Wiener and Walter Pitts] that the ultra-rapid computing machine, depending as it does on consecutive switching devices, must represent almost an ideal model of the problems arising in the nervous system. (Ibid., p. 14.)

The nervous system as a model for the computer:

> . . . the modern ultra-rapid computing machine was in principle an ideal central nervous system to an apparatus for automatic control . . . ." (Ibid., p. 26.)

Robotics:

> To sum up: the many automata of the present age are coupled to the outside world both for the reception of impressions and for the performance of actions. They contain sense organs, effectors, and the equivalent of a nervous system to integrate the transfer of information from the one to the other. They lend themselves very well to description in physiological terms. It is scarcely a miracle that they can be subsumed under one theory with the mechanisms of physiology. (Ibid., p. 43.)

Pattern recognition:

> How do we recognize the identity of the features of a man, whether we see him in profile, in three-quarters face, or in full face? How do we recognize a circle as a circle, whether it is large or small, near or far; whether, in fact, it is a plane perpendicular to a line from the eye meeting in the middle, and is seen as a circle, or has some other orientation, and is seen as an ellipse? (Ibid., p. 133.)

It is fair to say that here Wiener is not particularly successful, although he touches on a variety of approaches that have been explored by later students of pattern recognition. In fact, pattern recognition draws on some of the mathematical disciplines listed by Wiener as relevant to cybernetics— notably statistics, information theory, graph theory, and group theory.

Wiener even touches on artificial intelligence in the discussion of a chess-playing machine:

> I think it is possible to construct a relatively crude but not altogether trivial apparatus for this purpose. The machine must actually play—at high speed if possible—all its own admissible moves and all the opponent's admissible ripostes for two or three moves ahead. To each sequence of moves it should assign a certain conventional valuation. Here, to checkmate the opponent receives the highest valuation at each stage, to be checkmated, the lowest; while losing pieces, taking opponent's pieces, checking, and other recognizable situations should receive valuations not too remote from those which good players would assign them. The first of an entire sequence of moves should

receive a valuation much as von Neumann's theory would assign it. (Ibid., p. 165.)

Not at all a bad start on the problem, even though Wiener did not foresee that much more powerful computers (with the help of some programming ingenuity) would be made to search the move tree to greater depths than two or three.

To clarify this heterogeneous set of steps, I shall attempt a parsing of the sequence in Table 1. The last five ideas of Table 1 appear to define cybernetics according to Wiener. Most important, therefore, are two related insights. First, that there is an essential unity in the set of problems in communication, control, and statistical mechanisms (noisy phenomena), whether they are to be studied in the machine or in living tissue. Second, that "the computing machine must represent almost an ideal model of the problems arising in the nervous system." We shall return to this second issue.

RECEPTION OF WIENER'S IDEAS

Wiener went on to document by anecdotes the excitement and interest his idea engendered in a number of eminent scientists of widely different backgrounds and competence. In the second edition of his book [1961], he was able to add to the evidence for the widespread diffusion of the concepts embodied in the term *cybernetics*. Indeed, the concept was embraced eagerly by many scholars, especially in psychology and the social sciences; its acceptance was more muted in the purely physical sciences.

Wiener was himself uncertain about the applicability of his ideas to sociology and economics:

> It is certainly true that the social system is an organization like the individual, that it is bound together by a system of communication, and that it has a dynamics in which circular processes of a feedback nature play an important part. This is true, both in the general fields of anthropology and of sociology and in the more specific field of economics . . . . Drs. Gregory Bateson and Margaret Mead have urged me, in view of the intensely pressing nature of the sociological and economic problems of the present age of confusion, to devote a large part of my energies to the discussion of this side of cybernetics.

> Much as I sympathize with their sense of the urgency of the situation, and much as I hope that they and other competent workers will take up problems of this sort . . . I can share neither their feeling that this field has the first claim on my attention, nor their hopefulness that sufficient progress can be registered in this direction to have an appreciable therapeutic effect in the present diseases of society. (Ibid., p. 24.)

Wiener goes on to explain why he is pessimistic about the use of cybernetics in these fields. Wiener's argument is that "the main quantities affecting

Table 1

Studies				Ideas			
Development	Type[a]	Purpose	Type	Development	Type	Purpose	Type
1 Computing machines	T	Solution of differential equations	M				
2 Network analysis	M	Design of electrical networks	T				
3 TV scanning procedures	T	Representation of functions of several variables	M	1 Modern computers	T	(Doing mathematics)[b]	M
(1 + 2 + 3 lead to the first idea)							
4 Theory of prediction	M	Predicting aircraft flight	T	2 Control theory	M	Explaining neuromuscular behavior	B

5	Statistics of time series	M	Optimum prediction	T
6	Information theory	M	Communications engineering designs	T

(5 + 6 lead to the third idea)

3 The problems of control engineering and communications engineering are inseparable.

4	Control—communications theory	M	Explanation of metabolism, reproduction, irritability	B
5	(The mathematics) of[c] modern computers	M	Modeling the nervous system	B
6	Models of the nervous system	M	Developing purposeful and intelligent machines	T

[a] T, M, and B denote technology, mathematics, and biology, respectively.
[b] Wiener does not state this, but it would appear to be the correct inference.
[c] This is implicit in Wiener and follows from the first idea.

society are not only statistical, but the runs of statistics on which they are based are excessively short." He hints at the issues of ergodicity, stationarity, and changes of state:

> There is no great use in lumping under one head the economics of steel industry before and after the introduction of the Bessemer process, nor in comparing the statistics of rubber production before and after the burgeoning of the automobile industry and the cultivation of *Hevea* in Malaya. Neither is there any important point in running statistics of the incidence of venereal disease in a single table which covers both the period before and that after the introduction of salvarsan, unless for the specific purpose of studying the effectiveness of this drug. (Ibid., pp. 24–25.)

Curiously enough, he did not bring up the issue of purposiveness, which plays such a crucial role in the early paper of Rosenblueth, Wiener, and Bigelow [1943]. There, the authors argued for a particular restriction of the idea of "intrinsic purposive behavior," which they considered to be "teleological," and it was on this basis that they searched for certain restricted comparisons of living organisms and machines. Purposiveness is a slippery subject even within these two kinds of objects, but what can be said of purposive behavior in the social sciences?[4]

Nonetheless, in the decade of the 1950s and most of the 1960s, the cybernetics principles were taken up widely and many books were published. Titles of books in print in 1968 include, according to a book index,[5] *Philosophy and Cybernetics; Cybernetics and Management; The Social Impact of Cybernetics; Cybernetic Modelling: The Science of Art; Great Ideas in Information Theory, Language, and Cybernetics; Cybernetic Principles of Learning and Educational Design;* even *The Cybernetics of the Sacred* and *The Cybernetic ESP Breakthrough.* Only one book is avowedly a textbook for cybernetics: a book by Viktor M. Glushkov, *Introduction to Cybernetics* [1966].

Despite Wiener's caveats and those of others with respect to the inappropriate use of the concepts of cybernetics, it seems abundantly clear that the underlying ideas were so attractive that many scholars untrained in mathematics and statistics attempted to apply the techniques to which Wiener alluded in ways that were wildly inappropriate. By the late 1960s, the term *cybernetics,* though not the underlying concepts, had fallen into some disrepute. John F. Young, a British psychologist, attempted to clarify the psychological use of cybernetics, but in his book, *Cybernetics,* published in 1969, he felt impelled to justify himself:

---

[4] For a discussion of the philosophical aspects of their approach the reader may wish to consider the comments of Berlinski [1976].

[5] Nina R. Thompson, ed., *Cumulative Book Index 1967–1968* (New York: H. W. Wilson Co., 1971), vol. 1, p. 814.

It is unfortunate that many of the books on cybernetics which have been published fall into one of three categories. One type treats the reader as a moron who is to be astounded and so, it is hoped, impressed. Another treats the reader as though he were a potential employer who is to be baffled and so, it is hoped, impressed (and also, if possible, be made apprehensive and therefore generous). The third type of book includes the word 'cybernetics' in the title, but inside it apparently deals with an entirely different subject. It is hoped that the present book cannot be pigeon-holed into any of these categories.

A notable feature of cybernetics is the extent to which pseudo-mathematical tracts have appeared. Strangely, much of this writing has been produced not by mathematicians but by psychologists. Unfortunately, some of this 'mathematics' appears to be intended merely to impress and sometimes it has little relevance to any practical results which have been obtained. Possibly this is partly caused by the largely irrelevant mathematical chapters which Wiener inserted in his book on cybernetics. Whatever the reason, there has been a great deal of mathematical mumbo-jumbo associated with the subject. Fortunately, real mathematicians, physicists and engineers concerned with cybernetics have tended in general to be more restrained in their treatments.

The situation is by no means ideal, and there is a danger that cybernetics will become generally regarded as an up-to-date form of Black Magic, as a sort of twentieth century phrenology. If this unfortunately happens, then one whole field of research, at the border of many disciplines, will be robbed of the support it needs. (Young, 1969, pp. ix–x)

Fourteen years later, it must be said that the situation has not improved and that in large measure Young's melancholy prophecy in the last paragraph of his preface has been largely fulfilled.

Although I have not reviewed in more than a cursory way Russian literature available in English, it may be worth noting the somewhat different course of cybernetics in the Soviet Union. Wiener, who was a humanist and something of a socialist in his political leanings, was much disturbed by the original reception of his work in the Soviet Union. It appears to have been relegated to the category of bourgeois science and, hence, dismissed. However, following the defrocking of Stalin as a scientist, Wiener's cybernetic principles were firmly endorsed. In a manner that may be typical within Russia's science establishment, cybernetics—almost overnight—became a fundamental discipline; institutes were created, academic departments established, a journal was initiated, courses and textbooks were prepared. One striking difference remained. Western physical scientists and engineers rarely used *cybernetics* in titles of papers and referred, instead, to the mathematical name of the technique being applied to their research: control, time-series analysis, statistical communication theory, automata theory, and so forth. Russian literature tended to use *cybernetik* whenever any of these techniques were being applied. *Science Citation Index* for 1980 includes papers of Russian origin, with such titles as "Making Ultrasonic Inspection of Welded Joints More Efficient by Means of Cybernetics" and "Group

Identification of Materials in Gas Chromatography on the Basis of Cybernetic Models.''

Even in Russia the term is now not nearly so widely used as it was a decade ago. For example, in the *Science Citation Index* for 1980, there are only twelve papers indexed under *cybernetics* or one of its modifications. By contrast, entries under *cycles, cyclic processes,* and *cyclic* have more than 1600 citations.[6] Of the twelve papers cited under the keyword *cybernetics*, eight are from the Russian literature.

LIVING SYSTEMS

Putting aside the curious story of the linguistic depreciation of the word *cybernetics,* what of the ideas behind the term, especially with respect to mind and the nervous system? Every age compares life with its contemporary machinery.

Consider how interpreters of mind and nerve attempted to explain these phenomena. A central concept for Aristotle was *pneuma*. I draw the following quotations from the biologist, Thomas S. Hall, who has written what he calls a ''preliminary account'' of the ''difference between living and nonliving things.'' (Hall, 1969, p. viii.)

> How Aristotle viewed *pneuma* has occasioned considerable scholarly debate. . . . Its nature is partly suggested by Aristotle's reference to it as ''hot air'' or simply a ''hot substance''—but with the understanding that its heat is no ordinary fire-produced heat. . . .

> A. L. Peck supposes that Aristotle means to make *pneuma* a quite general intermediator between *psyche* and *soma,* a role which would give it great importance in life-matter relations. (Ibid., p. 115.)

Further, Hall writes:

> Diocles (ca. 300 B.C.) and Praxagoras (ca. 300 B.C.) had given the psychic *pneuma* its source in the heart whose arteries distribute it to the body generally whereas the veins carry blood. . . .

> It remained for Praxagoras' pupil Herophilus to take the giant stride of identifying the motor nerves and their role in efferent conduction, as well as the sensory nerves which he probably regarded as conductors of a sensory *pneuma*. The important point to note here is that Herophilus and his successor at Alexandria, Erasistratus, now returned the brain to the position of central organ of sensation and volition. Herophilus showed through dissection that nerves arise from the brain. Erasistratus's doctrine is already familiar to us.

---

[6]I chose *cycle* because the concept of cycles is important within cybernetics and made a correction for purely chemical terms such as *cyclic AMP. Science Citation Index,* part 10, permuterm subject index, columns 14496–14497, ISI Inc., Philadelphia, Pa. [1981].

The arteries distribute vital *pneuma* to the body generally, he said, including the brain. Here psychic *pneuma* is formed and travels outward over the nerves. Galen's ideas are notable especially because of the extent to which actual experimental evidence influenced his opinions. (Ibid., pp. 161–162.)

We are tempted to think that the Greeks purified their writings from the taint of technology much as modern mathematicians delete their marginalia and numerical examples, which detract from the elegance of their papers. Nevertheless, there is at least circumstantial evidence of a technological marker for *pneuma*. A few centuries after Aristotle, Hero of Alexandria, in his work *Pneumatica*, is reported to have given several examples of a kind of apparatus that may be the prototype of existing engines. Steam or steam-water-mixtures operated mechanisms that could move temple doors without human intervention. We may also note that Aristotle's use of *pneuma* is pure metaphor, but experimental findings were beginning to introduce their constraints on the model. "As for method, although Galen's experiments were often inconclusive, they were also numerous and relevant and were not to be matched in ingenuity until the seventeenth century." (Ibid., p. 163.)

The age-old vitalist/mechanist argument in biology is well known. But we are not here concerned with the argument per se but rather the role of the automata or pseudoautomata that have been known in history and myth as models for mechanistic thought.

An interesting point of scholarship is the extent to which mechanistically oriented physiologists were influenced, in constructing a new image of man, by the automated imitations of vital action familiar, as we have just noted, since earliest times. One recent careful student of this question, Derek J. de Solla Price, considers the connection a real and important one. (Ibid., pp. 223–224.)

Descartes was the most explicit early proponent of the mechanistic view. He closes his *Treatise of Man* with the following paragraph:

I desire that you should consider that all the functions that I have attributed to this machine [he here enumerates the functions] . . . *imitate* as perfectly as possible those of a *real* man; I desire, I say, that you should consider that all these functions follow quite naturally solely from the arrangement of its parts neither more nor less than do the movements of a clock or other automaton from that of its counterweights and wheels; so that it is not necessary to conceive in it any other principle of movement or of life than blood and spirits set in motion by the heat of the fire that burns continually in its heart and is of no other nature than all those fires that are in inanimate bodies. (Descartes in *Le Monde,* published posthumously 1664; as quoted by Hall, 1969, p. 262.)

Referring to Descartes, Harvey, and other seventeenth-century scientists, Hall writes:

. . . we need to realize that biology became mechanistic simultaneously on two levels, the meso- and micromechanical. At the *meso*mechanical level, the whole organism and its main working parts were viewed as machines. For Descartes (1635) the whole animal was an automaton and so were such working components as the heart and the various pairs of reciprocating muscles. Borelli (1685) had a comparable attitude toward the bird and its wings; the whole bird was a flying machine of which the wings are necessary working parts. Harvey, writing earlier than Descartes, compared the propulsion of blood through the heart to that of water through a water bellows.

At the *micro*mechanical level we encounter numerous devices, of which the most elaborate are, perhaps, those which Descartes imagined in the brain, apertures which, by opening and shutting and by being movable so as to face in various directions, control the flow of spirits between the ventricles and the nerves. In a somewhat more objective but still speculative spirit, Hooke (1665) suspected that his cells might be equipped with small mechanical contrivances.

Some theorists carried the mechanical analogy even beyond the level of things potentially visible through a microscope. Thus both Descartes and Giovanni Borelli . . . extended mechanical models all the way to the unit particle. (Hall, 1969, pp. 228–229.)

The sources of analogies for neurology or psychology have undergone no great changes from the seventeenth century to our own. In 1922, Knight Dunlap, professor of experimental psychology at the Johns Hopkins University, in a text entitled *The Elements of Scientific Psychology,* used two analogies: (1) the burning of a fuse to describe the production of nerve current and (2) a telephone exchange as the metaphor for the structure and perhaps function of brain and nerve.

If we have a series of neurons, with a fiber of the first in contact with a fiber of the second; a fiber of the second in contact with a fiber in the third, and so on; and if we stimulate the first neuron properly, it will stimulate the second, the second will stimulate the third, and so on. Obviously, some "process" passes through the neuron, passing into the cell body through one fiber, and out through another: because a neuron excited at the tip of one fiber will excite another neuron with which another of its fibers is in contact. This "process" is called "nerve current." Its exact nature is unknown, and is the subject of various theories, but it is analogous to the burning of the powder in a fuse. Suppose we lay a number of short pieces of fuse end to end, and light the free end of the first. The combustion process will run through the first piece, ignite the second, and so on through the whole line. Yet nothing travels, except the process of combustion. The chief differences between the action of this line of fuses, and the action of a chain of neurons are that the neuron has a rapid recovery, becoming quickly ready for another discharge; and that the neuron, in many cases, has numerous branches of its fibers in contact with many other neurons, and stimulates, at a given discharge, some of these without stimulating the others. (Dunlap, 1922, p. 177.)

The functioning of afferent and efferent neurons is relatively simple. Current due to stimulation of a given receptor can enter the cord or the brain stem at only one point. Current emerging from the cord or brain stem at a given point can go to only one effector or effector group. The central neurons, however, provide a multiple switching system, by which an afferent route can be connected with any one of several efferent routes. If we consider the cord, brain stem and hemispheres together, they may be compared to the exchange of a telephone system, through which any calling phone can be connected with any other phone. The difference is that the "sending" (receptors) and "receiving" (effectors) stations in the nervous system are distinct; whereas they are combined in the telephone system. The nervous system is a "one-way system." But within this system a given receptor can be connected with almost any effector, or with several at the same time; and conversely, a given effector may have connected to it any one of a wide range of receptors or various combinations of receptors. (Ibid., pp. 183–184.)

This was the state of affairs in neurology until the second half of the twentieth century. Mechanics was the metaphor, and contact between neurology and psychology was limited largely to the fact that behavior is the expression of nervous activity. Wiener, as we know, used the computer as a model.

THE COMPUTER ANALOGY FOR NEUROPHYSIOLOGY

Wiener was among the first to see the computer analogy, and he certainly contributed to its popular diffusion.

Let me now come to another point which I believe to merit attention. It has been clear to me that the modern ultra-rapid computing machine was in principle an ideal central nervous system to an apparatus for automatic control; and that its input and output need not be in the form of numbers or diagrams but might very well be, respectively, the reading of artificial sense organs, such as photoelectric cells or thermometers, and the performance of motors or solenoids. With the aid of strain gauges or similar agencies to read the performance of these motor organs and to report, to "feed back," to the central control system as an artificial kinesthetic sense, we are already in a position to construct artificial machines of almost any degree of elaborateness of performance. (Wiener, 1948 and 1961, pp. 26–27.)

Wiener cites a number of mathematicians, engineers, neurophysiologists, and physicians among his intellectual contributors and relates how he became acquainted with the work of Walter Pitts, who, together with Warren McCulloch, had made the mathematical connection between logic and the brain before him. [McCulloch and Pitts, 1943.] Wiener referred to their work in the following statement:

At that time [1943] Mr. Pitts was already thoroughly acquainted with mathematical logic and neurophysiology, but had not had the chance to make very many engineering contacts. In particular, he was not acquainted with Dr. Shannon's work, and he had not had much experience of the possibilities of electronics. He was very much interested when I showed him examples of modern vacuum tubes and explained to him that these were ideal means for realizing in the metal the equivalents of his neuronic circuits and systems. From that time, it became clear to us that the ultra-rapid computing machine, depending as it does on consecutive switching devices, must represent almost an ideal model of the problems arising in the nervous system. The all-or-none character of the discharge of the neurons is precisely analogous to the single choice made in determining a digit on the binary scale, which more than one of us had already contemplated as the most satisfactory basis of computing-machine design. The synapse is nothing but a mechanism for determining whether a certain combination of outputs from other selected elements will or will not act as an adequate stimulus for the discharge of the next element, and must have its precise analogue in the computing machine. The problem of interpreting the nature and varieties of memory in the animal has its parallel in the problem of constructing artificial memories for the machine. (Wiener, 1948 and 1961, p. 14.)

PSYCHOLOGY

The effect of cybernetic ideas may be illustrated by looking at the history of psychology in the twentieth century. Earlier, I described some of the metaphors used throughout the intellectual history of brain and behavior, and I cited a psychology text of 1922 that reveals the poverty of its analogic armamentarium. Kurt Lewin's closely reasoned program for a science of (gestalt) psychology gropes for the right mathematical framework without success. [Lewin, 1936.] No bridge to neurology is even hinted at. Lewin does not include adaptation, memory, information, transformations, computation, control, or any of their cognates among his definitions. He does talk of structure, spaces, and states (the idea of state space is implicit), but he is unable to achieve an integration that would support mathematical application.

In their introductory psychology text, Robert Woodworth and Donald Marquis make no use of such concepts as message, information, feedback, computation, or control. A discussion of neurology is included, but its relation to psychology does not go beyond the description given by Dunlap at least thirty-five years earlier. For these authors, the stimulus/response paradigm is preeminent. "The preceding chapter made clear that the environment acts on the individual by stimulating his receptors, and that the individual reacts to the environment by responses of various kinds. We learned that behavior also depends on the individual—his structure, his temporary state and his activities in progress." (Woodworth and Marquis, 1921 and 1949, p. 230.)

These fibers are conducting units like the insulated wires of a telephone cable. They illustrate the all-or-none theory of nerve transmission as Dunlap did: "[If] a charge of dynamite . . . explodes at all it explodes completely."

(Ibid., p. 238.) Woodworth and Marquis recognize the importance of organization but offer no means of investigating this property of the brain: "But these sensory data and motor responses must be organized if the individual is to deal effectively with the objective environment. Most of the cortex is concerned with this major job of organizing." (Ibid., p. 259.) We note again the analogic use of telephone cables and explosives. I find no reference to the analogy of the computer. Furthermore, in the chapter on perception, there is no bibliographic entry later than 1943. It is fair to conclude that the authors did not believe that perceptual research during the twenty-four years prior to this edition was of particular importance to beginning undergraduates.[7]

There is a notable instance of the converse situation, when a psychologist writing much earlier came very close to current concepts but did not have an apposite analogy at his disposal. In 1911, William MacDougall attacked the mechanistic view of mind. [MacDougall, 1911, rev. ed. 1961.]

> The history of thought upon the psycho-physical problem is in the main the history of the way in which Animism, the oldest and, in all previous ages, the most generally accepted answer to it, has been attacked and put more and more upon the defensive in succeeding centuries, until towards the end of the nineteenth century it was generally regarded in academic circles as finally driven from the field. I have therefore given to the historical chapters the form of a history of Animism. . . .

> The modern currency and usage of the word derives chiefly from Prof. Tyler's "Primitive Culture," and I use it with the general connotation given it in that celebrated treatise. The essential notion, which forms the common foundation of all varieties of Animism, is that all, or some, of those manifestations of life and mind which distinguish the living man from the corpse and from inorganic bodies are due to the operation within him of something which is of a nature different from that of the body, an animating principle generally, but not necessarily or always, conceived as an immaterial and individual being or soul. (Ibid., p. 14.)

The contemporary American psychologist Jerome Bruner has this comment on MacDougall's contribution in his 1961 introduction to a new edition of MacDougall's work:

> He [MacDougall] published a paper in 1901 in *Brain*, "On the seat of the psychophysical processes," in which it was plain that Mind acted not as a capricious organ of intervention but in a highly systematic way to set and alter the passage of neural impulses in the synapses of the central nervous system.

---

[7] My judgment has been made in light of the publishing history of this popular text. The copy available to me is a version of the twentieth edition that appeared in a new size in 1963 and was reprinted in 1967. The twentieth edition was copyrighted in 1949. However, the preface to the edition is dated February 26, 1947.

His argument is anatomical (that it is in the synapses between neurones that any shunting or selectivity of conduction must be determined), physiological (that the evidence of sensory adaptation and contrast and other sensory phenomena required a selective interaction in the brain), and psychological (that attention particularly required a theory of synaptic shunting). The paper is exquisitely argued and documented, and while it contains some bad guesses about eventual mechanisms of nerve transmission, the general outcome is still interesting. For what he is saying, to put it in ultramodern dress, is that if Body is the machine, Mind is the program that determines how the machine will process its data and one cannot equate the machine and the program. The series of three papers on such sensory phenomena as inhibition, facilitation, and contrast in visual sensation published in *Mind* in the 1890s make it quite clear that he is groping toward such a formulation. Mind, in short, *uses* the nervous system. To describe the nervous system, then, does not constitute a description or analysis of mind any more than the description of the use to which a man puts a hoe represented a description of the nervous system or the mind of the man that uses it. Mind, in effect, is the realm of purposes, plans, intentionality. He wished to get Mind as Program into Body as Machine. The misplaced concreteness of his solution is startling. The problem is real, and can be stated better today. (Bruner in MacDougall, 1961, pp. xiv–xv.)

But consider the psychology text by Floyd Ruch revised for the ninth edition in 1967. [Ruch, 1937 and 1967.]

The "knowledge explosion" in the area of physiological psychology in the last fifteen years has produced much that is of direct relevance to a science of behavior. So the discussion of this important area has been moved from the Reference Manual into the text itself. (Ruch, 1967, p. ii.)

The new analogies are beginning to be used.

Although psychologists and neurologists still have much to learn about our brains and nervous systems, they are sure that underlying every thought, every perception and every action is a pattern of neural activity. As we encounter stimulus situations of all kinds, messages are received, evaluated, integrated and stored, and other messages are sent out to the various organs of response. (Ibid., p. 41.)

Ruch cites Wiener for introducing the concept of servomechanism to biology. Moreover, the poverty of stimulus/response has been enriched to include stimulus, organization (which he credits to gestalt psychology), response, feedback. Hence:

While driving, you hear an automobile horn honking—*S*. Past experience causes you to seek an explanation—*O*. You glance in the rear view mirror—*R*—but your response does not stop at that point. You see another car following closely, and you respond by pressing harder on the accelerator. Your response of looking in the mirror supplied *sensory feedback*, which served as a new stimulus. Thus we see that our formula will not be really adequate unless we add the element of sensory feedback. (Ibid.)

During the last decade, teaching of general psychology has been turned upside down. Peter Lindsay and Donald A. Norman entitle their text *Human Information Processing: An Introduction to Psychology*. They begin the book with perception described in terms of pattern recognition, rules, and feature analysis. They describe "neural information processing" in terms of idealizations of the nervous system as logic elements and circuit diagrams. Feedback control enters even in their discussion of motivation. The terminology of cybernetics as construed by Wiener is on virtually every page, but neither Wiener nor cybernetics is mentioned. [Lindsay and Norman, 1972.]

BIOLOGY

It seems proper to conclude that the concepts of cybernetics have become internalized in many aspects of psychology; much the same can be said of neurology as well as other branches of biology. Biology remains largely an experimental science and finds little place for the mathematics underlying the cybernetic insights. Nonetheless, I cite a few examples from books I have at hand to defend this position. I quote from Manfred Zimmermann writing for a recent text in sensory physiology [Zimmermann in Schmidt, 1978]:

> The nerve fiber can be compared, from the point of view of its function, with a cable carrying information. The approach of the communications engineer— *information theory*—can also be applied to the nervous system. This body of knowledge, together with control theory, is often called *cybernetics;* especially in Europe, its application in biology is termed biocybernetics, though such general terms are used less in the United States. (Ibid., p. 68.)

Zimmermann then goes on to describe the rudiments of information theory and relate it to notions of stimulus threshold and sensitivity.

More elaborate uses of control theory have been made by Lawrence A. Stark in "The Control System for Versional Eye Movements." [Stark in Bach-y-Rita and Collins, 1971.] Control theory, including block diagrams and circuit models, but little mathematics, is used by Ernest R. Hilgard in a paper entitled "Pain Perception in Man." [Hilgard, 1978.] Indeed, the collection in which Hilgard's work is to be found begins with a series of five papers grouped under the heading "1. Basic Features, A. Feature Filters and Channels." Here, we find all the paraphernalia of communication theory: features, filters, channels, Fourier transformations (for space and time), autocorrelation, cross-correlation, and so forth. Later on in this book, a great deal of space is devoted to articles that require the notions of information and pattern recognition. [Held, Leibowitz, Teuber, 1978.] But since we have already seen them in introductory texts, there is no use belaboring the point.

Outside the domain of neurology or psychology, we find traces of the ideas of cybernetics in many corners of biology. Carl F. Rothe contributes a chapter to Selkurt's *Physiology,* which he entitles "Regulations of Visceral Function—B. Homeostasis and Negative Feedback Control." [Rothe in Selkurt, 1971.] He presents a block diagram for *a negative feedback-control* system but includes no mathematics.[8]

Brian C. Goodwin's book deals with a biological theory intended to provide insight into the basic formal organization of the highly evolved and elaborate forms of life. He casts much of his argument in terms of control models and makes heavy use of the mathematics of control theory and probability. [Goodwin, 1963.]

David Givol, an immunologist, begins a paper entitled "A Structural Basis for Molecular Recognition: The Antibody Case" [in Cuatrecasas and Greaves, 1976] with the sentence "Molecular recognition stands at the roots of biology. . . . Recognition via combining sites is a property of enzymes, antibodies, hormones, receptors, lectins and perhaps other classes of proteins." (Givol, 1976, p. 3.)[9]

Earlier in this collection, Melvyn Greaves writes of "biological communication"[10] as well as "signals and the cell surface." [Greaves in Cuatrecasas and Greaves, 1976.]

---

[8] For the nonbiologist, it may be worthwhile to explain the distinction between homeostasis and feedback-control. The concept of homeostasis is due to Walter B. Cannon. [Cannon, 1929.] Rothe defines it thus: "Homeostatic mechanisms operate to counteract changes in the internal environment which are induced either by changes in the (external) environment or by activity of the individual so as to maintain a constant and optimal internal environment." Rothe goes on— alas—to equate homeostasis with negative feedback-control. He is wrong. Feedback models in the physiology of organisms are instances of homeostasis, but the great bulk of homeostatic and adaptive models for the explanation of stability of composition and chemical activity in organisms rarely appeal to the notions of set-point, error function, and negative feedback. Of course, flow diagrams are put down, and (generally nonlinear) partial differential equations are used extensively, but the framework is that of physicochemical kinetics rather than control theory. We may regard homeostasis as the biological equivalent of LeChatelier's Principle augmented by the hypothesis that concentrations of material substances and the energetics of biological internal processes retain their constancy (in the common sense of that word) because the variation of any one is tied to very many, if not all, of the others.

[9] Molecular recognition draws on thermodynamics in order to give meaning to the notion of information. Molecular biologists measure affinity or association constants. The logarithm of this quantity is proportional to the (Helmholtz) free energy of binding. Very rarely, the entropy is evaluated, which would bring the concept into formal equivalence to the concepts of physical information originated by Leo Szilard [1929] and John von Neumann [1932 and 1955].

[10] The notion of specificity in the action of biologically active substances is at least seventy years old. Paul Ehrlich formed the concept of a receptor theory from immunological studies on toxin-

It is now widely appreciated that these processes [intercellular communication and recognition] play a crucial role in virtually all biological systems and functions. These encompass fertilization, embryonic development, infectious interactions, the activity of the nervous system, the regulation of growth and development by hormones and the immune response to foreign or "non-self" antigens. . . . In the last decade several major advances have led to a new level of understanding of the molecular basis of cellular recognition . . . . These studies have been paralleled by equally important insights into the general structure and organization of cell membranes and the possible ways in which signals arriving from the "outside" can be transduced across the cell surface membrane to induce or regulate the cells' programmed responses. . . . Many of us suspect intuitively that not only are intercellular recognition phenomena fundamental to all biological phenomena but that the codes and rules of the game will be few, and therefore similar in widely divergent cellular systems. (Cuatrecasas and Greaves, 1976, pp. vii–viii.)

CYBERNETICS IN APPLIED SCIENCE

So much for biology. The basic concepts of Wiener's cybernetics have become embedded in virtually every branch of scholarship. The notion that information can be handled as a mathematical quantity; that this quantity mediates the transmission of energy and, therefore, can be used to control it; that statistical uncertainty is itself a quantity related to (and degrading) information; that information can be used to guide decision-making and clarify our own descriptions of real-world phenomena; that information may be transformed by computation; and that information and control can be combined to create complex mechanisms that behave as if they were intelligent—these ideas, I maintain, are pervasive.

I feel it necessary to repeat that I am not commenting on the question of Wiener's priority in all his claims, nor is it relevant to my argument that the domain of cybernetics has changed with the times and now tends to exclude many of the ideas Wiener had included originally. Simply put, it seems to me that the ideas Wiener set down in his book and which *he* considered to be within cybernetics are now the common currency of science. It seems fruitless to attempt to prove my assertion. Mathematics—pure or applied—is there to be used whenever a scientist who has at least a nodding acquaintance with a particular subset of mathematics decides it is relevant to his problem. Moreover, because Wiener adjoined so much of mathematics to communication and control theory, we would be hard put to identify some area (not even differential topology or algebraic number theory) that could

---

antitoxin interactions. Even earlier Emile Fischer had attributed enzyme-substrate interactions to a lock-and-key (*schloss und schlussel*) mechanism. [Ehrlich, 1956, vol. 2, p. 178.] I wonder whether the introduction of the words *recognition* and *communication* helped. The fact remains that they are now part of the biologic vocabulary. [Cited in Greaves, 1976, p. 15.]

be excluded definitively. Nonetheless, the tools Wiener proposed to use in 1948 are still the tools of choice in many applications, although they have undoubtedly been refined during the last three decades.

COMPUTER SCIENCE AND ARTIFICIAL INTELLIGENCE

One area of technological development related to information and control, machine computation, has dominated all others in terms of number of participants and its influence on Western, especially American, society during the last twenty years. On the academic side, its practitioners prefer to call their discipline computer science rather than machine computation. Wiener included machine computation and emphasized its use as an analogy to the brain within the purview of cybernetics. Ironically, the concepts of cybernetics have played only a very minor role in the more recent growth of machine computation. The great majority of people working with computers, attempting to improve or to study their behavior, are interested in programming, computer architecture, computer languages, computational methods (algorithms), communication networking, computer system design and operations, and so forth.

It is only on the periphery of computer science that the special role Wiener has played is explicitly acknowledged. Marvin Minsky, who, with John McCarthy, coined the phrase *artificial intelligence,* discusses the place of cybernetics in artificial intelligence in a recent paper. [Minsky, 1979.] Whereas Minsky's comment exhibits a strong bias in favor of more recent work done under the banner of artificial intelligence rather than older work done under another rubric, it is an accurate picture of one highly publicized facet of current computer research indebted directly to the original concepts of cybernetics.

> The era of cybernetics was a premature anticipation of the richness of computer science. The cybernetic period seems to me to have been a search for simple, powerful, general principles upon which to base a theory of intelligence. Among the ideas it explored were the following
>
> *Negative feedback*   The psychological concept of goal was identified with the mechanism of setting up a generalized servomechanism to reduce the difference between an input goal parameter and an observed system parameter. This idea was exploited in various mathematical directions, but the secret of intelligence was not to be found in "optimal control" or similar knowledge-free theories. Nonetheless, the difference-reduction concept, reformulated in terms of a symbolic description of differences, finally became a key concept in artificial intelligence in the General Problem Solver system of Newell and Simon.
>
> *Pattern recognition*   The search for abstraction or invariance developed slowly, I think, because of the error of identifying the thing with itself; that is,

attempting to match image against image, rather than description against description. The issues raised in this exploration—how a global or gestalt characteristic of a situation is discerned from an ensemble of local features—slowly evolved into a very rich collection of theories of description and representation, so rich, in fact, that the subject is still difficult to survey and criticize.

Stochastic learning The secret of creativity was sought in the area of controlled random search, both in models of learning and in models of problem solving. The "stochastic learning models" of that era's mathematical psychology did not lead anywhere, nor did experiments on "programmed evolution" or "random neural networks." A somewhat later approach based on "perceptrons," which were self-adjusting learning devices, seemed more promising but subsequently died out. (Minsky, 1979, pp. 401–402.)

Nowadays, workers in artificial intelligence attempt to characterize tasks in terms of meaning and semantics. Their insights are drawn from linguistics and cognitive psychology rather than neurophysiology and psychophysics. Thus, their work is largely outside the area of cybernetics as it is ordinarily construed. They rarely use the sorts of applied mathematics Wiener thought to be important in cybernetics, and certainly their concepts of goals and directions are far from his notion of negative feedback or purposive control.

CYBERNETICS AS A SCIENTIFIC DISCIPLINE

Having concluded that the cybernetic hypotheses are part of the subconscious culture of science and technology, we are led also to the conclusion that cybernetics does not constitute a well-defined scholarly discipline nor does it connote a group of professionals with common technical problems and interests. There remain a few relatively minor journals whose names concatenate several terms; thus, *Journal of Cybernetics and Information Science; Biological Cybernetics, Biofeedback and Self-Regulation* (formerly published as *Kybernetik*); *Kybernetes: An International Journal of Cybernetics and General Systems;* and *Transactions of the IEEE Systems, Man and Cybernetics Society.* Occasionally symposia—also with concatenated titles—are held and their papers published; thus, *Progress in Cybernetics and Systems Research.* [Trappl and Hanika, 1975.] There is an International Association of Cybernetics.[11]

[11] There are some differences between terminology in the United States and Europe. The editors of the symposium just cited are president and vice president, respectively, of the Austrian Society for Cybernetic Studies. Professor Robert Trappl, the president, is also professor of biocybernetics and bioinformatics at the University of Vienna Medical School. The Technical University of Berlin has a cybernetic department (Fachbereich Kybernetik). I also note research groups on sociocybernetics in the computer science laboratory of Uppsala University and a Department of Cybernetics at Brunel University, England.

A search of U.S. college catalogs failed to turn up courses in cybernetics. I have referred earlier to the absence of mathematically oriented texts. Two institutions, San José State University and the University of California at Los Angeles, grant degrees in cybernetic systems. By contrast, thirty-four institutions of higher learning offer degrees in systems and information science, systems engineering, systems science, or systems technology. More than 300 universities offer degrees in computers, computer science, or equivalent titles; there are as yet no degrees available in artificial intelligence, pattern recognition, and the like.[12] Regular conferences are scheduled by the Institute of Electrical and Electronics Engineers (IEEE) Systems, Man, and Cybernetics Society. At a recent meeting (August 24–27, 1981), the list of topics included pattern recognition, artificial intelligence, man/machine systems, biomedical systems and biocybernetics, system design methodology, computer-aided design, and robotics. Each of these topics was explicitly referred to by Wiener in his second edition of *Cybernetics*.[13] In this sense, the interest of the field has remained stable. But virtually every one of these subjects has developed in large measure independently of the others, with its own journals, societies, and in some instances separate academic departments.

CYBERNETICS AND SYSTEMS THEORY

The Russian mathematical scientist Valentin F. Turchin has cast the ideas of cybernetics into a more formal mathematical way of looking at things than did Wiener. [Turchin, 1977.] For Turchin, cybernetics is based above all on the concept of the *system,* consisting of other objects called subsystems; so cybernetics considers the *relations* between systems and subsystems. A system or subsystem is characterized by its *state,* a concept that relies on our intuition of time; thus, cybernetics studies the organization of systems in space (real and abstract space) and time. Organization in time when it is purposive is called *control.* Finally, cybernetics tests the concept of *hierarchy;* the description at one hierarchical level will be different from that at another level. Hierarchical structure or subsystems are intended to *recognize* or classify concepts derived from lower levels. Hierarchies also establish the relations of goals and plans for the system by which recognition and the consequent control decisions are made.

When cybernetics is cast in this framework, it is easy to understand the growth in the use of the term *systems analysis* or *systems theory* as an

---

[12] *The College Blue Book, 18th Edition—Degrees Offered by College and Subject* (New York: Macmillan, 1981).

[13] Wiener devotes a significant portion of the pages of *Cybernetics* to mathematical discussions. We have the impression that the mathematics was introduced for illustration rather than for teaching the mathematics or its application.

equivalent to *cybernetics*. Many times the words are conjoined; for example, the largest society dealing with cybernetic issues per se is the IEEE Systems, Man and Cybernetics Society.

Systems theory is a domain of scholarship that exists in uneasy relation to that of cybernetics. The originator of the term *general system theory* and one of its major expositors, Ludwig von Bertalanffy, subsumes cybernetics within general systems theory. [Bertalanffy, 1968.] As with Wiener, Bertalanffy has no succinct definition for his newly coined phrase. It would appear that all problems not solvable by classical science are problems of general systems theory:

> The methodological problem of systems theory, therefore, is to provide for problems which, compared with the analytical-summative ones of classical science, are of a more general nature.

> As has been said, there are various approaches to deal with such problems. We intentionally use the somewhat loose expression "approaches" because they are logically inhomogeneous, represent different conceptual models, mathematical techniques, general points of view, etc.; they are, however, in accord in being "systems theories." (Ibid., p. 19.)

Later on, Bertalanffy particularizes slightly:

> Not only are general aspects and viewpoints alike in different sciences; frequently we find formally identical or isomorphic laws in different fields. In many cases, isomorphic laws hold for certain classes or subclasses of "systems," irrespective of the nature of the entities involved. There appear to exist general system laws which apply to any system of a certain type, irrespective of the particular properties of the system and of the elements involved.

> These considerations lead to the postulate of a new scientific discipline which we call general system theory. Its subject matter is formulation of principles that are valid for "systems" in general, whatever the nature of their component elements and the relations or "forces" between them. (Ibid., p. 37.)

Despite the lack of a formal definition, Bertalanffy, again as with Wiener, provides a definition by extension. His list of the systems theories comprises: classical system theory, computerization and simulation, compartment theory, set theory, graph theory, net theory, cybernetics (restricted to a theory of control systems—M. E.), information theory, theory of automata, game theory, decision theory, and queuing theory. He mentions, but does not discuss applied systems research, which includes systems engineering, operational research, linear and nonlinear programming. Later on, he adds factor analysis, lumps network and graph theory into topology or relational mathematics, and adds human engineering to applied systems research. (Ibid., p. 90.) Bertalanffy puts the origins of general systems theory earlier and in places different from those of cybernetics. His first publication with *general system theory* in the title was in proof when it was destroyed in World War II.[14]

The systems theorist George Klir holds a somewhat more restricted view of the general systems theory but includes cybernetics within systems theory. We are indebted to Klir for explicitly distinguishing between cybernetics as a science and cybernetics as a viewpoint. [Klir, 1970.] I could find in his work no suggestion that an analogous division of systems theory would be appropriate.

A currently active general systems theorist, Mihajlo Mesarović, offers another definition, one that stresses the mathematical nature of the theory:

> [The] conceptual basis for systems theory might be summarized in the following observation: Study of any real-life phenomena reveals two aspects—*informal*, dealing with the meaning, interpretations, significance, objectives, values and the like—and *formal*, dealing with the form (structure) in which the relationship between the attributes appears. Systems theory is concerned with the second, formal, aspect of the observations. Apparently, these formal relationships are invariant with respect to the specific nature of the phenomena under consideration.
>
> Systems theory, then, is based on the following fundamental premises:
>
> (a) *A theory of any real life phenomena (biological or otherwise) is always based on an image, termed a model.*
> (b) *Without introducing any constraints whatsoever the formal, invariant, aspects of the model can be represented as a mathematical relation. This relation will be termed a system.*
>
> A system (i.e., a mathematical model of a real-life phenomenon) is usually specified by means of a set of equations, e.g., difference equations, differential equations, etc. To comprehend the essence of the foundations of systems theory, it is important to appreciate, however, that a set of equations only *specifies* the given system and that the distinction should be made between a system and the set of equations that are used for its (constructive) specification. (Mesarović, 1968*b*, pp. 60–61.)

There is an obvious contradiction between Mesarović, who restricts systems theory to the formal relationships among the observable attributes of a real-life phenomenon, and Bertalanffy, who embraces logically different approaches, mathematical techniques, and general points of view as being systems theories. We face a procedural dilemma here that is equivalent to the one that exists for us in deciding how to describe cybernetics. Is systems theory what its generally acknowledged inventor says it is, or do we inter-

---

[14] The citation for this work appears to be missing from *General System Theory*, although there may be an inconsistency between the text (p. 14) and the bibliography. The text suggests the first paper was to appear in *Deutsche Zeitschrift für Philosophie*, while the bibliography, ordered chronologically, cites "Zu einer allgemeinen Systemlehre," *Blätter für Deutsche Philosophie* 3/4 (1945), extract in *Biologia Generalis* 19 (1949), 114–129. Are these one and the same?

pret it in terms of the (different) ways in which later workers describe its domain? Other domains of scholarship do not ordinarily pose such problems.

CYBERNETICS/SYSTEMS THEORY VIS-À-VIS CONTROL/COMMUNICATION THEORY

There is a direct line of descent in the history of control theory from Harry Nyquist through Wiener, followed by such control theorists as Richard Bellman, Rudolph Kalman, and onward to the present day. It is not implausible to suggest that James Clerk Maxwell would agree with his intellectual descendants as to the scope of a theory of governors that began with his work of 1868. [Maxwell, 1868.][15]

Very much the same argument can be made with regard to the history of information or communication theory. Claude Shannon in *The Mathematical Theory of Communication* asked and largely answered a question that was undoubtedly close to Wiener's problems with noise in stationary time-series analysis: "How is an information source to be described mathematically and how much information in bits per second is produced in a given source?" (Shannon and Weaver, 1949, p. 10.) Shannon thought of his work as an extension of the general theory of communication contained in the work of Nyquist [1924] and Ralph Hartley [1928] twenty years earlier. In a comment appended to Shannon's seminal paper, Warren Weaver acknowledges the contribution of several precursors.

Dr. Shannon's work roots back, as von Neumann has pointed out, to Boltzmann's observation, in some of his work on statistical physics (1894), that entropy is related to "missing information," inasmuch as it is related to the number of alternatives which remain possible to a physical system after all the macroscopically observable information concerning it has been recorded. L. Szilard (*Ztsch. f. Phys.*, Vol. 53, 1925) extended this idea to a general discussion of information in physics, and von Neumann (*Math. Foundation of Quantum Mechanics,* Berlin, 1932, chap. V) treated information in quantum mechanics and particle physics. Dr. Shannon's work connects more directly with certain ideas developed some twenty years ago by H. Nyquist and R. V. L. Hartley, both of the Bell Laboratories; and Dr. Shannon has himself emphasized that communication theory owes a great debt to Professor Norbert Wiener for much of its basic philosophy. Professor Wiener, on the other hand, points out that Shannon's early work on switching and mathematical logic antedated his own interest in this field; and generously adds that Shannon certainly deserves credit for independent development of such fundamental aspects of the theory as the introduction of entropic ideas. Shannon has natu-

---

[15] Maxwell writes: "I propose at present, without entering into any details of mechanism, to direct the attention of engineers and mathematicians to the dynamical theory of governors." (Maxwell, 1868, p. 106.)

rally been specially concerned to push the applications to engineering communication, while Wiener has been more concerned with biological application (central nervous system phenomena, etc.). (Shannon and Weaver, 1949, p. 95.)

For completeness, we note that Shannon also acknowledged the early use by Ronald A. Fisher of an information measure different from his: the quantity of information in a sample drawn from a density distribution with finite expectation. Colin Cherry carried the history back much further, but it need not concern us here. [Cherry, 1951.]

The appearance of Shannon's work had an explosive effect, not only in communications theory, but in sparking a multitude of attempts to apply his theory to all sorts of processes that appeared to be related to the transmission of objects with semantic content. How much of this efflorescence was due to Shannon and how much to Wiener is impossible to assess; the appearances of *Cybernetics* and "The Mathematical Theory of Communication" (as a paper) were contemporaneous [1948]. However, there are several important differences. Shannon presented a developed mathematical theory; he offered a transparently simple set of measures of information. He avoided entirely any allusion to the many kinds of transactions that people are likely to call informative. Rather, he asked how to measure information, and he set the ground rules for models that could conceivably use his measures.[16] Then, Shannon, in a simple example, showed how to estimate the entropy of a natural information source, the English language.

Information theory has developed much as any other branch of applied mathematics. Many applications have been developed for communication problems. Some of them led to newer, richer theory, and these were applied in their turn. And so on to the present.

This is not the place to elaborate on general systems theory, but we must distinguish between systems theory as a viewpoint and mathematical systems theory. The latter is quite clearly to be included within mathematics and continues to be an active area of mathematical development. It is in the direct line of descent of govenors, servomechanisms, feedback, and optimal control previously alluded to. Rudolf Kalman, Peter Falb, and Michael Arbib in the introduction to their text *Topics in Mathematical System Theory* lay emphasis on "the concepts of states, control, optimization and realization." [Kalman, Falb, and Arbib, 1969.] Suffice it to say that systems theorists and cyberneticians occupy the same turf. The choice of a name for a new domain of scholarship is a sociological rather than a scientific question. Scholars of the West tend to favor systems theory, the Eastern bloc appears to prefer cybernetics; there are some who will use both, and others who use neither, favoring instead more restricted labels to classify their work.

---

[16]This is by no means a trivial exercise. The probability distribution on an infinite set of possible messages must be properly defined or else the apparatus collapses. Wiener provided no handy mathematics; although at times he urges caution, he did not provide the apparatus for imposing restraint.

It is also worth noting that much as with cybernetics, systems theory is regarded by some workers—mathematicians in particular—as a field with many naive, ill-equipped, self-serving, and even fraudulent practitioners. The philosopher and student of mathematics, David Berlinski, furnishes a detailed critique of systems analysis from this point of view in an extravagantly polemical but still worthwhile book. [Berlinski, 1976.] He holds no higher opinion of cybernetics, though his blows at the latter are en passant. He describes his motivation thus: "It is the use of mathematical methods for largely ceremonial reasons that I deplore and denounce as pernicious." (Ibid., p. ix.)

CYBERNETICS/SYSTEMS THEORY VIS-À-VIS BIOLOGY AND OTHER THAN NATURAL SCIENCES

Biology, as was indicated earlier, has adopted the insights of cybernetics and many of the terms used in control theory, information theory, and computers. While I have attributed it to Wiener's influence, it may well have been due to the rise of systems theory. That is to say, biologists have presented their ideas in fora of both kinds. The Yale physiologist, Talbot Waterman, has put forward his view of the importance of systems analysis at a symposium on Systems Theory and Biology.

> Because of this multivariable and highly interconnected organization, living things require for their effective study some overall strategy like systems analysis. Such indeed is the fundamental thesis of this book. . . . my intention here is to indicate from an experimental biologist's point of view the relevance of the systems approach to understanding a living organism . . . .

> Organisms are self-regulating, adaptive systems capable of autoduplication. As such they must acquire energy from the environment and utilize it to do their biological work. To this end living things act thermodynamically as irreversible chemical machines. But to be self-regulating and adaptive, control and information are essential. Cybernetic mechanisms therefore must provide at once the basis for the organism's steady state and dynamic characteristics as well as the adaptedness required for its survival.

> As a consequence we have two major components to analyze for understanding biological systems. One of these comprises all the elements relating to the acquisition, transfer and utilization of *energy*. These permit the organism to grow, to move and in general to do work. The other consists of everything functioning in the detection, processing, retention, and utilization of *information*. These permit the control of what the organism does and how fast. Essential for the maintenance of life, both components are closely interrelated in jointly sustaining the steady state. (T. H. Waterman, 1968, p. 13.)

A few paragraphs later, Waterman turns his attention to the cybernetic component. It is not clear to me that he distinguishes between cybernetics and systems analysis except perhaps by intension:

. . . it is important to realize that the complete biological system comprises genetic (including, probably, developmental), synecological and evolutionary regulators as well. While control in all four (or five) of these realms shows certain fundamental similarities, physiological regulation has both the shortest time scale and usually its own characteristic machinery. Such control includes both the maintenance of the physiological steady state (homeostasis in Walter Cannon's sense of the word) . . . and the production of dynamic servocontrol exemplified by pursuit of prey or by adaptive synchronization of feeding and hibernation with the cycle of the seasons.

But homeostasis itself is truly dynamic in nature despite its proper distinction from the reference-input-following servo-type control. This is so because the physiological steady state is neither just a passive resistance to change nor a mere compliance to pattern imposed mainly from outside. Rather it results primarily from compensatory adjustments actively programmed within the organism in response to the total relevant information it has available. Thus in spite of an exquisite sensitivity to changes of many kinds, organisms maintain their stable state with remarkable thoroughness and precision. That they survive attests also to the reliability of their overall regulation despite failures or irregularities in detail. . . .

Systems Analysis. To resolve such an apparent paradox, systems analysis provides a powerful methodology. Not only in biology but in its engineering and other applications, systems analysis may be defined quite generally as the application of organized analytical and modeling techniques appropriate to explaining complex multivariable systems many of whose functional components may be initially quite imperfectly measured or even largely unidentified. Depending on the available data and the purpose of the analysis any, or more usually several, of a wide range of specific techniques may be employed ranging from the use of information theory and cybernetics to computer simulation or multivariable statistical analysis.

While this may seem a rather loosely defined recipe for advancing science, it does in fact provide a reasonably effective and increasingly appreciated array of interrelated disciplines appropriate in particular ways to the formidable problems in hand. (T. H. Waterman, 1968, pp. 3–4.)

One final fact completes this attempt to characterize the relation between cybernetics and systems theory; that is, the interest they have engendered in fields of study outside the natural sciences. Because these fields are not in my area of competence, I hesitate to venture a judgment as to the influence either cybernetics or systems theory has had. Nonetheless, there is little question that a number of distinguished social scientists, economists, and students of business administration have looked to these two fields for a source of ideas and tools relevant to their particular professional needs. For example, volume two of *Progress in Cybernetics and Systems Research* is comprised of papers in Socio-Economic Systems, Cognition and Learning, Systems Education, Organization and Management. [Trappl and Hanika, 1975.] A *Survey of Cybernetics,* published in 1969 and dedicated to the memory of Norbert Wiener, devotes the bulk of its pages to papers on Cybernetics and Artifacts (Information, Learning, and Teaching Systems; Models of Development; Artificial Intelligence Control), Cybernetics and Industry, Cybernetics and Society. [Rose, ed., 1969.] Stafford Beer provides the keynote introduction to the first collection just cited and the epilogue to the second. Beer, a pioneer in applying cybernetics to management and a prolific writer in the field, assigns an importance to applied cybernetics that transcends its role in explaining problems of communication and decision-making.

The reason for my defection [from the First Symposium on Cybernetics and Systems Research] was in fact an urgent recall to Santiago from the late President Salvador Allende of Chile. We had embarked six months earlier upon a program so ambitious as to have had at least a chance of revolutionizing the form of government on a cybernetic basis that would match the revolutionary political intentions of that democracy. This endeavor took precedence with me for two years, and I emerged from the experience very much changed. I changed in my awareness of myself, of my fellow men and of political realities; but these are not the topics that I shall discuss today. I changed also as a technologist, in terms of confidence. For I now know that it is possible to do what I have advocated for so many years—things which many used to say, and some still do say, are impossible.

But the changes that bear upon the nature of this symposium have to do with cybernetic insights themselves. There is of course no way of changing the laws by which large systems operate; but there can be a change in one's perception, and a change in the depth of understanding of principles we have known about all the time. It is of these matters that I speak today, because I know more clearly now what I am trying to say, and because I also know more about the direct practical relevance of these things to society at large. (Beer, 1975, p. 3.)

Wiener, writing twenty-eight years earlier, discussed the responsibilities of cyberneticians in the sphere of social activism. He shares much of Beer's view but paints his landscape in more sombre colors.

Those of us who have contributed to the new science of cybernetics thus stand in a moral position which is, to say the least, not very comfortable. We have contributed to the initiation of a new science which, as I have said, embraces technical developments with great possibilities for good and for evil. We can only hand it over into the world that exists about us, and this is the world of Belsen and Hiroshima. We do not even have the choice of suppressing these new technical developments. They belong to the age, and the most any of us can do by suppression is to put the development of the subject into the hands of the most irresponsible and most venal of our engineers. The best we can do is to see that a large public understands the trend and the bearing of the present work, and to confine our personal efforts to those fields, such as physiology and psychology, most remote from war and exploitation. As we have seen, there are those who hope that the good of a better understanding of man and society which is offered by this new field of work may anticipate and outweigh the incidental contribution we are making to the concentration of power (which is always concentrated, by its very conditions of existence, in the hands of the most unscrupulous). I write in 1947, and I am compelled to say that it is a very slight hope. (Wiener, 1948 and 1961, pp. 28–29.)

CONCLUDING REMARKS

To be sure, the analogies among such mechanical functions as information processing, computation, control, estimation, and the behavior of functioning organisms have been pushed quite far. Where experiments have permitted mathematical tests of mechanistic or probabilistic models for describing physiological or sensory-motor behavior, they have been well accepted, so much so that the terminology of computers and statistical signal processing has become part of the standard vocabulary of psychology and physiology. It is a tribute to Wiener that there are still a significant number of scientists who wish to preserve the word he used to define an intersection of many fields.

At the present time, it appears that cybernetics as a science in the terminology of Klir never really existed under that name, though many of the mathematical specialties co-opted by Wiener into cybernetics are flourishing. Cybernetics as a viewpoint has entered into the unconscious of workers in almost every branch of applied science and the sciences of man. It plays a role, though a minor role, in the reductionist domains of science and, hence, in virtually all of physics and chemistry, and much of biology.

Perhaps an explanation for the meteoric trajectory of cybernetics was prefigured in the very origin of Wiener's reason for inventing it.

> If the difficulty of a physiological problem is mathematical in essence, ten physiologists ignorant of mathematics will get precisely as far as one physiologist ignorant of mathematics, and no further. If a physiologist who knows no mathematics works together with a mathematician who knows no physiology, the one will be unable to state his problem in terms that the other can manipulate, and the second will be unable to put the answers in any form that the first can understand. (Wiener, 1948 and 1961, pp. 2–3.)

He softened this statement by adding:

> Dr. Rosenblueth has always insisted that a proper exploration of these blank spaces on the map of science could only be made by a team of scientists, each a specialist in his own field but each possessing a thoroughly sound and trained acquaintance with the fields of his neighbors; all in the habit of working together, of knowing one another's intellectual customs, and of recognizing the significance of a colleague's new suggestion before it has taken on a full formal expression. The mathematician need not have the skill to conduct a physiologi-

cal experiment, but he must have the skill to understand one, to criticize one, and to suggest one. The physiologist need not be able to prove a certain mathematical theorem, but he must be able to grasp its physiological significance and to tell the mathematician for what he should look. (Ibid., p. 3.)

Yet, the history of modern mathematics, applied science, and technology suggests that the first statement is still a more nearly true state of affairs; the second describes, at best, a transitional state. Mathematicians, scientists, engineers, and scholars continue to segregate into narrower and narrower specialties. The intersection of their interests, where it occurs, may well produce another specialty narrower still. When a physiologist is ignorant of the mathematics, his or her best course is to learn it. Someone may first be required to prepare the way by particularizing the mathematics for the physiological problem. This is a common precondition for much of applied mathematics. For example, the first courses taught to beginning electrical engineers are derived from the particularization of solutions of certain linear differential equations, the elements of graph theory, and a specialization of the propositional calculus. When the concepts for the physiological specialty are embedded in a mathematical framework shared by the community of specialists, there is no longer a need to acknowledge the specialist's indebtedness to the originator of the concept. After all, we would be quite surprised and not a little suspicious were an astrophysicist, say, to cite Newton or Leibniz for his or her use of the calculus.

Although many scholars have faith in the utility of the exchange of ideas among practitioners from different fields, the intersection of different disciplines remains an intersection and not a field of study itself, although with time it may be transformed into yet another specialty. The notions of cybernetics have permeated many disciplines—computer science, information theory, control theory, pattern recognition, neurophysiology, psychophysics, perceptual psychology, robotics, and the like. Having been integrated into them, cybernetics has performed the function for which it was proposed.

CYBERNETICS

Past and Present, East and West

Peter Elias

Eden gives an excellent commentary on the field of cybernetics, as introduced by Norbert Wiener in his book *Cybernetics*. [Wiener, 1948 and 1961.] I would like to add some terminological, historical, and geographical comments.

Cybernetics, or Control and Communication in the Animal and the Machine was published first by Hermann et Cie. in Paris in 1948. The internal evidence suggests that it was set in type and proofread (if at all) by people knowing neither English nor mathematics. The American edition, copublished by the Technology Press, John Wiley, and Hermann et Cie., was photo-offset from the original plates without correction: The numerous typographical errors were dealt with for the first time only in the second edition, published by the MIT Press in 1961.

In the preface and introduction to the second edition, Wiener gives some of the history of the field of cybernetics and mentions a series of conferences starting in 1944 and later sponsored by the Macy Foundation. The foundation sponsored ten such conferences in all. Five of these occurred after the publication of *Cybernetics*, and their proceedings were published by the foundation. [Josiah Macy Jr. Foundation, 1949–1953.]

1948 was also the year in which Shannon published his paper "A Mathematical Theory of Communication." [Shannon, 1948.] Wiener mentions Shannon's definition of information in his book. Shannon mentions Wiener's work on the prediction and filtering of noisy signals, which had appeared during World War II as a report from the Office of Scientific Research and Development entitled *The Extrapolation, Interpolation, and Smoothing of Stationary Time Series with Engineering Applications,* and which later appeared in book form under the same title [Wiener, 1949], but Shannon does not mention *Cybernetics* in his paper. In the United States, Shannon's theory and its later developments were not absorbed in cybernetics but acquired their own label, information theory. This label is still most commonly used in the same narrow way. However, the label is also the present title of a group within the Institute of Electrical and Electronics Engineers

(IEEE) whose *Transactions* are broader: They are devoted to theoretical work relevant to communications engineering, which includes, for example, not only extensions of Shannon's theory but also the filtering and detection of signals in noise and, in addition, algebraic coding theory—a field of discrete mathematics that is closely related to Shannon's work in both its origins and its applications, but has attained mathematical independence.

The same complex of ideas that captured the attention of Wiener and others in the United States was of great interest in England immediately after World War II. *Cybernetics* had a British audience, especially in neurophysiology. In fact, the earliest textbook of cybernetics that I have found is not the Glushkov volume of 1966 cited by Eden but a British volume published ten years earlier, complete with exercises for students [Ashby, 1956] by an author who had earlier written a book dealing enthusiastically with a cybernetic, homeostatic model of the human brain [Ashby, 1952]. Four symposia on information theory were held in London in 1950, 1952, 1955, and 1960; the first two organized by Willis Jackson and the last two by Colin Cherry (both professors of electrical engineering at Imperial College); proceedings were published. [Jackson, 1950, 1953; Cherry, 1956, 1961.] There were also two symposia in the United States, in 1954 and 1956, organized by the Information Theory Group of the IEEE and held at the Massachusetts Institute of Technology. [*IEEE Transactions,* 1954; 1956.] These symposia, and especially the ones in London, used a definition of information theory much broader than the narrow American usage I previously cited, which is still current in the United States. The papers presented dealt with a range of topics and fields of application as broad as, and quite similar to, those discussed by Wiener in *Cybernetics.* There was perhaps more emphasis on communication among people, and more interest by psychologists and linguists, in the London meetings than in Wiener's book, and less focus on the neuromuscular feedback loops in which Wiener and some of his early associates were particularly interested. However, a similar shift toward human studies and more complex problem domains is visible, for example, in the transactions of the tenth Macy meeting in 1955. The content of the London meetings together with Colin Cherry's book *On Human Communication* [1957 and 1966] may be taken to define what *information theory* meant in England during the period 1950–1960, and to some extent even later, while *cybernetics* was the correspondingly broad term widely accepted in the United States in the early 1950s.

In the United States, there is no present designation that has widespread professional acceptance and denotes approximately the particular mix of topics and techniques denoted by cybernetics here and by information theory in England in the early 1950s. The psychologists, linguists, neurophysiologists, and sociologists interested in communication within and between organisms, the biologists interested in genetic information, and others who might have called themselves cyberneticists in the early 1950s had mostly returned by the 1960s to their original disciplines, taking with them and integrating into those disciplines such concepts and techniques as had proved fruitful for their fields. In the Soviet Union, however, cybernetics became an important label just as its use was fading in the West.

There seems to have been no native development analogous to cybernetics in the Soviet Union before or during World War II. The necessary mathematical background, in mechanics for control theory and in probability and random-process theory for communications and stochastic control, was available because of the historic strength of Russian mathematics and the interest in applications of many of the best mathematicians, pre- and post-revolutionary. Kolmogorov, in fact, had done work related to Wiener's wartime work on filtering and prediction of random processes, and others also worked on random process problems. Kotelnikov, a talented communications engineer, submitted a doctoral thesis in 1947, which independently developed some of the new ideas about modulation that also appeared in the West after the war. [Kotelnikov, 1959.] But the high-quality work was almost all theoretical and mathematical in character and had little to do with the biological or behavioral sciences. The engineering development of sophisticated control, computer, and communications systems was much slower in the Soviet Union, even after the war. Most Russian engineers were educated in narrow engineering specialties and evidently did not experience the kind of interaction with behavioral scientists that occurred in the United States and Britain during wartime research and development. There were well-entrenched orthodoxies in the fields of linguistics, "higher nervous activity," psychology, and economics that were not receptive to new ideas, and researchers in these fields did not have access to the new instrumentation and computer resources that helped generate enthusiasm for cybernetic ideas in the West.

The first introduction of ideas from the neighborhood of cybernetics to the Soviet scientific community seems to have occurred from 1953 to 1956. Shannon's information theory was presented to the Soviet mathematical community by Aleksandr Khinchin, a distinguished mathematician, in two articles [1953; 1956] available in English. [Khinchin, 1957.] Khinchin emphasized the mathematical significance of the theory and not its potential for application to the social sciences and linguistics and gave it high praise. Khinchin was not alone: Kolmogorov, one of the world's great mathematicians, also showed early interest and has made a large number of fundamental contributions to questions arising from information theory since. The following passage from the 1956 article by Khinchin shows the enthusiasm of Soviet mathematicians for Shannon's work:

Information theory is one of the youngest branches of applied probability theory; it is not yet ten years old. The date of its birth can, with certainty, be considered to be the appearance in 1947–1948 of the by now classical work of Claude Shannon. Rarely does it happen in mathematics that a new discipline achieves the character of a mature and developed scientific theory in the first investigation devoted to it. Such in its time was the case with the theory of integral equations, after the fundamental work of Fredholm; so it was with information theory after the work of Shannon. [Khinchin, 1957, p. 30.]

At the same time, however, the 1956 philosophical encyclopedia of the Soviet Union defined cybernetics as a "reactionary pseudo-science, that arose in the United States after World War II and that has attained wide dissemination in other capitalistic countries . . . ." It was only gradually after Stalin's death that elements of Soviet society succeeded in taking steps to free more of science from ideological orthodoxies and constraints. Cybernetics became in a short time a highly positive concept in the Soviet Union and received a great impetus when Khrushchev at the 22nd Party Congress in 1961 said: "It is imperative to organize wider application of cybernetics, electronic computing, and control installations in production, research work, drafting and designing, planning, accounting, statistics and management."

The picture that Khrushchev and others presented was that cybernetics was the science of control and a socialist society could exploit such a science in organizing and planning the entire economic and social systems in ways ideologically impossible in capitalist countries. The result was the appearance of a flood of papers in a number of fields in the natural sciences, the social sciences, and engineering, which embodied new and often Western scientific approaches and did so under the banner of cybernetics. For a number of years, papers that were abandoning old orthoxodies cited Khrushchev and labeled themselves as cybernetic.

In the West, mathematical models for complex problem domains had been introduced in a number of fields under a variety of different names. Mathematical economics, operations research, input/output analysis, Monte Carlo techniques, information theory, game theory, system engineering, factor analysis, and other statistical techniques in the behavioral sciences all had origins prior to, and independent of, cybernetics in the United States. Mathematization and computer modeling in both engineering and the biological and behavioral sciences developed under all of those names. Even at its peak, cybernetics as a label was used in the United States by only a small subset of all of the users of computers and mathematical models. In the Soviet Union, however, such models had been much less developed and were not in significant use in the behavioral and social sciences. When the floodgates opened, all of these mathematical ideas useful in the analysis and computer modeling of complex systems—and indeed the very notion of doing such modeling—became identified with cybernetics.

CYBERNETICS AND SYSTEMS THEORY
A Search for Identity

Richard Mattessich

Murray Eden brings a wealth of historical material to bear on the task of clarifying relations between cybernetics and system theory as well as other connected areas. To disentangle those relations is an arduous task, since cybernetics, general system theory, operations research, systems analysis, computer science, communications theory, information science, artificial intelligence, automata theory, and so forth, all overlap with each other to a greater or lesser extent. This network of interrelations might be less complex were it not for the human urge to devise impressive labels and classification schemes and to cling tenaciously to one's own home-made categories. But this itself could be the consequence of our inability to come to grips with the universe as an indivisible entity. And, knowing no better, scholars proceeded, each in his or her own fashion, to chop reality into fairly arbitrary conceptual bits and pieces. However, the history of science assures us that in time, every paradigmatic storm settles down and a conceptual scheme emerges that appears fairly satisfactory even if not optimal. As some thirty years or more have passed since many of these areas have come into being, we should expect that most of the consolidation has taken place. This, indeed, seems to be the case, but perhaps not so definitely as to preclude some supplementation or moderate divergence of opinions.

As can be concluded from Eden's presentation, the term *cybernetics* has a narrow and a broad meaning. In the narrow and original sense, it represents "the science of control and communication in the animal and the machine." [Wiener, 1948 and 1961.] It is in this sense that it is usually understood in the Western Hemisphere, while in East European countries, as Eden points out, it is used in a much broader sense, which comes close to, or is identical with, our understanding of system theory. But the relation between cybernetics

Additional support from the Social Sciences and Humanities Research Council of Canada is gratefully acknowledged.

(in the narrow sense) and systems theory becomes clear only after grasping the reason why the former is only a part of the latter. This can best be demonstrated by discussing the major ideas and components that modern system theory consists of. And we may thus distinguish the following basic ideas and notions of the systems approach:

1. Organization and emergent properties.
2. Structure, hierarchy, and evolution.
3. Function and goal orientation.
4. Information, control, and feedback.
5. Environment and its influence.
6. System laws and mathematical homologies.

ORGANIZATION AND EMERGENT PROPERTIES

A major concern of Aleksandr Bogdanov [1913 and 1922; 1980] and Ludwig von Bertalanffy [1928 and 1933; 1950; 1968], the founders of system theory, was the reductionistic and atomistic attitude of the physical sciences and the related neopositivistic philosophy. Due to this attitude and to the fact that the biological and social sciences were about to borrow a good deal of their methodological inventory from the physical sciences, the phenomenon of emergent or holistic properties, especially those of living or social systems, was unduly neglected. But not even in physics and chemistry could those newly emergent properties be explained in terms of mere aggregation.[1] This initiated the quest for *principles of organization* within the framework of which the unique status of emergent properties could be given due recognition and which, in time, might even acquire explanatory powers. It is for this reason that Bogdanov's book [1913] was called *Tektologia* and bears the subtitle *The Universal Science of Organization* and why Bertalanffy [1968, p. 187] speaks of an *organismic revolution,* the core of which is supposed to be the notion of system. Closely connected with this is James G. Miller's [1978] hint that Alfred N. Whitehead, with his "philosophy of organism," might be the founder or precursor of system philosophy, and Miller's assertion that the "key concepts later accepted as basic to systems science occur in his [Whitehead's] writings." (J. G. Miller, 1978, p. xiii.)[2]

---

[1] For example, such holistic properties as the relatively harmless and useful properties of water or cooking salt that emerged from the combination of such explosive substances as hydrogen and oxygen or of no less dangerous substances as sodium and chloride, respectively.

[2] Personally, I am inclined to side with Wiener [1950, 1954, and 1967, pp. 27–28] in regarding Leibniz as the true precursor of the system approach. His monadology comes fairly close to a kind of system theory, although we believe that a monade is not to be identified with a system, but rather with *the reflective* (i.e., mental or quasimental) *aspect* of a system.

Of particular interest to us is the fact that Norbert Wiener—either in his books on cybernetics [1948 and 1961; 1950, 1954, and 1967] or in his later work [1949, 1964]—is *not* concerned with the problem of emergent properties and those organizational aspects that make this concern inevitable. Therefore, it seems that his cybernetics lacks the broad quest for principles of organization beyond those referring to control, homeostasis, and feedback information. It should be admitted, however, that Wiener's book *Cybernetics*, especially its last chapter, is concerned with several aspects of organization in the general sense.

SYSTEM STRUCTURE, HIERARCHY, AND EVOLUTION

Much of the literature of modern system theory is concerned with a concept very closely related to that of organization, the notion of structure or form as *the relation between elements*. Some system theorists go even so far as to regard a system as "an abstract relation on a set of objects" [see Mortazavian in this volume], thereby identifying and possibly confusing the structure of a system with the system itself [see footnote 7 and my comment on Mortazavian's paper].[3] Of special concern to system theorists are the hierarchical relations encountered in most systems and the fact that every system (except the cosmos seen as "the system of all systems") is embedded in an environment that also appears to be subjected to a further hierarchy. Thus, the concern with many system properties (such as open system, closed system, etc.) is characteristic for this approach. Our present world picture, formed by relatively recent insights into atomic and subatomic physics, astrophysics, and astronomy as well as the biophysical and biomolecular extension of evolution theory, conforms with such a hierarchy of open systems, in spite of the perennial uncertainty about the ultimate building stones of our universe. Here, too, Wiener's cybernetics does not seem to pay much heed to hierarchical relations (and many of their properties) that span the universe—whether we go from quarks to galactic clusters or through the hierarchic structure of a cell or larger organism. Might the reason for this neglect be the fact that Wiener, like many of us, realized only in the 1950s and 1960s that stars, galaxies, and the universe itself are subject to *evolutionary* changes—changes that ensure, on one side, the existence of structures and, on the other side, the impermanence of those structures? Only after such a realization might the notions of structure and hierarchy assume their full and pervasive significance.

---

[3] A more correct definition is presented by Oskar Lange: "Generally speaking, 'system' is taken to mean a set of elements together with the set of relations between the elements. The set of such relations (and their isomorphic transformations) is called the *structure* of the system." (Lange, 1962 and 1965, p. 17.)

FUNCTION AND GOAL ORIENTATION

One of the most crucial aspects found in system theory, but lacking among the concepts of traditional science, is the notion of goal orientation or purposiveness.[4] Physics and chemistry can get along without it fairly well (although the concept of *entropy* may weaken this statement), but there is growing evidence that the biological sciences and certainly the social sciences need the idea of goal orientation and the related notions of preference, value, efficiency, and so forth, most urgently. And it is no coincidence that the biochemical theory of the Nobel laureate Manfred Eigen [1971] introduces a value function into biology that has at least some affinity with the value function in economics.

Most of the approaches dealing with systems strongly emphasize the notions of purpose, goal orientation, efficiency and effectiveness of goal attainment, and so forth. But surprisingly enough (as Eden points out), Wiener does not deal with such notions in his cybernetics, in spite of the fact that he considered them in an earlier, coauthored paper. It is revealing for Wiener's thought process that the subject index of his work on cybernetics and society [1950, 1954, and 1967] contains only a single entry under *purpose,* and this pertinent passage must be taken as a rejection rather than an acknowledgment of this very notion: "Here I want to interject the semantic point that such words as life, *purpose,* and soul are grossly inadequate to precise scientific thinking." (Wiener 1950, 1954, and 1967, p. 45; emphasis added.) Such a radical attitude with regard to the notion of purpose is not typical for a general-systems theoretician, mainly because the applied and social sciences, and to some extent even the biological sciences (see Monod [1970 and 1971] and Jacob [1971] and their *project télénomique* possessed by every organism; see also Eigen [1971]) are in need of various notions of goal and goal attainment. But some proponents of the systems approach caution us by asserting that "biology does not have a single law statement, let alone theory, containing the concepts of plan (or design) and purpose." (Bunge, 1979a, p. 120.)

INFORMATION, CONTROL, AND FEEDBACK

The fact that cybernetics (in the narrow sense) is more or less limited to this area of control information, forms the strongest argument in favor of regarding cybernetics as a subset of systems research. The insights that (1) a control state is dependent on the pertinent information-flow and (2) the scientific laws governing control are universal, hence, independent of the traditional dichotomy between living and nonliving entities, seem to form

---

[4] And the hierarchy connected with this notion: state-maintaining, goal-seeking, multigoal-seeking, purposive, and purposeful. [Ackoff, 1971, p. 665.]

the essence of Wiener's cybernetics and undoubtedly are necessary conditions, though by no means sufficient conditions, of systems thinking. The application of the theory of information, homeostasis, and feedback to system theory constitutes a crucial achievement of applied mathematics, but this application is the natural consequence of a much broader set of empirical and philosophic ideas.

ENVIRONMENT AND ITS INFLUENCE

From the very beginning of system theory, the notion of environment has played an essential role. Apart from the fact that it represents the logical counterpart of the system notion, it performs important analytical and practical services in bounding a system and determining whether certain properties or phenomena (e.g., norms) are part of the system influencing the environment, or whether they impinge from outside on the system. [Mattessich, 1974*a*; 1978, chap. 2.] Distinctions—as those between internal versus external structure and relations; subsystem, system, and meta- or supersystem; and so forth—are consequences of this basic but perhaps artificial dichotomy between system and environment. There is little evidence that Wiener made any conscious use of this fundamental notion. And yet, the great analytical and pedagogic value of the system/environment dichotomy has become one of the hallmarks of the systems approach. We encounter it everywhere, whether we listen to a television program in which Jonathan Miller [1978] demonstrates the analogy between the *artificial inner environment* of a stratospheric airplane and the human bloodstream or whether we read a National Aeronautics and Space Administration report on the no less artificial environment afforded an astronaut by a space suit.

SYSTEM LAWS AND MATHEMATICAL HOMOLOGIES

An essential feature of systems theory is, or at least ought to be, the search for general laws underlying all systems and laws underlying more specific but still fairly general system-types. If at least a few such nontrivial laws can be found, the systems approach may, indeed, become a theory, although hardly an entire scientific discipline or a superscience. But if such laws prove to be elusive or fairly insignificant or too specific, then the systems approach will remain a mere methodology, the ideas and tools of which will be absorbed in time by the methodology of general science or some specific disciplines. At this moment, it seems that the latter alternative is more likely to occur. Although the systems approach belongs to empirical science [see my comment on Mortazavian's paper in this volume], the prospect of formulating fairly general and yet powerful empirical system hypotheses is not very bright; at best, we have *mathematical homologies,* which, however, do *not* make the systems approach an analytical discipline like logic or pure mathematics. Such homologies may best be illustrated by the isomorphism between a mechanical and an electrical oscillator. [Compare Rapoport, 1968*b*, p. 455.] From his introductory physics lessons, the reader may remember that the force $f(t)$ impacting a mechanical oscillator is

$$f(t) = m \frac{d^2x}{dt^2} + r \frac{dx}{dt} + kx,$$

where x is the spatial displacement of mass m, while r and k are coefficients of friction and elasticity, respectively (t stands for time and d and d^2 are the differential operators). Surprisingly, the impressed electromotoric force $E(t)$ of an electric oscillator (as used, for example, in radio and television) is expressed by the following relation *isomorphic* to the one previously stated:

$$E(t) = L \frac{d^2q}{dt^2} + R \frac{dq}{dt} + Cq,$$

where L stands for inductance, R for resistance, C for capacitance (and t and d or d^2 maintaining the previous meaning). This reveals significant structural homologies between mechanical and electromotoric force, mass and inductance, mechanical friction and electrical resistance, elasticity and electrical capacity. Perhaps the best evidence for the nonaccidental and empirical nature of these formal or mathematical homologies lies in the fact that the amount of heat produced by overcoming the mechanical friction is identical to that produced by overcoming the electrical resistance. Cybernetics and information theory did, indeed, produce such homologies, but again, they are fairly limited to feedback and homeostatic mechanisms, on one side, or analogies of entropy and negentropy, on the other side. While the present practice of system theory—especially applied system theory as practiced, for example, by the International Institute for Applied Systems Analysis (IIASA) in Laxenburg, Austria—operates on a much broader empirical basis but with homologies and system models of a lower level of generalization.

CONCLUSION

These few considerations will, I hope, help to sharpen our distinction between cybernetics and the more comprehensive systems approach. But Eden is quite correct in pointing out that in both areas "we face a procedural dilemma" that "other domains of scholarship do not ordinarily pose." To regard both of them as viewpoints and methodological tools instead of scientific disciplines might be the ultimate resolution. As regards the contradiction (to use Eden's expression) between Mesarović—who leans toward a purely analytical presentation of system theory (mathematical system theory)—and others, like Bertalanffy, who have a much broader vision of the systems approach, I may refer the reader to my comments on Mortaza-vian's contribution in this volume. There, it will become obvious why other domains do not ordinarily pose such a problem of contradiction. In physics, for example, there could be no doubt that such theoretical physicists and model-builders as John A. Wheeler, Murray Gell-Mann, and Stephen Hawk-ing are serving an empirical and not an analytical science, while some sys-tem theorists and model-builders, such as Mortazavian, seem to regard themselves as being in the service of an analytical discipline. The confusion and apparent contradiction is due to the failure of some mathematical-system theorists to stress two important and related facts, that (1) applied mathematics is the application of mathematics to *factual* sciences and (2) propositions represented by more or less *unrealistic* system models are still *empirical* propositions independent of their degrees of reliability and real-ity.[5] Thus, I wholeheartedly agree with Klir, Eden, and others that we must distinguish between "systems theory as a viewpoint" and "mathematical systems theory." But since there is a plurality of system theories, even of mathematical system theories, there is little justification for using the singu-lar for the entire area or subarea. Comprehending it as a viewpoint, we might talk about a systems approach, which implies its philosophic and especially its *methodological* aspects. [Mattessich, 1978.][6] We might also construct, as Bunge [1979a] does, a *systems framework* out of which various system theories may emerge through further interpretation. And for the purpose of empirical research as well as training scientists, the systems approach can-not be limited to the construction of mathematical models, but must include studying concrete systems and fitting abstract models to those concrete systems.

To conceive of an abstract system as a set of objects with one or more relations between at least two of those objects[7] seems at first glance to be a most simple or trivial methodological device. But the same holds true for Descartes's idea of representing algebraic functions by the geometric means of a coordinate system or Einstein's idea of transforming the *physical* phe-nomenon of the curvature of light (under the influence of mass) into the

---

[5]The renowned mathematician René Thom offers an interesting discussion about the distinction between the concrete (morphological) and the abstract (mathematical) notion of a system and points out that "from a mathematical viewpoint, the systemic approach leads to a rather sketchy theory." (Thom, 1980, p. 3.)

[6]This point of view comes close to that of Rapoport, who suggests that "general systems theory is best described not as a theory in the sense that this word is used in science but, rather, as a program or a direction in the contemporary philosophy of science." (Rapoport, 1968b, p. 452.)

[7]There is a crucial difference between this system definition and that of Mortazavian, admit-tedly based on that of Mesarović [1964a]. Apart from the fact that we distinguish between a concrete and an abstract system, our definition of the latter is first of all a special kind of *set of objects* and *not merely a set of relations* between those objects. As can already be seen from footnote 3, I respect the importance of this set of relations, but it represents the *structure* of the system, not the system itself.

geometric phenomenon of curvature of space or Gödel's idea of mapping all components of an axiomatic system into the system of natural numbers (Gödel numbers). The proof of the pudding does not lie in the degree of complexity of a methodological device, but in the consequences emerging from this device. Undoubtedly, the ideas of Descartes, Einstein, and Gödel have proved immensely fertile. But is this also true for the systems approach? Although the latter has gained much popularity, something still seems to be missing. This is not to deny that conceiving of reality as a hierarchy of interacting systems with emergent properties has certain methodological advantages; but we should ask two questions: How vast is the potential of this idea? And is there still a crucial step to be made in order to exploit the full power of this methodological device?

I have previously expressed the need for a formal or mathematical superstructure of system theory [Mattessich, 1978, pp. 18–24], and perhaps the solution lies in a comprehensive attempt to axiomatize system theory. The formalizations by mathematicians such as Kalman, Falb, and Arbib [1969], Mesarović, Macko, and Takahara [1970], and above all, Mesarović and Takahara [1975], are serious and meritorious attempts in this direction. The most comprehensive attempt is Bunge's [1979a] ontological framework of systemics, which I discussed in some detail elsewhere. [Mattessich, 1982.] Although at this stage it is difficult to assess the future potential of the system notion, the systems approach certainly is worth further exploration.[8]

---

[8]In connection with Eden's paper and my present comment, it is interesting to note that the British Journal *Kybernetes* (Thales Publications Ltd.) initiated the (1977) Norbert Wiener Competition under the closely related title, "The Unity between Cybernetics and General Systems Theory," published in its vol. 8 [1979] with pertinent contributions by Counelis (third prize), Gergely, Majumder (first prize), Mayne, Stanley-Jones, and Zeleny (second prize). I am grateful to George Gorelik, University of British Columbia, for drawing my attention to this particular publication.

CYBERNETICS IN THE INFORMATION DISCIPLINES

Manfred Kochen

Murray Eden concludes his essay on the history of cybernetics with the implication that the only function of cybernetics was to diffuse the principles of communication and control engineering into the culture of science and technology and to integrate itself into it. That has in fact been its primary effect. But it had more than one intended function. Another was to identify analogous or identical concepts in diverse fields and analyze those that are essentially mathematical by appropriate mathematics. It has not yet performed this function with equal success. The prospect of that happening in the next decade or two is the first point on which I would like to comment.

The second point concerns Dr. Rosenblueth's insistence on the need for teams of scientists to establish fruitful connections among principles of communication and control engineering and living systems, as reiterated by Wiener in *Cybernetics* and quoted by Eden. The need for teamwork is more urgent today than ever before, not only for interdisciplinary scientific research but for many survival-related activities. Despite the trend toward segregation into increasingly narrow specialties, as indicated by Eden, there are now techniques and signs of hope that this trend could be reversed.

My third point is stimulated by the phrase "the map of science" in the same quotation of Rosenblueth by Wiener. Cybernetics did not become a distinctive discipline or specialty as pointed out by Eden, though he hints that like other intersections of different disciplines, in time it might become yet another specialty. Under what conditions do new scientific specialties come into being, survive, wax or wane, merge with others, and die out? What is the likely role of cybernetics in the emerging information disciplines? A catalyst? One of them? A substrate?

It is quite possible that a new discipline of scientific planning to steer and manage complex human systems will emerge to perform one of the major intended functions of cybernetics: interdisciplinary teamwork in both scientific research and social development on a set of concepts related to synergetics. [Haken, 1980, p. 121.]

STIMULATING NEW MATHEMATICS AND COMPUTATIONAL ALGORITHMS

The attempt to link principles of communication and control to living systems by searching for essentially mathematical concepts common to the study of man-made and living systems can lead to new mathematics. One of the first such contributions came from Alan Turing's model of two interacting chemical species. [Turing, 1952.] This was a precursor to the theory of dissipative systems and more generally to the study of cooperative phenomena. [Nicolis and Prigogine, 1977; Eigen and Schuster, 1977, 1978; Thom, 1975.] It appears to have stimulated or at least reinforced the emergence of the mathematical specialty known as bifurcation theory. Though it had mathematical roots 200 years ago in Euler's time and was greatly advanced by Wiener's coauthor, Hopf, it has undergone vigorous development only recently. [Rollo May, 1973; Hopf, 1943; Sattinger, 1980; Stakgold, 1971; Arnol'd, 1972; Mittelmann and Weber, 1980.] It is the study of equations whose solutions bifurcate or branch out when a parameter in the equation is changed. Renewed interest in bifurcation theory was stimulated by results about cascading bifurcations and chaotic regimes.

It is not quite true, as asserted in the quotation of Minsky in Eden's paper, that the approach based on "perceptrons," or self-adjusting learning devices, has subsequently died out: A major effort on related lines of inquiry is underway at Rockefeller University. [Edelman, 1981; Edelman and Mountcastle, 1978.] It is based on the Darwinian notion that there must be sufficient preexisting diversity for self-selection of neuronal groups that respond to external patterns and whose success is reinforced by an amplification process. A second-order repertoire that operates selectionistically on the neuronal groups of the first-order repertoire is also postulated. Though this model is being analyzed with the help of a complex computer simulation, there appears to be a rather profound theorem underlying this, and this may stimulate the development of a mathematics of patterns of considerably greater sophistication than that which already exists.[1]

The mathematics underlying the study of pattern recognition appears to be in ferment. Not only are there promising signs of better understanding of the problem from novel psychological, engineering, and physiological perspectives [Uhr, 1982; Rosenfeld and Kak, 1976; S. R. Sternberg, 1980; Ermentrout and Cowan, 1980; Blaivas, 1977] but there are signs of new mathematics as well [Grenander, 1976; 1978].

The reliability of the human nervous system is remarkable. [Asratyan and Simonov, 1975.] It has been known for some time that large parts of a rat's brain can be extirpated without major behavioral deficits, suggesting that the brain acquires its reliability at the cost of redundancy. This is also what

---

[1] Marvin Minsky and Seymour Papert, *Perceptrons* [1969]. The invention of the perceptron was reported by Frank Rosenblatt [1958] and developed more fully in Rosenblatt, *Principles of Neurodynamics* [1962].

engineers have been doing in designing reliable computer systems. John von Neumann was the first to see the essentially mathematical problem common to both engineered and living systems, and this has led to a line of research, the full potential of which has yet to be developed. [von Neumann, 1956; Moore and Shannon, 1956; Kochen, 1959; S. Winograd and Cowan, 1963.]

Though the stimulus to several other promising areas of new mathematics could be traced to Wiener and cybernetics, only two will be mentioned. The first is the use of probabilistic and computational methods in even as pure a branch of mathematics as number theory.

To test whether a number n, less than, say, $2^{400} - 593$, is prime, select a random sample of 50 numbers $a_1, \ldots, a_{50}$, each less than n, and test if a_i is a witness to the nonprimality of n by checking that n does not divide a_i^{n-1} for each i. If all a_i fail this test, call n prime; the probability of error is less than $(1/4)^{50}$ or $(1/2)^{100}$. The computational complexity of such an algorithm is far less than that of a nonprobabilistic one. Somewhat similarly, the four-color conjecture has been settled with the help of a computer analysis of cases. While such methods are not universally accepted in the mathematical community, they are increasingly used by its leaders and may contribute to the way we think in mathematics. The idea of thinking stochastically is as profound as the Newtonian idea of thinking continuously or the Poincaré idea of thinking qualitatively. One of the roots of thinking stochastically is in a central tenet of Wiener's formulation of cybernetics: Our capacity to control is inherently incomplete and *necessitates* a statistical approach.

The same tenet may also have been a precursor to "fuzzy-set theory." Control engineers, interested in designing a system that could park a car, for example, did not believe that the classical mathematical concepts used in designing control systems were appropriate. [Zadeh, 1965; Lowen, 1981; Goguen, 1967; Smets, 1982.] A person performs the task in what seems to be a totally different way. He or she does not measure the variables fed back to the visual system with any greater precision than he or she specifies control variables with the motor system. Nor did probabilistic concepts appear to be fruitful. Instead, a new kind of mathematics was spawned that started from a generalization of the characteristic function of a set, replacing its two-valued range by the interval [0, 1]. Thus, the characteristic function of the set of large numbers for a particular judge was interpreted as the degree of membership in the class (fuzzy set) of large numbers assigned to any number x by that judge. For $x = 1$ to 10, it might be 0, for $x = 11$ to 50, 0.1; for $x = 51$ to 100, 0.2, and so forth; and for $x > 1000$, it might be 1. Fuzzy-set theory has stimulated contributions of a purely mathematical nature, though its future standing among the mathematical specialties cannot yet be forecast.

THE PROSPECTS FOR TEAMWORK

It would appear that contemporary young scientists are more broadly and deeply trained than their predecessors. Nearly every good science student encounters in undergraduate education more basic modern mathematics, physics, chemistry, and biology than was known when the previous generation attended school. This is the result of the doubling of knowledge every decade and the availability of ever better aids to learning. Thus, few physiologists today *ought to be* ignorant of mathematics and computation.

Yet, the very growth of knowledge has forced each contributor to confine attention to an increasingly narrow area of specialization in which he or she can keep up with all that is important to that area. In staying within the bounds of cognitive capacity, he or she has to decide not to keep up with what falls outside that specialty. This lack of keeping up may lead to loss of fluency, competence, confidence. Thus, a physiologist whose specialty is not mathematical physiology may be considered to be ignorant of mathematics.

Many of the tasks facing researchers as well as planners and decision-makers concerned with communications and control are increasing in complexity. Rapid progress in identifying neurobiochemical constituents, physiological functions, and anatomical structures of the nervous system has vastly increased the number of phenomena to be explained. Hormones, peptides, and opiates are made in the brain, and there are special receptors for them. The nervous system shows a remarkable degree of genetic predetermination and neuronal specificity.

The difficulties of controlling very large computer operating systems or dealing with many large, diverse databases or with the many incompatible parts of a large computer-communication system are being recognized. It is rare that one person can master the overall structure of a complex modern system.

The number of variables representing first-order effects has increased. What were higher order variables a few decades ago (e.g., air pollution from automobile exhaust) that could be neglected in an engineering approximation are now of first order. Interaction among variables is greater. The stakes are higher. There is more knowledge that must be sorted for relevance at the same time that there are fewer directly relevant experiences to guide us in coping with complex tasks.

We can cope by fragmenting the task or through teamwork. The trend has been toward reductionist analysis or fragmentation. As noted previously, each specialist is restricted to what he or she can cope with, and communicates at best with follow specialists. It is as if 49 blind men were grouped into 7 groups of specialists, each group thoroughly probing one part. Wiener and Rosenblueth realized that cybernetics, as a program, could not flourish in this way, and they insisted on a broader view of teamwork. The need has now become urgent.

The hope is that teamwork may now also become feasible. Despite the remarkable degree to which the scientific community responded with teamwork on a grand scale to the challenges of World War II, Wiener was not optimistic. There are perhaps fewer grounds for optimism today. But many people in all walks of life seem spontaneously to have become aware of a threat far greater than that of World War II: the extinction of mankind by nuclear holocaust. The corresponding challenge is disarmament followed by the replacement of national sovereignty in the international system. [Schell, 1982.] Grass-roots responses of a mass nature, from scientists and nonscientists alike, appear to be organizing themselves and may lead once again to cooperative teamwork toward insuring survival. The threat of irresponsible or accidental military action is not the only challenge. The possibility that information technologies will pervade all aspects of the economy and dramatically reduce the total world's need for human labor is another challenge requiring cooperative and perhaps equally radical responses. The threat to our biosphere and ecological balance is yet another major challenge that is being temporarily put aside.

The new technologies themselves, for example computer conferencing and computer networks, may help with team formation and maintenance. Trends toward decentralization may influence corresponding trends toward teamwork. [Kochen and Deutsch, 1980.] The possible leveling effects of computers on the distribution of power may generate changes in our reward system, shifting some of the emphasis from competition to cooperation. These are hopes, not expectations. But they are all we have.

A NICHE IN THE MAP OF SCIENCE?

It is now possible to display a "map of science" in graphic form. By defining the proximity of two published papers according to, for example, how many other papers each cited both of them, it is possible to group the papers as well as their authors into proximity clusters. It is curious that given the "distance" between every pair in a large sample of papers, the application of multidimensional scaling techniques results in a map for which just two dimensions suffice. [Small and Griffith, 1974.] It is then possible to see how this map changes from year to year; how some clusters break apart, move toward or away from others or fuse with others; and so on. Each such cluster can be interpreted as a specialty at some level.

If cybernetics were to re-emerge as yet another specialty, this method of mapping science would detect it, albeit with a great deal of interpretation. The American Society for Cybernetics has recently, under new leadership, experienced something of a renaissance. But that can also be said for various related areas discussed by Eden: systems theory, control theory, communication theory, and so forth. *Systems theory* and *communication theory* seem to have a greater variety of multiple meanings than does cybernetics. There are at least three disparate versions of systems theory and as many totally different connotations of communication theory. The information disciplines can be said to encompass all these areas; yet, cybernetics stands out as one of their major common ancestors.

CYBERNETICS
The View from Brain Theory

Michael A. Arbib

CYBERNETICS AN UMBRELLA TERM

Murray Eden starts his review with the sentence: "Norbert Wiener, in his book entitled *Cybernetics, or Control and Communication in the Animal and the Machine,* did not define explicitly the word he believed he had coined." Surely, the book's title *is*, at least implicitly, a definition. However, Eden is correct to stress that Wiener's book is intensely personal and brings together a vast array of hitherto disparate topics. He places Wiener's book in a historical perspective that goes back to Hero of Alexandria and reaches the present day via Descartes and Ampère, among others. I trace a similar history in my companion article ("Cognitive Science: The View from Brain Theory"), where I argue that the history of cybernetics is, in large part, also the history of cognitive science. This is consistent with Eden's discussion of the permeation of psychology by cybernetic concepts and counterbalances Pylyshyn's overemphasis on mathematical logic and artificial intelligence (AI) as driving forces in the development of cognitive science.

In our department at the University of Massachusetts at Amherst, we use the word cybernetics to refer to a conjoined study of brain theory and AI. [Lesser, 1981–1982.] However, there are many experts in AI who regard cybernetics as an outdated, outmoded term. They insist that there is no need for an umbrella term that relates AI to brain theory. Eden notes that others use the word *cybernetics* in the sense of any study of complex systems that is aided by a computer—a broad usage encompassing even mathematical economics. (This is particularly so in the Soviet Union, see [Arbib, 1966].) Finally, he suggests that, while some workers still use the word *cybernetics*,

This paper refers to research supported in part by NIH grant NS 14971 and NSF grant MCS 8005112 at the University of Massachusetts. Portions of the paper are adapted from a paper prepared for a symposium marking the 25th anniversary of the publication of Wiener's *Cybernetics*. [Arbib, 1975b.]

much of the original energy of the field has moved to a vast range of descendant disciplines. I think that this is true but still believe the umbrella term serves well to remind workers in different disciplines of the range of common concepts they share.

THE FATE OF WIENER'S CONCEPTS

In this section, I want to review briefly a number of topics in *Cybernetics* and discuss their appearance from a thirty-five-year perspective. I shall follow Eden in analyzing Wiener's book rather than analyze the other roots of cybernetics.

Statistical Mechanics

As Eden stresses, Wiener's book reflects strongly the influence of his rich experience in using *statistical* methods in control, communication, and filtering problems. In World War II, Wiener had studied problems of tracking, interpolation, smoothing, and prediction, particularly in relation to antiaircraft gunnery. The great insight of this study had been that we should not ask, "Here is a trajectory; now what is the best way of continuing it?" without having some information about what ensemble that trajectory belongs to. Having characterized an ensemble by the noise statistics of a stochastic process, we could make meaningful predictions, such as, "This is the proposed continuation of the trajectory to which the possible continuations will, in some well-defined statistical sense, come as close as possible." In his book, Wiener sought to unify these mathematical studies with his discussions with psychologists and physiologists, to lay the foundations for a new field, to be called cybernetics. Let me quote a passage from Wiener's book where he presents his views:

> . . . the theory of the sensitive automata is a statistical one. . . . To function adequately, [the automaton] must give a satisfactory performance for a whole class of inputs, and this means a statistically satisfactory performance for [the] class of inputs . . . which it is statistically expected to receive. Thus its theory belongs to the Gibbsian statistical mechanics . . . . (Wiener, 1961, pp. 43–44.)

Interestingly, many people working in cybernetics today (whatever their subdiscipline) do not hold this particular view. While workers continue to relate the study of brains, biological systems, or social systems with the study of mathematical and engineering systems, statistical methods are not of central importance. For example, the AI approach essentially ignores statistical questions, focusing on whether a heuristic or knowledge representation can help solve a problem most of the time. But this "most of the time" is not in any statistical sense, and there is no question of having an ensemble and using the techniques of statistical mechanics to estimate "the statistics of success."

Turning to brain theory, we find that models today are not statistical. We went through a period of glorious ignorance when, not knowing enough about the brain, we looked with awe at the great complexity of the neural net and said it must be random. Much work in the 1950s and 1960s sought information about the average activity of a statistically connected neural network, with hopes of explaining the alpha-rhythm from the statistics of such a network. In recent years, though, I would say that brain models have become more detailed and more deterministic as we have had much more detailed neurophysiological and neuroanatomical information. Those models that are statistical do not usually employ the techniques of Gibbsian statistical mechanics, but instead emphasize learning algorithms within the tradition of self-organization and pattern recognition. [Amari, 1974; Grossberg, 1976; Sutton and Barto, 1981; Widrow, 1964.]

I would say, then, that the Gibbsian statistical-mechanics approach is dead in the classic core of cybernetics. However, as I will discuss in the section on brain theory, cognate methods—the theory of competition and cooperation in neural nets—are now gaining increasing importance.

Feedback and State Variables

Wiener knew from his engineering experience that if the gain is too high in a feedback system, it will go into unstable oscillations. This led him to suspect that there might be a form of human brain damage that would cause the human's limb to go into violent oscillations when the patient tried to pick things up. Sure enough, that turned out to be the case—his clinician friends showed him such an effect in patients with cerebellar lesions. This is perhaps the root of the whole development of control-theoretic analysis of complex biological systems. [Milsum, 1966.]

Wiener's discussion of filtering, feedback, and stability does not use the idea of a state variable; rather, he discussed how, given the infinite history of the machine's input, we could specify the infinite story of its output. He did not ask such questions as "What is going on inside the box?" or "How can we relate the internal dynamics to the input/output behavior?" It is Rudolf Kalman, perhaps as much as anyone, who has made state-variable thinking mandatory in system theory. [Kalman, Falb, and Arbib, 1969.]

As Eden notes, Wiener suggested that "the computing machine must represent almost an ideal model of the problems arising in the nervous system." This might seem at cross-purposes with the previous emphasis on statistical mechanics. However, Kalman and Richard Bucy provide a rapprochement, for they showed how to replace the history-based statistical extrapolation method, known as the Wiener-Hopf filter, by the state-based recursive estimation technique, known as the Kalman-Bucy filter—which, implemented in computer hardware, is an integral part of guidance systems in today's planes, missiles, and spacecraft. [Kalman and Bucy, 1961.] Interestingly, the extrapolation problem has recently resurfaced in brain theory, with the look-ahead modules of Andras Pellionisz and Rodolfo Llinas, though, unfortunately, they have not tried to apply these earlier successful techniques from system theory. [Pellionisz and Llinas, 1979.]

Internal Models

When a system is carrying out some control task, its parameters may not be quite matched to its job. This suggests the need for what Wiener calls *informative feedback* and what most of us today would call either *model-referencing* or *feed-forward*. Here, we augment the core feedback-system by using an identification procedure to upgrade the parameters of the core system at the same time that it is locked into a feedback loop for ongoing control.

What is very interesting from our present perspective is that despite this feed-forward idea, there is no mention in Wiener's book of the work of the psychologist Kenneth Craik. Craik wrote perhaps the first work in cybernetic psychology—though, of course, not yet with that name. [Craik, 1943.] He looked at the nature of explanation and stressed the idea of our building in our heads a complex model of our world, not in the cardboard-and-glue sense, but, nonetheless, a model that could modulate our input/output behavior to match our experience of our world. This idea, not in n-dimensional differential-equation format, but in a very general data-structure format, has become crucial to much of the exciting work in artificial intelligence. We saw Shakey the robot using visual input to build an internal model of the world about which it will navigate [Nilsson and Raphael, 1967], while Terry Winograd based his approach to linguistics on having the computer able to refer to a model of its simple world of blocks on a table top when "disambiguating" sentences that it is using. [Winograd, 1972a.] The last ten years of AI have been dominated by a retreat from general methods and an increasing emphasis on techniques for representing specialized domains of knowledge—the so-called "expert systems." [R. Davis and Lenat, 1982; Shortliffe, 1976.]

So it goes on. We could relate the work in neurophysiology since 1948 to Wiener's interests; we could follow Wiener's notions on intermodality coding; and we could discuss at length the social problems that have become an inescapable reality since 1948. Nevertheless, here I must leave this retrospective look at Wiener's book. What I hope to have done is confirm Eden's demonstration that Wiener had a broad intellectual range and many of the questions Wiener raised are still very much alive, though transformed and enriched by the developments—both technical and conceptual—of the last 35 years.

BRAIN THEORY

A few years ago, I discussed two specific aspects of my research that may be viewed as having descended from Wiener's work (among others). [Arbib, 1975b.] First, I explored some contributions in modern system theory—the descendant of Wiener's control theory—by giving a nonmathematical prospectus for the highly mathematical study of "machines in a category" that Ernest Manes and I conducted at the University of Massachusetts (reviewed by [Arbib and Manes, 1980]) and, second, I turned to a discussion of brain theory. Rather than repeat here the discussion of machines in a category, I want simply to recall its conclusion. We concluded that our general insights into the functioning of systems had come about only because we could use category theory to build on the theories of sequential machines, linear systems, and tree automata. We had a sufficiently rich set of particular theories as examples, and we had a sufficiently general mathematical theory to provide the language for their unification. Brain theory, unlike mathematical systems theory, is only now building up a reasonable stock of good examples of theories of limited applicability, which may serve as a basis for developing powerful general techniques that can be brought to bear on a wide variety of specific problems relating the physiology and anatomy of neural circuitry.

For example, early studies of the role of lateral inhibition in, for example, contrast enhancement in sensory systems can now be related to models of mode selection, where emphasis is on directing attention to one mode, feature, or set of features of activity, rather than on preprocessing an array for further computation. [Ratliff, 1965.] These models are in turn part of a broad class of models dealing with competition and cooperation in neural nets.

One of the first models of decision-making in neural circuitry to explicitly opt for cooperative computation was the S-RETIC model. [Kilmer, McCulloch, and Blum, 1969.] It suggested how the reticular formation of the brain stem might switch the organism's gross state from one overall mode of behavior in the organism to another. Based on the anatomical work of Madge and Arnold Scheibel, Kilmer and McCulloch believed that a reasonable structural simplification of the system was a stack of poker chips. [Scheibel and Scheibel, 1958.] (The Scheibels' work may be cited as one of the earliest contributions to modules of neural structure intermediate between brain region and neuron. [Mountcastle, 1978.]) In the S-RETIC model, each module in the stack receives a sample of the overall system input and on the basis of that sampling, assigns weights that provide likelihood estimates for each of the different modes. Initially, these estimates are based only on a local sample. However, the modules are coupled in such a way that each module readjusts its weights on the basis of activity in other modules to which it is connected. Kilmer and McCulloch suggested a connection scheme that would lead to eventual consensus, with a majority of the modules assigning the greatest weight to a single mode—all without any executive control.

We now turn to the topic of segmentation of visual input from two eyes on the basis of depth cues. Bela Julesz designed random-dot stereograms in which each eye receives a totally random pattern but in which different regions in the two inputs are identical save for a shift in position, yielding a different disparity on the two retinas. [Julesz, 1971.] Although such a pattern for a naive subject can initially appear to be visual noise, disparity-matching takes place eventually, and the subject perceives surfaces at different depths. Neurophysiologists have found that cells in a cat's visual cortex are tuned for retinal disparity, and similar cells are posited in the human. What presumably causes the initial perception of visual noise is that in addition to the correct correlation of points in the two retinas, there are many spurious correlations, and computation is required to reduce them.

Parvati Dev was one of several workers to propose that the cells of a given disparity be imagined as forming a population arrayed in a spatial map corresponding to the map of visual direction. [Dev, 1975.] Connections between cells could then be arranged so that nearby cells of a given disparity would be mutually excitatory, whereas cells nearby in visual direction but different in disparity would have inhibitory interaction. In this way, the activity of the array would be organized into a pattern where cells of only one disparity-type would be highly active in each region of visual direction. As a result, the visual input would eventually be segmented into a number of distinct surfaces. (See David Marr's posthumously published magnum opus, *Vision*, for an influential approach to such problems. [Marr, 1982.])

In the stereopsis model, then, we have competition in the disparity dimension and cooperation in the other dimensions. We note the similarity to S-RETIC, where the cooperation dimension is the row of modules, and competition is between modes rather than disparities. Other workers have shown that a number of interesting features of visual psychophysics can be captured in a fairly simple neural network in which we have two interacting populations of cells—excitatory and inhibitory—with plausible interconnections. Such a model exhibits hysteresis, one of the most famous psychophysical manifestations of which is seen in fusion. Such hysteresis phenomena are also central to the study of stereopsis. Informal observations of this kind have laid the basis for rigorous mathematical analysis, which also subsumes an early model of frog prey-selection. (We note that these neural mechanisms are similar to the relaxation methods for segmentation and region labeling in machine vision. [Hanson and Riseman, 1978.]) A recent United States–Japan seminar brought together applied mathematicians, brain theorists, and neuroscientists to present a body of experimental and theoretical techniques in brain theory. The papers, collected by Amari and Arbib, give a good picture of both successes in building general theory and also the many strands of theory and experiment that still need to be tied together—or trimmed away completely. [Amari and Arbib, 1982.]

Another area of brain theory of continuing interest is the control of movement, including Nikolai Bernstein's theory of synergies (motor schemas)

[Bernstein, 1967; Gel'fand, Gurfinkel', Tsetlin, and Shik, 1971], but it is beyond the scope of this paper to review related studies of cerebellum and motor learning and studies of the role of optic flow in controlling locomotion. [See, for example, Arbib, 1981; Szentágothai and Arbib, 1974.]

Eden quotes Wiener's observation that the work of McCulloch and Walter Pitts linked neurophysiology and mathematical logic, using the all-or-none property of neuron firing to model the neuron as a binary discrete-time element. [McCulloch and Pitts, 1943.] This was a historically valuable observation, for it linked the study of effective computability to the study of neural nets and played a seminal role in the later development of automata theory. [Shannon and McCarthy, 1956.] However, modern brain theory no longer uses the binary model of the neuron, instead using continuous-time models that either represent the variation in average firing rate of the neuron or actually capture the time course of membrane potential. [Rall, 1964; Rinzel, 1978.] It is only by containing such correlates of measurable brain activity that brain models of the kind just discussed can really feed back to biological experiments. Such models also require the cybernetician to know a great deal of detailed anatomy and physiology as well as behavioral data. As I say elsewhere in this volume, I believe that the study of visuomotor coordination is one where the relation between brain theory and artificial intelligence is a very healthy one, for workers in both areas can fruitfully share ideas on how complex psychological functions may be distributed over an array of subsystems. We might then hope to break down these subsystems into neural terms rather than attempting to pass immediately from the overall organismic behavior to the activity of the individual neurons.

Cybernetics, at least in the areas of mathematical systems theory, brain theory, and artificial intelligence is alive and well. But, as Eden observes, whether or not scientists working in those areas care to call what they are doing *cybernetics* is an entirely different question.

CYBERNETICS

Closing the Loop

Murray Eden

In my paper, I have attempted to describe the place of cybernetics within the current constellation of scholarly disciplines by attending to Norbert Wiener's published statements and to two histories: that of the usage of cybernetics and the scientific fields Wiener included within cybernetics. Each of the commentors has added to the picture in ways largely complementary to mine and to one another. The differences between us are largely interpretative nuances.

Michael Arbib uses cybernetics "to refer to a conjoined study of brain theory and artificial intelligence." Indeed, in his comments on the lead paper by Pylyshyn, Arbib suggests that cognitive science is *Cybernetics Redux.* Having made this identification, Arbib discusses the influence of Wiener's ideas on studies of brain and behavior. He notes that some of the mathematical tools Wiener considered to be central have been superseded; new concepts and tools have transformed modern attempts to relate mathematical brain theory to observations by neurophysiologists, psychophysicists, and psychologists. Whereas Arbib is correct in discerning a direct line of descent from Wiener's cybernetics to current studies in artificial intelligence, his definition of cybernetics is too narrow, in that it appears to exclude communication *among* animals or humans. Wiener devotes the last chapter of *Cybernetics* to "Information, Language and Society." [Wiener, 1948 and 1961.] It is true that this chapter is, in large measure, a polemic against the venality of the free market, and the stupidity of the State, but before Wiener arrives at that point, he discusses the cybernetic aspects of intercommunication among social animals. Arbib's predilection leads him to the conclusion—a correct one given his definitions—"that the Gibbsian statistical-mechanics approach is dead in the classic core of cybernetics." But, as with artificial intelligence, theories intended to describe information exchange among humans or animals—for example, theories for explicating the social behavior of animals or theories of pattern analysis—exploit the common patrimony of cybernetics. Both are heavily statistical. Thus, we note that Manfred Kochen reports the studies of pattern recognition to be sources of better understanding and new mathematics. The work of the probability theorist Ulf Grenander to which Kochen refers, accords statistics a central role. [Grenander, 1976; 1978.]

Kochen observes that scientists who want to use cybernetics must begin by looking for matches between constructs in their fields of study and the concepts of cybernetics. The analogies will be fruitful if they lend themselves to mathematical description and can be analyzed by appropriate mathematics. Kochen's crucial point is that when suitable mathematics does not exist, it must be invented; hence, cybernetics can lead to new mathematics. This is hardly a function unique to cybernetics. Scientists borrow good concepts wherever they can find them; witness the older use of the notions of mechanics and kinematics in fields as disparate as economics (e.g., elasticity) and population genetics (e.g., selection pressure). Nonetheless, the point is well taken.

Kochen cites, as his earliest example, Alan Turing's remarkable model for generating morphological symmetries from a family of arbitrary but chemically plausible reactions. Kochen follows this thread to the theory of dissipative systems and bifurcation theory. He cites other progressions that are, historically speaking, largely autonomous—theories of learning machines, patterns, reliability, fuzzy sets, and number theory. Even if some of the connections to cybernetics are tenuous, this is an impressive list.

Richard Mattessich undertakes to demonstrate that cybernetics (in the narrow sense) is only a part of system theory. He argues that there are six ideas basic to systems thinking, of which only one is fundamental to cybernetics. Mattessich points out that Wiener was almost entirely unconcerned with the problems we must face in explaining such biological or social phenomena as the emergence of new properties, evolutionary change, hierarchical structures, the environment and its influences. He also states that Wiener did not deal with notions of purpose or goal orientation in his cybernetics. This latter statement is not precisely correct. Four years before *Cybernetics* appeared, Wiener coauthored a paper entitled "Behavior, Purpose and Teleology." [Rosenblueth, Wiener, and Bigelow, 1943.] Wiener later described its genesis; he and Bigelow, an engineer, had asked Rosenblueth, a physician and physiologist, the following question:

> Is there any pathological condition in which the patient, in trying to perform some voluntary act like picking up a pencil, overshoots the mark, and goes into an uncontrollable oscillation? Dr. Rosenblueth immediately answered us that there is such a well-known condition, that it is called purpose tremor, and that it is often associated with injury to the cerebellum.

> We thus found a most significant confirmation of our hypothesis concerning the nature of at least some voluntary activity. . . . This seemed to us to mark a new step in the study of that part of neurophysiology which concerns not solely the elementary processes of nerves and synapses but the performance of the nervous system as an integrated whole.

The three of us felt that this new point of view merited a paper, which we wrote up and published. (Wiener, 1948, p. 8.)

It would appear that even in this paper for philosophers of science, Wiener was concerned, not to explain nor use the concept of purpose, but to explain the manifestation of purpose by analogy to a control problem. In the larger sense, Mattessich is right; Wiener rejected *purpose* as a word "grossly inadequate to precise scientific thinking." Indeed, Wiener was not a general-systems theoretician.

I believe Mattessich is successful in his intention "to sharpen our distinction between cybernetics and the more comprehensive systems approach." As Mattessich points out, the founders of system theory were dissatisfied with reductionism as the scientific paradigm for explaining the phenomena of biological and social science. Therefore, they turned to a different set of ideas and components that, in Mattessich's view, comprise modern systems theory. Wiener approached science quite differently. Although Wiener in his early years was a student of philosophy and logic, by the time he occupied himself with the notions of cybernetics, he had become an applied mathematician. His interest was in quantitative science, the invention or use of mathematical theories that modeled a science with *empirical content*. He searched almost obsessively for analogies, in neurology for example, to test with his mathematical paraphernalia. Undoubtedly, much of what he considered needed to be treated at the phenomenalistic level, but I find no evidence in his writings that he believed ultimate reduction to mechanism was unlikely. Quite the contrary, he looked to statistical mechanics for the real answers. He may have been wrong in this particular view, but his approach is still well within the mainstream of current approaches in neurophysiology, psychophysics, and perceptual psychology.[1]

I suggest that Wiener's attitude toward science is the key to understanding his lack of concern with the problems that are central for systems theorists. In a few instances, as with *purpose*, he regarded them as nonproblems, because they were "inadequate to precise thinking." In other instances, for example, on issues of political or social science, he saw no prospect of success, because of technical reasons: The time series are too short and there are too many instabilities. He is quite explicit. He states:

I mention this matter because of the considerable, and I think false, hopes which some of my friends have built for the social efficacy of whatever new

---

[1] He is in good company. John von Neumann began his seminal paper on probabilistic logics with the statement: "Our present treatment of error is unsatisfactory and ad hoc. It is the author's conviction, voiced over many years, that error should be treated by thermodynamical methods, and be the subject of a thermodynamical theory, as information has been, by the work of L. Szilard and C. E. Shannon. The present treatment falls far short of achieving this, but it assembles, it is hoped, some of the building materials, which will have to enter into the final structure." (von Neumann, 1956, p. 43.)

ways of thinking this book may contain. They are certain that our control over
our material environment has far outgrown our control over our social environment and our understanding thereof. Therefore, they consider that the main
task of the immediate future is to extend to the fields of anthropology, of
sociology, of economics, the methods of the natural sciences, in the hope of
achieving a like measure of success in the social fields. From believing this
necessary, they come to believe it possible. In this, I maintain, they show an
excessive optimism, and a misunderstanding of the nature of all scientific
achievement. (Ibid., p. 162.)

We note that in the passage quoted, Wiener implied that *his* were "the
methods of the natural sciences."

Peter Elias has contributed a valuable addition to the brief history I have
presented. His comments on the Soviet response to the idea of cybernetics
are particularly welcome. His explanation of the difference between Soviet
and Western usage of the term *cybernetics* is both simple and plausible.
Elias points out that there were, almost from the beginning, different attitudes toward cybernetics in the United States and Europe. Sensitivities
with respect to terminology were heightened even within the community of
European workers. Elias cites W. Ross Ashby as the first author of a text on
cybernetics. [Ashby, 1956.] Curiously enough, Ashby, in his earlier *Design
for a Brain* makes only one reference to cybernetics. [Ashby, 1952 and
1960.] Colin Cherry, another early English worker in the field, much preferred the label *communication theory*. For him, a part of the theory was
"the theory of feedback (sometimes called cybernetics)." (Cherry, 1957, p.
21.) Later he writes:

> This wider field [communication theory and physics] . . . is referred to, at least
> in Britain, as *information theory*, a term which is unfortunately used elsewhere
> synonymously with communication theory. Again, the French sometimes refer
> to communication theory as *cybernetics*. It is all very confusing! (Ibid., p. 216.)

As a further example of the terminological dissonance, I am quoting from a
foreword that Meyer-Eppler, a German communication scientist and pho-
netician, wrote in his capacity as editor of a series on *Kommunikation und
Kybernetik*, in the first volume of that series, a book he had written himself:

> Max Bense has contrasted the classical (Archimidean) world emphasizing en-
> ergy and work with the nonclassical (Pascalian) world emphasizing information
> and communication. Although some aspects of the nonclassical world have
> been known for a long time, it has become accessible to systematic research,
> transcending all narrow overspecialization, only thanks to two essentially
> mathematical theories, *information theory* on the one hand and *theoretical
> cybernetics* on the other. . . . It is the task of *information theory* to open up to
> quantitative and structural comprehension either communication between per-
> son and person, as it manifests itself in *exchanges of symbols,* or communica-
> tion between man and the world, which essentially amounts to *observation*; by

contrast, *cybernetics* as "science of relations" (N. Wiener) employs mathematical methods to study regular patterns of behavior of highly complex energized systems, such as information-processing "machines," living organisms, and groups of organisms. (Meyer-Eppler, 1959, editor's foreword. Emphasis in the original. My own translation—M.Eden.)

The field of scholarship that the commentators and I are trying to characterize—I dare not try to assign it a name—appears to encourage terminological invention and yet greater confusion. For example, Kochen, disagreeing with Minsky as quoted by me, notes that perceptron-related work is being actively pursued. The work Kochen cites is quite close to work that Arbib includes within artificial intelligence. Minsky's definition is implied by the title of his book (with Papert), *Perceptrons—An Introduction to Computational Geometry*. [Minsky and Papert, 1969.] On the other hand, Rosenblatt, who coined the term *perceptron,* identifies it with a class of "brain models." [Rosenblatt, 1962.]

Mattessich has got it right when he attributes this tangle to "the human urge to devise impressive labels." I share with all four commentators a measure of regret that the taxonomy of the information sciences is still so ambiguous. Nevertheless, insofar as progress in scientific understanding is concerned, there is no great loss. Fortunately, whatever the global label, each particular research report is ultimately verified by the tests of the underlying domain of scholarship. To put it somewhat simplistically, if the work is mathematical, we check the theorems; if it is a model, we check to see whether it fits empirical observations. Perhaps we should be guided by Shakespeare: "What's in a name? That which we call a rose by any other name would smell as sweet."

SECTION 7

THIRTY YEARS OF INFORMATION THEORY

Myron Tribus

This paper is concerned with the impact of Shannon's 1948 paper "A Mathematical Theory of Communication," which was focused on the field of communications. [Shannon, 1948.] I especially wish to comment on the influence of Shannon's paper in fields other than communications. I approach the task with some hesitation: In 1961 Shannon, in a private conversation, made it quite clear to me that he considered applications of his work to problems outside communication theory to be suspect and he did not attach fundamental significance to them.

Despite Shannon's misgivings, as time goes on, his great contribution to the literature has made its existence felt in an ever-increasing number of fields. Shannon's clarification of the concepts of uncertainty and information and the ability to give a quantitative measure to these concepts has served as a powerful stimulant on the imagination of others. Of course, there have been numerous unjustified excursions in the name of information theory, but my studies show many solid accomplishments clearly inspired by this famous paper.

To test the spread of Shannon's influence, I thumbed through the *Engineering Index* and found that the first entry under the heading *Information Theory* occurred in 1951, only three years after his paper appeared. In 1952, there were eight entries; in 1953, there were thirteen entries, including three symposia and a reference to a bibliography containing over 1000 references to information theory. By 1958, ten years after Shannon's paper, the *Engineering Index* contained several pages of titles covering papers in the field of information. Many of the entries were references to symposia that themselves contained between fifteen and twenty papers on information theory. I can report also that the *Engineering Index* listing under the title *Information Theory* is incomplete. For example, in 1961, I prepared a paper on informa-

This is a slightly modified version of a paper first published as an article in Levine, Raphael D., and Tribus, Myron, eds., *The Maximum Entropy Formalism* (Cambridge, Mass.: MIT Press, 1979).

tion theory and thermodynamics. It was listed by the *Index* under *Thermodynamics* but not under *Information Theory*. There is, therefore, no easy way to track down all of Shannon's influence. For example, under the heading *Entropy*, the *Engineering Index* for 1961 merely says "See *Thermodynamics*." Once we know the field that was influenced, however, it is fairly easy to document the influence.

It is rather difficult to say where the field of information theory ends and other fields begin. Certainly, information theory overlaps significantly with many other fields. Define S = entropy, K = constant, p_i = probability of the truth of assertion i. For the purposes of this paper, I shall take the view that any field of inquiry that uses the function

$$S = -K \sum_i p_i \ln p_i \tag{1}$$

(or its continuous analog) in one of the following three ways is using information theory: (1) as a criterion for the choice of probability distributions; (2) to determine the degree of uncertainty about a proposition; and (3) as a measure of the rate of information acquisition.

Claude Shannon was not the first to use the function $-\Sigma_i p_i \ln p_i$, for this function (or its continuous analog) had been used as long ago as 1872 by Boltzmann. [Boltzmann, 1872.] What Shannon did was to give a universal meaning to the function $-\Sigma_i p_i \ln p_i$ and thereby make it possible to find other applications. Warren Weaver, in his popularization of Shannon's work, foresaw the widespread influence it was bound to have. Weaver understood that any paper that clarified our understanding of knowledge was certain to affect all fields that deal with knowledge.

In the 1961 interview with Shannon to which I referred, I obtained an anecdote worth recording here. I had asked Shannon what his personal reaction had been when he realized he had identified a measure of uncertainty. Shannon said that he had been puzzled and wondered what to call his function. *Information* seemed to him to be a good candidate as a name, but it was already badly overworked. Shannon said he sought the advice of John von Neumann, whose response was direct, "You should call it 'entropy' and for two reasons: First, the function is already in use in thermodynamics under that name; second, and more importantly, most people don't know what entropy really is, and if you use the word 'entropy' in an argument you will win every time!''

THERMODYNAMICS

A field in which Shannon's interpretation of entropy has had a profound effect is classical thermodynamics. [Tribus, 1958.] In this field, the entropy function has a long and involved history. Clausius coined the word *entropy* from the Greek language to mean transformation and defined it via the equation

$$dS = \frac{dQ}{T}, \tag{2}$$

where dQ = increment of energy added to a body as heat during a reversible process;

T = absolute temperature during the reversible heat addition;

dS = change in entropy.

The function as Clausius introduced it was, at the time, quite mysterious. It was an extensive property, like mass, energy, volume, momentum, charge and number of atoms of the chemical species. Unlike these quantities, however, entropy did not obey a conservation law. Instead, it showed a tendency to increase spontaneously. At a time so profoundly influenced by the success of the various conservation laws in physics, when determinism was at its peak, a measure that always *increased* was indeed mysterious and called for an explanation.

Among scientists and engineers, there are those who speak of *discovering* the laws of nature, and then there are those who speak of *inventing* these laws. The former are more numerous; they include the majority of teachers and, therefore, students. The chief difference between the two types lies in differing interpretations of what constitutes an *explanation*. The former would require that all mysteries be explained in terms of things already known or new axioms that square with the old. The latter are ready to rewrite and reorganize *all* human knowledge in their quest for consistency. To the latter, there are no explanations—merely consistent ways of tracing ideas to their common logical sources.

I have dwelt on the word *explanation* because the arguments that have raged in thermodynamics hinge greatly on this point. The information-theory approach raises a question in the following way. Shannon's measure gives, by ordinary differentiation,

$$dS = -K \sum_i (\ln p_i + 1) \, dp_i. \tag{3}$$

But since $\Sigma_i p_i = 1$, we have $\Sigma_i dp_i = 0$, and, therefore,

$$dS = -K \sum_i \ln p_i \, dp_i. \tag{4}$$

On the other hand, from classical thermodynamics, we have

$$dS = \frac{dQ}{T}. \tag{5}$$

How then are we to explain these two equations for dS?

In 1953, Brillouin formally stated the case for a close connection between these two entropies. [Brillouin, 1953.] He followed his early paper with several others and with his famous book on *Science and Information Theory*. [Brillouin, 1962.] In these publications, Brillouin showed there was an intimate connection between entropy and information, but he did not think it necessary to define one in terms of the other. Brillouin treated the field of thermodynamics as correct and preexisting, and he treated Shannon's information theory as a correct theory. He then proceeded to demonstrate a *consistency* between the two entropies.

As early as 1911, Van der Waals had proposed that there ought to be a connection between Bayes's equation in probability theory and the second law of thermodynamics. [Van der Waals, 1911.] As we now know, Shannon's measure can be derived through the use of Bayes's equation. [Tribus, Evans, and Crellin, 1964; Good, 1950.] In 1930, G. N. Lewis, in a discussion of irreversibility, had written "Gain in entropy means loss of information—nothing more." [Lewis, 1930.] As I mentioned earlier, Boltzmann had used the H-function as early as 1872.

In 1938, Slater based his book on the definition

$$S = -k \sum f_i \ln f_i, \tag{6}$$

choosing this expression for entropy over the more conventional one,

$$S = k \ln W, \tag{7}$$

which is used by most authors in statistical thermodynamics (f_i = fraction in microstate i; W = number of ways to realize a given macrostate). [Slater, 1938.]

With these historical antecedents, Brillouin evidently felt no need to take one concept as more primitive and felt no need to explain the others in terms of it. But he pointed the way.

It was E. T. Jaynes who first saw the complete answer and presented it in a sequence of brilliant and historical papers. [Jaynes, 1957a, b.] As shown in Equation (1), the entropy is defined by the probability. Jaynes turned it around: He proposed that Shannon's measure of uncertainty (entropy) be used to define values for probabilities. Prior to Jaynes's contribution, workers in statistical mechanics were forced to rely on classical thermodynamics for their ideas about entropy and develop statistical mechanics as "an analog." [Gibbs, 1948; Denbigh, 1955.] There had been no clear and unequivocal reason to define entropy in statistical mechanics other than the after-the-fact conclusion that since statistical mechanics works, it must be all right. Jaynes showed that by starting with the extremum of S [via Equation (1)] statistical mechanics was derived in a few lines. In 1961, after careful study of Jaynes's paper, I demonstrated that all of the laws of classical thermodynamics, and, in particular, the concepts of heat and temperature, could also be defined from Shannon's entropy using Jaynes's principle of maximum entropy. [Tribus, 1961*a*, *b*..] The debates engendered by this approach have been extensive and, on occasion, bitter. I have concluded from them that thermodynamics is as much a branch of theology as it is a branch of science! It is very comforting to be able to show that although Gibbs did not explain how or why he decided in 1901 to set the logarithm of the probability of a system linearly proportional to the energy and numbers of particles, thereby producing his "statistical analogs," he did say that the expected value of ln p is a minimum; that is, $-\int p \ln p \, dv$ is a maximum. [Gibbs, 1902; 1948.] So we may conclude that the Gibbs and Jaynes formalisms are essentially the same.

Using the information measure as a primitive idea, my colleague Robert Evans has been able to demonstrate that thermodynamic information is proportional to what has been called *availability* in thermodynamics. [R. B. Evans, 1966.] Actually, Evans has shown that a new function, which he calls "essergy" (and which is related to the function used in Germany under the name *Exergie*), is at once a measure of information and a measure of the potential work of systems. We have used the essergy function in the optimization of such thermal systems as sea-water-demineralization plants and steam-turbine generators. [El Sayed, 1968; El Sayed and Aplenc, 1968; El Sayed and Evans, 1968.] The original impetus for these developments came from Shannon's work.

STATISTICS

Jaynes has converted Shannon's measure to a powerful instrument for generating statistical hypotheses, and he has applied it as a tool in statistical inference. The mathematical aspects of Jaynes's use of Shannon's measure are straightforward. If the given information is in the form

$$\sum p_i = 1, \tag{8}$$

$$\sum p_i g_r(x_i) = <g_r>, \qquad r = 1, 2, \ldots m, \tag{9}$$

the minimally prejudiced (i.e., least presumptive) probability distribution is the set of p_i that obeys the $(m + 1)$ Equations (8) and (9) and maximizes

$$S = -K \sum_i p_i \ln p_i. \tag{10}$$

The resulting distribution is

$$p_i = \exp [-\lambda_0 - \lambda_1 g_1(x_i) - \lambda_2 g_2(x_i) \ldots], \tag{11}$$

where the λ's are Lagrangian multipliers. The entropy is

$$S = \lambda_0 + \sum_{r=1}^{m} \lambda_r <g_r>. \tag{12}$$

And the potential function, λ_0, is

$$\lambda_0 = \ln \sum_i \exp\left[-\sum_r \lambda_r g_r(x_i)\right]. \tag{13}$$

The Lagrange multipliers are related to the given data by the equation

$$-\frac{\partial \lambda_0}{\partial \lambda_r} = \langle g_r \rangle. \tag{14}$$

The higher moments are given by

$$\frac{\partial^2 \lambda_0}{\partial \lambda_r^2} = \text{var}\,(g_r) \quad \frac{\partial^2 \lambda_0}{\partial \lambda_r \partial \lambda_s} = \text{covar}\,(g_r g_s). \tag{15}$$

For other relations, see Jaynes or Tribus. [Jaynes, 1957b; Tribus, 1969.] Jaynes's principle shows that if Shannon's measure is taken to be *the measure* of uncertainty, not just *a measure*, the formal results of statistical-mechanical reasoning can be carried over to other fields.

Jaynes proposed, therefore, that in problems of statistical inference (which means problems for which the given data are inadequate for a deterministic prediction of what will [or did] happen), the probabilities should be assigned so as to maximize

$$S = -K \sum p_i \ln p_i \tag{16}$$

subject to

$$\sum_i p_i = 1 \tag{17}$$

and any other given information. Jaynes thus essentially *defines* probabilities via Shannon's measure. From this basis, we can see that any field that uses probability theory is a candidate to be influenced by Shannon's work.

I must confess that in 1957 I felt there was no explanation to be had and complained publicly that Shannon had confused things by calling two different ideas by the same name! I was forced to retract that ill-considered judgment in a footnote to my paper "Thermodynamics: A Survey of the Field" and wish now that I had retracted the whole paper! [Tribus, 1958.]

THERMODYNAMICS (AGAIN)

An explanation of the two entropies can be had only if we clarify our ideas about what we mean by (1) heat dQ, (2) temperature T, and (3) probability p_i.

What Shannon's work did, as interpreted by Jaynes, was to make it possible to take the information-based entropy as the *primitive* concept and explain dQ, T, and p_i in terms of S.

Jaynes's initial publication demonstrated that this approach permitted a derivation of statistical mechanics. He later went on to give illustrations of the use of this principle in decision theory [Jaynes, 1963], communication theory [Jaynes, 1957a, b], and transport theory [Jaynes and Scalapino, 1963].

RELIABILITY

It was also straightforward to use the same approach in reliability engineering. [Tribus, 1962.] In this case, the maximum-entropy principle was used with Bayes's equation to show how to form an initial estimate of reliability and then incorporate field-test and laboratory data as they become available.

STATISTICS (AGAIN)

Shannon's measure occurs in statistics, but unless we are attuned to its meaning, the significance of Shannon's function in any one case is apt to go unnoticed. For example, in hypothesis-testing, I demonstrated that the empirical fitting of experimental data to a probability distribution is expedited and rendered more accurate via maximum-entropy methods. [Tribus, 1969, chap. 7.]

I have also demonstrated that in the analysis of the contingency tables the first approximation to an exact Bayesian test for statistical dependence between attributes A_i and B_j is given by the measure

$$\Delta S^* = -N \sum_i f_i \ln f_i - N \sum_j f_j \ln f_j + N \sum_i \sum_j f_{ij} \ln f_{ij}, \qquad (18)$$

which simply tells us to compare the sum of entropies in the margins of the contingency table with the entropy of the center and see where the information resides. It is especially satisfying to be able to report that the first-order approximation to the right-hand side of Equation (18) is the familiar chi-square statistic. [Tribus, 1969, chap. 6.]

PSYCHOLOGY

Once the measure of uncertainty had been established, psychologists were quick to recognize its utility. In 1949, only a year after Shannon's article appeared, Miller and Frick published an article illustrating the relevance of the theory to psychology. [G. A. Miller and Frick, 1949.]

The first class of psychological problems to attract attention quite naturally centered on the human being as a communicator or receiver of information. Shannon had already given some impetus to the field by his analysis of the information content of symbols in the English language. Shannon's clever techniques provided brand-new tools for psychologists already attracted to engineering literature by Wiener's provocative publications on cybernetics, which had just appeared. Indeed, the appearance of popular treatments of feedback theory, decision theory, game theory, and information theory has had a profound effect on all of science. The impact on society of the computer and these theories was not only in the hardware and resulting increase in human ability to control and compute. They also had an effect on the way people thought about things. We all appreciate how looking back at the earth from space influenced our ability to think of "spaceship earth." But the introduction of the concepts of *feedback* and *signal-to-noise ratio* also influenced the way we thought about what we were doing. Physicians began to understand that the degree of feedback could influence our nervous systems. Psychologists in education began to see examinations as a form of feedback. The impact of the computer goes beyond its ability to do sums. No one who has ever written a computer program, especially one with branches in it, can fail to appreciate the idea of an algorithm. Such a person is likely to begin to apply it to, say, social decision-processes or political situations. A decision-tree is not only a way of portraying a method to describe uncertainty. It can also become normative and influence how people think about uncertainty and public risk-taking. Taken all together, these theories ushered in the age of *the knowledge worker* and *the information revolution*.

By 1954, William McGill was using differences in entropy between the margins and the center of a contingency table to measure a subject's response to stimuli. [McGill, 1954.] This work was unknown to me until I began to prepare for this assignment. It is interesting to note that we can *derive* Shannon's measure from a Bayesian analysis of contingency tables and then show the chi-square measure as its first approximation. [Tribus, 1969.] Fred Attneave uses the chi-square measure to see how significant the entropy difference is! Attneave lists 87 primary references to information theory in the field of psychology. [Attneave, 1959.] The range of topics considered is most impressive. Included are such titles as "Information Theory and Immediate Recall," "Information in Absolute Judgments," "Informational Aspects of Visual Perception," "Uncertainty and Conflict," "Model for Learning," "Information from Dot and Matrix Patterns," "Relation Between Error Variance and Information Transmitted in a Simple Pointing Task," and "Information in Auditory Displays."

Irwin Pollack investigated the information transmission when nine different musical tones were used and found 2.67 bits with and 2.19 bits without objective standard tones. [Pollack, 1953.] Attneave reports that Rogers tested a concert master of a symphony orchestra having absolute pitch and found he could transmit 5.5 bits!

NEUROLOGY

Measuring the ability of people and animals to transmit and receive information through various sensory channels is an obvious way of applying information theory, and Shannon's work could be taken over almost unchanged for this purpose. George Miller has pointed out, however, that the conceptual foundations of information theory have as much importance as the numerical measure. They provide a method for organization and patterning. Miller points out that concepts of gestalt psychology may be put to test via information-theoretic concepts. [Miller, 1953.] The view that psychoneural activity is the economical encoding of experience may also be attributed directly to Shannon's influence.

It may properly be said that the penetration of field X by field Y is complete when the concepts of field Y are used to prepare a textbook for students in field X. In this sense, the appearance of Wendell Garner's book in 1962, explaining psychological concepts via information theory, was a milestone. [Garner, 1962.]

SOCIAL SCIENCE

An economist, Alfred Kuhn, has used concepts of uncertainty, feedback, and decision analysis to produce a unified treatment of learning, motivation, language, culture, personality, personal transactions, organization, social systems, economics, public policy, and the political process. It is Kuhn's thesis that the concepts of engineering are to be subsumed as special cases in the concepts of these social sciences. [A. Kuhn, 1963.]

OTHER FIELDS

New applications of information theory in turbulence theory are emerging from the work of Silver and his colleague Tyldesley in Glasgow. [Tyldesley, 1962.]

John P. Dowds has developed his own method of applying the entropy concept to an examination of data from oil fields. Based on such an analysis, he purchased the rights to an abandoned oil well in Oklahoma, and, today, this well, which he christened Rock Entropy #1, is a producer sufficiently generous to support Mr. Dowds's further researches into the uses of entropy. [Dowds, 1964.]

My colleague Alvin Converse has also applied the entropy concept in a search technique, using entropy as a measure of the information obtained from each sample point in the search for the maximum of a function in a bounded interval. [Converse, 1967.]

The maximum-entropy principle has been used in land-use planning and predicting travel between different communities. [A. G. Wilson, 1969.]

There seems to be a growing use of information theory in medicine. I have searched, via machine techniques, for articles referring to Shannon's 1948 article and Jaynes's 1957 article and turned up papers on rheumatism, bacterial populations in the Beaufort sea [Kaneko, Atlas, and Krichevsky, 1977], information-processing of schizophrenics [Wijesinghe, 1977; Neufeld, 1977], molecular biology [Berger, 1977], diagnostic value of clinical tests, and the nature of living systems [J. G. Miller, 1976].

The ideas have also spread over the globe. J. O. Sonuga in Lagos, Nigeria, uses the entropy principle to analyze runoff. [Sonuga, 1976.] In the Netherlands, Van Marlen and Dijkstra use information theory to select peaks for retrieving mass spectra. [Van Marlen and Dijkstra, 1976.] At the Free University of Berlin, Eckhorn and Popel apply information theory to the visual system of a cat. [Eckhorn and Popel, 1974.] In Canada, Reilly and Blau use entropy in building mathematical models of chemical reacting systems [Reilly and Blau, 1974], as does Levine in Israel [Procaccia, Shimoni, and Levine, 1976]. And I suppose we can say the subject has really arrived when it is referenced by the U.S. Congress Office of Technology Assessment! [Coates, 1976.]

The future we can perceive but dimly. But surely Shannon's paper deserves to be read by future generations with the same sense of intellectual adventure that we associate with the great works of the past.

THE WIDER SCOPE OF INFORMATION THEORY

Donald M. MacKay

Tributes to the genius of Claude Shannon are well merited, and as one of his earliest admirers, I gladly echo those paid by Myron Tribus. My purpose now, however, is to say something about those aspects of the concept of information that Shannon's theory (for good and clearly stated reasons) chose to ignore. For it is, indeed, the case, as Shannon so often insisted, that his theory did not define the concept of information at all. [Shannon, 1951, p. 219.]

INFORMATION AND ITS UNEXPECTEDNESS

What Shannon's famous $\Sigma p_i \log (1/p_i)$ defines is the mean *statistical unexpectedness* of an item of information selected from a given ensemble; and this measure is benignly agnostic as to the *meaning* of the items of information selected in a communicative process except insofar as it affects their prior probabilities of selection.

For this reason, I am not so sanguine as Tribus in his paper that "Measuring the ability of people and animals to transmit and receive information through various sensory channels is an obvious way of applying information theory." The basic problem, of course, is that the probabilities p_i in Shannon's formula presuppose a well-defined ensemble; but in the case of a human subject, it is not at all obvious how we should define the operative ensemble, let alone its relative frequencies. It is still less clear that what we really want to understand about human information-processing is always illuminated by appeal to the particular measure of unexpectedness that Shannon developed for the assessment of communicative channel capacity. To try to translate every reference to information (whether in biology or elsewhere) into a statement about unexpectedness would be as inept, and as conceptually Procrustean, as translating all references to a house into statements about its size.

THE SCOPE OF INFORMATION THEORY

Information theory, in the more general sense it has developed over the past forty years, is concerned with all processes in which the spatio-temporal *form* of one set of objects or events (at *A*) determines the *form* of another set (at *B*) without explicit regard for the energetics involved. These are situations in which we say that information flows from *A* to *B*. In this operational context, then, we can define information as *that which determines form*, in much the same way as force is defined in physics as that which produces acceleration.

In all cases, information is operationally defined (like energy) by what it *does*. [MacKay, 1954b; 1969.] But whereas the work done by energy is physical in character, the work done by information is logical work. In talking about information, there is always a suppressed reference to a third party, since, as in the physical theory of relativity, we have to relate our definitions to an observer, actual or potential, before they become operationally precise.

In communication engineering, the form of a received message can be determined in one of two ways: (1) by a process of *construction*, as when the form of a television picture is built out of light-spots; or (2) by a process of *selection* from a range of *preconstructed* forms in obedience to a code signal, which has no necessary isomorphism with the form selected but merely specifies its address, as in Morse code.

Shannon's theory was concerned with processes of type (2), where the prime question is how many (or how few) elementary code signals can be sufficient (on average) to identify each form required to be selected. His answer—brilliantly conceived and elaborated—was that the average number of elementary signals required is proportional to the weighted mean unexpectedness $\Sigma p_i \log (1/p_i)$; but that in "noisy" situations, reliability can be increased by using more signals per selection and designing a redundant code to allow errors to be corrected automatically. One of Shannon's greatest achievements was to show in a precise sense that a given noise level could, in principle, be offset by introducing a corresponding degree of redundancy, so as to achieve practically error-free communication of sufficiently long messages.

An ingenious analogue of this theorem, due to Winograd and Cowan, has shown how structural redundancy in a computing network can be exploited to achieve error-free computation with unreliable elements. [S. Winograd and Cowan, 1963.] This has important implications for the theory of information-handling networks, including the central nervous system, where distributed processing may be organized so as to optimize reliability.

Processes of type (1), in which forms are not selected but constructed, are typical of scientific experimentation. For example, data are accumulated and processed into the form of a graph, or light is transmitted through a microscope or telescope and forms an image on a photographic plate. In this context, the possibility of information measurement had been recognized for some time before the publication of Shannon's papers. The English statistician Ronald A. Fisher described in 1935 an additive measure of the *amount of information* in a statistical sample, which reduced itself in the case of a Gaussian distribution to the invariance $1/\sigma^2$, and quantified in effect the sharpness of estimation. [Fisher, 1935, p. 188.] In 1946, Dennis Gabor, who later received the Nobel Prize for his work on holography, defined a quite different *quantum of information* in signal transmission, which he termed a "logon." The number of logons in a signal represented the number of degrees of freedom of its structure—the minimum number of independent measurements mathematically necessary to define its form under given limiting conditions of frequency bandwidth and duration. [Gabor, 1946.]

About the same time, I was independently groping after some abstract way of quantifying the information derived from a physical experiment. Two distinct measures of the process of form-construction emerged at an early stage. [MacKay, 1950; 1951; 1954b.] The first, analogous to Gabor's logon-content, has to do with the *number of degrees of freedom* of the constructive process: For example, the number of practically discriminable elementary areas within the field of view of a microscope. This is an *a priori* measure, which in an optical instrument is related to the notion of resolving power and defines the complexity or logical dimensionality of the framework within which construction of the form is to take place.

The second, analogous to Fisher's measure of amount of information, has to do with the *weight of evidence* associated with each degree of freedom of a constructive process. This is an *a posteriori* measure, closely related to the concept of signal-to-noise (power) ratio, and illustrated in the case of a photographic image by the density of the silver grains. I gave it the name of metron-content.

The details of this formalism do not matter here. The point is that for different purposes, the question "How much information?" may need to be answered in quite different ways, according to the quantifiable aspects of the process of form determination that are relevant. As a typical example, consider the recording of electrical signals from the scalp of a human subject—the electroencephalogram (EEG). A band-limited amplifier gives an output with a finite number of degrees of freedom $(1 + 2t\Delta f)$, where t is the duration and Δf the bandwidth of the amplifier. This is the logon-content of the signal. If signal-to-noise ratio is poor, the operator may deliberately narrow the bandwidth, reducing the logon-content for the sake of a greater signal-to-noise (power) ratio per degree of freedom, or metron-content. The latter measures the weight of physical evidence contributed as to the magnitude of the signal, and its total over a signal is invariant under such processes as averaging.

Although logon-content and metron-content are quantities that can be bartered for one another in the foregoing sense, each is clearly a measure of a different and important aspect of the ability of a signal to determine form.

Furthermore, in a generalized sense of the term, we can speak also of the logon-content of the *spatial* distribution of EEG activity over the scalp. The important informational question here concerns the number of *substantially independent spatial areas* of the scalp (from an electrical standpoint). This logon-content determines the maximum number of electrode-placements necessary and sufficient to record all the structural information present in the distribution of scalp potential.

By contrast with the foregoing measures, the familiar Shannon-Wiener measure of amount of information (for which selective information content, SIC, is a useful distinctive term) would fasten on the *mathematical improbability* of the signal and ignore its structure except insofar as it bears on its probability.

It would clearly be absurd to regard these various measures of amount of information as rivals. They are no more rivals than are length, area, and volume as measures of size. By the same token, it would be manifestly inept to take any of them as definitions of the concept of information itself.

At the time when Shannon's paper [Shannon, 1948] and Wiener's book [Wiener, 1948 and 1961] appeared, then, some progress had already been made with the quantification of processes of form-*construction*, to which Shannon's quantification of the statistics of form-*selection* was valuably complementary. By 1949, a group of us in England had set about organizing the First International Symposium on Information Theory, which was held in the rooms of the Royal Society in London in 1950. Shannon was a leading participant, as was Gabor; and Fisher chaired one of the main sessions. The need for complementary measures of information-content was illustrated in several papers, and the scope of the new concepts was explored in such diverse fields as psychology and optics. [*Proceedings,* 1950.]

INFORMATION THEORY AND THERMODYNAMICS

A major topic of discussion at the 1950 meeting was the relation between Shannon's measure and the thermodynamic concept of entropy, first introduced into the theory of heat engines in the nineteenth century as a measure of the unavailability of thermal energy. The expression, derived from the statistical theory of gas molecules as a measure of their nearness to thermal equilibrium (and, hence, of their inability to work a heat engine), contains $\Sigma\, p_i \log\,(1/p_i)$ as a factor. What it signifies here, as Tribus has explained, is the amount of information (in the Shannon-Wiener sense of selective information content), concerning the detailed microstate of the molecules, that remains *undeducible* from the macrodescription available (in terms of pressure, volume, temperature, etc.)—in short, the extent to which the microstate is underspecified.

Now, every unit of missing information (in this sense) means that a corresponding amount of energy cannot be pinned down to do work. It turns out that this amount of energy is proportional to the temperature, so we can say that each unit of missing information costs us (i.e., deprives us of the use of) one unit of *energy per unit of temperature*. The physicist's name for energy per unit of temperature is entropy, and the unit in which it is measured (when logs are taken to base e) is called Boltzmann's constant and written k. Thus, the entropy of a mass of gas molecules is written

$$k \sum p_i \log\left(\frac{1}{p_i}\right).$$

Unfortunately, although it is not the mathematical factor $\sum p_i \log(1/p_i)$ but the unit k that here brings in Clausius's notion of entropy, the habit has grown of attaching the label entropy to the mathematical factor. It is rather as if, having used the expression $M \times (\Sigma a_i n_i / \Sigma n_i)$ for the mean mass of a population of objects, n_i of which had mass $a_i \times M$, and so on, we were to forget about the factor M and call the expression $\Sigma a_i n_i / \Sigma n_i$ by the name *mass*. If, then, we later found someone using the latter expression to calculate the mean *income* of a population, we can imagine the confusion that would be caused by talking of his or her measure as mass. [MacKay, 1964b.]

But such, alas, is the state of our subject. If it is too late to clear up the muddle by dropping the use of *entropy* for the information measure, the best we can do may be to call the expression $k \sum p_i \log(1/p_i)$ physical entropy, and use some such term as mathematical entropy to distinguish the dimensionless expression $\sum p_i \log(1/p_i)$. To call the latter by some simple and descriptive name such as mean unexpectedness or statistical variety would, however, seem a better way of removing the recurrent confusion. It would have the further merit of reminding us of the essentially *relative* character of the mathematical measure, which clearly depends for its magnitude on the particular body of evidence (or if we like, the particular observer) by which the probabilities p_i are determined. Any convention that helps avoid the notion that information is a kind of absolutely measurable "stuff" (like water) might be worth a little trouble to secure.

Curiously enough, thermodynamic entropy also turns up in a key role in calculating the metrical information content (metron-content) of a physical measurement. The ultimate limit to the accuracy of determination of a signal amplitude, for example, is the thermal energy per degree of freedom (i.e., per logon), which is classically $\frac{1}{2}kT$ (k = Boltzmann's constant; T = absolute temperature). This provides a natural scale-unit in terms of which to quantify signal energy per logon. For a unit signal (1 metron) on this scale, the physical-entropy increase is thus $\Delta S = \frac{1}{2}kT/T$ or $\frac{1}{2}k$. In general, then, it is the limiting metron-content that is proportional to the increase in physical entropy brought about by a received signal. If the signaling system uses all discriminable signal levels with equal frequency, then the average selective information content per logon [Shannon's $\sum p_i \log(1/p_i)$] will be proportional only to the logarithm of the average physical-entropy increase. There is nothing paradoxical about this, once we remember that the relative probabilities p_i are defined by quite different considerations in the respective ensembles of the thermodynamic state-description and the communication engineer's repertoire; but it underlines the importance of not identifying Shannon's measure uncritically with physical entropy.

INFORMATION THEORY IN BIOLOGY

The early 1950s saw a rush of would-be applications of Shannon's measure in biological contexts. A pioneering example was the work of Hick on the influence of the selective information content of stimuli on reaction time, where the significant feature of stimulation was not the physical specification per se, but rather the *number of alternative forms that it might have assumed but did not*. [Hick, 1952.] The idea that the range of forms *not* taken by the input might be relevant to its specification is a characteristic contribution of information theory, and one that might not have been thought so obvious without it.

Again, the concept of the *redundancy* of an input pattern as an experimental parameter has suggested a class of stimuli (such as optical patterns of near-parallel lines) that have revealed interesting new phenomena and may throw light on the neural mechanisms that encode those features that are redundant. [MacKay, 1957a, b; 1960.]

At the other extreme, the use of random noise (acoustic or visual) to provide a stimulus of *minimal* redundancy has helped to uncover another class of phenomena rich in clues to neural processes. [MacKay, 1965.]

As Myron Tribus has mentioned, such concepts as economical encoding seemed at first to permit straightforward transfer. With hindsight, however, a snag becomes obvious. Concepts like economy or efficiency can be defined only in relation to specific criteria of *cost*, and the problem is to determine what counts as costly in a biological system. To an engineer, cost is normally at least proportional to (or may even rise more rapidly than) the number of elements in a network. In assessing a biological system that can multiply cells at a relatively small *genetic* cost, however, it is obvious that our criterion of economy or efficiency may have to be drastically modified. Moreover, since Shannon's measure was designed for a context in which the engineer must be able and willing to adjust his or her repertoire of code signals according to the known statistics of the traffic, and install correspondingly complex decoding processes ad hoc, it can here give a quite misleading idea of efficiency unless the biological cost (and likelihood) of implementing these processes is included in the calculation.

All this adds up to the suggestion that in the biological realm, theorems and concepts of information engineering can seldom, if ever, be transferred directly to make predictions. Their value, as we have seen earlier, lies in their power to suggest new questions from a new angle and with a new thrust. [MacKay, 1959; 1964b; 1965.] As always, it is from nature's answer to these questions, rather than from our armchair theorizing, that our knowledge grows. Equally clearly, it is the quality of our thinking in the armchair that will determine whether the questions we ask receive a worthwhile answer.

INFORMATION THEORY AND MEANING

As early as our 1950 Symposium on Information Theory, it was felt to be somewhat scandalous that the theory of information seemed to have so little working contact with such concepts as the *meaning* and *relevance* of information. Once the framework is widened from the simple source-channel-sink model to include the sender and recipient of messages as goal-directed agents, however, the links are not hard to find. [MacKay, 1954b; 1969.]

Briefly, the key is to think of the act of communication as goal-directed to bring about certain states of affairs in the recipient. The recipient at any given time has (1) a store of factual information, (2) a repertoire of skills, (3) a hierarchy (or heterarchy) of criteria of evaluation and priorities. These three interlock in a complex manner so as to set up at any given time a certain total state of conditional readiness (SCR) for all possible action, including planning and evaluating action. It is this SCR that can be thought of as the operational target of a communication.

The meaning (intended, received, or conventional) of a particular communication can now be defined as its readying function (intended, actual, or conventional) on the SCR of the recipient. Distinctions then emerge automatically between indicative, imperative, interrogative meaning, and so forth, according to the particular aspects of the SCR that are the target in each case. [MacKay, 1961b.] Functional criteria of meaningfulness (or meaninglessness) follow in obvious ways, and the *relative* nature of all the foregoing concepts, including that of information itself, becomes explicitly obvious. By quantifying the degrees of freedom of the SCR in its various aspects, it is in principle possible on these lines to attach numerical measures to the transfer of information between cognitive agents, in essentially the same way as in an inanimate context. [Ibid.]

CONCLUSION

It is undeniable that much of the popularity of the information-theoretical approach, especially in the 1950s, can be attributed to the seminal work of Claude Shannon and Norbert Wiener on the quantification of uncertainty. It may also be true that some of the later disillusionment with that approach, especially among psychologists, stems from an initial lack of public clarity about the scope and limits of Shannon's theory (despite his best efforts) and especially from a widespread failure to distinguish the concept of information per se from various measures of its amount. It should be added that some of the most generally useful qualitative concepts of information engineering cited by Tribus, such as feedback and feedforward, have quite independent origins and owe nothing to the mathematical theory of information-measurement. [MacKay, 1954b.]

This said, however, I agree with Tribus in expecting information-theoretical concepts, both qualitative and quantitative, to play an increasingly fruitful role in the construction, testing, and (doubtless) demolition of theories of brain function and kindred processes in a multitude of other contexts.

INFORMATION THEORY
IN PSYCHOLOGY

George A. Miller

Some enterprises are defeated by success. I like to think that the application of information theory to experimental psychology illustrates this oxymoron.

It is true that Shannon's measure of information—the mean value of the logarithmic probability [see Tribus's Equation (1)]—is seldom seen these days in psychological publications. It enjoyed a vogue in the 1950s, became widely known among experimental psychologists in the early 1960s, and disappeared by the 1970s. Students, noting this history, usually assume that it disappeared either because it was proven false or, worse, because the intellectual position it represents became uninhabited. Neither assumption is correct.

What students cannot appreciate is what life was like before information theory. Perhaps an example will help. I recall a series of experiments intended to determine the absolute threshold for the perception of visual form. Alternative shapes were displayed in near darkness, and illumination was gradually increased until viewers were able to identify the shape correctly. Different experimenters obtained wildly different results. Today, it is almost inconceivable that such experiments could have been run without controlling the viewer's expectations of what shapes might occur and without instructing the viewer on the acceptable set of alternative responses. No wonder the results were all over the lot!

The point is that before anyone tried to apply information theory to such experiments, there had been no reason to think of the viewer as a channel or of stimuli as inputs and responses as outputs. If you wanted to estimate the amount of information transmitted by such a channel, however, it immediately became apparent that you had to form a matrix with the stimuli as rows, the responses as columns, and the cells as the frequencies of occurrence of particular stimulus/response combinations. How many rows? How many columns? In order to estimate the probabilities that were required in order to compute the transmitted information, answers to such questions had to be fixed and known. One consequence of trying to apply information theory to psychology, therefore, was a principled increase in the rigor of psychological experimentation.

No one today wants to give up these conceptual and methodological advances. The notion that people are channels through which information flows into storage or behavior is today a familiar part of most introductory courses in psychology.

So, why has information measurement disappeared? For various reasons. For one thing, the basic ideas of information measurement are now part of the general culture. Everyone learns about bits and bytes as part of learning about computers, which are everywhere. Explanations in psychological journals or texts are no longer needed. For another, it has turned out that the probabilities themselves are psychologically more interesting than their logarithms. Mathematical psychology has increased greatly in sophistication since 1950, and interest now is less in measuring channel capacities than in characterizing the processes that limit them. Generally speaking, ideas first introduced to experimental psychology through information theory have now become foundational assumptions that everyone takes for granted, their historical origins now irrelevant to their present role.

Psychological interest was not confined to transmitted information. Redundancy, the extent to which the future of a message can be predicted from its past, was also important. Formally, redundancy is equivalent to transmitted information—both are best viewed as nonparametric measures of correlation; in one case, a correlation between the input and the output of a channel; in the other case, a correlation between the history of a message and its next symbol. Shannon illustrated his theory of the message source by computing upper and lower bounds for the amount of information per letter that is encoded in printed English messages, and the techniques he used introduced psychologists to some new ways of thinking about the sequential organization of behavior.

Shannon's assumption that the sequential statistics of printed messages can be regarded as the product of a stationary stochastic process—specifically, a higher order Markov process—was peripheral to the more fundamental ideas of information measurement, but it served to alert psychologists to theoretical possibilities they had not previously discovered. Language was not the only place where psychologists were concerned with the sequential aspects of behavior. Here, too, information theory fed the growth of mathematical psychology.

This peripheral assumption soon came under attack, however, and the impression some students have that information theory was somehow disproved may result from misinterpretations of that controversy. Chomsky argued that any device that generates sequences of message elements must be a grammar; he proved that Markov processes are not adequate grammars for natural languages. Shannon, of course, had not proposed that his stochastic generator should replace grammar—it was (and still is) a useful engineering approximation—and so he felt ill treated by implications that he had somehow failed in doing something that he had never tried to do. In any case, by 1960, the basic statistical parameters needed for that kind of approximation of English were known, and further research into that question was unnecessary. By 1960, therefore, psycholinguists had moved on to new research on the psychological reality of various types of generative grammars.

*   *   *

According to Shannon's measure of selective information, the less probable a message is, the more information it contains. This definition sometimes conflicts with one's notion of semantic information. Of the two sentences, *Rex is a dog* and *Rex is a mammal*, for example, the first is surely more probable in normal, conversational English. So, according to Shannon, *Rex is a mammal* must communicate more information than does *Rex is a dog*, which is more probable and therefore less informative.

Stated so baldly, it is apparent that something about Shannon's measure is odd. To say *Rex is a dog* implies that Rex is a mammal, but to say *Rex is a mammal* leaves it open whether Rex is a dog, cat, horse, elephant, or some other mammal. Semantically, therefore, *Rex is a dog* must communicate more information than does *Rex is a mammal*, which reverses the conclusion based on Shannon's measure.

At the very least, therefore, it must be admitted that Shannon's is not a measure of semantic information. It is sometimes referred to as a measure of selective information, since it has to do with selecting a transmitted message out of the set of all other messages that might have been transmitted instead.

Could a measure of semantic information be developed? In 1952, Rudolf Carnap and Yehoshua Bar-Hillel published a technical report from the Massachusetts Institute of Technology Research Laboratory of Electronics, entitled *An Outline of a Theory of Semantic Information*. In that report, they dealt with semantic information only insofar as it applies to declarative sentences, or statements. The general idea was that the content of a statement is given by the class of possible states of the universe that it excludes. *Rex is a dog* excludes more possible states of the universe than does *Rex is a mammal* and so has more content.

Detailed development of this idea is beyond the scope of this comment, but some of the more obvious consequences can be stated. If statement S_1 logically implies statement S_2, then the semantic information carried by S_1 includes the semantic information carried by S_2 and possibly more. If S_1 logically implies S_2 and S_2 logically implies S_1, then S_1 and S_2 contain equal amounts of semantic information. A tautology is logically implied by every statement and so contains no semantic information. A contradiction logically implies all other statements and so contains the maximum amount of semantic information. The amount of semantic information in the conjunction of two statements is equal to or less than the amount in the first plus the amount in the second, and so on.

An interesting question for a theory of semantic information is whether there is any equivalent for the engineer's concept of noise. For example, if a statement can have more than one interpretation and if one meaning is understood by the hearer and another is intended by the speaker, then there is a kind of semantic noise in the communication even though the physical signals might have been transmitted perfectly.

Semantic information never enjoyed the vogue among psychologists that selective information once did. It is worth reviving here only for the perspective it offers on Shannon's theory.

ENTROPY AND THE
MEASURE OF INFORMATION

Peter Elias

Information theory in Shannon's original technical sense as a mathematical theory of communication was derived in part from Shannon's work on cryptography during World War II and in part from earlier work on communications. The technical theory has had a considerable evolution since Shannon's early publications. [Shannon, 1948; 1949.] Key technical steps in that evolution appear in the volume of collected papers edited by Slepian. [Slepian, 1974.] The texts of Fano [1961], Gallager [1968], and McEliece [1977] give successive views of the field. Current work is published in many journals, but the greatest focus is in two, *IEEE Transactions* [1955] and *Problemy* [1965].

Tribus cites Shannon's feeling expressed in a 1961 conversation, that applications of information theory outside of the theory of communications are suspect and of no fundamental significance. I agree in part and will explain more precisely just why many such applications seem suspect to me. I feel that it is particularly important to get this point straight in the context of the present study. It is necessary to go into a bit of technical detail in order to make the more precise statement.

Entropy, the information measure that Shannon defined for communications purposes and Tribus discusses in his paper, is one of many possible measures of the width of a probability distribution. Any number of measures of this sort can be constructed. By the excercise of sufficient ingenuity, one can construct (as Shannon and others have) a set of axioms that any reasonable information measure must satisfy and then prove that entropy is the measure that satisfies them all and is uniquely determined by the axioms up to a multiplicative scale factor, the constant K in Tribus's Equation (1), which can be absorbed in the choice of a logarithmic base in that expression. (It is usual to choose the logarithmic base 2, set $K = 1$ in Equation (1), and call the unit of information in the resulting measure the bit [binary digit], the information required to select one of two equiprobable messages.) However, R. A. Fisher [1934] had come up earlier with a quite different measure of information, which uniquely satisfied some requirements that seemed to

Fisher to be natural to impose on an information measure to be used for some statistical purposes. The real basis on which Shannon—and later everyone else—concluded that entropy is the uniquely correct measure for the purposes of communications is not the fact that it satisfies some axioms but, rather, the fact that by adopting a new, intrinsically probabilistic model of communication and making use of his measure, he could prove two results that do not hold for other measures.

Shannon's model of an information source is a random process that generates an infinite sequence of messages. In the simplest case, which I assume for the purpose of explanation, that process just chooses the next message from a fixed set of messages, using a fixed probability distribution, independent of prior choices. His first result says, roughly, that if a source selects messages from a probability distribution that has an entropy of H bits then,

1. There is a uniquely decodeable encoding of sequences of N source symbols into sequences of binary digits that, for any e greater than 0 and all sufficiently large N, takes on the average no more than $N(1 + e)$ binary symbols to represent the N source symbols.

2. There is no uniquely decodeable encoding of sequences of N source symbols into sequences of binary digits that for any N takes on the average less than NH binary symbols to represent N source symbols.

Shannon's second result requires a channel model and some additional definitions. Shannon's model of a channel has an input alphabet and an output alphabet and a conditional probability distribution that gives the probability of receipt of each of the possible output symbols conditional on the transmission of each possible input symbol. If the transmitter uses different input symbols with a probability distribution known to the receiver, then the natural measure of how much information is transmitted per use of the channel, on the average, is the average difference between the entropies of the receiver's estimate of the probability distributions on the transmitted symbols before and after receipt of each symbol. That is, the average amount of information the channel should be credited with sending from transmitter to receiver is the average difference between two quantities: (1) the total amount of information the receiver initially needs in order to find the value of the next unknown transmitted symbol and (2) the amount of information the receiver still needs after a noisy version of that symbol has been received, in order to remove the uncertainty introduced by the noise in the channel and inform the receiver exactly what symbol was in fact transmitted. If the channel is noiseless, then the second entropy—the subtrahend—vanishes: On receipt of the output symbol, the receiver knows exactly what was sent. But when the channel is noisy, receipt of a symbol reduces the receiver's uncertainty about what was sent on the average, but not to zero.

This difference-of-entropies measure is called the mutual information between the transmitted and received symbols. Its value depends not only on the channel but on the probabilities with which different input symbols to the channel are used. If the transmitter chooses to send only one of the possible input symbols all the time, then the mutual information will, in fact, be zero, since the a priori and a posteriori distributions and entropies will be the same. If, instead, the transmitter chooses input symbols from the probability distribution that maximizes the mutual information, then that maximum value is called the capacity of the channel and is usually denoted by C and measured in bits per channel use.

Shannon's second result can now be stated. It says, roughly, that if a communications channel has capacity C bits per channel use (in the sense just defined), then for any positive e,

1. It is possible to encode sequences of N binary digits into sequences of at most $N/(C - e)$ channel input symbols in such a fashion that for all sufficiently large N, the receiver, knowing the encoding codebook, can decode the noisy sequence of received output symbols into a sequence of N binary digits that matches the original binary sequence perfectly with probability greater than $1 - e$.
2. If sequences of N binary digits are encoded into sequences of less than N/C channel input symbols, then any decoding procedure used by the receiver gives an output binary sequence that has probability at most e of matching the original binary sequence perfectly.

The first of these results was revolutionary when it was discovered. Its import is that lack of reliability in a channel does not limit the reliability of the information that can be received over the channel: It limits only the rate at which information of arbitrarily great reliability can be received. And unlike the result of repeating each message an arbitrary number of times to obtain arbitrarily reliable reception, which gives arbitrary reliability only at zero rate, Shannon's second result says that the rate at which information of arbitrarily great reliability can be received is, in fact, as large as the maximum rate at which unreliable information can be received.

Together, Shannon's two results allow the solution, in principle, of any problem of matching a message source to a communications channel, noisy or noiseless, in two stages. First, take the message source with entropy H and encode sequences of its messages into sequences of binary digits. Then, encode each sequence of binary digits into a sequence of channel-input symbols, and send it over the channel at the allowed rate, decoding the received noisy sequence into the input binary-digit sequence with probability near 1 and then decoding the input binary-digit sequence correctly into the original message sequence.

The net effect of these two results is to justify the use of a probabilistic model of communications for systems in which coding and decoding of messages is allowed and to demonstrate that in such a model, the entropy H

has a unique role as the measure of information. It is the common denominator between different message sources and between sources and channels. The entropy of a source determines how much in the way of channel resources must be devoted to its transmission, and no other information measure can make that claim.

The reason for looking with caution at the use of entropy and the rest of the formal apparatus of information theory in fields other than communications should now be obvious. Anyone who wants to use the measure is certainly free to do so, and some of those users—for example, Boltzmann—antedate Shannon. However, the fact that entropy has been proved in a meaningful sense to be the unique correct information measure for the purposes of communications does not prove that it is either the unique or a correct measure to use in some other field in which no issue of encoding or other changes in representation arises. The measure may, indeed, be useful or even unique for another application, but that fact must be demonstrated in the target field. The statement or implication that information theory has proved that entropy is the proper measure to use is not legitimate.

Psychology provides two interesting examples. Psychologists have used information-theoretic concepts in designing and analyzing experiments in human communication that clearly fit within Shannon's framework. [Attneave, 1959.] They (and Tribus) have also made use of the mutual information measure previously mentioned (and other related information-theoretic measures) to measure the degree of independence of two or more variables—especially when the variables are not number-valued but categorical, so that correlation coefficients cannot be computed. [McGill, 1954.] There is no case for uniqueness in that application. It is true that mutual information vanishes when (and only when) there is independence between the input and output but so do many other measures. Kendall gives an example of the kind of comparative discussion of a variety of information measures that is relevant for statistical purposes. [Kendall, 1973.]

The use of entropy in thermodynamics and statistical mechanics, as presented for example by Tribus [1961], has its own justifications, which antedate Shannon's work. In the related mathematical field of ergodic theory, entropy has been a subject of great recent interest, in part, because it is an invariant under a very broad class of transformations—that is, under any reversible encoding of one set of sequences into another. A recent book by Nathaniel Martin and James England presents developments in ergodic theory and other branches of mathematics that have evolved from Shannon's work and its extensions by Kolmogorov and Sinai. [Martin and England, 1981.] The fact that it is so easy to find the distribution that maximizes entropy subject to a set of constraints, as illustrated in the Tribus paper in Equations (8)–(11), is a great mathematical convenience and in the absence of other compelling reasons may itself be adequate justification for using this solution to the philosophically difficult problem of choosing prior distributions in fields other than thermodynamics. In thermodynamics, there is (at least in principle) an available independent experimental check by making measurements of temperature and heat flow. It is necessary to be careful in applying the technique of entropy maximization subject to constraints to the choice of probability densities in the case of continuous random variables, since the integral analog to the entropy expression takes a value that is not invariant under scale or other variable changes and is not itself an information measure. The difference of entropies that is the mutual information between two random variables is invariant under scale changes in the continuous case, however, and careful treatments of the continuous case are available; see Gallager [1968] and Pinsker [1964] for early careful versions.

In biology, Tribus lists some fairly recent papers; for historical interest, I will add references to two early symposia. [Quastler, 1955; and Yockey, 1958.] Some of the biological work deals with questions of the genetic storage of information—its transcription and translation into protein structure—and bit-counting seems highly relevant. Most of it, however, is of a statistical character coupled much more loosely, if at all, to Shannon's communications model.

In computer science, there have been various applications of information-theoretic ideas and answers to specific technical problems. In particular, there has been work on the economical storage and retrieval of information in computer memory by Peter Elias and Richard Flower, where bit-counting arguments are very relevant. [Elias and Flower, 1975.] Information theory has been used to prove the optimality of algorithms for one purpose or another, in particular, for demonstrating that sorting algorithms use a minimal number of comparisons. [Knuth, 1973, Section 5.3.] There has been work of commercial importance in the use of error-correcting codes (which arose in a communications context, although their later development has been more algebraic than information-theoretic) in providing reliable memories, both semiconductor main memories and magnetic tape and disk backup memories. Elwyn Berlekamp edited a collection of leading papers in this field and has recently summarized its current state. [Berlekamp, 1974; 1980.] There has also been some work of a different character of considerable philosophical interest, which makes use of a quite different information measure although it still gives bit-counting results. In this work (e.g., Solomonoff [1964], Kolmogorov [1965], and Chaitin [1977]), unlike Shannon's, an information value (possibly infinite) is defined for each particular sequence of symbols rather than being defined only on a probability distribution. The information in such a sequence is defined, roughly, to be the length (in bits) of the shortest Turing-machine program that can be used to generate the sequence.

Neither Shannon's measure nor the Solomonoff-Kolmogorov-Chaitin measure (sometimes called algorithmic information) seems to be of direct relevance for use in treating information as a commodity in economics. In both cases, for example, the amount of information contained in an edition of a million copies is the same as the information contained in one copy, and a bit of information that says that the price of a stock is going up rather than down has the same measure—one bit—independent of the size of the price change. It is possible, however, to consider channels where different input symbols not only define different conditional probability distributions on the received symbols but have different costs. [McEliece, 1977, chap. 2.]

THE ENTROPY FUNCTION
IN COMPLEX SYSTEMS

Elliott W. Montroll

Myron Tribus has clearly surveyed the evolution and numerous applications of information theory and maximum-entropy formalism. I elaborate on the theme by first making a few historical remarks on the early appearance of the expression

$$S = -\sum_j p_j \log p_j, \tag{1}$$

commonly called the entropy function. Then I display its appearance in certain observations on several sociotechnical systems.

HISTORICAL REMARKS

The combination $p \log p$ was apparently first published in de Moivre's *The Doctrine of Chances*, where we can learn how to calculate the odds of situations encountered in the popular eighteenth-century games of Bassette, Pharaon, Quadrille, Raffles, Hazard, and Piquet. [de Moivre, 1756.] The combinatorics relevant to those games were often expressed in terms of binomial coefficients, thus motivating de Moivre to estimate $n!$ for large n. On November 17, 1733, he distributed privately a few pages of his findings, containing what is now called Stirling's approximation. [Stirling, 1730.] Few copies of the small pamphlet have survived, but its contents are reprinted in the third edition of his book. James Stirling's minor role in the enterprise is mentioned. [de Moivre, 1756 and 1967, p. 244.]

De Moivre estimates $\log n!$, the binomial coefficients, and the ratio of a given term in the expansion of $(1 + 1)^n$ to the middle term in that expansion:

I have also found that the logarithm of the ratio, which the middle term of a high power (n) has to any distance from it by an interval l, would be denoted by a very near approximation, supposing $m = \frac{1}{2}n$, by the quantities (de Moivre, 1756, p. 244)

$$(m + l - \tfrac{1}{2}) \log (m + l - 1) +$$
$$(m - l + \tfrac{1}{2}) \log (m - l + 1) - 2m \log m + \log (m + 1)/m. \tag{2a}$$

For large $(m + l)$ and $(m - l)$, this combination is approximately

$$(m + l) \log (m + l) + (m - l) \log (m - l) - 2m \log m$$

$$= m \left[\frac{m + l}{m} \log \left(\frac{m + l}{m} \right) + \frac{m - l}{m} \log \left(\frac{m - l}{m} \right) \right] \qquad (2b)$$

$$= m \, (p_1 \log p_1 + p_2 \log p_2), \qquad (2c)$$

with $p_1 = (m + l)/m$ and $p_2 = (m - l)/m$.

Although the expression for $\log n!$ became widely applied in the next century, there seems to have been little interest in the combination in these equations until the publication of Boltzmann's famous paper "On the Relation between the Second Law of Thermodynamics and Probability Theory and the Laws of Thermal Equilibrium." [Boltzmann, 1877.] There, the expression corresponding to $-S$ of the entropy function appears in Boltzmann's derivation of the canonical energy-distribution function of statistical mechanics from an artificial model of kinetic-energy transfer by molecular collision.

In Boltzmann's first model, he postulated molecules to limit their kinetic energy to the set $0, \epsilon, 2\epsilon, \ldots, p\epsilon$. On collision, energy might be redistributed subject to energy conservation. Let w_j be the number of molecules of energy $j\epsilon$. Then the probability of a given state distribution is

$$\frac{n!}{\prod\limits_{0}^{p} w_j!}$$

with $\sum\limits_{0}^{p} w_j = n$ and total energy $= L = \sum j \, w_j.$ \qquad (3)

Boltzman sought the distribution of the total energy into its various states that maximized the state probability [minimized the denominator of the product in Equation (3) subject to the other restrictions in Equation (3)]. On taking logarithms of the product and applying Stirling's approximation to the logarithm of the factorials, the quantity he minimized was

$$M = \sum w_j \log w_j - n. \qquad (4)$$

Today, he would maximize $-M$, which is in the spirit of the entropy function [Equation (1)]. The combination $w_j \log w_j$ represents the analog of the terms in de Moivre's expression [Equation (2)] except that Boltzmann's terms followed from the multinomial coefficients in Equation (3), while de Moivre's came from binomial coefficients.

Boltzmann then let $w_j = f(j\epsilon)$, chose ϵ to be small, proceeded to the continuum $(\epsilon = 0)$ limit, let $p \to \infty$, and minimized

$$M' = \int_0^\infty f(x) \log f(x) \, dx \text{ (or maximize } -M') \text{ consistent with} \qquad (5a)$$

$$n = \int_0^\infty f(x) \, dx \quad \text{and} \quad L = \int_0^\infty x \, f(x) \, dx. \qquad (5b)$$

By exploiting the method of Lagrange multipliers, he found $f(x) = h \exp - hx$. This result is equivalent to the statement that the function $f(x)$ that maximizes an entropy integral $-M'$ under the restriction that the first moment of $f(x)$ is specified is a decaying exponential when $0 < x < \infty$.

Then Boltzmann considered real molecular systems and observed that if f were the Maxwell velocity distribution of perfect gas molecules that exist with equal probability anywhere in a container of volume V, the quantity

$$\Omega = -\int f \log f \, d^3v \, d^3x \qquad (6)$$

became proportional to the entropy of a perfect gas known from thermodynamics.

Notice that, if the variable x in Equation (5a) has the range $(-\infty, \infty)$ and $\sigma^2 = \int x^2 f(x) \, dx$, the second moment being specified, the various limits of integration go from $-\infty$ to ∞, and we find that the maximization of $-M'$ by Boltzmann's method yields the Gauss distribution

$$f(x) = c \exp (-x^2/2\sigma^2). \qquad (7)$$

As quantum theory became a starting point for statistical mechanics (following Planck, Einstein, Sommerfeld, etc.), one specified the energy states of a system by E_j. In an assembly of systems in contact with each other, the fraction of systems f_j in state E_j became determined by maximizing the entropy

$$S = -k \sum f_i \log f_i$$

with constraints $\sum f_i = 1$ and $E = \sum E_i f_i$. $\qquad (8)$

The f_i are then found to have the canonical distribution

$$f_i = c \exp \left(- \frac{E_i}{kT} \right).$$

As a student in the 1930s, I was introduced to this simple attractive style by John Slater's text. [Slater, 1938.] Since Slater was a popular lecturer at the Massachusetts Institute of Technology at that time, it must have become widely known to MIT students.

It was Claude Shannon's genius in elaborating the pioneering but more primitive ideas of Ralph Hartley and Harry Nyquist that identified the entropy function as an ideal measure of information transferred in communications systems. [Shannon, 1948.] Thus, through the strange manner in which scientific thought evolves, we find that a simple mathematical construct that appeared without special comment in de Moivre's gambling manual became a highly visible quantity in Boltzmann's kinetic theory of gases and eventually basic in the statistical-mechanical interpretation of the properties of gaseous and condensed matter. Surprisingly, it also emerged as the dominant mathematical structure for the optimization of human communication systems as they developed through the application of a century of engineer-

ing ingenuity. E. T. Jaynes was one of the first to attempt to unify information theory and statistical mechanics. [Jaynes, 1957a, b.]

THE ENTROPY FUNCTION IN SEVERAL SOCIOTECHNICAL SYSTEMS

Communication systems considered by Shannon were composed of mes-
sage-input elements, transmission channels, and message-output elements.
Since the entropy function appeared in a natural way for the information-
transfer rate in such systems, we might seek the importance of the function
in other sociotechnical systems composed of three analogous components.

Entropy Function in a Traffic Stream

A natural example is a highway-transportation system with an input provi-
sion for travelers and a road providing a channel for travel to exit points.
About twenty-five years ago, Robert Herman, Elliott Montroll, and colleagues at the General Motors Research Center performed car-following
experiments and made numerous observations on flow on single-lane roads
(and multilane highways under high-density conditions that prevented weav-
ing from one lane to another). [Chandler et al., 1958; Gazis et al., 1959;
Herman et al., 1959.] I now show that an entropy function evolves naturally
from the observed stimulus/response equation that describes car-following
in a platoon.

Let us consider a platoon of N cars identified as $1, 2, \ldots, N$ flowing along
a long single-lane highway void of traffic signals. An equation found to
describe with remarkable accuracy the response of a follower (identified by
$n + 1$) to the behavior of a leader (identified by n) is

$$\frac{dv_{n+1}(t + \Delta)}{dt} = \lambda_0 \left[\frac{v_n(t) - v_{n+1}(t)}{x_n(t) - x_{n+1}(t)} \right]. \tag{9}$$

Here, $v_n(t)$ is the speed of car n at time t, $x_n(t)$ is the location of the front end
of that car at time t, and Δ is the time lag between the stimulus provided by
the lead car and the response by the follower. The time lag Δ, which varies
from person to person, is about 1.5 sec. Equation (9) is a quantitative expression of the fact that the driver of the follower car ($n + 1$) accelerates when
his or her relative speed is too slow and decelerates when it is too fast. When
the driver being followed is far ahead, the response is not so sensitive as
when close.

Integration of equation (9) is the first step in the derivation of an equation
of state for traffic, a relation between vehicular flow-rate and density in
single-lane traffic:

$$v_{n+1}(t + \Delta) - \lambda_0 \log d_{n+1}(t) = \text{constant} \tag{10}$$

with

$$d_{n+1}(t) \equiv x_n(t) - x_{n+1}(t) \tag{11}$$

being the space available per car at location of nth car at time t. The traffic density at the location of car n, $\rho_n(t)$, is the reciprocal of the space per car: $\rho_n = 1/d_n =$ number of cars per unit-length. In a freely moving stable stream of traffic $v_n(t + \Delta)$ with $\Delta \simeq 1.5$ sec is approximately $v_n(t)$, and if ρ_c is bumper-to-bumper close-packing density at which $v_n = 0$, Equation (10) becomes

$$v_n(t) = -\lambda_0 \log \frac{\rho_n(t)}{\rho_c}. \tag{12}$$

The local-traffic-flow rate (dropping explicit dependence on time) is

$$q_n = \rho_n v_n = -\lambda_0 \rho_c \left(\frac{\rho_n}{\rho_c} \right) \log \left(\frac{\rho_n}{\rho_c} \right). \tag{13}$$

Notice that $0 < \rho_n/\rho_c \leq 1$ and that the dimensions of our variables might be cars per hour for q, cars per mile for ρ, and miles per hour for v. By averaging over N cars in a line of traffic, the mean flow rate is proportional to an entropy function in the variables (ρ_n/ρ_c). [Montroll, 1981.] Thus,

$$q = \lambda_0 \rho_c \left(-\frac{1}{N} \sum_{n=1}^{N} \frac{\rho_n}{\sigma_0} \log \frac{\rho_n}{\rho_c} \right) \tag{14}$$

$$= \lambda_0 \rho_c \log \frac{\rho_c}{\rho} + \rho \lambda_0 \left(\log \frac{1}{N} - \sum_{n=1}^{N} p_n \log p_n \right), \tag{15}$$

where ρ is the average traffic density and $p_n = \rho_n/\rho N$. While the variables ρ_n/ρ_c are not normalized, the set p_n is, so that $\Sigma p_n = 1$. The flow rate is a maximum at a given traffic density if all ρ_n are identical, so that $\rho_n = \rho$ and $p_n = 1/N$. Then the term in the bracket in Equation (15) vanishes. If drivers behave differently from each other (as of course they do), so that some ρ_n deviate from ρ, the entropy term in Equation (15) does not achieve its maximum value and the term in the parenthesis is negative, yielding a reduction in flow rate q.

Entropy in the Catalogs of Sears, Roebuck, and Company

Another important sociotechnical system is the merchandising system. Goods flow into a warehouse or distribution center of a retailing firm, remain temporarily as inventory, and finally flow to the consumer. A company's profit depends on the flow-through rate of goods and the pricing of the goods. The analogy between merchandising flows and communication and transportation flows suggests that the entropy function may appear in the process.

A further consideration of this idea requires merchandising data. By good fortune, the firm of Sears, Roebuck, and Company has provided a rich legacy of information on this subject in its annual catalogs, which form a magnificent database of Americana of the past 85 years.

The preparation of the catalogs was a major concern of Sears Roebuck. Basically, each page was audited to produce its share of the profit. [Emmet and Jeuck, 1950.] For example, in 1930 the goals set ranged from \$5,000 to \$20,000 per page, depending on the responsible merchandising department. Since the profit that year was \$14,300,000 and the catalog ran 1000–1500 pages, the profit per page averaged about \$10,000. Many pages reserved a small space for the tentative introduction of new products. Favorable public response motivated increased allocation the next year. With declining sales of an item, its space allocation decreased; sometimes it even disappeared from the catalog. Various department heads, anxious for raises and promotions, were very competitive in preparing pages that listed items that they hoped would outsell those of their colleagues. Robert Herman and I found the distribution function of prices by year listed in many of the catalogs. [Herman and Montroll, 1977.] Since prices ranged from a few cents to hundreds of dollars, we "expanded" the scale of low-cost items and "contracted" that of higher priced ones by recording the data as the logarithm of the price (to the base 2) $\log_2 P$. Of course, we were aware (as many before us dating back to Daniel Bernoulli) that $\log P$ is psychologically a more important variable than the price itself because we are especially sensitive to relative price changes $(\Delta P)/P \simeq \Delta \log P$.

Examining the price distribution from many catalogs indicates that, in a given catalog, the distribution of $\log_2 P_i$ (P_i being the price of the ith item) is very close to the normal distribution [Equation (7)]. Important distribution moments are

$$\log P = \langle \log_2 P \rangle = \frac{1}{N} \sum_{i=1}^{N} \log_2 P_i, \tag{16}$$

and

$$\sigma^2 = \frac{1}{N} \sum_{i=1}^{N} (\log_2 P_i - \log_2 P)^2. \tag{17}$$

The findings for $\langle \log_2 P \rangle$ and σ for eighteen years appear in Table 1. The quantity σ is the dispersion in the logarithm of prices relative to their mean value. The larger the σ, the broader the range of prices in the catalog.

The variation in $\langle \log_2 P \rangle$ over the years reflects changes in cost of living through the twentieth century. Catalog prices changed in two manners: (1) by the change in price of an invariant item such as a clothespin, a 1910 specimen being indistinguishable from one in 1940; and (2) by the change in the nature or quality of the item listed to reflect evolving technology and varying public taste. Many interesting deductions follow from changes in $\langle \log_2 P \rangle$, but it is to the third column σ of Table 1 that I wish to direct

Table 1.   Standard Deviation of $\log_2 P$ from Mean $\langle \log_2 P \rangle$ for Various Years in
the Period 1900–1976

Year[a]	$\langle \log_2 P \rangle$	σ	Year	$\langle \log_2 P \rangle$	σ
1900	0.150	2.43	1939–40	0.627	2.62
1902	0.212	2.34	1946–47	0.532	2.15
1908	−0.228	2.29	1948–49	1.336	2.37
1916	−0.068	2.38	1951–52	1.785	2.34
1924–25	0.422	2.32	1962	2.403	2.24
1929–30	0.998	2.26	1972–73	3.030	2.27
1932–33	0.691	1.91	1973–74	3.322	2.05
1934–35	0.673	2.22	1974–75	3.870	2.12
1935–36	0.537	2.39	1975–76	4.060	2.03

[a] An entry identified by a single year corresponds to a spring–summer catalog; an entry
identified by a number such as 1924–25 corresponds to a winter catalog.

attention. We have been as much impressed by the existence of an almost
invariant statistical quantity—an "economic constant of the motion"—for
the marketing operation. It is remarkable that for more than seventy-five
years, the dispersion σ [defined by Equation (17)] has hardly changed. The
average value of σ is 2.26 with $\langle (\sigma - \bar{\sigma})^2 \rangle^{\frac{1}{2}} = 0.17$.

Having observed the constancy of σ, let us construct a simple mathematical model to explain it. Let us suppose that in a given year the ith item in the
catalog experiences an inflation factor α_i, so that its price over the year
changes from P_i to $\alpha_i P_i$. Also, suppose that α is the mean inflation rate, so
that $\alpha_i = \alpha + \Delta \alpha_i$, where presumably $\Delta \alpha_i$ (with $\Sigma \Delta \alpha_i = 0$) may be treated as
a small number. Then, to first order in $(\Delta \alpha_i / \alpha)$, $\log P_i$ for one year is transformed in the next to

$$\log \alpha_i P_i \simeq \log P_i + \log \alpha + \left(\frac{\Delta \alpha_i}{\alpha} \right). \tag{18}$$

Hence, to second order, from Equation (17), σ^2 of one year transforms to

$$\sigma^2 + \frac{2}{N} \sum_{i=1}^{N} (\log_2 P_i - \log_2 \bar{P}) \left(\frac{\Delta \alpha_i}{\alpha} \right) + \frac{1}{N} \sum_{i=1}^{N} \left(\frac{\Delta \alpha_i}{\alpha} \right)^2. \tag{19}$$

The simplest assumption that might be made is that all items inflate in the
same manner, so that $\Delta \alpha_i = 0$ for all i. Then, σ^2 would remain completely
constant over the years. Table 1 indicates that this is almost but not precisely the case. If we were to assume that $\Delta \alpha_i$ were independent of the price
P_i, then the middle term in Equation (19) would vanish and σ^2 would increase
every year, which was not observed. If, however, we assume that low-
priced items were inflated more rapidly than high-priced ones, $\Delta \alpha_i$ would
be positive for small P_i and negative for large P_i, so that the middle term

in Equation (19) would be negative in order to cancel the contribution of the third term (a positive one) in Equation (19). This type of inflation is commonly experienced. Clearly, if σ^2 remains constant, so does its square root, σ.

It was observed in the text between Equations (6) and (7) that if a random variable has a range $(-\infty, \infty)$ and if its dispersion is given, then the entropy function is maximized by the Gauss or normal distribution. We have also observed that the dispersion σ^2 of the $\log_2 P_i$ distribution in Sears Roebuck catalogs has been essentially constant for seventy-five years. Since the distribution function of $\log P_i$ has been Gaussian, the entropy function associated with that variable has been maximized. Hence, in their marketing wisdom, Sears, Rosenwald, their staff, and their successors created a business based on catalogs with goods priced so that year after year the price distribution maximized the entropy function associated with $\log P_i$.

A broad log-normal price distribution represents a balance between high- and low-priced items, so that there is something of interest to all potential customers. Originally, Sears Roebuck attempted to make merchandise available in a medium-sized town to the farmer. They so well succeeded that they soon not only successfully competed with stores in such towns but also those in large cities. Circa 1910, several of the great department stores, including Macy's, Wanamaker's, and Filene's, unsuccessfully entered the catalog marketing field in competition with Sears. It has been observed that for a given type of merchandise, Sears stocked models that were cheaper and also more expensive (a broader distribution) than those listed in catalogs of the more traditional department stores. [Emmet and Jeuck, 1950.]

CONCLUDING REMARKS

The magnificent mathematical construct, the entropy function defined by Equation (1), made its first inconspicuous appearance in de Moivre's systematic investigation of developing a strategy for winning gambling games with the aid of probabilistic analysis. It was explicitly introduced by Boltzmann to furnish a probabilistic interpretation of the second law of thermodynamics, a law based on the thermal behavior of materials. After communications engineers devoted a century to inventing and improving communication systems, Claude Shannon showed that their drive toward optimization could be measured mathematically in terms of an entropy function with probabilities measured appropriately in terms of frequencies of coding symbols or in terms of Fourier components obtained by the Fourier decomposition of continuous signals. I have shown here that motor-car operators have developed a style of car-following in traffic platoons that yields a vehicular throughput that is measured in terms of an entropy function obtained from ratios of local-traffic density to close-packing traffic densities. Finally, one of the most carefully planned and financially rewarding retailing operations in the United States in the first half of this century seems to have evolved in a manner (unknown to the planners) that maximized an entropy function in distributing the logarithm of the item prices in its catalog, subject to dispersion in the square of the logarithm of the prices being specified and kept constant.

Notice that the last two examples have nothing to do with information theory or thermodynamic entropy. They seem to reflect the manner in which a group of people, trying to optimize their productivity, have unwittingly fallen into a behavior pattern that may be described by an appropriate entropy function. The diversity of examples of sociotechnical systems previously listed suggests that an astute observer should be able to find further examples of the entropy function in the complex systems generated by people who wish to optimize their productivity.

ENTROPY, PROBABILITY, AND COMMUNICATION

Myron Tribus

The main idea of my paper was that the entropy concept had been used not only as Shannon originally intended but in novel ways unforseen by him. Four distinct uses were detected in the literature:

1. To examine human communication processes within the nervous system as well as input/output processes of humans.

2. To consider how entropy assignments could be used to determine values and meanings for probabilities. Shannon defined entropy in terms of probabilities. Jaynes defined probabilities in terms of entropies, and this had led to new lines of inquiry in several fields not associated with information theory.

3. Defining entropy in a way devoid of concern with meaning has made it possible for problems of communication and information to be separated from problems of meaning, making it possible to discuss them either together or separately, with less confusion of concepts.

4. To define conditions for reproducibility in statistical physics.

The reviewers have added specific examples of some of these ideas and because of their specialized expertise and experience, have given us special insights. In each case, what makes Shannon's contributions so significant is the casting of old questions in a new and more interesting light.

I especially appreciate Donald MacKay's remark, "every unit of missing information . . . means that a corresponding amount of energy cannot be pinned down to do work." The essergy concept, derived in the paper, demonstrates just that. MacKay also brings out the importance of the constant K, which in the case of essergy is set equal to kT_0, just as he seems to suggest.

Although the editors have given me more space for a rejoinder, I do believe that in view of the reviewers' remarks, it is better to stop here and not increase the ratio of words to ideas.

SECTION 8

ON SYSTEM THEORY AND ITS RELEVANCE TO PROBLEMS IN INFORMATION SCIENCE

Hassan Mortazavian

My task is to offer explanatory remarks and present some questions, distinctions, and ideas that may be useful for a better understanding of system-theoretic concepts, in particular as they relate to problems in information science. My approach is entirely informal, although occasionally I shall have to provide formal definitions and technical details, partly in footnotes. The text should be intelligible to those without prior background in either system theory or information science. Writing a paper of this type is not an easy task. Perhaps one should not even attempt it, for there is no general agreement on the scope of either system theory or information science; and some issues on which consensus seems to have been approached cannot be accurately presented without using mathematical language.

SETS AND RELATIONS

A *set* is a collection of objects—sense-objects or thought-objects. If a set contains no objects, it is called *empty;* if it contains all objects of particular reference, it is called the *universal* set. When the number of objects contained in a set is finite, the set is called a *finite* set. If we consider the set of all human beings as the universal set of our particular concern, then the set of all male humans is a subset of the original set, and obviously it is finite. It is clear that a subset of a set is itself a set.

A *relation* defined on a set is nothing but a way of relating the elements or objects of the set to one another. For example, considering the set of all men, one may define a brotherhood relation and obtain a set of *pairs*, where the elements of every pair are brothers. Note that the same man can be a

Research for this paper was carried out while the author was on the staff of the Institut National de Recherche en Informatique et en Automatique, Paris, France, and he wishes to acknowledge the many useful comments received from his colleagues at INRIA.

member of more than one pair simply because he may have more than one brother. Imagine now that we relate men in terms of brotherhood, but we also want to distinguish between older brothers and younger brothers, excluding those who are twins. This amounts to first *partitioning* the elements of the set into two subsets, one consisting of all those men who are another man's older brother and the other consisting of all those who are another man's younger brother. Note that the same man then can be a member of both subsets, in that he may have both an older brother and a younger brother, hence, being also both an older and a younger brother himself. Therefore, membership in the two subsets need not be exclusive. After this partitioning is done, we relate every element of one subset to every element of the other subset with respect to the relation of brotherhood if such a relation exists between the two elements of concern. If the first subset consists of older brothers and the second subset of younger brothers and we choose the first element of every pair from the first subset and the second element from the second subset, what we get is a larger set consisting of what is referred to as a set of *ordered pairs*.

We need to define one more operation called the *Cartesian product* of two sets and denoted by $\times$ —the customary sign for multiplication. By the Cartesian product of two sets we mean a set consisting of all ordered pairs whose elements are chosen from the first and the second set, respectively. To be more precise, consider the two sets $U = \{$father, mother$\}$ and $Y = \{$son, daughter$\}$. Then the Cartesian product of U and Y is constructed as follows:

$$U \times Y = \{(\text{father, son}), (\text{father, daughter}), (\text{mother, son}),$$
$$(\text{mother, daughter})\}.$$

Note that the first element of every ordered pair of the product set belongs to the first set and the second element of every ordered pair of the product set belongs to the second; thus an ordering between elements is established.

A set S is said to be contained in a set T if every element belonging to S also belongs to T, and then one writes $S \subset T$. Conversely, we may say that T contains S.

These primitive concepts are sufficient for an elementary definition of the concept of system, meaning a relation defined on a family of sets.

Consider a simple example adopted from Casti with some modifications. [Casti, 1979.] Let U be a set of consumer items and Y a set of service facilities. For example,

$$U = \quad \{\text{bread}, \qquad \text{milk}, \qquad \text{stamps}, \qquad \text{shoes}\}$$
$$\qquad\qquad x_1 \qquad\qquad x_2 \qquad\qquad x_3 \qquad\qquad x_4$$

$$\qquad\qquad\qquad\qquad\qquad\qquad \text{department}$$
$$Y = \quad \{\text{market}, \qquad \text{store}, \qquad \text{bank}, \qquad \text{post office}\}$$
$$\qquad\qquad y_1 \qquad\qquad y_2 \qquad\qquad y_3 \qquad\qquad y_4$$

Let us define a relation R on the Cartesian product $U \times Y$ by the rule:

x$_i$ *is related to* y$_i$ *in the sense of relation* R *if and only if good* x$_i$ *may be obtained at facility* y$_i$.

Thus,

$$R = \{(x_1, y_1), (x_2, y_1), (x_3, y_4), (x_4, y_2)\}.$$

A convenient way to represent the relation R is by an *incidence* matrix:

R	y_1	y_2	y_3	y_4
x_1	1	0	0	0
x_2	1	0	0	0
x_3	0	0	0	1
x_4	0	1	0	0

where if the relation R exists between x_i and y_i, there is a 1 at the intersection of the ith row and the ith column; otherwise, there is a 0.

Now, considering that R as a relation is contained in the Cartesian product of the two sets U and Y, that is, $R \subset U \times Y$, the relation R may be considered to define a system in the most abstract sense of the term. (This is obviously not sufficient for characterizing most real-world systems, and a more mathematical structure is required, but we need not go into any detail concerning such technicalities.)

Now if we consider a decisionmaker who, after choosing the items he or she would like to obtain, determines the facilities that should be used to obtain every specific item chosen, then what we have previously described may as well be considered this person's decision-making system. (This elementary characterization of a system should not be generalized to more complex situations, although the basic idea remains the same.)

THE CONCEPT OF SYSTEM

There is no general agreement among system theorists about how to define this concept. The situation is not unlike the familiar one in mathematics where there is no consensus among mathematicians about the definition of such terms as *number, set, point,* or even *infinity*. We may argue, however, that the absence of a generally accepted definition of *number* in mathematics has not caused any significant delays in the progress of number theory or mathematics in general. Although we may not all agree on how to define *number*, for all practical purposes we all have a clear idea of what numbers are.

As long as we have no generally accepted definition of *system*, it suffices for all practical purposes to characterize and specify various instances of systems constructively. Progress in system theory depends for the most part on such constructive characterization. Before we say more about definition and constructive characterization, we need to clarify a few methodological issues.

It is clear that there is a difference between what is considered to be known and what is considered to be defined. Not all known objects are defined, and not all defined objects are necessarily known. By known objects I mean objects of which we have at least one example at hand. Thus, the number π as the ratio of the circumference to the diameter of a circle is a defined mathematical object. Its numerical value, however, is not completely known although it is known to certain degrees of approximation. On the other hand, a point in Euclidean geometry is not defined, but it is known. The definitions of *line, plane,* and *volume* depend on the primitive concept of *point*. Systems are known, and particular instances of systems may indeed be defined, but the very concept of *system* itself has not been defined to the satisfaction of most, let alone all, theorists.

This is what Bertrand Russell had to say about attempting to define number:

> Many philosophers, when attempting to define number, are really setting to work to define plurality, which is quite a different thing. *Number* is what is characteristic of numbers, as *man* is what is characteristic of men. A plurality is not an instance of number, but of some particular number. A trio of men, for example, is an instance of the number 3, and the number 3 is an instance of number; but the trio is not an instance of number. This point may seem elementary and scarcely worth mentioning; yet it has proved too subtle for philosophers, with few exceptions. (Russell, 1919, p. 11.)

Russell's remark is also relevant to our discussion of the definition of *system*. To see what system is, we have to study the characteristics of various instances of systems.

According to Russell's methodological position, a serious inquiry may proceed in two opposite directions. One may be called the *constructive* direction, toward gradually increasing complexity from deterministic systems to stochastic systems; from time-invariant systems to time-varying systems; from linear systems to nonlinear systems; and so on. The so-called *analytical* direction, on the other hand, proceeds to greater and greater abstraction and logical simplicity: For example, from concrete signal-flow representations of electrical circuits to graph-theoretical and topological representations of electrical circuits; from matrix representations of deterministic systems to algebraic representations of deterministic systems; and then to categorical representation of such systems. (By categorical representation of system, I mean the approach that uses category theory, a highly abstract branch of mathematics.) The choice between the two directions is not dictated by subject matter, but by the inclination of the investigator, the purposes of the research, and the state of development of a particular type of inquiry.

A definition of *system* is, as a rule, needed only when systems are pursued in the analytical direction. For merely constructive characterization, specific definitions of particular types of systems can be provided that suffice for all practical purposes. We should distinguish among:

1. A concrete system (i.e., an existing system in the real world or one to be constructed).
2. Various abstract (mathematical) systems or system-types.
3. The abstract (mathematical) concept of system.

By a concrete system, I mean any set of objects—sense-objects or thought-objects—that interact among themselves or are interrelated. In this sense, almost everything is a system of one kind or another. This broad notion of a system, however, is not the one with which system theory is concerned. Lack of clarity on this issue in the writings of some system theorists has caused misunderstandings and confusion among outsiders. System theory is not a theory of concrete systems in the sense just described. *System theory is the theory of (mathematical) models.* Rudolf Kalman made this issue clear when he wrote:

> "Does system theory deal with the real world?" To this obvious question the answer is *no*—that's quite simple. System theory studies models and does not accept responsibility for the accuracy or relevance of these models. That headache is reserved for the practitioners, and it should not be exaggerated. (Kalman, 1980, p. 7.)

This statement means that system theory deals with certain universal mathematical questions about (abstract or mathematical) models and as such is independent of particular fields of application. It contributes to other sciences by providing techniques for generating a class of models for any well-defined system at hand, based on data resulting from experiment, observation, and so forth. But it does not specify which model out of a class of models is *the* model for a particular concrete system.

In this sense, system theory is a theory that develops mathematical models for various abstract (mathematical) systems. Examples of such systems or system-types are: linear versus nonlinear systems, continuous versus discrete systems, deterministic versus stochastic systems, and so forth. These abstract systems can properly be defined only by appropriate mathematical tools. Nevertheless, I shall try to offer nonmathematical illustrations—at the risk of some inaccuracy.

To illustrate what a *linear* system is, consider the trajectory of the flight of an airplane. The plane is our system, and we assume that at every point of time there are only two controls or influences exerted on it: the wind and the control exerted by the pilot. Each one of these two inputs causes a particular change in the trajectory of the flight—a particular output. Now, this system is said to be linear if and only if the output corresponding to any linear combination of these two inputs is a linear combination of the outputs corresponding to those inputs. Otherwise, the system is said to be *nonlinear*. Roughly speaking, by a linear combination of two variables, we mean a combination performed only by addition (subtraction) and multiplication by a scalar. Note that according to this definition, it is not true that a system is nonlinear if it contains a nonlinear element. A linear system may indeed contain nonlinear elements.

A system is said to be *continuous* if its variables change continuously over time. A system is *discrete* if its variables change only at certain specific points in time. A car traveling on a road is an example of a continuous system; the number of people entering a shopping center is an example of a discrete system.

In computing control schemes for real-world continuous-time systems, in practice, we are forced to treat them, in some sense, as discrete-time systems. There are essentially two reasons for this: (1) We can make only a finite number of measurements of the output values in any time interval. (2) In computing an appropriate sequence of inputs (controls or decisions) to be applied to a system to control its behavior in some desired way, we generally use a digital computer, which is a discrete-time system, and can generate only distinct control signals at discrete times. The practical necessity of dealing with continuous-time systems as if they were discrete-time systems raises important questions about the treatment of *sampled-data systems,* that is, systems that should be considered as continuous-time but with which we can interact only at discrete times when samples of outputs are gathered and a sequence of discrete controls based on the sampled outputs is applied.

Before providing definitions for *deterministic* and *stochastic* systems, I ought to say a few words about determinism and causality. The word *determined* has often been used in an ambiguous way. In one sense, a quantity—say the output of a system—is determined when it is measured. In another sense, an event—say the occurrence of a specific sequence of outputs—is determined when it is caused. Although there are many reasons to believe in some principle of causality, it is not altogether easy to define the notions of *cause* and *causal laws*. It must be made clear, however, that what distinguishes deterministic systems from stochastic systems is not the assumption of causal relation between inputs and outputs or past and future behavior in one system to the exclusion of the other. Both deterministic and stochastic systems may or may not be considered as causal (although disbelief in causality causes many conceptual difficulties). Deterministic systems are determined, and stochastic systems are not determined, in the first sense, which is independent of the notion of causality.

These considerations suggest the following definitions:

Deterministic systems are those in which exact knowledge of outputs is ascertainable from exact knowledge of inputs. In other words, in deterministic systems, future behavior can be predicted with accuracy. Stochastic systems are those whose future behavior is not predictable.

Thus, roughly speaking, a system is stochastic if it exhibits no regularities in its behavior. These irregularities may be inherent in the internal mechanisms of the system; they may be caused by disturbances from the environment or simply a result of inaccuracies in our measurements, and so forth; or they may be a combination of these. In system theory, all such irregularities are referred to as noise. The word *noise* in this sense covers a much wider range of elements than in its electrical-engineering sense. In the present usage,

noise is equivalent to what cannot be accounted for or explained in the behavior of a concrete system by the deterministic part of a model adopted for that system.

Thus, for example, possible nonlinearities in a concrete system for which a linear model has been constructed are simply considered as noise. This point, though trivial, has proved too subtle for many practitioners.

At last we come to the concept of an abstract (mathematical) system. Various concrete systems, such as cars, cells, or trees, are instances of particular types of abstract (mathematical) systems, and these systems themselves are instances of system as a general concept. System theory is properly a theory of systems in this sense.

Mesarović defines a system as an abstract relation defined on a set of objects. [Mesarović, 1964a; 1970; 1975.] The objects can be anything. A system in this sense is a general notion, defined independently of any particular set of objects. The justification for the adoption of such a definition lies in the universal existence of *objects* and *relations,* and thus the definition is general enough to represent all sorts of systems. Starting from such a general notion of system, we proceed by assuming more structure for the objects and investigate the properties induced by various types of relations.

To clarify this definition, let us recall the example of obtaining certain consumer goods from different service facilities, given in the first part of this paper. In terms of this example, *decisions* to use the four different service facilities are the *inputs* to our shopping system, and the four consumer items obtained are the *outputs* (making the oversimplifying assumption that at every service facility, one and only one consumer item can be obtained).

This definition of system is the starting point of Mesarović's approach to system theory and what he calls general system theory. In his view, the latter is concerned with the most fundamental, abstract, and general aspects of various systems, whereas system theory, at least as reflected in the work of some authors, tends to deal with more specific questions about more specific types of systems (e.g., dynamical systems, automata, control systems, game-theoretic systems, etc.). The main reason for adopting the name *general system theory* has been to emphasize the point that system theory should be considered as a general theory, not as a theory of specific types of systems, for instance, control systems. In my view, the term *system theory* is comprehensive enough to capture all aspects of the field.

David Berlinski has criticized Mesarović's definition of a system as a relation defined on a set of objects on the grounds that this definition collapses the notion of a system into the notions of a sequence and a set. [Berlinski, 1976, pp. 28–29.] My response to Berlinski's criticism is that almost every abstract mathematical concept collapses into a few elementary notions such as sets, relations, points, and so on. The notion of a *graph*, for example, simply collapses to the notion of points and edges (or elements and relations between them), and yet *graph theory* is a powerful mathematical theory with a wide range of applications. An important advantage of this definition of system is that it stresses the structural characteristics of phenomena.

WHAT IS SYSTEM THEORY?

In the second part of this paper, I discussed the concept of system; now, I shall examine the essential questions of system theory, in particular: (1) What is system theory? (2) How and why did it emerge as a new discipline? (3) Why do we need to learn about its findings?

The terms *system, systems approach, system analysis, system science,* and so on, are so broadly used, and occasionally misused, that outsiders sometimes wonder what we really mean by *system theory.* Moreover, we often see *systems engineering, general system theory, mathematical system theory,* and so on. These terms all refer to various aspects of the same discipline, to wit, system theory.

System theory does not aim at unifying all or special types of scientific disciplines. It does, however, provide a methodological base for solving a number of problems common to various disciplines. Roughly speaking, system theory is the theory of phenomena that are "system-bound," "system-dependent," or "system-related." By this, I mean those phenomena that depend on the conditions of the environment in which they exist, interact with this environment, and thus cannot properly be studied in isolation.

Let us consider some examples of such system-dependent phenomena. The rate of growth of population in a country, for example, generally depends on such factors as average income of individuals, income-distribution patterns, age distribution of population, distribution of male and female populations, level of education, and so on. Therefore, a model of population growth for a country cannot be developed unless we also consider the relevant variables of socioeconomic environment in that country. Or, consider the problem of choice of an optimal energy policy for a nation. Such an optimal policy, if it exists, obviously depends on a number of national as well as global economic, political, environmental, natural, and other factors that should be specified for every particular nation.

All such phenomena are system-dependent, and the aim of system theory is to develop methods that can be used in analyzing, understanding, explaining, modeling, controlling, and predicting such system-dependent phenomena. But techniques of system theory are general in nature, not related by any means to the subject matter of specific disciplines. System theory aims at providing a common complement of methods that deal with such concepts as dynamics, stability, complexity, catastrophe, hierarchy, structure, and so on.

Dynamical systems are those that change their state over time. If the state of a dynamical system changes in the same way over time, it is called time-invariant, and if the way in which the state changes varies over time, it is called time-varying. Consider some specific examples: a traveling space vehicle, a home-heating system, an operating computer, a growing population, the flow of traffic on a road, genetic transference, ecological decay, and so forth. While each one of these examples refers to a specific dynamic behavior, the general concept of dynamics transcends all such particular situations. Countless examples of such dynamic situations in various areas can be supplied, but they can all be represented by a small number of mathematical models. System theory is concerned (among other things) with specifying all such general mathematical models that can represent dynamics in various situations. This is done by exploring that part of mathematics that is suitable for modeling dynamic behavior. It turns out that at least the elementary aspects of smooth dynamical systems can be almost completely studied by differential and difference equations—the first used when time is considered to be continuous, the second when time is considered to be discrete. The velocity of a car, or the flow of water into a tank, changes continuously; therefore, velocity and flow are modeled in continuous time, hence, by differential equations that relate the rate of change of a variable to its level at every point in time. The number of people entering a shopping center, on the other hand, changes discretely; therefore, it is modeled in discrete time, hence, by difference equations that relate the value of a variable at one time to values at adjacent times. That part of system theory that provides models for such dynamical phenomena, using mostly differential and difference equations, is called the theory of dynamical systems.[1] [Kalman, Falb, and Arbib, 1969; Brockett, 1971; Mesarović and Takahara, 1975; and Luenberger, 1979.]

---

[1]Of course, at a higher level of sophistication, the theory of dynamical systems requires a number of algebraic, geometrical, topological, and catastrophe-theoretic concepts as well.

In analyzing complex phenomena, we have to consider more than one variable at a time. Indeed, complex systems are characterized by interactions both among their variables, elements, or subsystems (all referring to the same thing) and with their environment. The ability to deal effectively with large numbers of interrelated variables is one of the most important characteristics of system theory. System theory provides mathematical tools for manipulating large numbers of simultaneous relations. Part of the definition of a complex system is that it is multistate. On the other hand, multi-input/multi-output systems are called multivariable, though multivariable systems are not necessarily complex.

Consider, for example, the problem of controlling air traffic at a modern airport. There are aircraft arriving, say, every five minutes. They have to be assigned a location in one of the available queues before they can land. Some of these flights obviously have priority over others; for example, international flights may have priority over domestic flights in landing. At the same time, a number of aircraft are queued up on the strips on the ground, waiting for their turn to take off. Again, some of these may have priority over others. Now, if the same strip is used for both landing and take-off, we have to coordinate two groups of queues, since no aircraft can land unless the take-off path is already cleared. The fact that there may be more than one queue for landing and take-off and that there are internal priority policies to be considered already makes the problem of coordinating and controlling landing and take-off schedules quite complicated. To be sure, there are at least a dozen more factors to be considered in a real situation. (For example, emergency situations may arise; too many aircraft may arrive at the same time; weather conditions may change unexpectedly; and so on.) The problem of control at an airport thus presents a number of theoretical problems to be solved by control theory, which is part of the discipline of system theory.

System-theoretic techniques thus have a wide range of applications, though system theory itself is essentially a theoretical discipline. Whenever we deal with a situation where there are too many variables, patterns of interrelations change over time, the value of a variable has to be predicted, a model has to be developed to represent a system, or a system is to be controlled in a specific manner to achieve a particular goal, system theory surely has something to contribute.

The following is a random list of fields that are or will have to be included in system theory: game theory, computer science, programming theory, cybernetics, operations research, computation theory, modeling, control theory, econometrics, optimization, artificial intelligence, pattern recognition, algebraic coding theory, and circuit theory.

How did system theory emerge? I submit that the following factors were involved:

1.   There was a general awareness among scientists in a variety of disciplines, mainly engineering, that the same types of problems are dealt with in

apparently unrelated areas. For example, goal-seeking behavior, communication, and control patterns were found to be common among machines, biological systems, and even organizational and social systems. This awareness led Norbert Wiener to the idea of cybernetics as a general theory of control and communication in machines and animals. [Wiener, 1948; 1950.]

2.   At the same time, Bertalanffy [1950] and others proposed the idea of a general system theory as a philosophy of science that transcends all academic disciplines, even mathematics. Even though Bertalanffy's idea had an influence on the later development of system theory, it was not successful, mainly because it rejected mathematics as the language of science. Consequently, what is presently referred to as system theory does not have much in common with Bertalanffy's general system theory.

3.   In the early 1960s, a new trend appeared, aimed at developing a mathematical theory of complex interactive phenomena, which led to the development of mathematical system theory. (I hasten to add that *system theory* and *mathematical system theory* refer to one and the same thing. There is no such thing as a nonmathematical system theory.) The major efforts in this direction are reflected in the works of a long list of researchers.[2] Although these authors have approached system-theoretic problems from different perspectives, using different analytical tools, they have all contributed to the development of system theory. As a result of these various contributions, and several other significant developments by others, system theory at the present time has found a more or less definitive form.

Although I cannot in the allotted space give more than only the sketchiest outline, I wish to emphasize that whenever we deal with complex interactive phenomena, we cannot avoid using the results of system theory, in the same way that we cannot avoid using the results of physics or chemistry when we want to study the nature of physical objects.

A system is a precise mathematical object and system theory a mathematical theory, though not entirely a branch of mathematics. Any attempt to apply system theory outside its mathematical context is then not proper. This remark makes it clear that much of what is considered as applications of system theory to various other disciplines, mainly social sciences, is not system-theoretic. (Not that system theory could not ideally be applied to

---

[2] Among the most important of the contributions are: Kalman, Falb, and Arbib [1969]; Bensoussan [1971]; Bensoussan and Lions [1978; 1981]; Bensoussan, Delfour, and Mitter [1982]; Bellman [1971]; Brockett [1971; 1978]; Brunovský [1970]; Byrnes and Falb [1979]; Fuhrman [1979]; Hazewinkel and Kalman [1976]; Hermann and Martin [1977]; Martin and Hermann [1978]; Kalman [1960a; 1960b; 1962; 1965; 1971; 1972; 1976; 1979; 1980; 1981; 1982]; Klir [1969]; Luenberger [1964; 1966; 1971; 1979]; Mesarović [1964]; Mesarović, Macko, and Takahara [1970]; Mesarović and Takahara [1975]; Pontryagin et al. [1962]; Popov [1972; 1973]; Rosenbrock [1970]; Rouchaleau and Sontag [1979]; Tannenbaum [1981]; Thom [1972; 1974; 1977; 1980]; Willems [1979]; Wonham [1967; 1974]; Zadeh and Desoer [1963]; Zadeh and Polak [1969].

social sciences; I am simply emphasizing the need for, but want of, appropriate applications.)

Before proceeding further, I would like to suggest the following definition for the discipline of system theory:

> *System theory (or system science) is the theory (science) of mathematical models of complex interactive systems.*

The true meaning of this definition, and the justification for its adoption, will become clear in the following pages.

In order to present some of the specific results of system theory, I need to return occasionally to the discussion of the specification of systems though this will involve some repetition. I will first take up a particular type of specification, called input/output description because the system is described in terms of inputs and outputs. If inputs and outputs of a concrete system are distinguishable, then it can be modeled or represented by an abstract (mathematical) input/output system.

Following the definition of a system as a relation (or relations) defined on a set, we may now partition the elements of the set into two object sets, one consisting of input elements, the other of output elements. In this way, a constructive definition of a system can be provided. A concrete input/output physical system is a part of the world isolated naturally or artificially from the rest of the world and considered as a box in which something (matter, energy, or information) enters at certain times and that itself puts out something at certain times. At each moment of time, the system, be it continuous or discrete, receives some input and produces some output. When the system produces output discretely, we assume that the output between two points of time is simply zero. We assume that values of the input are taken from a specific set, which for every system will be defined depending on the circumstances. For example, a country's imports are often restricted by both governmental regulatory policies and the conditions of the international-trade system. Or, another example, the amount of information a particular computer can process in every second is limited to the capacity of its central-processing unit (CPU). Such restrictions on inputs are quite natural and related either to bounds on inputs or the nature of the inputs. Thus, we define a set of permissible or allowable inputs to the system. In the same way, we define a set of permissible outputs from a system, though with much milder restrictions.

A philosophical justification for such an input/output description of a system helps make it clear that the notion of an input/output system is not simply a practical device. If we consider the system S contained in a specific domain D of the world with walls around it, then we need somehow to get inside this domain in order to be able either to control it or observe it. This remark paraphrases one made by René Thom:

. . . a system is never completely independent of us, human observers (if it was, we had better forget about it . . .); hence the walls of *D* have to be provided with windows, through which we may act on the system or, conversely, receive information about its inner state. This justifies introducing the notion of Input and Output of the system, or—in slightly different terms—of control parameters and of observables. (Thom, 1980, p. 3.)

In the input/output description of a system, the assumption is that we do not know anything about the internal structure of the system. All we observe (or know for sure) are the inputs and outputs. This type of description is also referred to as external description.

Now, an interesting and natural question arises. Can we say what the output of a system would be by just observing its input at the present time? The answer is generally no. In other words, we may also need to know the past history of the inputs of the system. Depending on the structure of the system, we may need to go back one time-point, two time-points, or more, in the past. Thus, the output of a system generally depends on both its present input and its past history, meaning some or all of its input/output pairs in the past. It is, however, best not to differentiate between present input and past input. The reason for this is that we would like to introduce a notion of *state* fundamental to our understanding of systems and containing those parts of the past and the present history of the system that are relevant to determining present and future outputs. We say, therefore, that the present output depends on the state of the system, and the (present) state of the system is informally defined as that part of the present and the past history of the system that is relevant to determining present and future outputs. The present state of a system, then, must be thought of as some (internal) attribute of the system at the present moment that determines the present output completely and affects future outputs. This idea is expressed in the following statement:

> Intuitively, the state may be regarded as a kind of information storage or memory or an accumulation of past causes. We must, of course, demand that the set of internal states of the system be sufficiently rich to carry all information about the history of the system needed to predict the effect of the past upon the future. We do not insist, however, that the state be the *least* such information, although this is often a convenient simplifying assumption. (Kalman, Falb, and Arbib, 1969, pp. 4–5.)

A system is finite-dimensional if its so-called state space is finite-dimensional. By this, we simply mean that the number of variables used to describe the state of the system at every point of time is a finite number. Most real-life systems are finite-dimensional. In large-scale systems, the number of such variables is relatively larger, but it is still finite. For example, the state of an economy can (supposedly) be described by a finite number of such variables as output rates of production sectors, consumption rates of consumption sectors, prices of various commodities, level of savings, and so on.

By a finite-state system, on the other hand, we mean a system that evolves in a finite number of states or takes only a finite number of states. An economy cannot be modeled as a finite-state system (i.e., as an automaton), whereas a sequential digital computer is a finite-state system.

Several more concepts of importance in system theory remain to be discussed: reachability, controllability, observability, realization, parameterization, identification, structure, and model. Since system-theoretic concepts are purely mathematical concepts, my attempts to make them comprehensible without using mathematical notations may prove unsuccessful. I should first recall the need to make three distinctions: (1) a "concrete" system, sometimes called a process or a plant; (2) an "abstract" or mathematical system, which is usually meant if *system* is used without a modifying adjective; and (3) an (abstract mathematical) "model" or "class of models" for a concrete system.

Suppose a concrete system is given or to be constructed. We describe this system by a set of mathematical equations. This set of equations defines a (mathematical) system and may be taken as a model for that particular concrete system. Therefore, our basic assumption here is that a mathematical model for a particular concrete system—existing or to be constructed—is already at hand. (I shall later return to the discussion of model building.)

We can think of all information-processing taking place inside a concrete system (or, equivalently, inside an abstract system that represents it) as expressed by transformations of states. Then, we may ask the following basic questions: (1) What effect does a specific input have on the state of the system? (2) What effect does the state have on output, or what do the outputs tell about the system? The answer to these two questions lies in the explication of two basic system-theoretic concepts: *reachability* and *observability*.

A system is (completely) reachable if every part of it is accessible to inputs. In other words, if any state can be produced by applying a suitable input, then the system is reachable.

For example, if we can change every significant situation in an economy by applying a suitable control policy (input or set of inputs), then the mathematical system-model representing the economy is said to be (completely) reachable.

On the other hand, as a dual of the concept of reachability, and with strictly dual reasoning, we can show that

if we can always determine the internal conditions of the system—that is, the instantaneous values of all its state variables—from the infor-

mation contained in the output, then the system is (completely) observable.

Observability of a system is an abstract mathematical concept and should not be mistaken for the ordinary process of observation. In the language of mathematical system theory, a system is said to be completely observable if its states can be inferred from the output structure. To determine the complete mathematical conditions of *reachability* and *observability* of all classes of systems is a fundamental question of system theory. The answer to this question has been found for several classes of systems.

In order to make these two abstract notions clear, consider a simple example (adapted from Rugh [1975]). A system of two water buckets, one above the other, consists of two *states*, one *control*, and one *output*. The two states are the depth of water in each bucket; the control is the water flow into the second bucket; and the output is the water flow out of the second bucket. This concrete system can be represented in an input/output form, depicting a single-input/single-output system. We need not assume knowledge of the (internal) states of the system.

If no water flows from the second bucket into the first, the depth of water in the first, that is, the first state-variable, cannot be influenced by inflow into the second bucket. Thus, we do not expect the mathematical system representing this system to be *completely reachable*. (Remember that we have reserved the concepts of reachability, observability, and so on, for mathematical systems representing concrete systems and shall not apply them to concrete systems themselves.) Thus, if the mathematical system representing a concrete system is not reachable, we conclude that the states of the concrete system should not be reachable either—assuming, of course, that the mathematical system is a correct representation of the concrete system. To repeat, system-theoretic concepts apply only to mathematical systems and have implications for concrete systems only in an indirect way.

In a different system, where water from the outside flows into the upper bucket and from there into the second bucket, and the output is the outflow from the upper bucket, we find a different situation. Since the output from the first bucket is not influenced by the water-level of the second—which implies that not every state of the system influences an output—the mathematical system representing this (concrete) system is not completely observable.

Reachability is a necessary condition for controllability of a system and thus it is the fundamental system-theoretic concept underlying all questions of control. Observability, on the other hand, is the fundamental concept underlying all questions of estimation of practically measurable variables. We sometimes undertake to estimate unmeasurable variables from their effects on measurable variables. Therefore, if the system is observable, unmeasurable variables can be deduced by computation from the measured ones.

Complete controllability (observability) means that all states are controllable (observable). The concepts of complete controllability and complete observability are fundamental theoretical notions, and many techniques of modern control design rely on satisfying these conditions. From a practical point of view, however, we do not always need to go through laborious formal calculations to check these conditions. The reason is that in practical applications, a good analyst can often decide from certain structural considerations whether a system is controllable (observable). I should mention that complete observability is also important in the context of system control. The reason is that we usually determine the controls to be applied to a system on the basis of measurements of available outputs. Inputs affect the states, and states affect the outputs; thus, the concepts of controllability and observability relate the input and output structure to the internal state mechanism. If the output structure is deficient in that it does not convey sufficient information about the internal state of a system, then it may not be possible to devise suitable control strategies to make the system behave in a desired way. Thus, in general, good control requires both the ability to get sufficient knowledge about the internal state of the system (observability) and the ability to change the values of states and thereby the behavior of the system (controllability).[3]

If a system is not reachable as presented, it can always be reduced to a reachable one by throwing away all its unreachable states. Likewise, if a system is not observable as presented, it can always be reduced to an observable one by throwing away all its nonobservable states.

The intimate relation of the concept of observability with the question of measurement of information in information sciences should be given proper consideration. If we apply both types of reductions just mentioned in a combined form, any system can be reduced to a form both reachable and observable. Such a form, or such a reduced-form system, is called canonical.

Neither the first nor the second bucket-system just described can have canonical mathematical representations, since these systems contained nonreachable or nonobservable states, unless we disregard such states. This means that in the first bucket-system we must disregard the depth of water in the first bucket, because it is not influenced by the control, which makes the system nonreachable. In the second bucket-system, we must disregard the depth of water in the second bucket, since it does not influence the only output of the system (that is, the outflow from the first bucket), which makes the system nonobservable. After such reduction is performed, the system is canonical in form. Thus, canonical means that a system is both reachable (every state can be reached from an input) and observable (every state can be observed from an output).

---

[3] For a more detailed discussion, see Luenberger's very instructive elementary textbook. [Luenberger, 1979.]

A third fundamental concept in system theory is realization. The problem of realization is the basic problem of identification, and, hence, modeling. Modeling is one of the main aims of system theory, with many implications for various fields of application from physics to econometrics.

Why do we need to develop models? Classical physical sciences dealt with situations where systems under study were relatively simple. The solar system, for example, with all its apparent complexity, is a much less complex system than a computer. The solar system can be studied using only the laws of physics. Although various parts of a computer obey the laws of physics, the functioning of a computer cannot be understood by these laws alone. It depends not only on the structure of its parts but also on the way these parts are interconnected. The same holds true for a biological system, such as the human brain, an economic system, a political system, and so on. Modeling is indispensable if complex systems are to be understood.

There are basically two approaches to modeling, each suitable to a particular type of modeling problem. The first approach is based on the assumption of laws governing the functioning of systems. The second is based on the assumption that the laws, if any, governing the functioning of a system are not known and, therefore, that a model must be constructed of the relevant data representing behavior of the concrete system to be modeled. The first approach is essentially theory-dominated, and the second approach is data-dominated. Both these approaches have advantages and disadvantages.

The first approach consists of writing down equations describing the functioning of a concrete system based on laws, such as Newton's law, Kirchoff's law, and so forth, and then fitting equations to data to determine values of the so-called free parameters that are not accessible to direct measurements or observation. Kalman has made interesting remarks about this approach (although he is essentially inclined toward the second approach), and I paraphrase him. [Kalman, 1974, pp. 496–500.]

1. Knowledge of physical laws is not enough, we must deduce their consequences in complicated situations. If the real system is too complex, we build a model. This allows deductions to be made more easily or more economically.

2. If the laws on which the model is based are valid, fitting the model to real data provides a method for determining values of parameters that are not accessible to direct measurement or observation. By means of the model, such parameters may be determined indirectly. If the model has no theoretical basis, then the parameters have no concrete meaning even if they have a well-determined, stable numerical value.

3. If model building is divorced from a priori laws, the existence of the model, however accurately it fits the data, has no implications beyond a kind of efficient tabulation of data.

4. It may be possible to contradict a law by the impossibility of fitting models based on it to real data. The converse situation occurs much less frequently: A well-fitting model does not establish the law on which it is based.

Kalman describes the main features of theory-dominated modeling; again, I paraphrase him:

1. The relevant behavior of a real system must be isolated and described in a formal mathematical way.
2. A class of models must be given, constructed on the basis of laws supposed to govern the relevant phenomenon and containing a sufficient number of free parameters to allow the behavior of the model to be fitted to real behavior.
3. The class of models must include the behavior in question (now interpreted as a model), so that we are assured a priori of a realization of the behavior within the given class of models.
4. Conceptually, models and real systems must be sharply distinguished. System theory is the study of the former, not the latter.

Kalman's main criticism of this philosophy of model construction is that the models developed are strongly dependent on laws, which has at least three implications. First, that laws built into a model usually constitute a more important body of quantitative data than the quantitative knowledge of the free parameters of the model, and, therefore, nothing essentially new can be learned from the model. The structure of the system is predetermined by the laws and only certain parameters have been estimated. This process should not be called system identification in the true sense of the term, since it basically consists of parameter estimation. The second limitation is that this type of modeling is not possible in areas of science where we do not know of any laws governing the behavior of systems. A third limitation of this modeling approach is that because it is theory-dominated and therefore disciplinary, the methodological principles developed cannot be easily carried from one discipline to another.

These considerations motivate the development of the second approach to modeling, which is basically data-dominated. Here, Kalman takes an approach that he admits to be purely Platonic. He believes that:

The only possibility of freeing the modeling process from over-dependence on "laws" is to convert the laws into purely mathematical axioms. Thus laws of physics ("acceleration proportional to force," "conservation of momentum") are replaced by mathematical statements ("linearity," "convexity"). As a consequence, the entire modeling process may be built up in a rigorous mathematical (hence "mechanizable") way. (Kalman, 1974, p. 500.)

A potential advantage of this approach would be that models are then no longer confined to the boundaries of rigidly separated disciplines and are equally applicable to physics, biology, computer science, economics, sociology, and so forth. This approach to modeling is based on the assumption that the fundamental concepts and structures (Kalman uses the word *universal underlying truths*, which I shall avoid for the sake of clarity) underlying all models of dynamical phenomena are purely mathematical in form, whatever the concrete embodiment of these phenomena (physical, biological, . . .). Kalman takes these mathematical laws to be certain algebraic rules (such as linearity).[4]

The second approach to modeling then conists of finding an equivalence class of models for a concrete system directly from input/output data (that is, behavior), which are assumed to have been generated by that system. Given a fixed amount of data and a specific type of model to be constructed for the system at hand, say a linear deterministic model, two main questions to be asked are (1) Could these data have been generated by a linear deterministic system? and (2) Does the class of all realizations constructed for the given data contain elements that are essentially different? These two questions are referred to as questions of the existence and uniqueness of realizations, respectively. The answer to both depends on many formal mathematical conditions. It can be shown that for finite-dimensional linear deterministic systems—assuming that the data are complete—a unique realization can always be constructed. When the data are not complete, the problem is more complicated, and the answer to this question is only partially known. Also, the problem of stochastic realization has a rich literature. For nonlinear systems, however, the problem of realization is very complicated and generally unsolved. To explain these abstract concepts, some degree of formalism would be indispensable; I therefore dispense with the explanatory exercise.

The realization problem for linear deterministic systems can be formulated in this question: "Given a complete external, or input/output, description of a system, can we determine a class of models for the internal structure of the system?" The answer is yes. More precisely, *given a fixed amount of input/output data about a (concrete) dynamical system, canonical realizations always exist; they depend on the data, and only on the data, and any two canonical realizations based on the same data are isomorphic.* (The reader will find detailed expositions of this classical result in many places. See, for example, the original paper of Kalman.) [Kalman, 1962.]

The next step is to define *model.* We must admit the possibility of only partial success in the process of identification, in that several different systems may have to be accepted as the model for a concrete system to be identified. The basic problem of identification is that of realizations. Identifi-

[4]For a dissenting view, see Thom [1972].

cation is limited only by the nonuniqueness of realizations. [Kalman, 1981, p. 5.]

Let us summarize our discussion of the second approach to modeling. The variables to be considered as the state variables of a specific concrete system are chosen by the modeler to begin with. This set of state variables, among other things, determines which data-set must be considered as representing the behavior of the concrete system to be identified (i.e., the concrete system for which a model is to be constructed). The realization of these data generates an equivalence class of models for the concrete system at hand. This stage of the modeling process is the system theorist's job. Then, it is the modeler's job to choose a model out of the equivalence class of models generated for this system.

Thus, the class of models identified for a concrete system is dependent on the data and only on the data describing the behavior of the concrete system at hand. Considering that the modeler chooses a specific data-set as the one describing the behavior of a concrete system according to his or her assumptions about the relevance of the data to the concrete system, and in view of the specific form of arrangement of the data (e.g., input/output form) and other assumptions, it is clear that the end result of the modeling process depends on the modeler's judgments.

The assumption of causality, for example, obviously lies behind all input/output descriptions of dynamical systems, inputs explicated ab initio as causes and outputs as effects. In many situations, however, and particularly in identifying socioeconomic systems, it may be argued convincingly that inputs and outputs are not distinguishable beforehand. Hence, "the identification of which variables constitute causes and which effects is itself a modeling question that should be dealt with on a conceptual level." (Willems, 1979, p. 72.) To be sure, the existence or nonexistence of causal relations cannot be ascertained from data. Yet, once such an assumption is made, identifying which variables constitute causes and which effects should be possible in principle, though only as part of the modeling process.

Several difficulties impede the second approach to modeling:

1. Complex systems, which contain the class of large-scale systems, cause serious difficulties. For such systems, it is not at all simple to construct a reduced model. Indeed, model reduction is an open area of active research. When the model is small (i.e., canonical), its construction does not depend on the computational procedure used. When the model is too large (i.e., not canonical), it will contain parts that do not depend on behavioral data and, therefore, not on the concrete system to be modeled, but on the method used to obtain the realization. This dependence is not trivial, nor is it trivial to recognize the canonical part of a noncanonical model. Indeed, it is not easy to decide whether a model is canonical or not. On the other hand, it is mathematically dangerous to try to describe the behavior of a system by a noncanonical model.

2. When sufficient behavioral data are not available (the word *sufficient* in this context is a well-defined term in realization theory), the class of constructed realizations among which a model is to be chosen becomes unreasonably large. Research in this area is in progress.

3. Data-dominated modeling is mathematically precise and safe, but to some extent, it lacks the transparency of theory-dominated modeling in the sense that it may not be easy to give concrete interpretation to the relations contained in the model. Whether or not this is to be considered a serious difficulty depends partly on the type of problem at hand and partly on the purpose of the modeling.

A final remark is pertinent at this point. It is extremely important to distinguish between a concrete system and a model representing it. Many practitioners, especially social scientists, including economists and econometricians, have not clearly distinguished between the two. This lack of clarity as to what is the system and what constitutes a model for it has led to much confusion. For example, we read in the text of Jan Tinbergen's Nobel lecture: "A first subject to be dealt with refers to the necessity to introduce the element of *space* into socioeconomic models." (Tinbergen, 1981, p. 19.) This use of the word *model* is not entirely consistent with our definition of model. All relevant variables of a concrete system, say, a specific socioeconomic system, must already be included in our description of that system, and, indeed, this is the only way we can talk about a system as a well-defined object. Once a system is well-defined, with all its state variables listed and sufficient information about them provided, a model, that is, a mathematical representation of that system, can be constructed. Thus, it is not correct to talk about introducing an element or a variable into a model. In our setting, the whole problem is reduced to providing the right description of a concrete system in terms of its state variables, which is the job of the specialist (in this case the social scientist), then constructing an equivalence class of models realizing that system, which is the job of the system theorist, and finally choosing a model from the equivalence class of models constructed and interpreting and using it, which is again the job of the specialist.

It is important to have the right description of a system before the modeling starts. Without this right description, modeling is bound to be a useless mathematical exercise. In our setting, then, providing the right description of a specific economic system is the job of the economist, and constructing the right mathematical model for that system is basically the job of the system theorist; thus, a basic part of econometrics becomes essentially a part of system theory. To many econometricians, this last remark may sound provocative if not absurd. Yet I shall argue, in line with earlier remarks in this paper, that the main objectives of econometric research, that is, identifying and modeling systems, belong to the domain of system theory. For, to repeat once more, system theory is the theory of mathematical models of (complex) systems.

Returning to the problem of realization, I wish to emphasize that for most deterministic systems, the realization problem has a unique solution, whereas for most stochastic systems, the solution of the realization problem is nonunique.[5] A deeper understanding of the problem of realization requires studying the problem of parameterization of data and model, but I can discuss it only briefly, with a reference to a more detailed discussion. [Kalman, 1981.]

A sharp distinction should be made between two types of parameters, descriptive and intrinsic ones. Descriptive parameters are only subject to *implicit* constraints, whereas the constraints on intrinsic parameters are *explicit*. Descriptive parameters specify the parameters of a particular system, whereas intrinsic parameters are concerned with only the equivalence class of realizations. Therefore, a basic problem of identification is specifying the intrinsic parameters of various classes of systems (e.g., linear deterministic systems that are finite-dimensional).

The *intrinsic parameters* of a class of systems should be characterized by two properties:

(i) There is one and only one parameter set corresponding to any system in the class.
(ii) The constraints on the parameters are explicit.

. . . so, in an oversimplified way, we have arrived at the conclusion that

Identification = Realization + Parameterization

(Kalman, 1981, pp. 13 and 19.)

To illustrate the difference between the descriptive and intrinsic parameters of a model, we consider the example of rotation on a plane (two-space). [Kalman, 1981.] Roughly speaking, the descriptive parameters of the model of a system involving rotation in space are functions of an angle. But the only intrinsic parameter of this model is the angle itself. This parameter is not free, but subject to an equivalence relation. "What has been generally referred to as 'structural parameters,' particularly in econometric literature, are the 'descriptive parameters,' whereas the truly structural parameters of a system are its unique intrinsic parameters." [Kalman, 1981.]

From our discussion of modeling based on input/output data, it should be clear that such modeling activities are intimately related to the study of properties of time-series data. However, the intrinsic properties of data—say, the patterns of jumps in time-series data—have not been discussed in time-series literature until recently. [Kalman, 1979.] A large number of open problems are to be investigated in the future. "At present even the preliminary question of parameterization of the data raises deep-seated theoretical

---

[5] Stochastic realization theory has a rich literature: Kalman [1965]; Rissanen and Kailath [1972]; Faurre [1973]; Akaike [1974]; Picci [1976; 1977]; Faurre et al. [1979]; Van Putten and Van Schuppen [1979].

questions. The entire literature of time-series analysis will have to undergo a certain revision . . . ." (Kalman, 1981, p. 38.) Intrinsic parameterization is a rather complicated topic, meriting detailed and technical discussions. [Kalman, 1982; Tannenbaum, 1981.]

THE CONCEPT OF INFORMATION

A proper discussion of the notion of information should begin with a distinction between the concepts of *information* and *amount of information*. The first concept generally refers to content, thus indicating what information a message or an experiment has supplied, whereas the second answers the question of how much information has been supplied. A second and most crucial distinction is that between the concepts of *semantic* and *nonsemantic* information; the latter has been called *physical* information.

A comprehensive discussion of the meaning of the concept of *information* lies outside the scope of this paper. One thing is certain from the literature: There is no consensus, no clarity, but plenty of confusion. Yet, it is perhaps possible to draw some distinctions among various denotations and interpretations of the term.

The central notion in the set of alternative concepts referred to as information is that of semantic information. According to Carnap [1950] and Bar-Hillel [1964], semantic information conveyed by a statement, which is referred to as the content of that statement, is the *"class of those possible states of the universe which are excluded by this statement*, that is, the class of those states whose being the case is incompatible with the truth of the statement."" (Bar-Hillel, 1964, p. 299.) If we replaced the word *states* by *state-description*, which is technically preferable, the definition for the content of a statement becomes *the class of all state-descriptions excluded by this statement*.

One basic advantage of this shift to state-description is the necessity of realizing the treatment with respect to given languages. (The word language is used in its logical sense, and in this sense, it contains both ordinary [natural] languages, such as English and French, and specialized [artificial] languages, such as computer languages, mathematical systems, and so on.)

A basic disadvantage of the work of Carnap and Bar-Hillel in defining semantic information on languages is that their approach is based on subjective probability versus empirical probability and apparently has not led to significant progress. More recently, it has been suggested that the concept of *information* is actually more fundamental than the concept of *probability*. [Ingarden and Urbanik, 1962; Forte and Kampé de Fériet, 1967; Černý and Brunovský, 1974.] Indeed, it has been suggested that probabilities exist only for special cases of information measures. [Cyranski, 1979.]

Based on such an assumption, a new approach to the idea of semantic information has been suggested, starting with a concept of system that corre-

sponds to the definition of the abstract notion of system previously discussed, meaning a relation defined on a set. [Ibid.] Thus, the basic assumption in this approach is that a system of objects is defined (i.e., completely
characterized) by some class of empirically definable relations on the family
of objects.[6] I cannot in this paper undertake to explain the concepts of
information and *measurement* and the attempts to extend and generalize
these classical notions.

I should not, however, ignore the question of the relation between the
theory of semantic information and the theory of communication or transmission of information or, even more appropriately called, the theory of
signal transmission, as originally developed by Shannon and Weaver. There
has been a deplorable confusion here due mainly to the misuse of terminology. The two theories have entirely distinct subject-matters and aims. The
theory of semantic information deals with the question of what and how
much content and meaning a proposition, sentence, statement, message,
signal, or observation has. In short, we may ask what and how much information is conveyed. The theory of communication or signal transmission, on
the other hand, is concerned with the question of what happens to a message, signal, or sentence when it is transferred through a channel from a
source to a receiver and what type of message can carry more content or
information. This latter theory is not concerned with the information or the
content of a message or sentence in itself and, thus, should not have been
called information theory.

Although the original writers on the mathematical theory of communication, or theory of (transmission of) information, have made it explicit that
they are not concerned with the semantics of communication, others have
failed to issue such a necessary warning. [Shannon and Weaver, 1949.]
Claude Shannon states, "These semantic aspects of communication are irrelevant to the engineering problem." (Ibid., p. 3.) And Colin Cherry said,
"It is important to emphasize, at the start, that we are not concerned with
the meaning or truth of messages; semantics lies outside the scope of mathematical information theory." (Cherry, 1951, p. 383.) Still, Cherry could not
help using this word *information* in a misleading way.

Although the mathematical theory of communication deliberately neglects semantic aspects of the process of communication, that is, the question of the meaning of messages, the underlying theoretical distinction
creates problems in application. The reason is that in most real-world situations, we are often concerned with almost all of such aspects simultaneously, and, therefore, a comprehensive theory of information dealing with
all these different aspects in a coherent manner is badly needed. Such a
theory does not exist at present. Bar-Hillel tried to develop a calculus of
information, with the aim of showing that it could be regarded as a common

---

[6]By "empirically definable relations," these authors mean those relations that can be established among objects as a result of measurements performed on them.

formal system containing both a theory of semantic information and the theory of signal transmission. [Bar-Hillel, 1964.] He was not entirely successful, mainly because his approach was based on subjective versus empirical probability. More recent efforts in this direction show that the problem can be approached without any probabilistic assumptions. This approach requires the use of a new type of mathematics that has not ordinarily been used in classical information theory; it may be considered as essentially system-theoretic though the authors have not made any explicit remark to this effect. [Černý and Brunovský, 1974; Cyranski, 1979.]

In the theory of communication (or signal transmission), we measure the relative rarity of each signal in a given set and in this way, find a measure of distortions in the content of what is carried by the signal; we sometimes call this the amount of information a signal can carry. This approach will be explicated by a simple example.

Imagine that a man who has two sons *A* and *B* finds a message on his desk indicating that his son had 'phoned him while he was away. If there is no other information, he would wonder which one of his sons had 'phoned. This message can indeed be considered as two potential messages, each referring to a distinct event: (1) *A* 'phoned; (2) *B* 'phoned. Since the event-set does not have a unique element, the information we can derive from it is obviously not maximum. In this case, the probability of the occurrence of any one of the two events is ½. If the man had three sons, the probability of the occurrence of any one of the events would have been ⅓, and the information conveyed by the message in this case would be less than in the previous case. Thus, we can say that the more improbable an event or signal, the more information it can carry. This is the sense in which the communication engineer uses the word *information* and relates it to the concept of probability in order to be able to measure the amount of information. The job of the communication engineer is, then, basically to design codes that can carry the maximum possible information.

But this is totally distinct from the problem of analyzing and measuring the meaning or the semantic information conveyed by messages or contained in them. It is, of course, also meaningful to compare the semantic information content of two messages. For example, we may assert that a statement such as *John is a translator* contains less semantic information than a statement such as *John translates from several languages;* similarly, *I will see you sometime next week* contains less semantic information than *I will see you next Monday.* But the communication engineer is only interested in the comparative rarity of statements of this kind expected to come from a certain source and would like to have a quantitative measure of these rarities. It must be perfectly clear, however, as Bar-Hillel has put it, that:

> *There is no logical connection whatsoever between these two measures, i.e., the amount of (semantic) information conveyed by a statement and the measure of rarity of kinds of symbol sequences . . . .*

Notice that *the concept of semantic information has intrinsically nothing to do with communication.* If an explication for this concept can be found, then the proposition that all apples are red will carry a certain amount of information entirely independently of whether a statement to this effect is ever transmitted . . . (Bar-Hillel, 1964, pp. 286–287.)

It is high time that we ask ourselves what we, and others, too, mean by the term *information science.* By information science, we mean the assemblage of systematic studies aimed at understanding, interpreting, analyzing, and measuring information; and modeling, organizing, and utilizing the process of transferring information, or more generally, knowledge—be it among humans, humans and machines, or only among machines. From this perspective, communication theory and the theory of semantic information are considered only as parts, though significant parts, of the broader discipline of information science.

SYSTEM THEORY AND INFORMATION SCIENCE

Throughout this paper, I have tried to point out the relations between system theory and information science. It may be helpful if I attempt a synthesis of my scattered remarks on this question.

An *information system* in the nonsemantic sense of the term is a special type of *relation* or *transformation* defined on two reference sets: inputs and outputs. In this case, information generated by the information source may be considered the input to the system and information derived from the system the output of the system. The information system can be defined in this manner if it is both *continuous* (e.g., nondigital measuring-devices such as a voltmeter; or devices for measuring pitch and amplitude of a sound wave, color and brightness of a graphic pattern, field strength of a radio emission, etc.) or *discrete* (e.g., a written language, a digital computer, etc.).

Also, as Thom remarked, there is a conceptual relation between an input/output representation of a system and the requirement to interact with the outside world (observe the outside world) in an information-theoretic sense. Indeed, Thom goes as far as relating the apparent time reversibility of physical laws with the concept of semantic information. Thom states:

I would claim—as a principle—that any phenomenon is associated with some kind of irreversibility: for a phenomenon has to *appear,* hence it has to emit something which can be seen (or detected through some apparatus amplifying human vision). Then the apparent time reversibility of physical laws only shows that these laws do not describe phenomena by themselves, but more accurately change of frames between observers. They describe, so to speak, how the same local irreversible phenomenon may be perceived by different observers . . . .

Putting things more abruptly, I would dare to say that the time reversibility of physical laws is probably no more than the expression of a sociological constraint, namely communication between several observers. For this constraint is nothing more than the linguistic constraint between members of the same linguistic community: when people speak the same language, they share the same semantic universe: because, to the same sentence, they have to put the same meaning (or at least, approximately the same). In fact, any observer has to communicate with himself—with his own past. Hence he needs to have the possibility of comparing his way of looking at the universe at time t_1 with the look he had at time $t_0 < t_1$; this requires a common standard of description, a permanent way of parameterizing the states of the world. Hence reversibility of the dynamics. (Thom, 1977, pp. 193–194.)

I cannot discuss here Thom's remarks and their far-reaching philosophical implications. I would like to emphasize that the questions of the relations between information science and system-theoretic concepts cannot be resolved without deep study of a number of extremely complex problems. For example, a theory of semantic information has to be developed in full consideration of automata theory, artificial intelligence, mathematical linguistics, hence, system theory as such.

The problem of modeling in system theory has turned out to be related to the question of deriving information about the state of a system from the given set of data. More specifically, two basic problems of information sciences, namely, the problem of analysis and measurement of the information content of a set of data derived from an experiment, and the problem of modeling information systems, have become intimately related to realization theory. I have discussed the significance of the results of realization theory in analyzing time-series data and concluded that the classical literature of time-series analysis needs an overall revision to incorporate the recent system-theoretic results. The problem of modeling should be considered as a very general problem. Models are used as tools for policy analysis and decision-making. They are also used to design information systems, and, therefore, they play a crucial role in providing us with proper information about a situation.

In the third part of this paper, I discussed the basic distinction between descriptive and intrinsic parameters of both models and data. This distinction implies another, namely, between two types of information that can be derived from the mathematical model developed for a concrete system, depending on whether this information is based on values of the descriptive or the intrinsic parameters. The former is called *descriptive information,* the latter *structural information.* Descriptive information derived from a system is relevant to only that particular system; structural information derived from a system is relevant to all members of the class of systems to which that particular system belongs. To illustrate, consider the class of all circles. Those properties of a particular member of this class that make it distinct from other circles (i.e., its radius) are descriptive and, hence, can provide us with only descriptive information about the circle. Those properties of a circle, on the other hand, that are common to all circles and make it distinct from anything that is not a circle are intrinsic and, hence, can provide us with structural information about the circle. The set of properties that distinguish circles from noncircles is invariant under changes in descriptive parameters. A similar argument applies to various classes of systems.

INFORMATION, SYSTEM STRUCTURE, AND MODELING

As society becomes complex, it requires more structure, organization, regulation, and information. Thus, the question of how information should be processed is becoming increasingly important. However, in order to deal with complex systems, we need to know how to capture complexity. Although it is perhaps impossible to provide a formal definition of complex systems, most of us have an intuitive idea of what a complex system is.

One fundamental requirement for identifying the structure of a complex system is the existence of a minimal information set concerning the structural aspects of that particular system. Without adequate information about inputs, outputs, processing, and location of books in a library, for example, we cannot develop a model of the operation of a library as a system. The question of what is the minimal information set required to identify the structure and develop a (structural) model of a system is, then, an extremely important but as yet open question. There is, at present, no general theory that determines such a (unique or nonunique) minimal information set. This is a fundamental problem in developing general-purpose problem-solving systems and beyond that, in developing a general theory of modeling. I believe that the development of such a theory of modeling must be pursued in the context, and as a natural continuation of (mathematical) system theory. System theory does have the capacity to represent systems of various forms regardless of their nature. The next step, then, would be to develop software that transforms mathematical representations into computer programs.

Although there is no causal link between a model and the reality that is supposed to be modeled, the selection of a model for a particular subject is not entirely arbitrary either. Therefore, a process of selecting relevant information is a necessary part of the process of modeling. The specific information set required to model a system depends entirely on the purpose of the modeling. There is no single model of any system in the world, be it mankind, history, or nature. Thus, there is no unique information set that can provide a comprehensive model of a system in its entirety. Moreover, there are no absolute criteria for preferring one model to another.

CONCLUSIONS

System theory applies to any branch of science in which we deal with complex interactive phenomena irrespective of the context in which the problem may arise. System theory is a mathematical discipline though not entirely a branch of mathematics. It is the theory of mathematical models and applies to various concrete situations by providing practitioners with tools and techniques to develop models for concrete systems. More specifically, if a concrete system is described in terms of a sequence of input/output data, the task of the system theorist is to provide answers to the following questions:

1. How can we construct a mathematical model, describing the internal structure of the system, for a given input/output sequence (i.e., data describing the behavior of a system over time), and where several models can be constructed, how can we obtain the simplest model? (This simplest model is not necessarily the true model, and it is the practitioner who has to choose a model out of the class of models to be constructed.)
2. Given a mathematical model that describes a concrete system and a set of admissible inputs, how can we determine the set of possible outputs of the system? In other words, how can we determine the set of possible behavioral modes of the system?
3. With a prescribed mode of performing measurements on the outputs of a system, is it possible to determine uniquely the (internal) state of the system at any time?
4. Given a criterion of performance for the behavior of a concrete system described by a mathematical model that uses a set of admissible inputs (i.e., controls), what is the best value that this criterion can be made to assume?

Answers to these questions are known for certain classes of systems. However, we are still far from being able to provide complete answers to all these and several other questions for all classes of systems.

Let us emphasize, however, that whenever we have to deal with complex interactive phenomena we cannot avoid using the results of system theory, in the same way that we cannot avoid using the results of physics or chemistry when we want to study the nature of physical objects.

SYSTEM THEORY, MATHEMATICS, AND QUANTIFICATION

Kenneth E. Boulding

Within its rather limited framework, Mortazavian's paper is very instructive. The argument is easy to follow, and I learned a good deal from it. It is, however, very narrow in scope, defining systems only in terms of mathematical models, and, as he says, general system theory goes far beyond this.

The distinction between semantic and nonsemantic information (what I myself call Bell Telephone or B.T. information of the Shannon and Weaver type) is obvious, but also very important, though I do not think the mathematics of semantics goes very far. The real trouble is that as we move into more complex systems, existing mathematics becomes more and more inadequate. It is remarkably deficient, for instance, in verbs. I confess I regard mathematics as one of the least developed of the sciences in terms of its potential. It is very inadequate at the present time for dealing with systems beyond at least the moderately simple. The human brain, for instance, is a system of complexity far beyond the scope of any known mathematics.

Classical mathematics, especially algebra and calculus, is fundamentally a generalization from the properties of numbers. Unfortunately, the real world does not consist of numbers or even very much of quantities. It consists of shapes, sizes, patterns, and "fittings"—that is, structures that fit into each other. I have sometimes said, I confess a little in jest, that there are not much more than a dozen numbers in the real world—e, pi, the velocity of light, Planck's constant, Eddington's mysterious 137, and a few things like that plus zero, 1, 2, 3, 4, 5, 6, 7 plus or minus 2, according to the psychologists. Beyond that, numbers are a figment of the human imagination or at least a crutch—though a useful and necessary crutch—to the human mind. The importance of numbers and numerical mathematics is that they can be mapped into topological structures, so that by their means we can analyze topological structures beyond the complexity with which our minds can deal. It is still topological structures, however, that are the real world, and the topology of n dimensions is still a fairly primitive science. Even Thom's catastrophe theory is still bound to continuous functions, whereas in the real world, we have system breaks, discontinuities, constant change of parameters, and innumerable relations for which there are no mathematical equivalents. The idea, therefore, that mathematization and quantification are the only hallmarks of science seems to be quite fallacious. It has done substantial damage even in the biological sciences, but especially in the social sciences. I was glad to have my attention called to a remarkable article by B. C. Brookes entitled "A New Paradigm for Information Science?" that discusses these considerations in more detail. [Brookes, 1976.]

In the early days of what is now called the Society for General Systems Research (of which I was a founding father and first president), I recall defining a system as anything that was not chaos, and I could hardly blame Mortazavian if he felt that such a definition was too broad and philosophical to be very useful. We did, I also recall, define a general system as any theoretical structure that was of interest to more than one academic discipline. This, perhaps, is a concept too sociological, especially in light of the rather accidental nature of the academic disciplines themselves, to have much prestige. Nevertheless, we cannot avoid the epistemological overtones of the systems concept; if system is equivalent to order (that is, nonchaos) or even some useful subset of things, structures, or relations that exhibit order, the critical question is how we come to perceive, recognize, or know about the order that presumably exists in the real world. This is nearly the same question as how do we get order—patterns and structures—inside our skins, and especially inside our skulls, that represent or map onto corresponding structures in the real world. The system of human learning is immensely complex and still very imperfectly understood, but we must know something about it or we would not be able to transmit the knowledge structures from one generation to the next, even though we do not know much about how these knowledge structures are coded inside the body.

In the formation of our knowledge structures, perhaps three processes can be identified. One is the building of knowledge structure in the nervous system by the genes, which used to be called *instinct*. The second is *thought*, that is, the internal building up of new knowledge structures by processes that involve consciousness. A very important element in this is the perception of identities—that is, relations that cannot be other than what they are. Mathematics has a peculiarly important role to play in perceiving identities; it might almost be defined, indeed, as the sophisticated pursuit of the obvious. Mathematical proof is simply the process of finding out what is indeed obvious, which is not always obvious at first. There is, indeed, a slight rattle from a skeleton in the closet here, partly from Russell and partly from Gödel, even perhaps partly from some Godot for whom we are still waiting and who might point out that what is obvious is not always true. It seems obvious to me that through a point we can draw only one line parallel to another line not going through the point, but it was not obvious to Riemann or Einstein. Similarly, it seems obvious that minus minus is plus, but I worry about the fact that not doing harm is a very different affair from doing good. It seems obvious, too, that infinity times zero is any finite number we like to name though this may involve definitions of both infinity and zero as things toward which we might travel hopefully but never arrive at, especially as infinity, and I presume also zero, has more addresses than we used to think. I worry though about calculating price indices when the price of a color television set in 1910 was infinite and the quantity was zero!

The third process in the formation of knowledge structures is *experience*, which represents a very complex structure of inputs into and outputs from the body, certainly involving B.T. information, but also involving much more than that in terms of structure, for instance, in language or even sense perception. We suspect that if information input is to change knowledge structure within the body, it must itself be structured in such a way that it "fits" into some internal pattern. (I believe strongly in the survival of the "fitting" rather than of the fittest!) If someone addresses a remark to me in Chinese, a language with which, I regret, I am unacquainted, it will have a very different impact from the same remark translated into English, even though both remarks may contain the same number of bits of B.T. information. Even the expression *B.T. information* will have a different impact on my reader in the last sentence than it would have had before reading the paper.

In the learning process, the impact of current inputs, whatever they are, depends on the existing structure of the mind, and this depends in no small measure on the existence of records of the past. We go to a familiar place and are able to find our way around it, because in our minds there is a structure (memory) that has recorded not only past inputs but past structures of knowledge. The success of science as a knowledge-expander depends in no small measure on that aspect of the scientific subculture that consists of keeping careful records of the past, whether this results in maps, the paths of the planets, national income statistics, or experimental results. Both observation and experience, the two great sources of the inputs of science, involve records of the past. Our perception of patterns in the records of the past is the foundation of both prediction and experiment, which is usually prediction of some future pattern of small contrived systems. Our ability to interpret such records and patterns, however, depends largely on whether they fit into previously discovered obvious relations, which are usually, though not always, mathematical in type. I have argued that the great laws of science are either truisms (mathematical identities) or near truisms, relations that we are almost sure have to be this way, which might rank as axioms. Much empirical work is devoted not to finding empirical laws, which are always unreliable, but in spotting where, in the empirical fields, the basic truisms apply. A good example is the principle of conservation, which simply says that if there is a fixed quantity of anything, any increase in one place or form must be offset by decreases in other places or forms. The empirical question is "What is there a fixed quantity of?" Energy? Matter? Money? And so on. A related identity is what I have called the "bathtub theorem"—that the increase in anything in a given period is equal to the additions minus the subtractions. Demography is based on this; so is Keynesian economics, which starts with the truism that everything that has been produced in a given period has either been consumed or is still around.

I know of no mathematical model that does not start off with truisms. To have properties, however, a model has to have behavioral relations, usually in the form of equations, though they can be more complex (inequalities, limits, set functions, etc.), that have constant parameters. Indeed, a parameter is defined as a constant of the system. One of the great problems of the real world, however, is that very few systems have constant parameters; indeed, about the only good example is the solar system and its parallels, which is why celestial mechanics has been so successful. Evolutionary and information systems, however, have constantly changing parameters. The ardent determinist chases rates of change and rates of change of rates of change in the usually vain quest for stable parameters, but the awful truth is that the real world has strong elements of inherent unpredictability. Stochastic models do not solve the problem, because probabilities also are unpredictable and variable. If the real world, as Ackoff has suggested, is a mess, it is a great mistake to be clear about it. Mathematicians, however, have a certain passion for clarity, being devotees of the obvious, which is why they should probably be kept on a suitable leash. Even the theory of fuzzy sets is about rather *nice* fuzzy sets.

Perhaps much of this discussion revolves around what is noise and what is not, as Mortazavian has hinted. Just as there are concepts beyond B.T. information in know-how, know-what, and even know-whether, so there must be concepts beyond B.T. noise, though I find it hard to identify them exactly. I am convinced, however, that the orderly loss of information, in some sense or another, is crucial to the human learning process just as selection—the moderately orderly loss of species—is crucial to the evolutionary process. The parallels between learning and evolution have, indeed, been pointed out many times. This is why we have to be extremely careful about the incautious application of the more traditional mathematical models. Decision processes are a good case in point. Mathematical models usually involve some kind of maximization of an objective variable or measure of value or utility. They not only easily lead to suboptimization (finding the best way to do something that should not be done at all), but they lead to a neglect of the agenda problem—that is, among what alternatives are we choosing? The elimination of agenda items, often by quite nonrational processes like boredom or anger—may be a much more important decision-making process than any kind of optimization with given agenda. Information overload and noise in the form of the seven deadly sins (pride, greed, sloth, etc.) may be much more important in actual decisions than rational optimization. Yet, these are systems, too, mixtures of order and chaos, even though they are intractable to mathematical treatment, at least with current methods. This, however, may be an argument for more and better mathematics rather than less!

CAN MATHEMATICAL SYSTEMS BE CONCRETE?

Richard N. Langlois

In a certain sense, Hassan Mortazavian's paper is as instructive for what it is not as for what it is. It is not about the relevance of system theory to problems in information science. Apart from a few stray tidbits about information (mostly repeated stern warnings not to confuse semantic and non-semantic information), the paper has virtually nothing whatever to say about the relevance of the former discipline to the latter. We might even be led to think that there *is* no connection between them. And that would be too bad. For it seems to me that the constructs of system theory actually provide us with some potentially useful insights into concepts like knowledge and information, meaning and information content.

What Mortazavian's paper *is* about is something called mathematical system theory. This is a well-defined (albeit tacitly defined) intellectual specialty. It has its own style, techniques, and attitudes, which Mortazavian's piece reflects quite accurately. Despite Mortazavian's desire to transform the phrase *mathematical system theory* into a pleonasm,[1] however, this specialty by no means includes all that system theory is conventionally held to contain. To many—particularly the so-called general systems theorists—system theory is a philosophical enterprise, an all-encompassing *Weltanschauung* and philosophy-of-the-Whole.[2] Nonetheless, there is some truth—descriptively if not normatively—to the contention that mathematical modeling is the sine qua non of system theory.

In fact, system theory operates by what I tend to think of as a kind of Platonism. We begin by assuming that there exist various concrete or real-world entities called systems. The system theorist's problem, like Plato's, is that we do not have direct knowledge of the behavior of these sensible things. But we can, instead, study various pure "forms"—in this case,

---

[1] "I hasten to add that *system theory* and *mathematical system theory* refer to one and the same thing. There is no such thing as a nonmathematical system theory." (Mortazavian in his paper in this volume.)

[2] I touch briefly on these issues in my own paper in this volume.

mathematical representations called models—in order to learn about concrete systems.

It is characteristic of system theorists to assume tacitly that the problems of connecting the model with the concrete are difficult in practice but not in principle. While shuttling in and out of the mathematician's cave successfully may require hard work and years of training, it is not a procedure that poses any inherent epistemological difficulties. To the system theorist, all the important questions are to be answered by interrogating the pure forms themselves, which, conveniently, can normally be done with mathematics.

In engineering (where simple realist ontologies always work the best), this approach has proven spectacularly successful. And, as a historical matter, most of the mathematics of system theory grew out of electrical engineering, principally circuit theory.

While it may be that there are as many conceptions of system theory as there are system theorists, it nonetheless seems to me that practitioners fall into two identifiable if overlapping groups: those who wish to leave the cave and those who do not.

One well-known manifestation of system theory goes by names like systems analysis, the systems view, or the systems approach. Broadly speaking, this version of system theory subsumes the discipline of operations research and is concerned with applying mathematical analysis to areas of military, business, and (yes) social management. It is in this guise that system theory has intruded most forcefully into modern thought; and I will resist the temptation to offer my own views on the subject.[3]

The second broad group of practitioners comprises those whose business it is to scrutinize the pure forms. Mortazavian is firmly in this camp. System theory, he says, is the theory of (mathematical) models. And he is quick to quote a warning that this theory "does not accept responsibility for the accuracy or relevance of these models." (Kalman, 1980, p. 7.) Yet, while insisting on the absolute mathematical purity of his discipline, Mortazavian wishes simultaneously to claim for it all-encompassing relevance. In consecutive paragraphs, we read both that "Any attempt to apply system theory outside its mathematical context is . . . not proper" and yet that "whenever we deal with complex interactive phenomena, we cannot avoid using the results of system theory, in the same way that we cannot avoid using the results of physics or chemistry when we want to study the nature of physical objects." The system theorist, it seems, is that most fortunate of people who can have his cake and eat it too; like Aphrodite ever-virginal, he can descend to embrace the worldly without endangering his mathematical purity.

---

[3]The literature here is voluminous and wide-ranging. For an intelligent defense of the systems view, see C. West Churchman [1968b] and for a hysterical one, see Simon Ramo [1969]. For representative critiques, see Laurence H. Tribe [1972] from a philosophical perspective and Ida Hoos [1972] from an empirical point of view.

This miraculous circumstance warrants a closer look, for it is the key to understanding much of Mortazavian's discussion. The solution to the mystery, I would argue, lies in recognizing how seriously mathematical system theorists (of the school Mortazavian represents) take their Platonism.

Apparently following Rudolf Kalman, Mortazavian discusses two approaches to modeling concrete systems. The first approach, he writes, "is based on the assumption of laws governing the functioning of systems. The second is based on the assumption that the laws, if any, governing the functioning of a system are not known, and, therefore, that a model must be constructed on the relevant data representing behavior of the concrete system to be modeled." This first approach appears to be nothing other than the hypothetico-deductive method, the approach that lies at the heart of the modern philosophy of science. This method views models or theories—or, indeed, paradigms or "research programmes"—as logical systems imposed by the mind to explain natural or social phenomena to that mind. Observed data are but one element—and not always the most important element—that goes into evaluating and modifying hypothetico-deductive models.[4] By contrast, the second approach described by Mortazavian implies a naive faith in data long ago renounced—with good reason—by the philosophy of science.

The important point to notice about this data-dominated approach to system theory is not its somewhat atavistic empiricism but the Platonism that is connected to it. The system theorist who adheres to this second approach sees the mathematical model not as a hazy adumbration of the concrete system, but as a more-or-less exact replica of it: The model is a sort of homunculus, identical in all essential ways to the concrete system. To put it another way, the Platonic system theorist believes that all concrete systems actually possess true, unique, knowable mathematical structures. The job of system *identification*—note the choice of word—is thus to interrogate the data and determine directly from these data which pre-formed homunculus (or at least which equivalence-class of acceptable homunculi) accurately captures the concrete system's true mathematical form.[5]

It should be clear why system theorists should prefer this latter view of the world: It serves in the quest to unify all sciences under the banner of system theory, and—not incidentally—it maximizes the role and importance of the system theorist in the scientific process. As Mortazavian explains, the role of the disciplinary scientist ("the specialist") in the Platonic

---

[4]On this growth-of-knowledge approach—which dominates the modern philosophy of science—see especially Imre Lakatos and Alan Musgrave [1970].

[5]It is in this context that much of Mortazavian's discussion and terminology must be understood. The notion of observability, for example, which sounds as if it has heavy epistemological meaning, actually has to do solely with the logic of mathematical models and not at all with the phenomenology of observing a system. The problem of observability is whether, once I already know all about a system and how it operates, I can always tell what the (known) state variables are doing just by watching the (known) output variables.

method is simply to *describe* the system with which he or she deals. The scientist is thus a handmaiden to the great generalist, a kind of graduate research assistant to the system theorist, whose task it is merely to provide the right description of the concrete system. It is the system theorist who performs the real scientific function, spinning the mathematical wheels to identify the correct equivalence-class of models, which is then given back into the grateful hands of the scientist.

Fortunately or unfortunately, however, we do not live in this simple Platonic world. Complex phenomena of nature, mind, and society (concrete systems) do not themselves possess variables; only mathematical models have variables. The job of the scientist is not to describe such phenomena in some nonproblematical fashion; rather, the scientist's task is one of active interpretation, mental construction. And mathematical models are often—but by no means always—useful tools in this creative process. Thus, the mathematical system theorist, who studies the logic of operation of such models, retains an important role in the scientific endeavor—even if it is the same role mathematics has always played in science rather than the supposedly new and distinctly baronial role the mathematical system theorist would wish to be assigned.

SYSTEM THEORY AND INFORMATION SCIENCE
Further Considerations

Richard Mattessich

The claim that system theory and mathematical system theory refer to one and the same thing, and the attempt to identify the broad discipline of system theory with one and only one of its many subareas, is bound to lead to confusion. Thus, it is important to realize that whenever Mortazavian, in his paper in this volume, speaks of system theory, he limits himself and his audience to the relatively narrow area of mathematical system theory. Although authors should be given freedom to choose their own terminology (or that of their circle), that freedom must be curtailed whenever convention is deeply enough rooted in a different meaning—otherwise misunderstanding is inevitable. But there might be more behind this narrow definition. Is it, perhaps, an attempt to declare everything beyond the mathematical part in system theory as trumpery or unscholarly endeavor?

SYSTEM THEORY AS AN EMPIRICAL AND METHODOLOGICAL CONCERN

Even if we were to accept Mortazavian's statement that Bertalanffy's idea of general system theory "was not successful," it can hardly be maintained that the system-theoretical works by Ackoff and Emery [1972], Boulding [1956a], Churchman [1961; 1968a; 1968b; 1971; 1979], Simon [1969 and 1981], J. G. Miller [1978], Bunge [1979a], and many others do not belong to system theory or are less successful than contributions by leading mathematical system theorists. And yet, Mortazavian, in his paper, asserts that "A system is a precise mathematical object and system theory a mathematical theory, though not entirely a branch of mathematics," thereby invoking

Additional support from the Social Sciences and Humanities Research Council of Canada is gratefully acknowledged.

Mesarović's definition according to which "a system is a relation $S \subseteq X \times Y$ on abstract sets X and Y." (Mesarović, Macko, and Takahara, 1970, p. 66.) But Mesarović seems to offer this definition strictly within a "framework of mathematical system theory" without identifying the latter with system theory in general. Mortazavian is quite correct when pointing out the importance of distinguishing between a *concrete system* and a *model* representing it. But instead of admitting that the study of concrete systems belongs to system theory or systems science, he compartmentalizes the academic division of labor in such a way that the empirical scientist's task is to provide the right description of a concrete system specifically for the system scientist, who, in turn, constructs an equivalence class of models into which this and similar models fit. But such an unconventional division of labor, and above all the exclusion of empirical, methodological, and philosophic aspects from the system approach is, I submit, unacceptable for the following reasons:

1. System theory cannot be derived from the type of a priori assumptions or intuitions that form the basis of logic and mathematics (for example, the assumption that the negation of a negation of an assertion is identical with the original assertion) and therefore cannot be part of pure mathematics. Furthermore, system theory cannot be conceived without factual observation and thus belongs to the realm of empirical science. This is not to deny that model building is an analytical concern; but the fact that those models might represent the phenomena of an empirical discipline in a somewhat unrealistic fashion does not convert the propositions expressed by such models into analytical ones. This would be too strong an attempt to make a virtue out of the shortcoming of being unrealistic. Any proposition that lends itself (in principle) to *refutation* (in Popper's sense), whether true or false, whether realistic or unrealistic, is an empirical proposition.

2. Just as theoretical physics, which also consists of (applied) mathematical theories (and likewise "is not entirely a branch of mathematics"), is first of all part of the empirical science of physics, so system theory remains meaningful only as part of one or more, or even all, of the empirical sciences apart from also belonging to applied mathematics. Let us remember that Albert Einstein was not a mathematician but a theoretical physicist with a strong philosophic bent. And if Bogdanov and Bertalanffy had insufficient appreciation for mathematics, we must not fall into the trap of reserving system theory for mathematicians, who lack training in the methodology of pure and applied empirical sciences. However, this is not meant as a rebuff to mathematics, which will always be a requisite for system theory.

3. To test whether a conceptual system "fits" a specific factual phenomenon is an indispensable and empirical-methodological concern of system theory. That is to say, the choice of fitting criteria requires scientific-empirical as well as normative-methodological expertise that can hardly be relegated to any other area but system theory and its philosophy.

4. A thorough study of the emergence and evolution of system theory offers clear evidence that the original impetus for this novel viewpoint arose from the inadequacy of the traditional atomistic and reductionistic approach when dealing with such factual phenomena as emergent (holistic) properties, environmental interactions, feedback information, and so forth. [Bogdanov, 1913 and 1922; Bertalanffy, 1928; 1950; 1968.] This inadequacy was hardly bothersome in physics but was strongly felt in the life sciences; and it is no coincidence that of the two pioneers of system theory, Bogdanov and Bertalanffy, one was a physician-philosopher, the other a biologist. The fact that both of them envisaged this new area as a superscience instead of mere methodology is unfortunate but affords no justification for mathematicians to usurp system theory and claim it entirely for themselves or deprive it of its empirical and methodological content.

5. The attempt to banish the factual and normative-methodological essence of system theory stands in crass contradiction to the present state of the sciences. System methodology has been so widely accepted that system theories not only evolve in operations research and applied mathematics, but emerge, in one form or another, in accounting theory, organization theory, and economics, the management sciences, electronic data processing, and engineering, and even in epistemology and ontology, of which Rescher's and Bunge's rigorous and integrative work are excellent examples. [Rescher, 1979; Bunge, 1979a.]

6. Finally, the system approach, due to its goal orientation, seems to be particularly suitable as a basis for formulating *instrumental hypotheses* (means/end relations), which are of special importance in the applied and social sciences. This entails the emergence of novel methodological and other epistemological problems, which I examined in a previously mentioned work. [Mattessich, 1978; 1974a; 1982.]

With regard to Mortazavian's suggestion to dispense with model-building when dealing with relatively simple systems, I propose he ask himself whether it was not model-building par excellence that led Johannes Kepler and later Isaac Newton to the discovery of fundamental laws of the solar system and of mechanics in general. Mortazavian's suggestion that "the solar system can be studied using only the laws of physics" would have been poor advice for Kepler and Newton, who still had to search for some of these laws. But even today, when the laws of mechanics and relativity theory are available, the scholars at NASA still do plenty of model-building in dealing with the solar system and its exploration. Thus, we might wonder about Mortazavian's or Kalman's distinction between the two approaches to model-building and how basic this distinction really is. Are we not dealing in both cases with the same process of model-building, in one case searching for fundamental relations, in the other case searching for less basic ones? *In both cases, the models are theory-dominated,* but in the first case, the theory is already well supported, while in the second case, it is either (1) a provisional hypothesis or (2) a mere conjecture that is not expected ever to fulfill the function of a scientific law.

Furthermore, the paragraphs devoted by Mortazavian to the genealogy of system theory leave something to be desired. Although Bertalanffy is briefly referred to, no mention is made of Bogdanov's more original work [1913 and 1922] nor of the contributions to this area by Ackoff [1963; 1971], Ackoff and Emery [1972], Bunge [1979a], Churchman [1964; 1968a; 1968b; 1971; 1979], Mattessich [1974a; 1978], J. G. Miller [1978], Simon [1969 and 1981], and many others. Indeed, even within the subarea of mathematical system theory, Mortazavian's references seem to be somewhat lopsided, since his bibliography contains only a single article from the important journal *Mathematical Systems Theory*.

All this is neither meant to deprecate contributions made by Mortazavian nor to deny the usefulness of mathematical system models. On the contrary, Bunge's ontological investigations, for example, provide a comprehensive axiomatic system-framework and thus acknowledge the importance of mathematical formulations in system theory. But Bunge, choosing the term *systemics*—as he holds that there is no single system theory but many of them—emphasizes that

> Systemics has two related motivations, one cognitive and one practical. The cognitive or theoretical rationale of systemics is, of course, the wish to discover similarities among systems of all kinds despite their specific differences. . . . The practical motivation for systemics is the need to cope with the huge and many-sided system characteristics of industrial societies. . . . (Bunge, 1979a, p. 1.)

Furthermore, it must be noted that among Bunge's sixty-three system postulates, there are not only analytical assumptions, but also many empirical and metaphysical (quasiempirical) assumptions. [Mattessich, 1982, p. 66.] Ackoff and Emery [1972] also emphasize their interest in *concrete systems* and, hence, in the empirical approach; and in a similar vein, I may quote Herbert Simon, who pleads for an empirical behaviorally oriented system theory:

> The research that was done to design computer time-sharing systems is a good example of the study of computer behavior as an empirical phenomenon. . . . To understand them, the systems had to be constructed, and their behavior observed. . . . Here again theoretical analysis must be accompanied by large amounts of experimental work . . . . (Simon, 1969 and 1981, pp. 24–25.)

Thus the definition of system offered by Mortazavian would be acceptable only (1) if the term *abstract system* were substituted for the term *system*, and (2) if it were supplemented by Mario Bunge's following definition of a concrete system: "An object is a *concrete system* iff it is composed of at least two different connected things.'' (Bunge, 1979*a*, p. 6.) Perhaps I should note that, for Bunge, a thing is always a *concrete* object and a connection is more than a mere relation, since "two things are *connected* (or *coupled* or *linked* or *bonded*) if at least one of them acts on the other.''

INFORMATION ECONOMICS, AN INDISPENSABLE PART OF INFORMATION SCIENCE

The somewhat narrow treatment by Mortazavian not only misses the empirical and methodological aspects of system theory, but equally neglects the important area of information economics. Such an omission appears to be particularly critical wherever an overall synthesis between system theory and information science is invoked, as it is by Mortazavian. His broad definition of information science gives no indication of excluding information economics and thus presumably would encompass it. But as Mortazavian neither discusses nor even mentions this important area, some pertinent remarks would be due in this paper. I shall, however, deal with information economics in connection with Richard Langlois's paper, "System Theory, Knowledge, and the Social Sciences," elsewhere in this volume.

PROBLEMS OF SYSTEMS THEORY

C. West Churchman

The lead papers in Sections 8 and 9, both of them on the topic of systems or the systems approach, illustrate a phenomenon common to academics who write from the point of view of different disciplines, namely, the ignoring of large hunks of literature on the same topic. I shall add to the confusion and, I hope, to the enlightenment by discussing still another systems approach, which both authors have largely ignored. An approach is toward something, I think (though in the case of the two papers, it seems as though *approach* is equivalent to *method*). The systems approach I want to discuss is an approach to planning.

Planning, a very old human activity, means the attempt to understand enough about a human social system to be able to formulate policies that, if implemented, will lead to an improvement in the system. This is not a definition of planning in a reductionist sense, since it uses such words as *understand, policies,* and *system,* which are at least as difficult to define as the word *planning* itself. But the description does indicate that we, the planners, are in the business of trying to help policymakers primarily, and only secondarily do we strive to excite the intellectual curiosity of people working in various academic disciplines.

The systems approach to planning is old. I date its first writings back to the *I Ching* (say 2000 B.C.),[1] which attempted to classify situations in which humans find themselves and to suggest attitudes about each of them that could create wisdom in action. Many other ancient and modern books may, or should, be cited, that I believe say some important things about planning and a systems approach to it.[2] The reader may notice that these books are written from an extraordinary variety of points of view and mathematics and economics are no more dominating than psychology, biology, law, psychoanalysis, political science, ethics, and epistemology.

[1]Compare Richard Langlois's estimate: "Economists . . . were the first systems theorists."
[2]The list should not omit the following: the *Bhagavad-Gita,* Plato, Aristotle, Lucretius, the *New Testament,* St. Augustinus, Hobbes, Spinoza, Kant, Bentham, Edgar Singer [1948], von Bertalanffy [1968], Emery [1969], Habermas [1970], Van Gigch and Hill [1971], Beer [1972], Ackoff and Emery [1972], Hoos [1972], Bateson [1972], Meadows et al. [1972], J. G. Miller [1978], Jantsch [1980], Checkland [1981].

Since the systems approach to planning is old, it would be ridiculous to judge it either a success or a failure; instead, it is a way of life for those of us who have dedicated our lives to trying to improve the human condition by means of the human intellect. For us, it is almost a platitude to say that we need to be comprehensive because policies carried into action have many ramifications outside the problem area first addressed, for example, all policies—energy, transportation, communication, military defense, and food—are tightly united to education. It is also a platitude to say that no matter how hard we try to be comprehensive, we are in for surprises our intellects completely missed. An example from recent years is the food system of the world: Planners concentrated their attention on such matters as food packages, green revolutions, and the like; we are now coming to realize that the problem of starvation (perhaps as many as one billion people in today's world are starving) is not a problem of food only, but also of world and national politics.

I should say that those of us who refrain from creating a discipline out of planning are scavengers, seeking ideas, methods, and knowledge that will enable us to increase our understanding of how to better the human condition. Most of us have learned to be quite wary because the garbage heap where we do our scavenging has many a nicely wrapped package with such attractive labels as organizational development, zero-based budgeting, control theory, management information system, or management science. We have learned long since that these labels are highly deceptive: organizational development leaves out most of the major issues in trying to redevelop an organization; management information systems are often computer-based databanks; zero-based budgeting does not start from scratch (it is zero distance from last year's budget); control theory says virtually nothing to a manager whose personnel are running amuck; and management science tends to be largely ignorant of what it is like to manage anything.

But often the most discouraging looking packages contain gems of understanding. Who would think that in a book discouragingly called *Foundations of the Metaphysic of Morals,* first published in English in 1799, Kant would write out the first clear ethical guide to systems design: "Never treat humanity, either in yourself or another, as means only but as an end withal." [Kant, 1799 and 1959.] This is a prescription badly needed in an age like ours, which shows strong political tendencies to design systems around utilitarian ethical ideas like productivity and wealth, and use people as means only in the pursuit of these goals.

Or, consider a more recent book by James Hillman, called *The Myth of Analysis.* [Hillman, 1972.] The analysis Hillman had in mind is not the systems analysis that Mortazavian describes in his paper, but rather psychoanalysis. But the myth (of real progress) applies equally well to either meaning of analysis.

Of course, being scavengers, some of us become fond of one kind of package, for example, linear (or nonlinear) programming, game theory, cybernetics, queuing theory, and so forth; so there are as many styles of the systems approach as there are practitioners. For the reader interested in applications, there is the journal *Interfaces*, which publishes applications together with an independent evaluation establishing that the application has worked. For a compendium of theoretical styles, see Peter Checkland's recent book *Systems Thinking, Systems Practice*. [Checkland, 1981.]

In the remainder of this comment, I shall consider two quite related topics that also appear in the papers by Richard Langlois and Hassan Mortazavian, namely, systems information and the relation between systems thinking and the logic of classes.

There is a fascinating aspect of the logic of planning for action, namely, that if someone does *x*, it follows that he or she does *not* do non-*x*, assuming that the descriptors of *x* are complete (i.e., that within a time span, all the relevant things he or she does have been enumerated). This statement is not really an axiom of systems planning because it is very close to being a tautology. What makes it fascinating is an axiom of all systems planning today:

Axiom 1. The class non-x not only is nonempty, but also contains a nonempty subset of actions that could have been taken by the decision-maker in the time span.

We even have a technical phrase for this nonempty set: "lost opportunities." The etymology of *to decide* is very appropriate, since the verb comes from the Latin *decidere*, which means *to cut, or to cut off.* Hence, if action *x* is taken during a time span, then the actor (decisionmaker) cuts off a nonempty set of lost opportunities—forever. That one or more of this set could be chosen later on does not change the fatality of the lost opportunity, especially in that large number of cases where timing is crucial. (In chess, for example, we cannot say to our opponent, "I failed to take your queen with my pawn on the last move, so now I would like to do it on this move even though you have moved your queen away.")

Why is the class of lost opportunities so fascinating to the systems planner? Because the characteristics of this class contain a most vital piece of information, namely, the cost of doing *x* rather than doing something in the class of lost opportunities. Now I need another axiom, perhaps not so self-evident as the previous one:

Axiom 2. For any action x taken over a specific time span, the class of lost opportunities can be ordered in terms of their value to a class of human beings.

Here, I need to point out that this ordering is no simple matter. In texts on decision-making, it is often assumed that an alternative action is like pulling the lever on a slot machine, where the action runs itself and we simply await the outcome. But if the action includes such matters as investing money, firing or hiring personnel, or selling property, we have to know how to do these things well or even optimally. Hence, in assessing the value of a lost opportunity, we have to understand how the opportunity can best be managed.

This is a crucial point in the systems approach to planning because in trying to determine how best to manage a lost opportunity, we are taken out of the original problem statement into other systems.

Definition.   The value of the correctly managed best lost opportunity is the "opportunity cost" of doing x *over the time space.*

Finally, if I can assume that the value scale that orders the lost opportunities is additive, then

Axiom 3.   In estimating the cost of doing x, *the planner should add the opportunity cost.*

This last axiom need not be so strongly stated; instead, we can use the more qualitative prescription: The planner must take full account of opportunity costs.

So much for formalism. Now, I would like to ask an epistemological question: "How do we come to know opportunity costs?" They are vital pieces of information for all planners who use the systems approach, and, hence (assuming my axioms hold), such planners should have an appropriate epistemology for them.

In the first place, it is clear that determining an opportunity cost is not empirical. The lost opportunities are all "counterfactual" (if y had been done instead of x, then . . .). Besides, it would be a hopelessly impractical task to test the consequences of each of the members of the correctly managed lost opportunities even if we knew what *correctly managed* meant. If this comment is valid, then it appears that what is called information theory, which assumes an empirical base for the information, is largely irrelevant as far as opportunity costs are concerned.

Rationalism would appear to be a more attractive epistemology with reference to Axiom 3. Suppose that the planner has a sufficiently strong theory to predict the cost of every possible action the decisionmaker could take over the time span. This, indeed, seems to be the case in linear programming. The geometry of linear programming is designed to map in multidimensional space all the possible costs for each set of possible actions. Actually, we do not normally find any discussion of opportunity costs in the literature of linear programming, perhaps because the authors think that their measurement is more or less automatically carried out.

In practice, the opportunity costs are all there, hidden by the method of estimating the parameters; for example, measures of the amount that a unit of an activity contributes to the measure of total cost. This very often is estimated empirically but without determining whether the unit that contributes to total cost was optimally managed or whether increasing or decreasing any particular output might lead to considerable organizational disruption.

The epistemological problem of estimating opportunity costs is more easily recognized if we turn to a very familiar system, inventory. Suppose my job is that of a purchasing agent for a retail store. How many white shirts, size 15½, 33, of a certain make should I order at one time? If I order too few, I run up ordering costs. If I purchase too many, I shall face obsolescence costs, and more to the point, I shall reduce liquid capital. The shirts sit on the shelf for a number of days and do not produce cash. What could best be done with the cash they cost me is the opportunity cost of capital, and we do try to use this number in estimating optimal order quantities. In other words, the correctly managed lost opportunity is a matter of correctly using the liquid capital.

But how do we obtain the estimate? Many textbooks on inventory control tell the student to use the interest that the cash could earn. Aside from the fact that there is no such thing as *the* interest in today's money markets, the suggestion is absurd at the policy level. If the best the retail store can do with liquid capital is to invest it in interest-earning accounts, then the store should liquify all its assets and set them to earning interest.

The question "What is the opportunity cost of holding inventory?" depends on determining the answer to another question, "What is the best use of liquid capital?" which depends on the answer to still another question, "What is the best use of any capital?" which asks for a total financial plan of the company.

I hope the reader can begin to see why systems information does not correspond to empirical information at all and why its acquisition is epistemologically mysterious. Far from being able to reduce the question of the appropriate opportunity cost to simpler questions, we find that it expands into questions about the larger system. The following is not an axiom, but more like a theorem:

The more we investigate how a system should work, the larger the system becomes; or

Under investigation, the boundaries of systems keep breaking outwards; or

The essence of the systems approach is the interconnection between systems.

I do not want to appear pessimistic about the matter of systems information. The excitement of all inquiry is its mysteries. Of course, we practice the systems approach even though the critical aspects remain a mystery. For example, another critical aspect of all social systems is the way people relate to each other; but despite years of studying human relations in psychology, sociology, organization theory, behavioral science, and so forth, we still know very little about how various kinds of relations are formed and how they influence what happens. Like any other profession, we make the best guesses we know how to, and we have plenty of hope.

In closing, I would like to make two comments, one more or less technical and relevant to the two papers, the other more general and germane to world systems. The technical question deals with the manner in which systems should be depicted. Here, it seems common sense to say that systems are made up of parts (components, departments, and the like) and that the systems-planning and management problem is to determine how the parts should work together for the good of the whole system (e.g., its goals). All this common sense suggests that the logic of parts and wholes is the appropriate beginning of systems theory: *Belongs to* is reflexive, nonsymmetric, transitive, and so forth. Also, if a belongs to b and b belongs to a, then a and b are the same.

However, if I want to justify an examination of part b when my interest is in part a, I would like to define *is a part of* somewhat as follows: b is a part of a if the way in which b operates influences strongly the performance of a. Please understand that this definition is epistemological and might more reasonably be posed as: Investigation of b is part of the investigation of a if . . . . But now, the part/whole logic will appear with an overall symmetry.

> *As investigation proceeds: Every part of any system becomes a part of every other part, and yet, despite this, the parts of a system do not become all the same.*

So my technical point is that the logic of classes is not the basis of systems theory, as Mortazavian seems to suggest.

My other point is based on the idea that we need to concentrate on systems interconnections. I think the point was made very well in the first book on world modeling, *The Limits to Growth*. [Meadows et al., 1972.] My chief interest in the past several years is in the social diseases called militarism and malnutrition. I and my colleagues at Berkeley have been trying to see in what sense these are related to each other. Seeing the relation does not necessarily solve every problem, but it may lead to more enlightenment. Here is the way we have been thinking about the interconnection:

1. There exist some sociopolitical structures for a nation that would enable the nation greatly to reduce starvation. (China seems to be an example though communism may not have the only example. Taiwan seems to have very little starvation.)

2. It serves the military (defense) interests of certain world powers to change countries that have adopted such sociopolitical structures (e.g., Chile) or stop countries from adopting such sociopolitical structures (e.g., Vietnam).

3. I conclude that the world food system and the world military system are interconnected.

MATHEMATICAL SYSTEMS THEORY AND INFORMATION SCIENCES

Mihajlo D. Mesarović

Much of what Hassan Mortazavian has written on systems in his paper I agree with—actually, almost all of it. I do not feel I should repeat what he has already said but rather will restrict myself to additions, comments, and reservations. Much of what I have to say actually is about what Mortazavian has chosen not to say. In other words, I am saying that the only criticism I have of Mortazavian's paper is that he has committed a sin of omission. This is fully understandable, as I will explain near the end of this comment. Mortazavian has given a very good account for a broad and sophisticated audience of the aspect of mathematical systems theory that is a somewhat glorified control theory (in particular, linear control theory), which is, in turn, what used to be called *modern control theory* in disguise.

In my view, the territory is much larger, particularly in the conceptual sense. As an illustration, we can simply refer to the journal *Mathematical Systems Theory* (which I founded more than ten years ago) to realize that mathematical systems theory is more than the theory of realization of linear systems, observability, and so forth. *Mathematical Systems Theory,* as a matter of fact, has published more articles on automata and models of computer systems than on anything else, and although I do not think that this is a good balance either, the fact illustrates a broad concern of mathematical systems theory.

I agree with Mortazavian that a system is a relation among objects. (How could I disagree with this definition, which I introduced more than ten years ago?) I also agree with Mortazavian that systems theory deals with *models* of specific, concrete systems rather than the systems themselves. However, I do not quite share Mortazavian's requirement that systems theory has to deal with complex interactive systems; in particular, my notion of complexity seems to be different from Mortazavian's. For example, dynamic systems are certainly complex, since they can have memory that can take them a finite or infinite number of steps back, so that even a one-input/one-output

567

system can be quite complex in the sense of being intricate. However, a system can be complex even without being dynamic. Complexity is due just as much to the disharmony among subsystems as to the intricacy in describing the behavior of a system and its time response. It is indeed peculiar that the least mathematical of all possible systems research, namely, that of Jay Forrester, is in full agreement with what is probably the most mathematically oriented research in systems theory, namely, that of Rudolf Kalman and his associates. Both of these schools basically adhere to the philosophy that systems theory is the theory of dynamics—and therefore, even though they use different methods, Forrester and Kalman have the same view on systems theory and what is the main problem in reality: the dynamics of behavior.

I agree with Mortazavian that systems theory should be mathematical—that is a position I have held for a long time and still consider valid. However, I do not think that the key problems in systems theory are those for which we can find relatively easy mathematical solutions (again, such as dealing with linear realization problems). The implication of what I have just said might become clearer at the end of this discussion.

Among the reservations I have about Mortazavian's paper is, before all, the issue of complexity. We cannot identify systems theory with the theory of models of complex systems and then talk about major findings in systems theory as they relate to the simplest systems we can imagine, namely, linear systems described by first-order differential equations. (Even if they are abstracted and couched in the framework of module theory, they are no more complex than their original description, that is, linear ordinary differential equations.) I would say that systems theory is indeed a theory of models or, if you like, a mathematical theory of models. But some models are simple while others are complex; and some models are simple models of complex systems, while others are complex models of complex systems. What is the nature of complexity? Here, of course, we would have to express a personal view because there is no agreement whatsoever as to how complexity ought to be defined. My approach to complexity is the following.

A system is complex if it consists of a family of interactive subsystems, each one of which operates autonomously under normal conditions. (This definition could be made mathematically precise—see my forthcoming book, coauthored with Yasuhiko Takahara.) The definition implies that there are two levels of systems behavior: the subsystem level and the overall systems level. Thus, my definition of complexity implies a hierarchy. Going back to Mortazavian's definition of system as a relation, I would say that whereas a system is a relation among sets, a *complex* system is a relation among systems themselves—that is, the complex system is a relation among the sets that in turn are systems themselves. This definition, though trivial, has significant implications in practice.

Just to illustrate this point, let us assume that we have to model an organization. Modeling an organization is just as legitimate a modeling task as modeling a rotating plane (an example Mortazavian used in his paper). An organization clearly has three characteristics:

1. It consists of a number of subsystems.
2. The subsystems are decision-making (or goal-seeking); that is, they can be most appropriately and most efficiently described in terms of their responses to any stimuli in reference to their pursuance of internal goals.
3. They are organized in a hierarchy; that is, there are decision-making subsystems that can modify, influence, or even control the behavior of the subsystems' units (on what are considered as lower levels).

Without going any further, it is quite clear that such a system as an organization can hardly be described by a set of first-order linear differential or difference equations or even by their module structure counterparts. Relations among the subsystems are far too complex for that. There are no identifiable state variables in the system as a whole, and the whole concept of state transition is not necessarily directly relevant. Notice that I have said not relevant (rather than impossible to introduce); concentration on time transition rather than other aspects of the system's functioning, such as conflict, would obscure the basic nature of the system and be a completely inadequate model of reality. The point I am making is that a system that in practice would be accepted as complex can hardly be described by a set of first-order (linear or nonlinear) differential equations.

Having said this, I have to admit that although I subscribe strongly to the notion that systems theory has to be mathematical, there is no mathematical theory as yet fully developed of the kind of complex systems described in the preceding example. Of course, I have to refer to our book *Theory of Hierarchical Multi-Level Systems,* which has not stimulated as much research over the last decade as I would have liked to see. [Mesarović, Macko, and Takahara, 1970.]

My second reservation regarding Mortazavian's paper concerns his inadequate emphasis on goal-seeking systems. A system is goal-seeking if its behavior can be best described with reference to the pursuance of a given goal. The simplest example is modeling a car moving on a highway. A Forrester/Kalman system-dynamic approach would describe this in terms of the car's acceleration and speed, that is, as a physical system. A goal-seeking description would require that the driver inside the car be identified and the moving point on the line representing the car on a highway be represented in terms of the strategy the driver uses in steering the vehicle along the road. A goal-seeking description, therefore, requires a description of a goal, a description of a strategy (how to pursue this goal), and a description of the environmental conditions in which this strategy is being pursued. All of these concepts could be, and indeed have been, defined mathematically. However, it is difficult to develop a full-scale theory starting from such a concept of a system, and this, of course, is the reason why progress in that direction is disappointingly slow.

My final reservation regarding Mortazavian's paper is its relegation of information sciences to Shannon's and Shannon-type mathematical constructs. Quite clearly, Shannon's notion of information refers only to the capacity for transmission. The concept of information is, of course, much richer. Actually, in my view, information cannot be defined without reference to the goal-seeking behavior of a system; therefore, information theory and systems theory are one and the same.

Elaborating further on this, it is my view that systems theory is not just mathematics. Systems theory is, indeed, a mathematical theory of models (not of real systems), but the functioning and behavior of systems and the importance of various issues with which the theory is concerned are not questions of mathematics but of the real world. This is why stability might be a more important consideration than finding a solution for equations. The crucial aspect of systems theory, and where it differs from mathematics, is that the importance of the problems with which a theory is designed to deal (in a precise, and therefore mathematical, manner) is defined outside of the theory itself. To repeat for emphasis, the importance of the problem comes from the real world. In the present state of development of systems theory, the underlying set of concepts for systems theory is from the decision-making and information-processing domains in a broad sense. Therefore, I would actually equate systems theory with information theory in an appropriately wider sense. In other words, to repeat this, too, systems theory goes beyond glorified control theory. Systems theory is a mathematical theory of models of real-life systems presented in terms of laws and concepts of decision-making and information-processing.

In conclusion, I wish to mention one more thing. The restrictiveness of Mortazavian's view of systems theory is perhaps best illustrated in the glorification of the problem and solution of the realization of linear systems. The theory of realization of linear systems is not necessarily mathematically very difficult. In a sense, it is a restatement of dependence in the set of linear equations. Even conceptually, it is not quite so important as Mortazavian seems to imply. To come back to the earlier example, let us assume that we are looking at an organization with many levels and numerous decisionmakers. Process identification really refers to identifying the levels and decisionmakers of which the system consists. It is not primarily a matter of identifying the proper number of state variables, that is, the proper linear structure in the sense of linear-systems theory. The problem of identification, therefore, is much more difficult than Mortazavian would make it appear.

Mathematical systems theory, in the sense I have advocated here, is very slow in developing. Whether this is in the nature of the problems involved, their difficulty, or whether it is so because of the scarcity of institutional and financial support for the required research or because of a lack of leadership in the scientific community, the future will show. At any rate, there is a danger that mathematical systems theory might have a fate somewhat like that of the attempt by Bertrand Russell to axiomatize mathematics.

Developing such a theory seems the right thing to do, but it may prove not to be possible. If it has taken us twenty years to come to the realization theory of linear dynamical systems, then it may take us another fifty to one hundred years to develop the theory of organizational systems with multi-level decision-making. If this is so and mathematical systems theory is to have an impact, then a somewhat different, more modest approach may be in order.

SYSTEM THEORY VERSUS SYSTEM PHILOSOPHY

Hassan Mortazavian

System theory is at present in a state of rapid development. Progress in system theory during the last two decades was more significant in the domain of finite-dimensional linear systems (deterministic or stochastic) that used, for the most part, the highly developed and already available tools of differential and difference equations, analysis, algebra, geometry, and probability theory. This was a great step forward. Many fundamental problems of system theory, however, still remain unsolved. In a sense, the unsolved problems are more challenging than the ones already solved. In my view, there are at least three reasons for this: First, the unsolved problems are generally more difficult. Second, the choice of the proper mathematics to be used or developed to formulate and solve these problems is far from trivial. Last, but not least, some of these problems are not even well understood at the conceptual level. For example, the concepts of complexity, structure, coordination, conflict, organization, goal-seeking behavior, information, and knowledge are poorly understood.

Advances in system theory are likely to be observed in the future in at least three directions: (1) Further development of the theory of nonlinear systems, systems with nonsmooth dynamics, as well as infinite-dimensional systems. (2) Elucidation and mathematical formulation of fundamental structural aspects of analysis, control, design, coordination, and organization of complex systems. (3) A more unified theory of the somewhat fragmented systemic disciplines, such as control theory, decision theory, automata theory, and computer science, with a view to the development of a higher level theory of analysis, control, and design, involving logic, abstract algebraic structures, and languages. This is particularly important because of the rapid development of cheap and flexible computer hardware. To be honest, at present, we have no satisfactory scientific answer to many questions involving the type of concepts just mentioned.

Mesarović is right that I have committed "a sin of omission." This was perhaps inevitable, as I decided to write about those aspects of system problems that we know something more or less definitive about, that could be explained in an informal way, and that can be directly applied to various disciplines where such system-theoretic problems arise.

Mesarović criticizes me on the grounds that, having identified system theory as the theory of models of complex systems, I then devoted much of my paper to the simple case of linear systems. I decided to write more about linear systems for two reasons: (1) The theory of linear systems is well developed; (2) it has been successfully used in many situations where a system is linear or can be linearized and thus can serve as a good example of the type of system-theoretic knowledge that has been applied. But certainly, system theory is not just "linear control theory."

I agree with Mesarović that "a system can be complex even without being dynamic." But I do not think that the definition of a complex system as one that "consists of a family of interactive subsystems, each one of which operates autonomously under normal conditions" is sufficiently inclusive. A family of interactive subsystems may be considered as complex even if some of the subsystems do not behave autonomously. Part of the complexity may indeed arise from the mode of interaction of the subsystems. Moreover, Mesarović's abstract definition of a complex system as a "relation among the sets that in turn are systems themselves" is, in my view, not exclusive. According to this definition, any relation on a family of sets that are themselves relations must be considered a complex system. I think more mathematical structure must be introduced to avoid the possibility that this relation becomes a trivial one.

Despite Mesarović's view that I have relegated "information sciences to Shannon's and Shannon-type mathematical constructs," I should like to mention that my definition of information sciences in my paper (at the end of the fourth section) was much broader. Shannon's theory was a theory of "statistics of highly improbable events" and was called information theory only for want of a better name. Information theory, in the sense of Shannon, has nothing to do with information in the semantic sense or even in the ordinary sense of the term. My discussion of Shannon's theory was mainly motivated by my attempt to point out some of these distinctions.

Boulding writes: "I confess I regard mathematics as one of the least developed of the sciences in terms of its potential. It is very inadequate at the present time to deal with systems beyond at least the moderately simple." I find myself in agreement with the first part of Boulding's remark. The reason is simple: Mathematics is only limited by the limitations of human imagination. But the inadequacy of present mathematics in dealing with complex systems is not the fault of mathematicians. Mathematicians were never truly devoted to understanding complexity. They were devoted to the search for truth, depth, generality, and simplicity. System theory, however, deals with complexity, and to do so, we may, indeed, be obliged to develop new types of mathematics. This new mathematics we may call *mathematics of systems*. This does not mean that the existing mathematics cannot be used to study systems. A fundamental application of mathematics—in particular, algebra, topology, and geometry—has been to invent an abstract conception of structure. In its more developed form, mathematics has been and ought to be used to treat more complex structures called systems.

Langlois writes that: ". . . most of the mathematics of system theory grew out of electrical engineering, principally circuit theory." Although many of the early system theorists were from electrical-engineering backgrounds—a fact that had a negative effect on the development of system theory, suggesting the idea that a system is a signal—none of the mathematics of system theory grew out of electrical engineering. Langlois's statement, in my view, would be equally surprising to mathematicians and electrical engineers. I wonder whether Langlois knows much about the nature of the mathematics used in system theory. At the present time, apart from calculus and linear algebra, system theorists use mathematical tools from various branches of mathematics: algebra, analysis, topology, algebraic geometry, differential geometry, combinatorial geometry, combinatorics, probability theory, and statistics and many other fields, none of which grew out of electrical engineering. It is by no means an exaggeration that a system theorist's progress is entirely dependent on how much mathematics he or she knows and how powerful his or her imagination is in making this mathematics directly applicable to system problems by discovering *isomorphisms* between mathematical constructs and various types of systems. As Richard Bellman put it, "mathematicians, as the keepers of abstractions, . . . hold the keys to the study of all systems." [Bellman, 1971*a*.]

Again, Langlois writes: "Practitioners fall into two identifiable if overlapping groups: those who wish to leave the cave and those who do not." And then he adds that Mortazavian firmly belongs to the second group, while those who leave the cave are, presumably among other things, "concerned with applying mathematical analysis to areas of military, business, and (yes) social management." I have many things to say about Langlois's statement but confine myself to two issues. (1) The notion of a practitioner who does not wish to leave the cave and "whose business is to scrutinize pure forms" is so evidently self-contradictory that I cannot but call it as meaningless as a square circle. (2) To leave or not to leave the cave is not the question. The question is to do honest scientific work. Incidentally, I do not believe in a rigid distinction between pure and applied mathematics, nor do I believe one is inferior to the other.

From Langlois's discussion of my remarks on modeling and the nature of system theory, it is clear that he has misunderstood me. When I wrote that "any attempt to apply system theory outside its mathematical context is not proper," I simply meant that system theory cannot be applied unless the general setting of a concrete problem is such that the numerical quantities that are put into the dynamics of the model or from which a model is to be constructed are mathematically well defined. In short, system theory must be applied mathematically.

Commenting on the second approach to modeling discussed in my paper, that is, modeling based on data not laws, Langlois finds that it "implied a naive faith in data long ago renounced—with good reason—by the philosophy of science." To be sure, observation alone, and thus modeling based on data alone, can never discover new laws or new theories. New laws can only be discovered by new theoretical analysis and new experimentation. What I said about the data-dominated approach to modeling does not amount to a "naive faith in data."

Langlois writes that Kalman's view of the world and to some extent my own view "serves in the quest to unify all sciences under the banner of system theory . . . ." I have said exactly the opposite in my paper when I wrote in the beginning of the third section, "system theory does not aim at unifying all or special types of scientific disciplines."

Contrary to Langlois's interpretation of my views, I do not regard the scientist as a handmaiden or "a kind of graduate research assistant to the system theorist." System theory is a science like any other science, and in science, there is no question of inferiority or superiority.

In a footnote, Langlois tried to clarify the special meaning of the term *observability* adopted by mathematical-system theorists. Langlois is right when he says that the notion of observability has nothing to do "with the phenomenology of observing a system." I said this myself in my paper: "*Observability* of a system . . . should not be mistaken for the ordinary process of observation." However, the rest of Langlois's footnote is partly misleading, partly wrong. The point is not that we "know all about a system," or find out "what the (known) state variables are doing." The question is whether we can measure the values of the state variables of a given system at every instant of time within a time interval from the measurement of its outputs.

I now turn to comments by Richard Mattessich. He warns the reader that whenever I speak of system theory I limit myself to "the relatively narrow area of mathematical system theory." I have argued in my paper that non-mathematical system theory does not and cannot exist and, therefore, that I take system theory and mathematical system theory to be identical. The term *mathematical system theory* was introduced, I think, for two reasons: One, to distinguish *true* system theory, which must be mathematical, from works that were not mathematical and yet were called system theory by their producers. Second, to distinguish the part of system-theoretic research that used more sophisticated mathematical tools from parts that used less sophisticated and sometimes poor mathematics. I cannot think of any system problem that can be solved without mathematics. If such a problem exists, it must be a trivial "nonproblem." I hasten to add two remarks: (1) System-theoretic ideas did not arise from mathematics, but rather from the practical necessity of dealing with complex concrete phenomena; (2) it is possible, and indeed quite probable, in any science to miss the real problem and fall into the trap of too much mathematical sophistication.

Mattessich criticized me for not having mentioned the works of Ackoff and Emery, Boulding, Bunge, Churchman, James G. Miller, and Herbert

Simon in my paper. These authors, in my view, have all contributed to what we may call *philosophy of systems*—a branch of philosophy dealing with problems centered around the notion of system.[1] Philosophy of systems, however, must be distinguished from system theory, which is the science of systems.

Now I shall consider Mattessich's six specific arguments against my view of system theory, one by one.

1. Contrary to Mattessich's view, system theory *is not* an empirical science. It is a mathematical theory. System-theoretic propositions can only be proved or disproved mathematically, but they cannot be tested empirically.

2. For these reasons, I entirely disagree with Mattessich's view that "system theory remains meaningful only as part of one or more or even all the empirical sciences." System theory is not part of any empirical science.

3. The choice of "fitting criteria" is partly a system-theoretic problem and has both mathematical and empirical aspects. The mathematical part is a basic concern of system theory, while the empirical part depends on the specialist's view of the constraints, specific purposes of modeling, degree of accuracy required, and so forth. It also raises certain philosophical problems, which must be dealt with in what I called philosophy of systems.

4. I entirely agree with Mattessich that the problems dealt with in system theory were hardly bothersome in physics. I do not believe, however, that mathematicians have ever claimed system theory for themselves. The fact that system theory is a mathematical theory has attracted many mathematicians to this field. I do not want to raise the controversial question whether by virtue of the fact that a system is a mathematical object and system theory a mathematical theory, system theorists may be considered as mathematicians in some rather broad sense.

5. Contrary to Mattessich's claim, I have made no attempt in my paper "to banish the factual and normative-methodological essence of system theory."

6. I do not find Mattessich's remark about the goal orientation of the systems approach relevant to the content of my paper.

I agree with Mattessich when he writes that "Mortazavian's suggestion that 'the solar system can be studied using only the laws of physics' would have been poor advice for Kepler and Newton, who still had to search for some of those laws." He has a point. I should not have said so without qualification.

---

[1] The scientific contribution of these authors, however, is by no means limited to this domain.

SECTION 9

SYSTEMS THEORY,
KNOWLEDGE,
AND THE SOCIAL SCIENCES

Richard N. Langlois

It is not too much of an overstatement, I think, to suggest that systems theory has not lived up to the great promise it has long been supposed to hold for the social sciences. Considering the magnitude of the claims, of course, disappointment was probably inevitable. Systems theory has been hailed by some as a way of unifying the methodology of all sciences. Others have intimated that this approach would finally endow the social sciences with that natural-science-like rigor and precision those disciplines allegedly lack. And others—more modestly—have looked to systems theory as a way of combatting the fragmentation and specialization of the sciences.

But systems theory has failed—at least so far—in its various attempts to bring all the disparate parts of inquiry under the sway of its organizing force. In fact, it is fairer to say that systems theory has itself *succumbed* to the diversity and complexity of modern scientific inquiry. Defining what we mean by systems theory or the systems approach is virtually impossible outside the context of a particular discipline, and we might almost say that there are as many versions of systems theory as there are would-be systems theorists.

In trying to be all-encompassing, systems theory has become unsystematic; and in trying to become systematic, it has become narrowly specialized. On the one hand, the attempt to describe at a broad level the system-theoretic approach to this or that inevitably ends up sounding like a Sears Roebuck catalog of vaguely connected concepts, models, and definitions. On the other hand, mathematical system theory[1]—the most rigorous and

This research was supported in part by the Division of Information Science and Technology of the National Science Foundation under grant IST-8110537. Note: Portions of this paper appeared under the title "Systems Theory and the Meaning of Information" in "Perspectives on Systems Methodology and Information Research," a supplement to the *Journal of the American Society for Information Science*, vol. 33 (November 1982), pp. 395–399.
[1] See Hassan Mortazavian's contribution to this volume.

tightly knit version of the systems approach—has coagulated out of the more general body of systems ideas to become a well-circumscribed mathematical specialty, even if one with certain imperialist pretensions.

I say this largely by way of apology—for I do intend in this paper to provide a perspective on systems theory. But because systems theory is, in fact, so multifarious, my portrayal of it will necessarily be selective, picking out those pieces that I find useful and letting the rest alone. This seems to me the only sensible compromise between the encyclopedic and the axiomatic.

My general concern will be with systems theory's relation to the social sciences, especially economics. More particularly, though, I will be concerned with the notions of knowledge and information and the ways in which systems theory can help illuminate those concepts. Indeed, I am hopeful that this essay might prove a useful preface to some research I am now beginning on the connection between the information sciences, broadly construed, and economic theory.

WHOLES AND PARTS

Perhaps the principal reason systems theory has failed to revolutionize scientific methodology is that at the broadest and most general level, it has nothing particularly revolutionary to offer.

At its most philosophical, systems theory is a confrontation with the age-old problem of *the whole and the parts*. Systems theorists discovered—or, rather, rediscovered—complexity. They saw the approach of the physical sciences, which is supposed to be analytic or reductionistic, as applicable only to phenomena of "organized simplicity." In dealing with the increasingly prevalent problems of "organized complexity," they argued, we cannot understand the parts in isolation from the whole. [Weaver, 1948.] Thus, we need to study the total system, to see the big picture. These are not new ideas, of course. In fact, it is striking the extent to which modern systems theorists—notably proponents of so-called general systems theory—have tended to retrace a lot of old footsteps in the long-standing debate over the doctrine of methodological holism. [D. C. Phillips, 1976, esp. pp. 46–67.]

Notwithstanding the holist rhetoric of most systems theorists, however, systems theory is not at all methodological holism in any strong sense. And at its best, systems theory is, in fact, a form of intelligent methodological individualism.

Since this is a somewhat unconventional thing to say, and since the individualism/holism debate is so frequently misunderstood, perhaps a brief digression is in order.

The conventional wisdom runs something like this. There is a doctrine in the social sciences called methodological individualism. It is a form of the analytic or reductionist method, and it therefore holds that knowing the properties of the parts—the individuals in society—is fully sufficient for grasping all there is to know about the whole—society. In other words, the properties of the whole can be deduced from the properties of the parts; or to put it in more familiar (and more naive) terms, the whole is just the aggregate or sum of the parts. This view is to be contrasted with methodological holism (or, sometimes, collectivism), which insists that wholes possess "emergent" properties that cannot be derived from the properties of constituent parts. To the holist, the whole is greater than the sum of its parts.

This is a familiar story. But, as is often the case with familiar stories, it is almost entirely wrong. There may well be some writers who espouse in principle this sort of naive methodological individualism. But no one can actually put such a view into practice. Consider the case of a neoclassical economist analyzing the effect of a tax suddenly placed on a certain commodity. In proper individualist fashion, he or she will instantly begin to model the choice problem faced by a representative economic agent, discovering, as always, that the individual will most likely consume less of the commodity than before. But this finding about individual demand tells the economist nothing about the whole—total demand—until he or she adds a global fact: that total demand is the sum of individual demand. In this (trivial) case, the whole *is* just the sum of the parts; but even here, the whole could not be deduced from the parts, since the relation among them— addition—is not logically contained in the individual-choice model itself. Moreover, there is nothing sacred about addition, and methodological individualists are quite willing to specify very different sorts of relations among the parts. In economics, for example, the aggregate result is very often exactly the opposite of what we would have expected from considering individual behavior alone.[2]

Far from denying the importance of emergent phenomena, the economist and philosopher Friedrich A. Hayek, widely (and correctly) cited as an archproponent of methodological individualism, reminds us that the entire *objective* of the social sciences is to explain how the behavior of individuals leads to orderly patterns and institutions that none had consciously planned—to explain, in other words, the emergent results of individual action. [Hayek, 1979, pp. 146–147.]

In sophisticated discourse, the question of emergent properties is in no way an issue between individualist and holist. *Both agree* that social phenomena must often be considered emergent wholes whose behavior cannot

---

[2] In his best-selling introductory textbook, Paul Samuelson (a methodological individualist in microeconomics, at least) finds it necessary to warn the student against fallacy-of-composition errors as early as page 11 of the text, where he presents a long list of such fallacies exploded by economic analysis. [Samuelson, 1980.] Indeed, Kenneth Arrow, Samuelson's fellow Nobel Laureate, has written that "the notion that through the workings of an entire system effects may be very different from, and even opposed to, intentions is surely the most important intellectual contribution that economic thought has made to the general understanding of social processes." (Arrow, 1968, p. 376.)

be entirely reduced to the behavior of individuals.[3] The issue is not whether we can deduce the nature of the whole from the properties of the parts; the issue is whether or not we should consult the parts *at all*. Holism is not the doctrine that we should study emergent phenomena; holism is the doctrine that we should somehow study wholes *directly* without considering the workings of the parts in a meaningful way.

It should be immediately clear that this position does not follow at all from a recognition of systemic interactions or emergent phenomena. The methodological individualist cannot deduce such phenomena from his or her knowledge of the parts; but—what is often overlooked—the holist is in no better position to understand such phenomena than is the individualist. The problem is simply a lack of knowledge about emergent properties, and calling oneself a holist does not instantly convey that knowledge. [D. C. Phillips, 1976, pp. 14–15.]

More to the point, adopting the holist stance arguably puts us in an epistemological position *inferior* to that of the individualist. The holist differs from the (sophisticated) individualist only in that the former insists on *throwing away* useful information. Here lies the real disagreement. The methodological individualist holds that the social scientist should always keep in the closest contact with the level of the parts (the individuals) and utilize fully whatever knowledge of the parts—however incomplete—he or she can bring to bear. [Machlup, 1969 and 1979b; Hayek, 1979, esp. chaps. 4, 6.]

The best way to appreciate this may be by analogy with literary criticism. No one would deny that a work of literature is more than the sum of the words and sentences it comprises. Yet the modern critic insists on studying these words and sentences carefully. Similarly, methodological individualism in social science is nothing more than an insistence on "sticking to the text," whereas holism is a license to engage in that most heinous of "lit-crit" solecisms, "reading in."

Although naive methodological individualism is probably impossible in practice, holism in this sense is not. Social science is rife with holistic formulations in which hypostatized concepts like *society, the capitalist class*, or *the public interest* take on operational significance in and of themselves—formulations in which, as Jacques Barzun said of Marx, the terms of reference become "entities stuffed with people but not composed of them." (Barzun, 1958, p. 182.) One result, ironically enough, is that holists are much more prone to fallacy-of-composition errors than are methodological individualists. For if we throw away information about the parts, we are inclined

---

[3] "The overall order of actions in a group is in two respects more than the totality of regularities observable in the actions of the individuals and cannot be wholly reduced to them. It is not so only in the trivial sense in which a whole is more than the mere *sum* of its parts but presupposes also that these elements are related to each other in a particular manner. It is more also because the existence of those relations which are essential for the existence of the whole cannot be accounted for wholly by the interaction of the parts but only in their interaction with an outside world both of the individual parts and the whole." (Hayek, 1967, pp. 70–71.)

directly to read in a logic of operation for the whole from some other source; and the logic of operation nearest at hand is that of the individual human. [Hayek, 1979, p. 101; Langlois, 1981, chap. 3.] The notion that, for example, a society permitting economic self-interest is therefore a greedy society is a bit of naive individualism characteristic of holists far more than of methodological individualists.

In order to make a plausible case for holism, we have to argue that less information is somehow better than more. This is no easy task. We might for instance invoke the *Gestalt* and assert that attention to the parts destroys our understanding of the whole. But this is to confuse perception and understanding. And, as my analogy with literary criticism was meant to suggest, the sophisticated methodological individualist has no compunction against stepping back to survey the *Gestalt*—so long as the (epistemologically more accessible) parts are also carefully analyzed. Historically, holists have taken a rather different (if not ultimately unrelated) line of attack. Hegel and his followers argued that the parts could not be studied in isolation because the parts acquire their very nature from their relation to the whole, which nature is necessarily altered if the parts are considered apart from that whole. But if taken at all seriously, this argument leads to logical absurdity, and it falls quickly apart when translated from the quasi-mysticism of essentialist rhetoric into a modern nominalist vocabulary. [D. C. Phillips, 1976, pp. 5–20.]

Proponents of general systems theory have unknowingly reinvented and invoked this Hegelian formulation in discussing the holism of systems theory. [Ibid., esp. pp. 45–50.] But most systems theorists—both mathematicians and practitioners alike—conceive of systems theory in a way *antagonistic* to this Hegelian view. They are certainly inclined to recite holist cant about "phenomena that depend on the conditions of the environment in which they exist, interact with this environment, and thus cannot be properly studied in isolation." (Mortazavian in this volume.) But all they mean by this is that the behavior of the whole cannot be understood without knowledge of the relations among the parts. The parts are conceived of as logically distinct elements of a mathematical set; those elements exist and are fully defined independently of any relations that might be specified. A system is just the set of parts plus a set of relations among the parts.[4] This is a formulation that would trouble a serious holist far more than it would a methodological individualist.

The philosopher Mario Bunge has recently transformed this set-theoretic definition of a system into a methodological position—*systemism*—that "combines the desirable features of individualism and holism." (Bunge, 1979a, p. 13.) To Bunge, a society (which he finds it necessary to call σ) may be represented as the ordered pair $\langle S, R \rangle$, where S is the set of individuals in

[4]Cf. Mihajlo Mesarović's "implicit (syntactical) definition" of a system in Mesarović [1964a, p. 7].

the society, and R is the set of relations among them. That systemism does in many ways combine the best of both worlds is, I believe, an entirely unobjectionable assertion. What is *not* true is that systemism somehow represents a new methodological alternative: The basic ideas of what Bunge calls systemism are essentially identical to what sophisticated methodological individualists have believed all along.[5]

It is important to notice that while Bunge's definition of society qua system is consistent with the general mathematical definition of a system [Mesarović, 1964a, p. 7], not all applications of systems theory are in accordance with the tenets of systemism understood as intelligent methodological individualism. The "parts" in Bunge's formulation are individuals in society, but this is by no means always the case in social science. The elements in a typical systems model are aggregate variables of one sort or another—dollars, commodity levels, energy use—that are represented as impinging directly on one another with no reference whatever to the existence of human beings. A good many systems models in the social sciences must, therefore, be classified as instances of naive holism; and while such models may often prove interesting and illuminating, they cannot—as is often claimed—serve as a general foundation for economics and other social sciences. This is a point to which I will return.

Perhaps I should apologize for the length of this digression. But, in a sense, perhaps this has not been a digression at all. After all, philosophical issues lie nearer to the surface in systems theory than they do in most intellectual endeavors, even if they are not for that reason more often perceived. More importantly, though, there is a sense in which it is methodological individualism that lies behind the systems-referential view of knowledge and information that I now wish to present.

SYSTEMS AND THE MEANING OF INFORMATION

There is a strain of thought on matters informational that I find somewhat disturbing. It is what I think of as the "oil-flow" model of information, with its attendant "oil-tank" model of knowledge. According to this (implicit) view, information is some sort of undifferentiated fluid that will course through the computers and telecommunications devices of the coming age much as oil now flows through a network of pipes; and the measure of our

---

[5] Bunge does admit that Hayek and other methodological individualists recognize "the reality of social relations" (p. 17), but he continues to paint them as naive individualists. "The individualist might not wish to dispute the systemist's thesis," says Bunge, "but, if he is consistent, he must insist that the structure of R is somehow 'contained' in, or deducible from, the properties of the individual members of society" (p. 19). But, as we saw (cf. again footnote 3), Hayek for one does *not* so insist, and I cannot see why he is therefore inconsistent in any way. Bunge is simply mistaken in his characterization of the individualist position. [Bunge, 1979a.]

knowledge in this world will be the amount of "info-fluid" we have managed to store up.[6]

This model of knowledge and information has some mutually reinforcing affinities with information theory in the well-known Shannon-Weaver sense, which developed for purposes of communications engineering a quantitative measure of something called information. [Shannon and Weaver, 1949.] Communications theorists are themselves quick to deny the connection between their concept of information and the term's everyday meaning, distinguishing not only between semantic and nonsemantic information but also between the concept of information itself and the notion of *amount of information*. The logic of systems can help illuminate these distinctions, I believe, and may even prove able to offer a conceptual model for information and knowledge alternative to the pipe and tank.

It is tempting to think that the distinction between the communications theorist's *information* and the more general sense of the term is at base a matter of mechanism versus antimechanism (the quantification of information is something appropriate to machines—to computers and switchboards, wires and transmitters), and that the very different character of information and knowledge in everyday experience arises from the distinctly non-mechanistic nature of the human system. There is more than a grain of truth in this, and I will later suggest that such a dichotomy between mechanistic and nonmechanistic systems is indeed in order. But, in the end, this view gives us only part of the picture. To a large extent, I believe, the real issues of information and knowledge actually cut across the mechanism/antimechanism dichotomy.[7]

To see what this means, let us look at how even the most mechanistic sorts of systems models use a concept of information.

Systems theorists often distinguish between terminal or causal systems and goal-seeking systems. [Mesarović, 1964a, p. 21; 1962, p. 13.] The former react to their environment according, as it were, to the logic of proximate cause: The environment affects the system's inputs, which, in turn, affect the behavior of the system in a strictly preprogrammed fashion. By contrast, goal-seeking systems operate according to something nearer the final cause. In this case, there are "certain invariable aspects of the system which reflect its goal" (Mesarović, 1962, p. 13); a teleological subsystem receives the system's inputs and guides its behavior in light of the goal. The distinction

---

[6]This oil-flow model is not without implications. More than one writer has suggested that information policy be predicated on the inevitable dependency of future society on this "info-substance" just as energy policy is supposed to deal with our dependence on oil. As a consequence, we should worry about the availability of "info-fluid" to disadvantaged groups like Chicanos much as we recently used to fret about the availability of heating oil to poor New Englanders.

[7]This is precisely the theme pursued by the British physicist Donald MacKay. [MacKay, 1969.] The next section of this paper will draw heavily on his ideas.

can perhaps best be illustrated using the familiar stimulus/response (S/R) model from behaviorist psychology. In the causal approach, we posit some direct mapping of the stimulus to the response; each stimulus directly causes a particular response. In the goal-seeking approach, we assume a slightly more sophisticated version of S/R in which an intermediate processing stage comes between stimulus and response.[8] The stimulus, of course, is the information with which we are concerned.

As a kind of objective correlative, we could think of a stimulus as involving a (weak) form of energy—a small electric current, a pattern of light, a sound wave—which elicits as response the release of another form of energy (often stronger or different in character).

In both causal and goal-seeking models, we can talk about the *meaning* of a piece of information. In the former case, the meaning of a signal is the response it elicits. In the latter, response is also the ultimate criterion of meaning, even if we cannot necessarily understand the meaning of a signal without first knowing the goal that the system is pursuing.

Now, it is important to notice that not all signals will be equally meaningful. A signal of the wrong form—the wrong voltage, frequency, or code, for example—cannot be understood by the system. At the same time, not all meaningful signals will have the same meaning. A small voltage may elicit a smaller response than—and thus have a meaning different from—that of a larger voltage. A message coded *ABCD* may have implications for achieving a system's goal that are very different from those of a message coded *DCBA*. And this provides a clue to the distinction between semantic information and the nonsemantic information of communications theory. The latter is concerned only with the extent to which a message is within the set of meaningful messages; it is not at all concerned with the message's implications for the system. For example, the messages *ABCD* and *DCBA*—which contain the same characters—would typically have identical information content in the communications-theory sense, even if they had very different meanings from the system's point of view.

To illustrate this, let me draw on an example from the (normative) theory of economic decision-making. Here we are dealing with a goal-directed system, one in which the "teleological subsystem" takes the form of a decisionmaker who maximizes profit (or, as we shall wish to introduce stochastic elements, who maximizes so-called expected profit, which is, in effect, profit weighted by probability).

Let us suppose that the decisionmaker is a farmer and that he has certain "decision variables" under his control, for example, the number of acres of wheat he can choose to plant. There are also variables—say, the weather—that are not within his grasp. The profit experienced by the decisionmaker depends on both the weather and the number of acres planted. If the de-

---

[8] Mesarović holds—correctly, I believe—that any mathematical system can be represented either way. A causal system can be modeled as if it were pursuing a goal; and a goal-directed system can be reduced to a direct mapping of inputs to outputs. [Mesarović, 1964*a*, p. 22.]

cisionmaker knows the weather—if he knows how much rainfall there will be—he can easily determine the acreage appropriate for maximum profit. If he is uncertain about the level of rainfall, he can articulate a probability distribution for that variable, which allows him to select the acreage that maximizes expected profit. But the decisionmaker who can anticipate the level of rainfall perfectly will very likely elect to plant an amount of acreage different from that selected by the farmer who is uncertain about the weather; more to the point, the better informed decisionmaker will realize a higher profit than his ill-informed counterpart.

If the decisionmaker who is uncertain can obtain some kind of information about the weather—divine revelation, perhaps, or the weather bureau's probability distribution for rainfall—then he can improve his acreage decision. But if this information is costly, the decision whether to acquire it can be represented as yet another decision-system of the same sort as the original acreage decision. In general, our profit-maximizing farmer should wish to acquire the information if its expected value exceeds its cost. [See, for example, Howard, 1966.]

This *expected value of information* is the interesting quantity. In order to examine it more closely, let us simplify our example even further. Suppose there are only two possibilities, heavy rain and light rain. The farmer must optimize his acreage planted in light of whatever information he might have about which of these two possibilities will occur; for example, he might consider the amount of rain experienced in past years or various freely available predictions by the Weather Bureau or the Department of Agriculture. On the basis of this imperfect information, the farmer estimates a probability of, say, 0.7 for heavy rain and 0.3 for light rain. Now, suppose that a fully reliable clairvoyant stands willing (for a stiff fee) to disclose which of the two alternatives nature actually has in store. How much is this revelation worth to our profit-maximizing decisionmaker? We have to consider how the new information would affect the farmer's acreage choice and, thus, his profits. If the clairvoyant says "heavy rain," he can optimize the acreage in a way that increases profits over the expected level. If the clairvoyant sends the message "light rain," he can also optimize acreage—in a different direction—to increase profit over the expected profit. In deciding whether to buy the clairvoyant's information, the farmer must decide if the increase in profit will be enough to justify the clairvoyant's fee—and he must decide *before he knows which message the clairvoyant will send.* So, the decision whether or not to buy the information must be based on the farmer's prior probability assessment of what the clairvoyant will say. Since the clairvoyant is merely revealing what nature will do, the farmer's weather forecast or other prior information is exactly as relevant to predicting the clairvoyant's message as to predicting nature's response—since the former is nothing but the latter moved forward in time.

Thus, the farmer must use his original probability assessment (0.7 chance of heavy rain; 0.3 chance light rain) in deciding whether to buy the information. And the expected value of perfect information is thus the sum of two magnitudes: the first is the increase in profits from adjusting to heavy rain if there will, in fact, be heavy rain, multiplied by 0.7, the probability that there will be (and, therefore, that the clairvoyant will say) heavy rain; the second is the increase in profits from optimizing for light rain given that there will, in fact, be light rain, times the probability that there will be (and, therefore, that the clairvoyant will say) light rain.[9] In other words, the expected value of perfect information (EVPI) is the sum of the value to the system of a set of possible messages weighted by the probability of occurrence of each message.

By contrast, the information measure of communications theory is oblivious to the value a message holds for the system that receives it: In analogy with the entropy measure of thermodynamics, the information content of the message *heavy rain* is, to the communications theorist, proportional only to the logarithm of the probability of that message being received.[10] Although the value measure and the entropy measure can move in the same direction, there is no general reason why this should be so.[11]

---

[9] The length of this sentence suggests that there are times when mathematics has its expository (or at least space-saving) advantages. Let $\Pi(a|w)$ be the (realized) profit from planting a acres under weather conditions w. The farmer's original problem is

$$\max\ [p\Pi(a|w = H) + (1 - p)\Pi(a|w = L)],$$

where H indicates heavy rain, L light rain, and p is the farmer's prior probability assessment on heavy rain. (The probability of light rain has to be $(1 - p)$ since there are only two possibilities.) Suppose that a^* is the value of a—the number of acres—that maximizes the quantity in brackets. Then,

$$\text{EVPI} = p[\Pi(a_H^*|H) - \Pi(a^*|H)] + (1 - p)[\Pi(a_L^*|L) - \Pi(a^*|L)],$$

where p is the farmer's assessed probability that the clairvoyant will call for heavy rain (which is necessarily identical to his original assessment of the probability of heavy rain), a_H^* is the optimal choice of acreage under conditions of heavy rain, and a_L^* is the optimal acreage under light rain conditions.

[10] In the notation of footnote 9, the (nonsemantic) information content of the message *heavy rain* is proportional to $-\log_2 p$. The information content or entropy of the light-rain/heavy-rain information system is the information content of each possible message weighted by its probability,

$$H = -[p\log_2 p + (1 - p)\log_2(1 - p)].$$

[11] In our now familiar example, it happens that the two measures are closely related: Information content is high when value is high and vice versa. (The reason is that a high-entropy [low "info-content"] message is one with a high probability. If a farmer anticipated heavy rain with a high probability, then a^* is likely to be already near a_H^*, and $[\Pi(a_H^*|H) - \Pi(a^*|H)]$ is low. Similarly, the more unexpected message would have both a higher information content and a higher value, since a^* would be less close to a_L^*. I believe this monotonicity can be shown rigorously to hold if the profit function is concave.) But such a connection is merely fortuitous. Consider an industrial research laboratory, for example, in which one experiment has a very high "info-content" (e.g., the experiment has a 50-50 chance of resulting in the message *success*) but low profit implications for the company, while a second experiment has a low "info-content" (e.g., a 90 per cent chance of success) but big profit implications. The research manager who used entropy as a decision-making criterion would be sorely misguided.

MEANING AND STRUCTURE

Stimulus/response systems—what we could call cybernetic systems in a broad sense[12]—are mechanistic systems in that action alone matters. It is not so much that action—response—has taken the place of meaning; rather, meaning itself is *defined* solely in terms of the action released or controlled by the action in question.[13] In the case of our agricultural decision-system, for example, the meaning of a message about the weather is the acreage the decisionmaker chooses to plant. Now, because this is a goal-directed system, we can interpret the relation between message and action in light of the goal, and since the goal is a simple quantitative one, we can even measure the value of the message for the goal's achievement.[14] Nonetheless, all meaning is ultimately reflected in the system's behavior, in its output.

Yet, if we look at the question of meaning in a slightly different way, we may be able to generalize beyond simple stimulus/response systems. Another way to say that the meaning of a message within a cybernetic system arises from the action that message brings about is to say that the meaning is defined *by the system itself*. What makes the message *rain will be heavy* comprehensible to our decision-system—and the message *tea tonight at eight* meaningless to it—is that, by virtue in this case of its very structure, the system is ready to respond to the one and not the other. Furthermore, notions of information and meaning seem as applicable to complex and arguably nonmechanistic systems (such as brains) as to simple cybernetic systems.

In general, then, we might follow Donald MacKay in speaking of a system's structure as defining "conditional states of readiness." It is the overall configuration—not any particular response in isolation—that determines the meaning of a message.

> It isn't until we consider the range of other states of readiness, that *might have been considered but weren't*, that the notion of meaning comes into its own. A

---

[12] By a cybernetic system in a broad sense, I mean any system that is concerned with information and control. In a narrower sense, cybernetics is concerned specifically with feedback systems, where a monitoring signal is sent from output back to input in order to control that output and bring the system into an equilibrium condition called "homeostasis." The locus classicus here is Norbert Wiener's *Cybernetics*. [Wiener, 1948 and 1961.]

[13] "Depuis longtemps, le pragmatisme et le behaviourisme ont appris aux psychologues à mettre l'accent sur l'action plutôt que sur la conscience. La cybernétique adopte rigoureusement ce point de vue: le sens, la conscience dans l'information, n'a rien d'essentiel; ou plus exactement, le sens d'une information n'est rien d'autre que l'ensemble des actions qu'elle déclenche et contrôle." (Ruyer, 1954.)

[14] Here, I think, we need to make the distinction between the (1) meaning, (2) meaningfulness, and (3) value of a message. A message to the decisionmaker reading *keep doing what you're already doing* is fully meaningful even though it does not entail a different action or necessarily result in a level of goal achievement higher than would have occurred in its absence. (Of course, a strict behaviorist would be unable to distinguish a meaningless message from a meaningful message to maintain the status quo, but this is not a problem in a goal-directed model.)

change in meaning implies a different selection from the range of states of
readiness. A meaningless message is one that makes no selection from the
range. An ambiguous message is one that could make more than one selection.
(MacKay, 1969, p. 24; emphasis original.)

MacKay offers the metaphor of a railroad switching yard in which the
configuration of tracks and switches stands ready to direct the trains passing
through it. By sending the right electronic signal—or, in older yards, by
inserting the correct key in a switch box—we can rearrange the configuration of tracks. The meaningfulness of a message thus depends on its form—
the shape of the key. And that meaning consists of the change the message
effects in the arrangement of the yard, the selection it makes from the set of
all possible configurations. (Notice that this example is somewhat less behavioristic than that of the decision-making farmer, in that the reception of a
meaningful message does not, in this case, imply action. Although the selection operation implies *potential* action—the shunting of a train in one direction instead of another—it is meaningful even in the absence of action; it is a
property of the system itself.) This view of information and meaning seems
to me exceedingly suggestive and points to some implications we can generalize without, I think, much embarrassment.

The first implication is that meaning must always be defined in terms of
the system—or person—receiving the signal. Meaninglessness, MacKay
notes, "is a relative concept, and a precise definition of meaning would be
useless unless it automatically reminded us of this." (MacKay, 1969, p. 86.)
The meaning of a message to a cybernetic system—a robot, a spacecraft, an
economic decision-system—depends on the system's structure and the message's form; and, while the human system is of a very different order, it
remains that meaning cannot be defined independent of that system—the
apprehending mind. "Meaning is always meaning *to someone*." (MacKay,
1969, p. 36; emphasis original.)[15] This may sound reasonable, but it is not an
entirely noncontroversial view, for it stands in opposition to numerous attempts to define meaning entirely in extrapersonal empirical and logical
terms.[16]

A correlative implication is that—perhaps surprisingly—this view tends
to blur rather than sharpen the distinction between semantic and nonsemantic information. If we speak of information as involving a selection operation
on the states of readiness of a system, then we can speak of the selective
information-content of a signal as somehow measuring the extent or mag-

---

[15] And here, in an important sense, is where methodological individualism comes back into the
picture.

[16] This is true of Wittgenstein in the *Tractatus logico-philosophicus* and also of the later logical
empiricists. [Wittgenstein, 1922; Carnap, 1950; Bar-Hillel and Carnap, 1953b; Bar-Hillel, 1964.]
I should also note that it was this attempt to eliminate the personal and (contra Mortazavian in
this volume) *not* the use of subjective probability that was the ultimate problem with the
positivist approach. It was a problem of too *little* subjectivism, not too much.

nitude of the selection operation performed. The expected value of information developed in the agricultural example is precisely this sort of measure. How does it differ from the entropy measure of communications theory?

> The communications engineer measures the selective information-content of ... signals, not in terms of the selective operation performed by the symbol on the ensemble of states of readiness of the ... receiver, but in terms of the selective operation performed by the signal on the *ensemble of signals*. The symbols are represented in this ensemble in the proportions in which they normally occur, the most frequently used occupying the largest space and being most easily selected. (MacKay, 1969, p. 75; emphasis added.)

Thus, the entropy measure of communication theory is not so much a measure of nonsemantic information content as it is a measure of the semantic (i.e., selective) information content of operations on one particular system, albeit a system different from the one actually receiving the signal; it is a value-of-information measure for a system in which value and probability (or, rather, improbability) are identical.[17]

Another, more significant, aspect of this view—which we might call the system-referential view of information—is, it seems to me, that it argues strongly against the oil-flow model. Information is not homogeneous; meaning is a matter of form not of amount; and the value or significance of a message depends as much on the preexisting form of the receiver as on the message itself. More to the point, this view suggests that information is stored as knowledge in a system not as oil is stored in a tank, but by virtue of the change that information makes in the very organization of the system itself. In a fundamental sense, knowledge and organization are identical.

I will postpone some of the more resonant implications of this last, rather provocative, statement. For the moment, let me try to illustrate what such a connection between knowledge and organization might mean.

We are all accustomed to thinking of memory as a function that takes place in some isolated part of a system—a computer memory bank or a human brain, for instance. But information is not stored in those places like relics in an attic; information submitted to a system's memory changes the organization of that subsystem: The arrangement of magnetic elements in a

---

[17] We can see this clearly by comparing the equations in footnotes 9 and 10. For the value-of-information measure, we had

$$\text{EVPI} = p\,\Delta\Pi(w = H) + (1 - p)\Delta\Pi(w = L),$$

where $\Delta\Pi$ is shorthand for the expression in brackets in footnote 9. For the entropy measure, we had

$$H = -[p\log_2 p + (1 - p)\log_2(1 - p)].$$

In the first case, the probabilities weight terms that measure the effect of a message on the system; in the second case, the probabilities weight terms referring only to the selection of a message from the set of messages.

core memory, for example, is changed when data are stored. Furthermore, the memory bank is not the only locus of memory in the system. In an important sense, the entire organization of the system—hardware plus software, mind and body—contains functional knowledge to guide behavior. I do not think this is a new or particularly controversial way of putting things.

At the risk of a charge of idiosyncrasy, let me go beyond this to suggest a distinction between structural information and parametric information. The former is information that operates on—that changes—the basic structure of the system; the latter is information that operates on parameters of the system—on elements that adjust or calibrate the workings of the system within the dictates of, but without altering, its underlying structure.

I apologize if this all sounds a little vague. But the nature of form and structure is a problem that has animated philosophy since the Presocratics, and I make no pretense of trying to solve it. At an intuitive level, the notion of a system's structure is fairly clear: A system has various fixed (or relatively slow changing) attributes that define its form, that set the scope, ground rules, and boundary conditions for the system's more variable aspects. (This may have a physical correlative in hardware as distinct from software, but it need not; even within the software of a computer program, the mental representations of a human mind, or indeed any system in the abstract, we can speak of an underlying structure.) If we restrict ourselves to the mathematical realm, we can make the notions of structural and parametric information more precise, if in the end perhaps no less metaphoric.[18]

The agricultural decision-system again provides a clear example. Here, the model's structure lies in the form of the profit function; that function specifies a parameter, weather conditions, that can be altered by reception of an appropriate message. Our decisionmaker is able to obtain only parametric information and thus to gain only parametric knowledge from a signal. As the problem is formulated, no signal can change his profit function or any of the basic givens of the situation he faces.

In the modern mathematical "economics of information" [Hirshleifer and Riley, 1979], the focus is exclusively on parametric information of this sort. For a long time, the mainstream of economics had concentrated on "perfect-information" models, where the decisionmakers were portrayed as having full knowledge of all aspects of the decision-situations they faced. In newer

---

[18] Mesarović offers a definition of systems structure that, as best I understand it, is consistent with what I have in mind. The organization of a system consists in the systems relation that maps one set of parts into another. This relation R "can be considered as defined by an abstract relation and the specific values of the unspecified constituents, the so-called relational constituents; $R = \{T, \zeta\}$, where T = systems structure, ζ = set of relational constituents." (Mesarović, 1964a, p. 10.) As Mesarović further suggests (in Equation 9), these relational constituents can take the form of parameters of the system. Thus, my distinction between structural and parametric seems in accord with his view. Also see Mortazavian's paper in this volume.

models, the decisionmakers retain full structural knowledge of the problems they face; but now there are certain key parameters—such as weather conditions—obscured from their vision. As we might guess, the myopic decisionmakers invariably choose less efficiently than their better informed counterparts, a situation that has proven a boon to the legions of modern economists who take pleasure in identifying causes of what they term market failure much as nineteenth-century paleontologists delighted in unearthing new species in fossil. Meanwhile, the importance of imperfect *structural* knowledge—with its very different economic implications—has escaped widespread attention.

KNOWLEDGE, STRUCTURE, AND ECONOMICS

It is fair to conclude, I think, that systems theory and the theory of knowledge and information (broadly defined) must ultimately be related in a fundamental way. Both are concerned with form and organization. And it is little wonder that communications theory, with its entropylike measure of information content, has held a singular fascination for systems theorists. An organized entity is a nonrandom entity, one whose organization is unexpected in some sense, and it is unexpectedness—negative entropy—that communications theory measures.

Although, as we saw, the derivation of a scalar measure of organization is possible only in the very special case with which communications theory is concerned, it nonetheless remains that the knowledge content of a system is closely bound up with that system's organization—with its structure.

We have already seen two logics of organization identified by systems theorists: causal systems and goal-directed systems. I would now like to suggest that these two are not the whole story.

A causal system is an instance of what we might call a "mechanical" structure. The movements of the parts are causally related to one another within the dictates of a fixed structure. The centuries-old example is the mechanical clockwork. Each gear moves by virtue of the force impressed on it by a previous gear; and each carries out its function within the pattern ordained by the designer. Once cut loose from its creator, the mechanical system cannot increase its level of organization. Indeed, any change in structure (other than those effected by the ministrations of the designer) must lower the level of system organization, thus increasing entropy in some sense.

Information and control are closely related concepts in systems theory. In a strictly causal system, the only way to change behavior is by reprogramming the system; often, this can be accomplished by adjusting various control variables to modify the system's structure—much as we manipulate the steering wheel and foot pedals to alter the behavior of an automobile. This is called open-loop control, in that the controlling information comes entirely from outside the boundaries of the system.

The mechanical-control model has not been absent from economics. The various models of stabilization policy, now happily somewhat out of fashion, have long portrayed the economy as a system of aggregate variables (national income, consumption, investment, etc.), which the government—viewed as an entirely exogenous entity—could regulate by suitable manipulation of its control variables, for example, government expenditures.

As we have seen, goal-directed systems (or cybernetic systems, in the narrow sense of the term) work somewhat differently. These systems also have a fixed structure, but now there are certain manipulable variables that can be altered by information generated within the system itself. The system possesses a goal; and, by means of an information-feedback loop, it is able to compare its situation with that goal and make appropriate adjustments toward it. Among control theorists, this is called closed-loop control.[19]

I have already suggested that there is a definite congruence between causal systems and goal-directed ones, and while perhaps less horological than the former, the latter are not necessarily less mechanical in the everyday sense of the term. (An ordinary mechanical thermostat is a cybernetic device.) But there remains a tendency to see cybernetic systems as somehow more organic than causal systems. This is, I believe, largely because many bodily systems also operate in a cybernetic fashion.[20]

Rather than settling at a mechanical equilibrium point—like a clock running down or gas molecules coming to terms with the surrounding temperature—a cybernetic system achieves a condition of dynamic balance called homeostasis. Like a mechanical system, though, a cybernetic system in homeostasis is struggling to maintain a fixed level of organization. Any change in the system's state is, therefore, potentially dangerous, and prolonged changes represent worrisome imbalances that threaten to destroy the system. Indeed, many who take cybernetics seriously as a general metaphysics of order soon develop an attitude I tend to call thermodynamic Manichaeism—the implicit belief that every trend, every economic or social

---

[19] I should also mention here the branch of systems theory called optimal-control theory. The optimal-control theorist seeks the best way to control a system in order to achieve some goal. For example, we might wish to calculate that trajectory of a rocket between two points that minimizes flight time, fuel consumption, or some other objective. (And, as a matter of fact, it was precisely such aerospace problems that formed much of the early subject matter of this theory.) Mathematically, the optimal path is found using the calculus of variations (and something called the Pontryagin Maximum Principle) or the (closely related) technique of dynamic programming. Once found, this optimal trajectory can be imposed directly by open-loop control or implemented through a feedback system to create goal direction and closed-loop control. [See generally Bryson and Ho, 1968.] Optimal-control theory has found its way into economics, especially in economic-growth models (not unrelated to the simple stabilization policy models already mentioned) [Burmeister and Dobell, 1970, chapter 11] and in the theory of resource extraction [Sweeney, 1977]. See also Kamien and Schwartz [1981] and Aoki [1976].

[20] Human biology was, in fact, an early inspiration for cybernetics. [Cannon, 1939.]

innovation is a potential victory for the forces of entropy and disorder over the forces of homeostasis. [Langlois, 1981, chap. 2, esp. pp. 73–82.] And it is thus probably no surprise that systems theorists [Mesarović and Pestel, 1974] and cybernetically oriented biologists [Hardin, 1977] are prominent among the new Malthusians who see dangerous social and ecological imbalances in the world's future.

In economics, there has been some effort afoot, especially by so-called post-Keynesians, to close the loop on the macroaggregate models of economic stabilization. These economists, as one observer correctly notes, ". . . might wish to replace the Newtonian-clockwork model by something they call a 'cybernetic' model, which may be an improvement (if it could ever be devised), but a shift from mechanical statics to sophisticated mechanical dynamics is no radical conceptual revolution." (Kristol, 1981, p. 212.)

What is the alternative to the mechanical causal and cybernetic models? The answer is best found by leaving the level of aggregate dynamics and returning to consideration of the parts—the human agents. A human being—at least in part or at times—is a goal-directed system. This is the basis of the ideal type—*homo economicus*—that underlies much of mainstream economic modeling. Yet everyone this side of B. F. Skinner recognizes that the flesh-and-blood human being does not operate with the stimulus/response compulsiveness of a simple goal-directed cybernetic system. There is something more, or perhaps different, at work.

One major school of thought holds, at least implicitly, that differences between the human mind and a mechanical cybernetic system are ones of degree rather than of kind. The mind is an immensely complex thing, and if we could only construct a cybernetic system—that is to say, a digital computer, the apotheosis of the mechanical cybernetic system—with sufficient complexity, we could largely replicate much of what the mind can do. Adherents to this view take heart from the old saying attributed to Marx that quantitative change allowed to go on long enough inevitably becomes qualitative change.

There are dissenters from this viewpoint, of course. Most notable among these is Hubert Dreyfus, whose analysis continues to stir controversy in the field of artificial intelligence. [Dreyfus, 1979.] In a significant sense, Dreyfus's thesis rests on the system-referential view of knowledge already articulated. Human knowledge, he argues, is very much tied to the biologically and culturally evolved structure of the human organism. What is meaningful to a human is meaningful only in reference to that structure, and meaning cannot be reduced to the system of explicit, extrapersonal, context-free statements that a computer, by virtue of its own structure, must employ. It is for this reason, Dreyfus argues, that no artificial intelligence program has yet been (or could be) written in which the important functions of discriminating meaning and significance are not preprogrammed by the human designer.

However this be resolved, it is clear that the human mind operates differently from *simple* cybernetic systems. The human mind is an example of a system in which information can result not merely in parametric but in structural knowledge. Unlike our simple cybernetic decisionmaker, the flesh-and-blood human is able, both spontaneously and as the result of signals, to change the problem formulation, rearrange the structure of his or her expectations, to alter his or her states of readiness. In Kantian terms, we might say that the human system is able to "evolve categories of description beyond those built into its design . . . ." (MacKay, 1969, p. 55.)

The lexicon of systems theory has a couple of words that sound as if they were intended to articulate a conception of the metamechanistic or the metacybernetic; these are *open system* and *self-organizing system*. The first is of thermodynamic origin and refers to a system that is not isolated and thus is able to exchange matter or information with an outside environment. A self-organizing system—by one definition, at least [Mesarović, 1964*a*, pp. 11–13]—is a system that can change its structure in response to the environment.[21] Clearly, a human system is both open and self-organizing. But I am not entirely persuaded that these terms by themselves fully capture our intuitive sense of the distinction between a mechanistic and nonmechanistic (or metamechanistic) system. Openness and self-organization are certainly necessary but perhaps not sufficient conditions to qualify a system for the latter category. Indeed, these distinctions do not seem to rule out various sorts of robots or things like "perceptrons" and "heuristic programs." [Ibid.][22] Perhaps the best distinction, despite its greater generality, is that between a "morphostatic" and a "morphogenetic" system. [Buckley, 1967, pp. 58–59.]

Models in the mainstream of economics—including, as I have suggested, those in the mathematical economics of information—portray the economic agent as a passive cybernetic reactor, a morphostatic system that responds to changes in data according to the logic of the economic problem programmed into it by the economist. As Fritz Machlup has long and patiently explained, this approach is not a statement about human psychology but a perfectly reasonable and justifiable technique of analysis—particularly for the sorts of economic problems to which the basic tools of partial-equilibrium comparative statics are normally applied. [Machlup, 1967.] But even granting all this, there remains a wide range of problems that demand a more active, morphogenetic ideal-type of the economic agent—one who can acquire structural knowledge and change the economic problem he or she faces.[23]

---

[21] Ludwig von Bertalanffy's definition of this term seems a bit different and comes nearer to the distinction I am looking for. He describes a self-organizing system as one capable of "evolving from a less to a more differentiated state." (Bertalanffy, 1968, p. 68.)

[22] The reason for this, I believe, is that Mesarović is willing to classify systems as self-organizing if they change their structure within the dictates of a fixed higher level structure; that is, if they "change their structure by using a relation from the set Ω_R." (Mesarović, 1964*a*, p. 11.)

[23] Morphogenetic man has not been entirely neglected in economics. Under the title of entrepre-

If economic agents are cybernetic reactors, they can adjust the economic mechanism in light of changed circumstances, but they cannot thereby increase the organization (decrease the entropy) of that mechanism. And any imperfection in the agent's knowledge (that is, any lack of correspondence between the economic problem perceived by the agents and the "true" economic problem) can lead to a bad equilibrium, a market failure. But if economic agents can alter the problem they face, if they can bring new *structural* knowledge into the system, then elaboration of, and increased differentiation in, the economic system becomes possible. Far from causing disorder or chaos, apparent departures from homeostatic equilibrium can actually result in an *increase* in system organization and a *decrease* in entropy. This is the phenomenon of "spontaneous order" [Hayek, 1967, p. 77] or, in technical jargon, "deviation-amplifying mutual causal effects." [Maruyama, 1963.][24]

Recognizing the existence and importance of morphogenetic processes has a number of far-reaching implications for both systems theory and economics, but this is not the place to explore them, I am afraid. Instead, let me close with some brief observations on relations between these two disciplines.

Systems theorists of my acquaintance are sometimes inclined to the opinion that economics lacks an adequate systems perspective and its scientific development would be rapidly enhanced by a complete subsumption of that discipline into systems theory. This viewpoint is not without its ironies. In an important sense, it was economists who were the first systems theorists. Moreover, the founders of economics were concerned with a fully morphogenetic version of systems theory. [Hayek, 1967.] Adam Smith's conception of economic growth based on the increasing division of labor is very much a theory about the evolution of economic structure from a less to a more differentiated state. [A. Smith, 1776 and 1936.] And, indeed, it is now widely recognized that the theory of evolution, known to us through the biological theory of Darwin, was articulated at least a century earlier in the social sciences.[25]

Of course, modern systems theory is also concerned with questions of morphogenesis, but mathematical systems theory—in the guise of nonequilibrium thermodynamics [Prigogine, 1971] and topology [Thom,

---

neur, he has been studied by Joseph Schumpeter and more recently, Israel Kirzner, among others. [Schumpeter, 1934; Kirzner, 1973.]

[24] Another name for this class of phenomena is autopoiesis, an area that is apparently attracting increasing interest among systems theorists. For a bibliographic introduction, see Zeleny [1981].

[25] David Hume, who numbered economics and social thought in general among his philosophical interests, adumbrated a genuinely Darwinian view of evolution in his *Dialogues Concerning Natural Religion*, first published in 1779 but written in 1759, a hundred years before *The Origin of Species*. [Hume, 1961, especially p. 478.]

1975][26]—is just beginning to grapple with these problems. In practice, the systems theorists who wish to bring economics under their wing are the control theorists and cyberneticians (in the narrow sense), the builders of naive-holist macromodels of the economy. In this sense, then, a subsumption of economics into systems theory is a step backwards—a step back in the direction of the French physiocrats, whose ideas Adam Smith transcended in founding the discipline of economics.[27] The problem is not a lack of high-powered systems mathematics in economics: Modern economists have not been slow in the least to adopt whatever new mathematical techniques emerge from systems theory. Indeed, if there is any need to make economics more system-theoretical, it is a need not to give it over to the cybernetic modelers but to return the discipline to the more sophisticated version of systems thought on which it was founded.

[26]This work by Thom, which presents the notion of catastrophe theory, has attracted a large following in a number of disciplines and remains something of a cause célèbre in mathematical systems theory. It promises mathematical interpretations of some of the most ancient and vexing problems of philosophy—the nature and origin of form and structure—and the text alternates enticing intimations of the profound with an utterly impenetrable formalism, thereby applying a time-tested formula for attracting a cult following.

[27]On the similarities between physiocrats and certain modern systems models of the economy, see Almarin Phillips [1955].

SIGNALS, MEANING, AND CONTROL IN SOCIAL SYSTEMS

Walter Buckley

There are three main topics in Langlois's paper on which I would like to comment. One is his philosophical critique of systems theory involving "emergentism." Second is his discussion of information and meaning in relation to social science. Last is the question of control theory, again as it may apply to social science.

I shall not dwell long on the first topic since, in my view, Langlois has erected a straw man in arguing that systems theory, in its concern for the whole and its emergent properties, tends to ignore the components. None of the founding theorists or important contributors have held such a view. The mistake perhaps derives from the emphasis given to emergent properties and behaviors of the whole in the attempt to offset the strong reductionist tendencies in most of the sciences. This issue has been well reviewed by Anatol Rapoport in his contrast of the traditional *analytical* methodology of physics with the glaring need for *synthetic* methods in the biological and social sciences. [Rapoport, 1968a.]

Langlois's characterization of intelligent or sophisticated methodological individualism wipes out any significant differences with emergentism and does away with important issues that still need to be thrashed out in principle. In practice, however, since we cannot begin to explain or predict the properties or behaviors of complex dynamic wholes from a knowledge of the parts, it seems wise to study both and try to understand how each interacts with and influences the other.

In discussing communication theory, it is, of course, important to distinguish and define signals, information, and meaning and distinguish as well their relevance to simple systems as compared to complex systems that decide or choose different behaviors. Soon after Shannon published his theory of information, it became widely recognized that it was actually a theory of signals, and he himself recognized that it did not deal with informa-

601

tion in the semantic sense. Langlois is correct to point to the mechanistic implication of signal theory, though there is no need to deny that complex systems such as computers are indeed information processors—as long as that does not imply that the information has meaning for them. The example that Langlois gives of "a slightly more sophisticated version of S/R" theory doing duty as a goal-seeking system with the stimulus being the information and having an "intermediate processing stage" gives too much to S/R theory. A distinction that might be helpful here has been made by automata theorists and others between simple systems with constant internal states and systems with varying internal states. For the former, the outputs are a function only of the inputs, and given a particular input at any time, the output must always be the same. For the latter, the outputs are a function of both the inputs and the internal state at a particular time, and, thus, the same input may result in different outputs at different times or vice versa. All systems capable of making a choice, or selecting different outcomes even if the input is the same, depend on this feature—this means all living systems and some that are man-made. Simple systems, including S/R systems, do not "process information," but only react to signals.

Signals are varying objects or physical processes and may or may not convey information. Information is not an object or entity, but is inherently relational, a mapping between two or more sets of events. When we seek information from a statistical analysis of our research data, we are looking for such a mapping. Information, if it properly maps to the internal states of a system, can selectively trigger sets of behaviors. If the system has constant internal states, it behaves predictably; if not, it is capable of novelty.

I was glad to see Langlois's reference to the work of Donald MacKay, which has been a unique contribution too little recognized and not sufficiently built on. His notion of information changing the conditional probabilities underlying a person's readiness to act in certain ways should help to extend the application of modern communication theory to the psychological and social sciences. Given his definition of information as that which does logical work on an organism to keep its field of purposive activity matched to the requirements of its environment, he goes on to define the *meaning* of an item of information as its selective function on the range of the organism's possible states of orientation. MacKay notes that this is also a relational concept. On this basis, communication becomes a process whereby some of this selective organizing work of one organism is induced via symbols in another organism. This is a deeper way of saying that organisms can learn from the experiences of others without having to risk direct confrontation with the environment themselves. In return, however, there is the risk of false or incomplete information (or mapping).

Though Langlois has recognized the merit of MacKay's work, some of Langlois's discussion is misleading or mistaken. It is not helpful to speak of the *meaning* of a piece of information for what he calls causal or goal-seeking systems. (Here it is necessary to distinguish goal-seeking from purposeful systems. [Ackoff and Emery, 1972.] Modern weapons as well as thermostats are goal-seeking.) Nor is it felicitous to speak of voltages being meaningful and understood by such systems. And once again it is inept to identify S/R systems with cybernetic systems.

More importantly, it is an oversimplification of MacKay's concept of meaning to define it "solely in terms of the action released" and thus identify it with a conditioned, hence, mechanical response. Langlois comes closer to the mark when he later points out that what identifies the realm of meaning is the overall configuration of potential behaviors from which selections might be made rather than any particular response in isolation. The manner in which he presents the example of the agricultural decision-system makes it more appropriate to a narrower signal or information theory. The meaning of the input information about the possibility of rain is not simply the acreage chosen for planting, but rather, it is the mapping between the learned properties of rain and the range of possible consequences of rain for the farmer's particular goals and interests at the moment. If those goals, interests, or other internal states change, the mapping—hence, the meaning—of rain may change. These various properties, consequences, goals, and values interact in the farmer's mind to lead to the choice strategy he settles on. The meaning cannot be narrowly defined in terms of the final action resulting from the decision process.

Also it is misleading to suggest that the meaning of a message does not exist until the action occurs, and, hence, it is the action that generates the meaning. There may be confusion here with the process whereby a meaning comes to be generated in the first place. George Herbert Mead's theory of the social genesis of mind, self, and social institutions contributed greatly to our understanding here. [Mead, 1934.] For Mead, meaning comes to be established in social interactional settings through the association of gestures and symbols with particular acts. Thus, a symbol comes to mean the tendency to act in a way called out by the object symbolized. For Mead, the meaning of the symbol *chair* was the tendency to sit down in one. (This, too, comes close to an overly simplified identification of meaning and an act it might call out, representing a weakness in his views, deriving perhaps from his behaviorist and pragmatist background and environment.)

Taking a more or less standard decision-model, we can see the many different intermediate points at which input information may have a bearing on—play a selective role in—determining some final behavioral outcome:

1. Input information may help select which of several problems we should now make a decision about.
2. It may help select the set of potential strategies of action that might be put to bear on the selected problem or goal.
3. It may help select a particular strategy from the set of potential ones.
4. Finally, it may help select an initial act in carrying out the strategy or plan.

An important implication of this viewpoint is that a set of signals or information that is meaningful (that maps part of the world) for one person or group may only be, literally, noise for another (as when I hear Chinese spoken). Furthermore, people using the same language may talk past one another when the words and phrases are mapped to very different social or cultural worlds. Mead tried to show in great detail that the social bond, which makes possible permanently organized social and cultural life, involves an empathic interpenetration of minds and perspectives on the world. This is generated through a long socialization process based on symbolically induced self-images, other images, and common meanings, which thus make it possible to coordinate activities with others by taking the role of the other and orienting behavior toward a collective *generalized other*. A better understanding of the process is essential to an assessment of why it breaks down.

In turning to control theory, especially as applied to economics, Langlois offers the rather startling thought that Adam Smith was a founding father of a more advanced theory of cybernetic control and self-organizing systems.[1] All of this requires a more precise discussion of control theory than Langlois, or I, can muster in a short space. I will try, however, to fill in some gaps and resolve some ambiguities as I see them. At a minimum, not only must open-loop and closed-loop control be defined more carefully, but the notion of uncontrolled stabilizing system should be introduced.

If we conceptualize a control system as consisting, at minimum, of a controlling element that outputs control variables to the controlled system, a major problem of control is how the controlling system determines what values of the control variables to output in order to keep the system on the goal-track. This implies, also, that for a system to be able to control (or regulate), it must have a reasonably well-specified goal.

In closed-loop control, such as our standard thermostat, an auto-pilot, or a driver controlling a car down the middle of the lane, the information required to determine the control variables is derived from the representation of the goal-state in the system and from feedback information about the system's actual behavior—which, in turn, implies information about the disturbances acting on it and causing it to deviate.

In open-loop control, this feedback information is lacking, possibly because the system takes too long to respond to control or has not yet been affected by expected disturbances but must prepare for them. The control information must then come from direct assessment of the acting or impending disturbances and previously learned or currently theorized knowledge of what control actions are required to cancel the effects of the disturbances and maintain the goal-track. An example of a tentative and still half-hearted attempt at open-loop control is recent governmental activity aimed at introducing control measures to head off anticipated societal (and global) dis-

[1] See Wassily Leontief's recent critique of academic economics and its nonempirical foundation. [Leontief, 1982.]

turbances stemming from energy-resource depletion, pollution, population growth in underdeveloped societies, and so forth. The effort is especially disconcerting for Western societies, since there is an obvious inherent contradiction between the required societal and global control of relevant economic and other activities on the one hand and an economic ideology of no-control (laissez faire) derived from—yes, Adam Smith.

This brings us to the notion of uncontrolled but sometimes stabilizing systems. [Alfred Kuhn, 1974.] As already stated, control (or regulation) implies some clear representation in the system of a goal-state, whether programmed in by adaptation and evolution or by a human being, or learned from experience by a sentient being. Consider a simple ecological system of rabbits and foxes and their interlocked niches. Given certain initial populations of each in a certain stable environment, the population sizes of each may (or may not) stabilize and remain relatively constant over long periods as long as only relatively small disturbances occur. This stability is due to mutual relations among the variables, but these are not error-bearing feedback relations relative to some system goal. For there is no overall goal represented anywhere in the system, although component organisms have their own evolved goal-states (physiological needs). We speak of ecological systems as maintaining a delicate balance, because they are not control systems—not self-regulating. If internal or external environmental changes begin to occur, the system will easily be disrupted if not permanently destroyed—as is occurring, for example, with most of the world's rain forests.

The Adam Smith conception of an economic system translates into basically the same as that previously outlined—an uncontrolled system that sometimes stabilizes under rather ideal environmental conditions. Had Smith acquired modern conceptions of cybernetics and control theory, he could never have seriously introduced his notion of the "invisible hand" or the market place as a control or regulating mechanism. Western economic systems have demonstrated throughout history their delicate balance and consequent vulnerability to internal or external change. They have come under increasing attempts at public control but never sufficiently to override the noise in the system generated by the independent goal-actions of many actors. Modern collective decision theory has amply conceptualized and demonstrated how the collective as well as individual goals of all may be frustrated by the independent self-interested goal-behaviors of each. The "tragedy of the commons" is built into classical economic theory, which is currently reaping its dividends with special vengeance.

Langlois begins his paper with a critique of systems theory. I heartily agree that there are many things wrong with the movement (and the people involved in the Society for General Systems Research have recently been strongly self-critical), though I do not think Langlois mentions the core problem. Systems theory is widely recognized by most of its serious proponents as not a theory (except for the mathematician), but a set of conceptual and methodological tools along with a number of guiding principles. It cannot by itself provide a theory for any particular substantive area of study. To be useful, it must be integrated into the conceptual and empirical materials of a discipline. There are too few who have mastered it sufficiently well to apply it knowledgeably to their social-scientific field of study, especially empirical study. Most systems researchers are not social scientists and vice versa. Consequently, many attempted applications of systems theory to aspects of society are either poor social science or poor systems research. It is asking a lot to expect someone to master another field of study such as systems research, especially when the latter itself draws from a number of disciplines. But some of its important concepts are being quietly assimilated by various social sciences, though substantial progress may have to wait for the development of institutes and programs designed to integrate systems research and substantive studies.

It is my belief, however, that the promise of systems research for the social sciences is still great and has much more to offer in the areas of communication and social control than we have yet seen. The two need only engage in more intensive and empirically relevant interaction.

TOWARD A SYSTEM-BASED UNIFIED SOCIAL SCIENCE

Robert D. Beam

We often hear that "one man can no longer cover a broad enough field" and that "there is too much narrow specialization" . . . . We need a simpler, more unified approach to scientific problems, we need men who practice science—not a particular science—in a word, we need scientific generalists.

(Bode, Mosteller, Tukey, and Winsor, 1949, p. 553.)

Richard Langlois's paper reflects the opinion that systems theory has failed to bring about interdisciplinary synthesis of, and integrated education in, the social sciences. I would like to present a quite different relation between systems theory and the social sciences. In contrast to Langlois's position, I would like to suggest a means by which systems theory *can* "unify . . . the methodology of all sciences, . . . endow the social sciences with that natural-science-like rigor," and combat the "fragmentation and specialization" of social-science knowledge. (Langlois in this volume.) It is my opinion that systems theory has much to offer at the basic and most general level of social science, because, and again in contrast to Langlois, I feel it has *succeeded* in bringing "all disparate parts of inquiry under the sway of its organizing force." (Ibid.) Systems theory has provided a framework for social theory, a framework that allows for unification of the behavioral and social sciences on an analytic-deductive basis. Such a unified social science is built on systems concepts from the ground up, and the chief objective of my comment is to provide a brief outline of this discipline as it relates to a selected few of Langlois's remarks.

I would first like to articulate a model that makes a clear distinction between the servomechanism responding to environmental stimuli in a pre-programmed fashion and the human system as a complex controlled system capable of effecting *conscious* learned responses to environmental stimuli. This distinction is, I believe, one that Langlois also considers to be required. A complex controlled human system seems to me to be analogous to what he terms a metacybernetic system. This is a model that seeks to accomplish for social science what the model of "economic man" accomplishes for economic science. In contrast to the cybernetic-reactor model of economic man, this model enables the agent to *alter* the environment or his or her relation to it.

Since all behavior of analytic relevance to social science is learned behavior, this model focuses only on behavior that is directed *from* the nervous system *toward* some goal. The present model also assumes that all information that can be used to direct behavior is stored in the form of concepts (images) to be retrieved from storage through perceptions, memory, or communications.

The simple cybernetic model includes three logically irreducible ingredients for purposive behavior selection: a detector that acquires and processes information about the system's environment; a selector that chooses responses on the basis of the system's goal-state; and an effector that effectuates the overt behavioral response. The nature of control is the system's internal ability to detect deviance from a preferred state and correct its own behavior so as to restore, or move back toward, the "preferred" position. All purposive behavior requires negative feedback for both servomechanisms and organisms, including the human system.

But unlike other controlled systems, humans possess conscious awareness of, or information about, the system states of their detector, selector, and effector (DSE) subsystems. The more complex model of the human system contains sub-DSE controls for each of the main-level DSEs. Mechanical man-made servomechanisms, even computers, do not possess these types of sub-DSE controls.[1] The complex cybernetic model presented here provides a conceptually simple explanation of consciousness, even though it is not yet firmly established where in the brain consciousness resides or how it functions. Although the human biological system is responsible for effectuating overt behavior, it is the method of behavior selection that is of interest to social science. Thus, it is the control system of humans, as opposed to the biological system, that formulates and guides the execution of behavior relevant to psychological and social analysis.

The terms *detector*, *selector*, and *effector* have strictly functional definitions. The detector encompasses all sensory, cognitive, and intuitive processes by which humans form, identify, and modify both real and imaginary concepts about themselves and their environment. The selector spans the entire range of emotions, pleasures, pains, fears, loves, desires, and so forth—all things to which positive and negative valences can be attached, a valence being a property of the nervous system that produces pleasant or unpleasant feelings that reinforce approach responses or avoidance responses, respectively. The effector includes all neural connections that di-

---

[1] For a more complete presentation of the human system as a complex controlled system, see Alfred Kuhn [1974, pp. 60–102; 1975, pp. 49–73]. The contents of this paper draw heavily on the model of unified social science, as developed in these two volumes.

rect behaviors as diverse as splitting wood, singing an aria, or dancing the tango. Nothing in this model precludes one DSE subsystem from modifying the other two, as when detector modifies selector (we want what we believe is possible, and we do not want what we believe is impossible), selector modifies detector (we sometimes see what we want to see and hear what we want to hear), or some other combination.

MEANING, INFORMATION, AND KNOWLEDGE IN THE DETECTOR

In this model, the detector deals with cognition and perception, which are essentially the processes of learning and using patterns. Cognition, or pattern learning, involves the processes by which pattern concepts are organized and stored in the detector. Perception involves the use of incoming sensations as cues to identify (match) events in the environment with concept images (referents) of those events retrieved from storage. More specifically, signal inputs from the environment activate sensory receptors that modulate sensory nerves. This is the detection stage in which information received is without *meaning*. Information acquires meaning only after the detector *codes* or organizes sensory and linguistic inputs into concepts or patterns of concepts by categorizing the inputs by their similarities and differences. The detector can organize information into its own concepts or it can adopt the organized concepts of others through communication. The detector forms new concepts by abstraction (inductively forms new "emergent" concepts through the essentially morphogenic process of random variation and selective retention or intersection (acquires new concepts by deduction and discrimination, usually in the form of semantic communications). Knowledge in the detector is thus organized information, and this, I take it, is what Langlois means by his statement that knowledge and organization are identical.

If cognition in the detector is the process of *coding* and storing information in conceptual bins, perception is the process of *decoding* or retrieving coded information from storage. Perception is the process by which the detector matches primary patterns of incoming sensations with secondary patterns of previously stored images (knowledge) to infer information about presently experienced reality that is not contained in either primary or secondary form alone. Perception thus involves the receipt and use of primary information as *cues* to identify or activate secondary information in the form of previously stored concept-images. Matching uncoded sensory inputs with previously coded (learned) and stored concepts is known as pattern recognition. A signal input does not become a stimulus in the detector until it has been decoded or identified, and strictly speaking, it is not the signal itself, but the identification that constitutes the stimulus. A meaningful signal input is one whose cues are sufficient to activate a stored channel of concept images in the detector, or in MacKay's terminology, to select from the range of all possible "states of readiness." MacKay's metaphor of the railroad switching yard aptly describes this decoding process in the detector.

MOTIVATION IN THE SELECTOR

The selector subsystem reflects the control system's preferences, goals, values, and inner tendencies. Learning occurs in this subsystem as well as in the detector. The inborn (unlearned) components of this subsystem are its primary motives or the pleasant or unpleasant valences that certain emotions or sensations activate. Primary motives are oriented toward physical survival. The learned components of the selector are known as secondary motives and are conditioned connections between a learned concept and an inborn valence. We cannot *appreciate* or *like* economics until we have formed some previous concept(s) of what economics is about. Pattern learning thus involves learning a concept in the detector and (simultaneously) attaching a valence to that concept in the selector. Valences about concepts can be modified with experience or through additional concept learning.

Pattern using in the selector occurs whenever choices are made on the basis of learned secondary motives. The strength of a secondary motive depends on the degree of pleasantness or unpleasantness of the attached valence. Whereas concepts constitute detector states, motives constitute selector states that reinforce approach responses or avoidance responses to concepts that set them off. Both the detector and the selector learn and use primary and secondary levels of information and motives in selecting overt behavior to be executed by the effector.

BEHAVIOR EXECUTION IN THE EFFECTOR

For the individual human, all decision processes are confined to the detector and the selector. Effector processes are confined to the muscular execution of previously selected behavior. Pattern learning in the effector involves learning new performance skills, while pattern using involves their exercise. Less emphasis is placed on the effector in understanding directed behavior in humans, since social science is concerned more with the *what* and *why* of behavior selection than the *how*.

A person's behavior is guided toward his or her goals by decisions that reflect the interrelated detector, selector, and effector states of his or her control system. Decision theory deals with response selection in humans under conditions of complexity, particularly with respect to the conscious content of all DSE subsystems. The adaptive behavior process can be viewed in this model as involving two stages, a performance stage and a feedback stage. During the performance stage, the detector identifies an *opportunity function* of perceived alternative responses consonant with the capabilities of the effector. The selector ranks these responses in a *preference function* according to their likelihood of achieving a given goal or set of goals. A decision occurs when the most highly valued alternative is selected from the opportunity function and carried out by the effector. A feedback or learning stage follows in which the detector receives feedback information about the success of the previous action. The selector compares the new state of the environment with the goal-state and elects to continue or change the response, and the effector receives new instructions from the selector and carries them out but at a level different from that of the control system itself. A single stream of behavior is manifested in which the feedback stage of a previous action melds imperceptibly with the performance stage of the next. Learning occurs when through experience or a change of goals, a given stimulus-input of information elicits a different output-response than it did before. Directed behavior in humans is the result of decisions that interrelate perceived alternatives in the detector with secondary motives in the selector.

This DSE model of behavior selection provides a "proper scientific explanation" of "willed" or goal-oriented behavior [Alfred Kuhn, 1981], an explanation that until the development of cybernetics had sharply divided the goal-and-future-oriented soft sciences from the antecedent-cause hard sciences. Such an explanation occurs when the purposive action to be explained, the *explicandum*, is deduced from pieces of information that constitute the explanation, the *explicans*. [Homans, 1967, p. 25; Brown, 1963, p. 122; Hempel, 1963, p. 50.] To illustrate, using Langlois's decisionmaker:

Explicans

Premise 1 (detector) *if:* our decisionmaker perceives that planting acreage A_1 will yield a profit of \$100,000.00 and that planting acreage A_2 will yield a profit of \$75,000.00,

Premise 2 (selector) *and if:* his dominant motive is to maximize profits,

Explicandum

Conclusion (effector) *then:* he *will* plant acreage A_1.

This example illustrates why economics is the most theoretically precise of all the social sciences. The model of economic man makes explicit assumptions about detector and selector states for each person. The detector contains complete and accurate information. The selector's goal-state is unambiguous maximization of profit or utility. The behavioral response is unequivocally prescribed as soon as alternatives are compared with the goal. If we introduce uncertainty in the detector into the analysis, we may complicate the decision process, but not its basic logic of formulating the scope of the decision and listing alternatives to be considered within the set. Viewed as a cybernetic system, a decision's components are the costs and values of various alternatives, and the governor is the motive system of the decisionmaker. The selector will be unable to formulate a preference-ordering of responses until expected costs and benefits of each have been assessed, either through probability distributions or by buying the service of the clairvoyant. In either case, if the information needed to eliminate uncertainty in the detector is costly, the decision to acquire it will be made only if the expected value of this information exceeds its cost *to* the decisionmaker.

THE INTRASYSTEM/INTERSYSTEM AXES OF CONTROLLED SYSTEMS

All disciplines in the social sciences deal with types of social systems, yet their specialized concepts bear little resemblance to one another. There exist, however, some basic social mechanics that underlie all social science in the same sense that principles of the lever, inclined plane, and pulley underlie all mechanical contrivances. [Alfred Kuhn and Beam, 1982.] The intrasystem/intersystem axes of controlled systems shown in Figure 1 reveal basic system-based concepts of social interaction that underlie not only the core disciplines of economics, political science, and sociology, but also such related areas as small group theory, social psychology, management theory, and organization theory. The rectangles in Figure 1 show two goal-oriented systems, to wit, two individuals or two formal (controlled) organizations of individuals. Within each system are listed the three logically irreducible ingredients for purposive behavior: detector, selector, and effector. Behavior selection is separated into a decision stage and an effectuation stage with feedback. An intrasystem view consists of analysis of the behavior of a given system as a function of the DSE states of its control system. Since social science deals with interactions among two or more goal-oriented systems, an *intersystem* view is used to analyze interactions of their detector subsystems (communication), their selector subsystems (transaction), and their effector subsystems (organization).

Communication is the process of transferring patterns between systems. It both reflects and affects their detector states. Transaction transfers things of value between systems and reflects and affects their selector states. Organization carries out joint behavior by two or more systems and reflects and affects their effector states. Typically, systems theorists have analyzed linkages (social interactions) among humans with the analytic tools in information and communication theory. [Cadwallader, 1959; Haberstroh, 1960.] Matter/energy interactions—for example, sexual union or physical combat—are typically categorized in a different conceptual bin. [Buckley, 1967, p. 48.] The intersystem view of Figure 1 separates interactions analytically into the science of pattern transfers and the science of value transfers across controlled systems. Although considered the sine qua non of interaction, communications are viewed in this model as the facilitators of transactions that reflect the values people attach to their matter/energy transfers, and not the matter/energy transfers themselves. Thus, communications and transac-

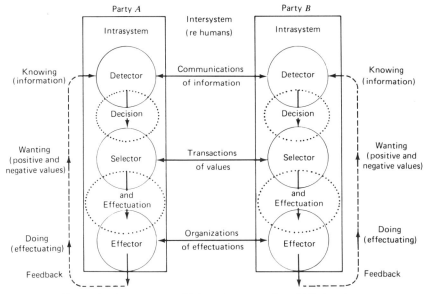

Figure 1. Intrasystem and intersystem axes of controlled systems.

tions are the interactions between humans that parallel the information and matter/energy interactions between living systems. I am not at all certain how Langlois would respond to the contention that a tight and coherent model of social interaction should include *both* the science of communication and the science of transaction,[2] each of which can be briefly outlined as follows. [Alfred Kuhn, 1974, chaps. 7–11.]

Communications

The Shannon-Weaver mathematical theory of communication is directed primarily at measuring the accuracy with which symbols used in communication can be transmitted. [Shannon and Weaver, 1949.] The theory is based on a mathematical theory of information that postulates a source to generate signals of a given variety and a receiver who can make use of this variety. [G. A. Miller, 1953.] The theory assumes that both the source and receiver possess similar concept-referents, which they attach to the signs they use to communicate messages. The communication theorist thus assumes that the signs transmitted during the communication process have the same meaning to the sender and the receiver. Since output depends on input and noise, accuracy in communication refers to the extent to which input to the communication channel resembles output from the channel. The theorist is not

---

[2] A more extensive coverage of the propositions relating to these basic sciences can be found in Alfred Kuhn [1974], chaps. 7–11.

concerned with the semantic level of communication, but with the amount of information measured in binary digits that can be accurately transmitted through the channel.

By contrast, the communication model in Figure 1 assumes that the channel is capable of accurately transmitting information—signals—and is interested instead in the accuracy with which (1) the coded pattern to be transferred is clear in the detector of the sender, (2) the message is detected by the receiver, and (3) the concept-referents that the transmitted signs select in the receiver's head correspond to patterns in the sender's head. Analytic interest is here directed to the effect of the communication on the detector states of the interacting parties, and not on the channel capacity of the transmission-medium or its levels of noise or redundancy.

I believe this view of semantic pattern-transfer is in accord with Mac-Kay's framework as Langlois describes it. It is an alternative to the oil-flow model of information, which, like the systems-referential view, might argue that information is not like "hardware products to be delivered through obstacles with minimum damage at least cost." (Nevitt, 1981, p. 595.) The core of the semantic problem of communication for social science lies in the proper selection of signs, such that they serve as cues sufficient to enable the receiver's detector to decode their meaning. The mathematical theory of communication, with its emphasis on bit-counts, noise, entropy, redundancy, and so forth, has much to contribute to binary computers, telecommunications, and other areas. But it has little to say about the manner in which humans match signs with concept images or recombine these images through sign communications to form new images. Although bit-count analysis can apply to information transmissions below the social level, it does not determine *how much meaning* is transferred by a given sign. The meaning of the sign depends on the concept-referent of that sign as it exists in the head of the sender at the moment of transmission and within the context in which the sign is used. The communication model in Figure 1 is concerned with the transfer of patterns *across* detectors of separate individuals, and not with transmission of information in bits. Hence, a discussion of bit-counts when referring to pattern transfers is not directly relevant to the analysis.

Transactions

At the intrasystem level, an individual's decisions reflect the comparison of benefits and costs among alternatives, a selected behavior being one whose expected benefits exceed its cost. When faced with two mutually exclusive alternatives X and Y, the cost of acquiring Y is the forfeited value of X, and the cost of acquiring X is the forfeited value of Y. At the intersystem level, we deal with situations in which party A is in possession of X, party B holds Y, and an exchange is contemplated by both parties. An exchange involves two separate but mutually contingent decisions. A will give up X for Y if and only if he values Y over X. B will give up Y for X if and only if she values X

over Y. Whereas successful communications between parties require similar detector-states with respect to the patterns exchanged, matter/energy exchanges are successful to the extent that the parties' selector states are *dissimilar* (have reverse preference orderings) for the things exchanged. Although the term *exchange* seems to fit the transfer of goods and services between parties, the general principles that derive from such exchanges can be extended to cover other events, such as blackmail, boycotts, hijackings, wars, strikes, and peer-group pressures, and so forth, all of which lack a matter/energy base and do not fit the formal conception of an exchange.

The more general term that includes all of these value-based interactions is known as a *transaction*, the analysis of which relies heavily on the concepts of *power* (the ability to induce wanted behaviors in others regardless of the overt terms of trade), and *bargaining power* (the ability to get good terms for oneself in transactions with others). Power and bargaining power are system variables that change according to the parties' selector-states for the things exchanged and mold the success and terms of a given transaction. These same variables operate regardless of the context—social, political, or economic—in which they occur. Such a broadened and systematized theory of selector-based transactions between humans provides the conceptual base for a science of power that has heretofore been scattered throughout the literatures of game theory, organization theory, community power structures, conflict theory, social psychology, international and domestic politics, bilateral monopoly, collective bargaining, and social exchange theory.

Cybernetics has been defined as the science of communication and control. [Wiener, 1948 and 1961.] With respect to the interaction between parties A and B in Figure 1, communication is necessary if A is to get B's detector to know *what* A wants. The aspect of control, however, lies in understanding *why* B complies with A's demands, by examining the ways in which A provides inducements to B's selector. [Alfred Kuhn, 1981, p. 587.] Detector-based interactions are logically separated from selector-based interactions. Every real interaction involves both communication and transaction, and a tight and logically rigorous nomothetic science of social interaction can be achieved only if the two are separated analytically. This is because no propositions about pure communication also apply to propositions about pure transaction. Langlois appears to consider all interactions as instances of communication only. However, in this model, communication is viewed as the indispensable *medium* of interaction, while its *content* is mostly transactional.

Organizations

Whenever a continuing and reasonably stable pattern emerges from the joint effects of the separately decided behaviors of two or more parties, the relation they form is called an *organization*. An organization is a social system of interacting subsystems of human components. It is an emergent social phenomenon in that it is a higher level system than its component members. The whole of an organization is more than the *sum* of its parts, where sum is taken to mean *not* their numerical addition, but their unorganized aggregation. [Buckley, 1967, p. 48.]

Just as an analytic need arose to separate interactions into communications and transactions, so there is also an analytic need to separate an organization by its structure and its process. Its *structure* is described in terms of its subsystems and their interrelated roles, a role being a set of DSE states and actions of a subsystem, including its specified communications and transactions with other subsystems. A role is thus a pattern-set of expectations about the behavior of the individual who occupies that role, and the structure of roles is analogous to the blueprint of the organization. The organization *process* describes the interactions of the role occupants themselves, particularly the way in which their actual communications and transactions constitute the joint effects of the organization as a whole.[3] [A. Kuhn and Beam, 1982, chaps. 8–9.]

As social systems, organizations span the analytic gamut from purely controlled (formal) organizations to purely uncontrolled (informal) organizations, with a continuum of mixtures (semiformal organizations) in between. Formal organizations, such as governments or business enterprises, possess a controlled subsystem that acts on behalf of the whole system and has the capacity to communicate with, induce motivations of, and instruct its subsystem role-occupants to behave in the way it (the control system) desires. [Ackoff, 1957–1958.] Formal organizations are thus oriented around the consciously coordinated behaviors of parts into behavior of the whole. Conscious coordination plus whole-system goals distinguish formal organization from its conceptual opposite, an informal organization. An informal organization such as a pure market economy is an ecological social system that has no control subsystem, no whole-system goals, and does not behave as a unit. Each subsystem pursues its own self-oriented goals, and any coordination that produces a joint effect of their interactions involves morphogenic processes that are wholly unplanned and undirected at the main-system level. The main identifying criteria of informal organization are absence of conscious coordination and presence of attention to subsystem goals. A semiformal organization such as the sociocultural system is informal in the sense that it does not behave as a unit but formal in that selected subsystems that do behave as units seek to modify their own behavior as well as the behaviors of other subsystems in ways they believe are in the best interests of the organization as a whole. Thus, to repeat, the main identifying characteristics of semiformal organization are absence of conscious coordination and presence of attention to whole-system goals by subsystems.

---

[3] See the relation between an organization as an acting system and a pattern system, in Alfred Kuhn and Robert Beam [1982], chaps. 8–9.

THE INTEGRATION OF SOCIAL SCIENCE KNOWLEDGE

Every discipline in the social sciences is a set of lenses and a set of blinders. Our academic institutions have been quite successful in providing specialized lenses but have been less successful in removing the blinders. The intrasystem/intersystem axes of controlled systems in Figure 1 are a tight, logical way to unify the methodology of all social science disciplines. Regardless of the specific context in which it occurs, the study of behavior-selection in humans can focus on the three irreducible components of goal-oriented behavior: detector, selector, and effector, or DSE. Coordinated action among humans is possible only by linking together their control systems via their detectors (through communication), their selectors (through transaction), their effectors (through organization), or some combination of these. Communication, transaction, and organization are the most basic building blocks of social analysis. When used as modular units, these general-purpose conceptual basics can be assembled into a vast variety of special-purpose configurations that lie scattered throughout the conventional social science disciplines.

For example, supply-and-demand curves in economics can be derived from the transaction model by adding parties to each side of an initial transaction. [Alfred Kuhn, 1974; Beam, 1979.] Conflict and cooperation are configurations of communication and transaction. Transaction has also been successfully used as a framework for labor negotiations. [E. E. Herman and A. Kuhn, 1981, chaps. 11–12.] The symbolic interaction process is a configuration of communication, transaction, and perceptual-detector processes. Authority is a unique transactional interaction within the context of formal organization. Decision theory is the study of complex DSE processes under conditions of uncertainty. The theory of government, as modified by conditions of sovereignty, all-purpose goals, involuntary membership, and legitimacy, is a special-purpose configuration of the formal organization model. [Alfred Kuhn, 1975, chap. 13.] Group decision-making is achieved through communication (persuasive influence), transaction (trade-off or compromise), or a particular transactional configuration known as dominant coalition. In each case, the same few basic components are fitted together as modular units to form special-purpose configurations previously viewed as the exclusive domain of specialists in each of the social science disciplines.

The purpose of this approach is not to undercut the disciplines, but to provide them with a common set of system-based analytic underpinnings. The integration of social science knowledge is not to be achieved by setting more and more areas of specialized knowledge side by side under some thematic interdisciplinary umbrella. [Bowler, 1981, p. 214.] Integration is achieved, rather, by developing more efficient conceptual structures that allow the human mind to deal with larger amounts of information by means of a smaller number of general concepts. It is achieved with a structure that reaches across specialized vocabularies and methodology to bring all "disparate parts of inquiry under the sway of its organizing force" (Langlois) by transforming the myriad fragments of social and behavioral science into a coherent whole. This is the great promise that systems theory has long been supposed to hold for the social sciences: The promise of a unified social science that (to borrow a phrase from James G. Miller) "discerns the pattern of a mosaic which lies hidden in the cluttered, colored marble chips of today's empirical facts." (J. G. Miller, 1978, p. 42.)

SYSTEMS, INFORMATION, AND ECONOMICS

Richard H. Day

I have been greatly stimulated by Langlois's remarks on systems and information in relation to economics. Rather than take issue with small points of disagreement I would like to augment his ideas and relate them to a very general, dynamic view of information in economic development. First, I try to identify the economizing of scientific information that is the basis of systems thinking. I then argue for a relativist view regarding the individualist/holist controversy. Next comes a brief illustration of Langlois's equation of knowledge and organization. I further try to make somewhat more precise the idea of a morphogenetic agent, arguing that a nonanalytic faculty of mind, creative intelligence, plays a fundamental role in generating structural information. Finally, I suggest that if economic systems are globally unstable, this faculty would be a necessary condition for the continuing evolution of human culture.

SYSTEMS THINKING: SUCCESS OR FAILURE

No field should be judged by its failure to accomplish everything to which its most ardent advocates aspire, for then we should have to judge every field to be a failure—just as we would have to judge to be a failure everyone among us whose grasp fell short of his or her reach. No, a field must be judged by the ability of its contributors to identify principles and organize them into a coherent system of thought that compels attention, invites use, and stimulates refinement, generalization, and application. From this point of view, systems thinking has been a success.

If we look at the early pioneers alone (Lotke, Cannon, and Ashby are my favorites), we find already firmly established the important fact that structure and process, once carefully identified and described for a given range of phenomena, are similar, perhaps identical, to those of quite a different range of phenomena. This enables results developed in one field to have immediate application to another.

A striking example is the use of concepts of negative-feedback control in engineering (servomechanisms), economics (behavioral adjustment processes), biology (homeostasis) and, indeed, systems dynamics, generally. Here is a primal concept of great utility in a diversity of settings.

Other examples abound. Several years ago, I began considering the existence of erratic fluctuations in deterministic economic processes; how this happened is germane to our discussion. I was led to the work of Edward Lorenz, a meteorologist, by Kenneth Cooke, a mathematician who was a fellow participant at a small working conference on simulation in archeology. [Sabloff, 1981.] I had described my ideas on adaptive economics and recursive programming, which I used as a framework for simulating economic development and technological change in modern agriculture and industry. [Day, 1975; Day and Cigno, 1978.] But for this occasion, I illustrated the ideas with models of the prehistoric transition from hunting to agriculture and from feudal manorialism to a market-based agriculture. [Day, 1981a.] Cooke observed that Lorenz's concept of deterministic, nonperiodic flow could be applied to some of the equations in my models. A few days later, I told Jess Benhabib, a colleague then at the University of Southern California, of this work. He had already run across it quite independently in collaborating with another of our colleagues, Kazuo Nishimura, on the existence and stability of cycles in economic growth. We began a collaboration on the topic, in the course of which we made use of related literature in biology, classical mechanics, and chemical thermodynamics, just to mention a few. [Robert May, 1976; Moser, 1973; Prigogine, 1971.]

The key idea that unifies research in these varied fields is that of the complicated implications of *nonlinear* dynamic systems (difference or differential equations). Others, too, emphasized this important principle. [Samuelson, 1948; Forrester, 1962.] Its nature is still only partly understood and the subject of intense investigation.

I was especially intrigued by results concerning a quadratic difference equation that had arisen in some of my earlier studies. I had noticed the complicated possibilities that equation possessed, but I had set the work aside. [Day, 1967.] In the meantime, the same equation had been investigated intensely in connection with totally different lines of work. [For a review, see Day, 1982.] It was eventually found by Mitchell Feigenbaum to exemplify properties common to a large class of nonlinear functions. [M. J. Feigenbaum, 1980.]

These observations also shed some light on the nature of information. Indeed, the structural-information content of phenomena may be described by an abstract, dynamical system that seems to manifest salient features of those phenomena. In this sense, the idea of a system is analogous to that of a strategy or policy. A system represents all its possible implications in response to all conceivable applications, "parameterizations," and calibrations just as a strategy represents all actions that respond to all conceivable decision inputs. Systems thinking is, therefore, a way of expressing compactly as much as we know and can find out rigorously about classes of disparate phenomena. *In short, systems thinking is a means for economizing thought.*

No one should appreciate such a point of view more than economists. The principle is economic. Its application is in no field better exemplified than in economics. I have in mind Samuelson's *Foundations of Economics*, which did so much to identify and clarify the small number of principles that lay at the heart of economic thought as it had evolved in its many branches.

INDIVIDUALISM, HOLISM, AND AGGREGATION

Langlois is correct in emphasizing that complete understanding of emergent phenomena must involve attention to the individual parts that make up a given whole. His examples, drawn from economics, are good ones, and it would behoove systems scientists to devote more attention to insights from that field. A certain amount of handslapping (if somewhat self-righteous) may be salutary here.

But there is a nontrivial problem in the individualist point of view. There are parts and there are parts, and parts within parts at various levels. It is true that macroeconomics lacks even now an adequate microeconomic foundation, but we do macroeconomics anyway because we must. Governments exist; they make policy, and there is a manifest need for reasonable policy. Until really good microtheory of individual action and reaction can be developed, less satisfactory macromodels will have to be relied on as primary tools for carrying on debates on economic policy.

The problem goes deeper. Just as there are subatomic particles of which atoms are composed, so the business firm is, in fact, an organization of individual humans. It is not at all clear that an understanding of emergent macroeconomic phenomena can be understood without reference to the structure of relations among individuals within all the basic units of economic life, household, government, firm, bank, and so forth. And further, can we really say that we understand the rationality of individuals until we understand how and to what extent optimal choice emerges from the various emotional drives and other diverse components of the mind? If economics has made progress in the cause of the individualist methodology, it has surely not made enough and only scratched the surface of this fundamental problem.

My own opinion is that this problem can never really be solved. We can only hack away at it: "What cannot possibly be completed remains nevertheless a task," said Karl Jaspers. (Jaspers, 1961, p. ix.) We must then pursue understanding at many levels: Some must examine the parts (at a given level) narrowly; others may investigate a system with parts defined in some aggregate way in a more holistic fashion. We explore alternative aggregations, alternative specifications of detail. And at all times we must retain some uncertainty (and a healthy level of skepticism) about just what the meaning is of abstract systems when used to represent what we understand of phenomena.

THE MEANING OF INFORMATION

When Langlois considers the role of information in systems, he gets to the root of the issue when he asserts the systems-referential view:

> Information is not homogeneous; meaning is a matter of form not of amount; and the value or significance of a message depends as much on the preexisting form of the receiver as on the message itself. . . . [I]nformation is stored as knowledge in a system not as oil is stored in a tank, but by virtue of the change that information makes in the very organization of the system itself. In a fundamental sense, knowledge and organization are identical. (Langlois in his paper in this volume.)

The McCulloch-Pitts model of the neuron and nerve nets provides a nice illustration of this idea. [Shannon and McCarthy, 1956.] A nerve net is a system of on-off threshold switches. An external input turns the input switches on or off or leaves them unchanged. A sequence of messages (pulses, signals) then flows from unit to unit altering the state of the system by altering the state in each constituent element. Very simple examples of such nets exhibit behavior analogous to memory and learning.

Whatever such a system may lack as a model of the brain, it may nonetheless exhibit something profound about the nature of meaning in Langlois's systems-referential sense, how meaning emerges from a cascade of interconnected individuals capable of only elemental stimulus/response behavior and where every meaning has an exact organizational analog.

STRUCTURAL AND PARAMETRIC INFORMATION: THE MORPHOGENIC AGENT

The distinction Langlois makes between parametric information and structural information is important. Let me elaborate and illustrate. Imagine a mathematical system represented by difference or differential equations. Let us suppose that a subset of equations represents states of an actor or agent. A second subset represents the agent's environmental states. The former can be thought of as the agent's policy. The complete system represents the behavior of the agent-environment pair. Imagine that parameters of the agent equations change. Then environmental states, as generated by the environmental equations, which have remained fixed, will elicit modified behavior. Parametric information has changed.

Suppose that an actor can respond to environmental cues in accordance with two quite different sets of equations, that is, two alternative policies. He is now faced with a choice in addition to stimulus/response at the level of elemental states. He must choose a policy. If for a given set of states a policy switch occurs, *structural* information has changed.

Next, imagine that our agent senses environment (external) and agent (internal) states and on the basis of these chooses a policy. Given this policy, stimulus/response occurs. Suppose this choice can be represented by equations, too. The overall system is expanded to include a morphogenetic component. Structure changes endogenously; form evolves. Elsewhere, I have shown how models of this kind can represent essential features of economic development and provide an endogenous theory of structural change. [Day, 1981*a, b.*]

CREATIVE INTELLIGENCE

Notice that in modeling the selection of policies by a new set of state-transition equations, a structural change becomes formally like a parametric change. This formal similarity disguises the point, however. There is a big difference in nature between behavior of amoeba, which have quite fixed patterns of S/R, and those of humans, who can, according to a highly elaborated socio-politico-economic system, switch monetary and fiscal policies from, say, Keynesian equations to Friedmanian ones.

Moreover, there seems to be a nonanalytic type of morphogenesis, the essence of which is poorly represented by equations of any kind so far as I know: Humans *create* structure. In shifting from one organization to another, we sometimes invent something new, something that did not exist before. Why should we have this capability? No other creatures have it in more than a rudimentary form.

Before suggesting the answer, let us emphasize how important creativity is. Economists, focusing as they so often do on equilibrium and comparative-static theory and influenced as they are by politicians' demands for the analysis of immediate effects of policy, forget that the essence of life (and very likely of stellar existence, too) is evolution: The progression of things through a variety of forms; new forms emerge where none like them existed. If conditions are favorable, they grow and flourish. Inevitably, they decline and die out.

All of this suggests that given forms are globally unstable: Their equations of motion ultimately carry them outside their bounds of homeostasis. Nature handles this problem by variation and selection. Conscious individuals, however, do not wish to be bound by this profligate, merciless process. If, when *their* systems and the world about them begin to go awry, they could only *create* something new, something that would set them working again so to speak, then *they* would continue to exist. Nature need not kill her children if only they can create. To contrast this property with economic rationality in the usual sense, I prefer to use the term *creative intelligence*. If it did not exist, we would not.

UNSTABLE SYSTEMS

From the long view, evolution, not "stationarity," is the fundamental fact of life. When individuals cannot adapt, they are killed; when organizations cannot adapt, they are disassembled. When societies cannot adapt, they are destroyed, swept aside, covered with sand, swallowed by jungle, or trampled under by a new regime. Humans are destroying virtually all mammal species with whom they lack a symbiotic tie. Industrialized societies are destroying the last vestiges of paleolithic man. The internal-combustion engine has driven away the horse, the oxygen process has eliminated the Bessemer process. Everywhere and at every level, we see evidence that economic systems are globally unstable and that in any given form they eventually stop working. Just now, concern arises about the instability of the contemporary world economy. The emergent phenomenon that becomes most crucial for us is the next form of economic policy. From where does it come?

It must come from the same attribute of mind that guided the subtle hand of those stone-chippers of so many centuries ago who invented the spearhead. The attribute that makes it possible to create an image, to set in place a form in some way unlike any that came before. This attribute creates a menu of possible ways of life from which policies can be selected and behavior carried on. Once in existence itself and perpetuated within the species, it always operates.

When something new is created, since structural information is changed, its full implications are seldom perceived. The hunting band may have led some innovative tribe to a flourishing culture, rich in food, ceremony, and leisure. Eventually, however, when the last woolly mammoth was butchered, the last herd of giant bison driven over a cliff, a way of life came to an end. The inventors of fine spears, bows and arrows unleashed a new spiral of progress, but one that eventually also succumbed in unexpected ways.

The implications are that: (1) Intelligence creates new forms that at crucial times make possible a continuation of certain living groups; (2) with changes in structure, a people may persist for a while; (3) the ultimate consequences of adaption are unknown, and the new system is also (always?) unstable, so that new forms must repeatedly be found. Morphogenetic man is thus an active participant in evolution, matter that has come not only to reflect on itself, but also to design the new forms it will occupy in its trajectory through space and time.

INFORMATION ECONOMICS,
TEAM THEORY,
AND AGENCY THEORY

Richard Mattessich

This paper should be taken as a supplement rather than a commentary to the preceding paper by Richard Langlois. Some of these pages were originally written as a second part of my commentary on Hassan Mortazavian's paper in this volume. A request from the editors initiated its conversion into a separate discussion dealing more directly with the relation between systems theory and economics. I cannot, under the constraint of time and space, take a thorough, critical position to Langlois's point of view. But since his paper does not deal with the special area of information economics and its extensions, one may with justification regard my contribution as complementary to his. However, one point of criticism of Langlois's view ought to be expressed at this stage.

METHODOLOGICAL SYSTEMISM VERSUS
METHODOLOGICAL INDIVIDUALISM

I agree with Langlois when he asserts that "systems theory is not at all methodological holism in any strong sense." Indeed, in a recent comparison between Bunge's important work [Bunge, 1979a] and my own systems methodology, I expressed this view:

> Bunge is anxious of not appearing to be a holist. This is understandable in the face of the absurdity of an absolute or extreme holistic Weltanschauung à la Hegel. But how can one defend the systems approach (where the interrelations between system and environment are so prominently emphasized) without being a relative or moderate neo-holist? To escape this dilemma, Bunge distinguishes *three* philosophic attitudes: On one extreme he sees *atomism* together with *ontological reductionism*, which both of us, Bunge as well as myself, reject. The middle ground is occupied by what Bunge calls *systemics* or *systemism*, which I addressed (mainly for esthetic reasons) as *relative holism* or

Additional support from the Social Sciences and Humanities Research Council of Canada is gratefully acknowledged.

neo-holism. The other extreme is addressed by Bunge shortly as holism, which I prefer to call absolute or extreme holism, the basic idea of which is again rejected by both of us. But what is the essence behind systemism or relative holism? I fully agree with Bunge (1979, pp. 1–3, 39–43) when he says that it has both, a *cognitive* motive to discover similarities between systems, as well as a *practical* motive to cope with the complexities of modern industrial societies. Its philosophic justification is to be found in the fact that "both systemics experts and ontologists are interested in the properties common to all systems irrespective of their particular constitution, and both are intrigued by the peculiarities of extremely general theories, which are methodologically quite different from specific theories (p. 3). (Mattessich, 1982, pp. 53–54.)

But whether this is identical to saying, as Langlois does, that "systems theory is in fact a form of intelligent methodological individualism" depends very much on what one means by this expression. As pointed out by Lukes, "methodological individualism acquires a range of different meanings in accordance with how much of 'society' is built into the explanatory 'individual'." (Lukes, 1973, p. 601.) Most interpretations of methodological individualism attribute to it the view that emergent properties of social institutions are explainable solely in terms of the behavior of individuals making up those institutions.[1] A systems theorist might object to this view by pointing out that just as the properties of water cannot be *explained* by the individual properties of hydrogen and oxygen, so the behavioral properties of many social institutions must be taken as *basic* and cannot be derived entirely from the behavior of their individual constituents. For example, methodological individualism, which dominated neoclassical economics for over a century, was hardly in a position to anticipate the social costs and dreadful ecological consequences of modern superindustrialism, precisely because some of these costs and other consequences are *emergent* properties of this particular, novel kind of system. In these environmental abuses lie the reason why more holistic trends emerged and why the study of ecology and the entire ecological movement became so prominent. The abuses also explain why systems thinking, slumbering for over four decades—from its inception by Aleksandr Bogdanov [1913 and 1922] to the 1950s or 1960s—became the rage in many quarters and why neopositivism, not to be identified with methodological individualism, has experienced such a decline. If, in the past three decades, the maxims of systemism had been heeded as much as those of methodological individualism, mankind might have been spared the disastrous ecological dilemma it is presently confronted with. In summary, to identify the systems approach with methodological individualism, as commonly understood, means misunderstanding an important aspect of the systems approach: namely, the acceptance of emergent properties as basic and irreducible.

---

[1] The definitions of methodological individualism offered in the two most important standard works [Dray, 1967, pp. 53–58; Lukes, 1973, pp. 600–601] seem to corroborate this interpretation.

As I pointed out elsewhere [Mattessich 1978, pp. 53–103, 247–248], traditional science offers plenty of evidence of individual aspects of system thought; in economics, Walras's general-equilibrium analysis is an example par excellence. In general, however, traditional economics *disregarded* such important system-methodological insights as, for example, the distinction between *renewable* and *nonrenewable* resources—a distinction crucial for a more holistic theory of income as well as price and capital formation. It is the merit of the systems approach to have awakened many areas and disciplines to the need for a better understanding of emergent properties and, hence, a fuller or more systematic treatment of the relation between system and environment. And in this, methodological individualism seems to have failed.

THE ADVENT OF INFORMATION ECONOMICS

According to Lamberton, "the economics of information and knowledge . . . analyzes the processes by which information is produced, diffused, stored, and used." (Lamberton, 1971, p. 7.) The pioneers of this broadly conceived economics of information *and knowledge* are Kenneth Boulding [1956a; 1966], Fritz Machlup [1962], Jacob Marschak [1954; 1964; 1974, vol. 2], George Stigler [1961], and others. But information economics (IE) in the more narrow sense[2]—particularly relevant to a rigorous systems approach—originated with Marschak and was further developed by other authors, for example, Marschak and Roy Radner [1972], Gerald Feltham [1972], Joel Demski [1972 and 1980], and Demski and Feltham [1972; 1976; 1983]. In this narrow sense, IE pivots on the evaluation of information systems (and thus, by necessity, on the evaluation of particular information signals). In other words, the following question becomes crucial: "Which information system among alternatives ought to be chosen for a particular information purpose or situation?" Although IE is far from being capable of answering these questions in the complex environment of actual practice, important theoretical insights have been gained for simplified situations. The principal idea on which IE rests is relatively simple; it emerges from statistical decision theory as naturally as does a butterfly from the pupa's cocoon. To reveal this, a minor modification of the traditional decision model suffices. The latter[3] expresses the expected utility value $E(a_i)$ of action $a_i (i = 1, \ldots, n)$ as the sum total of all utility values $u(a_i, s_j)$ attributed to each action a_i at state $s_j (j = 1, \ldots, m)$ multiplied by the probability $p(s_j)$ with which each state s_j is expected to occur. And the optimal action a_0 to be chosen among the n

---

[2] It seems to be advantageous to make a distinction between *information* (as evidence) and *knowledge* (as hypothesis) and, hence, between *information economics* and *knowledge economics*. [Mattessich, 1974a; 1978, pp. 226–233.]

[3] $E(a_i) = \displaystyle\sum_{j=1}^{m} u(a_i, s_j) \cdot p(s_j)$ and $E(a_0) = \max_i E(a_i)$.

alternatives results from selecting the highest among the n expected values $E(a_i)$, hence, from maximizing the latter over $i = 1, \ldots, n$. The modification or conversion of the decision model into an information-economic model now consists in making the previously hidden or implicit information signal y_k explicit by substituting the *conditional* probability $p(s_j|y_k)$—that is, probability of event s_j after receiving message y_k—for the previous probability value $p(s_j)$. Then the expectations of actions a_i (or a_{0k} in case of the optimal action, given signal y_k) must also be formulated in terms of signal y_k.[4]

Thus, the expected value of action a_i, given signal y_k, amounts to the sum total of the products of the utility $u(a_i,s_j)$ attributed to each action a_i at state $s_j(j = 1, \ldots, m)$ multiplied by the conditional probability $p(s_j|y_k)$ of state s_j occurring, *provided* signal $y_k(k = 1, \ldots, r)$ is received. The expected value $E(a_{0k},y_k)$ of the optimal action a_{0k}, given signal y_k, is formed by an analogous maximization choice. But note that first for each signal there may be a different optimal action (for this reason, the action must now also bear the subscript of the signal) and second, that a_{0k} need not be identical to a_0, otherwise a systematic information system would hardly be required.

But in IE the emphasis obviously cannot be on the optimal action of a specific *single* signal y_k but must be on an action optimal under all signal possibilities. Furthermore, one is interested only in the *excess* or differential utility that the information system yields over the expected value of the optimal action $E(a_0)$, that is, compared with a situation employing an ordinary *decision model*. Finally, it has to be taken into consideration that the use of the information system involves some costs C_I, either by operating it (say, in a market-research department) or by buying the information from outside the firm (say, subscribing to a forecast service). Hence, the expected net value E_I of the information system I can be formulated as the summation of each optimal expected action for each signal *minus* the expected value of the optimal action $E(a_0)$, that is, without the employment of any information system, *minus* the operating cost C_I of the information system.[5] But since there may be many alternative information systems $(I = 1, \ldots, N)$, the expected net value E_0 of the *optimal* information system must be expressed as maximum among each of the expected net values E_I, that is, for each of the N information systems feasible.[6] This requires that the calculation for E_I be made for each of the N information systems.[7]

---

[4] $E(a_i y_k) = \sum\limits_{j=1}^{m} u(a_i,s_j) \cdot p(s_j|y_k)$ and $E(a_{0k},y_k) = \max\limits_{i} E(a_i,y_k)$.

[5] $E_I = \sum\limits_{k=1}^{r} E(a_{0k},y_k) \cdot p(y_k) - E(a_0) - C_I$.

[6] $E_0 = \max\limits_{I} E_I$.

[7] I have elsewhere offered an illustration of such a calculation for an agricultural weather-forecasting system. [Mattessich, 1978, pp. 219–224.]

THE SIGNIFICANCE OF TEAM THEORY AND AGENCY THEORY

Of course, as valuable as the evaluation of information systems is for designers and users of such systems, it is merely one aspect of IE. The interconnection with system and organization theory (and thus with the supersystems served by information systems) manifests itself in many ways. Marschak and Radner's *team theory* is one such manifestation:

> The economic theory of teams attacks a middle ground. We study the case in which several persons perform various tasks including those of gathering and communicating information and of making decisions; but they have common, not divergent, interests and beliefs. Hence the optimality requirement is easily defined, just as in the case of a single person. But the single person's problem of optimizing his information instrument and its use is replaced by that of optimizing the allocation of tasks among the members of the team.
>
> We have equated *economical* and *efficient* to denote an arrangement that is most desirable (or, in the general case of organization, one that is viable), under given feasibility constraints. These constraints include the limitations of human capacities for communication and good decision-making (and analogous limitations of inanimate instruments). While our concern is a practical, purposive, prescriptive one, the general solutions we discuss would depend, when applied to any concrete case, on data supplied by workers in descriptive fields—the names of R. Cyert, J. March, and H. Simon come to mind![8]—psychological or sociological data along with those of natural technology. On the other hand, our results may prove of some value to descriptive theorists of human organization by pointing to those data, quantitative and otherwise, that would be of most importance if one wanted to increase the efficiency of a given organization. (Marschak and Radner, 1972, pp. 4–5.)

Another, more recent and perhaps more fashionable manifestation of the interface of information economics with organizational and even contractual aspects, is the broad area of *agency theory*. [Jensen and Meckling, 1976; Hirshleifer and Riley, 1979; Baiman, 1980–1984; Feltham, 1984.] Originally, this theory may have been regarded as merely one of the more recent attempts in the perennial search for a more realistic theory of the firm.[9] But the widespread response it is presently receiving in several quarters of applied science, such as accounting theory, finance, management science, and so forth, seems to secure it a special position. Agency theory is concerned with relations between control and information for the purpose of determining the most preferable feasible contract between a *principal* (who could be either the shareholders of a company or its single owner or a manager vis-à-vis his or her subordinates or even an insurance company) and his or her *agent* (management vis-à-vis the owners, a subordinate, or an insured) en-

---

[8]See, for example, Cyert and March [1963] and March and Simon [1958].
[9]For former attempts and the controversy surrounding them, see Machlup [1967; 1978, chap. 16, pp. 391–423.]

tering into a mutual agency contract that delegates to the agent the management of some kind of entity in compensation for which he or she receives a portion of the entity's profit. Depending on the contract, the portion may range from a fixed amount to a percentage of the profit, with possible penalties for imperfect fulfillment of the contract establishing some risk-sharing between principal and agent. Both of them are supposed to work toward a common goal, but since each of them is trying to maximize his or her own profit or utility (possibly at the cost of the other party), a conflict of interest is likely to emerge.

For this reason, an information system is required that informs principal and agent about the entity's total profit and supplies further information to facilitate the agent's managerial task and the principal's control of the agent. As long as the principal can observe the agent's activities, no *moral hazard* arises, and the optimal contract stipulates a fixed remuneration to the agent with penalties whenever he or she is found to be remiss in his or her duties. Often the principal's monitoring of the agent's activity is too expensive or cumbersome. In this case, the ultimate profit shares of principal and agent may not only depend on the total profit, but also on the particular differentiated information available to each of the two parties.

Applied to the situation of a newly formed company, this means that the cost of raising equity capital (and the expected return) may be considerably influenced by the kind of control-and-information system available to shareholders. Thus, it may be in the interest of promoters and managers to have either a voluntary or institutionally enforced system of accounting and auditing regulations imposed on them, because the lack of directly monitoring their activity otherwise results in higher shareholders' risk. Such regulations could lower the cost of raising capital and increase management's own portion of the profit. Hence, the combination of agency theory and information economics may well be relevant to such practical issues as the ongoing legislative or quasilegislative activity of the Financial Accounting Standards Board of the United States.

For these reasons, agency theory fits well into the general program of information economics, since the value of individual information as well as the entire information system plays a crucial role in this theory. The theory also constitutes an obvious link between the information system and the systemic or organizational structure of the entity involved. Here again, one encounters rigorous mathematical presentations in the service of an empirical discipline with the ultimate aim of creating testable or at least refutable hypotheses.[10]

---

[10]The pertinent literature is vast, and the bibliography arranged by Demski and Feltham [1981] comes close to a thousand articles and books. But to be more specific, I list the following relevant publications (beyond those previously indicated): Atkinson and Feltham [1980]; Arrow [1974]; Barnea, Haugen, and Senbet [1981]; Dickson, Senn, and Chervany [1977]; Fama [1980]; Hilton [1981]; Holstrom [1979]; Itami [1977]; Mattessich [1975; 1983 forthcoming]; Ng and Stoeckenius [1979], and Zmud [1979].

ON THE RECEPTION OF NOISE
A Rejoinder

Richard N. Langlois

It is in many ways comforting to an author when the response his work elicits is wildly divergent in perspective, focus, and tone. The comprehending responses weigh against the misunderstanding ones; the supportive balance the critical; the polite counteract the not-so-polite. And, at the very least, the diverse set of responses my paper has called forth suggests that the paper's deficiencies were not entirely systematic ones.

What this diversity of response also illustrates, I believe, is that there are indeed as many versions of systems theory as there are systems theorists. If C. West Churchman is right, systems theory includes everything this side of the *I Ching*.[1] Such diversity is really all I was trying to emphasize in my evidently provocative suggestion that systems theory had failed in its supposed quest to unify all of the social sciences.

There are, of course, a few common themes of criticism among my commentators, and I will turn to these shortly. Let me begin with the happier—but, as is usually the case, briefer—task of discussing those commentators who have largely agreed with me.

Foremost among these is Richard Day, whose analysis I can endorse almost without reservation. He explains very clearly a number of ideas I was struggling to express. Of particular importance is Day's treatment of the form of nonanalytic morphogenesis that arises from creative intelligence; this is a topic to which I will return before this rejoinder is over.

I also found much to agree with in Robert Beam's piece. Unlike Walter Buckley,[2] he does seem to understand what the example of the "cybernetic

---

[1] Although Churchman's piece is printed as a comment on Mortazavian, it also refers to my paper; so it does seem appropriate to include Churchman peripherally in this rejoinder.

[2] Since I do not deal with this aspect of Buckley's comment elsewhere, perhaps a few lines are in order here. I find little to disagree with in Buckley's paragraphs dealing with information and meaning—except his characterization of my own position. If one were to read Buckley and not my original paper he or she would think I am some sort of behaviorist with a mechanistic conception of meaning. In fact, my whole point in saying that meaning in very simple systems—whether one wishes to call them stimulus/response, cybernetic, or whatever—is reducible to

farmer" was all about, and his discussion is a successful if slightly jar-gonized expansion of what I was trying to say. Also, his treatment of the important and often-neglected distinction between formal and informal or-ganizations is excellent, even if, with Friedrich Hayek, I would prefer to avoid confusion and call the latter not an organization at all but an "order." [Hayek, 1973, pp. 36–40.]

Beam asks whether I would concur that models of social interaction should involve both "the science of communication and the science of trans-action." Absolutely. The economics of information, in particular, should be precisely a study of both communication and transaction. I am a little trou-bled, though, with the idea that the analysis of transactions should rest heavily on the concept of power. If anything, it seems to me, it should be the other way around: Power, insofar as it appears as a social phenomenon, is something that needs to be explained in terms of the structures of transac-tions involved. Economics has lately turned renewed attention to the idea of the transaction as a unit of analysis, a trend that has opened up some inter-esting new areas of inquiry. [O. E. Williamson, 1979; 1980.]

Now, let me turn to those who found more fault with my presentation.

Both Buckley and Richard Mattessich are still bothered by an issue I was trying to defuse: whether systems theory differs from methodological indi-vidualism in its desire to consider the whole greater than the sum of the parts. I probably should have realized that my negative answer would raise some hackles; there is much intellectual capital invested in the proposition that systems theory is less reductionistic than methodological individualism and more attentive to emergent phenomena. There may, in fact, be subtle distinctions to be worked out in principle, but the important issues will continue to lie elsewhere.

Systemism and methodological individualism are not (necessarily) identi-cal. (I had thought I was clear on this point.) But what distinguishes them is not a debate about whether properties of the whole can be deduced solely from properties of the parts; rather, it is a debate about *what shall be consid-ered the parts*. This way of putting things should raise even more hackles. For the methodological individualist's response—that in the social sciences the only acceptable parts are the knowledge, expectations, intentions, and actions of human beings—calls into serious question whole classes of fash-

---

action is to illustrate the extent to which it *cannot* be so reduced in more complicated systems. Some of the confusion may have arisen from my portrayal—for heuristic reasons—of the decision-making farmer as a real person. What I was actually trying to illustrate was the ideal type of an economic agent as portrayed in a mathematical maximization model. In such a model, meaning is indeed "the mapping between the learned properties of rain and the range of possible consequences of rain for the farmer's particular goals and interests at the moment"; but in the *model* farmer, this is exactly a mapping of acreage into expected profit, because the way in which I have constructed the model *rules out* any changes in internal states or values and goals. I heartily agree that this is too narrow a definition of meaning in economics: That is one of the central points of my paper.

ionable systems models in which physical quantities impinge directly on one another as if without the intervention of human minds.

One way to see the issue is to recognize, as Mattessich and Buckley apparently do not, that prediction and explanation are not identical, at least not in the social sciences. While it is certainly true that one cannot *predict* the behavior of water solely from the properties of hydrogen and oxygen considered separately, it is nonetheless true that, contra Mattessich,[3] one can—in fact must—*explain* water with reference to hydrogen and oxygen.[4] That is what chemists always do; there *is* no other way to explain water. Similarly, the social sciences are concerned almost exclusively with phenomena that are the unintended (emergent) byproducts of human intention. But those phenomena, once recognized, can and must be explained in terms of human intention even if their behavior could not have been predicted from considering the individual's intention alone.[5]

This has some fairly radical implications. Casting the problem in these terms makes it clear that far from being *less* reductionistic than methodological individualism, systems theory is often in danger of being far *more* reductionistic. Although the methodological individualist believes that social wholes must be explained (though not predicted) in terms of human actions, he or she does not believe that such wholes should be explained in terms of more basic or more material components such as energy, dollars, or even homogenized "labor value."

As a consequence, methodological individualism is skeptical of the many system models that take this materialistic and—yes—reductionistic approach. Good examples of such models are the various energy-analysis models that attempt to draw conclusions about the allocation of resources and the value of various commodities solely by considering something called "embodied energy content." (Costanza, 1980.)[6]

Mattessich suggests that methodological individualism somehow missed the "important system-methodological distinction" between renewable and nonrenewable resources. In the first place, system theory per se is a very general theory and has nothing whatever to say about whether in a particular application one should distinguish between the renewable and the non-

---

[3] Buckley also seems to confuse explanation and prediction in this way when he writes that "we cannot begin to explain or predict the properties or behaviors of complex dynamic wholes from a knowledge of the parts. . . ."

[4] For a good discussion of exactly this hydrogen and oxygen example, see Dennis C. Phillips [1976, pp. 14–15, 32–33].

[5] It is in this explanatory sense that the social sciences, as Buckley suggests, should be synthetic rather than analytic. But Anatol Rapoport was not the first to argue this position. In words first published in the 1940s, Hayek wrote that: "While the method of the natural sciences is . . . analytic, the method of the social sciences is better described as compositive or synthetic." (Hayek, 1941 and 1979, pp. 66–67.)

[6] I have referred to Robert Costanza's article as an example because it was certainly considered system-theoretic in some circles, as evidenced by the fact that it was reprinted in the *General Systems Yearbook* series.

renewable. In order to claim the necessity of this distinction, one would have to invoke some ancillary methodological doctrine. For example, methodological individualism added to systems theory might point to the importance of various distinctions about the knowledge possessed by social agents. By analogy, it is not systems theory by itself but something like methodological resourcism or methodological ecologism that Mattessich is implicitly invoking. And, again, this is not *more* holistic than individualism but *less*, since it calls for the reduction of social phenomena to natural resources, that is, for the explanation of social phenomena in terms of natural resources.

In the second place, methodological individualists are by no means unable to deal with emergent phenomena like "the social costs and dreadful ecological consequences of modern superindustrialism." Economics has a well-developed theory of external costs—in fact, I am aware of no other field that has a similar theory. [See, for example, Baumol and Oates, 1975.] Economics tackles these emergence problems head on—it simply comes up on occasion with answers different from those the methodological resourcist would like. Indeed, some economists might even go so far as to question what Mattessich seems to view as an established fact if not as a self-evident truth—the existence of a "disastrous ecological dilemma" facing mankind.

In a certain sense, I do agree that the methodological doctrine one adheres to colors the way one sees a problem or a phenomenon. As Buckley put it, what is meaningful to one person—say, Chinese—may be noise to another who has not studied Chinese. Similarly, someone who studies social phenomena with a particular set of parts in mind will very likely see the behavior of other parts as mere noise. The danger is least when the parts are human beings, since, if one builds the models right, whatever is important to human beings—be it resources, pollution, or whatever—should find its way into the models through them. But if the parts are something like resource flows, then there is serious danger of neglecting human elements altogether: For while humans may care about resources, resources care very little about humans.

And this is why economic and other individualistic models are frequently far less apocalyptic than their materialist counterparts: They take into account human ability to adapt and innovate, a capacity that Day described so well. Humanist models have a resource that resource-minded models invariably overlook.

> The impact of man in the evolutionary process arises because of the capacity of his images—that is, the knowledge present in his mind—to grow by a kind of internal breeder reaction: the imagination. It is this which has given the human nervous system such a fantastic social-evolutionary potential, a potential of which we have probably hardly used up one per cent in the brief history of the human race. (Boulding, 1964, p. 141.)

Which brings us to Adam Smith, another source of raised hackles among my commentators. The notion that Smith anticipated modern cybernetics is scarcely novel to me. The biologist Garrett Hardin—who made popular the idea of a "tragedy of the commons" [Hardin, 1968]—also suggested that

> long before Claude Bernard, Clerk Maxwell, Walter B. Cannon, or Norbert Wiener developed cybernetics, Adam Smith has just as clearly used the idea in *The Wealth of Nations*. The "invisible hand" that regulated prices to a nicety is clearly this idea. In a free market, says Smith in effect, prices are regulated by negative feedback. (Hardin, 1961, p. 54.)

In fact, what *I* was trying to say is something rather different. What Smith was getting at in his conception of an "invisible hand" is *not* the idea that given an appropriate set of legal institutions, the market will produce homeostasis governed by negative feedback. What Smith argued was that given an appropriate set of institutions, the free exchanges of individuals will lead to the production of wealth—to continual and cumulative change in organization and technology. [Böhm, 1982.] For Smith, the unintended consequences of individual action within what he called "the system of natural liberty" would be in the nature of evolutionary morphogenesis. [Adam Smith, 1776 and 1936, p. 651.]

As I tried to emphasize in my paper, it is important to get straight which kind of a system one thinks the economy is. If one does not conceive of it as an evolving order but as a cybernetic system in need of central direction, then one is likely to interpret change and innovation not as morphogenesis but as chaos and disorder.

But the choice of which lens one uses to view the economy (or society more generally) is not arbitrary. As a historical matter, Buckley is dead wrong when he says that Western economic systems have been generally feeble and unstable. It may or may not be true that the economicopolitical system is unstable. The free institutions on which the market economy is based are the exception not the rule in history. But when those institutions were more or less firmly in place—as in Western Europe and America during most of the last 200 years—the result, as even Marx recognized, was the greatest outpouring of human creative intelligence and energy in the history of mankind. There were certainly recessions and depressions (some of which were arguably caused or aggravated by attempts at central control), but it is a perversity of perspective to call the system feeble or unstable.[7]

---

[7]I was pleased in this context to see Churchman point out the fallacy of seeing world poverty and starvation as basically a food problem. The problem is an institutional one—a problem of setting up in Third World countries the kinds of social and economic institutions conducive to the production of wealth. But I was distressed at his explanation in terms of superpower politics, although the difficulty may have arisen from the brevity with which he expressed himself. As stated, his explanation is an instance of what Karl Popper called "the conspiracy

The tragedy of the commons can indeed be a significant phenomenon in free economic systems. But far from being endemic in the institutions Smith advocated, the tragedy of the commons results precisely when those institutions are *absent*.[8] Economists have recognized clearly for at least 20 years that tragedy-of-the-commons problems and so-called externality problems more generally can always be traced to problems in the existence and definition of property rights. [Coase, 1960.] The implication is that such externalities by no means imply the necessity of central direction or control; they may in most cases simply call for the creation, clarification, or redefinition of property rights.

But Buckley's point is not merely that a more-or-less free economy—with or without adequately defined systems of property rights—will produce bad outcomes (like too much pollution or too much grazing of rangeland). Buckley's claim is that such an economy is unstable. It is in putting the matter this way that Buckley betrays the attitude I called thermodynamic Manichaeism. He likens the economy to a predator/prey system, which he describes as uncontrolled. This, he says, explains the increasing attempts at central economic and social control, which, however, have been largely frustrated by the noise of the independent goal-actions of individuals. I am afraid I find this explanation of economic reality nothing short of chilling.

---

theory of society," a mode of social explanation more primitive than most forms of theism. [Popper, 1966, pp. 94–95.] The reason this mode of explanation fails, as Popper notes, is that we live in a complex world in which the prevalence of unintended consequences makes power a complicated affair and a generally implausible explanation. It is not clear that countries would all know what to do—or could do it if they knew—in the absence of superpowers. Neither is it clear that superpowers can prevent nations so determined from setting up wealth-producing (or at least starvation-preventing) systems. There are a number of countries (Taiwan and South Korea) that are certainly the focus of superpower attention but have nonetheless been able to set up fairly successful wealth-producing institutions. And there are dozens of forgotten countries entirely unable to change their behavior patterns in the face of starvation.

[8]The political order Smith advocated was never literally laissez faire; it was, in fact, based on a common-law framework involving property rights and a strong conception of justice. His claim was that when these institutions are in place, people left to themselves will produce good social outcomes. In more system-theoretic terms, Smith was arguing that good social outcomes would be the emergent result of individual action within the constraints of certain boundary conditions. If the catch-phrase laissez faire meant anything, it meant that the economic system should not be viewed as requiring external central control in the manner of an aircraft or spaceship. This is the control-theoretic content of the old slogan "a government of laws and not of men." Moreover, Smith's advocacy of the "system of natural liberty" was based on its justice properties; that it led to good economic outcomes was for Smith simply a happy coincidence. [Buchanan, 1979.] The justice properties of Smith's system, incidentally, are closely related to those implied in the Kantian imperative cited by Churchman. I was very pleased to see this reference to Kant, but I was also a little surprised to see this imperative discussed favorably in an article extolling rationalist planning—since, to most philosophers, the Kantian imperative is taken as implying individual rights that, if not exactly inconsistent with rationalist planning, are nonetheless conceived of precisely as strong constraints to, or protections against, the centralized implementation of rationalist plans. [Nozick, 1974; Fried, 1978; Dworkin, 1978.]

The predator-prey uncontrolled system is simply the wrong lens through which to view a more-or-less free economic society. Aspects of the system may behave in the predator/prey fashion; in particular, competition among business firms (or, more generally, among ideas or patterns of economic behavior) may usefully be cast in terms of ecological niches. But while any particular firm (or idea or pattern of behavior) may fail to adapt to change, the economic system as a whole is not therefore any more unstable or nonadaptive than is the whole process of biological evolution when a particular species fails to survive a change. Systems-dynamic models of the predator/prey sort are often useful, but they do not accurately capture the full logic of an evolutionary system. [Boulding, 1978.]

That someone should see the economy or society as an unstable or uncontrolled system is so frightening precisely because—as Buckley unabashedly puts it—the free choices of individuals do not appear to him as consistent with order; they are mere noise. I doubt that I need elaborate on the political implications of such a perception.

All of this illustrates, once again, the extent to which one's methodological starting-point influences the results of the final analysis. If one reacts to the words and phrases of spoken Chinese as if they were mere noise, it is quite probably because one has not studied Chinese. And if one sees the independent goal-actions of men as mere noise, it may well be for the analogous reason.

EPILOGUE

SEMANTIC QUIRKS IN
STUDIES OF INFORMATION

Fritz Machlup

Semantic and methodological discussions are to the ears of some scientists what symphonic and chamber music is to the tone-deaf. They do not hear anything that makes sense or seems to matter. Composers have not attempted to dedicate tone poems to the tone-deaf; not-so-wise students of the philosophy of science have not given up their ambition to write for scientists who disdain what they regard as "splitting hairs." There are probably degrees of methodophobia; as an optimist, I continue to believe that a lively exposition can succeed in convincing some doubters that there may, after all, be something to these quibbles about quirks.

The quirks on which I intend to quibble in these pages are semantic but also methodological. A discussion, for example, of the meanings of "science" and "scientific" cannot help being a mélange of semantic decisions about methodological positions. In general, whereas purely historical semantics may do without methodology, analytical semantics of scientific terms will usually contain a large dose of methodology.

My remarks are organized under three main headings: What They Mean by Information; What They Mean by Science; and What They Mean by Computing.

WHAT THEY MEAN BY INFORMATION

The pronoun "They" in this heading does not refer just to the members of the diverse cultures interested in the study of information but it refers to all who use the word. If a scholar adopts a word from everyday life to denote

This manuscript was unfinished at the time of Fritz Machlup's death; it was prepared for publication by Una Mansfield, to whom he had handed over the completed parts. Missing subsections are indicated by an Editor's Note at the point where they would have appeared in the section "What They Mean By Science." Fortunately, the subjects missing from this text have been treated elsewhere by Machlup, and scholars interested in knowing more of his views should consult the volume *Knowledge and Knowledge Production*. [Machlup, 1980.]

some specific "designata" different from the common meanings, the latter are not thereby extinguished. They remain in the dictionary and we have no right to disregard them.

Dictionary Definitions

The original meaning of the word "information" in several modern languages comes from Latin, where *informare* means "to put into form"; thus, according to the *Oxford English Dictionary,* the verb "to inform" means "to form (the mind, character, etc.) esp. by imparting learning or instruction"; but more frequently, "to impart knowledge of some particular fact or occurrence to;[1] to tell (one) of something." The noun "information" has essentially two traditional meanings: (1) "the action of informing; the action of telling or [the] fact of being told of something," and (2) "That of which one is apprised or told; intelligence, news." Any meanings other than (1) the *telling of something* or (2) *that which is being told* are either analogies and metaphors or concoctions resulting from the condoned appropriation of a word for something that had not been meant by earlier users.

Many definitions of information are the result of limiting the something that is being told to something previously unknown to the person or persons getting informed or previously known with less confidence. Accordingly, information may become equivalent to news, directions, instructions, advice, confirmation, or reconfirmation. Such restrictions to novelty, surprise, or more assuredness, however, are quite arbitrary; this becomes clear as soon as one realizes that besides *new* information, there may be *old* information, *repeated* information, and *expected* information, and therefore no logical justification for excluding these by dictatorial or persuasive definitions.

Information and Knowledge

Teachers of information science and computer science have sometimes found it suitable to their purposes to instruct students to observe a hierarchy—in ascending order—within the triad: data, information, and knowledge. Historical semantics gives only qualified support to such proposals.

A close and firm link between information and knowledge has always existed, and most dictionaries define information as a certain kind of knowledge. Some have the word information denote "a transfer of knowledge" or "a form of knowledge" or "a piece of knowledge." Distinctions between information and knowledge have been proposed chiefly on three scores: (1) Information is piecemeal, fragmented, particular, whereas knowledge is

---

[1] Lest the slightly archaic word "to impart" is misunderstood, its definition is "to give a part or share of; to bestow, communicate as knowledge or information; to make known, tell, relate . . . ." Hence, it always refers to an activity, not just an opportunity of being observed. Learning about something by looking should not be confused with learning by being told.

structured, coherent, and often universal. (2) Information is timely, transitory, perhaps even ephemeral, whereas knowledge is of enduring significance. (3) Information is a flow of messages, whereas knowledge is a stock, largely resulting from the flow, in the sense that the "input" of information may affect the stock of knowledge by adding to it, restructuring it, or changing it in any way (though, conceivably, information may leave knowledge unchanged).[2] These distinctions are mutually compatible, though they often relate to different aspects of the cognitive processes or states involved.

None of the distinctions relates to practical usefulness; neither knowledge nor information needs to be useful or valuable to merit its designation. Indeed, the fact that people speak of "useless information" and "useless knowledge" indicates that usefulness is no definitional criterion. [Machlup, 1982, pp. 8–11.] Nor is it a requirement of normal language use that information be correct and knowledge be true. Indeed, we all have learned that information may be misleading or downright incorrect or false; and philosophers of science have taught us that we must never accept empirical knowledge as definitely true. For a few decades linguistic philosophers dominated the philosophy departments of some great universities and preached the "justified true belief" definition of knowledge. [Machlup, 1980, pp. 37–38, 43, 114–120.] This definitional requirement clashed with the more sensible verdict of other philosophers that "all human knowledge is uncertain, inexact, and partial." (Russell, 1948, p. 507.) To assume that scientific knowledge is always true is to violate a truly scientific attitude.

Another difference between information and knowledge may deserve em-

---

[2]This third distinction has been most interestingly elaborated by Boulding: ". . . we cannot regard knowledge as simply the accumulation of information in a stockpile, even though all messages that are received by the brain may leave some sort of deposit there. Knowledge must itself be regarded as a structure, a very complex and frequently quite loose pattern, . . . with its parts connected in various ways by ties of varying degrees of strength. Messages are continually shot into this structure; some of them pass right through its interstices (. . .) without effecting any perceptible change in it. Sometimes messages 'stick' to the structure and become part of it. . . . One of the most interesting questions in educational theory and practice is under what conditions does information 'stick' in this way, and under what conditions does it fail to 'take hold' of the structure of knowledge. . . . Occasionally, however, a message which is inconsistent with the basic pattern of the mental structure, but which is of such a nature that it cannot be disbelieved hits the structure, which is then forced to undergo a complete reorganization." (Boulding, 1955, pp. 103–104.)

Manfred Kochen made a statement about "[w]ays to integrate the growing body of information into a commonly shared fabric of knowledge." (Kochen, 1970, p. 44.) This may sound as if it were the same as Boulding's view but really is not. Kochen evidently thinks of a *social* "body [stock] of information" and a *social* "fabric of knowledge," as if the sum of individual minds could be hypostatized into an "aggregate mind" of the whole society, or perhaps an "electronic encyclopedia" that includes all fragmented and obsolete piecemeal messages that once conveyed timely information of transitory relevance. There is no growing *body* of information, for what is not integrated into knowledge is thrown out or forgotten. There is, of course, a growing *flow* of information and some of it is put into storage in computer systems. Whether the eventual output is information or knowledge depends on the individual users.

phasis: Information is acquired by being told, whereas knowledge can be acquired by thinking. In a way, this notion is implied in the third of the listed distinctions, with the restructuring of knowledge induced by new information. The point, however, is that the rethinking may be only unconsciously related to information previously received or it may be entirely unrelated to received information. Any kind of experience—accidental impressions, observations, and even "inner experience" not induced by stimuli received from the environment—may initiate cognitive processes leading to changes in a person's knowledge. Thus, *new knowledge can be acquired without new information being received*. (That this statement refers to subjective knowledge goes without saying; but there is no such thing as objective knowledge that was not previously somebody's subjective knowledge.)

Going back to the three earlier distinctions, one may ask whether the featured differences can be identified at the time information is received or only after some thinking about it. When school children are told that there will be no school tomorrow, this news item is immediately cast as information and will ordinarily not be characterized as new "knowledge," although, of course, the children "know" it. When they are told that $7 \times 8 = 56$, this will usually be characterized as an integral part of a coherent and enduring knowledge structure. But the borderline is sometimes blurred. When people are told about an epidemic disease, a new virus, and available vaccination, they receive both information and knowledge. When a new discovery or a new theory is announced in newspapers and news broadcasts, this will be information to most recipients but new knowledge to specialists in some fields of inquiry. Still another possibility is that what someone first regards as a fragmented piece of information of only transitory relevance will eventually, perhaps much later, turn out to have initiated a significant change in his or her knowledge structure.

To sum up, information in the sense of telling and being told is always different from knowledge in the sense of knowing: The former is a process, the latter a state.[3] Information in the sense of that which is being told *may* be the same as knowledge in the sense of that which is known, but *need not* be the same. That even in everyday parlance people sense a difference can be seen from the fact that in railroad stations, airports, department stores, and large public buildings we expect to find a booth or counter marked *Information* but never one marked *Knowledge*. Similarly, in our modern economy we find many firms selling information services, not knowledge

---

[3] In an earlier discussion of the "Uses, Value, and Benefits of Knowledge," I used the analogy of a transport and delivery service in relation to the object transported and delivered: "To use information—a process, mind you—is to listen, to look at, to read; in short, it is its reception and, if possible, the full or partial understanding by the recipient. The use of the knowledge conveyed is something else. The act of delivering is one thing, the object delivered is another . . . . Use of mode of transportation and use of the transported object are different things. Likewise, use of a mode of information should not be confused with the use of the message or knowledge conveyed." (Machlup, 1979*b*, pp. 63 and 65.)

services. On the other hand, we would frown on education programs that fill the student's head with loads of information: We want them to disseminate knowledge of enduring value and to develop a taste or thirst for more knowledge, not just information.[4]

Information and Observation

Many a scientist uses *observation* and *information* as equivalent terms. It is easy to understand that an observer may feel that his observation, or the object of his observation, "tells" him something; most of these objects, however, are dead, and neither able nor willing to tell anything to anybody. To speak of information in this case is just a metaphor. If the object of observation is a human artifact, genuine information may be involved if, for example, an old inscription invites deciphering. The inscription was evidently designed to inform; hence, an attempt to read and interpret it is part of a process of information. Information takes at least two persons: one who tells (by speaking, writing, imprinting, pointing, signaling) and one who listens, reads, watches.

The metaphoric use of "interrogation" and "information" for "experimentation" and "observation" has been frequently proposed. For example: "I see no reason why what is learned by direct observation of the physical environment should not be regarded as *information* just as that which is learned by observing the marks on a document . . . . The primary *source* of scientific information is nature itself." (Brookes, 1974, pp. 142–143. Emphasis in the original.) I, for one, see strong reasons for rejecting a confusion between "observing" and "reading" or "being told."

The reference to reading invites comment on another source of confusion: Readings from instruments in a scientist's laboratory, the reading of data from his records of observation, and the reading of a report he has prepared on his work, findings, or conclusions, are three different things. Only the last of these three instances of reading constitutes information in the basic sense of telling about something. The first, the *instrument readings,* are only metaphoric information: They are part of the observation of pointers in apparatuses designed on the basis of preconceived theories; neither the instruments nor the pointers are "telling" anything, though their reading may furnish valuable clues to the observer and analyst. The second instance, the *reading of the data,* may be part of a process of information, namely, if the data were developed by others, as, for example, when technicians tell the investigator what they have observed. If, however, the scientist reads his own data, his own notes, this reading is part of his work as observer and interpreter. It would be misleading to say that he tells something to himself, or that the data tell him anything: In actual fact, he merely looks, thinks,

[4]The last paragraph reproduces what I wrote in chapter 1 of volume 3 of my projected ten-volume series. [Machlup, 1984.]

rethinks, interprets, infers. Only when he tells his fellow scientists about his work—by word of mouth, by a written report, or by a published paper—is genuine information (in the original sense of the word) being conveyed.

To use the words information and observation as synonyms is bad linguistic practice; it leads to confusion between different sources of knowledge and is therefore epistemologically and methodologically unsound. The fact that eminent scientists have sometimes been semantically imperceptive and have metaphorically used the term information in lieu of observation is no good reason for emulating them.[5]

Information and Data

The use and misuse of the term *data* is due, in part, to linguistic ignorance. Many users do not know that this is a Latin word: *dare* means "to give"; *datum,* "the given" (singular); and *data,* "the givens" (plural). Data are the things given to the analyst, investigator, or problem-solver; they may be numbers, words, sentences, records, assumptions—just anything given, no matter in what form and of what origin. This used to be well known to scholars in most fields: Some wanted the word data to refer to facts, especially to instrument-readings; others to assumptions. Scholars with a hypothetico-deductive bent wanted data to mean the given set of assumptions; those with an empirical bent wanted data to mean the records, or protocol statements, representing the findings of observation, qualitative or quantitative. With this background of historical semantics, a reader of recent definitions of, or statements about, data cannot help being appalled.

There are writers who insist that data consist entirely of numbers.[6] That this restrictiveness is (fortunately) exceptional can be inferred from the fact that the majority qualifies the noun and speaks of numerical data and statistical data where the givens are sets of numbers. Such numbers are rarely *given* in nature, but instead have to be produced by employing sophisticated techniques using instruments that sometimes are built on the basis of rather complex theories. A good deal of prior knowledge has gone into the construction of measuring devices that are to furnish the numerical data wanted. Yet, we often read of "raw data" being used to produce information and

---

[5] Among the metaphoric users is Claude Bernard: "We must observe without any preconceived idea; the observer's mind must be passive, must hold its peace; *it listens to nature and writes at its dictation.*" (Bernard, 1865 and 1927, p. 22. Emphasis added.) The statement is wrong in more than one respect, but especially in the phrase I emphasized.

As a curiosum I may cite a phrase that compounds the confusion by speaking of "macroscopically observable information," where "information" evidently stands for "phenomena." The same writer "informs" us wrongly that "entropy is related to 'missing information' "; what is missing is the possibility of observation. [Shannon and Weaver, 1949.]

[6] "The corpus of information . . . consists of two types of information—non-data and data. Non-data is non-numeric . . . . Data, on the other hand, is numeric, highly formatted and results from analysis." (Dolan, 1969, p. 41.)

eventually knowledge.[7] Perhaps raw data are only relatively raw, in that they are inputs for the production of more highly fabricated kinds of information.[8] Many writers prefer to see data themselves as a type of information, while others want information to be a type of data.[9]

One can probably find quotations supporting all possible combinations of the three terms or of the concepts they are supposed to denote.[10] Each is said to be a specific *type* of each of the others, or an *input* for producing each of the others, or an *output* of processing each of the others. This semantic muddle, however, need not cause any serious trouble, because the arguments in which data, whatever they are, play a central role are relatively simple: Data entry, data storage, data retrieval, data processing, data services, and all the rest, refer simply to things fed into a computer. These things, now data from the point of view of the programmers, operators, and users of the computer, *need not be data in any other sense*. Drafts of a manuscript for a learned monograph (or of a mystery story, for that matter) may have been typed into the computer; or the subject index for a textbook; a bibliography of writings on the history of French painting; detailed statistics of the gross national income of the United States from 1940 to 1980; expert knowledge for the diagnosis of diseases of various kinds; graphs and images of all sorts; or what not. Most of these inputs, now in the memory of the computer system, are very far from being raw data in the sense of empirical scientific analysis. Whether they are pieces of fragmented information—say, the football scores of American college teams for Saturday, November 13—or whether they are elaborate compendia of systematic knowledge in some discipline, for the users of these materials accessible in the computer memory they are data stored and data retrieved.

Of course, these materials are not stored in the form in which they were typed, with words and numbers; instead, they are encoded by means of digital data representation. Data transmitted from a computer are "represented by the presence or absence of an electrical impulse (representing a bit 'on' or a bit 'off')." (Shelly and Cashman, 1980, p. 86.) Thus, there may be a slight source of semantic confusion between data and data representation,

---

[7] Thus we read about "transformations that result in data becoming information and knowledge." (Kent, 1982, p. 315.)

[8] For example, information is defined as "the result of processing of data, usually formalized processing." (Hayes, 1969, p. 218.)

[9] Manfred Kochen cites approvingly a statement he attributes to West Churchman: "Information . . . is essentially raw data. Knowledge is interpreted data." (Kochen, 1970, p. 48.) Thus both information and knowledge are said to be data; and information is said to be raw, though in fact it may be thoroughly processed and well-done.

[10] "In more elaborate versions of the . . . model the analyst can request the synthesist to synthesize a new CKS [contingent knowledge structure] . . . that may change the effective information that the analyst obtains from the raw input data. . . . The contingent knowledge structure (CKS) is a data structure which represents the understander's knowledge of the state of the world." (R. J. Bobrow and Brown, 1975, pp. 115–117.)

but this can easily be avoided by using terms such as *impulse* or *signal,* or even *symbols.*[11]

Why all this has caused so many writers in information science to stumble over their attempts to define data and information in terms of one another is probably explained by their ambition to sound more sophisticated than the problems warrant. There is no need to establish either a hierarchy or a temporal sequence in discussing data and information. Apart from computer systems, the two words may be equivalents—say, "we have the information" or "we have the data needed for a particular inquiry"—or they may be otherwise related—say, "our data do not furnish the information wanted in this case." On the other hand, in a computer system, data are what has been fed into the memory of the system and is now available for processing.

This oversimplified presentation on "what they mean by data" has disregarded some differences of possible importance. Take, for example, three possible outputs: (1) a printout that gives us exactly what has been fed into the memory of the computer, the same words and numbers in just the order in which they have been stored; (2) a new arrangement of the data, after a programmed process of sorting and re-ordering of the stored materials (chronological or alphabetical ordering, or selecting on the basis of detailed instructions); and (3) an output different from the stored data as a result of an analysis made by the computer in accordance with involved instructions specified, step by step, in a highly sophisticated program.[12]

Since the writers on computer and information sciences are arguing about the question whether the results of such high-degree processing should still be called data or should be referred to as information, I submit that—in this case—the name does not make a bit of difference for any reasonable purpose. From the point of view of the computer operator, one may still say the data are in the memory and the output is something else. From the point of view of the user of the output, data and information are equivalent terms. The people selling management information systems (MIS) feel better if they call the output of their system *information,* that is, something of a higher order. Some people in management-decision theory prefer to say that the MIS output is not yet all that is needed for a decision, that more analysis

---

[11] "Sometimes a distinction is made between the mechanistic representation of the symbols, which is called 'data,' and the meaning attributed to the symbols, which is called 'information'." (Teichroew, 1978, p. 658.)

[12] Examples of the two higher degrees of data-processing may be helpful: (1) Input: reservations by passengers of an airline made on particular dates for particular flights on particular days; Output: an alphabetized list of all passengers who have reserved space on a particular flight, or a list of the reservations a particular passenger has made for consecutive flights. (2) Input: numerical series of business information considered relevant for analyses leading to reports helpful to management decisions about the operations of the business firm; (MIS Information) Output: sales report showing fluctuations in the demand for product model X over a period of Y years.

and, especially, more judgment is needed, and hence that the output supplied to the decisionmakers is still in the "lower" category of *data*. I repeat that this quibbling is of no consequence.

As a relief from the dreariness of this discussion, I want to end it with a quotation from the paper by Jesse Shera in this volume. He exclaimed: "Data, data everywhere and not a thought to think."

Decisions, Actions, Uncertainty

With this business of the semantic or operational links between data and information out of the way, we may return to our survey of meanings of the word information. We shall find that numerous proposals for restrictive definitions have been made and, for better or worse (more often, for worse), widely adopted.

There are those who link, by definition, information to decision-making and action.[13] This is one of the many instances in which a word that has a wide meaning is appropriated for use with a very narrow meaning. For these definers, information, to be information, has to have value, has to be *used for decision-making,* and has to be designed to *lead to action.* I submit that more than 90 per cent of all information received during a day (week, month, year) by people in all walks of life is not related to any decisions or impending actions. Just think of the sports sections of newspapers and broadcasts, or of the general news reports day after day! Most recipients of such information do not entertain any thought that it may help them in making decisions for practical actions. Even on the highest level of thinking, information need not be in the service of pragmatics.

Another restriction built into proposed definitions of information is that it must *reduce uncertainty* on the part of those getting informed. This issue is complicated by the fact that uncertainty means different things in the discussion of physical phenomena, processes, and measurements on the one hand, and in the discussion of human behavior and cognitive processes, on the other. Since I am still talking about information in the sense of telling something to somebody, I may at this point confine myself to uncertainty as it bears on persons receiving information and to the definitional contention that information is not information unless it reduces uncertainty. This restriction by definition has been imposed by eminent representatives of the behavioral and social sciences, especially psychologists and economists. [Garner, 1962; Arrow, 1979.] For the moment I need not say more than that this definition is at variance with the common usage of the word. Countless

---

[13] "Information is data of value in decision-making." (Yovits and Abilock, 1974, p. 163.) The perpetrators of this definition proceed to the statement that: "The information contained in a decision state is related to the mean square variance of the expected values of the courses of action." (Ibid., p. 166.)

numbers of messages that convey information in the ordinary sense are received by people without any effect on their uncertainty; and some news items may even raise uncertainty in several respects.

Linguistics and Language Philosophy

Students of linguistics use the term information not always for what one person tells another by some form of explicit message but rather for explaining the relations among words in a sentence. In this formulation, information, in a very special sense, is something implicit in verbal expression; it is not an action, process, or piece of knowledge, but it is what identifies the meaning of words. This usage has the interesting result that meaning is defined as information whereas, ordinarily, information is viewed as conveying meaning and as having a "meaning-content." This apparently contradictory interrelation is duplicated in another instance: A message is often said to contain information, and information is said to consist of messages. One way to overcome such inconsistencies may be to distinguish information from representations of information and from transmission of information.

In order to avoid confusion between the transmission of physical signals and the meaning-content of messages or statements, Bar-Hillel and Carnap adopted the term *semantic information.* As if there could be such a thing as nonsemantic information! Yet, it was probably necessary to use that glaring pleonasm in conferences with representatives of the statistical theory of signal communication who had appropriated the word information to denote "signal apart from meaning." Bar-Hillel and Carnap, emulating the communication theorists' efforts at measurement, proceeded to search for a *unit* of semantic information; after analyzing the notion of an *atomic statement* they proposed a unit of measurement, called semantic *content-element.* [Bar-Hillel and Carnap, 1953b, pp. 148–149.] In any case, for these philosophers of language and inductive (probabilistic) inference, information is defined in terms of semantic content-elements of verbal statements.[14]

For many logicians and philosophers, information consists of statements, and the amount of information contained in a statement is determined by the relative number of excluded alternatives. If a statement predicates one thing and thereby denies or excludes many alternatives, it is said to constitute *more* information than a statement that excludes only a few other possible states of the world. These considerations may make good sense in scientific testing, where alternative outcomes are not too numerous; but in primitive pieces of news the number of alternatives excluded by the statement may be indefinite. It would depend on the expectations the recipient of the informa-

---

[14] Inductive inference is used by Carnap in contradistinction to deductive inference; and inductive probability is distinguished from statistical probability.

tion entertained before he or she received it; the number of alternative possibilities may well be unlimited.

The notions of uncertainty and of probability are, of course, related, and both play important roles in various definitions or characterizations of information. "Two alternative notions of semantic information are *reduction in uncertainty* and *change in belief*. . . . Information is defined in terms of probabilities . . . ." (Jamison, 1970, pp. 28–29.) With two notions of semantic information and three views of probability—statistical, logical, and subjectivist—we are confronted with "six alternative theories of information." (Ibid., p. 29.) The quoted author, Dean Jamison, is inclined toward "a definition of information that is adequate from a subjective point of view." (Ibid., p. 53.)

Cognitive Information Summarized

All meanings and definitions just reviewed were of information in the general sense of something being told to somebody, where this somebody was supposed to grasp what was being told. In other words, it was meaningful (semantic, cognitive) information; either it was the act (or process) of telling or it was that which was being told. Some definitions, however, were restrictive, refusing the designation information to some types of (what others call) information. Thus, to list the restrictions most often proposed, information is *not* recognized as information according to (any particular) proposed definition unless (1) it is about something previously unknown to the recipient; or (2) it is about something previously less assuredly known to the recipient; or (3) it affects the stock or structure of the recipient's knowledge; or (4) it consists only of raw data, not yet interpreted; or (5) it is useful to the recipient in some way; or (6) it is used in decision-making by the recipient; or (7) it bears on actions contemplated, considered, or actually taken by the recipient; or (8) it reduces the recipient's uncertainty; or (9) it helps identify the contextual meanings of words in sentences; or (10) it excludes some alternatives to what is predicated in a statement; or (11) it changes some belief held by the recipient, particularly with respect to the distribution of probabilities in the recipient's view.

This is surely not an exhaustive list of alternative definitions of information directed to a human mind; but it suffices to show that many analysts prefer to make things true by definition and to save words to modify a more broadly defined term. For example, instead of saying *new* information or *unexpected* information, some choose to omit the adjective and decree that novelty or unexpectedness is a necessary characteristic of information.

We now turn to metaphoric uses of the word. We shall, in the next subsections, discuss uses of the term information in connection with descriptions or models of processes or phenomena pertinent to living humans or, more generally, "living systems."

Information Within Living Systems: The Nervous System

Not all writers on nervous systems deem it necessary to use the term information in describing what goes on when sensory impulses or signals are conveyed to the central nervous system or when motor controls are exercised by it over muscles or other organs. In scanning some of the texts and handbooks of neurophysiology I have found that some writers can do quite well without the term information; perhaps they have decided that it is better to avoid the (often misleading) metaphor.[15] Other writers, however, seem to have concluded that the nervous system can be more easily explained if communication systems such as telegraph and telephone are taken as analogies.[16] From analogy to metaphor is only a short step and users of a metaphor may become so used to it that they adopt the term as the genuine designation of the phenomena or processes they wish to describe or explain. It is not always clear whether the writers on sensory physiology, psychophysics, and cognate subjects want the word information to refer to its content or only to the process of transmission. When neurophysiologists describe nerve-communication in terms of firings from one neuron to the next, they can easily avoid references to "information being passed on." However, they have a much harder time when they want to describe tactile sensations from mechanical stimulation being picked up by receptors in the skin and sent on to reach a central neuron. Is the pin-prick or the tickle a stimulus, an impulse, or perhaps a piece of information encoded by cutaneous receptors and decoded by central neurons? To judge from the literature, it seems to be difficult to dispense with the use of the term information.[17]

---

[15] "Neurophysiology deals with functional aspects of the nervous system, with transmission of nerve impulses, motor control, reflexes, and even perception, emotion, and mentation." (Ochs, 1965, p. 9.) "[T]he means of propagation of the nerve signal itself is electrical in nature." (Ibid., p. 11.)

[16] "The nerve fibre can be compared, from the point of view of its function, with a cable carrying information." (Zimmermann, 1978, p. 68.) This writer proceeds to discuss information transmission in the nervous system and to employ the term information not only for the transmission process but also for measuring the amount of information in the sense used in the mathematical theory of communication.

[17] Analysts of the sensibility of the skin distinguish among several types of "receptors of cutaneous sensations" and report on mechano-reception (the skin's sensibility to touch and pressure), thermo-reception (the skin's sensibility to heat and cold), and nociception (the skin's sensibility to pain). [R. F. Schmidt, 1978, p. 81.] The process of transmission from the receptor to the receiving end of the neural string—yes, the receptors in these instances are the senders—is similar for different sensations. The question of just what is being transmitted is difficult to answer; one can understand the analysts' terminological promiscuity in the exposition of various sensibilities, when they rather indiscriminately dally with impulses, stimuli, sensations, inputs, signals, and information. In his discussion of vibration receptors in the skin, Robert Schmidt states that "[t]his receptor can transmit no *information* about the depth of skin indentation." (Schmidt, 1978, p. 91. Emphasis added.) But "mechano-receptors . . . can *signal* the position of a joint . . . ." (Ibid., p. 96. Emphasis added.) However, "signals" deriving "from the central motor systems . . . appear to send a *'memo'* (efference *copy* . . .) of their *signals* to the

Perhaps we should not worry so much about proper word use, and accept the fact that *information* has become an all-purpose weasel-word. Even a writer as careful and lucid as Michael Arbib, in a passage in this volume, manages to use the word information in three senses: as a process, as a current (specific) content, and as the accumulated content of several previous messages.[18] Lest the reader get the impression that the metaphoric use of the term information in neurophysiology began only with the emergence and dramatic growth of the theory of information, I should mention that many earlier instances can be found in the literature.[19]

Brain research is another subdiscipline in which some writers are fond of using the term information while others seem to avoid it. We find this difference in linguistic preference in different reports on the split brain and the "interhemispheric communication" between the two halves of the brain. [Sperry, 1965, 1982; Gazzaniga, 1970, 1981.] Thus, we read that after severing the connections between the hemispheres "information learned by one half-brain did not transfer to the other." (Gazzaniga, 1981, p. 517.) The two halves were no longer on speaking terms, so to speak.

Before I proceed to the next group of habitual users of the term information in biology, the geneticists, I may point to an interesting difference in metaphoric use. Writers on neurophysiology are essentially concerned with what once was discussed in terms of stimulus and response and is now discussed in terms of signals and information; the analogy here refers to brief ad hoc messages, telling in a few spoken words, as it were. On the other hand, writers on genetics, with their models of a genetic code, refer to long sets of long-term instructions, specifications with a blueprint for future performance, hence, telling in a long written scroll. Thus the metaphor "information" alludes to "spoken messages" within the *nervous* system, but to

---

muscles, to interact centrally with the sensory *input* from proprioceptors. These efference *copies give advance information* about the intended muscle activity and the movements that will result." (Ibid., p. 99. Emphases added.) Even more metaphorically, "Pain . . . *informs* us of threats to our bodies, for it is activated by noxious (tissue-damaging) stimuli." (Ibid., p. 111. Emphasis added.)

[18] In his paper in Section 2 of this volume, Arbib has two sentences where all three senses are alluded to: "Information picked up modifies the perceiver's anticipations of certain kinds of information that, thus modified, direct further exploration and prepare the perceiver for more information." Arbib admits, however, that we do not know yet "how the organism can be committed to an overall action by a population of neurons, none of which has global information about which action is appropriate." Global information, we assume, refers to accumulated experiences (perhaps knowledge).

[19] "We know that when the eye sees, all the consequent information is transmitted to the brain by means of electrical vibrations in the channel of the optic nerve . . . . The impulses which flow in the arm nerves of a typist convey to her fingers the translated information which reaches her eye or ear, in order that the fingers may be caused to strike the proper key." (Bush, 1945, p. 58.) I understand that more recent descriptions would not be in terms of electrical vibrations, but the point in offering the quotations was to show the early use of the word information for neurophysiological signals.

"written directions" within the *genetic* system. (I probably merit a severe scolding for this "outrageous flirting with the potentially disastrous consequences of false analogies," against which George Miller warns in such delightful language in his paper on "Informavores" in this volume.) In any case, I have found little, if any, resistance to the metaphoric use of the word information in either neurophysiology or in molecular biology. And even information scientists condone the practice.[20]

Information Within Living Systems: The Genetic System

Responsibility for introducing into literature on genetics expressions like "information in writing" rests with the biologists. Biochemists discovered the genetic code, a kind of written language with equivalents for letters, words, and sentences (and even punctuation marks), formed by "nucleotide base symbols or characters." (Nirenberg, 1963, p. 80.)[21] According to George W. Beadle, there are five billion nucleotide bases (of four different types) in the nuclear chromatin of a human cell. The so-called codons (each consisting of three bases) "could convey more than 300,000,000 words of written prose." This corresponds to 600,000 pages of 500 words each, or to 1,000 volumes of books with 600 pages each. "That is a set of genetic specifications for making one of us out of an egg cell . . . ." (Beadle, 1963*a*, pp. 3–4.) In the formulation by James Watson, "the fertilized egg contains all the information necessary for the growth and development of an adult . . . animal." (Watson, 1965, pp. 10–11.)

[20] For example, after talking about the documentary sense of information, Bertram C. Brookes, a distinguished writer in information science, made this pronouncement: "Clearly, they [the geneticists] are not using 'information' in its documentary sense and it is a far cry from documentary 'marking' and 'parking' to the biochemical processes of a living cell. But while the information analogy is helpful to microbiologists I see no reason why it should not be used." (Brookes, 1974, p. 146.)

[21] The genetic code is made up by four nucleotide bases (symbols, characters, letters), conventionally denoted by the letters A, T, G, and C. Pairs (or doublets) of letters would allow coding of only 4^2, or 16, "words," which would be insufficient to specify 20 amino acids. Sequences of three letters (triplets) allow coding of 4^3, or 64 words, or codons, and thus permit a good deal of redundancy. The "sequence of nucleotides in DNA carries the genetic information that orders (codes) the sequence of amino acids in proteins." (Watson, 1965, p. 99.) "The molecule's message written in nucleic acid code" may represent *structural* genes, controlling *"how* molecules of specific amino acids are combined to form a particular protein, programming the pattern of spatial organization of that protein, ..." Other messages written in the same code represent *regulatory* genes, programming "the pattern of temporal organization, determining *when* syntheses of protein molecules shall occur by controlling rates of synthetic processes." (J. G. Miller, 1978, p. 221. Emphases in the original.)

The allusion, in the text above, to punctuation marks refers to termination or the end of a chain of triplets. "Termination is not a random process, but is highly controlled by special 'full-stop' or termination codons. Recent studies have shown that certain triplets or codons (called 'nonsense codons') in the mRNA [messenger RNA] chain automatically bring about termination of the peptide chain at that point. The nonsense codons are UAA, UAG, and UGA. When the ribosome reaches a nonsense codon, the bond between the final amino acid and the tRNA [transfer RNA] molecule to which it is attached is hydrolyzed." (Baker and Allen, 1982, p. 561.)

It may be worthwhile seeing how researchers in molecular biology, cytogenetics, and phylogenetics (evolutionary biology) have come to deal with different kinds and forms of information in several different contexts. Besides the information "stored" in the genes, or "imprinted" in the DNA by sequences of nucleotides, there is the "transcription," or "copying," of DNA information into an RNA "transcript," and then the "translation" of nucleic-acid information into protein information. There is also translation of the information encoded in the message in the cytoplasm, a "backward flow of genetic information" from RNA to DNA, resulting in "DNA copies of messenger RNAs, which have become inserted in the genome." [The quoted phrases are from "Research News" published in *Science,* vol. 212 (1981), p. 313, and vol. 216 (1982), p. 969.] I wonder whether, in these and similar formulations, information as a *content* of meaning in terms of action or effect is sufficiently distinguished from physical representations of information. In addition to the phenomena and processes involving the written genetic code, there are other kinds of information in the geneticists' scenario, for example, a hypothesis of a "cross-talk" between adjacent chromosomes, and hypotheses of "extrinsic generic instructions," or "information" from the environment, that may account for phylogenetic patterns in evolution. [*Science,* vol. 214 (1981), p. 1334, and vol. 217 (1982), p. 1239.]

Information Within Social Systems: Society, Polity, Economy

If we were to follow the sequential order prescribed by James G. Miller in his book on *Living Systems,* we would have to move up from the cell and the organism to the group and the organization before we came to society. [J. G. Miller, 1978.] For our purposes—reviewing what is meant by the term information—Miller's sequence would not be useful, because it plays down or conceals the one issue that matters most: The difference between information in a metaphoric sense where no minds and no cognitive processes are involved, and information in the original and traditional sense where meaningful perceptions and thoughts reach a mind that receives and interprets them. Not the organism but the individual plays this role in an appropriate model of received information, no matter whether the individual is regarded as standing alone or as thinking, acting, and reacting as a member of a group, an organization, or a society.[22] These points were made and elaborated by Talcott Parsons in a review article on Miller's book. [Parsons, 1979.] As a matter of fact, these issues have been clear to all social scientists who understood the principles of methodological individualism—and therefore

---

[22] For James Miller, "A society is a large, living, concrete system with organizations and lower levels of living systems as subsystems and components." Miller explicitly rejects Toynbee's view of looking at society as "a product of the relations between individuals," and likewise the definition by Parsons, Shils, and others, of a social system as "interactive relationships of a plurality of individual actors." (J. G. Miller, 1978, p. 747.) Here is one of Miller's explicit statements on information (or perhaps a proposed definition): "Information is the patterning of matter-energy in systems." (Ibid., p. 1030.)

did not confuse it with political individualism—and who rejected the myths of romantic holism—not to be confused with the holistic aspect of general system theory. Some of the papers in Sections 8 and 9 of this volume deal with the problems in question and generate heat and light in the process. (The reader may enjoy both these outputs.)

What the word information means to individual members of groups, organizations, and society, and also to analysts of these social systems, is not different from what the dictionary definitions say. On all these levels, information has or is a meaningful content. In the analysis of information flows, of the possible relations between information and decision, of possible effects of information upon mass action, and of several other problems, specialists in the study of organizations may emphasize other aspects than do the students of economic society or political society; some writers may find it expedient to make different specifications with regard to degrees of uncertainty or changes in beliefs, or with regard to revisions of expectations or even of goals; still, *the fundamental notion of information is the same in all social sciences.*

There have been writers who were fascinated by notions of *social* information and *social* knowledge, in the senses of new information acquired or total knowledge possessed by society—where society was supposed to be something quite different from the individuals that compose it.[23] The basic ideas of system-thinking seem to foster a belief in the reality of a *whole* apart from its components and their interactive relations. If information is something that reaches a mind, or several or many minds, it ought to be clear that *the whole does not have a mind of its own* and can neither receive nor process the information that has reached its members. To be sure, some special decisionmakers, say, members of legislatures, administrations, public agencies, and so forth, may have the right and the power to act upon received information (collectively) issuing laws, decrees, and regulatory orders controlling, constraining, inducing, or prohibiting certain kinds of ac-

---

[23] Norbert Wiener has in his *Cybernetics* a chapter on "Information, Language, and Society," in which he tries to differentiate the "intelligence of society" or "community" from the intelligence of its members. [Wiener, 1948 and 1961, p. 162.] He states that there is "no necessary relation in either direction between the amount of racial, or tribal, or community information and the information available to the individual." (Ibid., p. 158.) Not all references, however, to social and individual knowledge are naive or fallacious. On sensible distinctions between social and individual knowledge, proposed by Bertrand Russell, Alfred Schutz, Thomas Luckmann, and others, see my book on *Knowledge and Knowledge Production.* [Machlup, 1980, pp. 161–162, 167–173.] However, the contributions of system theorists to the flows of information into the system and among its components are, by and large, rather confusing. Thus, for example, James Miller speaks of a "special form [of information flow], the flow of money, which is one sort of information." (J. G. Miller, 1978, p. 1027.) Miller may possibly be thinking of prices emerging in commodity markets and interpreted as giving signals or information to producers and consumers. But this has nothing to do with the circulation of money; and it surely does not support the notion that flows of money are flows of information. It is not a useful analogy—just a fallacy.

tions. Still, both the controllers and the controlled are individuals, even if the controllers may claim to be acting on behalf of society. Moreover, mass actions by individuals not entitled or empowered to legislate or to govern may well exercise powerful influences on governors and controllers. The titles and constitutional functions assigned to particular components of a social system do not necessarily determine their effectiveness; the controlling forces may be widely diffused, independent of any official organization chart.

Information Within Man-Made Systems: Machines

Interactions among parts of man-made apparatuses are sometimes referred to as intercommunication or information flows. Let us recall that Norbert Wiener gave to his book *Cybernetics* the subtitle "Control and Communication in the Animal and the Machine." He proposed the term *feedback* for the "chain of the transmission and return of information" and showed that "there are . . . feedback chains in which no human element intervenes." His first examples for a "purely mechanical feedback system" were the thermostat and the steam engine. "The information fed back to the control center tends to oppose the departure of the controlled from the controlling quantity." (Wiener, 1948 and 1961, pp. 96–97.)

The similarity of the working of homeostatic feedbacks in physiological and in man-made systems makes the use of the term information in both living and nonliving systems acceptable *as long as one does not forget that the term is used as a metaphor*. Real information can come only from an informant. Information without an informant—without a person who tells something—is information in an only metaphoric sense.[24]

I wonder why so many scientists have found it permissible to overlook, disregard, or minimize the differences between information and those types of causation that have nothing to do with signs, meanings, and mental processes. Among possible reasons may be the use of algebraic expressions in lieu of literary statements. If $Y = f(X)$, writers and readers of such a function are led to shut out any questions of whether X is a mechanical, electrical, anorganic-chemical, organic-chemical effector or a sign conveying to some mind or minds a meaningful message that may influence the recipients in their considerations, decisions, and actions. Colin Cherry regarded the difference in the responses of man and of machine as essential: quasi-

---

[24] One of the few specialists who was sufficiently perceptive to see the difference was Colin Cherry: "All communication proceeds by means of *signs*, with which one organism affects the behavior [or *state*] of another. . . . In certain cases it is meaningful also to speak of communication between one machine and another as, for example, the control signals which pass between a guided missile and a ground radar." Cherry proceeds to consider the question how to "distinguish between communication proper, by the use of spoken language or similar empirical signs, and other forms of causation." (Cherry, 1957, p. 219.)

voluntary versus semiautomatic. "If I push a man into the lake, he inevitably goes in; if I tell him to jump in, he may do one of a thousand things."
(Cherry, 1957, p. 220.) To be sure, the question whether X was a push or a
sign may be of little interest to a scientist who wants to explain the state Y of
the man, dead or alive, but surely wet. However, to a scientist not satisfied
with algebra it will make a difference whether X was a physical force or
rather a sequence of signs in gestures or words. Indeed, some scientists may
wish to inquire what kind of meaningful information has induced our man to
jump in the lake: a command, an advice, a threat of worse consequences, a
bet, an offer of a bribe, a report of a sad event? If any of these messages and
any acts of physical force can be indiscriminately called *information,* this
term has lost much of its usefulness.

Despite this grave charge, I concede that, with the degree of discernment
that one should expect from any academically trained person, the probability of confusion caused by metaphoric uses of the term is not intolerably
great.

Information as an Alias for Signal Transmission

We now come to the last group of users of the term information; it is a rather
special case: They use *information* and *amount of information* in a sense that
has so little to do with any traditional or metaphoric meanings of the word
that one can only wonder why the scientific community has allowed it to
continue. In the Prologue to this volume, especially in the subsection on
"Information Theory," it was pointed out why the misnaming has been
infelicitous, misleading, and disserviceable, and also why frequent attempts
to correct this state of terminological affairs have been unsuccessful. At the
present juncture I merely wish to state just what the information theorists (or
rather the expositors of the mathematical theory of communication or signal
transmission) meant when they said information.[25]

Information in the sense used in (narrow) information theory refers
neither to the process of telling something to somebody nor to the something
that is being told; indeed, it has nothing to do with meaning, not even in a
metaphoric sense. Instead, it is the statistical probability of a sign or signal
being selected from a given set of signs or signals. This probability is of
significance for the design of communication systems, for determining the
optimal size of a communication channel, for measuring its capacity for
signal transmission, for appraising the efficiency of a system (existing or
proposed), and for other purposes. Expressions such as "information in the
technical sense," "statistical sense," "mathematical sense," or "engineering sense," have become customary in order to distinguish this concept from

---

[25] As Donald MacKay writes in his paper in Section 7 of this volume, "[Shannon's] theory did
not define the concept of information at all."

information in a meaningful or semantic sense. Kenneth Boulding speaks of "Bell Telephone or B.T. information" and, like hundreds before him, dismisses the notion as irrelevant for the social and behavioral sciences. (See his paper in this volume.)

It is difficult, perhaps impossible, to formulate a clear definition of so-called information in the statistical sense. It surely is not information nor is it signals transmitted. As a matter of fact, few writers have attempted a definition; what they set out to define was a "*measure* of information," or a "*rate* of information," or a "statistical *relation* between *signs*." (Cherry, 1957, p. 226.) In Cherry's words, "Shannon's measure of the selective information rate of signals in terms of their statistical rarity" is at best *one* of several things one may want to measure. (Ibid., p. 229.) The adjective *selective* modifying the noun *information* can remind us of the close relation to probability theory but it does not inform us of the meaning of the thus modified noun. Moreover the terms *measure, rate,* and *relation* must refer to some specified object or objects, and it is not clear just what the object, misnamed information, is meant to be. We still have to be told *what* is being measured.

One might, paraphrasing several information theorists, try to define information in the technical sense as "the coding and transmission of signals contained in a given repertoire [or set]." Although this would make sense, it is not what Shannon's formula expresses. The reference to probability theory, of which this kind of information theory is an application, is too indirect; the word "selection" does better in this respect. The old definition by Ralph Hartley, saying in effect that information is the successive selection of signs or words from a given list, is among the clearest; he rejected all meaning as a "mere subjective factor," and insisted that "it is the signs that we transmit, or physical signals; we do not transmit their meaning." (Hartley, 1928, quoted from Cherry, 1957, p. 43.) More descriptive expressions were suggested in the introductory essay of this volume: *activating impulses* are transmitted through the communication channel, designed to make the receiver pick out the intended signs from a given ensemble (repertoire, alphabet). *Activation rate* is measurable and easily correlated with the notion of channel capacity. *Activation* and *amount of activation* are meant when communication theorists speak of information and amount of information.

That we should stress the (measurable) physical signals rather than their meanings is reasonable for communication engineers designing telegraph, telephone, and other transmission channels. At the level of personal oral communication, we would, to be consistent with their terminology, have to define information as vibrations of the air, measurable by amplitudes and frequencies; and at the level of hand-written communication, we would have to define information in terms of ink-marks or pencil-strokes. This would be possible, of course, but it would be a wasteful use of the word information; it would not be what people meant by it.

Information as Negative Entropy

In discussing the unfortunate use of *information* as an alias for signal transmission or activation, I have not mentioned the term *entropy,* often employed to illuminate (or obscure) information theory. The relation between the terms merits separate discussion, but unfortunately space limitations preclude such discussion here.

To be sure, there are those who consider entropy and information as semantically related terms. Thus the physicist Gilbert N. Lewis stated that "gain in entropy always means loss of information, and nothing more." (Lewis, 1930, p. 573.) And Warren Weaver, in his interpretation of Shannon's theory, said first that "information is measured by entropy"—which would presume that they are different things—then went on to say that "entropy is related to 'missing information'," and finally that "entropy and information" were equivalent concepts. [Shannon and Weaver, 1949.] Still, although one can find instances in which information and entropy are made equivalent terms, the relationship is more interesting from the point of view of methodology.

A Compendium of Meanings

At the beginning of this discourse on "What They Mean by Information" we looked into dictionary definitions; they all referred to *telling* something or to the *something* that is being told. Information is addressed to human minds and is received by human minds, though the recipient need not always be chosen by the informant or transmitter. Pieces of information carry meanings and are interpreted by cognitive processes, but not necessarily by all intermediaries. A thoughtful analysis of this basic sense of information would probably make the informants' intention to inform a criterion of information.

Starting from this fundamental concept we have noted several restrictive definitions of information in the basic sense: Restrictions were imposed by users of the term for purposes of their theoretical tasks. The requirement of truth or correctness should exclude false or incorrect messages; the requirement of value or usefulness should exclude messages not helpful in decisions and actions; the requirement of novelty should exclude repeated or redundant messages; the requirement of surprise should exclude messages that the recipient expected; the requirement of uncertainty-reduction should exclude messages that leave the recipient's state of uncertainty unchanged or increased; and so forth. No exhaustive enumeration of persuasive or dictatorial restrictions is here intended. Specialists in several disciplines—psychology, economics, decision theory, linguistics, and others—have imposed restrictions when it suited their purposes and have thereby made it harder for nonspecialists to understand what was meant.

Information is used in some metaphoric senses if, though some characteristics of the basic concept are missing, other essentials are present and suggest *transmission* of meaningful messages from transmitters to recipients. The major metaphoric uses occur in the description of the operation of living systems. Writers on the nervous system, on brain research, and on the genetic system have been the chief employers of the metaphor. The characteristics of information in the basic sense that are missing from information in any of the metaphoric senses are, chiefly, the involvement of a mind and of cognitive processes. These characteristics can help the social scientist to distinguish between genuine and metaphoric information when he analyzes the operation of social systems. If his analysis includes individuals, transmitting and receiving signals and messages and making up their minds before they act or refrain from acting, he is concerned with information in the basic sense. However, if he resorts to systems of nondeliberating organisms or to a society as a whole, which cannot have a mind of its own, he is at best indulging in metaphoric uses of information, more likely with alleged forces that are not information in any sense. What makes the metaphoric uses of the word information acceptable is that, although the processes involved are physical (electrical, chemical) and biological (neurological, molecular) rather than cognitive, one can think of nerve cells "telling" something and of genes "telling" various other cells of the body what to do and when to do it.

This fiction can hardly be sustained in the case of man-made apparatuses and machines. To use the word information for actions and interactions, feedforwards and feedbacks, of the different parts of a nonliving (though still goal-directed) system, comes close to a caricature. Too many cyberneticists have accepted the antropomorphic expression that machine-part *A* "tells" something to machine-part *B*. The word "information" in this sense stands for "effectuation." No intention, no mind, no cognitive action is involved.

The use of the word information where only observation and analysis are involved, is just a confusion. Those who believe that observation of physical reality or "consultation" of data "tell" us anything have misunderstood the basic lessons of methodology.

Finally, to speak of information when information theorists explain their system is a sad misuse of language; they explicitly abstract from a meaning-content of the signals the transmission of which they describe. Their system does not care about telling anything, directing or advising anybody, arousing anybody's interest, or inducing any decisions or emotions. Appropriate words to use in the context would be signal transmission, actuation, or activating impulses. The use of the word information in this sense has led to unending confusion and should no longer be condoned.

WHAT THEY MEAN BY SCIENCE

This second piece about semantic quirks should not take nearly as much space as the previous one. Not that the word science has been used in fewer diverse meanings than the word information; but the differences in the meanings of science can be more easily explained.

Dictionary Definitions

The Latin noun *scientia,* derived from the verb *scio, scire* (to know), means knowledge (both knowing-what and knowing-how), awareness, cognition, insight, skill, and science in the widest sense. Some writers, Caesar among them, spoke of *scientia atque usus militum,* which alludes to a possible differentiation between theoretical knowledge and practical experience in military matters, but a broad sense of "knowledge" was the more common meaning of *scientia.*

The *Oxford English Dictionary* gives the following meanings: (1) The state of fact of knowing; knowledge or cognizance. (2) Knowledge acquired by study. b. Trained skill. (3) A particular branch of knowledge or study; a recognized department of learning. (4) A branch of study which is concerned either with a connected body of demonstrated truths or with observed facts systematically classified . . . under general laws. (5) The kind of knowledge or intellectual activity . . . . What is taught in the Schools, or may be learned by study. b. In modern use often 'Natural and Physical Science'. c. The portions of philosophy, logic, etc., included in the course of study in the Oxford School of Literae Humaniores.

Note the division of Entry (5) into (a) any discipline taught, (b) natural and physical sciences, and (c) humanistic studies, where (b) is given as the modern use and (c) as having become obsolete in the twentieth century. This list reflects a history of semantic change but does not do justice to it: It is a history of arbitrary restrictions imposed by successive schools of thought, each trying to exclude the teachings of its opponents as unscientific. I have elsewhere presented a brief sketch of this semantic development, but I think that a still more concise statement here will be helpful. [Machlup, 1980, pp. 62–70.]

The sequence of exclusions has some similarities to a game of musical chairs. For the playful the game may be good fun; in actual fact, however, it has caused, and continues to cause, a waste of scientists' time as each tries to secure for himself a safe chair—instead of doing more important work.

Excluding Empirical Knowledge

The first exclusion was of empirical knowledge or any kind of knowledge that could be doubted or had to be tested by experience. Science was supposed to be perfect knowledge, derived from unquestionable principles; it was abstract knowledge demonstrable with mathematical certainty. This concept of science goes back to Aristotle, but was dominant until the seventeenth century, remaining strong for the next two centuries, and was still preferred by some exceptional philosophers in the twentieth century.

Limiting references to a minimum, I cite only three: The French philosopher Descartes held in 1644 that "any knowledge that can be questioned ought not to be called 'science'." The British astronomer Sir John Herschel, in 1831, formulated the definition of science as abstract logically demonstrable knowledge. And the Italian Benedetto Croce is one of those who held out for this classical position when he wrote, in 1913: "But we cannot rest satisfied with asserting the right of Logic to be recognized as a science: we must make the further demand that Philosophy alone—and not empirical sciences—be admitted as science in the strict sense of the word." (Croce, 1913, p. 201.)

In this statement, however, philosophy was given its modern meaning, for until the nineteenth century philosophy was the name for what today are the empirical sciences: "Astronomers and physicists did not feel degraded by being called natural philosophers rather than scientists; nor did historians, political economists and other students of human society take offense at being called moral philosophers." (Machlup, 1980, p. 64.)

Excluding Nonsystematic Knowledge

The next stage in the semantic development was really one of liberalization, in that the exclusion of empirical knowledge was lifted to the extent that such knowledge was systematized according to stated principles. The German philosopher Immanuel Kant was among the leaders in making science less exclusive; he still reserved the designation "science proper" for bodies of knowledge formulated in propositions of apodictic certainty, that is, purely analytic propositions. And metaphysics was still "the science of the first principles of human cognition." (Kant, 1848, p. 581.) But what had previously been natural philosophy and moral philosophy became two categories of empirical sciences, along with the formal sciences.

Excluding All But the Natural Sciences

The next turn in the sequence of exclusions took place in mid-nineteenth century England and affected the semantic development in all English-speaking countries. The natural scientists, only recently admitted to the society of scientists, "threw out" those who had previously excluded them—the rationalists and all who relied on speculative arguments. First the natural scientists meant to expel only those professing metaphysics, but soon they went further and excluded all but the laboratory scientists, the experimentalists. Thus, the designation *science* was to be reserved for the natural sciences to the exclusion of social sciences, history, philosophy, logic, ethics, literature—in short, all the scholars who do most of their work at a desk, in a library.

One of the consequences of this radical change of word-meaning was a language barrier between English-speaking countries and the rest of the world. None of the equivalents of the word science in languages other than English has that particular restrictive meaning. The academies of sciences everywhere but in the English-speaking world retained their divisions for historical sciences, juridical sciences, philosophical sciences, and so forth; how can one translate these words into English without contradiction in terms? (The phrase "arts and sciences" is often called in for the purpose.) And how should "scientists" in the restrictive sense be translated into French, German, Italian, Japanese, or Russian? (It can be done, of course, by adding some additional words to modify the noun.) Far more serious than the task of translation have been the countless confusions when partners in learned discussion erroneously confounded the exclusive designation with the wider meanings of science.[26]

Excluding Laymen's and Practitioners' Knowledge

On the continent of Europe and in other non-English-speaking countries the restriction of the meaning of "science" to natural sciences or experimental sciences has never been accepted. However, since definitions are inherently restrictive, they must exclude something: If the *genus proximum* of science is knowledge, the *differentiae specificae* are (1) the systematic organization of that knowledge on the basis of stated principles, (2) the acquisition of that knowledge in arduous study and honest research, and (3) the use of that knowledge for the sake of knowing, disseminating, or adding to it in further research. The last two specific criteria are usually stated negatively in the form of two exclusions: of laymen's knowledge (which is not acquired in arduous study) and of practitioners' knowledge (which is used for a practical purpose other than in teaching, writing, and researching).

No other exclusions besides those of unsystematic knowledge, laymen's knowledge, and practitioners' knowledge are promulgated by this cosmopolitan sense of science; no restrictions apply with regard to subject matter, research technique, modus operandi, or form of presentation. References to this meaning of science can be culled from encyclopedias and dictionaries in virtually all languages except English. [Machlup, 1980, pp. 67–70.]

---

[26]The title of Max Weber's essay "Wissenschaft als Beruf" was rendered in English as "Science as a Vocation." Since Weber meant by science all disciplines or branches of learning, the translator should have rendered it as "academic disciplines" or "science and other scholarship," or some other awkward phrase. Titles of editions of the scientific papers of eminent lawyers, art historians, or theologians in Europe could not be translated into English before checking whether the papers were in the authors' own fields or perhaps on subjects of natural science. After all, in Germany or France a lawyer's paper on a legal issue prepared for publication in a law journal is a *scientific* paper; if it were a brief for the court's consideration, it would be of direct practical usefulness and hence "nonscientific." Erudition and purpose—not the subject and not the method—determine what is science in cosmopolitan usage.

Excluding Philosophy

A second round of the elimination contest between science and philosophy began at the end of the nineteenth century but, almost hilariously, after a complete semantic turn-around. The earlier exclusion of philosophy had been the exclusion of empirical disciplines, such as physics and biology, anthropology, and politics, then known as natural and moral philosophy, respectively. Now these philosophies had become the sciences, and the universal systems of analytical propositions, based on axioms and logical implications, had become philosophy. As if in a comedy of errors in which characters exchange their clothes and their names, we find scientists throwing out philosophers—only that in the first act the evicted ones were the searchers for truth by experience, in the second act they were searchers for truth by ratiocination.

Not that everybody agreed with the expulsion of philosophy. From the supreme position in science—*philosophia prima* in Francis Bacon's classification of the sciences, and the "science of the sciences" in the schemes of the academies—philosophy was to be outcast as a nonscience! Not unexpectedly, the philosophers protested most loudly. "We cannot refuse the name science to logic . . . ", said Morris Cohen. (Cohen, 1931, p. 89.) Benedetto Croce's strong claim on behalf of philosophy was cited above. Rudolf Carnap reserved to the "formal sciences" and to "knowledge based on common sense" prominent places in the *Logical Foundations for the Unity of Science*. (Carnap, 1939 and 1969, p. 145.)

Anglo-American scientists, on the other hand, seem determined not to tolerate the company of philosophers, and even Anglo-American philosophers seem to justify segregation, and even discrimination. Bertrand Russell is often quoted among those who draw a firm dividing line between science and philosophy: "[P]hilosophy consists of speculations about matters where exact knowledge is not yet possible . . . and for that reason questions are perpetually passing over from philosophy into science as science advances." Moreover, philosophy keeps us "aware of how much that seemed like knowledge isn't knowledge." (Russell, 1960, pp. 11–12.)

Most contributors to this volume appear to share the view that philosophy should be excluded from the concept of science. Hassan Mortazavian shows this tenet even in the title of his paper, "System Theory versus System Philosophy"; and in its text he elaborates by saying that "philosophy of systems—a branch of philosophy dealing with problems centered around the notion of system. . . must be distinguished from system theory, which is the science of systems."

The separation of philosophy from science has been deeply deplored by some of our great scientists. Thus, Louis de Broglie, the physicist, wrote: "In the nineteenth century there came into being a separation between scientists and philosophers. The scientists looked with a certain suspicion upon the philosophical speculations . . . . The philosophers, in turn, were no longer interested in the special sciences because their results seemed too narrow. This separation, however, has been harmful to both philosophers and scientists." (de Broglie, 1941, pp. 26–27.) Philipp Frank, although he could not, as a teacher at Harvard, insist that philosophy was a science, did write about "science as a fragment of philosophy, [and] how 'science' can become philosophy." (Frank, 1957, pp. 28, 32.) In a section on speculative science he vigorously denied that philosophy is "concerned with hypotheses of a more speculative nature than those found in science . . . , since all hypotheses are speculative. No distinction can be made between scientific and speculative hypotheses." (Ibid., p. 37.)

Excluding Nontested and Nontestable Knowledge

Some may think that the exclusion of philosophy is tantamount to the exclusion of nontestable knowledge. This is not so. The concept of science that excludes philosophy may still include many hypotheses and propositions of a hypothetico-deductive character as well as models containing "intermediate" variables that are nonmeasurable and nonobservable. A concept of science that excludes nontested and nontestable knowledge-claims is, therefore, more restrictive than the one that excludes philosophy.

[*Editor's Note (U.M.):* This subsection was unfinished at the time of Professor Machlup's death. Also missing from the manuscript were the following subsections listed in his outline for inclusion at this point: *Excluding Nonempirical Knowledge; Excluding Nontheoretical, Nonnomological Knowledge; Excluding Knowledge of Man and Society; Excluding Ideographic and Historical Knowledge; Excluding Literary Scholarship in the Humanities; Excluding Evaluative and Prescriptive Knowledge;* and *Excluding Nonquantitative Knowledge.* The manuscript continued with the subsection, *Excluding Art.*]

Excluding Art

Occasional remarks by teachers and writers about some discourse or endeavor being "not science but merely art" or "as yet only art but gradually developing into science" cause me to comment briefly on this issue.[27] I have done so on earlier occasions and can therefore be very brief. [Machlup, 1969, pp. 106–108; 1978, pp. 432–434; 1980, pp. 90–92.]

Most attempts to separate science from art (chiefly practical arts, not fine arts) suffer from insufficient attention to nuances both in science and in art. Only Jeremy Bentham's distinction can avoid problems of making arbitrary divisions in the spectrum from "pure thought" to "actual performance," since Bentham decided to contrast *thinking* and *doing,* or "thought" and

---

[27] One example: "If computer programming is to become an important part of computer research and development, a transition of programming from an art to a disciplined science must be effected." (Bauer, Juncosa, and Perlis, 1959, pp. 121–122.)

"action." (Bentham, 1816, p. 9.) Even with these categories there are difficulties, in that the scientist too *does* something—experimenting, writing, teaching—and the performer ordinarily *thinks* when using the special knowledge needed for the attainment of a task.

Another distinction was proposed by John Stuart Mill: "Science is a collection of truths; art, a body of rules, or directions for conduct." (John Stuart Mill, 1836 and 1844, p. 124.) This seems clear until we realize that rules for conduct could easily be translated into general propositions of cause and effect, and vice versa. As we look for criteria to distinguish science and art, we will find it necessary to subdivide each. The distinction between basic and applied science is unavoidable; as to art, we ought to realize that (1) general teaching of rules for performance, (2) precepts for concrete situations, (3) directives for immediate action, and (4) execution of such directives are all different things. [Machlup, 1980, p. 92.] In this division of the spectrum, the line that separates applied science from art as a body of general rules for possible performance is by no means hard and fast. This is not necessarily a disadvantage; sometimes it is better not to impose arbitrary demarcation lines where differentiation is a matter of judgment.

In his Turing Award lecture in 1974, Donald Knuth addressed himself to the question of "Computer Programming as an Art." He clearly disassociated himself from the opinion "that there is something undesirable about an area of human activity that is classified as an 'art'; it has to be a science before it has any real stature." (Knuth, 1974a, p. 667.) One of his theses was that programming was also "an art *form,* in an aesthetic sense." Programming "can be like composing poetry or music," it can give aesthetic pleasure to the programmer as well as to the user, it can be "a beautiful thing." (Ibid., pp. 670, 672.) Of course, programming is also an art in the technical sense, in that it takes know-how and skill to write a good program for a task to be executed by the computer. On the other hand, the required knowing-how is based on a goodly measure of scientific knowing-that, and the program is designed to assist in finding other pieces of knowing-that. Even the purest scientist needs to have various skills; to comprehend, to reason, to see previously overlooked problems, to ask the right questions, to devise relevant experiments, to interpret the findings intelligently, and so forth. In other words, the scientific researcher needs a lot of know-how—and this is art. Undoubtedly, the mixture of know-how, know-that, and know-what-to-find-out is different for different tasks and different researchers; there may be tasks for which routine skills are the chief ingredients. On the whole, assessments of the share of art and the share of science in research are questionable. To some extent, such assessments enter into job descriptions and the choice of staff titles, for example, in the distinction between professional and technical personnel; but I doubt that this is what people have in mind when they proclaim that some activity is only art, not science.

Moreover, I cannot help, when I hear such a pronouncement, asking the rude question "So what?" If programming, modeling, experimenting, forecasting, and similar activities are art, not science, what bearing does this have on the activity so demoted? Perhaps the assessor has some dictum in mind like "science is true" whereas art is not aiming at truth. The answer, then, would be that the mentioned activities are engaged in the service of finding, or approaching, the truth, even if no scientist can ever be sure to have captured it.

Excluding Technology

Among dictionary meanings of the word technology are "applied science" and "industrial science." More formally, technology may be defined as the science of techniques and their uses, (originally) in the transformation of materials into products but (lately) also in any kind of operation, even purely mental activity. Thus, technology is a practical science in the sense that its theoretical and descriptive propositions can be applied in practical pursuits.[28] The idea that technology is formulated in the imperative mood, like a cookbook, is obsolete; most imperative, normative, or prescriptive statements can be reformulated as declarative sentences.[29]

It follows that science and technology are *not* opposites; the relation is that of genus and species. The misconception that they are opposites may be due to historical reasons. Institutes of technology in continental Europe have long been separated from traditional universities. This separation was not because of a distinction between scientist and professional; indeed, the ancient professional schools—law, medicine, and theology—training the learned professions, were regarded as the superior faculties of the universities. The different status of technology was perhaps due to the fact that students of technology did not need, and rarely had, knowledge of Latin and no one so "uneducated" could be admitted to a university. Even the secondary schools preparing students for higher education were separated—in location as well as ideology: A classical curriculum was required for those preparing for university, a modern-realistic curriculum for those preparing for higher schools of technology. By now much of this is past history but the ideological separation seems to survive.

[28] The concept of "practical science" goes back to Aristotle and held an important place in the system of four "orders of science" distinguished by Thomas Aquinas—natural philosophy, rational philosophy, moral philosophy, and practical sciences. Aquinas used "mechanical arts" as a synonym for "practical sciences." As examples he listed medicine, shipbuilding, and strategy. [Machlup, 1982, pp. 26–27.]

[29] This statement seems to contradict the contention of Pearson and Slamecka in their paper to the effect that "one of the distinguishing features of science and technology concerns the essential role played in science by declarative sentences and in technology by imperative sentences." This point holds equally for a handbook of medicine: Handbooks and reference books in medicine and in technology (computer technology, fibre technology, mining technology, and so forth) are not actually written in the imperative mood. Only their pragmatic applications are closer to those in the foundation sciences, and to emphasize this, some philosophers have resorted to the cookbook analogy.

Some writers on the relation between science and technology like to stress the place of science as a *prerequisite* of technology, referring to the fact that technologists and engineers, to do their job well, must know enough physics, chemistry, and a few other disciplines to use or apply these bodies of knowledge. This would make science a source of supply for the production of technology—another rather naive conception, which disregards the important intellectual feedback from technology to various other disciplines including the basic natural sciences. The essential point is that the universe of learning includes many disciplines, all coherent and systematically ordered arrangements of knowledge—and hence sciences—and many overlapping or interdependent. Included in this class is the science of technology.[30]

Is there a difference between technology and engineering? Again the contrast between science as knowledge and art as performance is relied upon as a distinguishing characteristic. Engineering is the activity of designing and constructing artifacts, often works of public utility; and technology is the general knowledge required for that activity. Technology, according to the dictionary, is the "discourse or treatise" dealing with the known possibilities of transforming available inputs into desired outputs. Thus, the distinction between technology and engineering makes it even clearer that technology is a branch of science—the most practical branch perhaps—developed with ultimate "action-orientation" or "mission-orientation."[31]

WHAT THEY MEAN BY COMPUTING

Some people are very proud of the continuing changes of their language as old words acquire new meanings. They take this as a sign of progress: Theirs is a living language, which flexibly adapts itself to changes in the environment, particularly in technology. They are not disturbed by the fact that some of the new meanings of old words are largely due to ignorance of the original meanings or to laziness, avoiding the task of coining new words that

---

[30] A subtle comment on the triple relationship among science, philosophy, and technology may be quoted here: "The union between science and philosophy was possible only during a period of separation between science and technology. Modern science was born when technology became scientific. The union of science and technology was responsible for the separation between science and philosophy." (Philipp Frank, 1957, p. 29.)

[31] In discussing the alleged juxtaposition of science, on the one hand, and practical arts, technology, and engineering, on the other, one may ask, as Saul Gorn does in his lead paper in this volume, why the words *academic* and *practical* are so often used as mutual insults. The reason, I submit, is that people often like to explain their career choices by appeals to higher principles: The academic looks down on the practical man who is obtuse to the eternal values of the search for learning for the sake of learning; the man of practice looks down on the long-haired "college prof" who wastes his time on merely "academic" matters and is oblivious to practical affairs. Both groups may be happy in their "superior wisdom."

would express what is actually meant.[32] The word "computing" acquired a new meaning when it was realized that the electronic computer could do other things than what it had originally been designed for.

Dictionary Definitions

The word "to compute" is a direct derivation from the Latin *computare,* where it has the same meaning as in English: "[T]o determine by computation; to reckon, count; to take account of; [and] to make computation." Its synonym is "to calculate."

The computing engine or computing machine, later called the computer, was designed for *number* manipulation by means of *symbol* manipulation. Charles Babbage (1792–1871), realizing that his machine could do more than numerical calculations, called his device an analytical engine.[33] The electronic machines developed in the twentieth century, though capable of manipulating symbols of any sort, were nevertheless designated as computers, since the primary use for which they were intended was numerical computation.

Multipurpose Machines

It did not take long for nonnumerical tasks to develop, to grow, and to overtake the numerical ones. Some enterprising people might have come forth with a new name for that miraculous machine that could do so many things besides computing—but this did not happen or, at least, any new names suggested were not accepted. So the noun "computer" stuck even after it was generally known that the computer was capable of doing scores of things other than computing. As a matter of fact, many computer experts began to extend the meaning of the verb "computing" to make it comprise virtually everything that can be done with a computer. This semantic expansion has caused some, though not serious, obstacles in professional and scientific communication.

Now a Multipurpose Word

The logic of the semantic change is a little primitive: If a computer is a device for computation, then anything that is done by a computer should be

---

[32] Among the stock examples of a long time ago are *manufacture* (meaning made by hand, now used for the opposite, made by machine) and *manuscript* (meaning written by hand, now including the opposite, a typescript).

[33] "Meanwhile . . . he [Babbage] was at work on . . . his Analytical Engine, a grander, bigger, all-purpose calculating machine. It would not only be capable of arithmetic calculations, but it would also be capable of analysis and of tabulating any function whatever." (McCorduck, 1979, pp. 25–26.)

called computation. It is easy to understand why more conservative semanticists object to this peculiar logic. For it leads to possible confusion by intelligent readers who have not yet been brainwashed; for example, when they read a sentence or clause to the effect that "mental processes are computational processes," they are most likely to think of processes of numerical computation—but would be wrong.

Several writers in this volume take it for granted that computing means symbol manipulation. Allen Newell says that when the artificial intelligence community emphasizes symbol manipulation, they do not mean nonnumerical processing but only that prominence of many nonnumerical tasks "make[s] the characterization of computers as number manipulators no longer ring true." Avron Barr's paper carries the title "Artificial Intelligence: Cognition as Computation"; he does not even mention the possibility that readers may associate computation with numbers. To the writers on cognitive science it is quite obvious that computational psychology and computational linguistics do not deal with numerical computations but only with programs for and processes by the computer.

The traditionalist, who does not like semantic changes that could with just a little care be avoided, will regret the expansion of the intension of *computing* and *computation*. Are those who want to use these words in their original meanings now forced to add *number* or *numerical* as modifiers to indicate what they mean? They feel robbed by the appropriation of their terms by a "gang of wordlifters."[34]

Incidentally, the expansion of the meaning of the word computing did not go all the way to having it include *everything* that can be done with a computer. The most notable exceptions refer to processes where symbol manipulation seems more prominent: Word-processing has not yet become text computation; composing of music has not yet become music computation; composing of camera-ready copy for the printer has not become computational composition. That may still come. The expansion that has already taken place has reached the point of no return. Readers will have to accept the notion of nonnumerical computation.

---

[34] When I requested Zenon Pylyshyn's view on this semantic question, he replied: "Although the term does have its roots in early calculating machines, my impression is that in psychology, philosophy of mind, and certainly computer science it is viewed as an entirely neutral term which designates what computers do—i.e., manipulate symbols. The public, of course, still equates that with calculation over numbers, but in this case it is the public's idea which will change, rather than the term." (Pylyshyn in private correspondence, August 20, 1982.)

CUMULATIVE LIST OF REFERENCES

ABELSON, ROBERT P., "Computer Simulation of 'Hot' Cognition," in Tompkins, Silvan S., and Messick, Samuel, eds., *Computer Simulation and Personality: Frontier of Psychological Theory* (New York: Wiley, 1963), pp. 277–298.

ABELSON, ROBERT P., "The Structure of Belief Systems," in Schank, Roger C., and Colby, Kenneth M., eds., *Computer Models of Thought and Language* (San Francisco: W. H. Freeman, 1973), pp. 287–339.

ACKOFF, RUSSELL L., "Towards a Behavioral Theory of Communication," in *Management Science,* vol. 4 (1957–1958), pp. 218–234.

ACKOFF, RUSSELL L., "General Systems Theory and Systems Research—Contrasting Conceptions of System Science," in *General Systems,* vol. 8 (1963), pp. 117–124.

ACKOFF, RUSSELL L., "Towards a System of System Concepts," in *Management Science,* vol. 17 (July 1971), pp. 661–671.

ACKOFF, RUSSELL L., AND EMERY, FRED E., *On Purposeful Systems* (Chicago: Aldine-Atherton, 1972).

ACM CURRICULUM COMMITTEE ON COMPUTER SCIENCE, "An Undergraduate Program in Computer Science—Preliminary Recommendations." A Report from the ACM Curriculum Committee on Computer Science, in *Communications of the ACM,* vol. 8 (Sept. 1965), pp. 543–552.

ACM CURRICULUM COMMITTEE ON COMPUTER SCIENCE, "Curriculum 68: Recommendations for Academic Programs in Computer Science," in *Communications of the ACM,* vol. 11 (Mar. 1968), pp. 151–197.

ADA Reference Manual (Washington, D.C.: U.S. Department of Defense, July, 1980; rev., summer 1982).

AKAIKE, HIROTUGU, "Stochastic Theory of Minimal Realization," in *IEEE Transactions on Automatic Control,* vol. AC-19 (Dec. 1974), pp. 667–674.

AMAREL, SAUL, "On Representations of Problems of Reasoning about Actions," in Michie, Donald, ed., *Machine Intelligence 3* (Edinburgh: Edinburgh University Press, 1968), pp. 131–172.

AMAREL, SAUL, "Computer Science," in *Encyclopedia of Computer Science* (New York: Petrocelli/Charter, 1976), pp. 314–318.

AMARI, SHUN-ICHI, "A Method of Statistical Neurodynamics," in *Kybernetik,* vol. 14 (1974), pp. 201–215.

AMARI, SHUN-ICHI, AND ARBIB, MICHAEL A., eds., *Competition and Cooperation in Neural Nets* (New York: Springer-Verlag, 1982).

AMPÈRE, ANDRÉ-MARIE, *Essai sur la philosophie des sciences, ou Exposition analytique d'une classification naturelle de toutes les connaissances humaines* (Paris: Bachelier, 1834; seconde partie [ed. Jean Jacques Ampère], Paris, 1838, 1843; another ed., Bruxelles: Culture et Civilisation, 1966).

ANDERSON, JOHN R., *Language, Memory, and Thought* (Hillsdale, N. J.: Lawrence Erlbaum, 1976).

ANDERSON, JOHN R., AND BOWER, GORDON H., *Human Associative Memory* (Washington, D.C.: V. H. Winston, 1973).

AOKI, MASANAO, *Optimal Control and Systems Theory in Dynamic Economic Analysis* (New York: North-Holland, 1976).

ARBIB, MICHAEL A., "A Partial Survey of Cybernetics in Eastern Europe and the Soviet Union," in *Behavioral Science,* vol. 11 (1966), pp. 193–216.

ARBIB, MICHAEL A., *The Metaphorical Brain: An Introduction to Cybernetics as Artificial Intelligence and Brain Theory* (New York: Wiley-Interscience, 1972).

ARBIB, MICHAEL A., "Artificial Intelligence and Brain Theory: Unities and Diversities," in *Annals of Biomedical Engineering,* vol. 3 (Sept. 1975*a*), pp. 238–274.

ARBIB, MICHAEL A., "Cybernetics After 25 Years: A Personal View of System Theory and Brain Theory," in *IEEE Transactions on Systems, Man, and Cybernetics,* vol. SMC-5 (1975*b*), pp. 359–363.

ARBIB, MICHAEL A., "Perceptual Structures and Distributed Motor Control," in Brooks, Vernon B., ed., *Handbook of Physiology: Section 1: The Nervous System, Vol. II: Motor Control* (Bethesda, Md.: The American Physiological Society, 1981), pp. 1449–1480.

ARBIB, MICHAEL A., "Modeling Neural Mechanisms of Visuomotor Coordination in Frog and Toad," in Amari, Shun-ichi, and Arbib, Michael A., eds., *Competition and Cooperation in Neural Nets* (New York: Springer-Verlag, 1982), pp. 342–370.

ARBIB, MICHAEL A.; CAPLAN, DAVID; AND MARSHALL, JOHN C., eds., *Neural Models of Language Processes* (New York: Academic Press, 1982).

ARBIB, MICHAEL A., AND MANES, ERNEST G., "Machines in a Category," in *Journal of Pure and Applied Algebra,* vol. 19 (Dec. 1980), pp. 9–20.

ARDEN, BRUCE W., ed., *What Can Be Automated? The Computer Science and Engineering Study (COSERS)* (Cambridge, Mass.: MIT Press, 1980*a*).

ARDEN, BRUCE W., "COSERS Overview," in Arden, Bruce W., ed., *What Can Be Automated? The Computer Science and Engineering Study (COSERS)* (Cambridge, Mass.: MIT Press, 1980*b*), pp. 3–31.

ARISTOTLE, *The Nicomachean Ethics of Aristotle,* with English notes by J. S. Brewer (Oxford, England: Henry Slatter, 1836; another ed., New York: G. P. Putnam Sons, 1926). [1st ed., 1513]

ARMER, PAUL, "Attitudes Toward Intelligent Machines," in Feigenbaum, Edward A., and Feldman, Julian, eds., *Computers and Thought* (New York: McGraw-Hill, 1963), pp. 389–405.

ARNOL'D, V. I., "Lectures on Bifurcations in Versal Families," in *Russian Mathematical Surveys,* vol. 27 (Sept./Oct. 1972), pp. 54–123.

ARROW, KENNETH J., "Economic Equilibrium," in Sills, David L., ed., *International Encyclopedia of the Social Sciences,* vol. 4 (New York: Macmillan and Free Press, 1968), pp. 376–388.

ARROW, KENNETH J., *The Limits of Organization* (New York: W. W. Norton, 1974).

ARROW, KENNETH J., "The Economics of Information," in Dertouzos, Michael L., and Moses, Joel, eds., *The Computer Age: A Twenty-Year View* (Cambridge, Mass.: MIT Press, 1979), pp. 306–317.

ASHBY, W. ROSS, *Design for a Brain: The Origin of Adaptive Behaviour* (New York: Wiley, 1952; 2nd ed., rev., 1960).

ASHBY, W. ROSS, *An Introduction to Cybernetics* (London: Chapman and Hall, 1956).

ASRATYAN, G. E., AND SIMONOV, P., *How Reliable is the Brain?* (Moscow: Mir, 1975).

ATKINSON, ANTHONY A., AND FELTHAM, GERALD A., "Information in Capital Markets: An Agency Theory Perspective," Working Paper, Faculty of Commerce and Business Administration, University of British Columbia, Vancouver, B.C., 1980.

ATTNEAVE, FRED, *Applications of Information Theory to Psychology: A Summary of Basic Concepts, Methods, and Results* (New York: Holt, 1959).

AUGUSTINUS, AURELIUS, *St. Augustine's Confessions* (Cambridge, Mass.: Harvard University Press, 1950–1951).

BACKUS, JOHN, et al., "The FORTRAN Automatic Coding System," in *Proceedings of the Western Joint Computer Conference,* sponsored by the Institute of Radio Engineers, the American Institute of Electrical Engineers, and the Association for Computing Machinery and held [in Los Angeles] Feb. 26–28, 1957; pp. 188–198.

BACKUS, JOHN, "Can Programming Be Liberated From the von Neumann Style? A Functional Style and Its Algebra of Programs" [the 1977 ACM Turing Award Lecture], in *Communications of the ACM,* vol. 21 (Aug. 1978), pp. 613–641.

BAIMAN, STANLEY, "Agency Research in Managerial Accounting: A Survey," in *Journal of Accounting Literature,* vol. 1 (spring 1980), pp. 154–213; reprinted in Mattessich, Richard, et al., *Modern Accounting Research: History, Survey, and Guide* (Vancouver, B.C.: Canadian Certified General Accountants Research Foundation, forthcoming 1984).

BAKER, JEFFREY J. W., AND ALLEN, GARLAND E., *The Study of Biology* (Reading, Mass.: Addison-Wesley, 4th ed., 1982).

BALLARD, DANA H., AND BROWN, CHRISTOPHER M., *Computer Vision* (Englewood Cliffs, N.J.: Prentice-Hall, 1982).

BARALT-TORRIJOS, JORGE, "A Programmatic Interpretation of Combinatory Logic" (Ph.D. diss., Georgia Institute of Technology, 1973).

BAR-HILLEL, YEHOSHUA, *Language and Information* (Reading, Mass.: Addison-Wesley, 1964).

BAR-HILLEL, YEHOSHUA, AND CARNAP, RUDOLF, "Semantic Information," in Jackson of Burnley, Willis Jackson, Baron, ed., *Communication Theory*. Papers read at a symposium on Applications of Communication Theory, held [at the Institution of Electrical Engineers, London] Sept. 22–26, 1952 (London: Butterworths, 1953*a*), pp. 503–512.

BAR-HILLEL, YEHOSHUA, AND CARNAP, RUDOLF, "Semantic Information," in The *British Journal for the Philosophy of Science,* vol. 4 (Aug. 1953*b*), pp. 147–157.

BARKER, ROGER G., AND WRIGHT, HERBERT F., *The Midwest and Its Children: The Psychological Ecology of an American Town* (Evanston, Ill.: Row, Peterson, 1954; New York: Harper and Row, 1955).

BARNEA, AMIR; HAUGEN, ROBERT A.; AND SENBET, LEMMA W., "Market Imperfections, Agency Problems, and Capital Structure: A Review," in *Financial Management,* vol. 10 (summer 1981), pp. 7–22.

BARR, AVRON; BENNETT, JAMES S.; AND CLANCEY, WILLIAM J., *Transfer of Expertise:*

A Theme for AI Research (Stanford University, Heuristic Programming Project, Working Paper No. HPP-79-11, 1979).

BARR, AVRON, AND FEIGENBAUM, EDWARD A., eds., *The Handbook of Artificial Intelligence*, vols. 1, 2 (Los Altos, Calif.: William Kaufmann, 1981).

BARTLETT, FREDERIC C., *Remembering: A Study in Experimental and Social Psychology* (Cambridge: Cambridge University Press, 1932).

BARZUN, JACQUES, *Darwin, Marx, Wagner* (Garden City, N.Y.: Anchor Doubleday, 2nd ed., 1958).

BATESON, GREGORY, *Steps to an Ecology of Mind* (New York: Ballantine Books, 1972).

BAUER, WALTER F.; JUNCOSA, MARIO L.; AND PERLIS, ALAN J., "ACM Publication Policies and Plans," in *Communications of the ACM*, vol. 6 (Apr. 1959), pp. 121–122.

BAUMOL, WILLIAM J., AND MARCUS, MATITYAHU, *Economics of Academic Libraries* [prepared for the Council on Library Resources by Mathematica Inc.] (Washington, D.C.: American Council on Education, 1973).

BAUMOL, WILLIAM J., AND OATES, WALLACE, *The Theory of Environmental Policy* (Englewood Cliffs, N.J.: Prentice-Hall, 1975).

BEADLE, GEORGE WELLS, *Genetics and Modern Biology* (Philadelphia: American Philosophical Society, 1963a).

BEADLE, GEORGE WELLS, *The New Biology and the Nature of Man* [the Dewey F. Fayerburg Memorial Lecture, 1963], in *Phoenix* (Ann Arbor: University of Michigan, 1963b), vol. 1.

BEAM, ROBERT D., "Testing the Integrated Social Science Hypothesis: An Economic Approach" (Ph.D. diss., University of Cincinnati, 1979).

BECKER, JOSEPH D., "Reflections on the Formal Description of Behavior," in Bobrow, Daniel G., and Collins, Allan, eds., *Representation and Understanding: Studies in Cognitive Science* (New York: Academic Press, 1975), pp. 83–102.

BEER, STAFFORD, *Brain of the Firm* (London: Allen Lane, 1972).

BEER, STAFFORD, "Progress in Cybernetics and Systems," in Trappl, Robert, and Hanika, Francis de Paula, eds., *Progress in Cybernetics and Systems Research, Vol. II: Socio-Economic Systems, Cognition and Learning, Systems Education, Organization and Management.* Papers presented at a symposium organized by the Austrian Society for Cybernetic Studies and held [in Vienna] Apr. 1974 (New York: Halsted Press, 1975), introduction.

BELL LABORATORIES, "UNIX Time-Sharing System," in *Bell System Technical Journal,* vol. 57, no. 6 (July–Aug. 1978), pp. 1897–2312, part 2.

BELLMAN, RICHARD, *Introduction to the Mathematical Theory of Control Processes,* 2 vols. (New York: Academic Press, 1971a).

BELLMAN, RICHARD, *Mathematics, Systems and Society: An Informal Essay* (Stockholm: Swedish Natural Science Research Council [NFR], report no. 2, 1971b).

BENSOUSSAN, ALAIN, *Filtrage optimal des systèmes linéaires* (Paris: Dunod, 1971).

BENSOUSSAN, ALAIN; DELFOUR, M.; AND MITTER, S. K., *Control of Infinite Dimensional Systems* (Cambridge, Mass.: MIT Press, 1982).

BENSOUSSAN, ALAIN, AND LIONS, JACQUES LOUIS, *Applications des inéquations variationnelles en contrôle stochastiques* (Paris: Dunod, 1978).

BENSOUSSAN, ALAIN, AND LIONS, JACQUES LOUIS, *Contrôle impulsionnel et inéquations quasi variationnelle* (Paris: Dunod, 1981).

BENTHAM, JEREMY, *Introduction to the Principles of Morals and Legislation* (Oxford: Oxford University Press, 1789).

BENTHAM, JEREMY, *Chrestomathia* (London: Payne and Foss, 1816).

BERGER, J., "A Comment on Information Theory and Central Dogma of Molecular Biology," in *Journal of Theoretical Biology*, vol. 65 (Mar. 1977), pp. 393–395.

BERLEKAMP, ELWYN R., *Key Papers in the Development of Coding Theory* (New York: IEEE Press, 1974).

BERLEKAMP, ELWYN R., "The Technology of Error-Correcting Codes," in *Proceedings of the IEEE*, vol. 68 (May 1980), pp. 564–593.

BERLINSKI, DAVID, *On Systems Analysis: An Essay Concerning the Limitations of Some Mathematical Methods in the Social, Political and Biological Sciences* (Cambridge, Mass.: MIT Press, 1976).

BERNARD, CLAUDE, *Introduction to the Study of Experimental Medicine* (first published in French, 1865; English trans. H. D. Greene, London: Macmillan, 1927).

BERNARD, CLAUDE, *Leçons sur les phénomènes de la vie communs aux animaux et aux végétaux* (Paris: J. B. Baillière et fils, 1878–1879), 2 vols.

BERNSTEIN, JEREMY, "Profiles: Marvin Minsky," in The *New Yorker,* Dec. 14, 1981, pp. 50–126.

BERNSTEIN, NIKOLAI A., *The Coordination and Regulation of Movement* (New York: Pergamon Press, 1967). Translated from the Russian.

BERTALANFFY, LUDWIG VON, *Kritische Theorie der Formbildung* (Berlin, Borntraeger, 1928).

BERTALANFFY, LUDWIG VON, *Modern Theories of Development: An Introduction to Theoretical Biology* (London: Oxford University Press, 1933; New York: Harper Torchbooks, 1962). Translation and adaptation by J. H. Woodger of *Kritische Theorie der Formbildung,* Berlin: Borntraeger, 1928.

BERTALANFFY, LUDWIG VON, "Zu einer allgemeinen Systemlehre," *Blätter für deutsche Philosophie,* vol. 18, nos. 3/4 (1945). Reprinted in *Biologia Generalis,* vol. 19 (1949), pp. 114–129.

BERTLANFFY, LUDWIG VON, "An Outline of General System Theory," in The *British Journal for the Philosophy of Science,* vol. 1 (May 1950), pp. 134–165.

BERTALANFFY, LUDWIG VON, *Robots, Men, and Minds* (New York: Braziller, 1967).

BERTALANFFY, LUDWIG VON, *General System Theory: Foundations, Development, Applications* (New York: Braziller, 1968).

BERWICK, ROBERT C., AND WEINBERG, A., *The Grammatical Basis of Linguistic Performance* (Cambridge, Mass.: MIT Press, 1983).

BEVER, THOMAS G., "The Cognitive Basis for Linguistic Structures," in Hayes, John R., ed., *Cognition and the Development of Language* (New York: Wiley, 1970), pp. 279–352.

BEVER, THOMAS G., "Broca and Lashley were Right: Cerebral Dominance is an Accident of Growth," in Caplan, David, ed., *Biological Studies of Mental Processes*, proceedings of a Conference on Maturational Factors in Cognitive Development and the Biology of Language, held [at MIT] June 1978 (Cambridge, Mass.: MIT Press, 1980*a*), pp. 186–230.

BEVER, THOMAS G., "Normal Acquisition Processes Explain the Critical Period for Language Learning," in Diller, Karl C., ed., *Individual Differences and Universals in Language Learning Aptitude* (Rowley, Mass.: Newbury House, 1980*b*), pp. 176–198.

BEVER, THOMAS G., AND HURTIG, R. R., "Detection of a Non-Linguistic Stimulus is Poorest at the End of a Clause," in *Journal of Psycholinguistic Research,* vol. 4 (1975), pp. 1–7.

Bhagavad-Gita, The, trans. Christopher Isherwood (London: Phoenix House, 1947).

BINET, ALFRED, AND SIMON, THEODORE, *The Development of Intelligence in Children: The Binet-Simon Scale,* trans. Elisabeth S. Kite (Baltimore: Williams and Wilkins, 1916).

BITZER, DONALD, "The Wide World of Computer-Based Education," in Rubinoff, Morris, and Yovits, Marshall C., eds., *Advances in Computers,* vol. 15 (New York: Academic Press, 1976), pp. 239–284.

BLACK, MAX, "The Definition of Scientific Method," in Stauffer, Robert C., ed., *Science and Civilization* (Madison: University of Wisconsin Press, 1949), pp. 67–95.

BLAIVAS, ALEXANDER, "Visual Analysis," in *Mathematical Biosciences,* vol. 28 (1977), pp. 101–149.

BLOOMFIELD, LEONARD, *An Introduction to the Study of Language* (New York: Holt, 1914).

BLOOMFIELD, LEONARD, *Language* (New York: Holt, 1933).

BLOOMFIELD, LEONARD, "Linguistic Aspects of Science," in *International Encyclopedia of Unified Science,* vol. 1, no. 4 (Chicago: University of Chicago Press, 1939).

BLUMENTHAL, ARTHUR L., *The Process of Cognition* (Englewood Cliffs, N.J.: Prentice-Hall, 1977).

BOBROW, DANIEL G., "Dimensions of Representation," in Bobrow, Daniel G., and Collins, Allan, eds., *Representation and Understanding: Studies in Cognitive Science* (New York: Academic Press, 1975), pp. 1–34.

BOBROW, DANIEL G., ed., Special Issue on Non-Monotonic Logic, *Artificial Intelligence,* vol. 13 (Apr. 1980), pp. 1–172.

BOBROW, DANIEL G., AND COLLINS, ALLAN, eds., *Representation and Understanding: Studies in Cognitive Science* (New York: Academic Press, 1975).

BOBROW, DANIEL G., AND RAPHAEL, BERTRAM, "New Programming Languages for Artificial Intelligence Research," in *ACM Computing Surveys,* vol. 6 (Sept. 1974), pp. 153–174.

BOBROW, ROBERT J., AND BROWN, JOHN SEELY, "System Understanding: Synthesis, Analysis, and Contingent Knowledge in Specialized Understanding Systems," in Bobrow, Daniel G., and Collins, Allan, eds., *Representation and Understanding: Studies in Cognitive Science* (New York: Academic Press, 1975), pp. 103–129.

BODE, HENDRIK; MOSTELLER, FREDERICK; TUKEY, JOHN; AND WINSOR, CHARLES, "The Education of a Scientific Generalist," in *Science,* vol. 109 (June 1949), pp. 553–558.

BODEN, MARGARET A., *Purposive Explanation in Psychology* (Cambridge, Mass.: Harvard University Press, 1972).

BODEN, MARGARET A., *Artificial Intelligence and Natural Man* (New York: Basic Books, 1977).

BODEN, MARGARET A., *Minds and Mechanisms: Philosophical Psychology and Computational Models* (Ithaca, N.Y.: Cornell University Press, 1981*a*).

BODEN, MARGARET A., "The Case for a Cognitive Biology," in Boden, Margaret A., *Minds and Mechanisms: Philosophical Psychology and Computational Models* (Ithaca, N.Y.: Cornell University Press, 1981*b*), pp. 89–112.

BOGDANOV [MALINOVSKII], ALEKSANDR ALEKSANDROVICH, *Vseobshchaia organization-naia nauka, tektologiia [Tektology: The Universal Science of Organization]*, 3 vols. (St. Petersburg: Izdatelstvo, 1913; 2nd ed., Moscow: Izdatelstvo, 1922).

BOGDANOV [MALINOVSKII], ALEKSANDR ALEKSANDROVICH, *Allgemeine Organisations-lehre—Tektologie* (Berlin: Organisationsverlagsgesellschaft GmbH, 1926). Translation from Russian to German of vols. 1 and 2 of *Vseobshchaia organizationnaia nauka, tektologiia,* 1913 and 1922.

BOGDANOV [MALINOVSKII], ALEKSANDR ALEKSANDROVICH, *Essays in Tektology,* trans. and ed. George Gorelik (Seaside Calif.: Intersystems Publications, 1980).

BOGUSLAW, ROBERT, *The New Utopians: A Study of System Design and Social Change* (Englewood Cliffs, N.J.: Prentice-Hall, 1965).

BÖHM, STEPHAN, "Das Biespiel der 'unsichtbaren' Hand," in Acham, Karl, ed., *Gesellschaftliche Prozesse* (Graz, Austria: Academia, 1982).

BOLTZMANN, LUDWIG VON, "Weitere Studien über das Wärmegleichgewicht unter Gasmolekülen," in *Kaiserliche Akademie der Wissenschaften* [Vienna] *Sitzungsberichte,* II Abteil 66 (1872), pp. 275–370.

BOLTZMANN, LUDWIG VON, "Über die Beziehung zwischen dem zweiten Hauptsatze der mechanischen Wärmetheorie und der Wahrscheinlichkeitsrechnung respektive den Sätzen über das Wärmgleichgewicht" ["On the Relation between the Second Law of Thermodynamics and Probability Theory and the Laws of Thermal Equilibrium"], in *Kaiserliche Akademie der Wissenschaften* [Vienna] *Sitzungsberichte,* II Abteil 76 (1877), pp. 373–435.

BOLTZMANN, LUDWIG VON, "Der zweite Hauptsatz der mechanischen Wärmetheorie," a paper written in 1886, reproduced in Boltzmann, Ludwig, *Populäre Schriften* (Leipzig: Johann Ambrosius Barth, 1905*a*), pp. 25–50.

BOLTZMANN, LUDWIG VON, "Über statistische Mechanik," a paper delivered at a congress in St. Louis, 1904, reproduced in Boltzmann, Ludwig, *Populäre Schriften* (Leipzig: Johann Ambrosius Barth, 1905*b*), pp. 345–363.

BONGARD, MIKHAIL MOISEEVICH, *Pattern Recognition,* ed. Joseph K. Hawkins, and trans. Theodore Cheron (Rochelle Park, N.J.: Hayden, Spartan Book, 1970).

BOOKSTEIN, ABRAHAM, "The Bibliometric Distributions," in The *Library Quarterly,* vol. 46 (Oct. 1976), pp. 416–423.

BOOLE, GEORGE, *An Investigation of the Laws of Thought, on which are Founded the Mathematical Theories of Logic and Probabilities* (London: Walton and Maberly, 1854. Republished as vol. 2 of George Boole's *Collected Logical Works,* Chicago: Open Court, 1916; New York: Dover ed., 1961).

BOULDING, KENNETH E., "Notes on the Information Concept," in *Explorations* [Toronto], vol. 6 (1955), pp. 103–112.

BOULDING, KENNETH E., *The Image: Knowledge in Life and Society* (Ann Arbor: University of Michigan Press, 1956*a*).

BOULDING, KENNETH E., "General Systems Theory—The Skeleton of Science," in *Management Science,* vol. 2 (Apr. 1956*b*), pp. 197–208.

BOULDING, KENNETH E., *The Meaning of the Twentieth Century* (New York: Harper, 1964).

BOULDING, KENNETH E., "The Economics of Knowledge and the Knowledge of Economics," in *American Economic Review,* vol. 56, no. 2 (1966), pp. 1–13.

BOULDING, KENNETH E., *Eco-dynamics: A New Theory of Societal Evolution* (Beverly Hills, Calif.: Sage Publications, 1978).

BOWLER, T. DOWNING, *General Systems Thinking: Its Scope and Applicability* (New York: Elsevier/North-Holland, 1981).

BRACHMAN, RONALD J., AND SMITH, BRIAN C., eds., Special Issue on Knowledge Representation, *SIGART Newsletter,* vol. 70 (Feb. 1980), pp. 1–138.

BRANSCOMB, LEWIS M., "Information: The Ultimate Frontier," in *Science,* vol. 203 (12 Jan. 1979), p. 143.

BRESNAN, JOAN, "A Realistic Transformational Grammar," in Halle, Morris; Bresnan, Joan; and Miller, George A., eds., *Linguistic Theory and Psychological Reality* (Cambridge, Mass.: MIT Press, 1978), pp. 1–59.

BRIET, SUZANNE, *Qu'est-ce que la documentation?* (Paris: Editions Documentaires Industrielles et Techniques, 1951).

BRILLOUIN, LEON, "Negentropy Principle of Information," in *Journal of Applied Physics,* vol. 24 (Sept. 1953), pp. 1152–1163.

BRILLOUIN, LEON, *Science and Information Theory* (New York: Academic Press, 1956; 2nd ed. 1962).

BROCKETT, ROGER W., *Finite Dimensional Linear Systems* (New York: Wiley, 1971).

BROCKETT, ROGER W., "The Geometry of Partial Realization Problems," in *Proceedings of a Conference on Decision and Control* organized by the Institute of Electrical and Electronics Engineers (New York: IEEE Press, 1978).

BROGLIE, LOUIS DE, "L'Avenir de la physique," in Broglie, Louis de, et al., *L'Avenir de la science* (Paris: Plon, 1941), pp. 1–35.

BROGLIE, LOUIS DE, *La cybernétique: théorie du signal et de l'information* (Paris: Editions de la Revue d'Optique Théorique et Instrumentale, 1951), p. v.

BROOKES, BERTRAM C., "Robert Fairthorne and the Scope of Information Science," in *Journal of Documentation,* vol. 30 (June 1974), pp. 139–152.

BROOKES, BERTRAM C., "A New Paradigm for Information Science," in The *Information Scientist,* vol. 10 (Sept. 1976), pp. 103–111.

BROWN, ROBERT R., *Explanation in Social Science* (Chicago: Aldine-Atherton, 1963).

BRUNOVSKÝ, P., "A Classification of Linear Controllable Systems," in *Kybernetika,* vol. 6 (1970), pp. 176–188.

BRYSON, ARTHUR, AND HO, Y. C., *Applied Optimal Control* (New York: Halsted Press, 1968).

BUCHANAN, JAMES, "The Justice of Natural Liberty," in O'Driscoll, Gerald P., Jr., ed., *Adam Smith and Modern Political Economy: Bicentennial Essays on The Wealth of Nations* (Ames: Iowa State University Press, 1979) pp. 117–131.

BUCKLAND, MICHAEL K., *Library Services in Theory and Context* (New York: Pergamon Press, 1983).

BUCKLEY, WALTER, *Sociology and Modern Systems Theory* (Englewood Cliffs, N.J.: Prentice-Hall, 1967).

BUNGE, MARIO, *Treatise on Basic Philosophy, Vol. IV, Ontology II: A World of Systems* (Dordrecht, Holland, and Boston: D. Reidel, 1979*a*).

BUNGE, MARIO, "A Systems Concept of Society: Beyond Individualism and Holism," in *Theory and Decision,* vol. 10 (Jan. 1979*b*), pp. 13–30.

BURKS, ARTHUR W., ed., *Essays on Cellular Automata* (Urbana: University of Illnois Press, 1970).

BURMEISTER, EDWIN, AND DOBELL, A. RODNEY, *Mathematical Theories of Economic Growth* (New York: Macmillan, 1970).

BUSH, VANNEVAR, "As We May Think" (1945). Reprinted in Pylyshyn, Zenon W., ed., *Perspectives on the Computer Revolution* (Englewood Cliffs, N.J.: Prentice-Hall, 1970), pp. 47–59.

BUTLER, PIERCE, *An Introduction to Library Science* (Chicago: University of Chicago Press, 1933).

BUTTERFIELD, HERBERT, *The Origins of Modern Science 1300–1800* (London: Bell, 1949; New York: Macmillan, 1951; Toronto: Clark, Irwin and Co., 1957).

BYRNES, C., AND FALB, PETER L. "Applications of Algebraic Geometry in System Theory," in *American Journal of Mathematics,* vol. 101 (1979), pp. 337–363.

CADWALLADER, M., "The Cybernetic Analysis of Change in Complex Social Organizations," in *American Journal of Sociology,* vol. 65 (1959), pp. 154–157.

CANNON, WALTER B., "Organization for Physiological Homeostasis," in *Physiological Reviews,* vol. 9 (July 1929), pp. 399–431.

CANNON, WALTER B., *The Wisdom of the Body* (New York: W. W. Norton, 1939).

ČAPEK, KAREL, *R.U.R. (Rossum's Universal Robots)* (Garden City, N.Y.: Doubleday, Page and Co., 1923).

CARNAP, RUDOLF, "Foundations of Logic and Mathematics," in Neurath, Otto; Carnap, Rudolf; and Morris, Charles, eds., *Foundations of the Unity of Science: Toward an International Encyclopedia of Unified Science,* vol. 1 (Chicago: University of Chicago Press, 1939*a*; bound ed., 1969), pp. 139–214.

CARNAP, RUDOLF, "Logical Foundations of the Unity of Science," in Neurath, Otto; Carnap, Rudolf; and Morris, Charles, eds., *Foundations of the Unity of Science: Toward an International Encyclopedia of Unified Science,* vol. 1 (Chicago: University of Chicago Press, 1939*b*; bound ed., 1969).

CARNAP, RUDOLF, *Logical Foundations of Probability* (Chicago: University of Chicago Press, 1950).

CARNAP, RUDOLF, AND BAR-HILLEL, YEHOSHUA, *An Outline of a Theory of Semantic Information* (Cambridge, Mass.: MIT Research Laboratory of Electronics Technical Report, 1952). Reprinted as chap. 15 in Bar-Hillel, *Language and Information: Selected Essays on Their Theory and Application* (Reading, Mass.: Addison–Wesley, 1964).

CARROLL, C. EDWARD, *The Professionalization of Education for Librarianship* (Metuchen, N.J.: Scarecrow Press, 1970).

CASTI, JOHN L., *Connectivity, Complexity, and Catastrophe in Large-Scale Systems* (New York: Wiley, 1979).

Cataloguing Rules: Author and Title Entries. Compiled by Committees of The Library Association and of the American Library Association (London: The Library Association, 1908).

ČERNÝ, J., AND BRUNOVSKÝ, P., "A Note on Information Without Probability," in *Information and Control*, vol. 25 (June 1974), pp. 134–144.

CHAITIN, GREGORY J., "Algorithmic Information Theory," in *IBM Journal of Research and Development*, vol. 21 (July 1977), pp. 350–359.

CHANDLER, ROBERT E.; HERMAN, ROBERT; AND MONTROLL, ELLIOTT W., "Traffic Dynamics: Studies in Car Following," in *Operations Research*, vol. 6 (Mar./Apr., 1958), pp. 165–184.

CHASE, WILLIAM G., AND SIMON, HERBERT A., "The Mind's Eye in Chess," in Chase, William G., ed., *Visual Information Processing*, proceedings of the Eighth Symposium on Cognition, held [at Carnegie-Mellon University, Pittsburgh] in 1972 (New York: Academic Press, 1973), pp. 215–281.

CHECKLAND, PETER, *Systems Thinking, Systems Practice* (Chichester, England: Wiley, 1981).

CHERRY, COLIN, "A History of the Theory of Information," in The *Proceedings of The Institution of Electrical Engineers*, vol. 98 (Sept. 1951), pp. 383–393. Reprinted with minor changes as "The Communication of Information (An Historical Review)," in *American Scientist*, vol. 40 (Oct. 1952), pp. 640–664.

CHERRY, COLIN, ed., *Information Theory*, proceedings of the Third Symposium on Information Theory, held [in London] 1955 (London: Butterworths, 1956).

CHERRY, COLIN, *On Human Communication: A Review, A Survey, and A Criticism* (Cambridge, Mass.: MIT Press, 1957; 2nd ed., 1966).

CHERRY, COLIN, ed., *Information Theory*, proceedings of the Fourth Symposium on Information Theory, held [at the Royal Institution, London] Aug. 29–Sept. 2, 1960 (London: Butterworths, 1961).

CHOMSKY, NOAM, *Syntactic Structures* (The Hague, Netherlands: Mouton, 1957).

CHOMSKY, NOAM, "A Review of *Verbal Behavior* by B. F. Skinner," in *Language*, vol. 35 (1959), pp. 26–58.

CHOMSKY, NOAM, "Formal Properties of Grammar," in Luce, Robert Duncan; Bush, Robert R.; and Galanter, Eugene, eds., *Handbook of Mathematical Psychology*, vol. 2 (New York: Wiley, 1963), chap. 12, pp. 323–418.

CHOMSKY, NOAM, *Aspects of the Theory of Syntax* (Cambridge, Mass.: MIT Press, 1965).

CHOMSKY, NOAM, *Cartesian Linguistics: A Chapter in the History of Rationalist Thought* (New York: Harper and Row, 1st ed., 1966).

CHOMSKY, NOAM, *Language and Mind* (New York: Harcourt, Brace, and World, 1968; enlarged ed., Harcourt, Brace, Jovanovich, 1972).

CHOMSKY, NOAM, "Conditions on Transformations," in Anderson, Stephen R., and Kiparsky, Paul, eds., *A Festschrift to Morris Halle* (Englewood Cliffs, N.J.: Prentice-Hall, 1973).

CHOMSKY, NOAM, *The Logical Structure of Linguistic Theory* (New York: Plenum Press, 1975a).

CHOMSKY, NOAM, *Reflections on Language* (New York: Pantheon, 1975*b*).

CHOMSKY, NOAM, "On Cognitive Structures and Their Development: A Reply to Piaget," in Piatelli-Palmarini, Massimo, ed., *Language and Learning: The Debate between Jean Piaget and Noam Chomsky* (Cambridge, Mass.: Harvard University Press, 1980*a*), pp. 35–54.

CHOMSKY, NOAM, *Rules and Representations* (New York: Columbia University Press, 1980*b*).

CHOMSKY, NOAM, *Lectures on Government and Binding* (Dordrecht, Holland: Foris, 1981).

CHOMSKY, NOAM, *Some Concepts and Consequences of the Theory of Government and Binding,* Linguistic Inquiry Monograph 6 (Cambridge, Mass.: MIT Press, 1982).

CHOMSKY, NOAM, AND HALLE, MORRIS, *The Sound Pattern of English* (New York: Harper and Row, 1968).

CHOMSKY, NOAM, AND MILLER, GEORGE A., "Introduction to the Formal Analysis of Natural Languages," in Luce, Robert Duncan; Bush, Robert R.; and Galanter, Eugene, eds., *Handbook of Mathematical Psychology,* vol. 2 (New York: Wiley, 1963), chap. 11, pp. 269–321.

CHURCH, ALONZO, *The Calculi of Lambda-Conversion* (Princeton, N.J.: Princeton University Press, 1941).

CHURCHLAND, PAUL M., *Scientific Realism and the Plasticity of Mind* (Cambridge: Cambridge University Press, 1979).

CHURCHMAN, C. WEST, *Predictions and Optimal Decision—Philosophical Issues of Science of Values* (Englewood Cliffs, N.J.: Prentice-Hall, 1961).

CHURCHMAN, C. WEST, "An Approach to General Systems Theory," in Mesarović, Mihajlo D., ed., *Views on General Systems Theory* (New York: Wiley, 1964), pp. 173–176.

CHURCHMAN, C. WEST, *A Challenge to Reason* (New York: McGraw-Hill, 1968*a*).

CHURCHMAN, C. WEST, *The Systems Approach* (New York: Dell, 1968*b*).

CHURCHMAN, C. WEST, *The Design of Inquiring Systems* (New York: Basic Books, 1971).

CHURCHMAN, C. WEST, *The Systems Approach and Its Enemies* (New York: Basic Books, 1979).

CHURCHWELL, CHARLES D., *The Shaping of American Library Education* (Chicago: American Library Association, 1975), ACRL Monograph 36.

CLARK, MARGARET, AND FISKE, SUSAN, eds., *Affect and Cognition* (Hillsdale, N. J.: Lawrence Erlbaum, 1982).

COASE, RONALD, "The Problem of Social Cost," in *Journal of Law and Economics,* vol. 3 (1960), pp. 1–14.

COATES, J. F., "Technology Assessment—Tool Kit," in *Chemical Technology,* vol. 6, no. 6 (1976), pp. 272–383.

COHEN, MORRIS R., *Reason and Nature: An Essay on the Meaning of Scientific Method* (New York: Harcourt, 1931).

COHEN, PAUL R., "Models of Cognition: Overview," in Cohen, Paul R., and Feigenbaum, Edward A., eds., *The Handbook of Artificial Intelligence,* vol. 3 (Los Altos, Calif.: William Kaufmann, 1982), pp. 1–10.

COLLINS, ALLAN, "Why Cognitive Science?" in *Cognitive Science,* vol. 1 (Jan. 1977), pp. 1–2.

CONVERSE, ALVIN O., "The Use of Uncertainty in a Simultaneous Search," in *Operations Research,* vol. 15 (Nov./Dec. 1967), pp. 1088–1095.

COPINGER, WALTER ARTHUR, "On the Necessity for the Formation of a Bibliographical Society of the United Kingdom and Suggestions as to its Operations," in The *Library,* vol. 4 (Jan./Dec. 1892), pp. 1–7.

COSTA, SERPIL DE, "Foundation and Development of IFLA, 1926–1939," in The *Library Quarterly,* vol. 52 (Jan. 1982), pp. 41–58.

COSTANZA, ROBERT, "Embodied Energy and Economic Valuation," in *Science,* vol. 210 (12 Dec., 1980), p. 1224.

COUNELIS, JAMES S., "Cybernetics and General Systems—A Unitary Science (Information and the Unity of General Systems Theory and Cybernetics)," in *Kybernetes,* vol. 8 (1979), pp. 25–32.

COWAN, W. MAXWELL, ed., *Annual Review of Neuroscience* (Palo Alto, Calif.: Annual Reviews Inc., 1981).

CRAIK, KENNETH J. W., *The Nature of Explanation* (Cambridge: Cambridge University Press, 1943).

CROCE, BENEDETTO, "The Task of Logic," in *Encyclopaedia of the Philosophical Sciences, Vol. 1: Logic* (London: Macmillan, 1913).

CUATRECASAS, PEDRO, AND GREAVES, MELVYN F., eds., *Receptors and Recognition,* series A, vols. 1, 2 (London: Chapman and Hall, 1976).

CYERT, RICHARD M., AND MARCH, JAMES G., *A Behavioral Theory of the Firm* (Englewood Cliffs, N. J.: Prentice-Hall, 1963).

CYRANSKI, JOHN F., "Measurement, Theory, and Information," in *Information and Control,* vol. 41 (June 1979), pp. 275–304.

DAVIS, MARTIN D., ed., *The Undecideable: Basic Papers on Undecideable Propositions, Unsolvable Problems, and Uncomputable Functions* (Hewlett, N. Y.: Raven Press, 1965).

DAVIS, RANDALL, "Applications of Meta-Level Knowledge to the Construction, Maintenance, and Use of Large Knowledge Bases," in Davis, Randall, and Lenat, Douglas, *Knowledge-Based Systems in Artificial Intelligence* (New York: McGraw-Hill, 1982), pp. 229–390.

DAVIS, RANDALL, AND LENAT, DOUGLAS, *Knowledge-Based Systems in Artificial Intelligence* (New York: McGraw-Hill, 1982).

DAVIS, WATSON, "Regarding the Name: Documentation Institute of Science Service" (Washington, D.C.: Documentation Institute of Science Service, 11 July 1935), mimeographed.

DAWKINS, RICHARD, *The Selfish Gene* (New York and London: Oxford University Press, 1976).

DAY, RICHARD H., "A Microeconomic Model of Business Growth, Decay and Cycles," in *Unternehmensfusching* Band 11, Heft 1 (1967), pp. 1–20.

DAY, RICHARD H., "Adaptive Processes and Economic Theory," in Day, Richard H., and Groves, Theodore, eds., *Adaptive Economic Models,* proceedings of a Symposium on Adaptive Economics, held [at the University of Wisconsin, Madison] Oct. 21–23, 1974 (New York: Academic Press, 1975).

DAY, RICHARD H., "Dynamic Systems and Epochal Change," in Sabloff, Jeremy A., ed., *Simulations in Archeology* (Albuquerque: University of New Mexico Press, 1981*a*).

DAY, RICHARD H., "Unstable Economic Systems," in *Economic Notes*, vol. 10, no. 3 (Siena, Italy: Monte dei Pasche di Siena, 1981), pp. 3–15.

DAY, RICHARD H., "Chaos in Recursive Economics," in *Journal of Economic Behavior and Organization* (forthcoming 1983).

DAY, RICHARD H., AND CIGNO, A., *Modelling Economic Changes: The Recursive Programming Approach* (Amsterdam: North-Holland, 1978).

DEBONS, ANTHONY; KING, DONALD W.; MANSFIELD, UNA; AND SHIREY, DONALD L., *The Information Professional: Survey of an Emerging Field* (New York: Marcel Dekker, 1981).

DE BROGLIE, LOUIS [see "Broglie, Louis de"].

DE COSTA, SERPIL [see "Costa, Serpil de"].

DE GROOT, ADRIAAN D. [see "Groot, Adriaan D. de"].

DE MOIVRE, ABRAHAM [see "Moivre, Abraham de"].

DEMSKI, JOEL S., "Information Improvement Bounds," in *Journal of Accounting Research* (spring 1972).

DEMSKI, JOEL S., *Information Analysis* (Reading, Mass.: Addison-Wesley, 1972; 2nd ed., 1980).

DEMSKI, JOEL S., AND FELTHAM, GERALD A., "Forecast Evaluation," in The *Accounting Review,* vol. 47 (July 1972), pp. 533–548.

DEMSKI, JOEL S., AND FELTHAM, GERALD A., *Cost Determination—A Conceptual Approach* (Ames: Iowa State University Press, 1976).

DEMSKI, JOEL S., AND FELTHAM, GERALD A., "References in Information Economics," Working Paper, Faculty of Commerce, University of British Columbia, Vancouver, B.C., 1981.

DEMSKI, JOEL S., AND FELTHAM, GERALD A., *Economic Returns to Accounting Information in a Multi-Person Setting* (preliminary title; forthcoming in the series Studies in Accounting Research of the American Accounting Association, Sarasota, Florida: AAA, 1983).

DENBIGH, KENNETH G., *The Principles of Chemical Equilibrium, with Applications in Chemistry and Chemical Engineering* (Cambridge: Cambridge University Press, 1955).

DENNETT, DANIEL C., *Brainstorms: Philosophic Essays on Mind and Psychology* (Montgomery, Vt.: Bradford Books/MIT Press, 1978*a*).

DENNETT, DANIEL C., "Intentional Systems," in Dennett, Daniel C., *Brainstorms: Philosophic Essays on Mind and Psychology* (Montgomery, Vt.: Bradford Books/MIT Press, 1978*b*), pp. 3–22.

DENNING, PETER J., "Working Sets Past and Present," in *IEEE Transactions on Software Engineering,* vol. 6 (Jan. 1980), pp. 64–84.

DENNIS, JACK B., AND MISUNAS, DAVID P., "A Preliminary Architecture for a Basic Data-Flow Processor," in *Proceedings of the Second Annual Symposium on Computer Architecture,* held [in Houston] by the IEEE Computer Society and the Association for Computing Machinery, in cooperation with the University of Houston, Jan. 20–22, 1975 (New York: Institute of Electrical and Electronics Engineers, 1975), pp. 126–132.

DESTUTT DE TRACY, ANTOINE LOUIS CLAUDE, *Projet d'éléments d'idéologie à l'usage des écoles centrales de la République francaise,* 4 vols., Paris, an IX [1801]–1818 (Paris: 3rd ed., Courcier, 1817).

DEUTSCH, KARL, "The Nerves of Government," in *General Systems Yearbook,* vol. 21 (1963), pp. 125–176.

DEV, PARVATI, "Perception of Depth Surfaces in Random-Dot Stereograms: A Neural Model," in *International Journal of Man-Machine Studies,* vol. 7 (July 1975), pp. 511–528.

DEWEY, JOHN, *The Quest for Certainty: A Study of the Relation of Knowledge and Action* [the Gifford Lectures, University of Edinburgh] (New York: Minton, Balch, and Co., 1929).

DEWEY, MELVIL, *Classification and Subject Index for a Library* (Amherst, Mass.: 1876; 18th ed., Lake Placid Club, New York: Forest Press, 1971).

DICKSON, GARY R.; SENN, JAMES A,; AND CHERVANY, NORMAN L., "Research in Management Information Systems: The Minnesota Experiments," in *Management Science,* vol. 23 (May 1977), pp. 913–923.

DIJKSTRA, EDSGER W., "Notes on Structured Programming," in Dahl, Ole-Johan; Dijkstra, Edsger W.; and Hoare, C. A. R., *Structured Programming* (London and New York: Academic Press, 1972).

DIJKSTRA, EDSGER W., *A Discipline of Programming* (Englewood Cliffs, N. J.: Prentice-Hall, 1976).

DOLAN, F. T., "The Role of the Information Scientist," in *International Journal of Man-Machine Studies,* vol. 1 (1969), pp. 39–50.

DOWDS, JOHN P., "Application of Information Theory in Establishing Oil Field Trends," in Parks, George A., ed., *Computers in the Mineral Industries* (Stanford, Calif.: School of Earth Sciences, Stanford University, 1964).

DRAY, WILLIAM H., "Holism and Individualism in History and Social Science," in *Encyclopedia of Philosophy,* vol. 4 (New York: Macmillan and Free Press, 1967), pp. 53–58.

DRESHER, B. ELAN, AND HORNSTEIN, NORBERT, "On Some Supposed Contributions of Artificial Intelligence to the Scientific Study of Language," in *Cognition,* vol. 4 (Dec. 1976), pp. 321–398.

DRESHER, B. ELAN, AND HORNSTEIN, NORBERT, "Reply to Schank and Wilensky," in *Cognition,* vol. 5 (June 1977a), pp. 147–149.

DRESHER, B. ELAN, AND HORNSTEIN, NORBERT, "Reply to Winograd," in *Cognition,* vol. 5 (Dec. 1977b), pp. 379–392.

DREYFUS, HUBERT L., *What Computers Can't Do: A Critique of Artificial Reason* (New York: Harper and Row, 1972; rev. paperback ed., 1979).

DRIESCH, HANS, *The History and Theory of Vitalism* (London: Macmillan, 1914). Translated from the German.

DUNLAP, KNIGHT, *The Elements of Scientific Psychology* (St. Louis: C. V. Mosby Company, 1922).

DWORKIN, RONALD, *Taking Rights Seriously* (Cambridge, Mass.: Harvard University Press, 1978).

ECKHORN, R., AND POPEL, B., "Rigorous and Extended Application of Information

Theory to Afferent Visual Systems of a Cat," in *Kybernetik*, vol. 16, no. 4 (1974), pp. 191–200.

EDELMAN, GERALD M., "Group Selection as the Basis for Higher Brain Function," in Schmitt, Francis O.; Worden, Frederic G.; Adelman, George; and Dennis, Stephen G., eds., *The Organization of the Cerebral Cortex*, proceedings of a colloquium held [at Woods Hole, Mass.] (Cambridge, Mass.: MIT Press, 1981).

EDELMAN, GERALD M., AND MOUNTCASTLE, VERNON B., *The Mindful Brain: Cortical Organization and the Group-Selective Theory of Higher Brain Functions* (Cambridge, Mass.: MIT Press, 1978).

EGAN, MARGARET E., AND SHERA, JESSE H., "Foundations of a Theory of Bibliography," in The *Library Quarterly*, vol. 22 (Apr. 1951), pp. 125–137.

EHRLICH, PAUL, *The Collected Papers of Paul Ehrlich*, 2 vols., comp. and ed. F. Himmelweit (London and New York: Pergamon Press, 1956).

EIGEN, MANFRED, "Self-Organization of Matter and the Evolution of Biological Macromolecules," in *Naturwissenschaften*, vol. 58 (Oct. 1971), pp. 465–528.

EIGEN, MANFRED AND SCHUSTER, PETER, "The Hypercycle: A Principle of Natural Self-Organization. Part A: Emergence of the Hypercycle," in *Naturwissenschaften*, vol. 64 (Nov. 1977), pp. 541–565.

EIGEN, MANFRED, AND SCHUSTER, PETER, "The Hypercycle: A Principle of Natural Self-Organization. Part B: The Abstract Hypercycle," in *Naturwissenschaften*, vol. 65 (Jan. 1978*a*), pp. 7–41.

EIGEN, MANFRED, AND SCHUSTER, PETER, "The Hypercycle: A Principle of Natural Self-Organization. Part C: The Realistic Hypercycle," in *Naturwissenschaften*, vol. 65 (July 1978*b*), pp. 341–369.

ELIAS, PETER, "Coding and Information Theory," a paper written in 1959, reprinted in Evans, C. R., and Robertson, A. D. J., eds., *Cybernetics* (Baltimore: University Park Press, 1968), pp. 253–266.

ELIAS, PETER, AND FLOWER, RICHARD A., "The Complexity of Some Simple Retrieval Problems," in *Journal of the Association for Computing Machinery*, vol. 22 (July 1975), pp. 367–379.

EL SAYED, Y., *On the Use of Exergy and Thermoeconomics in the Design of Desalination Plants* (Hanover, N.H.: Thayer School of Engineering, Dartmouth College, Jan. 1968).

EL SAYED, Y., AND APLENC, A., *Application of the Thermoeconomic Approach to the Analysis and Optimization of a Vapor Compression Desalting System* (Hanover, N.H.: Thayer School of Engineering, Dartmouth College, Sept. 1968).

EL SAYED, Y., AND EVANS, ROBERT B., *Thermoeconomics and the Design of Heat Systems* (Hanover, N.H.: Thayer School of Engineering, Dartmouth College, Oct. 1968).

EMERY, FRED E., *Systems Thinking* (Harmondsworth, England: Penguin Books, 1969).

EMMET, BORIS, AND JEUCK, JOHN E., *Catalogues and Counters: A History of Sears, Roebuck, and Company* (Chicago: University of Chicago Press, 1950).

EMONDS, JOSEPH E., "Root and Structure Preserving Transformations" (Ph.D. diss., Massachusetts Institute of Technology, 1970).

ERMENTROUT, G. B., AND COWAN, JACK D., "Large-Scale Spatially Organized Activity in Neural Nets," in *SIAM Journal on Applied Mathematics,* vol. 38 (Feb. 1980), pp. 1–21.

ERNST, GEORGE W., AND NEWELL, ALLEN, *GPS: A Case Study in Generality and Problem Solving* (New York: Academic Press, 1969).

EVANS, ROBERT B., "Basic Relationships Among Entropy, Exergy, Energy, and Availability," in Spiegler, K. S., ed., *Principles of Desalination* (New York: Academic Press, 1966), pp. 44–66.

EVANS, THOMAS G., "A Program for the Solution of Geometric-Analogy Intelligence Test Questions," in Minsky, Marvin L., ed., *Semantic Information Processing* (Cambridge, Mass.: MIT Press, 1968), pp. 271–354.

EWERT, JÖRG-PETER, *Neuroethology: An Introduction to the Neurophysiological Fundamentals of Behavior* (Berlin and New York: Springer-Verlag, 1980).

FALB, PETER L., "Linear Systems and Invariants" (Lecture Notes, Control Group, Lund University, Sweden, 1974).

FAMA, EUGENE F., "Agency Problems and the Theory of the Firm," in *Journal of Political Economy,* vol. 88 (Apr. 1980), pp. 288–307.

FANO, ROBERT M., *Transmission of Information* (Cambridge, Mass., and New York: MIT Press and Wiley, 1961).

FARRADANE, JASON E. L., "The Institute: The First Twelve Years," in The *Information Scientist,* vol. 4 (Dec. 1970), pp. 143–151.

FAURRE, P., "Réalisations markoviennes de processus stationnaires," *Research Report No. 13, INRIA* (Rocquencourt, France: Institut National de Recherche en Informatique et en Automatique, 1973).

FAURRE, P.; CLERGET, M.; AND GERMAIN, F., *Opérateurs rationnels positifs: Application à l'hyperstabilité et aux processus aléatoires* (Paris: Dunod, 1979).

FEIGENBAUM, EDWARD A., "The Simulation of Verbal Learning Behavior," in *Extending Man's Intellect,* proceedings of the Western Joint Computer Conference, held [in Los Angeles] by the Institute of Radio Engineers, the American Institute of Electrical Engineers, and the Association for Computing Machinery, May 9–11, 1961, vol. 19, pp. 121–132.

FEIGENBAUM, EDWARD A., "Artificial Intelligence: Themes in the Second Decade," in Morrell, A. J. H., ed., *Information Processing 68,* proceedings of the IFIP Congress 1968, organized by the International Federation for Information Processing [Edinburgh, Scotland] Aug. 5–10, 1968 (Amsterdam: North-Holland, 1969), pp. 1008–1024.

FEIGENBAUM, EDWARD A., "The Art of Artificial Intelligence, I: Themes and Case Studies of Knowledge Engineering," in *IJCAI-77: Proceedings of the Fifth International Joint Conference on Artificial Intelligence,* held [at the Massachusetts Institute of Technology, Cambridge, Mass.] by the International Joint Conference on Artificial Intelligence, Aug. 22–25, 1977 (Pittsburgh: Carnegie-Mellon University), vol. 2, pp. 1014–1029.

FEIGENBAUM, EDWARD A., AND FELDMAN, JULIAN, eds., *Computers and Thought* (New York: McGraw-Hill, 1963).

FEIGENBAUM, MITCHELL J., "Universal Behavior in Nonlinear Systems," in *Los Alamos Science,* vol. 1 (summer 1980), pp. 4–27.

FEINSTEIN, AMIEL, *Foundations of Information Theory* (New York: McGraw-Hill, 1958).

FELDMAN, JEROME A., AND SUTHERLAND, WILLIAM R., eds., "Rejuvenating Experimental Computer Science—A Report to the National Science Foundation and Others," in *Communications of the ACM,* vol. 22 (Sept. 1979), pp. 497–502.

FELDMAN, JULIAN, "Simulation of Behavior in Binary Choice Experiment," in *Extending Man's Intellect,* proceedings of the Western Joint Computer Conference, held [in Los Angeles] by the Institute of Radio Engineers, the American Institute of Electrical Engineers, and the Association for Computing Machinery, May 9–11, 1961, vol. 19, pp. 133–144.

FELTHAM, GERALD A., "The Value of Information," in The *Accounting Review,* vol. 43 (Oct. 1968), pp. 684–696.

FELTHAM, GERALD A., *Information Evaluation* (Sarasota, Florida: American Accounting Association, 1972).

FELTHAM, GERALD A., "Financial Accounting Research: Contributions of Information Economics and Agency Theory," in Mattessich, Richard, et al., *Modern Accounting Research: History, Survey, and Guide* (Vancouver, B.C.: Canadian Certified General Accountants Research Foundation, forthcoming 1984).

FIENGO, ROBERT, "Semantic Conditions on Surface Structure" (Ph.D. diss., Massachusetts Institute of Technology, 1974).

FISHER, RONALD A., "Probability Likelihood and Quantity of Information in the Logic of Uncertain Inference," in *Proceedings of the Royal Society,* series *A,* vol. 146 (Aug. 1, 1934), pp. 1–8.

FISHER, RONALD A., *The Design of Experiments* (London: Oliver and Boyd, 1935).

FLEXNER, ABRAHAM, "Is Social Work a Profession?" in *School and Society,* vol. 1 (June 1915), pp. 902–906.

FLOOD, MERRILL M., "The Systems Approach to Library Planning," in *Intellectual Foundations of Library Education,* proceedings of the Twenty-Ninth Annual Conference of the Graduate Library School (Chicago: University of Chicago Press, 1965), pp. 38–50.

FODOR, JERRY A., "Methodological Solipsism Considered as a Research Strategy in Cognitive Psychology," in The *Behavioral and Brain Sciences,* vol. 3 (Mar. 1980), pp. 63–109.

FODOR, JERRY A., *Representations: Philosophical Essays on the Foundations of Cognitive Science* (Cambridge, Mass.: Harvard University Press, 1981).

FODOR, JERRY A.; BEVER, THOMAS G.; AND GARRETT, MERRILL F., *The Psychology of Language: An Introduction to Psycholinguistics and Generative Grammar* (New York: McGraw-Hill, 1974).

FODOR, JERRY A., AND GARRETT, MERRILL F., "Some Syntactic Determinants of Sentencial Complexity," in *Perception and Psychophysics,* vol. 2 (1967), pp. 289–296.

FORRESTER, JAY W., *Industrial Dynamics* (Cambridge, Mass.: MIT Press, 1962).

FORRESTER, JAY W., *World Dynamics* (Cambridge, Mass.: Wright-Allen, 1971).

FORTE, B., AND KAMPÉ DE FÉRIET, J., "Information et probabilité," in *C. R. Acad. Sci.* [Comptes Rendus de l'Academie de Sciences (Paris)], séries *A,* vol. 265 (1967), pp. 110–114, 142–146, 350–353.

Frank, Philipp, *Philosophy of Science: The Link between Science and Philosophy* (Englewood Cliffs, N.J.: Prentice-Hall, 1957).

Frederiks, J. A. M., "Disorders of the Body Schema," in Vinken, P. J., and Bruyn, G. W., eds., *Handbook of Clinical Neurology, Disorders of Speech, Perception, and Symbolic Behavior* (Amsterdam: North-Holland, 1969–), vol. 4, pp. 207–240.

Frege, Friedrich Ludwig Gottlob, *Begriffsschrift, eine der arithmetischen nachgebildete Formelsprache des reinen Denkens* (Halle A/S, Germany: L. Nebert, 1879).

Freidin, Robert A., "Cyclicity and the Theory of Grammar," in *Linguistic Inquiry*, vol. 9 (1978), pp. 519–550.

Fried, Charles, *Right and Wrong* (Cambridge, Mass.: Harvard University Press, 1978).

Fromkin, Victoria A., et al., *Speech Errors as Linguistic Evidence* (The Hague, Netherlands: Mouton, 1973).

Fuhrman, P., "Functional Models, Factorizations, and Linear Systems"—talks given at the NATO-AMS Advanced Study Institute on Algebraic and Geometric Methods in Linear System Theory (Cambridge, Mass.: Harvard University, 1979).

Furth, Hans G., "The Operative and Figurative Aspects of Knowledge and Information," in Debons, Anthony, ed., *Information Science: Search for Identity*, proceedings of the 1972 NATO Advanced Study Institute in Information Science, held [in Seven Springs, Champion, Penn.] Aug. 12–20, 1972 (New York: Marcel Dekker, 1974), pp. 21–27.

Gabor, Dennis, "Theory of Communication," in *Journal of the Institution of Electrical Engineers*, vol. 93, no. 3 (1946), pp. 429–457.

Gallagher, Robert G., *Information Theory and Reliable Communication* (New York: Wiley, 1968).

Galvin, Thomas J., "The Challenge of Technology in the Eighties," lecture presented at Ann Arbor, University of Michigan, "Issues and Challenges of the Eighties: A Michigan Libraries Forum," 1981.

Gardner, Beatrice T., and Gardner, R. Allen, "Two-Way Communication with an Infant Chimpanzee," in Schrier, Allan M., and Stollnitz, Fred, eds., *Behavior of Non-Human Primates: Modern Research Trends*, vol. 4 (New York: Academic Press, 1971), pp. 117–184.

Garfield, Eugene; Malin, Morton V.; and Small, Henry, "Citation Data as Science Indicators," in Elkana, Yehuda, et al., eds., *Toward a Metric of Science: The Advent of Science Indicators* (New York: Wiley, 1978).

Garner, Wendell R., *Uncertainty and Structure as Psychological Concepts* (New York: Wiley, 1962).

Gatlin, Lila L., *Information Theory and the Living System* (New York: Columbia University Press, 1972).

Gauld, Alan, and Shotter, John, *Human Action and Its Psychological Investigation* (London and Boston: Routledge and Kegan Paul, 1977).

Gazis, Denos C.; Herman, Robert; and Potts, Renfrey B., "Car Following Theory of Steady-State Traffic Flow," in *Operations Research*, vol. 7 (July/Aug. 1959), pp. 499–505.

GAZZANIGA, MICHAEL S., *The Bisected Brain* (New York: Appleton-Century-Crofts, 1970).

GAZZANIGA, MICHAEL S., "1981 Nobel Prize for Physiology or Medicine," in *Science*, vol. 214 (30 Oct. 1981), pp. 517–518.

GEL'FAND, IZRAIL' MOISEEVICH; GURFINKEL', V. A.; TSETLIN, M. L.; AND SHIK, M. L., eds., *Models of the Structural-Functional Organization of Certain Biological Systems*, trans. Carol R. Beard (Cambridge, Mass.: MIT Press, 1971).

GERGELY, TAMÁS, "On the Unity Between Cybernetics and General System Theory," in *Kybernetes*, vol. 8 (1979), pp. 45–49.

GIBBS, JOSIAH WILLARD, *Elementary Principles in Statistical Mechanics: Developed with Especial Reference to the Rational Foundation of Thermodynamics* (New York: Scribners, 1902; 2nd ed. New York: Dover Publications, 1960).

GIBBS, JOSIAH WILLARD, *The Collected Works of J. Willard Gibbs*, vol. 2, chap. 2, theorem 5 (New Haven, Conn.: Yale University Press, 1948). Original publication 1906, under the title *The Scientific Papers of J. Willard Gibbs*, pp. 20–25.

GIGLEY, HELEN, *A Computational Neurolinguistic Approach to Processing Models of Sentence Comprehension: COINS Technical Report 82-9* (Amherst: University of Massachusetts at Amherst, Dept. of Computer and Information Science, 1982).

GIVOL, DAVID, "A Structural Basis for Molecular Recognition: The Antibody Case," in Cuatrecasas, Pedro, and Greaves, Melvyn F., eds., *Receptors and Recognition*, vol. 2 (London: Chapman and Hall, 1976), series *A*, pp. 1–42.

GLASS, ARNOLD L.; HOLYOAK, KEITH J.; AND SANTA, JOHN L., *Cognition* (Reading, Mass.: Addison-Wesley, 1979).

GLUSHKOV, VIKTOR MIKHAILOVICH, *Introduction to Cybernetics*, trans. by Scripta Technica Inc., (New York and London: Academic Press, 1966).

GOGUEN, JACK, "L-Fuzzy Sets," *Journal of Mathematical Analysis and Applications*, vol. 18 (Apr. 1967), pp. 145–174.

GOLDSTEIN, IRA, AND PAPERT, SEYMOUR, "Artificial Intelligence, Language, and the Study of Knowledge," in *Cognitive Science*, vol. 1 (Jan. 1977), pp. 84–124.

GOLDSTEIN, KURT, *Language and Language Disturbances: Aphasic Symptom Complexes and Their Significance for Medicine and Theory of Language* (New York: Grune and Stratton, 1948).

GOOD, IRVING J., "Weighing Evidence," in Good, Irving J., *Probability and the Weighing of Evidence* (London: Charles Griffin and Co.; New York: Hafner, 1950), chap. 6.

GOODWIN, BRIAN C., *Temporal Organization in Cells; A Dynamic Theory of Cellular Control Processes* (London and New York: Academic Press, 1963).

GORN, SAUL, "The Computer and Information Sciences: A New Basic Discipline," in *SIAM Review*, vol. 5 (Apr. 1963), pp. 150–155.

GORN, SAUL, "The Individual and Political Life of Information Systems," in Heilprin, Laurence B.; Markuson, Barbara E.; and Goodman, Frederick L., eds., *Education for Information Science*, proceedings of a symposium held at Airlie House, Virginia, 1965 (Washington, D.C.: Spartan Books, 1965), pp. 33–40.

GORN, SAUL, "The Computer and Information Sciences in the Community of Disciplines," in *Behavioral Science*, vol. 12 (Nov. 1967), pp. 433–452.

GORN, SAUL, "The Identification of the Computer and Information Sciences: Their Fundamental Semiotic Concepts and Relationships," in *Foundations of Language: International Journal of Language and Philosophy,* vol. 4 (Nov. 1968), pp. 339–372.

GREAVES, MELVYN F., "Cell Surface Receptors: A Biological Perspective," in Cuatrecasas, Pedro, and Greaves, Melvyn F., eds., *Receptors and Recognition,* vol. 1 (London: Chapman and Hall, 1976), series *A,* pp. 1–32.

GREGORY, RICHARD L., "On How So Little Information Controls So Much Behavior," in Waddington, Conrad H., ed., *Towards a Theoretical Biology, Vol. 2: Sketches,* proceedings of an IUBS Symposium (Chicago: Aldine-Atherton, 1969), pp. 236–247.

GREIBACH, SHEILA A., "Formal Languages: Origins and Directions," in *Symposium on the Foundations of Computer Science,* proceedings of the Twentieth Annual Symposium on Foundations of Computer Science, held [in San Juan, Puerto Rico] by the IEEE Computer Society's Technical Committee on Mathematical Foundations of Computing (New York: Institute of Electrical and Electronics Engineers, 1979), pp. 66–90.

GRENANDER, ULF, *Lectures in Pattern Theory, Vol. 1: Pattern Synthesis* (New York: Springer-Verlag, 1976).

GRENANDER, ULF, *Lectures in Pattern Theory, Vol. 2: Pattern Analysis* (New York: Springer-Verlag, 1978).

GROOT, ADRIAAN D. DE, *Thought and Choice in Chess* (The Hague, Netherlands: Mouton, 1965).

GROSSBERG, STEPHEN, "Adaptive Pattern Classification and Universal Recoding: I. Parallel Development and Coding of Neural Feature Detectors," in *Biological Cybernetics,* vol. 23, no. 2 (1976), pp. 121–134.

GUNDERSON, KEITH, *Mentality and Machines* (Garden City, N.Y.: Doubleday, 1971).

HABERMAS, JÜRGEN, *Toward a Rational Society: Student Protest, Science, and Politics,* trans. Jeremy J. Shapiro (Boston: Beacon Press, 1970).

HABERSTROH, CHADWICK J., "Control as an Organizational Process," in *Management Science,* vol. 6 (Jan. 1960), pp. 165–171.

HAKEN, HERMANN, *Synergetics: An Introduction: Nonequilibrium Phase Transitions and Self-Organization in Physics, Chemistry, and Biology* (Berlin and New York: Springer-Verlag, 1977; 2nd ed., 1978).

HAKEN, HERMANN, "Synergetics: Are Cooperative Phenomena Governed by Universal Principles?" in *Naturwissenschaften,* vol. 67 (Mar. 1980), pp. 121–128.

HALL, THOMAS STEELE, *Ideas of Life and Matter: Studies in the History of General Physiology 600BC–1900AD, Vol. I: From Pre-Socratic Times to the Enlightenment* (Chicago: University of Chicago Press, 1969).

HANSON, ALLEN R., AND RISEMAN, EDWARD M., eds., *Computer Vision Systems,* proceedings of a Workshop on Computer Vision Systems, held [at the University of Massachusetts, Amherst] 1977 (New York: Academic Press, 1978).

HARDIN, GARRETT, *Nature and Man's Fate* (New York: Mentor, 1961).

HARDIN, GARRETT, "The Tragedy of the Commons," in *Science,* vol. 162 (1968), p. 1243.

HARDIN, GARRETT, *Exploring New Ethics for Survival* (New York: Viking Press, 1977).

HARRIS, ZELLIG S., *Methods in Structural Linguistics* (Chicago: University of Chicago Press, 1951).

HARRIS, ZELLIG S. "Co-occurrence of Transformation in Linguistic Structure," in *Language,* vol. 33 (1957), pp. 283–340.

HARTER, STEPHEN P., " 'Information' in Every Name," in *Bulletin of the American Society for Information Science,* vol. 9 (Oct. 1982), pp. 40–41.

HARTLEY, RALPH V. L., "Transmission of Information," in *Bell System Technical Journal,* vol. 7 (July 1928), pp. 535–563.

HARTMANIS, JURIS, "Observations about the Development of Theoretical Computer Science," in *Symposium on the Foundations of Computer Science,* proceedings of the Twentieth Annual Symposium on Foundations of Computer Science, held [in San Juan, Puerto Rico] by the IEEE Computer Society's Technical Committee on Mathematical Foundations of Computing (New York: Institute of Electrical and Electronics Engineers, 1979), pp. 224–233.

HARTMANIS, JURIS, "Quo Vadimus: Computer Science in a Decade," in *Communications of the ACM,* vol. 24 (June 1981), pp. 351–369.

HAUGELAND, JOHN, "The Nature and Plausibility of Cognitivism," in The *Behavioral and Brain Sciences,* vol. 1 (June 1978), pp. 215–260.

HAYEK, FRIEDRICH A., "The Counter-Revolution of Science," in *Economica,* N.S. vol. 8 (1941). Reprinted in *The Counter-Revolution of Science* (Glencoe, Ill.: The Free Press, 1952; also Indianapolis: Liberty Press, 1979).

HAYEK, FRIEDRICH A., "Notes on the Evolution of Systems of Rules of Conduct," in *Studies in Philosophy, Politics, and Economics* (Chicago: University of Chicago Press, 1967).

HAYEK, FRIEDRICH A., *Law, Legislation, and Liberty, Vol. I: Rules and Order* (Chicago: University of Chicago Press, 1973).

HAYES, PATRICK J., "Some Comments on Sir James Lighthill's Report on Artificial Intelligence," in *AISB Study Group European Newsletter,* Issue 14 (July 1973), pp. 36–53.

HAYES, PATRICK J., "The Naive Physics Manifesto," in Michie, Donald, ed., *Expert Systems in a Microelectronic Age* (Edinburgh: Edinburgh University Press, 1979), pp. 463–502.

HAYES, ROBERT M., "Information Science in Librarianship," in *Libri,* vol. 19, no. 3 (1969), pp. 216–236.

HAZEWINKEL, M., "Moduli and Canonical Forms for Linear Dynamical Systems II: The Topological Case," in *Mathematical Systems Theory,* vol. 10 (1977), pp. 363–385.

HAZEWINKEL, M., AND KALMAN, RUDOLF E., "On Invariants, Canonical Forms and Moduli for Linear, Constant, Finite Dimensional, Dynamical Systems," in *Proceedings of the CNR-CISM Symposium on Algebraic System Theory,* held [at Udine] 1975 (Heidelberg, Germany: Springer-Verlag, 1976), pp. 48–60.

HEILPRIN, LAURENCE B., "Operational Definitions," in Debons, Anthony, ed., *Information Science: Search for Identity,* proceedings of the 1972 NATO Advanced Study Institute in Information Science, held [in Seven Springs, Champion, Penn.] Aug. 12–20, 1972 (New York: Marcel Dekker, 1974), pp. 115–138.

HELD, RICHARD; LEIBOWITZ, HERSCHEL W.; AND TEUBER, HANS-LUKAS, eds., *Hand-*

book of Sensory Physiology, Vol. VIII: Perception (Berlin, Heidelberg, and New York: Springer-Verlag, 1978).

HEMPEL, CARL G., "Fundamentals of Concept Formation in Empirical Science," in Neurath, Otto; Carnap, Rudolf; and Morris, Charles, eds., *Foundations of the Unity of Science: Toward an International Encyclopedia of Unified Science,* vol. 2 (Chicago: University of Chicago Press, 1939; bound ed., 1969), pp. 651–746.

HEMPEL, CARL G., *Philosophy of Natural Science* (Chicago: Aldine-Atherton, 1963).

HERMAN, E. EDWARD, AND KUHN, ALFRED, *Collective Bargaining and Labor Relations* (Englewood Cliffs, N.J.: Prentice-Hall, 1981).

HERMAN, ROBERT, AND MONTROLL, ELLIOTT W., "Some Statistical Observations from a 75 Year Run of Sears Roebuck Catalogues," in Landman, Uzi, ed., *Statistical Mechanics and Statistical Methods in Theory and Application: A Tribute to Elliott W. Montroll,* proceedings of a Symposium on Statistical Mechanics and Statistical Methods in Theory and Research, held [at the University of Rochester, N.Y.] Nov. 4, 1976 (New York: Plenum Press, 1977), pp. 785–803.

HERMAN, ROBERT; MONTROLL, ELLIOTT W.; POTTS, RENFREY B.; AND ROTHERY, RICHARD W., "Traffic Dynamics: Analysis of Stability in Car Following," in *Operations Research,* vol. 7 (Jan./Feb. 1959), pp. 86–106.

HERMANN, ROBERT T., AND MARTIN, CLYDE F., "Applications of Algebraic Geometry to System Theory, Part I," in *IEEE Transactions on Automatic Control,* vol. AC-22 (Feb. 1977), pp. 19–25.

HESSE, HERMANN, *Magister Ludi (Das Glasperlenspeil)* [the Nobel Prize novel], trans. Mervyn Savill (New York: Holt, 1949).

HICK, W. EDMUND, "On the Rate of Gain of Information," in *Quarterly Journal of Experimental Psychology,* vol. 4 (Feb. 1952), pp. 11–26.

HILGARD, ERNEST R., "Pain Perception in Man," in Held, Richard; Leibowitz, Herschel W.; and Teuber, Hans-Lukas, eds., *Handbook of Sensory Physiology, Vol. VIII: Perception* (Berlin, Heidelberg, and New York: Springer-Verlag, 1978), pp. 849–875.

HILGARD, ERNEST R., AND BOWER, GORDON H., *Theories of Learning* (New York: Appleton-Century-Crofts, 1948; 4th ed., 1975).

HILLMAN, DONALD J., "Knowledge Transfer Systems," in Weiss, Edward C., ed., *The Many Faces of Information Science* (Boulder, Colo.: Westview Press, 1977), pp. 75–103.

HILLMAN, JAMES, *The Myth of Analysis: Three Essays in Archetypal Psychology* (Evanston, Ill.: Northwestern University Press, 1972).

HILTON, RONALD W., "The Determinants of Information Value: Synthesizing Some General Results," in *Management Science,* vol. 27 (Jan. 1981), pp. 57–64.

HINTON, G. E., "Shape Representation in Parallel Systems," in *Proceedings of the Seventh International Joint Conference on Artificial Intelligence* [Vancouver, B.C., 1981], pp. 1088–1096.

HIRSHLEIFER, JACK, AND RILEY, JOHN G., "The Analytics of Uncertainty and Information—An Expository Survey," in *Journal of Economic Literature,* vol. 17 (Dec. 1979), pp. 1375–1421.

HOBBES, THOMAS, *Leviathan, or, The Matter, Form and Power of a Commonwealth Ecclesiastical and Civil* (London: Andrew Cooke, 1651).

HOFSTADTER, DOUGLAS R., *Gödel, Escher, Bach: an Eternal Golden Braid* (New York: Basic Books, 1979).

HOFSTADTER, DOUGLAS R., "Metamagical Themas: How Might Analogy, the Core of Human Thinking, be Understood by Computers?," in *Scientific American,* Sept. 1981, p. 18.

HOFSTADTER, DOUGLAS R., *Who Shoves Whom Around Inside the Careenium?* (Bloomington: Indiana University Computer Science Department Technical Report No. 130, July 1982*a*; forthcoming in *Synthese*).

HOFSTADTER, DOUGLAS R., "Metamagical Themas: Can Inspiration Be Mechanized?" in *Scientific American,* Sept. 1982*b*, p. 16.

HOFSTADTER, DOUGLAS R., "Metamagical Themas: On Variations on a Theme as the Essence of Imagination," in *Scientific American,* Oct. 1982*c*, p. 20.

HOFSTADTER, DOUGLAS R., *The Tumult of Inner Voices* (forthcoming, Southern Utah State College, 1982*d*).

HOFSTADTER, DOUGLAS R.; CLOSSMAN, GRAY A.; AND MEREDITH, MARSHA J., *Shakespeare's Plays Weren't Written by Him, But by Someone Else of the Same Name: An Essay on Intensionality and Frame-Based Knowledge Representation Systems* (Bloomington: Indiana University Computer Science Department Technical Report No. 96, July 1980).

HOFSTADTER, DOUGLAS R., AND DENNETT, DANIEL C., eds., *The Mind's I: Fantasies and Reflections of Self and Soul* (New York: Basic Books, 1981).

HOLSTROM, BENGT R., "Moral Hazard and Observability," in *Bell Journal of Economics,* vol. 10 (spring 1979), pp. 74–91.

HOLZNER, BURKART, AND MARX, JOHN H., *Knowledge Application: The Knowledge System in Society* (Boston: Allyn and Bacon, 1979).

HOMANS, GEORGE C., *The Nature of Social Change* (New York: Harcourt, Brace, and World, 1967).

HOOS, IDA R., *Systems Analysis in Public Policy: A Critique* (Berkeley: University of California Press, 1972).

HOPCROFT, JOHN E., AND ULLMAN, JEFFREY D., *Introduction to Automata Theory, Languages, and Computation* (Reading, Mass.: Addison-Wesley, 1979).

HOPF, EBERHARD, "Abzweigung einer periodischen Lösung von einer Stationären Lösung eines Differentzialsystems," in *Berichte über die Verhandlungen Sächsischen Akademie der Wissenschaften zu Leipzig,* Mathematisch-Naturwissenschaftliche Klasse, vol. 95 (1943), pp. 3–22.

HOWARD, RONALD A., "Information Value Theory," in *IEEE Transactions on Systems Science and Cybernetics,* vol. SSC-2 (Aug. 1966), pp. 22–26.

HUME, DAVID, *Dialogues Concerning Natural Religion* (1779), in Green, T. H., and Grose, T. H., eds., *A Treatise on Human Nature* (London: Longmans, Green, and Coy., new ed., 1878, vol. II), pp. 380–468; reprinted in *The Empiricists* (Garden City, N.Y.: Doubleday, 1961).

I Ching, or Book of Changes, trans. Richard Wilhelm and Cary F. Baynes (Princeton, N.J.: Princeton University Press, Bollingen Series 19, 1951).

IEEE Transactions on Information Theory (New York: Institute of Electrical and Electronics Engineers, 1954, 1956).

INGARDEN, R., AND URBANIK, K., "Information Without Probability," in *Colloquium Mathematicum,* vol. 9 (1962), pp. 131–149.

INSTITUTE OF RADIO ENGINEERS, *IRE Transactions on Information Theory,* vol. IT-1 (New York: IRE Professional Group on Information Theory, Sept., 1954).

INSTITUTE OF RADIO ENGINEERS, *IRE Transactions on Information Theory,* vol. IT-2 (New York: IRE Professional Group on Information Theory, Sept. 1956).

ITAMI, HIROYUKI, *Adaptive Behavior: Management Control and Information Analysis* (Sarasota, Florida: American Accounting Association, 1977).

JACKENDOFF, RAY S., *Semantic Interpretation in Generative Grammar* (Cambridge, Mass.: MIT Press, 1972).

JACKSON OF BURNLEY, WILLIS JACKSON, BARON, ed., *Proceedings* of Symposium on Information Theory, held [at the Royal Society, London] 1950 (London: Ministry of Supply, 1950).

JACKSON OF BURNLEY, WILLIS JACKSON, BARON, ed., *Communication Theory,* papers read at a symposium on "Applications of Communication Theory," held [at the Institution of Electrical Engineers, London] Sept. 22–26, 1952 (London: Butterworths, 1953).

JACOB, FRANÇOIS, *La logique du vivant: Une histoire de l'hérédité* (Paris: Gallimard, 1971), trans. by Betty E. Spillmann as *The Logic of Living Systems* (London: Allen Lane, 1974).

JAKOBSON, ROMAN, *Selected Writings,* vol. 1: *Phonological Studies* (The Hague, Netherlands: Mouton, 1962).

JAKOBSON, ROMAN, *Selected Writings,* vol. 2: *Word and Language* (The Hague, Netherlands: Mouton, 1971).

JAMISON, DEAN, "Bayesian Information Usage," in Hintikka, Jaako, and Suppes, Patrick, eds., *Information and Inference* (Dordrecht, Holland: Reidel, 1970), pp. 28–57.

JANTSCH, ERICH, *The Self-Organizing Universe; Scientific and Human Implications of the Emerging Paradigm of Evolution* (Oxford, England: Pergamon Press, 1980).

JASPERS, KARL, *The Future of Mankind,* trans. E. B. Ashton (Chicago: Chicago University Press, 1961).

JAYNES, EDWIN T., "Information Theory and Statistical Mechanics," in The *Physical Review,* vol. 106, 2nd series (May 1957a), pp. 620–630.

JAYNES, EDWIN T., "Information Theory and Statistical Mechanics," in The *Physical Review,* vol. 108, 2nd series (Oct. 1957b), pp. 171–190.

JAYNES, EDWIN T., "Note on Unique Decipherability," in *IRE Transactions on Information Theory,* vol. IT-5 (Sept. 1959), pp. 98–102.

JAYNES, EDWIN T., "New Engineering Applications of Information Theory," in Bogdanoff, John L., and Kozin, Frank, eds., *Proceedings of the First Symposium on Engineering Applications of Random Function Theory and Probability* (New York: Wiley, 1963), pp. 163–203.

JAYNES, EDWIN T., AND SCALAPINO, D., "Non-Local Transport Theory," a paper presented at the first meeting of the Society for Natural Philosophy [Baltimore], Mar. 25, 1963.

JENSEN, MICHAEL C., AND MECKLING, WILLIAM H., "Theory of the Firm: Managerial Behavior, Agency Cost and Ownership Structure," in *Journal of Financial Economics,* vol. 3 (Oct. 1976), pp. 305–360.

JEWETT, CHARLES C., "A Plan for Stereotyping Catalogues by Separate Titles; and for Forming a General Stereotyped Catalogue of Public Libraries in the United States," in *Proceedings of the American Association for the Advancement of Science*, vol. 4 (1851), pp. 165–176.

JOHNS, ADA WINIFRED, *Special Libraries: Development of the Concept, their Organizations, and their Services* (Metuchen, N.J.: Scarecrow Press, 1968).

JOSIAH MACY JR. FOUNDATION, *Cybernetics*, proceedings of the Sixth Conference (1949) to the Tenth Conference (1953) (New York: Josiah Macy Jr. Foundation, last pub. 1955).

JULESZ, BELA, *Foundation of Cyclopean Perception* (Chicago: University of Chicago Press, 1971).

KALMAN, RUDOLF E., "A New Approach to Linear Filtering and Prediction Problems," in *Transactions of the American Society of Mechanical Engineers, Journal of Basic Engineering*, series *D*, vol. 82*D* (Mar. 1960*a*), pp. 35–45.

KALMAN, RUDOLF E., "On the General Theory of Control Systems," in *Proceedings of the First IFAC Congress*, held [in Moscow] 1960 (London: Butterworths, 1960*b*), vol. 1, pp. 481–491.

KALMAN, RUDOLF E., "Canonical Structure of Linear Dynamical Systems," in *Proceedings of the National Academy of Sciences (USA)*, vol. 48 (1962), pp. 596–600.

KALMAN, RUDOLF E., "Linear Stochastic Filtering Theory—Reappraisal and Outlook," in Fox, J., ed., *Proceedings of a Symposium on System Theory* (Brooklyn, N.Y.: Polytechnic Institute of Brooklyn, 1965), pp. 197–205.

KALMAN, RUDOLF E., "On Minimal Partial Realizations of a Linear Input/Output Map," in Kalman, Rudolf E., and De Claris, N., eds., *Aspects of Network and System Theory* (New York: Holt, Rinehart, and Winston, 1971), pp. 385–408.

KALMAN, RUDOLF E., "Kronecker Invariants and Feedback," in Weiss, L., ed., *Proceedings of the 1971 NRL-MRC Conference on Ordinary Differential Equations* (New York: Academic Press, 1972), pp. 459–471.

KALMAN, RUDOLF E., "Comments on the Scientific Aspects of Modeling," in Marois, M., ed., *Towards a Plan of Action for Mankind* (Amsterdam: North-Holland, 1974), pp. 492–505.

KALMAN, RUDOLF E., "Realization Theory of Linear Dynamical Systems," in *Control Theory and Functional Analysis* (Vienna: International Atomic Energy Agency, 1976).

KALMAN, RUDOLF E., "On Partial Realizations, Transfer Functions, and Canonical Forms," in *Acta Polytechnica Scandinavica*, Mathematics and Computer Science Series no. 31 (1979), pp. 9–32.

KALMAN, RUDOLF E., "A System-Theoretic Critique of Dynamic Economic Models," in *International Journal of Policy Analysis and Information Systems*, vol. 4 (1980), pp. 3–22.

KALMAN, RUDOLF E., "Identifiability and Problems of Model Selection in Econometrics"—invited paper presented at the Fourth World Congress of the Econometric Society, held [in Aix-en-Provence, France] 1980 (rev. version, Jan. 1981).

KALMAN, RUDOLF E., "Finitary Models for Time Series and the Identification of

Dynamics," in Krishnaiah, Paruchuri R., ed., *Developments in Statistics* (New York: Academic Press, 1982).

KALMAN, RUDOLF E., AND BUCY, RICHARD S., "New Results in Linear Prediction and Filtering Theory," in *Transactions of the American Society of Mechanical Engineers, Journal of Basic Engineering,* series *D,* vol. 83*D* (Mar. 1961), pp. 95–108.

KALMAN, RUDOLF E.; FALB, PETER L.; AND ARBIB, MICHAEL A., *Topics in Mathematical System Theory* (New York: McGraw-Hill, 1969).

KAMIEN, RALPH, AND SCHWARTZ, NANCY, *Dynamic Optimization: The Calculus of Variations and Optimal Control in Economics and Management* (New York: Elsevier, 1981).

KANEKO, TATSUO; ATLAS, RONALD M.; AND KRICHEVSKY, MICAH, "Diversity of Bacterial Populations in Beaufort Sea," in *Nature,* vol. 270 (Dec. 1977), pp. 596–599.

KANT, IMMANUEL, *Foundations of the Metaphysic of Morals* (London: 1st ed. in English, 1799; another ed., Indianapolis: Bobbs-Merrill, 1959).

KANT, IMMANUEL, *Critick of Pure Reason* (London: William Pickering, 1848).

KAPLAN, ABRAHAM, "The Age of the Symbol—A Philosophy of Library Education," in The *Library Quarterly,* vol. 34 (Oct. 1964), pp. 295–304.

KARETZKY, STEPHEN, *Reading Research in Librarianship: A History and Analysis* (Westport, Conn.: Greenwood Press, 1982).

KARMILOFF-SMITH, ANNETTE, "Micro- and Macrodevelopmental Changes in Language Acquisition and Other Representational Systems," in *Cognitive Science,* vol. 3 (Apr./June 1979), pp. 91–117.

KARMILOFF-SMITH, ANNETTE, AND INHELDER, BÄRBEL, "If You Want to Get Ahead, Get a Theory," in *Cognition,* vol. 3, no. 3 (1975), pp. 195–212.

KATZ, JERROLD J., *Underlying Reality of Language and Its Philosophical Import* (New York: Harper and Row, 1971).

KATZ, JERROLD J., AND POSTAL, PAUL M., *An Integrated Theory of Linguistic Descriptions* (Cambridge, Mass.: MIT Press, 1964).

KENDALL, D. G., "Entropy, Probability, and Information," in *International Statistical Review,* vol. 41 (1973), pp. 59–68.

KENT, ALLEN, "Field Definition—Information Science," in Section 7: "Computer and Information Sciences," *Peterson's Guides to Graduate Study,* Book 5, 1982.

KEYSER, SAMUEL J., AND O'NEIL, WAYNE, "The Evolution of the English Plural," in *Linguistic Research,* vol. 1, no. 2 (1980).

KHINCHIN, ALEKSANDR I., *Mathematical Foundations of Information Theory,* trans. R. A. Silverman and M. D. Friedman of two pieces: "The Entropy Concept in Probability Theory" (1953) and "On the Fundamental Theorems of Information Theory" (1956) (New York: Dover, 1957).

KILMER, WILLIAM L.; MCCULLOCH, WARREN S.; AND BLUM, JAY, "A Model of the Vertebrate Central Command System," in *International Journal of Man-Machine Studies,* vol. 1 (July 1969), pp. 279–309.

KING, DONALD W., "Thoughts for ASIS Members," in *Bulletin of the American Society for Information Science,* vol. 6 (Aug. 1980), pp. 3–4.

KING, DONALD W.; KRAUSER, CHERI; AND SAGUE, VIRGINIA M., "Profile of ASIS Membership," in *Bulletin of the American Society for Information Science,* vol. 6 (Aug. 1980), pp. 9–17.

KING, GILBERT W., et al., *Automation and the Library of Congress* (Washington, D.C.: Library of Congress, 1963).

KIRZNER, ISRAEL M., *Competition and Entrepreneurship* (Chicago: University of Chicago Press, 1973).

KLEENE, STEPHEN C., "Origins of Recursive Function Theory," in *Symposium on the Foundations of Computer Science,* proceedings of the Twentieth Annual Symposium on Foundations of Computer Science, held [in San Juan, Puerto Rico] by the IEEE Computer Society's Technical Committee on Mathematical Foundations of Computing (New York: Institute of Electrical and Electronics Engineers, 1979), pp. 371–381.

KLIMA, EDWARD S., AND BELLUGI, URSULA, *The Signs of Language* (Cambridge, Mass.: Harvard University Press, 1979).

KLING, ROB, "Social Analyses of Computing: Theoretical Perspectives in Recent Empirical Research," in *Computing Surveys,* vol. 12 (Mar. 1980), pp. 61–110.

KLIR, GEORGE JIRI, *An Approach to General System Theory* (New York: Van Nostrand Reinhold, 1969).

KLIR, GEORGE JIRI, "On the Relation Between Cybernetics and General Systems Theory," in Rose, John, ed., *Progress of Cybernetics,* proceedings of the First International Congress of Cybernetics, held [in London] 1969 (London and New York: Gordon and Breach Science Publishers, 1970), vol. 1, pp. 155–165.

KNUTH, DONALD E., *The Art of Computer Programming, Vol. 1: Fundamental Algorithms* (Reading, Mass.: Addison-Wesley, 1968).

KNUTH, DONALD E., *The Art of Computer Programming* (Reading, Mass.: Addison-Wesley, 1973–1981), 3 vols.

KNUTH, DONALD E., "Computer Programming as an Art" [the 1974 ACM Turing Award Lecture], in *Communications of the ACM,* vol. 17 (Dec. 1974a), pp. 667–673.

KNUTH, DONALD E., "Computer Science and Its Relation to Mathematics," in *American Mathematical Monthly,* vol. 81, no. 4 (1974b), pp. 323–343.

KOCHEN, MANFRED, "Extension of Moore Shannon Model for Relay Circuits," in *IBM Journal of Research and Development,* vol. 3 (Apr. 1959), pp. 169–186.

KOCHEN, MANFRED, *Some Problems in Information Science* (Metuchen, N.J.: Scarecrow Press, 1965).

KOCHEN, MANFRED, ed., *The Growth of Knowledge: Readings on Organization and Retrieval of Information* (New York: Wiley, 1967).

KOCHEN, MANFRED, "Stability in the Growth of Knowledge," in Saracevic, Tefko, ed., *Introduction to Information Science* (New York and London: Bowker, 1970), pp. 48–55.

KOCHEN, MANFRED, "WISE: A World Information Synthesis and Encyclopaedia," in *Journal of Documentation,* vol. 28 (Dec. 1972), pp. 322–343.

KOCHEN, MANFRED, "Views on the Foundations of Information Science," in Debons, Anthony, ed., *Information Science: Search for Identity,* proceedings of the 1972

NATO Advanced Study Institute in Information Science, held [in Seven Springs, Champion, Penn.] Aug. 12–20, 1972 (New York: Marcel Dekker, 1974), pp. 171–187.

KOCHEN, MANFRED, ed., *Information for Action,* proceedings of a symposium organized by the American Association for the Advancement of Science (New York: Academic Press, 1975).

KOCHEN, MANFRED, "Paper as a Medium of Communication: Trends in Alternate Technologies," in *International Forum on Information and Documentation* (forthcoming 1982).

KOCHEN, MANFRED, AND DEUTSCH, KARL W., *Decentralization: Sketches Towards a Rational Theory* (Cambridge, Mass.: Ogilvie-Hill Press, 1980).

KOFFKA, KURT, *Principles of Gestalt Psychology* (New York: Harcourt, 1935).

KÖHLER, WOLFGANG, *Gestalt Psychology: An Introduction to New Concepts in Modern Psychology* (New York: Liveright, 1929; rev. ed., 1947; paperback ed., New York: New American Library, 1947, 1961).

KOLMOGOROV, A. N., "Three Approaches to the Quantitative Definition of Information," in *Problems of Information Transmission,* vol. 1 (Jan./Mar., 1965), pp. 1–7. English trans. of the Russian *Problemy Peredachi Informatsii.*

KORNFELD, W. A., AND HEWITT, CARL E., *The Scientific Community Metaphor* (Artificial Intelligence Laboratory, M.I.T., Report No. AIM-641, 1981).

KOSSLYN, STEPHEN M.; PINKER, STEVEN; SMITH, GEORGE E.; AND SHWARTZ, STEVEN P., "On the Demystification of Mental Imagery" [with peer commentaries], in The *Behavioral and Brain Sciences,* vol. 2 (Dec. 1979), pp. 535–581.

KOTELNIKOV, VLADIMIR A., *The Theory of Optimum Noise Immunity,* trans. R. A. Silverman (New York: McGraw-Hill, 1959).

KOWALSKI, ROBERT, *Logic for Problem Solving* (New York: North-Holland, 1979).

KRISTOL, IRVING, "Rationalism in Economics," in Bell, Daniel, and Kristol, Irving, eds., *The Crisis in Economic Theory* (New York: Basic Books, 1981).

KUHN, ALFRED, *The Study of Society: A Unified Approach* (Homewood, Ill.: Irwin-Dorsey Press, 1963).

KUHN, ALFRED, *The Logic of Social Systems* (San Francisco: Jossey-Bass, 1974).

KUHN, ALFRED, *Unified Social Science* (Homewood, Ill.: Dorsey Press, 1975).

KUHN, ALFRED, "Let's Bring the Skeleton Out of the Closet," in Lasker, E. G., ed., *Applied Systems and Cybernetics* (New York: Pergamon, 1981).

KUHN, ALFRED, AND BEAM, ROBERT D., *The Logic of Organization* (San Francisco: Jossey-Bass, 1982).

KUHN, THOMAS S., *The Structure of Scientific Revolutions* (Chicago: University of Chicago Press, 1962*a*; 2nd enlarged ed., 1970).

KUHN, THOMAS S., "The Historical Structure of Scientific Discovery," in *Science,* vol. 136 (Apr./June 1962*b*), pp. 760–764.

KUHN, THOMAS S., "Second Thoughts on Paradigms," in Suppe, Frederick, ed., *The Structure of Scientific Theories* (Urbana: University of Illinois Press, 1974), pp. 459–482.

KUHN, THOMAS S., *The Essential Tension: Selected Studies in Scientific Tradition and Change* (Chicago: University of Chicago Press, 1977).

LAFERRIÈRE, DANIEL, "Making Room for Semiotics," in *Academe*, vol. 65 (Nov. 1979), pp. 434–440.

LAKATOS, IMRE, "Falsification and the Methodology of Scientific Research Programmes," in Lakatos, Imre, and Musgrave, Alan, eds., *Criticism and the Growth of Knowledge*, proceedings of the International Colloquium in the Philosophy of Science, London, 1965 (Cambridge: Cambridge University Press, 1970), vol. 4, pp. 91–195.

LAKATOS, IMRE, AND MUSGRAVE, ALAN, *Criticism and the Growth of Knowledge* (Cambridge: Cambridge University Press, 1970).

LAKOFF, GEORGE, "Some Remarks on AI and Linguistics," in *Cognitive Science*, vol. 2 (1978), pp. 267–275.

LAKOFF, GEORGE, AND ROSS, JOHN R., "Is Deep Structure Necessary?" in McCawley, James D., ed., *Syntax and Semantics: Vol. 7: Notes from The Linguistic Underground* (New York: Academic Press, 1976), pp. 159–164.

LAMBERTON, DONALD M., ed., *Economics of Information and Knowledge* (Harmondsworth, England: Penguin Books, 1971).

LANGE, OSKAR, *Wholes and Parts: A General Theory of System Behaviour*, trans. Eugeniusz Lepa of *Całość i rozwój w świetle cybernetyki* [Warsaw: Polish Scientific Publishers, 1962] (Oxford, England: Pergamon Press, 1965).

LANGEFORS, BÖRJE, "Information Systems Theory," in *Information Systems*, vol. 2, no. 3 (1977), pp. 207–219.

LANGENDOEN, D. TERRENCE, AND POSTAL, PAUL M., "The Vastness of Natural Language" (1982).

LANGER, SUSANNE K., *Philosophical Sketches* (Baltimore: Johns Hopkins Press, 1962).

LANGLOIS, RICHARD N., "Knowledge, Order, and Technology" (Ph.D. diss., Stanford University, 1981).

LASHLEY, KARL S., "The Problem of Serial Order in Behavior," In Jeffress, Lloyd A., ed., *Cerebral Mechanisms in Behavior*, proceedings of the Hixon Symposium, held [at the California Institute of Technology, Pasadena] 1948 (New York: Wiley-Interscience, 1951), pp. 112–136.

LEES, SIDNEY, "Uncertainty and Imprecision," in *Transactions of the American Society of Mechanical Engineers, Journal of Basic Engineering*, series D, vol. 88 (June 1966), pp. 369–378.

LEES, SIDNEY, "On Measurement," *Applied Mechanics Reviews* (forthcoming 1983).

LENAT, DOUGLAS, *The Heuristics of Nature* (Stanford University, Heuristic Programming Project, Working Paper No. HPP-81-22, 1981).

LENNEBERG, ERIC H., *Biological Foundations of Language* (New York: Wiley, 1967).

LEONTIEF, WASSILY, "Academic Economics," letter to the editor, *Science*, vol. 217 (9 July 1982).

LESSER, VICTOR, "AI and Brain Theory (BT) Research at the University of Massachusetts at Amherst," in *AI Magazine* (winter 1981–1982), pp. 16–20.

LESSER, VICTOR, AND ERMAN, LEE, "A Retrospective View of the Hearsay-II Architecture," in *Proceedings of the Fifth International Joint Conference on Artificial Intelligence* (Cambridge, Mass.: MIT Artificial Intelligence Laboratory, 1977), pp. 790–800.

LEVY, J., "Lateral Specialization of the Human Brain: Behavioral Manifestations and Possible Evolutionary Basis," in Kiger, John A., Jr., ed., *The Biology of Behavior* (Corvallis: Oregon State University Press, 1972), pp. 159–180.

LEWIN, KURT, *Principles of Topological Psychology,* trans. Fritz Heider (New York and London: McGraw-Hill, 1936).

LEWIS, GILBERT N., "The Symmetry of Time in Physics," in *Science,* vol. 71 (6 June 1930), pp. 569–577.

LICKLIDER, J. C. R., "Man-Computer Symbiosis," in *IRE Transactions on Human Factors in Electronics,* vol. HFE-1 (1960), pp. 4–11.

LIEBERMAN, PHILIP, "Primate Vocalizations and Human Linguistic Ability," in *Journal of the Acoustical Society of America,* vol. 44 (1968), pp. 1574–1584.

LINDSAY, PETER H., AND NORMAN, DONALD A., *Human Information Processing: An Introduction to Psychology* (New York: Academic Press, 1972; 2nd ed., 1977).

LINDSAY, ROBERT; BUCHANAN, BRUCE; FEIGENBAUM, EDWARD A.; AND LEDERBERG, JOSHUA, *Applications of Artificial Intelligence for Organic Chemistry: The DENDRAL Project* (New York: McGraw-Hill, 1980).

LIONS, JACQUES LOUIS, *Contrôle optimal de systèmes gouvernés par des equations aux dérivées partielles* (Paris: Dunod, 1968).

LIONS, JACQUES LOUIS, *Function Spaces and Optimal Control of Distributed Systems* (Paris: Collège de France, 1977).

LOCKE, JOHN, *An Essay Concerning Humane Understanding* (London: Thomas Basset, 1690; 32nd ed., W. Tegg, 1860).

LOCKE, WILLIAM NASH, AND BOOTH, A. DONALD, eds., *Machine Translation of Languages: Fourteen Essays* (Cambridge, Mass., and New York: Technology Press of MIT and Wiley, 1957).

LOEBNER, EGON E., "Subhistories of the Light-Emitting Diode (LED)," in *IEEE Transactions on Electron Devices,* vol. 23 (1976), pp. 675–699.

LOEBNER, EGON E., AND BORDEN, H. "Ecological Niches for Optoelectronic Devices," in *WESCON,* vol. 13, session no. 20 (1969), pp. 1–8.

LORENZ, EDWARD, "Deterministic, Non-periodic Flow," in *Journal of Atmospheric Sciences,* vol. 82 (Mar. 1963), pp. 985–992.

LORENZ, KONRAD, *Evolution and Modification of Behavior* (Chicago: University of Chicago Press, 1965).

LOTKE, ALFRED J., *Elements of Mathematical Biology* (New York: Dover, 1924; another ed. 1956).

LOWEN, R., "Compact Hausdorff Fuzzy Topological Spaces are Topological," in *Topology and Its Applications,* vol. 12 (Jan. 1981), pp. 65–74.

LUCRETIUS, TITUS LUCRETIUS CARUS, *On the Nature of Things* (in six books), trans. J. S. Watson (London: H. G. Bohn, 1851; 1st ed. in Latin, Verona, 1486).

LUENBERGER, DAVID G., "Observing the State of a Linear System," in *IEEE Transactions on Military Electronics,* vol. MIL-8 (Jan. 1964), pp. 74–80.

LUENBERGER, DAVID G., "Observers for Multivariable Systems," in *IEEE Transactions on Automatic Control,* vol. AC-11 (Apr. 1966), pp. 190–197.

LUENBERGER, DAVID G., "An Introduction to Observers," in *IEEE Transactions on Automatic Control,* vol. AC-16 (Dec. 1971), pp. 596–602.

LUENBERGER, DAVID G., *Introduction to Dynamic Systems* (New York: Wiley, 1979).

LUKES, STEVEN, "Types of Individualism," in *Dictionary of the History of Ideas*, vol. 2 (New York: Scribner's, 1973), pp. 594–604.

MACDOUGALL, WILLIAM, *Body and Mind; A History and a Defense of Animism* (Boston: Beacon Press, 1961; 1st ed., London: Methuen and Co., 1911).

MACHLUP, FRITZ, *The Production and Distribution of Knowledge in the United States* (Princeton, N.J.: Princeton University Press, 1962).

MACHLUP, FRITZ, *Essays in Economic Semantics* (Englewood Cliffs, N.J.: Prentice-Hall, 1963).

MACHLUP, FRITZ, "Theories of the Firm: Marginalist, Behavioral, Managerial," in *American Economic Review*, vol. 57 (Mar. 1967), pp. 1–33.

MACHLUP, FRITZ, "If Matter Could Talk," in Morgenbesser, Sidney; Suppes, Patrick; and White, Morton, eds., *Philosophy, Science, and Method* (New York: St. Martin's Press, 1969*a*), pp. 286–305. Reprinted in Machlup, Fritz, *Methodology of Economics and Other Social Sciences* (New York: Academic Press, 1978), pp. 309–332.

MACHLUP, FRITZ, "Positive and Normative Economics: An Analysis of the Ideas," in Heilbroner, Robert L., ed., *Economic Means and Social Ends: Essays in Political Economics* (Englewood Cliffs, N.J.: Prentice-Hall, 1969*b*), pp. 99–129. Reprinted in Machlup, Fritz, *Methodology of Economics and Other Social Sciences* (New York: Academic Press, 1978), pp. 425–450.

MACHLUP, FRITZ, *Methodology of Economics and Other Social Sciences* (New York: Academic Press, 1978).

MACHLUP, FRITZ, "Meeting Review: An Economist's Reflections on an Institute for Advanced Study of Information Science," in *Journal of the American Society for Information Science*, vol. 30 (Mar. 1979*a*), pp. 111–113.

MACHLUP, FRITZ, "Uses, Value, and Benefits of Knowledge," in *Knowledge*, vol. 1 (Sept. 1979*b*), pp. 62–81.

MACHLUP, FRITZ, *Knowledge: Its Creation, Distribution, and Economic Significance, Volume I: Knowledge and Knowledge Production* (Princeton, N.J.: Princeton University Press, 1980).

MACHLUP, FRITZ, *Knowledge: Its Creation, Distribution, and Economic Significance, Volume II: The Branches of Learning* (Princeton, N.J.: Princeton University Press, 1982).

MACHLUP, FRITZ, *Knowledge: Its Creation, Distribution, and Economic Significance, Volume III: The Economics of Information and Human Capital* (Princeton, N.J.: Princeton University Press, 1984).

MACHLUP, FRITZ; LEESON, KENNETH; AND ASSOCIATES, *Information Through the Printed Word: The Dissemination of Scholarly, Scientific, and Intellectual Knowledge, Vol. 1: Book Publishing* (New York: Praeger, 1978*a*).

MACHLUP, FRITZ; LEESON, KENNETH; AND ASSOCIATES, *Information Through the Printed Word: The Dissemination of Scholarly, Scientific, and Intellectual Knowledge, Vol. 2: Journals* (New York: Praeger, 1978*b*).

MACHLUP, FRITZ; LEESON, KENNETH; AND ASSOCIATES, *Information Through the Printed Word: The Dissemination of Scholarly, Scientific, and Intellectual Knowledge, Vol. 3: Libraries* (New York: Praeger, 1978*c*).

MACHLUP, FRITZ; LEESON, KENNETH; AND ASSOCIATES, *Information Through the Printed Word: The Dissemination of Scholarly, Scientific, and Intellectual Knowledge, Vol. 4: Books, Journals, and Bibliographic Services* (New York: Praeger, 1980).

MACKAY, DONALD M., "Quantal Aspects of Scientific Information," in *Philosophical Magazine,* vol. 41 (1950), pp. 289–311.

MACKAY, DONALD M., "The Nomenclature of Information Theory," in *Proceedings of the First International Symposium on Information Theory,* held [in London] Sept., 1950, sponsored by the American Institute of Radio Engineers. Lithoprinted, 1953. Reprinted in Foerster, Heinz M. von, ed., *Cybernetics,* transactions of the Eighth Conference sponsored by the Josiah Macy Jr. Foundation (New York: Josiah Macy Jr. Foundation, 1951*a*).

MACKAY, DONALD M., "In Search of Basic Symbols," in Foerster, Heinz M. von, ed., *Cybernetics,* transactions of the Eighth Conference sponsored by the Josiah Macy Jr. Foundation (New York: Josiah Macy Jr. Foundation, 1951*b*), pp. 181–221.

MACKAY, DONALD M., "On Comparing the Brain with Machines," in *American Scientist,* vol. 42 (Apr. 1954*a*), pp. 261–268.

MACKAY, DONALD M., "Operational Aspects of Some Fundamental Concepts of Human Communication," in *Synthese,* vol. 9 (1954*b*), pp. 182–198.

MACKAY, DONALD M., "Moving Visual Images Produced by Regular Stationary Patterns," in *Nature,* vol. 180 (Oct. 26, 1957*a*), pp. 849–850.

MACKAY, DONALD M., "Some Further Visual Phenomena Associated With Regular Patterned Stimulation," in *Nature,* vol. 180 (Nov. 23, 1957*b*), pp. 1145–1146.

MACKAY, DONALD M., "Information Theory: Its Uses and Abuses," in *Bulletin of the British Psychological Society,* vol. 38 (1959), pp. 70–71.

MACKAY, DONALD M., "Interactive Processes in Visual Perception," in Rosenblith, Walter A., ed., *Sensory Communication* (Cambridge, Mass., and New York: MIT Press and Wiley, 1960), pp. 339–355.

MACKAY, DONALD M., "Information and Learning," in Billing, H., ed., *Learning Automata* (Munich: Oldenbourg, 1961*a*), pp. 40–49.

MACKAY, DONALD M., "The Place of 'Meaning' in the Theory of Information," in Cherry, Colin, ed., *Information Theory,* papers read at a symposium on Information Theory, held [at the Royal Institution, London] Aug. 29–Sept. 2, 1960 (London: Butterworths, 1961*b*), pp. 215–225. Reprinted in MacKay, Donald M., *Information, Mechanism and Meaning* (Cambridge, Mass.: MIT Press, 1969), pp. 79–93.

MACKAY, DONALD M., "The Informational Approach," in *Cybernetics of Neural Processes, La ricerca scientifica, 31* (Rome: Consiglio Nazionale delle Ricerche, 1964*a*), pp. 123–128.

MACKAY, DONALD M., "Information Theory in the Study of Man," in Cohen, John, ed., *Readings in Psychology* (London: Allen and Unwin, 1964*b*), pp. 214–235.

MACKAY, DONALD M., "Information in Brains and Machines," in Kalenich, Wayne A., ed., *Proceedings of the IFIP Congress 1965,* organized by the International Federation for Information Processing [New York] May 24–29, 1965 (Washington, D.C.: Spartan Books; London: Macmillan, 1965), vol. 2, pp. 637–643.

MacKay, Donald M., *Information, Mechanism and Meaning* (Cambridge, Mass.: MIT Press, 1969).

Majumder, D. Dutta, "Cybernetics and General Systems—A Unitary Science?" in *Kybernetes,* vol. 8 (1979), pp. 7–15.

Marais, Eugène N., *The Soul of the White Ant,* trans. Winifred De Kok (New York: Dodd, Mead, 1937; Kraus reprint, 1969).

March, James G., and Simon, Herbert A., *Organizations* (New York: Wiley, 1958).

Marcus, Mitchell P., *A Theory of Syntatic Recognition for Natural Language* (Cambridge, Mass.: MIT Press, 1980).

Marr, David C., "Approaches to Biological Information Processing," book review of Conrad, Michael; Güttinger, W.; and Dal Cin, M., eds., *Physics and Mathematics of the Nervous System,* proceedings of a summer school organized by the International Centre for Theoretical Physics, Trieste, and the Institute for Information Sciences, University of Tübingen, held [in Trieste, Italy] Aug. 21–31, 1973 (Berlin and New York: Springer-Verlag, 1974), in *Science,* vol. 190 (Nov. 1975), pp. 875–876.

Marr, David C., "Early Processing of Visual Information," in *Philosophical Transactions of the Royal Society of London,* vol. 275 (1976), pp. 483–534.

Marr, David C., "Artificial Intelligence—A Personal View," in *Artificial Intelligence,* vol. 9 (Aug. 1977), pp. 37–48.

Marr, David C., *Vision: A Computational Investigation into the Human Representation and Processing of Visual Information* (San Francisco: W. H. Freeman, 1982).

Marr, David C., and Poggio, T., "From Understanding Computation to Understanding Neural Circuitry," in *Neurosciences Research Program Bulletin,* vol. 15 (1977), pp. 470–488.

Marschak, Jacob, "Towards an Economic Theory of Organization and Information," in Thrall, R. M.; Coombs, C. H.; and Davis, R. L., eds., *Decision Processes* (New York: Wiley, 1954), pp. 187–220.

Marschak, Jacob, "Problems in Information Economics," in Bonini, C. P.; Jaedicke, R. K.; and Wagner, H. M., eds., *Management Controls: New Directions in Basic Research* (New York: McGraw-Hill, 1964), pp. 38–90.

Marschak, Jacob, *Economic Information, Decision and Interpretation—Selected Essays,* vols. 1–3 (Dordrecht, Holland, and Boston: D. Reidel, 1974).

Marschak, Jacob, and Radner, Roy, *Economic Theory of Teams* (New Haven, Conn.: Yale University Press, 1972).

Martin, Clyde F., and Hermann, Robert, "Applications of Algebraic Geometry to Systems Theory: The McMillan Degree and Kronecker Indices of Transfer Functions in Topological and Homomorphic Invariants," in *SIAM Journal of Control and Optimization,* vol. 16 (1978), pp. 743–755.

Martin, Natiianiel F. G., and England, James W., *Mathematical Theory of Entropy* (Reading, Mass.: Addison-Wesley, 1981).

Martin, Paul E., "What Can Cybernetics Do For Industry?" in *Austria Today,* no. 2 (1981), pp. 11–14.

Maruyama, Magoroh, "The Second Cybernetics: Deviation-Amplifying Mutual Causal Processes," in The *American Scientist,* vol. 51 (June 1963), pp. 164–179.

MATTESSICH, RICHARD, "The Incorporation and Reduction of Value Judgments in Systems," in *Management Science,* vol. 21 (Sept. 1974*a*), pp. 1–9.

MATTESSICH, RICHARD, "Informations- und Erkenntnisekonomik: Treffpunkt von Philosophie und Wirtschaftswissenschaft," in *Zeitschrift für betriebswirtschaftliche Forschung,* vol. 26 (Dec. 1974*b*), pp. 777–784.

MATTESSICH, RICHARD, "Information Economics and the Notion of 'MIS'," in Grochla, E., and Szyperski, N., eds., *Information Systems and Organizational Structure* (New York: Walter De Gruyter, 1975), pp. 342–364.

MATTESSICH, RICHARD, *Instrumental Reasoning and Systems Methodology—An Epistemology of the Applied and Social Sciences* (Dordrecht, Holland, and Boston: D. Reidel, 1978).

MATTESSICH, RICHARD, "Axiomatic Representation of the Systems Framework: Similarities and Differences between Mario Bunge's World of Systems and My Own Systems Methodology," in *Cybernetics and Systems,* vol. 13 (1982), pp. 51–75.

MATTESSICH, RICHARD, ed., *Modern Accounting Research: A Survey and Guide* (Vancouver: Research Foundation of the Canadian Certified General Accountants' Association, forthcoming 1983).

MATURANA, HUMBERTO R., "Biology of Language: The Epistemology of Reality," in Miller, George A., and Lenneberg, Elizabeth, eds., *Psychology and Biology of Language and Thought: Essays in Honor of Eric Lenneberg* (New York: Academic Press, 1978), pp. 27–63.

MAXWELL, JAMES CLERK, "On Governors," in *Proceedings of the Royal Society of London,* vol. 16 (Mar. 1868), pp. 270–283. Reprinted in Niven, William Davidson, ed., *The Scientific Papers of James Clerk Maxwell* (Cambridge: Cambridge University Press, 1890; New York: Dover, 1965), vol. 2, pp. 105–120.

MAY, R., "The Grammar of Quantification" (Ph.D. diss., Massachusetts Institute of Technology, 1977).

MAY, ROBERT, "Simple Mathematical Models with Very Complicated Dynamics," in *Nature,* vol. 261 (1976), pp. 459–467.

MAY, ROLLO, *Stability and Complexity in Model Ecosystems* (Princeton, N.J.: Princeton University Press, 1973).

MAYNE, A. J., "Cybernetics and General Systems—A Unitary Science?" in *Kybernetes,* vol. 8 (1979), pp. 39–43.

McCARTHY, JOHN, "Programs with Common Sense," in *Mechanization of Thought Processes* (London: HMSO, 1959).

McCORDUCK, PAMELA, *Machines Who Think: A Personal Inquiry into the History and Prospects of Artificial Intelligence* (San Francisco: W. H. Freeman, 1979).

McCULLOCH, WARREN S., "A Historical Introduction to the Postulational Foundations of Experimental Epistemology," in McCulloch, Warren S., *Embodiments of Mind* (Cambridge, Mass.: MIT Press, 1965), pp. 359–372.

McCULLOCH, WARREN S., AND PITTS, WALTER H., "A Logical Calculus of the Ideas Immanent in Nervous Activity," in *Bulletin of Mathematical Biophysics,* vol. 5 (1943), pp. 115–133.

McELIECE, ROBERT J., *The Theory of Information and Coding* (Reading, Mass.: Addison-Wesley, 1977).

McGill, William J., "Multivariate Information Transmission," in *Psychometrika,* vol. 19 (June 1954), pp. 97–116.

McRae, Robert, "The Unity of the Sciences: Bacon, Descartes, and Leibniz," in *Journal of the History of Ideas,* vol. 18 (Jan. 1957), pp. 27–48.

Mead, George Herbert, *Mind, Self, and Society* (Chicago: University of Chicago Press, 1934).

Meadows, Donnella H., et al., *The Limits to Growth: A Report for the Club of Rome's Project on the Predicament of Mankind* (New York: Universe Books, 1972).

Mehra, Raman K., and Lainiotis, Dimitri G., eds., *System Identification: Advances and Case Studies* (New York: Academic Press, 1976).

Merton, Robert K., *The Sociology of Science: Theoretical and Empirical Investigations,* ed. Norman W. Storer (Chicago: University of Chicago Press, 1973).

Mesarović, Mihajlo D., "On Self-Organizational Systems," in Yovits, Marshall C.; Jacobi, George T.; and Goldstein, Gordon D., eds., *Self-Organizing Systems,* proceedings of a conference on self-organizing systems, held [in Chicago] 1962 (Washington, D.C.: Spartan Books, 1962), pp. 9–36.

Mesarović, Mihajlo D., ed., *Views on General Systems Theory,* proceedings of the Second Systems Symposium, held [at Case Institute of Technology] 1963 (New York: Wiley, 1964*a*).

Mesarović, Mihajlo D., "Foundations for a General Systems Theory," in Mesarović, Mihajlo D., ed., *Views on General Systems Theory,* proceedings of the Second Systems Symposium, held [at Case Institute of Technology] 1963 (New York: Wiley, 1964*b*), pp. 1–24.

Mesarović, Mihajlo D., ed., *Systems Theory and Biology,* proceedings of the Third Systems Symposium at Case Institute of Technology (New York: Springer-Verlag, 1968*a*).

Mesarović, Mihajlo D., "Systems Theory and Biology—View of a Theoretician," in Mesarović, Mihajlo D., ed., *Systems Theory and Biology,* proceedings of the Third Systems Symposium at Case Institute of Technology (New York: Springer-Verlag, 1968*b*), pp. 59–87.

Mesarović, Mihajlo D.; Macko, Donald; and Takahara, Yasuhiko, *Theory of Hierarchical, Multi-Level Systems* (New York: Academic Press, 1970).

Mesarović, Mihajlo D., and Pestel, Eduard, *Mankind at the Turning Point: The Second Report to the Club of Rome* (New York: Dutton, 1974).

Mesarović, Mihajlo D., and Takahara, Yasuhiko, *General Systems Theory: Mathematical Foundations* (New York: Academic Press, 1975).

Meyer, Jean, "Essai d'application de certains modèles cybernétiques à la coordination chez les insectes sociaux," in *Insectes Sociaux,* vol. 13, no. 2 (1966), p. 127.

Meyer-Eppler, Werner, "Vorwort des Herausgebers," *Grundlagen und Anwendungen der Informationstheorie* [*Kommunikation und Kybernetik in Einzeldarstellungen,* Band 1, Herausgegeben von W. Meyer-Eppler] (Berlin: Springer-Verlag, 1959).

Michalski, Ryszard S.; Carbonell, Jaime; and Mitchell, Tom, eds., *Machine Learning—An Artificial Intelligence Approach* (Palo Alto, Calif.: Tioga Press, 1983).

MILL, JOHN STUART, "On the Definition of Political Economy; and on the Method of Investigation Proper to It," in *London and Westminster Review,* October, 1836; reprinted in Mill, John Stuart, *Essays on Some Unsettled Questions of Political Economy* (London: John W. Parker, 1844).

MILL, JOHN STUART, *Essays on Some Unsettled Questions of Political Economy* (London: John W. Parker, 1844; 1st ed. 1836).

MILLER, GEORGE A., *Language and Communication* (New York: McGraw-Hill, 1951).

MILLER, GEORGE A., "What Is Information Measurement?" in *American Psychologist,* vol. 8 (Jan. 1953), pp. 3–11.

MILLER, GEORGE A., "The Magical Number Seven, Plus or Minus Two: Some Limits on our Capacity for Processing Information," in *Psychological Review,* vol. 63 (Mar. 1956), pp. 81–97.

MILLER, GEORGE A., "Some Psychological Studies of Grammar," in *American Psychologist,* vol. 17 (1962), pp. 748–762.

MILLER, GEORGE A., AND CHOMSKY, NOAM, "Finitary Models of Language Users," in Luce, Robert Duncan; Bush, Robert R.; and Galanter, Eugene, eds., *Handbook of Mathematical Psychology,* vol. 2 (New York: Wiley, 1963), chap. 13, pp. 419–492.

MILLER, GEORGE A., AND FRICK, FREDERICK C., "Statistical Behavioristics and Sequences of Responses," in *Psychological Review,* vol. 56 (Nov. 1949), pp. 311–324.

MILLER, GEORGE A.; GALANTER, EUGENE; AND PRIBRAM, KARL H., *Plans and the Structure of Behavior* (New York: Holt, Rinehart, and Winston, 1960).

MILLER, GEORGE A., AND JOHNSON-LAIRD, PHILIP N., *Language and Perception* (Cambridge, Mass.: Belknap Press, 1976).

MILLER, JAMES G., "The Nature of Living Systems," in *Behavioral Science,* vol. 21 (Sept. 1976), pp. 295–319.

MILLER, JAMES G., *Living Systems* (New York: McGraw-Hill, 1978).

MILLER, JONATHAN, *The Body in Question* (New York: 1st American ed., Random House, 1978).

MILLER, LAURENCE, "Has Artificial Intelligence Contributed to an Understanding of the Human Mind? A Critique of Arguments For and Against," in *Cognitive Science,* vol. 2 (Apr./June 1978), pp. 111–127.

MILSUM, JOHN H., *Biological Control Systems Analysis* (New York: McGraw-Hill, 1966).

MINSKY, MARVIN L., "Steps Toward Artificial Intelligence," in Feigenbaum, Edward A., and Feldman, Julian, eds., *Computers and Thought* (New York: McGraw-Hill, 1963), pp. 406–450.

MINSKY, MARVIN L., ed., *Semantic Information Processing* (Cambridge, Mass.: MIT Press, 1968).

MINSKY, MARVIN L., "A Framework for Representing Knowledge," in Winston, Patrick H., ed., *The Psychology of Computer Vision* (New York: McGraw-Hill, 1975), pp. 211–277.

MINSKY, MARVIN L., "Computer Science and the Representation of Knowledge," in

Dertouzos, Michael L., and Moses, Joel, eds., *The Computer Age: A Twenty-Year View* (Cambridge, Mass.: MIT Press, 1979), pp. 392–421.

MINSKY, MARVIN L., AND PAPERT, SEYMOUR, *Perceptrons: An Introduction to Computational Geometry* (Cambridge, Mass.: MIT Press, 1969).

MITTELMANN, H. D., AND WEBER, H., eds., *Bifurcation Problems and Their Numerical Solution*. [Workshop on Bifurcation Problems and Their Numerical Solution, University of Dortmund, Jan. 15–17, 1980] (Basel, Switzerland, and Boston: Birkhäuser, 1980).

MOIVRE, ABRAHAM DE, *The Doctrine of Chances; or, a Method of Calculating the Probability of Events in Play* (London: 1718; 3rd ed. 1756; photo. reproduction of 3rd ed. together with the biography by Helen M. Walker, New York: Chelsea Press, 1967).

MONOD, JACQUES, *Chance and Necessity: An Essay on the Natural Philosophy of Modern Biology,* trans. Austryn Wainhouse [of *Le hasard et la nécessité: Essai sur la philosophie naturelle de la biologie moderne,* Paris: Editions du Seuil, 1970] (New York: 1st American ed., Knopf, 1971).

MONTROLL, ELLIOTT W., "Theory and Observations of the Dynamics and Statistics of Traffic on an Open Road," in Bogdanoff, John L., and Kozin, Frank, eds., *Proceedings of the First Symposium on Engineering Applications of Random Function Theory and Probability* (New York: Wiley, 1963), pp. 231–269.

MONTROLL, ELLIOTT W., "On the Entropy Function in Sociotechnical Systems," in *Proceedings of the National Academy of Sciences,* vol. 78 (Dec. 1981), pp. 7839–7843.

MOORE, EDWARD F., AND SHANNON, CLAUDE E., "Reliable Circuits Using Less Reliable Relays," in *Journal of the Franklin Institute,* part 1, vol. 262 (Sept. 1956), pp. 191–208; part 2, vol. 262 (Oct. 1956), pp. 281–297.

MORRIS, CHARLES W., "Foundations of the Theory of Signs," in Neurath, Otto; Carnap, Rudolf; and Morris, Charles, eds., *Foundations of the Unity of Science: Toward an International Encyclopedia of Unified Science*, vol. 1 (Chicago: University of Chicago Press, 1939; bound ed., 1969), pp. 77–137.

MOSER, JÜNGEN, *Stable and Random Motions in Dynamical Systems* (Princeton, N.J.: Princeton University Press, 1973).

MOSES, JOEL, "Symbolic Integration" (Ph.D. diss., Massachusetts Institute of Technology, 1967).

MOUNTCASTLE, VERNON B., "An Organizing Principle for Cerebral Function: The Unit Module and the Distributed System," in Edelman, Gerald M., and Mountcastle, Vernon B., *The Mindful Brain* (Cambridge, Mass.: MIT Press, 1978), pp. 7–50.

NALIMOV, VASILII V., "The Penetration of the Humanities into Other Fields of Knowledge," in Colodny, Robert G., ed., *Faces of Science* (Philadelphia: ISI Press, 1981; 1st pub. in Russian in the journal *Znanie-sila,* no. 5 [1979]).

NAUR, PETER; RANDELL, BRIAN; AND BUXTON, JOHN N., eds., *Software Engineering: Concepts and Techniques,* proceedings of the NATO conferences (New York: Petrocelli/Charter, 1976). Part I reports on the conference held [in Garmisch, Germany] by the NATO Science Committee, Oct. 7–11, 1968; Part II on the conference held [in Rome] by the NATO Science Committee, Oct. 27–31, 1969.

NEISSER, ULRIC, "Decision-time without Reaction-time: Experiments in Visual Scanning," in *American Journal of Psychology,* vol. 76 (Sept. 1963), pp. 376–385.

NEISSER, ULRIC, *Cognitive Psychology* (New York: Appleton-Century-Crofts, 1967).

NEISSER, ULRIC, *Cognition and Reality* (San Francisco: W. H. Freeman, 1976).

NEUFELD, RICHARD W. J., "Response-Selection Processes in Paranoid and Non-Paranoid Schizophrenia," in *Perceptual and Motor Skills,* vol. 44 (Apr. 1977), pp. 499–505.

NEUMANN, JOHANN VON, *Mathematische Grundlagen der Quantenmechanik* (Berlin: Julius Springer, 1932).

NEUMANN, JOHN VON, *Mathematical Foundations of Quantum Mechanics,* trans. Robert T. Beyer (Princeton, N.J.: Princeton University Press, 1955; German ed., 1932).

NEUMANN, JOHN VON, "Probabilistic Logics and the Synthesis of Reliable Organisms from Unreliable Components," in Shannon, Claude E., and McCarthy, John, eds., *Automata Studies* (Princeton, N.J.: Princeton University Press, 1956), pp. 43–98.

NEUMANN, JOHN VON, *The Computer and the Brain* (New Haven, Conn.: Yale University Press, 1958).

NEVITT, BARRINGTON, "The Complementarity of Art and Science in General Systems," in Lasker, G. E., ed., *Applied Systems and Cybernetics* (New York: Pergamon, 1981), pp. 592–596.

NEWELL, ALLEN, "Remarks on the Relationship Between Artificial Intelligence and Cognitive Psychology," in Banerji, Ranan B., and Mesarović, Mihajlo D., eds., *Theoretical Approaches to Non-Numerical Problem Solving,* proceedings of the Fourth Systems Symposium, held [at Case Western Reserve University] 1968 (New York: Springer-Verlag, 1970), pp. 363–400.

NEWELL, ALLEN, "Production Systems: Models of Control Structures," in Chase, William G., ed., *Visual Information Processing,* proceedings of the Eighth Annual Carnegie Symposium on Cognition, held [at Carnegie-Mellon University, Pittsburgh] May 19, 1972 (New York: Academic Press, 1973a), pp. 463–526.

NEWELL, ALLEN, "You Can't Play Twenty Questions With Nature and Win: Projective Comments on the Papers of this Symposium," in Chase, William G., ed., *Visual Information Processing,* proceedings of the Eighth Annual Carnegie Symposium on Cognition, held [at Carnegie-Mellon University, Pittsburgh] May 19, 1972 (New York: Academic Press, 1973b), pp. 283–310.

NEWELL, ALLEN, "Artificial Intelligence and the Concept of Mind," in Schank, Roger C., and Colby, Kenneth M., eds., *Computer Models of Thought and Language* (San Francisco: W. H. Freeman, 1973c), pp. 1–60.

NEWELL, ALLEN, "One Final Word," in Tuma, David T., and Reif, F., eds., *Problem Solving and Education: Issues in Teaching and Research,* proceedings of a conference held [at Carnegie-Mellon University, Pittsburgh] Oct. 9–10, 1978 (Hillsdale, N.J.: Lawrence Erlbaum, 1980a), pp. 175–189.

NEWELL, ALLEN, "Physical Symbol Systems," in *Cognitive Science,* vol. 4 (Apr./June 1980b), pp. 135–183.

NEWELL, ALLEN, "The Knowledge Level," in *AI Magazine,* vol. 2 (1981), pp. 1–20.

NEWELL, ALLEN, AND ERNST, GEORGE, "The Search for Generality," in Kalenich,

Wayne A., ed., *Proceedings of the IFIP Congress 1965*, organized by the International Federation for Information Processing [New York] May 24–29, 1965 (Washington, D.C.: Spartan Books; London: Macmillan, 1965), vol. 1, pp. 17–24.

NEWELL, ALLEN; PERLIS, ALAN J.; AND SIMON, HERBERT A., "Computer Science," letter to the editor, *Science,* vol. 157 (22 Sept., 1967), pp. 1373–1374.

NEWELL, ALLEN, AND SHAW, JOHN C., "Programming the Logic Theory Machine," in *Proceedings of the Western Joint Computer Conference,* sponsored by the Institute of Radio Engineers, the American Institute of Electrical Engineers, and the Association for Computing Machinery and held [in Los Angeles] Feb. 26–28, 1957, pp. 230–240.

NEWELL, ALLEN; SHAW, JOHN C.; AND SIMON, HERBERT A., "Empirical Explorations of the Logic Theory Machine: A Case Study in Heuristics," in *Proceedings of the Western Joint Computer Conference,* sponsored by the Institute of Radio Engineers, the American Institute of Electrical Engineers, and the Association for Computing Machinery and held [in Los Angeles] Feb. 26–28, 1957, pp. 218–230.

NEWELL, ALLEN, AND SIMON, HERBERT A., *Human Problem Solving* (Englewood Cliffs, N.J.: Prentice-Hall, 1972).

NEWELL, ALLEN, AND SIMON, HERBERT A., "Computer Science as Empirical Inquiry: Symbols and Search" [the 1976 ACM Turing Award Lecture], in *Communications of the ACM,* vol. 19 (Mar. 1976*a*), pp. 113–126.

NEWELL, ALLEN, AND SIMON, HERBERT A., "Symbol Manipulation," in *Encyclopedia of Computer Science* (New York: Petrocelli/Charter, 1976*b*), pp. 1384–1389.

NEWMEYER, FREDERICK J., *Linguistic Theory in America: The First Quarter Century of Transformational Generative Grammar* (New York: Academic Press, 1980).

NG, DAVID S., AND STOECKENIUS, JAN, "Auditing: Incentives and Truthful Reporting," in *Journal of Accounting Research,* vol. 17 (supplement 1979), pp. 1–24.

NICOLIS, GEORGE, AND PRIGOGINE, ILYA, *Self-Organization in Nonequilibrium Systems: From Dissipative Structures to Order through Fluctuations* (New York: Wiley, 1977).

NILSSON, NILS J., *Problem Solving Methods in Artificial Intelligence* (New York: McGraw-Hill, 1971).

NILSSON, NILS J., "Artificial Intelligence," in Rosenfeld, J. L., ed., *Proceedings of the IFIP Congress,* vol. 4 (New York: American Elsevier, 1974), pp. 778–801.

NILSSON, NILS J., *Principles of Artificial Intelligence* (Palo Alto, Calif.: Tioga Press, 1980).

NILSSON, NILS J., "Artificial Intelligence: Engineering, Science or Slogan?" in *AI Magazine,* vol. 3 (Jan. 1982), pp. 2–9.

NILSSON, NILS J., AND RAPHAEL, BERTRAM, "Preliminary Design of an Intelligent Robot," in *Computer and Information Sciences,* vol. 2 (1967), pp. 235–259.

NIRENBERG, MARSHALL W., "The Genetic Code: II," in *Scientific American,* vol. 208 (Mar. 1963), pp. 80–94.

NISBETT, RICHARD, AND ROSS, LEE, *Human Inference: Strategies and Shortcomings of Social Judgment* (Englewood Cliffs, N.J.: Prentice-Hall, 1980).

NORMAN, DONALD A., "Memory, Knowledge, and the Answering of Questions," in

Solso, Robert L., ed., *Contemporary Issues in Cognitive Psychology: The Loyola Symposium on Cognitive Psychology* [Chicago] 1972 (Washington, D.C.: Winston, 1973), pp. 135–165.

NORMAN, DONALD A., "Twelve Issues for Cognitive Science," in *Cognitive Science*, vol. 4 (Jan./Mar. 1980), pp. 1–32.

NORMAN, DONALD A., "Categorization of Action Slips," in *Psychological Review*, vol. 88 (Jan. 1981), pp. 1–15.

NOZICK, ROBERT, *Anarchy, State, and Utopia* (New York: Basic Books, 1974).

NYQUIST, HARRY, "Certain Factors Affecting Telegraph Speed," in *Journal of the American Institute of Electrical Engineers*, vol. 43 (Feb. 1924), pp. 124–130.

OCHS, SIDNEY, *Elements of Neurophysiology* (New York: Wiley, 1965).

OFFRAY DE LA METTRIE, JULIEN JAN, *Man a Machine* (London: 2nd ed., G. Smith, 1750; ed. with notes by Gertrude Carman Bussey, La Salle, Ill.: Open Court Publishing Company, 1961). Translated from the French.

OTLET, PAUL, "Les sciences bibliographiques et la documentation," in *Institut International de Bibliographie Bulletin 8* (1903), pp. 121–147.

OTLET, PAUL, AND GOLDSCHMIDT, ROBERT, *Sur une forme nouvelle du livre: le livre microphotographique* (Brussels: Institut International de Bibliographie, 1906). Publication 81.

OTTEN, KLAUS, "Basis for a Science of Information," in Debons, Anthony, ed., *Information Science: Search for Identity*, proceedings of the 1972 NATO Advanced Study Institute in Information Science, held [in Seven Springs, Champion, Penn.] Aug. 12–20, 1972 (New York: Marcel Dekker, 1974), pp. 91–106.

OTTEN, KLAUS, AND DEBONS, ANTHONY, "Opinion Paper: Towards a Metascience of Information: Informatology," in *Journal of the American Society for Information Science*, vol. 21 (Jan./Feb. 1970), pp. 89–94.

PAPERT, SEYMOUR, Paper given at the NUFFIC [Netherlands Universities Foundation for International Cooperation] Summer School, 1972 (The Hague, Netherlands: NUFFIC, 1972).

PAPERT, SEYMOUR, *Mindstorms: Children, Computers, and Powerful Ideas* (New York: Basic Books, 1980).

PARSONS, TALCOTT, "Concrete Systems and 'Abstracted' Systems," in *Behavioral Science*, vol. 25 (Jan. 1980), pp. 46–55. Reproduced from *Contemporary Sociology*, 1979.

PEARSON, CHARLS, "Towards an Empirical Foundation of Meaning" (Ph.D. diss., Georgia Institute of Technology, 1977).

PEARSON, CHARLS, AND SLAMECKA, VLADIMIR, *Semiotic Foundations of Information Science*. Report of the School of Information and Computer Science, GIT-ICS-77-01 (Atlanta: Georgia Institute of Technology, 1977).

PEIRCE, CHARLES SANDERS, "On a New List of Categories," in Hartshorne, Charles, and Weiss, Paul, eds., *Collected Papers of Charles Saunders Pierce, Vol. I: Principles of Philosophy* (Cambridge, Mass.: Harvard University Press, 1931), chap. 6, pp. 287–305. [Originally published in *Proceedings of the American Academy of Arts and Sciences*, vol. 7 (May 1867), pp. 287–298.]

PELLIONISZ, ANDRAS, AND LLINAS, RODOLFO, "Brain Modelling by Tensor Network

Theory and Computer Simulation. The Cerebellum: Distributed Processor for Predictive Coordination," in *Neuroscience,* vol. 4 (1979), pp. 323–348.

PERITZ, BLUMA C., "The Methods of Library Science Research: Some Results from a Bibliometric Survey," in *Library Research,* vol. 2 (1980–1981), pp. 251–268.

PERLIS, ALAN J., "Computer Science Is Neither Mathematics nor Electrical Engineering," in Finerman, Aaron, ed., *University Education in Computing Science,* proceedings of a conference on Graduate Academic and Related Programs in Computing Science, held [at the State University of New York, Stony Brook] June 1967 (New York: Academic Press, 1968), pp. 69–79.

PERLIS, ALAN J., "Current Research Frontiers in Computer Science," in Dertouzos, Michael L., and Moses, Joel, eds., *The Computer Age: A Twenty-Year View* (Cambridge, Mass.: MIT Press, 1979), pp. 422–436.

PHILLIPS, ALMARIN, "The Tableau Économique as a Simple Leontief Model," in *Quarterly Journal of Economics,* vol. 69 (Feb. 1955), pp. 137–144.

PHILLIPS, DENNIS C., *Holistic Thought in Social Science* (Stanford, Calif.: Stanford University Press, 1976).

PIAGET, JEAN, *Genetic Epistemology,* trans. Eleanor Duckworth (New York: Columbia University Press, 1970).

PIAGET, JEAN, *Biology and Knowledge: An Essay on the Relations between Organic Regulations and Cognitive Processes,* trans. Beatrix Walsh (Edinburgh, Scotland: Edinburgh University Press, 1971).

PIAGET, JEAN, "The Psychogenesis of Knowledge and Its Epistemological Significance," in Piatelli-Palmarini, Massimo, ed., *Language and Learning: The Debate between Jean Piaget and Noam Chomsky* (Cambridge, Mass.: Harvard University Press, 1980), pp. 23–34.

PIATELLI-PALMARINI, MASSIMO, ed., *Language and Learning: The Debate between Jean Piaget and Noam Chomsky* (Cambridge, Mass.: Harvard University Press, 1980).

PICAVET, FRANÇOIS JOSEPH, *Les idéologues: essai sur l'histoire des idées et des théories scientifiques, philosophiques, religieuses, etc. en France depuis 1789* (Paris: F. Alcan, 1891; reprint, New York: Burt Franklin, 1971).

PICCI, G., "Stochastic Realization of Guassian Processes," in *Proceedings of the IEEE,* vol. 64 (1976), pp. 112–122.

PICCI, G., "Some Connections Between the Theory of Sufficient Statistics and the Identifiability Problem," in *SIAM Journal of Applied Mathematics,* vol. 33 (1977), pp. 383–398.

PIERCE, JOHN R., *Symbols, Signals, and Noise: The Nature and Process of Communication* (New York: Harper, 1961; Torchbook ed., 1965).

PINSKER, M. S., *Information and Information Stability of Random Variables and Processes,* trans. Amiel Feinstein (San Francisco: Holden-Day, 1964).

PITTS, WALTER H., AND McCULLOCH, WARREN S., "How We Know Universals: The Perception of Auditory and Visual Forms," in *Bulletin of Mathematical Biophysics,* vol. 9 (1947), pp. 127–147.

PLATO, *The Republic* (Glasgow, Scotland: 1st ed. in English, 1763; another ed., Oxford: Oxford University Press, 1955).

POLANYI, MICHAEL, *Personal Knowledge* (Chicago: University of Chicago Press, 1958).

POLLACK, IRWIN, "The Information of Elementary Auditory Displays," in *Journal of the Acoustical Society of America,* vol. 25 (July 1953), pp. 765–769.

PONTRYAGIN, L. S.; BOLTYANSKIL, V. G.; GAMRELIDZE, R. V.; AND MISHCHENKO, E. F., *The Mathematical Theory of Optimal Processes* (New York: Wiley, 1962).

POOLE, WILLIAM FREDERICK, *An Index to Periodical Literature* (Boston: 3rd ed., J. R. Osgood, 1882; 1st ed. 1848; reprinted with five supplements covering the literature from 1802–1906, Gloucester, Mass.: Peter Smith, 1963).

POORE, JESSE H.; BARALT-TORRIJOS, JORGE; AND CHIARAVIGLIO, LUCIO, *On the Combinatory Definability of Hardware and Software* (Atlanta: Georgia Institute of Technology, 1971). Research Report GITIS-71-04.

POPOV, V. M., "Invariant Description of Linear Time-Invariant Controllable Systems," in *SIAM Journal of Control,* vol. 10 (1972), pp. 252–264.

POPOV, V. M., *Hyperstability of Control Systems* (New York: Springer-Verlag, 1973; Roumanian ed., Bucharest, 1966).

POPPER, KARL R., *The Logic of Scientific Discovery* (London: Hutchinson, 1959; Torchbooks, 1965), trans. author with the assistance of Julius Freed and Lan Freed, from *Logik der Forschung: Zur Erkenntnistheorie der modernen Naturwissenschaft* (Vienna, 1935).

POPPER, KARL R., *Conjectures and Refutations: The Growth of Scientific Knowledge* (New York: Basic Books, 1962).

POPPER, KARL R., *The Open Society and its Enemies,* vol. 2 (Princeton, N.J.: Princeton University Press, 5th ed., 1966).

POPPER, KARL R., "Epistemology Without a Knowing Subject," in Popper, Karl R., *Objective Knowledge: An Evolutionary Approach* (Oxford: Clarendon Press, 1972*a*), pp. 106–152.

POPPER, KARL R., *Objective Knowledge: An Evolutionary Approach* (Oxford: Clarendon Press, 1972*b*; rev. ed., Oxford University Press, 1979).

POPPER, KARL R., AND ECCLES, JOHN C., *The Self and Its Brain* (Berlin and New York: Springer International, 1977).

PREMACK, DAVID, *Intelligence in Ape and Man* (Hillsdale, N.J.: Lawrence Erlbaum, 1976).

PRIGOGINE, ILYA, "Unity of Physical Laws and Levels of Description," in Grene, Marjorie, ed., *Interpretations of Life and Mind* (New York: Humanities Press, 1971).

Problemy Peredachi Informatsii, published since 1965 in Moscow in Russian. English trans., *Problems of Information Transmission,* pub. Consultant's Bureau, 227 West 17th Street, New York, N.Y. 10011.

PROCACCIA, I.; SHIMONI, Y.; AND LEVINE, R. D., "Entropy and Microscopic Disequilibrium: Isothermal Time Evolution with Application to Vibrational Relaxation," in *Journal of Chemical Physics,* vol. 65 (Oct. 1976), pp. 3284–3301.

Proceedings of the First International Symposium on Information Theory, held [in London] Sept. 1950, sponsored by the American Institute of Radio Engineers. Lithoprinted, 1953.

PUTNAM, HILARY, "Minds and Machines," in Hook, Sidney, ed., *Dimensions of Mind* [a symposium, New York University Institute of Philosophy, 1959] (New York: New York University Press, 1960).

PYLYSHYN, ZENON W., ed., *Perspectives on the Computer Revolution* (Englewood Cliffs, N.J.: Prentice-Hall, 1970).

PYLYSHYN, ZENON W., "Computational Models and Empirical Constraints" [with peer commentaries], in The *Behavioral and Brain Sciences,* vol. 1 (Mar. 1978), pp. 93–127.

PYLYSHYN, ZENON W., "Complexity and the Study of Artificial and Human Intelligence," in Ringle, Martin, ed., *Philosophical Perspectives in Artificial Intelligence* (New York: Humanities Press, 1979), pp. 23–56.

PYLYSHYN, ZENON W., "Computation and Cognition: Issues in the Foundations of Cognitive Science," in The *Behavioral and Brain Sciences,* vol. 3 (Mar. 1980), pp. 111–169.

PYLYSHYN, ZENON W., *Computation and Cognition: Issues in the Foundations of Cognitive Science* (Cambridge, Mass.: Bradford Books/MIT Press, forthcoming 1984).

QUASTLER, HENRY, ed., *Information Theory in Psychology: Problems and Methods,* proceedings of a conference on the Estimation of Information Flow, held [in Monticello, Ill.] July 5–9, 1954 (Glencoe, Ill.: Free Press, 1955).

QUILLIAN, M. ROSS, "Semantic Memory," in Minsky, Marvin L., ed., *Semantic Information Processing* (Cambridge, Mass.: MIT Press, 1968), pp. 216–270.

QUINE, WILLARD VAN ORMAN, "The Problem of Meaning in Linguistics," in Quine, Willard van Orman, *From a Logical Point of View* (Cambridge, Mass.: Harvard University Press, 1953).

RALL, WILFRED, "Theoretical Significance of Dendritic Trees for Neuronal Input-Output Relations," in Reiss, Richard F., et al., eds., *Neural Theory and Modeling,* proceedings of the 1962 Ojai Symposium, held [in Ojai, Calif.] Dec. 4–6, 1962 (Stanford, Calif.: Stanford University Press, 1964), pp. 73–97.

RALSTON, ANTHONY, *Introduction to Programming and Computer Science* (New York: McGraw-Hill, 1971).

RAMO, SIMON, *Cure for Chaos: Fresh Solutions to Social Problems through the Systems Approach* (New York: D. McKay, 1969).

RAPHAEL, BERTRAM, "The Relevance of Robot Research to Artificial Intelligence," in Banerji, Ranan B., and Mesarović, Mihajlo D., eds., *Theoretical Approaches to Non-Numerical Problem Solving,* proceedings of the Fourth Systems Symposium [at Case Western Reserve University] 1968 (New York: Springer-Verlag, 1970), pp. 455–466.

RAPOPORT, ANATOL, *Operational Philosophy: Integrating Knowledge and Action* (New York: Harper and Row, 1953; 2nd printing, Wiley, 1967).

RAPOPORT, ANATOL, "Foreword," in Buckley, Walter, ed., *Modern Systems Research for the Behavioral Scientist* (Chicago: Aldine-Atherton, 1968a).

RAPOPORT, ANATOL, "Systems Analysis—General Systems Theory," in Sills, David L., ed., *International Encyclopedia of the Social Sciences* (New York: Macmillan and Free Press, 1968b), vol. 15, pp. 452–458.

RAPOPORT, ANATOL, "General Systems Theory: A Bridge Between Two Cultures"

[Third Annual Ludwig von Bertalanffy Memorial Lecture], in Report of the SGSR [Society for General Systems Research] Annual Meeting, Feb. 18–21, 1976, pp. 9–16.

RATLIFF, FLOYD, *Mach Bands: Quantitative Studies on Neural Networks in the Retina* (San Francisco: Holden-Day, 1965).

RAYWARD, W. BOYD, *Systematic Bibliography in England: 1850–1895* (Urbana: University of Illinois Graduate School of Library Science, 1967a). Occasional Paper 84.

RAYWARD, W. BOYD, "UDC and FID: A Historical Perspective," in The *Library Quarterly,* vol. 37 (July 1967b), p. 259–278.

RAYWARD, W. BOYD, *The Universe of Information: The Work of Paul Otlet for Documentation and International Organization* (Moscow: VINITI, 1975), Fédération Internationale de Documentation Publication No. 520.

RAYWARD, W. BOYD, "Subject Access to the *Catalogue of Scientific Papers, 1800–1900,*" in Rayward, W. Boyd, ed., *The Variety of Librarianship: Essays in Honour of John Wallace Metcalfe* (Sydney: Library Association of Australia, 1976), pp. 146–170.

RAYWARD, W. BOYD, "Some Developments in Nineteenth-Century Bibliography: Great Britain," in *Libri,* vol. 27 (June 1977a), pp. 97–107.

RAYWARD, W. BOYD, "IFLA-FID: Is it Time for Federation?" in *IFLA Journal,* vol. 3, no. 3 (1977b), pp. 278–280.

RAYWARD, W. BOYD, "International Library and Bibliographic Organization," in *ALA World Encyclopedia of Library and Information Services* (Chicago: American Library Association, 1980a), pp. 264–268.

RAYWARD, W. BOYD, "The Problems of Professional Knowledge in Librarianship," in *Changes and Exchanges; Australian Viewpoints* (Sydney, Australia: Kuringgai College of Advanced Education, 1980b), pp. 135–154.

RAYWARD, W. BOYD, "The Evolution of an International Library and Bibliographic Community," in *Journal of Library History,* vol. 16 (spring 1981a), pp. 449–462.

RAYWARD, W. BOYD, "The Perils of Bibliography: Four 19th-Century Experiences," in *Wilson Library Bulletin,* vol. 56 (Oct. 1981b), pp. 110–115.

REDDY, D. RAJ, *Working Papers in Speech Recognition (IV): The HEARSAY II System* (Carnegie-Mellon University Computer Science Department Technical Report, Feb. 1976).

REILLY, PARK M., AND BLAU, G. E., "The Use of Statistical Methods to Build Mathematical Models of Chemical Reacting Systems," in *Canadian Journal of Chemical Engineering,* vol. 52 (June 1974), pp. 289–299.

REITMAN, WALTER R., *Cognition and Thought: An Information-Processing Approach* (New York: Wiley, 1965).

Report of the Royal Commission Appointed to Inquire into the Constitution and Government of the British Museum (London: His Majesty's Stationery Office, 1850). Minutes of Evidence, Minute 9751.

RESCHER, NICHOLAS, *Cognitive Systematization: A System-Theoretic Approach to a Coherentist Theory of Knowledge* (Totowa, N.J.: Rowan and Littlefield, 1979).

RICHARDSON, JOHN, *The Spirit of Inquiry in Library Science: The Graduate Library*

School at Chicago, 1921–1951 (Chicago: American Library Association, 1982). ACRL Monographs in Librarianship, no. 42.

RINZEL, JOHN, "Integration and Propagation of Neuroelectric Signals," in Levin, Simon A., ed., *Studies in Mathematical Biology, Part 1: Cellular Behavior and the Development of Pattern* (Washington, D.C.: Mathematical Association of America, 1978), pp. 1–66.

RISSANEN, J., AND KAILATH, T., "Partial Realization of Random Systems," in *Automatica,* vol. 8 (1972), pp. 389–396.

ROBERTS, LAWRENCE G., "Machine Perception of Three-Dimensional Solids," in Tippett, James T., et al., eds., *Optical and Electro-Optical Information Processing.* Symposium on Optical and Electro-Optical Information Processing Technology [Boston] 1964 (Cambridge, Mass.: MIT Press, 1965), pp. 159–197.

ROBERTSON, GEORGE; McCRACKEN, DANIEL D.; AND NEWELL, ALLEN, "The ZOG Approach to Man-Machine Communication," in *International Journal of Man-Machine Studies,* vol. 14 (May 1981), pp. 461–488.

ROBINSON, ALAN J., "A Machine-Oriented Logic Based on the Resolution Principle," in *Journal of the Association for Computing Machinery,* vol. 12 (Jan. 1965), pp. 23–41.

ROSE, JOHN, ed., *Survey of Cybernetics—A Tribute to Dr. Norbert Wiener* (London: Iliffe Books, 1969).

ROSEN, SAUL, "Software," in *Encyclopedia of Computer Science* (New York: Petrocelli/Charter, 1976), pp. 1283–1285.

ROSENBLATT, FRANK, "The Perceptron: A Probabilistic Model for Information Storage and Organization in the Brain," in *Psychological Review,* vol. 65 (Nov. 1958), pp. 386–408.

ROSENBLATT, FRANK, *Principles of Neurodynamics: Perceptrons and the Theory of Brain Mechanisms* (Washington, D.C.: Spartan Books, 1962).

ROSENBLUETH, ARTURO; WIENER, NORBERT; AND BIGELOW, JULIAN, "Behavior, Purpose and Teleology," in *Philosophy of Science,* vol. 10 (Jan. 1943), pp. 18–24.

ROSENBROCK, H. H., *State-Space and Multivariable Theory* (London: Nelson and Sons, 1970).

ROSENFELD, AZRIEL, AND KAK, AVINASH C., *Digital Picture Processing* (New York: Academic Press, 1976).

ROTHE, CARL F., "Regulations of Visceral Function—B. Homeostasis and Negative Feedback-Control," in Selkurt, Ewald E., ed., *Physiology* (Boston: Little, Brown, 3rd ed., 1971).

ROUCHALEAU, Y., AND SONTAG, E., "On the Existence of Minimal Realizations of Linear Dynamical Systems Over Neotherian Integral Domains," in *Journal of Computer and System Sciences,* vol. 18 (1979), pp. 65–75.

RUCH, FLOYD LEON, *Psychology and Life: A Study of the Thinking, Feeling, and Doing of People* (Glenview, Ill.: Scott, Foresman, 1937; 9th ed., rev., 1967).

RUGH, WILSON J., *Mathematical Description of Linear Systems* (New York: Marcel Dekker, 1975).

RUSSELL, BERTRAND, *Introduction to Mathematical Philosophy* (New York: Simon and Schuster, 1919).

RUSSELL, BERTRAND, *Human Knowledge: Its Scope and Limits* (New York: Simon and Schuster, 1948).

RUSSELL, BERTRAND, *Bertrand Russell Speaks His Mind* (London: Arthur Barker, 1960).

RUYER, RAYMOND, *La cybernétique et l'origine de l'information* (Paris: Flammarion, 1954).

SABLOFF, JEREMY A., *Simulations in Archeology* (Albuquerque: University of New Mexico Press, 1981).

SAGER, NAOMI, "Information Structures in the Language of Science," in Weiss, Edward C., ed., *The Many Faces of Information Science* (Boulder, Colo.: Westview Press, 1977), pp. 53–73.

SALTON, GERARD, "Information Retrieval," in *Encyclopedia of Computer Science* (New York: Petrocelli/Charter, 1976), pp. 649–656.

SAMUEL, ARTHUR L., "Some Studies in Machine Learning Using the Game of Checkers," in *IBM Journal of Research and Development,* vol. 3 (July 1959), pp. 210–229.

SAMUELSON, PAUL A., *Foundations of Economic Analysis* (Cambridge, Mass.: Harvard University Press, 1948).

SAMUELSON, PAUL A., *Economics* (New York: McGraw-Hill, 11th ed., 1980).

SARACEVIC, TEFKO, ed., *Introduction to Information Science* (New York: R. R. Bowker, 1970).

SATTINGER, D. H., "Bifurcation and Symmetry Breaking in Applied Mathematics," in *Bulletin (New Series) of the American Mathematical Society,* vol. 3 (Sept. 1980), pp. 779–819.

SAUSSURE, FERDINAND DE, *Cours de linguistique générale* (Lausanne and Paris, 1916). English trans., *Course in General Linguistics* (New York: Philosophical Library, 1959).

SCHANK, ROGER C., "Identification of Conceptualizations Underlying Natural Language," in Schank, Roger C., and Colby, Kenneth M., eds., *Computer Models of Thought and Language* (San Francisco: W. H. Freeman, 1973), pp. 187–247.

SCHANK, ROGER C., *Dynamic Memory: A Theory of Reminding and Learning in Computers and People* (Cambridge: Cambridge University Press, 1982).

SCHANK, ROGER, AND ABELSON, ROBERT P., *Scripts, Plans, Goals, and Understanding: An Inquiry into Human Knowledge Structures* (Hillsdale, N.J.: Lawrence Erlbaum, 1977).

SCHANK, ROGER C., AND NASH-WEBBER, BONNIE, eds., *Theoretical Issues in Natural Language Processing,* proceedings of the first conference on Theoretical Issues in Natural Language Processing (prepared by Bolt, Beranek and Newman, Inc., Cambridge, Mass., 1975).

SCHANK, ROGER C., AND WILENSKY, ROBERT, "Response to Dresher and Hornstein," in *Cognition,* vol. 5 (June 1977), pp. 133–145.

SCHEIBEL, MADGE E., AND SCHEIBEL, ARNOLD B., "Structural Substrates for Integrative Patterns in the Brain Stem Reticular Core," in Jasper, H. H., et al., eds., *Reticular Formation of the Brain* (Boston: Little, Brown, and Co., 1958), pp. 31–68.

SCHELL, JONATHAN, "The Fate of Mankind," in The *New Yorker,* Feb. 1, 1982, pp. 8, 15.

SCHMIDT, ROBERT F., "Somatovisceral Sensibility," Section 3 of Schmidt, Robert F., ed., *Fundamentals of Sensory Physiology,* trans. Marguerite A. Biederman-Thorson (New York: Springer-Verlag, 1978; 2nd, corrected ed., 1981), pp. 81–125.

SCHRADER, ALVIN M., "In Search of a Name: Information Science and Its Conceptual Antecedents," in *Library and Information Science Research,* vol. 6 (spring 1984).

SCHRÖDINGER, ERWIN, *What is Life? The Physical Aspect of the Living Cell* (Cambridge, England: The University Press; New York: Macmillan, 1945).

SCHULTZ, CLAIRE, K., AND GARWIG, PAUL L., "History of the American Documentation Institute—A Sketch," in *American Documentation,* vol. 20 (1969), pp. 152–160.

SCHUMPETER, JOSEPH A., *The Theory of Economic Development,* trans. Redvers Opie (Cambridge, Mass.: Harvard University Press, 1934).

SCHUTZ, ALFRED, AND LUCKMANN, THOMAS, *The Structures of the Life-World,* trans. Richard M. Zaner and A. Tristram Engelhardt, Jr. (Evanston, Ill.: Northwestern University Press, 1973).

Science, "Research News," in *Science,* vol. 212 (1981), p. 313
"Research News," in *Science,* vol. 214 (1981), p. 1334
"Research News," in *Science,* vol. 216 (1982), p. 969
"Research News," in *Science,* vol. 217 (1982), p. 1239

SEARLE, JOHN R., "Minds, Brains, and Programs" [with peer commentaries], in The *Behavioral and Brain Sciences,* vol. 3 (Sept. 1980), pp. 417–457.

SEARLE, JOHN R., "Minds, Brains, and Programs," in Hofstadter, Douglas R., and Dennett, Daniel C., eds., *The Mind's I: Fantasies and Reflections on Self and Soul* (New York: Basic Books, 1981), pp. 353–373.

SEARLE, JOHN R., "The Myth of the Computer." Book review of Hofstadter, Douglas R., and Dennett, Daniel C., eds., *The Mind's I: Reflections on Self and Soul* [New York: Basic Books, 1981] in The *New York Review of Books,* vol. 29 (29 Apr. 1982*a*), pp. 3–6.

SEARLE, JOHN R., "Response to Dennett" in the letters section of The *New York Review of Books,* June 24, 1982*b*.

SEBEOK, THOMAS A., *Contributions to the Doctrine of Signs* (Bloomington: Indiana University and Peter de Ridder Press, 1976).

SEIFFERT, HELMUT, *Information über die Information; Verständigung im Alltag—Nachrichtentechnik—Wissenschaftliches Verstehen—Informationssoziologie—Das Wissen des Gelehrten* (München: C. H. Beck, 1968).

SELLEN, BETTY-CAROL, ed., *What Else You Can Do With A Library Degree* (Syracuse, New York: Gaylord, 1980).

SHANNON, CLAUDE E., "A Mathematical Theory of Communication," in *Bell System Technical Journal,* vol. 27 (July and Oct. 1948), pp. 379–423; 623–656.

SHANNON, CLAUDE E., "Communication Theory of Secrecy Systems," in *Bell System Technical Journal,* vol. 28 (1949), pp. 656–715.

SHANNON, CLAUDE E., Contribution to the discussion, in Foerster, Heinz M. von, ed., *Cybernetics,* transactions of the Eighth Conference sponsored by the Josiah Macy Jr. Foundation (New York: Josiah Macy Jr. Foundation, 1951), p. 219.

SHANNON, CLAUDE E., AND McCARTHY, JOHN, eds., *Automata Studies* (Princeton, N.J.: Princeton University Press, 1956).

SHANNON, CLAUDE E., AND WEAVER, WARREN, *The Mathematical Theory of Communication* (Urbana: University of Illinois Press, 1949).

SHELLEY, MARY WOLLSTONECRAFT, *Frankenstein; or The Modern Prometheus* (1818 text), ed. James Rieger (Indianapolis: Bobbs-Merrill, 1974).

SHELLY, GARY B., AND CASHMAN, THOMAS J., *Introduction to Computers and Data Processing* (Fullerton, Calif.: Anaheim, 1980).

SHERA, JESSE H., "Emergence of a New Institutional Structure for the Dissemination of Specialized Information," in *American Documentation,* vol. 4 (1953), pp. 163–173.

SHERA, JESSE H., "Of Librarianship, Documentation, and Information Science," in *UNESCO Bulletin for Libraries,* vol. 22 (Mar./Apr. 1968), pp. 58–65.

SHERA, JESSE H., AND CLEVELAND, DONALD B., "History and Foundations of Information Science," in Williams, Martha E., ed., *Annual Review of Information Science and Technology* (White Plains, N.Y.: Knowledge Industries Publications [for the American Society for Information Science], 1977), vol. 12, pp. 249–275.

SHERA, JESSE H., AND EGAN, MARGARET E., "Introduction," in Bradford, Samuel Clement, *Documentation* (London: Crosby Lockwood, 2nd ed., 1953; 1st ed., 1948).

SHERA, JESSE H., AND EGAN, MARGARET E., *Bibliographic Organization,* papers presented before the fifteenth annual Conference of the Graduate Library School, 1950 (Chicago: University of Chicago Press, 1951).

SHORTLIFFE, EDWARD H., "MYCIN: A Rule-Based Computer Program for Advising Physicians Regarding Antimicrobial Therapy Selection" (Ph.D. diss., Stanford University, 1974).

SHORTLIFFE, EDWARD H., *Computer-Based Medical Consultations: MYCIN* (New York: American Elsevier, 1976).

SILVERMAN, L., "Realization of Linear Dynamical Systems," in *IEEE Transactions on Automatic Control,* vol. AC-16 (1971), pp. 554–567.

SIMON, HERBERT A., *Models of Man, Social and Rational: Mathematical Essays on Rational Human Behavior in a Social Setting* (New York: Wiley, 1957).

SIMON, HERBERT A., "Modelling Human Mental Processes," in *Extending Man's Intellect,* proceedings of the Western Joint Computer Conference, held [in Los Angeles] by the Institute of Radio Engineers, the American Institute of Electrical Engineers, and the Association for Computing Machinery, May 9–11, 1961, vol. 19, pp. 111–120.

SIMON, HERBERT A., *The Sciences of the Artificial* [the Karl Taylor Compton Lecture, 1968] (Cambridge, Mass.: MIT Press, 1969; 2nd enlarged ed., 1981).

SIMON, HERBERT A., "Information Processing," in *Encyclopedia of Computer Science* (New York: Petrocelli/Charter, 1976), pp. 647–649.

SIMON, HERBERT A., "Information Processing Models of Cognition," in *Annual Review of Psychology,* vol. 30 (1979), pp. 363–396.

SIMON, HERBERT A., "Cognitive Science: The Newest Science of the Artificial," in *Cognitive Science,* vol. 4 (Jan./Mar. 1980), pp. 33–46.

SIMON, HERBERT A., "Studying Human Intelligence by Creating Artificial Intelligence," in *American Scientist,* vol. 69 (May–June, 1981), pp. 300–309.

SIMON, HERBERT A., AND FEIGENBAUM, EDWARD A., "An Information-Processing Theory of Some Effects of Similarity, Familiarization, and Meaningfulness in Verbal Learning," in *Journal of Verbal Learning and Verbal Behavior,* vol. 3 (Oct. 1964), pp. 385–396.

SIMON, HERBERT A., AND KOTOVSKY, KENNETH, "Human Acquisition of Concepts for Sequential Patterns," in *Psychological Review,* vol. 70 (Nov. 1963), pp. 534–546.

SINGER, EDGAR A., JR., *In Search of a Way of Life* (New York: Columbia University Press, 1948).

SKINNER, BURRHUS F., *The Behavior of Organisms* (New York: Appleton-Century-Crofts, 1938).

SKINNER, BURRHUS F., *Verbal Behavior* (New York: Appleton-Century-Crofts, 1957).

SLAGLE, JAMES R., "A Heuristic Program that Solves Symbolic Integration Problems in Freshman Calculus," in Feigenbaum, Edward A., and Feldman, Julian, eds., *Computers and Thought* (New York: McGraw-Hill, 1963), pp. 191–203.

SLAGLE, JAMES R.; DIXON, J. K.; AND JONES, T. L., "List Processing Languages," in *Encyclopedia of Computer Science* (New York: Petrocelli/Charter, 1976), pp. 778–785.

SLAMECKA, VLADIMIR, "The Science and Engineering of Information," in Finerman, Aaron, ed., *University Education in Computing Science,* proceedings of a conference on Graduate Academic and Related Research Programs in Computing Science, held [at Stony Brook] by the State University of New York, 1967 (New York: Academic Press, 1968), pp. 81–92.

SLAMECKA, VLADIMIR, AND GEHL, JOHN, eds., "Information Sciences at Georgia Institute of Technology: The Formative Years 1963–1978," in *Information Processing and Management,* vol. 14, no. 5 (1978), pp. 320–361.

SLAMECKA, VLADIMIR, AND PEARSON, CHARLS, "Information Science," in *Encyclopedia of Computer Science* (New York: Petrocelli/Charter, 1976), pp. 656–657.

SLAMECKA, VLADIMIR, AND PEARSON, CHARLS, "The Portent of Signs and Symbols," in Weiss, Edward C., ed., *The Many Faces of Information Science* (Boulder, Colo.: Westview Press, 1977), pp. 105–128.

SLATER, JOHN C., *Introduction to Chemical Physics* (New York: McGraw-Hill, 1st ed. 1938).

SLEEMAN, DEREK E., AND BROWN, JOHN SEELY, eds., *Intelligent Tutoring Systems* (New York: Academic Press, 1982).

SLEPIAN, DAVID, ed., *Key Papers in the Development of Information Theory* (New York: IEEE Press, 1974).

SLOAN FOUNDATION, ADVISORS OF THE ALFRED P., "Cognitive Science 1978." Report of the State of the Art Committee (New York: Alfred P. Sloan Foundation, Oct. 1978).

SLOBIN, DAN I., *Psycholinguistics* (Glenview, Ill.: Scott, Foresman, and Co., 1971; 2nd ed., 1979).

SLOMAN, AARON, *The Computer Revolution in Philosophy: Philosophy, Science, and Models of Mind* (New York: Humanities Press, 1978*a*).

SLOMAN, AARON, "Intuition and Analogical Reasoning," in Sloman, Aaron, *The Computer Revolution in Philosophy: Philosophy, Science, and Models of Mind* (Hassocks, England: Harvester Press, 1978*b*), pp. 144–176.

SMALL, HENRY, AND GRIFFITH, BELVER C., "The Structure of Scientific Literatures. I: Identifying and Graphing Specialties," in *Science Studies,* vol. 4 (Jan. 1974), pp. 17–40.

SMETS, PHILIPPE, "Probability of a Fuzzy Event: An Axiomatic Approach," in *Fuzzy Sets and Systems,* vol. 7 (1982), pp. 153–164.

SMITH, ADAM, *An Enquiry into the Nature and Causes of the Wealth of Nations* (London: W. Strahan and T. Cadell, 1776; another ed., New York: Modern Library, 1936).

SMITH, REID G., "A Framework for Problem Solving in a Distributed Processing Environment" (Ph.D. diss., Stanford University, 1978).

SNOW, CHARLES P., *The Two Cultures and the Scientific Revolution* [the Rede Lecture, 1959] (Cambridge, England: The University Press, 1959).

SNOW, CHARLES P., *The Two Cultures and a Second Look. An Expanded Version of the Two Cultures and the Scientific Revolution* (Cambridge, England: The University Press, 1964).

SOLOMONOFF, R. J., "A Formal Theory of Inductive Inference," in *Information and Control,* vol. 7 (Mar. 1964), pp. 1–22.

SONTAG, EDUARDO D., *Polynomial Response Maps* (Berlin and New York: Springer-Verlag, 1979).

SONUGA, J. O., "Entropy Principle Applied to the Rainfall-Runoff Process," in *Journal of Hydrology,* vol. 30 (May 1976), pp. 81–94.

SPERLING, GEORGE, "The Information Available in Brief Visual Presentations," in *Psychological Monographs* no. 11, vol. 74 (1960).

SPERRY, ROGER W., "Mind, Brain, and Humanist Values," in Platt, John R., ed., *New Views of the Nature of Man* (Chicago: University of Chicago Press, 1965), pp. 71–92.

SPERRY, ROGER W., "Mental Unity Following Surgical Disconnection of the Cerebral Hemispheres" [Harvey Lectures], vol. 62 (1968), p. 293–322.

SPERRY, ROGER W., "Some Effects of Disconnecting the Cerebral Hemispheres" [Nobel Prize Lecture, 1981], *Science,* vol. 217 (24 Sept. 1982), pp. 1223–1226.

SPINOZA, BENEDICTUS DE, *On the Improvement of the Understanding* (New York: Dutton, 1963; 1st English trans., 1883).

SRIDHARAN, N., *Prototype Deformation* (Rutgers University Computer Science Department Technical Report, New Brunswick, N.J., 1980).

STAKGOLD, IVAR, "Branching of Solutions of Nonlinear Equations," in *SIAM Review,* vol. 13 (July 1971), pp. 289–332.

STANLEY-JONES, DOUGLAS, "Cybernetics and General Systems—A Unitary Science?" in *Kybernetes,* vol. 8 (1979), pp. 25–32.

STARK, LAWRENCE, "The Control System for Versional Eye Movements," in Bach-y-Rita, Paul, and Collins, Carter C., eds., *The Control of Eye Movements,* proceedings of a Symposium on the Control of Eye Movements, held [in San Francisco] Nov. 10–11, 1969 (New York: Academic Press, 1971), pp. 363–428.

STEINER, GEORGE, *After Babel: Aspects of Language and Translation* (New York and London: Oxford University Press, 1975).

STERNBERG, SAUL, "High-Speed Scanning in Human Memory," in *Science,* vol. 153 (5 Aug., 1966), pp. 652–654.

STERNBERG, STAN R., "Language and Architecture for Parallel Image Processing," in Grisema, E. S., and Kanal, L. N., eds., *Proceedings of the Conference on Pattern Recognition in Practice* (Amsterdam: North-Holland, 1980).

STIGLER, GEORGE J., "The Economics of Information," in *Journal of Political Economy,* vol. 69 (1961), pp. 213–225.

STIRLING, JAMES, *Methodus differentialis sive tractatus de summatione et interpolatione serierum infinitarum* (London: 1730; another ed., London, 1764).

STRACHEY, CHRISTOPHER, "Computer," in Bullock, Alan, and Stallybrass, Oliver, eds., *The Harper Dictionary of Modern Thought* (New York: 1st U.S. ed., Harper and Row, 1977), p. 122.

STRACHEY, CHRISTOPHER, "Computing Science," in Bullock, Alan, and Stallybrass, Oliver, eds., *The Harper Dictionary of Modern Thought* (New York: 1st U.S. ed., Harper and Row, 1977), p. 124.

SUSSMAN, GERALD JAY, *A Computer Model of Skill Acquisition* (New York: American Elsevier, 1975).

SUTHERLAND, IVAN E., "SKETCHPAD: A Man-Machine Graphical Communication System," in *AFIPS Conference Proceedings, Vol. 23: 1963 Spring Joint Computer Conference,* organized by the American Federation of Information Processing Societies and held [in Detroit] May 1963 (Washington, D.C.: Spartan Books, 1963), pp. 329–346.

SUTTON, RICHARD S., AND BARTO, ANDREW G., "Towards a Modern Theory of Adaptive Networks: Expectation and Prediction," in *Psychological Review,* vol. 88 (1981), pp. 135–170.

SWANK, RAYNARD C., *A Unifying Influence* (Metuchen, N.J.: Scarecrow Press, 1981).

SWANSON, DON R., "Introduction," in *Intellectual Foundations of Library Education,* proceedings of the twenty-ninth annual Conference of the Graduate Library School (Chicago: University of Chicago Press, 1965), p. 2.

SWANSON, DON R., "Introduction to the Conference," in *The Role of Libraries in the Growth of Knowledge,* proceedings of the fortieth Conference of the Graduate Library School (Chicago: University of Chicago Press, 1980a).

SWANSON, DON R., "Libraries and the Growth of Knowledge," in *The Role of Libraries in the Growth of Knowledge,* proceedings of the fortieth Conference of the Graduate Library School (Chicago: University of Chicago Press, 1980b), pp. 112–134.

SWEENEY, JAMES L., "The Economics of Depletable Resources: Market Forces and Intertemporal Bias," in *Review of Economic Studies,* vol. 64 (Feb. 1977), pp. 125–142.

SZENTÁGOTHAI, JANOS, AND ARBIB, MICHAEL A., "Conceptual Models of Neural Organization," in *Neurosciences Program Research Bulletin,* vol. 12, no. 3 (1974), pp. 310–479.

SZILARD, LEO, "Über die Entropieverminderung in einem thermodynamischen System bei Eingriffen intelligenter Wesen," in *Zeitschrift für Physik,* vol. 53 (1929), pp. 840–856.

TANNENBAUM, A., *Invariance and System Theory: Algebraic and Geometric Aspects,* Lecture Notes in Mathematics No. 845 (Berlin, Germany: Springer-Verlag, 1981).

TATE, VERNON D., "Introducing *American Documentation,*" in *American Documentation,* vol. 1 (Jan. 1950), pp. 3–7.

TAUBE, MORTIMER, *Computers and Common Sense: The Myth of Thinking Machines* (New York: Columbia University Press, 1961).

TAYLOR, ROBERT S., "Professional Aspects of Information Science and Technology," in Cuadra, Carlos A., ed., *Annual Review of Information Science and Technology* (New York: Wiley [for the American Documentation Institute], 1966), vol. 1, pp. 15–40.

TEICHROEW, D., "Information Systems," in *Encyclopedia of Computer Science* (New York: Petrocelli/Charter, 1978), pp. 657–660.

TERMAN, LEWIS MADISON, *The Measurement of Intelligence: An Explanation of and a Complete Guide for the Use of the Stanford Revision and Extension of the Binet-Simon Intelligence Scale* (Boston and New York: Houghton Mifflin, 1916).

TERRACE, HERBERT S.; PETITTO, L. A.; SANDERS, R. J.; AND BEVER, THOMAS G., "Can an Ape Create a Sentence?" in *Science,* vol. 206 (1979), p. 891.

THOM, RENÉ, *Stabilité structurelle et morphogénèse* (Reading, Mass.: Addison-Wesley, 1972; trans. as *Structural Stability and Morphogenesis,* 1975).

THOM, RENÉ, *Modèles mathématiques de la morphogénèse, séries* 10/18 (Paris: Union Générale d'Editions, 1974).

THOM, RENÉ, *Structural Stability and Morphogenesis: An Outline of a General Theory of Models,* trans. D. H. Fowler (Reading, Mass.: 1st English ed., W. A. Benjamin, 1975).

THOM, RENÉ, "Structural Stability, Catastrophe Theory, and Applied Mathematics" [the John von Neumann lecture, 1976], in *SIAM Review,* vol. 19 (Apr. 1977), pp. 189–201.

THOM, RENÉ, "Systemic versus Morphological Approach in General Systems Theory," in Pichler, Franz R., and Hanika, Francis de Paula, eds., *Progress in Cybernetics and Systems Research, Vol. VII: General Systems Methodology, Organization and Management, Cognition and Learning,* papers presented at a symposium organized by the Austrian Society for Cybernetic Studies and held [in Vienna] Apr. 1974 (Washington, D.C.: Hemisphere Publishing Company, 1980).

TINBERGEN, JAN, "The Use of Models: Experience and Prospects" [Nobel Prize lecture delivered Dec. 1969], in The *American Economic Review,* vol. 71 (Dec. 1981), pp. 17–22.

TORDA, CLARA, *Information Processing by the Central Nervous System and the Computer (A Comparison)* (Berkeley, Calif.: Walters, 1982).

TRAPPL, ROBERT, AND HANIKA, FRANCIS DE PAULA, eds., *Progress in Cybernetics and*

Systems Research, Vol. II: Socio-Economic Systems, Cognition and Learning, Systems Education, Organization and Management, papers presented at a symposium organized by the Austrian Society for Cybernetic Studies and held [in Vienna] Apr. 1974 (New York: Halsted Press, 1975).

TREMBLAY, JEAN-PAUL, AND SORENSON, PAUL G., *An Introduction to Data Structures with Applications* (New York: McGraw-Hill, 1976).

TRIBE, LAURENCE H., "Policy Science: Analysis or Ideology?" in *Philosophy and Public Affairs,* vol. 2 (fall 1972), pp. 66–110.

TRIBUS, MYRON, "Thermodynamics: A Survey of the Field," in *Recent Advances in the Engineering Sciences: Their Impact on Engineering Education,* proceedings of a conference on Science and Technology for Deans of Engineering, Purdue University, Lafayette, Ind., Sept. 9–12, 1957 (New York: McGraw-Hill, 1958).

TRIBUS, MYRON, *Thermostatics and Thermodynamics: An Introduction to Energy, Information, and States of Matter, with Engineering Applications* (Princeton, N.J.: Van Nostrand, 1961*a*).

TRIBUS, MYRON, "Information Theory as the Basis for Thermostatics and Thermodynamics," in *Journal of Applied Mechanics,* ASME Transactions, series *E,* no. 83 (Mar. 1961*b*), pp. 1–8.

TRIBUS, MYRON, "The Use of the Maximum Entropy Estimate in Reliability Engineering," in Machol, Robert E., and Gray, Paul, eds., *Recent Developments in Information and Decision Processes,* proceedings of the Third Symposium on Information and Decision Processes, held [at Purdue University] 1961 (New York: Macmillan, 1962).

TRIBUS, MYRON, *Rational Descriptions, Decisions, and Designs* (New York: Pergamon Press, 1969).

TRIBUS, MYRON; EVANS, ROBERT; AND CRELLIN, GARY L., "The Use of Entropy in Hypothesis Testing," in *Proceedings* of the Tenth National Symposium on Reliability and Quality Control, Jan. 7–9, 1964.

TURCHIN, VALENTIN FEDOROVICH, *The Phenomenon of Science,* trans. Brand Frentz (New York: Columbia University Press, 1977).

TURING, ALAN M., "On Computable Numbers, with an Application to the Entscheidungsproblem," in *Proceedings of the London Mathematical Society,* vol. 42, no. 2 (1936), pp. 230–265.

TURING, ALAN M., "Computing Machinery and Intelligence," in *Mind,* vol. 59 (Oct. 1950), pp. 433–460.

TURING, ALAN M., "The Chemical Basis of Morphogenesis," in *Philosophical Transactions of the Royal Society of London,* vol. 237 (Aug. 1952), pp. 37–72.

TURNBULL, GEORGE HENRY, *Hartlib, Drury and Comenius: Gleanings from Hartlib's Papers* (Liverpool, England: University Press of Liverpool, 1947).

TYLDESLEY, JOHN R., "A Thermodynamic Approach to Turbulence Phenomena" private communication, Dept. of Mechanical Engineering, Glasgow University (1962).

UHR, LEONARD M., "Computer Arrays and Networks" (1982).

VAN DER WAALS, JOHANNES, D., "Über die Erklärung der Naturgesetze auf statistisch-mechanischer Grundlage," in *Physikalische Zeitschrift,* no. 13 (July 1911), pp. 547–549.

VAN GIGCH, JOHN P., AND HILL, RICHARD E., *Using Systems Analysis to Implement Cost-Effectiveness and Program Budgeting in Education* (Englewood Cliffs, N.J.: Educational Technology Publications, 1971).

VAN MARLEN, GEERT, AND DIJKSTRA, AUKE, "Information Theory Applied to Selection of Peaks for Retrieval of Mass Spectra," in *Analytical Chemistry,* vol. 48 (1976), pp. 595–598.

VAN PUTTEN, C., AND VAN SCHUPPEN, J. H., "On Stochastic Dynamical Systems," in *Proceedings of the Fourth International Symposium on the Mathematical Theory of Networks and Systems* (Delft, Netherlands: North-Holland, 1979).

VON BERTALANFFY, LUDWIG [see "Bertalanffy, Ludwig von"].

VON NEUMANN, JOHN [see "Neumann, John von"].

WANG, HAO, "Toward Mechanical Mathematics," in *IBM Journal of Research and Development,* vol. 4 (Jan. 1960), pp. 2–22.

WAPLES, DOUGLAS, "The Graduate Library School at Chicago," in The *Library Quarterly,* vol. 1 (Jan. 1931), pp. 26–36.

WATERMAN, DONALD A. "Generalization Learning Techniques for Automating the Learning of Heuristics," in *Artificial Intelligence,* vol. 1 (spring 1970), pp. 121–170.

WATERMAN, DONALD A., AND HAYES-ROTH, FREDERICK, eds., *Pattern-Directed Inference Systems.* Report of a Workshop on P-D I Systems [Honolulu] 1977 (New York: Academic Press, 1978).

WATERMAN, TALBOT H., "Systems Theory and Biology—View of a Biologist," in Mesarović, Mihajlo D., ed., *Systems Theory and Biology,* proceedings of the Third Systems Symposium at Case Institute of Technology (New York: Springer-Verlag, 1968), pp. 1–37.

WATSON, JAMES D., *Molecular Biology of the Gene* (New York: Benjamin, 1965).

WATSON, JOHN B., "Psychology as the Behaviorist Views It," in *Psychological Review,* vol. 20 (Mar. 1913), pp. 158–177.

WEAVER, WARREN, "Science and Complexity," in The *American Scientist,* vol. 36 (Oct. 1948), pp. 536–544.

WEAVER, WARREN, "The Mathematics of Information," in *Automatic Control* (New York: Simon and Schuster, 1955), pp. 100–104.

WEBB, EUGENE J.; CAMPBELL, DONALD T.; SCHWARTZ, RICHARD D.; AND SECHREST, LEE, *Unobtrusive Measures: Nonreactive Research in the Social Sciences* (Chicago: Rand McNally, 1966).

WEBER, DAVID C., "The Changing Character of the Catalog in America," in The *Library Quarterly,* vol. 34 (Jan. 1964), pp. 20–33.

WEBSTER, CHARLES, ed., *Samuel Hartlib and the Advancement of Learning* (London: Cambridge University Press, 1970).

WEGNER, PETER, "Three Computer Cultures, Computer Technology, Computer Mathematics, and Computer Science," in Alt, Franz L., and Rubinoff, Morris, eds., and Freiberger, Walter, guest editor, *Advances in Computers* (New York: Academic Press, 1970), vol. 10, pp. 8–78.

WEGNER, PETER, "ADA Education and Technology Transfer Activities," in *ADA Letters* (Aug. 1982).

WEGNER, PETER, ed.; Dennis, Jack; Hammer, Michael; and Teichroew, D., assoc. eds., *Research Directions in Software Technology* (Cambridge, Mass.: MIT Press, 1979).

WEINREICH, URIEL, "Semantics and Semiotics," in *International Encyclopedia of the Social Sciences* (New York: Macmillan and Free Press, 1968), vol. 14, pp. 164–169.

WEISS, EDWARD C., ed., *The Many Faces of Information Science* (Boulder, Colo.: Westview Press, 1977).

WEIZENBAUM, JOSEPH, *Computer Power and Human Reason: From Judgment to Calculation* (San Francisco: W. H. Freeman, 1976).

WELLISCH, HANS, "From Information Science to Informatics," in *Journal of Librarianship,* vol. 4 (July 1972), pp. 164–187.

WERTHEIMER, MAX, *Drei Abhandlungen zur Gestalttheorie* (Neuherausgabe, Erlangen: Philosophische Akademie, 1925).

WESTERN JOINT COMPUTER CONFERENCE, *Extending Man's Intellect,* proceedings of the Western Joint Computer Conference, held [in Los Angeles] by the Institute of Radio Engineers, the American Institute of Electrical Engineers, and the Association for Computing Machinery, May 9–11, 1961, vol. 19.

WHEELER, WILLIAM MORTON, "The Ant Colony as an Organism," in *Journal of Morphology,* vol. 22, no. 2 (1911), pp. 307–325.

WHITE, CARL M., *A Historical Introduction to Library Education* (Metuchen, N.J.: Scarecrow Press, 1976).

WHITEHEAD, ALFRED NORTH, AND RUSSELL, BERTRAND, *Principia Mathematica* (Cambridge: Cambridge University Press, 1910–1913; 2nd ed. 1925–1927; paperback ed. 1962).

WHITTEMORE, BRUCE J., AND YOVITS, MARSHALL C., "A Generalized Concept for the Analysis of Information," in Debons, Anthony, ed., *Information Science: Search for Identity,* proceedings of the 1972 NATO Advanced Study Institute in Information Science, held [in Seven Springs, Champion, Penn.] Aug. 12–20, 1972 (New York: Marcel Dekker, 1974), pp. 29–45.

WIDROW, BERNARD, "Pattern Recognition and Adaptive Control," in *IEEE Transactions on Applications and Industry,* vol. 83 (1964), pp. 269–277.

WIENER, NORBERT, *Cybernetics, or Control and Communication in the Animal and the Machine* (Cambridge, Mass.: MIT Press, 1948; 2nd ed., MIT Press and Wiley, 1961).

WIENER, NORBERT, *Extrapolation, Interpolation, and Smoothing of Stationary Time Series with Engineering Applications* (Cambridge, Mass.: Technology Press of the Massachusetts Institute of Technology, 1949).

WIENER, NORBERT, *The Human Use of Human Beings—Cybernetics and Society* (Boston: Houghton Mifflin, 1950 and 1954; 2nd ed., Boston: Avon, 1967).

WIENER, NORBERT, *God and Golem, Inc.: A Comment on Certain Points Where Cybernetics Impinges on Religion* (Cambridge, Mass.: MIT Press, 1964).

WIJESINGHE, O., "The Effect of Varying the Rate of Presentation on the Information Transmission of Schizophrenic and Control Group," in *British Journal of Psychiatry,* vol. 130 (May 1977), pp. 509–513.

WILLEMS, J. C., "System-Theoretic Models for the Analysis of Physical Systems," in Ricerche di automatica, vol. 10 (Dec. 1979), pp. 71–105.

WILLIAMSON, CHARLES CLARENCE, "The Place of Research in Library Service," in The *Library Quarterly*, vol. 1 (Jan. 1931), pp. 1–19.

WILLIAMSON, OLIVER E., "Transaction-cost Economics: The Governance Contractual Relations," in *Journal of Law and Economics*, vol. 22, no. 2 (1979), pp. 233–261.

WILLIAMSON, OLIVER E., "The Organization of Work," in *Journal of Economic Behavior and Organization*, vol. 1 (1980), pp. 5–38.

WILSON, ALAN G., "A Statistical Theory of Spatial Distribution Models," in *Transportation Research* (New York: Pergamon Press, 1967), vol. 1, pp. 253–269.

WILSON, ALAN G., "The Use of Entropy-Maximizing Models in the Theory of Trip Distribution, Mode Split, and Route Split," in *Journal of Transport Economics and Policy*, vol. 3 (Jan. 1969), pp. 108–126.

WILSON, EDWARD OSBORNE, *The Insect Societies* (Cambridge, Mass.: Harvard University Press, 1971).

WILSON, PATRICK, "Limits to the Growth of Knowledge: The Case of the Social and Behavioral Sciences," in The *Library Quarterly*, vol. 50 (Jan. 1980), pp. 4–21.

WILSON, T. D., "Sociological Aspects of Information Science," in *International Forum on Information and Documentation* (Moscow), vol. 6 (1981), pp. 13–18.

WINDELBAND, WILHELM, "The Principles of Logic," in Ruge, Arnold, et al., *Encyclopaedia of the Philosophical Sciences, Vol. 1, Logic* (London: Macmillan, 1913), pp. 7–66.

WINOGRAD, SHMUEL, AND COWAN, JACK D., *Reliable Computation in the Presence of Noise* (Cambridge, Mass.: MIT Press, 1963).

WINOGRAD, TERRY, "Procedures as a Representation for Data in a Computer Program for Understanding Natural Language" (Ph.D. diss., Massachusetts Institute of Technology, 1971).

WINOGRAD, TERRY, *Understanding Natural Language* (New York: Academic Press, 1972a).

WINOGRAD, TERRY, "Understanding Natural Language," in *Cognitive Psychology*, vol. 3 (Jan. 1972b), pp. 1–191. [Special issue]

WINOGRAD, TERRY, "On Some Contested Suppositions of Generative Linguistics About the Scientific Study of Language," in *Cognition*, vol. 5 (1977), pp. 151–179.

WINOGRAD, TERRY, "Beyond Programming Languages," in *Communications of the ACM*, vol. 22 (July 1979), pp. 391–401.

WINSTON, PATRICK H., "Learning Structural Descriptions from Examples" (Ph.D. diss., Massachusetts Institute of Technology, 1970).

WINSTON, PATRICK H., ed., *The Psychology of Computer Vision* (New York: McGraw-Hill, 1975).

WISDOM, JOHN OULTON, "The Hypothesis of Cybernetics," in *British Journal for the Philosophy of Science*, vol. 2 (May 1951), pp. 1–24. Reprinted in Pylyshyn, Zenon W., ed., *Perspectives on the Computer Revolution* (Englewood Cliffs, N.J.: Prentice-Hall, 1970).

WITTGENSTEIN, LUDWIG VON, *Tractatus logico-philosophicus* (London: K. Paul, Trench, Trubner, 1922; another ed., trans. D. F. Pears and B. F. McGuinness, London: Routledge and Kegan Paul, 1969).

WONHAM, W. MURRAY, "On Pole Assignment in Multi-Input Controllable Linear Systems," in *IEEE Transactions on Automatic Control,* vol. AC-12 (1967), pp. 660–665.

WONHAM, W. MURRAY, *Linear Multivariable Control: A Geometric Approach* (Berlin, Germany: Springer-Verlag, 1974, 1979).

WOODS, WILLIAM A., "Transition Network Grammars for Natural Language Analysis," in *Communications of the ACM,* vol. 13 (Oct. 1970), pp. 591–606.

WOODS, WILLIAM A., "What's in a Link: Foundations for Semantic Networks," in Bobrow, Daniel G., and Collins, Allan, eds., *Representation and Understanding: Studies in Cognitive Science* (New York: Academic Press, 1975), pp. 35–82.

WOODWORTH, ROBERT SESSIONS, AND MARQUIS, DONALD G., *Psychology; A Study of Mental Life* (New York: Holt, 1921; 20th ed., 1949; reprinted Methuen and Company, 1967).

WRIGHT, H. CURTIS, "The Wrong Way To Go," in *Journal of the American Society for Information Science,* vol. 30 (Mar. 1979), pp. 67–76.

WRIGHT, H. CURTIS, "Professionalism and the Socratic Paradox," in *Scholar and Educator* (spring 1980), pp. 5–15.

WRIGHT, H. CURTIS, "The Instrumentality of Data," in *National Library Association Newsletter,* vol. 6 (May 1981), pp. 4–5.

WUNDT, WILHELM, *Sprachgeschichte und Sprachpsychologie, mit Rücksicht auf B. Delbrücks "Grundfragen der Sprachforschung"* (Leipzig, Germany: W. Engelmann, 1901).

YOCKEY, HUBERT P., ed., *Proceedings of a Symposium on Information Theory in Biology,* held [in Gatlinburg, Tenn.] Oct. 29–31, 1956 (New York: Pergamon Press, 1958).

YOUNG, JOHN FREDERICK, *Cybernetics* (New York: American Elsevier, 1969).

YOUNG, ROBERT M., *Mind, Brain, and Adaptation in the Nineteenth Century: Cerebral Localization and its Biological Context from Gall to Ferrier* (Oxford, England: Clarendon Press, 1970).

YOVITS, MARSHALL C., AND ABILOCK, JUDITH G., "A Semiotic Framework for Information Science Leading to the Development of a Quantitative Measure of Information," in Zunde, Pranas, ed., *Information Utilities,* proceedings of the thirty-seventh ASIS Annual Meeting, vol. 11 (Washington, D.C.: American Society for Information Science, 1974), pp. 163–168.

YOVITS, MARSHALL C.; JACOBI, GEORGE T.; AND GOLDSTEIN, GORDON D., eds., *Self-Organizing Systems,* proceedings of a Conference on Self-Organizing Systems [Chicago] 1962 (Washington, D.C.: Spartan, 1962).

YOVITS, MARSHALL C.; ROSE, LAWRENCE; AND ABILOCK, JUDITH, "Development of a Theory of Information Flow and Analysis," in Weiss, Edward C., ed., *The Many Faces of Information Science* (Boulder, Colo.: Westview Press, 1977), pp. 19–51.

ZADEH, LOFTI A., "Fuzzy Sets," in *Information and Control,* vol. 8 (June 1965), pp. 338–353.

ZADEH, LOFTI A., AND DESOER, CHARLES A., *Linear System Theory* (New York: McGraw-Hill, 1963).

ZADEH, LOFTI A., AND POLAK, E., *System Theory* (New York: McGraw-Hill, 1969).

ZELENY, MILAN, "Cybernetics and General Systems—A Unitary Science?" in *Kybernetes,* vol. 8 (1979), pp. 17–23.

ZELENY, MILAN, *Autopoiesis: A Theory of Living Organization* (New York: Elsevier, 1981), General Systems Research Series, vol. 3.

ZIFF, PAUL, "The Feelings of Robots," in *Analysis,* vol. 19 (Jan. 1959), pp. 64–68.

ZIMMERMANN, MANFRED, "Neurophysiology of Sensory Systems: The Sensory System in the Light of Information Theory," in Schmidt, Robert F., ed., *Fundamentals of Sensory Physiology,* 3rd ed. of *Grundriss der Sinnesphysiologie,* trans. Marguerite A. Biederman-Thorson (New York: Springer-Verlag, 1978), pp. 68–80.

ZLOOF, MOSHÉ M., "Query-by-Example: A Data Base Language," in *International Business Machines Systems Journal,* vol. 16, no. 4 (1977), pp. 324–343.

ZMUD, ROBERT W., "Individual Differences and MIS Success: A Review of the Empirical Literature," in *Management Science,* vol. 25 (Oct. 1979), pp. 966–979.

ZUNDE, PRANAS, AND GEHL, JOHN, "Empirical Foundations of Information Science," in Williams, Martha E., ed., *Annual Review of Information Science and Technology* (White Plains, N.Y.: Knowledge Industries Publications [for the American Society for Information Science], 1979), vol. 14, pp. 67–92.

INDEX